The Cambridge Handbook of Kinship

Presenting twenty-nine original chapters – each written by an expert in the field – this handbook examines the history of kinship theory and the directions in which it has moved over the past few years. Using examples from across the globe (Africa, India, South America, Malaysia, Asia, the Pacific, Europe, and North America), this handbook highlights the power of kinship theory to address questions of broad anthropological significance. How have recent advances in reproductive medicine fundamentally altered our understanding of biological properties? How has globalization brought in its wake new ways of imagining human relatedness? What might recent shifts in state welfare policies tell us about those relations of power that define the difference between "functional" versus "dysfunctional" families? Addressing these and many other timely concerns, this volume presents the results of cutting-edge research and demonstrates that the study of kinship is likely to remain at the core of anthropological inquiry.

SANDRA BAMFORD is Associate Professor of Anthropology at the University of Toronto. Her main area of expertise focuses on the analysis of kinship and family ties. Her previous books include *Biology Unmoored: Melanesian Reflections on Life and Biotechnology* (2007) and *Kinship and Beyond: The Genealogical Model Reconsidered* (2009, coedited with James Leach).

CAMBRIDGE HANDBOOKS IN ANTHROPOLOGY

Genuinely broad in scope, each handbook in this series provides a complete state-of-the-field overview of a subdiscipline or major topic of anthropological study and research. Grouped into broad thematic areas, the chapters in each volume encompass the most important issues and themes within each subject, offering a coherent picture of the latest theories and findings. Together, the volumes will build into an integrated overview of the discipline in its entirety.

The Cambridge Handbook of Kinship

Edited by
Sandra Bamford
University of Toronto

CAMBRIDGE
UNIVERSITY PRESS

CAMBRIDGE
UNIVERSITY PRESS

Shaftesbury Road, Cambridge CB2 8EA, United Kingdom

One Liberty Plaza, 20th Floor, New York, NY 10006, USA

477 Williamstown Road, Port Melbourne, VIC 3207, Australia

314–321, 3rd Floor, Plot 3, Splendor Forum, Jasola District Centre, New Delhi – 110025, India

103 Penang Road, #05–06/07, Visioncrest Commercial, Singapore 238467

Cambridge University Press is part of Cambridge University Press & Assessment, a department of the University of Cambridge.

We share the University's mission to contribute to society through the pursuit of education, learning and research at the highest international levels of excellence.

www.cambridge.org
Information on this title: www.cambridge.org/9781107697744

DOI: 10.1017/9781139644938

First published 2019
First paperback edition 2023

A catalogue record for this publication is available from the British Library

Library of Congress Cataloging-in-Publication data
Names: Bamford, Sandra C., 1962– editor.
Title: The Cambridge handbook of kinship /
edited by Sandra Bamford.
Description: Cambridge; New York, NY:
Cambridge University Press, 2019. |
Series: Cambridge handbooks in anthropology |
Includes bibliographical references and index.
Identifiers: LCCN 2018048914 | ISBN 9781107041189
(hardback : alk. paper) | ISBN 9781107697744 (pbk. : alk. paper)
Subjects: LCSH: Kinship–Handbooks, manuals, etc.
Classification: LCC GN480 .C34 2019 | DDC 306.83–dc23
LC record available at https://lccn.loc.gov/2018048914

ISBN   978-1-107-04118-9   Hardback
ISBN   978-1-107-69774-4   Paperback

Contents

Figures

Tables

Contributors

Sandra Bamford Associate Professor, Anthropology, University of Toronto.

Zsuzsa Berend Instructor and Academic Administrator, Departmental Honors Program, Sociology, University of California, Los Angeles.

Daphna Birenbaum-Carmeli Associate Professor, Nursing, University of Haifa.

Deborah A. Boehm Professor, Anthropology and Gender, Race, and Identity, Anthropology, University of Nevada, Reno.

Fenella Cannell Associate Professor/Reader, Anthropology, London School of Economics.

Janet Carsten Professor of Social and Cultural Anthropology, School of Social and Political Science, University of Edinburgh.

Isabelle Clark-Decès Anthropology, Princeton University (Deceased).

Nicole Constable Research Professor, UCIS; Professor of Anthropology and Gender, Sexuality and Women's Studies, University of Pittsburgh.

Carol Delaney Associate Professor, Emerita, Anthropology, Stanford University.

Janet Dolgin Dicker Distinguished Professor of Law, Maurice A. Deane School of Law, Hofstra University; Professor of Science Education, Zucker School of Medicine, Hofstra/Northwell; Director, Gitenstein Institute of Health Law and Policy (Hofstra Law); Co-Director, Hofstra Bioethics Center.

Lieba Faier Associate Professor, Geography, University of California, Los Angeles.

Gillian Feeley-Harnik Professor (Emerita), Anthropology, University of Michigan, Ann Arbor.

Sarah Franklin Professor of Sociology, Sociology, University of Cambridge.

Christine Ward Gailey Anthropology, University of California, Riverside.

Tine M. Gammeltoft Professor, Anthropology, University of Copenhagen.

Kathryn E. Goldfarb Assistant Professor, Anthropology, University of Colorado, Boulder.

Zeynep B. Gürtin Lecturer in Women's Health, Institute for Women's Health, University College London.

Valerie Hartouni Professor, Communication, University of California, San Diego.

Signe Howell Professor (Emerita), Social Anthropology, University of Oslo.

Marcia C. Inhorn William K. Lanman, Jr. Professor, Anthropology and International Affairs, Yale University.

Tsipy Ivry Senior Lecturer, Chair of the Graduate Program in Medical and Psychological Anthropology, Anthropology, University of Haifa.

Eleana Kim Associate Professor, Anthropology, University of California, Irvine.

Gail Landsman Associate Professor (Emerita), Anthropology, University at Albany, State University of New York.

James Leach Directeur de recherche, CNRS. Professor of Anthropology, Centre de Recherche et de Documentation sur l'Océanie (CREDO), Aix-Marseille Université/University of Western Australia.

Jessaca Leinaweaver Professor, Anthropology, Brown University.

Ellen Lewin Professor in the Departments of Gender, Women's and Sexuality Studies and Anthropology, University of Iowa.

Susan McKinnon Professor Emerita, Anthropology, University of Virginia.

Hollis Moore Visiting Assistant Professor, The School of Justice Studies, Eastern Kentucky University.

Sarah Pinto Professor, Anthropology, Tufts University.

Koreen M. Reece Postdoctoral Research Fellow, Anthropology, University of Edinburgh.

Elly Teman Senior Lecturer in Anthropology, Behavioral Sciences, Ruppin Academic Center, Israel.

Soraya Tremayne Research Associate, Institute of Social and Cultural Anthropology, University of Oxford.

Noa Vaisman Assistant Professor, Anthropology, Aarhus University, Denmark.

Mary Weismantel Professor, Anthropology, Northwestern University.

Mary Elena Wilhoit Assistant Professor of Anthropology, Lyon College.

1

Introduction: Conceiving Kinship in the Twenty-First Century

Sandra Bamford

1.1 Beginnings

In September 2016, Dr. John Zhang – a New York fertility specialist – made an announcement which was seen by some as holding out incredible promise, while for others spelled impending doom. Using a novel technique known as mitochondrial replacement therapy (MRT), he created a baby using the DNA of three people. In an interview, Zhang told *New Scientist* that he had performed the procedure for a Jordanian couple and that the resulting embryo was born in April of 2017 (Reardon 2016). According to published accounts, the boy's mother carried a "rare genetic condition known as Leighs syndrome: a neurological disorder which is caused by faulty mitochondria" (Mullin 2017) which are passed on exclusively through women. Although the embryo was created in New York City, it was transferred to the mother's uterus in Mexico in order to circumvent US regulatory procedures which currently prohibit the creation of genetically modified embryos.

MRT was developed to prevent the transmission of hereditary diseases "caused by mutations in the mitochondrial genome": the cells energy-producing structures (Knoppers et al. 2017). The Mitochondrial Disease Foundation in Pittsburgh, Pennsylvania states that between 1,000 and 4,000 children are born each year in the United States alone with significant mitochondrial conditions (Shoot 2015). While mitochondrial diseases affect relatively few families, the results can be catastrophic. Some of the more common mitochondrial conditions include heart problems, muscular dystrophy, vision loss, and stroke-like episodes (Shoot 2015). Many children who have inherited these conditions die within their first few years of life (Shoot 2015; cf. Wrigley, Wilkinson and Appleby 2015).

Mitochondrial Replacement Therapy has the potential of allowing parents who are at risk of transmitting a mitochondrial disorder to their offspring to have a healthy child, and one to whom they are both genetically related (Wrigley, Wilkinson and Appleby 2015). The version of MRT that Dr. Zhang used is referred to as Maternal Spindle Transfer (MST).[1] The procedure begins by obtaining a healthy egg from a donor and removing that egg's nucleus. Into this enucleated (i.e., hollowed-out) egg are injected the chromosomes of the intending mother (Mullin 2017). The reconstituted egg is then fertilized, and the resulting embryo is implanted into the womb of the intending mother. The mitochondria provided by the donor give energy to the cells, but do not code for physical traits such as eye and hair color, skin tone, stature, IQ, etc. (Shoot 2015). What this means is that roughly 99 percent of the resulting egg's genetic material comes from the mother who intends to raise the baby.

While MRT has the potential to eliminate a variety of debilitating conditions, the technique remains controversial and is currently banned in most countries. Because the long-term consequences of the procedure are unknown, emerging ethical guidelines suggest that if the technique were to become widely available, it should be carried out only on male embryos who would be incapable of passing on the donated mitochondria to future generations (Reardon 2016). Some commentators have also flagged social and ethical concerns: should children born through this technique have the right to know the identity of the egg donor (Lioke and Reame 2016; Newson, Wilkinson and Wrigley 2016: 589)? Although the resulting child would receive only a small percentage of their overall genetic makeup from the donor (i.e., 37 genes of an estimated 20,000 total), some studies have suggested that mitochondrial genes may play a role in mental illness so the genetic contribution from the egg donor is not irrelevant (Lioke and Reame 2016).

For his part, Dr. Zhang sees a bright future for MRT. Buoyed by his success with the Jordanian couple, Zhang has decided to pursue the commercial applications of MRT and has opened up a company called Darwin Life with a decidedly bold mission – to assist older women in becoming pregnant by having their DNA transferred to a younger woman's eggs (Mullin 2017; cf. Bhattacharya 2017).[2] Zhang claims that this will be a "cure for infertility" (Mullin 2017) and says Darwin Life will offer the service to women in their mid to late forties.[3] The procedure will cost US$80,000–120,000 per cycle and Zhang estimates that it will generate over two billion dollars in sales per year (Mullin 2017). Because the technique remains illegal in the US, Zhang says that Darwin Life will continue to make embryos in the US but will perform the embryo transfer at his New Hopes clinic in Guadalajara, Mexico, or in other countries that do not have the same regulatory red tape. In an interview, Zhang stated: "For now our nuclear transfer technique is very much like an iPhone that is designed in California but assembled in China" (Mullin 2017).

***

In January of 2018, the Associated Press published an article with the following title: "Gay Couple Married in Canada sues U.S. Government for Denying Citizenship to Child" (Melley 2018). The article went on to describe the plight of Aiden and Ethan Dvash-Banks – 16-month-old twins, "born only minutes apart from the same womb and to the same fathers" (Fadel 2018). Like most twins, Aiden and Ethan have much in common, but there is one thing that they do not share: Aiden has been granted US citizenship while Ethan has not. This discrepancy has recently become the basis of a legal suit which is winding its way through the US court system and is highlighting in the process the significant social inequalities that continue to exist for members of the LGBTQ community, notwithstanding the recent legalization of same-sex marriage.

The fathers of the twins, Andrew and Elad Dvash-Banks, met ten years ago while both were attending university in Tel Aviv (Levin 2018). Andrew was a US citizen and Elad an Israeli. After dating for several years, they got married in Canada in 2010 – at a time when same-sex marriage was still illegal in the United States. The couple were hoping to have children and to eventually move to California where Andrew was raised and where his family still lived (Levin 2018). Their twins were born to a surrogate in September 2016 and according to the pending lawsuit, both boys should have been eligible by birth to apply for US citizenship since each had a father who had been born in the United States. The boys had been conceived by the same surrogate using donor eggs and sperm donated from each father (Melley 2018).

It was only when the Dvash-Banks family went to the US consulate in Toronto to obtain passports for their sons that they realized a problem existed. According to Andrew, at the time of their application, the couple were asked a series of "invasive and embarrassing" questions having to do with how their sons had been conceived (Fadel 2018; cf. Melley 2018). The consular officer refused to process their applications without a DNA test to confirm biological paternity for each child. A few months later, two packages arrived. The one addressed to Aiden contained a passport along with a note saying, "Congratulations on your U.S. citizenship." Ethan's envelope contained a different message: "We regret to inform you that your application for U.S. citizenship has been denied" (Fadel 2018). When asked for clarification, the State Department claimed that it "could not comment on pending lawsuits," but drew attention to a clause on its website which reads: "at least one biological parent must have been a U.S. citizen when the child was born for the child to qualify for birthright citizenship" (BBC News 2018).

While awaiting their case to be heard, the Dvash-Banks family has since moved to Los Angeles having acquired a temporary tourist visa for Ethan, which has since lapsed (Melley 2018). The family of four is challenging the decision of the State Department claiming that it discriminates against LGBTQ people by "denying birthright citizenship to the children of gay couples based on blood relationships" (Levin 2018). Even though both fathers are listed on the boys' birth certificates, the fact that Ethan's father was born in Israel is enough to disqualify his son from being granted American citizenship. Heterosexual couples are not subject to the same level of scrutiny, and their children would not be denied citizenship on the basis of having bi-national parents. "The message is that you are not fully equal. Your family is less than other families," said Andrew Dvash-Banks in a recent interview (Levin 2018).

Immigration Equality – a gay rights advocate group – has launched a lawsuit in the Supreme Court on behalf of the Dvash-Banks family. A second suit has been filed, under identical circumstances, on behalf of a lesbian couple, Allison Blixt and Stefania Zaccari. According to Aaron Morris, the executive director of Immigration Equality, "the State Department is treating same sex couples as if they were not married and are disenfranchising their children" (Levin 2018). Morris further contends that the problem emerged under the Obama administration after the Defense of Marriage Act (DOMA) was overturned, thereby opening the door to same-sex marriage. As stated in the suit, this decision violates the Immigration and Nationality Act, which states that children "born abroad are U.S. Citizens at birth when one of the child's parents is married to a U.S. citizen" (BBC News 2018). It is expected that the resolution of this case will have far-reaching implications with respect to gay and lesbian rights, not to mention the definition of citizenship in the United States.

***

Inga Whatcott thought she hit "pay-dirt" when at the age of 12 she was adopted from overseas. Having grown up in a Russian orphanage after having been abandoned by her biological mother who worked in the sex trade, Inga was adopted by an American couple – Pricilla and Neal Whatcott in 1997. Interviewed in 2013, Inga remembers thinking to herself: "I'm gonna' have a family, I'm gonna' go to school, I'm gonna' have friends" (Twohey 2013d). Only a few months after bringing her to the United States, Inga's adoptive parents gave up trying to raise her. The Whatcotts claim that the agency who handled the adoption failed to inform them that Inga had significant emotional and behavioral issues: that she "suffered from depression, post-traumatic stress disorder, that she smoked" and that she had been previously abused and was functionally illiterate (Twohey 2013d). The Whatcotts' claim they tried to find a solution to their difficulties through counseling and support groups. They also contacted a Russian judge in an effort to nullify the adoption. When all things failed, Neil and Patricia turned to what Pricilla now calls the "underground network" (Twohey 2013d). They posted an ad on the Internet in an effort to find a new home for their daughter. This would be the second time that Inga was abandoned, but it wouldn't be the last. Over the next six months, Inga was profiled online by the Whatcotts three additional times. No one wanted to keep her and no governmental agency played any role in tracking her whereabouts whatsoever.

An investigative report published by Reuters in 2013 helped to expose a growing and disturbing phenomenon that has come to be known as "private rehoming" in child welfare circles. Through Yahoo! and Facebook groups (sometimes even Craigslist and Kijiji) parents who have come to regret an adoption advertise their unwanted children online and pass them on to persons they have never met (Twohey 2013a, 2013c). According to the Reuters report, loopholes in custody transfer laws allow parents to give away their children through online message boards with little or no government screening or oversight (Davidson and Whalen 2014). When the underground network is used, the only persons who vet the child's new home are the parents who want to nullify the adoption in the first place. In the words of one mother who was completely at her wits' end: "I was so sick of this kid that I would have given her to a serial killer" (Twohey 2013b).

As the victim of a "disrupted adoption," Inga's experiences are not unique. In their investigative report, Reuters analyzed over 5,000 online messages about rehoming in North America dating from September 2007 to September 2012. On one Yahoo! forum alone – Adoption from Disruption – a child was offered up for rehoming approximately once a week for five years (Twohey 2013a). Most of the online posts described the children as having "special needs," including Reactive Attachment Disorder (RAD), emotional or physical disabilities, fetal alcohol syndrome, and/or autism. After learning about the results of the Reuters report, Yahoo! closed down Adoption from Disruption (Twohey 2013a). The company also shut down five additional Internet forums that Reuters brought to their attention (Twohey 2013a). In the wake of these closures, rehoming sites have moved more deeply underground where they can be accessed on a "members only" basis (Davidson and Whalen 2014). The unregulated nature of this market makes it particularly dangerous. Although some children have ended up in stable home environments, many others have been thrown into very dark places and have become the undocumented victims of sexual, emotional, and physical abuse. Born through the rapid proliferation of social media platforms, private rehoming exists in a gray zone between informal adoption and child trafficking.

***

The three vignettes which open this handbook have all recently captured the popular imagination and have made headline news in many parts of the world. Despite their diversity, all of these cases share in common one important feature – they help to highlight the sweeping changes that have been taking place with respect to how kin connections are imagined, formed, and administered in the twenty-first century. An interest in kinship has long been central to the discipline of anthropology. Indeed, anthropology emerged as a distinct academic field in the mid-nineteenth century when scholarly attention began to focus on comparative kin relations. Well over a century later, the study of kinship continues to occupy a privileged place within the discipline. In what was once a highly popular introductory text on the topic, Robin Fox writes: "Kinship is to anthropology what logic is to philosophy, or the nude is to art; it is the basic discipline of the subject" (1967: 10). This handbook will help to highlight why kinship has often been said to hold this pride of place.

This collection is a state-of-the-field survey that captures the many important contributions that the study of kinship has made to anthropology – both as a fledgling discipline in the mid-nineteenth century, and continuing on through more recent years. Consisting of 29 original chapters, each written by a specialist in the field, this collection explores the history of kinship studies and the many different directions in which it has moved over the past few decades. Drawing upon research undertaken across the globe (Africa, India, South America, Malaysia, the Middle East, Asia, the Pacific, Europe, and North America), the chapters in this handbook demonstrate the continuing power of kinship theory to address many questions of broad anthropological concern, and to cast light on some of today's most pressing social issues: How have recent advances in reproductive medicine fundamentally altered our understanding "life" and different biological forms? How has globalization, coupled with the spread of late capitalism, brought in its wake new ways of imagining human relatedness? How might recent shifts in state welfare policies (particularly with the rise of neoliberalism in many parts of the globe) impacted how families operate on a day-to-day basis? How do recent shifts in global capitalism, coupled with the emergence of new political forms, both inform and take their inspiration from kin relations? Addressing these, and a wealth of other questions, this collection presents the results of cutting-edge research and helps to demonstrate why it is that the study of kinship is likely to remain at the core of anthropological inquiry in the years to come.

In November 2017, at the annual meetings of the American Anthropological Association (held that year in Washington DC), I had the opportunity to meet up with a cherished colleague whom I hadn't seen for quite some time. He is a fellow anthropologist, but his area of specialization lies far outside the field of kinship studies. As we talked about recent developments in the field, he confessed to me that he often feels ill-equipped to advise any of his own graduate students when they come to him with questions about kinship. He, like many of his students, has only the sketchiest knowledge about kinship studies, let alone how the field has changed over time. He then recounted to me his own truncated understanding of the field, one that I have subsequently come to realize is shared by the vast majority of non-specialists. Evolutionary theorists like Morgan (1870, 1877) and Maine (1861) helped to put kinship studies on the map. During the 1930s, 1940s, and 1950s, anthropologists (most of whom were trained in the structural-functionalist vein, and who worked in Africa) imported many of their own ethnocentric Euro-American assumptions about kinship into their own purportedly objective ethnographic accounts. David Schneider, in his two most celebrated works, *American Kinship* (1968) and *A Critique of the Study of Kinship* (1984), offered up a devastating critique of these works in which he revealed that previous studies of kinship were flawed in that they were little more than an imposition of Euro-American folk ideas about relatedness upon the social worlds of other people. In the wake of Schneider's publications, kinship studies all but disappeared. There has only – and very recently – been a renewed interest in the field, prompted in large part by the advent of new reproductive technologies (NRTs) in the West.

One very important aim of this handbook is to serve as a corrective to this history which errs on several counts. It assumes: (1) that there is a hard and fast distinction between what is sometimes called the "old" and "new" kinship studies, (2) that kinship studies all but vanished in the wake of Schneider's work and only very recently have become the subject of renewed scholarly interest, and (3) that studies of NRTs constitute, for the most part, what has taken place in the field of kinship studies over the past few decades.

The chapters in this collection serve as an eloquent testament to the immense breadth that characterizes contemporary kinship studies. While studies of NRTs have certainly contributed immeasurably to the field of kinship studies and have precipitated a radical re-questioning of what it means to be "related" to other persons and other species (and not only in the West but across the globe as well), the chapters which follow aptly demonstrate the incredible diversity that characterizes contemporary kinship scholarship. Recent studies in the field deal not only with NRTs, but also with the challenges that often accompany family-making in an increasingly globalized world. Another key focus has to do with the "politics of reproduction" and the degree to which the state (and or other powerful actors/agencies) play a role in legitimizing what relationships can count as "kinship." The degree to which biological reproduction plays a role in defining relatedness (and if so, how, and to what degree) resurfaces as a theme in many of the following chapters, including how such interpretations have changed (and continue to change) over time. What will be immediately apparent is that contemporary kinship studies deal with a wide range of topics and themes, which go well beyond the social and ethical impact of NRTs.

We shall also see throughout this collection that the distinction between what has sometimes been called "old" and "new" kinship studies is not quite so hard and fast as it seems. Throughout this handbook, it will become evident that several continuities exist between "traditionalist" and "revisionist" works in the field. Far from leaving our theoretical roots behind, contemporary and cutting-edge works are often very much informed by many of the questions and issues that were raised in the past. Several chapters in this handbook also look back upon the history of the field and offer up new insights concerning previous debates and theoretical schools. Through the lens of contemporary works, it becomes possible to view the contributions and limitations of older works in a new light, and to gain an appreciation for how previous scholarship has continued to influence newer works and will likely continue to do so in the future. In the process, important continuities and disjunctures are revealed in the history of anthropological theorizing and new directions for future research are suggested.

In order to set the stage for the chapters which follow, I turn my attention in the next section to a necessarily abbreviated history of the role that kinship studies played in the development of anthropological theory.

1.2   Kinship Studies and Anthropology

Attempting to capture the breadth of kinship studies from an historical perspective is a daunting, if not impossible task, and certainly not one that I aspire to in the following pages. What I offer up instead is a highly truncated and selective intellectual history in which many significant figures and scholarly debates will be left out. There are several full-length books that do an admirable job in discussing kinship studies from an historical perspective. These include, Robert Parkin's *Kinship: An Introduction to Basic Concepts* (1977); Adam Kuper's *The Invention of Primitive Society* (1988); Ladislav Holý's *Anthropological Perspectives on Kinship* (1996); and Janet Carsten's *After Kinship* (2004). Furthermore, as noted above, many of the chapters that follow also address the intellectual history of the field. Thus, the following short account is by no means comprehensive: what I strive to do is to highlight some of the key texts or debates which played an important role in how the field developed.

Anthropology's fascination with kinship first took root in the mid to late nineteenth century. The publication in 1861 of *Ancient Law* by Sir Henry Sumner Maine played a key role in getting the conversation under way. Trained as a lawyer, Maine was interested in the "patriarchal joint family" – an extended kinship group consisting of a despotic father and his sons holding property in common. This type of family was common in many parts of India, and Maine believed it represented the original (i.e., primordial) family form throughout much of the world. In *Ancient Law*, Maine was interested in setting forth the argument that as societies moved from being "simple" to "complex," there was a corresponding movement from being based on "status" to being based on "contract." For Maine, the term "status" referred to the ascribed rights and duties that flowed from being a member of a family. The world of "status" was juxtaposed to the world of "contract" wherein individuals were seen to be autonomous agents free to enter into contracts and to form associations with whomever they pleased. As Maine describes his vision of social history:

> The movement of the progressive societies has been uniform in one respect. Through all its course, it has been distinguished by the gradual dissolution of family dependency and the growth of individual obligations in its place. The individual is steadily substituted for the Family, as the unit of which civil laws take account.
>
> *(1861: 163)*

According to Maine, it was the practice of incorporating waifs and strays into the extended patriarchal joint family through adoption (i.e., legal fictions) which eventually led to its dissolution. While these new additions to the family initially strengthened the unit, in time, the "hereditary members of the inner core" (Kuper 1988: 26) began to discriminate against members of the group who were not related to it by blood. As the population of these marginalized citizens continued to grow, they banded together on the basis of their similar interests and developed an alternative logic of civil society. This paved the way for the growth of modern, state-based social forms. As we shall witness in several of the chapters that follow (see in particular the contributions by McKinnon, Reece, and Cannell), Maine's work was to have a lasting impact on anthropology. In particular, he popularized the idea that so-called "primitive" societies were organized on the basis of kinship, while so-called "modern" ones were based on "contract."

The work of Lewis Henry Morgan (1870, 1877) gave further impetus to the early development of an interest in kinship. Born in upper state New York, Morgan began to visit a local Iroquois reservation as a young man, where he collected ethnographic information. Over the course of his research, Morgan noticed that the Iroquois method of classifying kinspersons was markedly different from that which characterized his own society. The term "father," for example, was applied not only to one's male biological parent, but was extended to many other men in the community as well. The word for "mother" was used in a similarly expansive way. To make sense of this phenomenon, Morgan began to collect kinship terminologies from different parts of the world and from reports of societies that existed in classic antiquity (1877). Morgan noticed that many societies, separated in time and space, had similar ways of classifying kin (Fox 1967: 19). On the basis of this insight, he drew a distinction between what he called "classificatory" and "descriptive" kinship systems. Classificatory systems grouped "distinct" biological relatives together (for example, one's "father" and "father's" brother may be referred to by the same kinship term); descriptive systems, by contrast, used distinct terms for "different" categories of biological kin.[4] Operating with the assumption that kin terms were used to refer to biological relatives, Morgan postulated a theory to account for these different systems of nomenclature. If a terminological system designated many men as "father," then perhaps this indicated that in the not so distant past, the society in question practiced a form of group marriage in which many men could conceivably be the biological father of the child. Like Maine, Morgan then put his theory into an evolutionary framework wherein "simple" (or ancient) societies progressed through a series of stages from "primitive promiscuity" to a system based on monogamy, wherein biological paternity could be fairly certain. Occurring in tandem with these shifting social changes were changes in subsistence practices and the rise of private property (Morgan 1877).

Like Maine, Morgan's ideas were to leave a lasting legacy on the future of kinship studies. A distinction between "social" (i.e., classificatory) versus "biological" (i.e., descriptive) kinship came to be mapped onto a corresponding distinction between "primitive" vs. "modern" society. As Sarah Franklin and Helena Ragoné have pointed out, many nineteenth-century accounts of comparable social organization focused much of their attention on documenting diverse cultural beliefs about procreation, or what Euro-Americans "colloquially called the 'facts of life'" (Franklin and Ragoné 1998a: 1). For many early kinship theorists, acquiring "accurate" (i.e., bio-scientific) knowledge of how offspring were produced signaled a critical stage in the transition from "savagery" to "civilization," characterized by the triumph of "reason" over "nature" (Franklin 1998: 102). Emerging amid the intellectual furor that accompanied the publication of *The Origin of Species* (Darwin 1859), biology came to be seen as the "true" basis of kinship giving kin ties a seemingly "real" and "primordial" basis.

The publication of W. H. R. Rivers' essay, "The Genealogical Method of Anthropological Inquiry" in 1910, further solidified the attention that was given to reproductive knowledge as the basis of cross-cultural comparison. As Mary Bouquet has argued, Rivers intended nothing less than to establish ethnography as a science "as exact as physics or chemistry" (Bouquet 1993: 114). Toward this end, he enjoined fieldworkers to obtain "basic information on relatedness," by collecting genealogical data as a standard component of ethnographic research.

As proposed by Rivers, the genealogical method entailed two essential tasks. First, the fieldworker collected a "pedigree" consisting of the proper names of relatives of a particular individual. Next, the local terms for addressing these persons (i.e., a set of kinship terms) was collected. Rivers contended that through the use of this technique it would be possible to discern the thought process through which individuals in the culture being studied classified kinspersons within their social universe. Having grasped the cultural logic that informed reproductive arrangements, it was then possible to examine how this conceptual framework organized the society in question: how it structured the formation of local groups, marriage arrangements, domestic relations, and broader political processes. Rivers described the utility of this method in "The Genealogical Method of Anthropological Inquiry." Here he notes: "By means of the genealogical method, it is possible with no knowledge of the language and with very inferior interpreters, to work out with the utmost accuracy systems of kinship so complicated that Europeans who have spent their whole lives among the people have never been able to grasp them" (1910: 107).

The development of the genealogical method was to significantly influence the history of anthropology thinking. Seeming to offer up the promise of scientific objectivity, this toolkit was enthusiastically adopted by field researchers for many years to come. As Mary Bouquet has noted in an influential essay, Rivers' focus on pedigree as the paramount tool of cross-cultural research "paved the way for kinship to become the center-piece of British social anthropology during the first half of the twentieth century" (Bouquet 1993: 208). Whatever else an ethnographer might seek to document in his or her research, a description of the kinship system was an essential component of anthropological inquiry (see Bamford and Leach 2009 for a detailed discussion concerning the importance of genea-logical thinking in the history of anthropology).

In the decades immediately following the publication of Rivers' influ-ential essay, generations of anthropologists set off for distant parts of the globe, armed with a methodological tool kit with which they thought they could build a truly comparative science of humankind. During the 1920s, 1930s, and 1940s, the work of Malinowski (1922, 1929), A. R. Radcliffe-Brown (1922, 1931, 1940, 1952), E. Evans-Pritchard (1940, 1951), and Meyer Fortes (1945, 1949) proved to be particularly influential in championing the study of kinship (defined largely in genealogical terms) as a necessary component in the analysis of non-Western societies. As Adam Kuper (1988) has pointed out, taken together, these works (along with others) eventually shored up an interest in understanding how "stateless" societies were organized on the basis of descent groups, and how these groups were defined and perpetuated through time. Even as late as 1967, J. A. Barnes described the collection of genealogical infor-mation as "part of the ethnographer's minimum obligation for making fieldwork intelligible to others" (quoted in Bouquet 1996: 43). (See Feeley-Harnik – Chapter 3 – this volume, for a detailed look at many of these works.)

French alliance theory – associated predominately with the work of Claude Lévi-Strauss – existed as something of a theoretical outlier to those works described above. For structural functionalists, whose primary con-cern was the workings of descent groups, marriage was significant only insomuch as it provided a means of producing legitimate offspring who were needed to perpetuate the kin group through time. The publication of Lévi-Strauss' *Les structures élémentaires de la parenté* in 1949 (translated into English as *The Elementary Structures of Kinship* in 1969) raised an entirely different set of questions. Lévi-Strauss begins his massive tome by asking why it is that all societies the world over have some kind of prohibition on incest. After dispelling some of the most common explanations for the taboo (including that inbreeding produces degenerative offspring), he concluded that marrying outside one's immediate group forces men to enter into relationships of exchange with other men building those broader social connections that are constitutive of culture or society. A man must renounce his sister as a possible spouse because she is his point of entry into alliances with other men:

> Exchange – and consequently the rule of exogamy that expresses it – has in itself a social value. It provides the means of binding men together and superimposing on the natural links of kinship, the henceforth artificial links ... of alliance governed by rule.
>
> *(Lévi-Strauss 1949 [1969]: 480)*

In his text, Lévi-Strauss drew upon a massive amount of evidence to support his conclusion that different ways of circulating women to men in marriage have different consequences with respect to the overall integration of society. For Lévi-Strauss, the real difference between societies the world over lay not in how they conceptualized and acted upon relationships of descent, but rather how they structured matrimonial arrangements. From this perspective, the task that lay before ethnographers had little to do with charting parent–child ties, but rather documenting different patterns of marriage.

David Schneider played a significant, although by no means exclusive, role in bringing the existing house of cards tumbling down. He did this by questioning the foundation upon which nearly a century of anthropological research had been based. In his first major work, *American Kinship: A Cultural Account* (1968), Schneider strove to illuminate the cultural assumptions that informed North American kinship configurations. He argued that North American kinship logic rested on a distinction between what he called the "order of nature" and the "order of law." He argued that in the worldview of North Americans, one can be related "by blood" (that is, in nature), or one can be related "in law" (that is, by marriage/social conventions). Schneider further argued that coitus operated as a core symbol in American kinship insomuch as it provided a bridge between these two seemingly distinct domains:

> The family is defined by American culture as a "natural" unit which is "based on the facts of nature ..." The fact of nature which is the cultural construct of the family is that of sexual intercourse. This figure provides all of the cultural symbols of American kinship. This figure is formulated in American culture as a biological entity and a natural act. Yet throughout each element which is culturally defined as

"natural" is at the same time augmented and elaborated, built upon and informed by the rule of human reason, embodied in law and morality.

(Schneider 1968: 40)

To the degree that Schneider documented that Euro-American understandings of kinship were culturally constructed, the implications of his study were far reaching. Schneider suggested that Euro-Americans drew upon a distinction between "social" and "biological" kinship to classify different kinspersons in their social universe. Even more significantly, he suggested that because these categories had informed research abroad, anthropology had failed as a "science" to grasp much of anything about the world. For many years, cultural anthropology had defined itself as occupying a unique place in the social sciences by virtue of its seemingly "obsessive" interest in matters pertaining to kinship and succession (Franklin and Ragoné 1998a: 1). Any particular kinship system was seen to be a cultural elaboration on the basic "facts" of human reproduction. It was the task of sociocultural anthropology to document the different interpretations that each society placed on procreative arrangements. But if the distinction between "social" versus "biological" kinship was a culturally specific one, then what exactly was it that fieldworkers had been studying?

In his second major work, *A Critique of the Study of Kinship* (1984), Schneider confronted this question in detail. He suggested that what anthropologists had been studying (or thought they had been studying), for well over a century was little more than a reflection of our own cultural assumptions taken to different parts of the globe. The very idea that people everywhere drew upon the "facts" of human heterosexual reproduction as a basis for classifying kin said more about the symbolic logic of Euro-American kinship than it did about the cultures that ethnographers claimed to be studying.

In the course of destabilizing the universal basis of kinship, Schneider simultaneously dismantled kinship as an independently existing analytical domain (Weston 1995: 89). Having cast aside the subfield's procreative basis, Schneider challenged the foundations upon which kinship as a domain of theorizing rested. He did so by showing that kinship was not the "same thing" in all cultures. If this was the case, then the comparative mission of anthropology had been called into question (Carsten 2000: 25) since "like" was not being compared with "like." Having lost its procreative underpinnings, the study of kinship seemed to lose its place as an object of analytical inquiry.

While Schneider is often credited with dismantling orthodox approaches to kinship, he was not entirely alone in this endeavor. Ernest Gellner (1957) and Rodney Needham (1960) had also voiced concerns about the many unexamined assumptions that framed existing accounts of kinship

(Franklin and McKinnon 2001: 3). Furthermore, as Sarah Franklin points out, feminist scholars had long been troubling the use of an essentialized biological framework as the basis for grounding a system of sexual differences. "Not only had feminist anthropologists been critiquing the natural basis of gender (and even the idea of there being a natural basis for anything) long before Schneider examined the cultural role of biology in American kinship systems, but they had also done so in more depth" (Franklin – Chapter 4 – this volume). The publication in 1980 of *Nature, Culture and Gender* (edited by MacCormack and Strathern) – four years before the appearance of Schneider's *Critique* – furnishes concrete evidence that a burgeoning wave of feminist anthropologists had already begun to trouble the essentializing qualities of biological discourse. Both the editors and the contributors to this anthology called into question the putative universality of the conceptual linkage of men and culture, women, and nature. Foreshadowing Schneider's later critique, they probed "the epistemological status of analytical models, and their relationship(s) to folk models in anthropological discourse" (Poole 1982: 593).

The publication of *Gender and Kinship: Essays toward a Unified Analysis* (1987), edited by Jane Collier and Sylvia Yanagisako, further destabilized the idea that kinship could be approached as an independently existing analytical domain. What the editors called for in this work was nothing short of a reorienting of anthropological approaches to kinship and gender. What had been taken as two distinct analytical domains must be approached as an integrated totality – a "social whole." Through a careful and insightful review of the history of these fields, they demonstrated that studies of gender and kinship had begun with precisely the same underlying assumption: namely, that innate (or natural) differences existed between people, and that these underlying distinctions form the basis upon which human creativity goes to work. Analysis then proceeds by examining how various rights and duties, along with their cultural meanings, map on to these existing biological differences. At the heart of this approach lies Euro-Americans' unquestioned acceptance concerning the biological basis of sexual reproduction. For Westerners, it is sexual intercourse that acts as the analytic fulcrum between male and female as gendered units on the one hand, and the units of kinship – the genealogical grid – on the other. In their concluding remarks, Yanagisako and Collier (1987) call for a unified frame of analysis, which would put an end to treating gender and kinship as separate analytical domains. Both fields rest on a singular assumption: the physiological basis of reproduction. Sexual intercourse becomes the analytic pivot that turns biological differences between male and female into offspring whose precise place can be plotted on a genealogical grid. Thus, "what have been conceptualized as two distinct fields of study constitute a single field that has not succeeded in freeing itself from notions about natural differences between people" (Yanagisako and Collier 1987: 15).

In the collection *Naturalizing Power* (1995), Yanagisako and Delaney (eds) took many of the aforementioned themes to their logical conclusion. The editors begin by noting that *American Kinship* paid virtually no attention to social inequalities (an issue that Schneider, himself, recognized). *Naturalizing Power* was centrally concerned with documenting how a wide variety of social inequalities – including those based on class, ethnicity, race, and gender – are naturalized in the discourses and practices of kinship, in the law, in the rhetoric of nationalism and religion, and in the stories Euro-Americans tell themselves about the "natural" world. In the words of the editors: "Inequality and hierarchy come already embedded in symbolic systems, as well as elaborated through contextualized material practices" (1995: ix–x). Put somewhat differently, the same discourses that inform Euro-American understandings of kinship inform a wide variety of seemingly unrelated fields. It follows that kinship, like all of the other cultural "domains" that have captured the interest of anthropologists (i.e., politics, religion, economics, etc.), is human-made, and only appears to be a given in the "natural order" of things.

In the wake of these burgeoning critiques, scholars were left with a dilemma: they could either abandon the study of kinship altogether, or they could embrace a far wider definition of the concept than had been used in earlier accounts. Over the past few decades, an attempt has been made in the latter direction. One important move has drawn attention to the notion of "relatedness" (Carsten 2000) in an effort to define kinship as a "process," rather than as a state of being. Scholars working in this vein have focused on creating embodied links through "purposeful acts of feeding, caring, loving, sharing and remembering" (Viveiros de Castro 2009: 257). Here, the overwhelming emphasis is on the "socially created" nature of consanguineal relations (2009: 257); on the ability to generate bonds of corporeal consubstantiality through conscious human effort (see Bamford & Leach 2009 for a fuller description of this trend).

Janet Carsten's (1995, 1997) research on the Maylays of Southeast Asia did much to put this intellectual approach on the map. In several highly influential publications, she argued that people on the island of Langkawi become "kin" through living and consuming together in houses. "Bodily substance," she notes, "is not something with which Maylays are simply born and remains forever unchanged … [instead] it gradually accrues and changes throughout life as a parson participates in social relationships." Mary Weismantel (1995) took a similar approach in her study of kinship among the Zumbagua of highland Ecuador where she demonstrated that intentional acts of feeding and sharing create embodied links between persons not otherwise connected through reproductive substance (cf. Leinaweaver 2008). These works did much to demonstrate that kin ties do not necessarily flow from biological reproduction – there are many other ways to form families and to ground kin connectedness. Studies of gay and lesbian kinship (Lewin 1993, 1998; Weston 1991, 1995; Hayden 1995) along with those of adoption (Gailey 2010; Modell 1994, 2002) also furnished important examples of how kinship can be created outside of the "ruling sign of biology" (Franklin and McKinnon 2001: 6).

Freed from its earlier emphasis on biological reproduction, contemporary studies of kinship have moved in a number of different directions. One important line of inquiry has examined how recent advances in biotechnology have prompted Euro-Americans (and more recently, persons the world over) to reflect on the social and ethical implications of what it means to create life in a clinic or laboratory setting, independent of a process of sexual intercourse. Marilyn Strathern's pioneering work *Reproducing the Future* (1992a) did much to show just how productive this line of inquiry could be. Inspired by the advent of new reproductive technologies (NRTs), coupled with the rise of Margaret Thatcher's "enterprise culture" in the United Kingdom, Strathern asks how we might think about a new "legal and social object in the world in the form of a human embryo in the very early stage of development, alive but outside the parental body" (1992a: 4). What kind of future follows from "increasingly sophisticated techniques of intervening" (1992a: 4) in the process of human reproduction? How does technological intervention potentially alter the social relationships that flow from procreation (see also Strathern 1992b)? Sarah Franklin expanded the scope of inquiry by examining the experiences of women and couples actually undergoing fertility treatments at two British IVF (in vitro fertilization) clinics. In *Embodied Progress* (1997) she documents the way in which IVF "takes over" and becomes "a way of life" for couples seeking a solution to involuntary childlessness (see also Andrews 1999; Davis-Floyd and Dumit 1998; Edwards et al. 1993; Edwards 2000; Hartouni 1997; Konrad 2005; Ragoné 1994; Thompson 2005, to name but a few). More recent studies have examined how these technologies have been taken up in a variety of non-Western settings, and the social, ethical, legal, and political complications that often arise as a consequence of their adoption (Clark 2009; Deomampo 2016; Inhorn 2012; Ivry 2010; Kahn 2000; Nahman 2013; Roberts 2012; Teman 2010).

Another highly productive move in recent years has been to examine kin connections that cross national and transnational boundaries. Changes in the global economy have precipitated significant shifts with respect to how love, intimacy, family life, and reproduction are imagined, negotiated, and lived on a day-to-day basis. Ginsburg and Rapp's anthology *Conceiving the New World Order: The Global Politics of Reproduction* (1995a) played a pivotal role in putting many of these issues on the table. Using the politics of reproduction as a lens through which to examine social life, the authors in this collection showed how individuals create or challenge significant aspects of their culture through their reproductive behavior. Several chapters in this volume examined the impact of global processes on reproduction and showcased a growing awareness of the "transnational inequalities on which reproductive practices and policies" (Ginsburg and Rapp 1995b: 1) are often based. Colen's article on "stratified reproduction," wherein she highlighted how some categories of persons are empowered to reproduce at the expense of others, proved to have incredible staying power and inspired many scholars in the years to come (Colen 1995). This collection was followed, almost a decade later, by *Global Women: Nannies, Maids, and Sex Workers in the New Economy* (Ehrenreich and Hoschild 2002), which further highlighted the importance of examining kinship within a global context. The chapters in this volume detail the lives of female migrants who are filling a growing care vacuum in many Euro-American countries. As First World women have entered the labor market in significant numbers, Third World women have been filling the gap that their departure creates in domestic labor, largely because First World men have refused to take on additional domestic work to any significant degree.

The publication in 2013 of *Vital Relations: Kinship as a Critique of Modernity* (McKinnon and Cannell) represents yet another significant intervention in the field of kinship studies, and returns us to some of the themes that were introduced by nineteenth-century thinkers. As we have seen, Euro-American ideas about modernity have long rested on the supposition that a contrast exists between "small-scale" and "modern" societies, wherein kinship is assumed to be of central importance in the former and to have receded and/or been subsumed by more powerful social formations in the latter. Put somewhat differently, the assumption has been that as societies move from being "simple" to "complex," kinship essentially withers away as an organizing principle and is replaced by relations organized on the basis of more powerful social forms (such as contract) (Maine 1861). Both the editors and contributors to this anthology challenge this system of ideas. Through nuanced case studies we are introduced to the important role that kinship plays in precipitating social, religious, legal, political, and social change. Far from being confined to the domestic sphere, kinship occupies a vital place in the workings of the modern nation-state, and it does so in multiple ways. A second important insight to emerge from this collection concerns the degree to which many of the ideas that informed nineteenth-century evolutionary theory continue to hold purchase in contemporary ethnographic accounts. This anthology serves as an important reminder of the need for ongoing reflexivity in anthropological reading, writing, and practice.

The chapters in this handbook provide a detailed analysis of these and many other significant developments. If it once looked as though kinship studies were doomed to obsolescence by virtue of their inability to move beyond the ethnocentric assumptions of Euro-American researchers, it now seems clear that there remains much to be done at both a theoretical and ethnographic level. "Kinship" is no longer what it appeared to be in the nineteenth and early twentieth centuries: how kin connections are constructed and lived on a day-to-day basis is subject to ongoing change (both in the West and the world over), as are the analytical and methodological tools employed by anthropologists to make sense of these arrangements. As the following chapters eloquently demonstrate, it is clear there remains much work to be done.

1.3   The Contents of This Book

This handbook is divided into six parts, each of which explores a key theme in contemporary kinship studies. The division into parts is, in some ways, artificial. Many of the chapters could easily fit into more than one part. The chapter by Boehm, for example, which explores Mexican families divided by the US–Mexico border, casts light not only on the nature of transnational kinship (Part IV), but also the role of the state in both making and breaking kin connections (Part VI). Similarly, the chapter by Franklin, which provides a detailed analysis of the different ways in which biology has been theorized (both within and outside the discipline of anthropology), could find a home in Part I, which focuses on theoretical trends, or Part II which examines the degree to which biology remains relevant (or not relevant) in contemporary discussions of kinship. Hence, while the chapters in each part "speak" to one another in important ways, there are also many productive "cross-cutting" conversations that take place between the different sections of this book.

Although the chapters in this handbook deal with a broad range of topics, certain themes run through the collection as a whole. First, it becomes clear in many of the studies that follow that kin relations are not always "warm and fuzzy," but can also be characterized by marked ambivalence. Until fairly recently, the dominant view in anthropology has been that kin connections are characterized by positive sentiments; they entail ties of mutual support and cooperation. This sentimentalized view of the family has much in common with David Schneider's findings in *American Kinship* (1968), wherein he demonstrated that North Americans tend to view kinship as entailing relationships of "diffuse, enduring, solidarity." More recently, Marshall Sahlins (2013) also focused on the amicable dimension of kin relations. Kinship, in his view, entails a "mutuality of being" (2013: 2), whereby "kinsfolk are members of one another, intrinsic to each other's identity and existence" (2013: 62). Both meaningfully and emotionally, "relatives live each other's lives and die each other's death" (2013: ix). Several of the chapters in this collection challenge the view that kinship is necessarily (or, even predominately) harmonious and conflict-free. This theme of disjuncture and/or exclusion surfaces, in one way or another, in the chapters by Goldfarb, Vaisman, Pinto, Gammeltoft, Constable, Landsman, and Reece.

A second insight that weaves through many of the chapters that follow concerns the utility of examining kin connections through time. As Janet Carsten notes (Chapter 6 – this volume), there has been a tendency in both older and newer studies of kinship to "focus on procreation and birth rather than other moments or processes such as death or succession." Holding the entire life course in view allows us to see certain dimensions of kinship which have previously been given short shrift. Carsten helpfully coins the terms "thickening" and "thinning" to describe the way in which kin connections may coalesce or dissolve through time. The chapters by Weismantel and Wilhoit, Constable, Faier, Boehm, Kim, and Moore are particularly helpful in documenting the degree to which kin ties ebb and flow through time.

A final theme that unites several chapters in this collection concerns the extent to which the state plays an active role in shaping the dynamics of family life. This is readily apparent in those chapters which examine the promulgation of policies that regulate the growing use of NRTs (see, Hartouni, Dolgin, Teman and Berend, and Ivry and Teman) not to mention the legal wranglings that often take place when the parentage of a particular child is under dispute (Hartouni, Dolgin). The chapters that deal with adoption and foster care in this handbook (Gailey, Leinaweaver, Kim, and Goldfarb) also provide striking examples of how the state makes certain kin-based connections visible while rendering others invisible and/or obsolete. The contributions by Vaisman, Gammeltoft, Boehm, Kim, McKinnon, Moore, Reece, and Cannell highlight a veritable host of additional ways in which the state is implicated in family life, including through the regulation of marriage and the active promotion of a given set of state-defined "family values."

In addressing these themes, along with many others, this collection unfolds in the following way.

Part I: Opening Frameworks examines the intellectual history of kinship studies in anthropology including how it has significantly shaped the overall trajectory of the discipline. The aim of this section is to present a balanced picture of both classical and more recent theoretical trends which not only examine some of the shortcomings in earlier studies, but also the many positive contributions they made in putting kinship studies on the map. More than simply constituting one topic among the many others that anthropology pursues, kinship has figured prominently in how anthropologists have conceptualized cultural difference, and has been used to distinguish anthropology as an academic discipline from other social sciences.

The first chapter in this section, written by Carol Delaney, examines the intersection of gender, kinship, and religion. Since the nineteenth century, kinship and religion have been understood to be separate social domains: one had to do with the "natural" world, the other with the "spiritual" one (see also Cannell, Chapter 30 – this volume). Through a careful analysis of both ethnographic and text-based material, Delany demonstrates the degree to which Euro-American theories of gender and procreation are intertwined with Biblical conceptions in such a way that the emerging framework naturalizes and legitimates a system of gender asymmetries. More specifically, the idea that males beget children by "planting their seed" in a fertile woman assigns men (but not women) an active and creative role in the elicitation of kin relations. This contribution helps to highlight how anthropological accounts of social life are often informed by a set of cultural assumptions seemingly far afield from the "domain" under investigation (cf. Yanagisako & Delaney 1995).

Chapter 3, written by Gillian Feeley-Harnik, is a detailed and nuanced account of the history of descent theory. More than simply trudging through a genealogy of key theorists, Feeley-Harnik analyzes the broader social and political context within which those ideas that informed descent theory were first formulated. She shows, for example, how the human manipulation of plants and animals brought about significant shifts with respect to how descent was imagined. Feeley-Harnik's contribution also importantly highlights the fact that theories of descent are never value neutral: they resonate with political agendas and furnish a metatheory that plays a key role in defining who should live and die.

In the next chapter, we turn our attention from the topic of descent to that of marriage. Isabelle Clark-Decès provides us with a compelling retrospective account of French alliance theory, including how it came to be caught up in anthropological interpretations of the gift. After reviewing the work of several key theorists (including Claude Lévi-Strauss and Louis Dumont) she documents how the orthodox model of alliance fails to capture the realities of South Indian kinship. In the process, she problematizes the degree to which it is possible to draw any hard and fast distinction between affines and consanguines (persons related by marriage and persons related by blood) – a distinction which informed much of classical kinship theory.

In the chapter which follows, Sarah Franklin provides a detailed analysis of the work of David Schneider. While acknowledging the significance of his insights to the development of anthropological theory, Franklin also demonstrates that his work was limited in several important ways. By failing to consider the critiques of biology that were being developed by feminist theorists at the same time (or even earlier), Schneider limited his project to a deconstruction of cultural categories, and failed to pursue the political implications that his work possibly engendered.

Chapter 6 by Janet Carsten concludes this section of the handbook. In a far-reaching and evocative exploration of recent works on kinship, Carsten outlines some of the more important directions in which kinship studies have moved in the past few years. A key theme to emerge throughout this chapter concerns how kinship is "made and dissolved through time": a process she refers to as "thickening" and "thinning." She also examines the different materials and processes through which this making and unmaking occurs. Her chapter offers up a wealth of ideas concerning where kinship studies may profitably venture in the future.

Having set out the historical and theoretical context within which kinship studies emerged, Part II: The (Non)Biological Basis of Relatedness, examines the extent to which biology serves (or does not serve) as the basis of human relatedness. This theme has been extensively debated within anthropological circles and was particularly relevant in the years that immediately followed the publication of David Schneider's (1968, 1984) work. The chapters in this section explore the potentially broad range of criteria upon which kin connections can be brought into being. The sharing of food, labor, or a common attachment to land may all serve as the origin of kinship relations. This section also looks at practices of adoption and the formation of LGBTQ families and the degree to which they are modeled upon or challenge orthodox Euro-American kin ideologies.

In Chapter 7, Kathryn Goldfarb examines how an *absence* of meaningful kin ties comes to be embodied in both children and adults in quite a literal sense. Focusing on children who have moved through the Japanese welfare system, she shows how their bodies are understood by institutional caregivers to express accumulated histories of both nurture and neglect (cf. Becker 1995). Anthropologists have long argued that relatedness can emerge through continuing acts of caregiving which create an embodied tie between a child and his or her caregiver. Goldfarb shows that the reverse is also true: temporally extended absences of care and/or neglect also leave physical traces upon the body. This chapter elegantly highlights the need for anthropologists to look for not only relevant "inclusions" in kin ties, but also significant "exclusions" as well.

The chapter by Mary Weismantel and Mary Elena Wilhoit is a sweeping and comprehensive survey of Andean kinship configurations and the different theoretical approaches that anthropologists have used to make sense of these configurations. An important insight to emerge from this chapter is that, "kin relations initiated as adults are on par with those established at birth." Put somewhat differently, processes of conception and birth should not be privileged over postnatal modes of eliciting relatedness.

In Chapter 9, James Leach draws our attention to the creativity of the landscape and the role it plays in the construction of kin ties. Focusing on the Reite people of Papua New Guinea, he documents the way in which kin connections emerge in tandem with the creation of meaningful places in the landscape. According to Leach, Reite people share substance by being fed from crops and other resources that derive from the same place. In this way, it is impossible to separate kin ties from the broader relationships that people form with the environment including nonhuman species.

If the previous three chapters explored sociality in non-Western settings, the next two focus the bulk of their attention on Euro-American kin configurations.

Chapter 10 by Christine Ward Gailey examines the many different faces that practices of adoption can take, both in Euro-American settings as well as those abroad. She argues that examining adoption through both an historic and an ethnographic lens provides us with a unique opportunity to view a variety of kin ties "unhampered by ideas of 'natural relationships.'" One important insight to emerge from her analysis concerns the degree to which adoption in both Europe and North America is inflected by multiple hierarchies of social difference, including those based on race, class, and gender.

In Chapter 11, Ellen Lewin examines how gays and lesbians make claims to kinship in contemporary North America. A key concern in her paper is to address a question that has been raised repeatedly in the existing academic literature: are gay and lesbian families inherently subversive, or do they adhere to normative constructions of the kin relations? After reviewing a host of literature, along with the results of her own firsthand research, Lewin concludes that LGBTQ families can be *both* subversive and modeled on mainstream configurations, depending on a number of factors, including the presence or absence of dependent children.

Part III: Reproducing Society: Gender, Birth, and Power examines the degree to which kinship and reproduction are embedded in a series of power relations, whether generated by the state and its legal apparatus, or by the deployment of authoritative systems of knowledge, such as biomedicine. Childbirth and reproduction are often highly politicized events at the level of the household and more broadly at the level of the nation. This section investigates how states often intervene to shape the fabric of family life. The following chapters explore (among other things) how birth, reproduction, and the assignment of parental rights become sites upon which the state asserts its authority over the bodies and subjectivities of its citizens. We also examine how differentially valued systems of knowledge can play an important role in shaping the overall contours of family life.

The contribution of Noa Vaisman (Chapter 12) brings many of the aforementioned themes to light and in a startlingly dramatic way. Based on research carried out with Argentina's adult "living disappeared," Vaisman documents how the state first intervened during a time of military rule to separate children from biological parents who had been defined by the state as politically "subversive." These children were then quietly placed in other families to be raised by different parents. Decades later, but now under a new and purportedly democratic regime, the state is intervening once again – and often against the wishes of those most affected – to reunite formerly "disappeared" children with their previous biological kin. We see through this lens the marked ambivalence that many now experience in attempting to make sense of kin relations, both past and present. Her chapter also documents the degree to which violence and disconnection are at the heart of contemporary family politics in Argentina.

Sarah Pinto's evocative and poetic contribution (Chapter 13) highlights how kinship intersects with the fields of health and medicine. Affliction in the area of India where Pinto lived and worked is both surprisingly common and also frequently attributed to the will of dead affines – more often than not, women. As structural "outsiders" to the conjugal homes they entered at marriage, the existence of spirit possession makes vivid the vulnerability of their position in the household. This chapter helps to highlight how discourses of medicine and health are deeply embroiled with those of both gender and kinship.

In Chapter 14, Valerie Hartouni investigates the role that legal technologies play in preserving traditional family values in the wake of a climate of sweeping social change. The fodder for her analysis is a series of surrogacy cases that went awry over the past few decades and were in need of legal resolution. While the specific details of each of these cases were markedly different from one another (some involved traditional surrogates, others gestational ones; some were contracted on a commercial basis, others were altruistic in nature; in some cases the intending parents were gay, in others they were heterosexual), Hartouni documents how the legal machinery churns along to maintain, as best it can a stable and unchanging vision of the social world which perpetually seems to be on the verge of collapse.

The final chapter in this section (Chapter 15), by Tine Gammeltoft examines sex-selective abortion practices in Vietnam. Although the Vietnamese state officially condemns the practice of sex selection, it ironically also promotes "traditional" family ideologies that perpetuate a cultural preference for sons. Gammeltoft's insightful analysis unpacks the state's contradictory and ambivalent messages, and strives to understand how local residents make sense of and respond to these contradictory edicts.

Part IV: Transnational Connections examines kinship within a global context. Here we shall see that in a world characterized by global and transnational ties, social relationships can no longer be viewed as an exclusively local phenomenon, but often cross national, cultural, and ethnic boundaries. In addition to investigating the social and political implications of transnational adoption (is it a new form of colonialism or grounded in an expanding global humanitarian ethic?), we also explore the movement of domestic workers across national boundaries and query what this movement entails. This section highlights that the growing occurrence of transnational families is no longer something that can be seen as exceptional and warrants the development of new approaches to the study of kinship and social life on the part of anthropologists.

In Chapter 16, Nicole Constable examines the lives of foreign domestic workers (FDW) in Hong Kong and the many different roles they play in families. These women often migrate from Indonesia or the Philippines and it is not uncommon for them to enter into sexual/romantic relationships with men while abroad and to form new family connections, sometimes on a permanent, but more often on a temporary, basis. Constable provides a nuanced account of how family dynamics may work when kin are stretched across national and international boundaries.

In the following chapter, Jessica Leinaweaver draws our attention to the topic of transnational adoption. A key insight to emerge from her analysis is that the "transnational" component of transnational adoption is "unevenly distributed." The families in the receiving countries use the metaphor of transnationalism to render sensible the transracial and cross-class relationships they have created through the adoption of a child from overseas. From the perspective of the birth mother and other kin in the sending country, however, the transnational component of the adoption is far less relevant insomuch as it cannot be used to form any type of ongoing relationship with persons in the receiving country. Leinaweaver's analysis thus brilliantly highlights the many inequities that characterize adoption when it takes place across national boundaries.

In Chapter 18, Lieba Faier brings us back to the theme of sexual and romantic encounters within a transnational context. More specifically, Faier examines how Filipina migrants married to Japanese men both perpetuate and subtly redefine what it means to be *oyomesan* – a "traditional Japanese bride and daughter-in-law." Significantly, they do so while still maintaining a strong sense of their Filipina identity along with vibrant and enduring kinship ties with family members back home. Faier documents the social and economic forces at play, along with what motivates Filipina women to marry in this way.

In the next chapter Deborah Boehm deals with undocumented Mexican migrants living and working within the United States. The author presents several case studies and first person accounts that help to highlight how families are "made" and "unmade" (and where possible, "made again"), in response to processes of migration and deportation. Her chapter is a moving and poignant account of both the precarity and resilience of family life when it is lived across international borders.

The last chapter in this section, by Eleana Kim, interrogates the role of paperwork in the production of kinship knowledge and subjectivity among Korean-born transnational adoptees. Since 1953, approximately 200,000 South Korean infants and children have been adopted by families in Europe and North America. Through a careful analysis of the contents of adoption files, Kim documents how legal technologies operate to remove a child from his or her network of natal kinship relationships and to reinscribe them as an "orphan" available for adoption overseas. In Kim's words, "legal fictions produce desirable, unencumbered children [eligible for placement with] wealthy Western families." Kim's analysis serves as an eloquent illustration of Carsten's suggestion in Part I of this handbook, that we would all do well to attend to the different materials (in this case paperwork) through which kin ties are cemented and negated.

Part V: Technological Conceptions pays attention to the ways in which innovations in science and technology along with reproductive medicine have impacted how kinship is created and experienced. Since the birth of the first "test-tube" baby in 1978, the last few decades have witnessed spectacular innovations in the area of artificial conception. It is now possible to artificially create in a clinic what was previously understood to be the province of innate biology. Four out of the five chapters in this section examine how the new reproductive technologies (NTRs) are restructuring ideas about procreation, parenthood, and family life (and three of these contributions explore different questions related to surrogacy). The remaining chapter deals with a variety of therapeutic technologies that have been developed to treat childhood disabilities.

Janet Dolgin's contribution (Chapter 21) examines four surrogacy cases that were deliberated in US courts between 1987 and 2013. Through a painstaking analysis of the decisions rendered, she demonstrates that North American understandings of the family have slowly been changing over the past few decades, along with the place that children are understood to occupy within it (compare to Hartouni's analysis in Chapter 13 as described above). If custody disputes were once decided on the basis of a child's "best interests," some of the most recent cases have allowed contract agreements to trump "best interests" in determining the custody of a child. Once set in stark opposition to the world of contract (Maine 1861), the dividing line between "status" (the family) and "contract" (the free market) has become increasingly difficult to shore up in the face of these changes.

In Chapter 22, Inhorn, Birenbaum-Carmeli, Tremayne, and Gürtin provide a compelling analysis of how NRTs are being variously incorporated within different Middle Eastern cultures. Undertaking a four-way comparison between Israel, Iran, Turkey, and the Arab world, they highlight both the similarities and differences in matters pertaining to kinship and the use of NRTs in the region. One of their key findings is that the use of third-party reproductive assistance (i.e., creating a child through either egg or sperm donation) is a particularly contentious issue in the Middle East. While allowed in Shia-dominant Iran and in Israel, it is disallowed throughout the Sunni Muslim world. This chapter furnishes a wonderful illustration of how religious ideologies interpenetrate in significant ways with kinship configurations (a point also taken up by Delaney and Cannell in this volume).

In Chapter 23, written by Elly Teman and Zsuzsa Berend, we return to the practice of surrogacy, but with a different set of questions in mind. This chapter offers up a comparative analysis of how surrogates interpret kinship (primarily with respect to the child they are carrying) in two different sociopolitical settings: Israel and the United States. Teman and Berend demonstrate that American and Israeli surrogates have much in common; they both describe surrogacy as a "journey of love," and they both insist that they do not bond with the child they are carrying. However, it appears that one important difference exists: the degree to which surrogates view genes as being relevant to the status of parenthood. Israeli surrogates, it seems, make a sharp distinction between gestation and genetics. In their view, the former is neutral in value while the latter is the basis of motherhood. US surrogates, on the other hand, do not see genes as being constitutive of motherhood. Teman and Berend link this finding to relevant sociopolitical factors: Israel is a Jewish state wherein both kinship and citizenship is passed on through women. Within this context, genes are important as a symbol not just for kinship but as an important symbol of national continuity.

Landsman opens Chapter 24 with a provocative set of questions that frame her analysis: "Who counts as a member of the family? Which characteristics threaten eligibility for kinship and belonging?" She goes on to document how the diagnosis of a childhood disability can diminish personhood and radically alter the dynamics of family life. In a compelling and thought provoking analysis, she highlights how parents of disabled children often turn to a variety of therapeutic technologies and treatments in an effort to intervene in the development of the child. She further highlights that both assistive technology (such as a wheelchair) and/or ongoing caregiving efforts may, in turn, transform the subjectivity of family members by redefining "dependency" as "connectivity" and by calling into question the idea of an autonomous and bounded self.

The contribution by Tsipy Ivry and Elly Teman (Chapter 25) wraps up this section of the handbook. In this chapter, the authors argue that scholars of kinship have erred in the past by not giving due attention to unpaid gestational labor (or what they call "ordinary pregnancy"). In the existing literature, anthropologists have focused on high-tech modes of reproduction and have tended to ignore how normal pregnancies are managed and experienced. This chapter is offered up as a corrective to this omission. Through a detailed examination of paid and unpaid gestational labor in Israel (with a comparative focus on Japan), the authors demonstrate that ordinary pregnancy and surrogacy are mutually constituted and both are informed by the same underlying system of meanings.

The final section of this handbook (Part VI) is entitled Kinship and the Nation-State. As we have seen, a key assumption in classical kinship theory was that "small-scale" (i.e., non-Western) societies were organized in terms of an "idiom" of kinship, while modern nation-states were structured in such a way that kinship played only a minor (and largely individualistic) role. The chapters in this section challenge that assumption through a set of studies that reveal the importance of kinship to the social, economic, and political workings of the nation-state.

Chapter 26 by Susan McKinnon addresses many of the aforementioned themes. In contrast to the dominant narrative of modernization theory, which sets kinship apart from political and economic relations, this chapter eloquently highlights the important ways in which differing kinship and marriage constellations are central to imagining (and contesting) different forms of governance, not to mention ideas about what constitutes a "modern" nation-state. McKinnon's focus throughout this chapter is on marriage and how it has undergone several significant shifts in the history of the United States. She demonstrates that during the second half of the nineteenth century, Americans expended considerable effort to bring about the prohibition of several key social institutions including slavery, polygamy, cousin marriage, and nepotism, whose reliance on the values of hierarchy, inequality, family privilege, and divine law were seen to be inconsistent with the ethos of a modern nation-state. Thus, changes in marriage practices took place in tandem with shifting understandings of what constitutes a modern nation. McKinnon also highlights how a conceptual pairing between monogamy and secular democracy continues to structure how Euro-Americans see other societies the world over and in the process re-legitimates the evolutionary framework of nineteenth-century theorists.

In Chapter 27, we turn our attention to the prison system in Brazil. Hollis Moore begins her contribution by describing the seemingly unimaginable sentiments of a loving mother who is relieved that her adult daughter is incarcerated in the local penitentiary. How can we make sense of her response? How can it be that a mother's love is demonstrated by a desire to see her daughter in jail? In this chapter, Moore is concerned with explaining why it is that Andreia's reaction makes a great deal of sense. The reader is introduced to a world in which making ends meet is precarious; to one where violence is an everyday fact of life, and the police, rather than offering protection from harm, actually exacerbate the climate of danger. We are also introduced to a world in which the state offers little to its citizens, in the form of either social services or welfare. Within this context, prison may be experienced as a site of safety, resource availability, stability, and certainty. In unpacking these themes, Moore demonstrates that while families are turning to the prison as a carceral "safety net" of sorts, they are also contributing to the informal economy that structures prison life. The reproduction of families is fully enmeshed with the reproduction of state penitentiaries.

The chapter written by Signe Howell is a comparative analysis of the interface between kinship and politics. Howell focuses on three different ethnographic settings: the Chewong of the Malay rainforest, the Lio of Indonesia, and the modern democratic nation of Norway. Through an investigation of kinship and political forms in each of these locations, Howell calls into question several oppositions which have long had purchase in Western thought: the distinction between public/private; traditional/modern; and state/non-state. Howell concludes by noting that while there is no predictive correlation between a particular kinship order and a particular mode of sociopolitical organization, kinship and politics are nonetheless mutually constituted.

In Chapter 29, Koreen Reece draws our attention to the intersection between kinship, globalization, and humanitarian organizations as they come together in Botswana to deal with the ravages of HIV/AIDS. Following the lead of McKinnon and Cannell (2013) in *Vital Relations*, Reece documents the "persistent life of kinship in economic, political, and religious projects of the nation state," and she does so in a number of different ways. First, she explores the shifting boundary between kinship and the nation-state. Reece does this by charting the bureaucratization of the family on the one hand and the domestication of the work place on the other. What we see is a blurring of the state and the family at the same time that the "work" of reiterating this distinction is repeatedly emphasized. Reece demonstrates that although the family in Botswana is the purported target of a vast array of interventions (by government agencies, NGOs, and other international constituencies), at the end of the day, the work of these organizations is geared more towards acts of state-making (in particular, the reproduction of these organizations themselves) rather than actually serving the needs of Setswana families. An interesting insight to emerge from Reece's chapter is that as the various organizations and agencies intersect with one another, there are a series of unintended consequences. Perhaps most strikingly, an implicitly evolutionary framework is reinscribed and legitimized: Setswana families are marginalized and demonized, while the West is portrayed as a source of love and salvation. Acting in the name of "needy children," what gets reproduced and naturalized is a system of global inequalities.

The final chapter in this section (and in the handbook as a whole) is written by Fenella Cannell. In this contribution Cannell uses data on Mormonism to challenge several assumptions in modernization theory: namely that modernity is characterized by compartmentalized domains in which kinship is trivialized and the secular realms of politics and economics are seen to be the most critical components of social life. Cannell also argues that anthropological theories of kinship have erred in assuming that modern nation-states are, for the most part, secular in nature. Drawing on original ethnographic material, Cannell demonstrates that Mormon teachings refuse to make a hard and fast distinction between kinship and religion. "While an individual person can attain life everlasting, the real joy of heaven and the purpose of human existence resides in the attempt to get to heaven with all your family. If every person does his or her part, every kinship relation can be eternalized and given everlasting life." Cannell's chapter serves as an important cautionary tale: we must refrain from assuming that the so-called "modern world" necessarily entails a decline in either kinship or religions engagement. Moreover, we cannot take for granted that religion and kinship are separate analytical domains: for some people they are mutually constituted.

Taken together, these chapters reveal the breadth and scope of contemporary kinship studies. They remind us of the pivotal place that the analysis of kinship has always played in the discipline of anthropology and help to highlight why it is that such studies will continue to be relevant in the future. Rich in analytical insights and ethnographic detail, these chapters showcase the power of an anthropological perspective when it comes to understanding the fabric of social life and challenging many of our taken for granted assumptions about the world.

Acknowledgments

A few select portions of the material presented in this Introduction have appeared previously in Sandra Bamford, *Biology Unmoored: Melanesian Reflections on Life and Biotechnology* 2007 (The Regents of the University of California. Published by the University of California Press) and in the "Introduction" to *Kinship and Beyond: The Genealogical Model Reconsidered* (Berghahn Books), coedited with James Leach.

Notes

1. There is a second technique that is sometimes used to replace faulty mitochondrial DNA (mtDNA) known as pronuclear transfer (PNT). PNT involves creating an embryo using the intended parents' egg and sperm and removing the pronuclei. The pronuclei is then transferred into an early embryo that had been created using the intended father's sperm and a donor egg and allowed to develop (Newson, Wilkinson and Wrigley 2016). Some have argued that PNT may be a more ethical/socially acceptable form of MRT in that it entails treating an existing embryo known to suffer from a particular condition, rather than engaging in selective reproduction (Wrigley, Wilkinson and Appleby 2015).
2. Zhang calls this procedure HER IVF – Human Egg Reconstitution In Vitro Fertilization.
3. Scientists are still unclear about the cause of age-related infertility, but many (including Zhang) believe it has to do with faulty mitochondria in older women.
4. As Schneider (1984) was later to note, it is clear that Morgan brought to his analysis an understanding of kinship that was thoroughly grounded in Euro-American ideas: kinship was, first and foremost, a biological relationship wherein distinct relatives occupied different places on a genealogical grid.

References

Andrews, Lori. 1999. *The Clone Age: Adventures in the New World of Reproductive Technology*. New York: Henry Hold.

Bamford, Sandra and James Leach. 2009. "Introduction: Pedigrees of Knowledge, Anthropology and the Genealogical Method." In *Kinship and Beyond: The Genealogical Model Reconsidered*, ed. Sandra Bamford and James Leach, 1–23. New York: Berghahn Books.

Barnes, John. 1967. "Genealogies." In *The Craft of Social Anthropology*, ed. Arnold Leonard Epstein, 101–127. London: Social Sciences Paperbacks in Association with Tavistock.

BBC News. 22 Jan. 2018. "Lesbian Couple Sues for Son's U.S. Citizenship."

Becker, Anne. 1995. *Body, Self, and Society: The View from Fiji.* Philadelphia, PA: University of Pennsylvania Press.

Bhattacharya, Shaoni. 19 June 2017. "Controversial Doctor to Use MRT Technique for Over 40s Fertility." *BioNews* 905.

Bouquet, Mary. 1993. *Reclaiming English Kinship: Portuguese Refractions of British Kinship Theory.* Manchester: Manchester University Press.

1996. "Family Trees and Their Affinities: The Visual Imperative of the Genealogical Method." *Man* (n.s.) 2(1): 43–66.

Carsten, Janet. 1995. "The Substance of Kinship and the Heat of the Hearth: Feeding, Personhood, and Relatedness among Malays in Pulau-Langkawi." *American Ethnologist* 22(2): 223–241.

1997. *The Heat of the Hearth: The Process of Kinship in a Malay Fishing Community.* Oxford: Clarendon Press.

ed. 2000. *Cultures of Relatedness: New Approaches to the Study of Kinship.* London: Cambridge University Press.

2004. *After Kinship.* Cambridge: Cambridge University Press.

Clarke, Morgan. 2009. *Islam and New Kinship: Reproductive Technology and the Shariah in Lebanon.* New York: Berghahn Books.

Colen, Shellee. 1995. "'Like a Mother to Them': Stratified Reproduction and West Indian Childcare Workers and Employers in New York." In *Conceiving the New World Order: The Global Politics of Reproduction*, ed. Faye Ginsburg and Rayna Rapp, 78–102. Berkeley, CA: University of California Press.

Collier, Jane and Sylvia Yanagisako, eds. 1987. *Gender and Kinship: Essays Toward a Unified Analysis.* Stanford, CA: Stanford University Press.

Darwin, Charles. 1859 (1979). *The Origin of Species.* New York: Gramercy Books.

Davidson, Allya and Julia Whalen. 2014. "Online Adoption 'Rehoming': Legal Loopholes Allow Children to Be Given Away." *CBC News.*

Davis-Floyd, Robbie and Joseph Dumit, eds. 1998. *Cyborg Babies: From Techno-Sex to Techno-Tots.* New York: Routledge.

Deomampo, Daisy. 2016. *Transnational Reproduction: Race, Kinship and Commercial Surrogacy in India.* New York: New York University Press.

Edwards, Jeanette. 2000. *Born and Bred: Idioms of Kinship and New Reproductive Technologies in England.* Oxford: Oxford University Press.

Edwards, Jeanette, Sarah Franklin, Eric Hirsch, Francis Price and Marilyn Strathern. 1993. *Technologies of Procreations: Kinship in the Age of Assisted Conception.* New York: Routledge.

Ehrenreich, Barbara and Arlie Hoschild. 2002. *Global Woman: Nannies, Maids, and Sex Workers in the New Economy*. New York: Henry Holt and Co.

Evans-Pritchard, Edward. 1940. *The Nuer: A Description of the Modes of Livelihood and Political Institutions of a Nilotic People*. Oxford: Oxford University Press.

1951. *Kinship and Marriage among the Nuer*. Oxford: Oxford University Press.

Fadel, Leila. 26 Jan. 2018. "Same-Sex Couples Sue U.S. Government for Kids' Citizenship." Transcript of *All Things Considered*, NPR.

Fortes, Meyers. 1945. *The Dynamics of Clanship among the Tallensi*. Oxford: Oxford University Press.

1949. *The Web of Kinship among the Tallensi*. Oxford: Oxford University Press.

Fox, Robin. 1967. *Kinship and Marriage: An Anthropological Perspective*. Cambridge: Cambridge University Press.

Franklin, Sarah. 1997. *Embodied Progress: A Cultural Account of Assisted Conception*. London: Routledge.

1998. Making Miracles: Scientific Progress and the Facts of Life." In *Reproducing Reproduction: Kinship, Power and Technological Innovation*, ed. Sarah Franklin and Helena Ragoné, 102–117. Philadelphia, PA: University of Pennsylvania Press.

Franklin, Sarah and Susan McKinnon, eds. 2001. *Relative Values: Reconfiguring Kinship Studies*. Durham, NC: Duke University Press.

Franklin, Sarah and Helena Ragoné. 1998a. "Introduction." In *Reproducing Reproduction: Kinship, Power and Technological Innovation*, ed. Sarah Franklin and Helena Ragoné, 1–14. Philadelphia, PA: University of Pennsylvania Press.

Franklin, Sarah and Helena Ragoné, eds. 1998b. *Reproducing Reproduction: Kinship, Power and Technological Innovation*. Philadelphia, PA: University of Pennsylvania Press.

Gailey, Christine. 2010. *Blue Ribbon Babies and Labors of Love: Race, Class and Gender in U.S. Adoption*. Austin, TX: University of Texas Press.

Gellner, Ernest. 1957. "Ideal Language and Kinship Structure." *Philosophy of Science* 24: 235–242.

Ginsburg, Faye and Rayna Rapp, eds. 1995a. *Conceiving the New World Order: The Global Politics of Reproduction*. Berkeley, CA: University of California Press.

1995b. "Introduction: Conceiving the New World Order." In *Conceiving the New World Order: The Global Politics of Reproduction*, ed. Faye Ginsburg and Rayna Rapp, 1–18. Berkeley, CA: University of California Press.

Hartouni, Valeria. 1997. *Cultural Conceptions: On Reproductive Technologies and the Remaking of Life*. Minneapolis, MN: University of Minnesota Press.

Hayden, Cori. 1995. "Gender, Genetics, and Generation: Reformulating Biology in Lesbian Kinship." *Cultural Anthropology* 10(1): 41–63.

Holý, Ladislav. 1996. *Anthropological Perspectives on Kinship*. London: Pluto Press.

Inhorn, Marcia. 2012. *The New Arab Man: Emergent Masculinities, Technologies and Islam in the Middle East*. Princeton, NJ: Princeton University Press.

Ivry, Tsipy. 2010. *Embodying Culture: Pregnancy in Japan and Israel*. New Brunswick, NJ: Rutgers University Press.

Kahn, Susan. 2000. *Reproducing Jews: A Cultural Account of Assisted Conception in Israel*. Durham, NC: Duke University Press.

Knoppers, Bartha, Arthur Leader, Stacey Hume, Eric Shoubridge, Rosario Isasi, Forough Noohl, Ubaka Ogbogu, Vardit Ravitsky and Erika Kleiderman. 2017. "Mitochondrial Replacement Therapy: The Road to the Clinic in Canada." *Journal of Obstetrics and Gynaecology Canada* 39(10): 916–918.

Konrad, Monica. 2005. *Nameless Relations: Anonymity, Melanesia and Reproductive Gift Exchange between British Ova Donors and Recipients*. New York: Berghahn Books.

Kuper, Adam. 1988. *The Invention of Primitive Society*. New York: Routledge.

Leinaweaver, Jessaca. 2008. *The Circulation of Children*. Durham, NC: Duke University Press.

Lévi-Strauss, Claude. 1949. *Les structures élémentaires de la parenté*. Paris: Presses Universitaires de France.

    1969. *The Elementary Structures of Kinship*. Boston, MA: Beacon Press.

Levin, Sam. 24 Jan. 2018. "One Ruled a U.S. Citizen, the Other Not: Gay Couple's Twins Face Unusual Battle." *The Guardian*.

Lewin, Ellen. 1993. *Lesbian Mothers: Accounts of Gender in American Culture*. Ithaca, NY: Cornell University Press.

    1998. *Recognizing Ourselves: Ceremonies of Lesbian and Gay Commitment*. New York: Columbia University Press.

Loike, John and Nancy Reame. 22 Dec. 2016. "Opinion: Ethical Considerations of 'Three-Parent' Babies." *The Scientist*.

MacCormack, Carol and Marilyn Strathern. 1980. *Nature, Culture and Gender*. Cambridge: Cambridge University Press.

McKinnon, Susan and Fenella Cannell, eds. 2013. *Vital Relations: Modernity and the Persistent Life of Kinship*. Santa Fe, NM: School for Advanced Research Press.

Maine, Henry. 1861. *Ancient Society*. London: John Murray.

Malinowski, Bronislaw. 1922. *Argonauts of the Western Pacific*. London: G. Routledge and Sons.

    1929. *The Sexual Life of Savages*. London: Routledge and Kegan Paul.

Melley, Brian. 23 Jan. 2018. "Gay Couple Married in Canada Sues U.S. Government for Denying Citizenship to Child." *The Associated Press*.

Modell, Judith. 1994. *Kinship with Strangers: Adoption and Interpretations of Kinship in American Culture*. Berkeley, CA: University of California Press.

    2002. *Sealed and Secret Kinship*. New York: Berghahn Books.

Morgan, Lewis. 1870. *Ancient Society*. New York: Holt and Co.

1877. *Systems of Consanguinity and Affinity of the Human Family*. Washington DC: Smithsonian Institution.

Mullin, Emily. 13 June 2017. "The Fertility Doctor Trying to Commercialize Three-Parent Babies." *MIT Technology Review*.

Nahman, Michal. 2013. *Extractions: An Ethnography of Reproductive Tourism*. Basingstoke: Palgrave Macmillan.

Needham, Rodney. 1960. "Discussion: Descent Systems and Ideal Language [Response to Gellner]." *Philosophy and Science* 27: 96–101.

Newson, Ainsley, Stephen Wilkinson and Anthony Wrigley. 2016. "Ethical and Legal Issues in Mitochondrial Transfer." *EMBO Molecular Medicine* 8(6): 589–591.

Parkin, Robert. 1977. *Kinship: An Introduction to Basic Concepts*. Oxford: Blackwell.

Poole, Fitz. 1982. "Review of *Nature, Culture and Gender*." *American Ethnologist* 9(3): 593–595.

Radcliffe-Brown, Alfred. 1922. *The Andaman Islanders: A Study in Social Anthropology*. Cambridge: Cambridge University Press.

1931. "Social Organization of Australian Tribes." *Oceania* 1(3): 322–341.

1940. "On Joking Relationships." *Africa* 13(3): 195–210.

1952. *Structure and Function in Primitive Society*. Cohen and West.

Ragoné, Helena. 1994. *Surrogate Motherhood: Conception in the Heart*. Boulder, CO: Westview Press.

Reardon, Sarah. 28 Sept. 2016. "'Three-Parent Baby' Claim Raises Hopes – and Ethical Concerns." *Nature*.

Rivers, William. 1910. "The Genealogical Method of Anthropological Inquiry." In *Kinship and Social Organization*, ed. W. H. R. Rivers, 97–112. New York: The Athlone Press.

Roberts, Elizabeth. 2012. *God's Laboratory: Assisted Reproduction in the Andes*. Berkeley, CA: University of California Press.

Sahlins, Marshall. 2013. *What Kinship Is – and Is Not*. Chicago, IL: University of Chicago Press.

Schneider, David. 1968. *American Kinship: A Cultural Account*. Englewood Cliffs, NJ: Prentice Hall.

1984. *A Critique of the Study of Kinship*. Ann Arbor, MI: University of Michigan Press.

Shoot, Brittany, 28 Feb. 2015. "3-Parent IVF: Why Isn't It Available in the United States?" *The Guardian*.

Strathern, Marilyn. 1992a. *Reproducing the Future: Essays on Anthropology, Kinship, and the New Reproductive Technologies*. Manchester: Manchester University Press.

1992b. *After Nature: English Kinship in the Late Twentieth Century*. Cambridge: Cambridge University Press.

Teman, Elly. 2010. *Birthing a Mother: The Surrogate Body and the Pregnant Self*. Berkeley, CA: University of California Press.

Thompson, Charis. 2005. *The Ontological Choreography of Reproductive Technologies*. Cambridge, MA: The MIT Press.

Twohey, Megan. 09 Sept. 2013a. "The Child Exchange Part 1: Americans Use Internet to Abandon Children Adopted from Overseas." *Reuters Investigates*.

09 Sept. 2013b. "The Child Exchange Part 2: In a Shadowy Online Network, a Pedophile Takes Home a 'Fun Boy.'" *Reuters Investigates*.

10 Sept. 2013c. "The Child Exchange Part 3: With Blind Trust and Good Intentions, Amateurs Broker Children Online." *Reuters Investigates*.

11 Sept. 2013d. "The Child Exchange Part 5: Orphaned in Russia, Brought to America and Then Abandoned Time and Again." *Reuters Investigates*.

Viveiros de Castro, Eduardo. 2009. "The Gift and the Given: Three Nano-Essays on Kinship and Magic." In *Kinship and Beyond: The Genealogical Model Reconsidered*, ed. Sandra Bamford and James Leach, 237–268. New York: Berghahn Books.

Weismantel, Mary. 1995. "Making Kin: Kinship Theory and Zumbagua Adoptions." *American Ethnologist* 22(4): 685–704.

Weston, Kath. 1991. *Families We Choose: Lesbians, Gays, Kinship*. New York: Columbia University Press.

1995. "Forever Is a Long Time: Romancing the Real in Gay Kinship Ideologies." In *Naturalizing Power: Essays in Feminist Cultural Analysis*, ed. Sylvia Yanagisako and Carol Delaney, 87–110. New York: Routledge.

Wrigley, Anthony, Stephen Wilkinson and John Appleby. 2015. "Mitochondrial Replacement: Ethics and Identity." *Bioethics* 29(9): 631–638.

Yanagisako, Sylvia and Jane Collier. 1987. "Toward a Unified Analysis of Gender and Kinship." In *Gender and Kinship: Essays Toward a Unified Analysis*, ed. Sylvia Yanagisako and Carol Delaney, 14–50. Stanford, CA: Stanford University Press.

Yanagisako, Sylvia and Carol Delaney. 1995. *Naturalizing Power: Essays in Feminist Cultural Analysis*. New York: Routledge.

Part I

Opening Frameworks

2

The Seeds
of Kinship Theory

Carol Delaney

> I will bless thee, and in multiplying I will multiply thy seed as the stars
> of the heaven, and as the sand which *is* upon the seashore.

(Genesis 22: 17)

It may seem odd to begin a chapter about kinship with a biblical quotation. Yet, as will become clear, I believe that early kinship theory, unwittingly perhaps, developed from assumptions about gender, family, and
kinship that are deeply embedded in the Bible. Although anthropologists
have been trained to understand people in their cultural context, rarely
have we analyzed how the Euro-American cultural context contributed to
our theoretical frameworks. Since the nineteenth century, at least, when
anthropology was beginning to emerge as a distinct intellectual discipline, religion and kinship were treated as separate areas of exploration –
one had to do with the spiritual and the other with the natural and rarely
did (or do) the twain meet. Yet for hundreds of years, even millennia,
the Euro-American worldview, values, laws, and institutions, including
family and kinship, were heavily influenced by the Bible. Because the
biblical notions of family and kinship were seen as natural, obvious, and
true, it was difficult for kinship theorists to gain perspective on their
own, let alone very different kinship systems.

The above quotation from Genesis occurs directly after Abraham
was prepared to sacrifice his son at God's command. Although he was
reprieved at the last moment, he is revered for his willingness to comply.
Indeed, for his obedience to God, Abraham became known as the "father
of faith" at the foundation of the three "Abrahamic" religions, namely
Judaism, Christianity, and Islam. "Because thou hast done this thing, and
hast not withheld thy son, thine only son, I will bless thee … and in thy
seed shall all the nations of the earth be blessed" (Genesis 22: 16, 18).

Several things need to be noted at once: God asked only Abraham to sacrifice his son; He did not also ask Sarah, his wife. Implied is that the son belonged to Abraham in a way he did not belong to Sarah; second, Isaac was *not* Abraham's only son. His firstborn, Ismail, was conceived by Hagar, who was not his wife. Thus, *marriage* was the bond that legitimated a child and created the bond of kinship.

For me, however, the most important conspicuous assumption has been overlooked, and that is the word *seed*. Though as A. I. Hallowell said long ago, "The most fundamental assumptions of any religious system are the least transparent" (quoted in M. F. Ashley Montague [1937] 1974: 387), even if in plain view. Because the word *seed*, inscribed in sacred texts, has long been part of the discourse, few have thought to explore its meanings and ramifications. However, in some recent translations of the Bible, the word *seed* has been changed to *progeny*, but as a result, the very assumptions that undergird the patriarchal structure embedded in that text, namely, notions of gender and procreation, are disguised.

While seed did mean progeny, only men had seed, only the man could *beget* a child, thus it should not be surprising that the child was thought to belong to the man. Women were thought to provide the nurturing medium, the "soil," in which the seed was planted. Women were (and still are) also described as either "fertile" or "barren," words that further identify them with the earth, while "potent" or "impotent" are used to describe men, thus highlighting power. Only men passed on seed, thus, boy children were valued more highly than girl children, for they were the only ones to continue the line. All the lineages in the Bible are patrilineages. Seed was imagined to incorporate the essence, the identity, and the soul of a person. Girls and women had souls, of course, but they were bequeathed by the father.

This ancient theory is inscribed not only in the Bible but also in the Qur'an. There Allah (God) speaks to men: "Women are given to you as fields, go therein and sow" (Sura 2: 223). These ideas are also found in Aristotle's *Generation of Animals* and other ancient and medieval texts. In Christianity, this theory became even more pronounced: God is called Father, who sends his "only begotten" son, depicted in medieval paintings as a whole baby descending on beams of light, to be born from the body of Mary. This is what I have called a "monogenetic" theory of procreation – the principle of creation comes from only one source – comparable, I suggest, to the monotheistic view of the male-imaged Creator (Delaney 1998).

Meanings of "father" and "mother" were constructed long before the modern scientific theory of procreation in which male and female contribute the same kind of material, namely *genes*, to the formation of an embryo. In *addition*, of course, women also provide nurture both inside and outside the womb and the labor of childbirth – yet those are the only aspects that have traditionally defined the word *mother*. The modern genetic theory did not become widely known until the mid-twentieth century and then only to certain segments of the population. Even so, the age-old cultural theory persists because the two theories are separated into different semantic contexts.

The older, folk-biblical, theory was the way I, an American born in 1940, was first told about how babies come into being, namely "the Daddy plants his seed," and I still hear references to it today. Indeed, because it is so deeply ingrained I began to repeat it when my daughter asked that perennial question! Mid-sentence, I stopped and realized in shock its implications. That moment was the inspiration for all my academic work. "Father" still means the one who "begets," who is *the* procreator, and "mother" is the one who bears the child and nurtures it. (Check your dictionaries!) Thus, it is extremely important to acknowledge the way language constitutes how we think about these issues. That the terms "mother" and "father" incorporate the ancient, erroneous, ideas can be seen when they are used for cultural processes far removed from physical procreation such as in "to father something" vs. "to mother something," or "the father of state" and "mother nature." So too, the use of the word "reproduction" instead of "procreation" to describe the process of bringing a unique, sentient being into the world is not only associated with women but also serves to devalue the process as if it were akin to something a photocopy machine does. To date, our language has not changed to adjust our modern understanding of the process. Furthermore, to take the terms "father" and "mother" as natural and therefore universal not only distorted the way anthropologists have perceived other cultures' notions of relatedness but also continues to obscure our own.

In order to further investigate my burgeoning thoughts on this issue, I first went to Harvard Divinity School, to do research on the Bible, particularly the story of Abraham, and on other, surrounding, Near Eastern cultures. There I learned that in Sumerian culture the primary deity was Inanna, Queen of Heaven and women were priests. Women could also adopt children in their own name and hold property. The Hurrians who lived in the area around Harran, where Abraham is supposed to have migrated after leaving Ur, had a very different kinship system from the one in the biblical text, at least as can be gleaned from their kinship terminology. Thus, I began to wonder whether all peoples of the world had the same notions of gender and procreation as we do. This propelled me to do doctoral research in cultural anthropology, and fieldwork in a culture influenced by Islam, the "Abrahamic" religion I knew least about, and in a place where the modern genetic theory of procreation was likely to be unknown.

I chose to go to Turkey, where I had worked previously on an archaeology project. I lived in a remote Turkish village for two years (1980–1982) where I quickly had to learn the proper kinship terms to address individuals. After I was well integrated in the village, I began to ask people how they were related and how babies come into being. All were adamant that the man was the *creator* by means of his seed (*tohum* or *döl*) and thus, they were his, they belonged to him. There was no word for the female contribution, only *dölyatağı* – literally, "seedbed," that is the womb. These beliefs about procreation were a major disincentive for a woman to leave her husband and seek a divorce, even in an unhappy or abusive marriage, because she would not get custody of the children.

"Girls are like the leaves on a tree, they fall off; they are the end of the line, boys are the trunk." Since a boy child was necessary to continue the line, women were expected to continue to have children until a boy was produced. If she did not produce a male heir, she was blamed. She was "not able to hold onto the seed." They had no idea about the roles that x and y chromosomes in the sperm played in conception. The lack of a male heir was also the reason a man could divorce his wife or, in some cases, take a second wife even though that was forbidden in Turkey.

Michael Meeker, another anthropologist who worked in Turkey, quoted his villagers as saying: "If you plant wheat, you get wheat, if you plant rye, you get rye, the man plants the seed, the woman is like the field in which it is planted" (1970: 157), reinforcing the idea that identity comes from the man. The villagers among whom I lived, agreed. Thus, it is not surprising that my book resulting from this fieldwork was titled, *The Seed and the Soil: Gender and Cosmology in Turkish Village Society* (1991). I used the word "cosmology" rather than religion, because I wanted to direct attention to worldview and notions of "coming into being" rather than just on the way Islam was practiced in that village.

While anthropologists have traditionally asked about origin myths, unfortunately, those interested in kinship have rarely asked people about how babies originate, that is, about their beliefs concerning procreation, because they assumed the process was natural, obvious, and universal. It was Bronislaw Malinowski whose work among the Trobriand Islanders brought the issue to anthropological attention. Before turning to his work, I wish to step back a bit and turn to Lewis Henry Morgan who is generally credited as the founding "father" of kinship studies as an academic field.

2.1   Lewis Henry Morgan

While living in upper New York state, Lewis Henry Morgan, a lawyer, became acquainted with the Iroquois and noticed that they had a kinship system that was very different from the one he was familiar with, at least in terms of its nomenclature. For example, where we have two different words for "father" and "father's brother," namely "father" and "uncle," the Iroquois had only one. For Morgan, it seemed obvious that family relationships must be the same everywhere since they rest on the same biological facts of sex and reproduction, established through marriage and constituted by the streams of blood. So he struggled to learn what could explain the Iroquois system and wondered whether all Native American groups had a similar system. He devised a questionnaire that he took when he visited other groups. He also sent it to missionaries, explorers, and government officials who were working in different societies around the world. He asked them to fill in the native term that corresponded to *our* relationships of mother, father, sister, brother, aunt, uncle, cousin, grandmother, etc., which seems logical. Yet, forcing other peoples' terms onto the grid used by Morgan and Euro-Americans, greatly distorted their kinship systems, and it took some time for anthropologists to figure out what these other systems represented.

I cannot possibly cover the various systems in Morgan's huge volume, *Systems of Consanguinity and Affinity* (1871),[1] but hopefully one example will illustrate the problem. In a number of cases he found that the same term was applied to several different women, clearly not all of whom could be the birth mother and, similarly with the terms for men, not all of whom could be the father. He called such a system "classificatory" and assumed, at first, that the people were not pair bonding but engaging in promiscuous intercourse and group marriage. Given his belief that always and everywhere kinship terms reflected biological relations, he assumed that these groups simply didn't know the "facts of life." He classed them as "primitive" and placed them at the bottom of the cultural evolutionary scale. The Euro-American system was, naturally, the epitome, the most advanced, civilized system because it was:

> based on a true and logical appreciation of the natural outflow of the streams of blood … (and) proceeds upon the existence of marriage between single pairs, and of the certainty of parentage through this marriage relation.
>
> *(1871: 468–469)*

He called the Euro-American systems "descriptive" because each relative has a distinct term, even though in English, unlike Turkish, one term is used for both the brother of one's father and the brother of one's mother, namely "uncle," and similarly for the female siblings of both, namely "aunt." In Turkish, however, there is a different term for each – *amca* for father's brother and *daya* for mother's brother, similarly, *hala* for father's sister and *teyze* for mother's sister. By Morgan's definition, the Turkish system was more "descriptive" than the Euro-American one and, therefore should have been considered the most advanced. That does not mean, however, that there was or is gender equality in the Turkish system, far from it.

John McLennan, a Scotsman, critiqued Morgan's analysis, claiming that he had made two major mistakes: "He did not steadily contemplate the main peculiarity of the system – its classification of connected persons" and thus "did not seek the origin of the system in the origin of the classi-fication" (1896: 269). His second mistake "was to have so lightly assumed the system to be a system of blood-ties" (1896: 269). Ultimately, McLennan suggested, instead, that a kinship terminological system was a way to incorporate, and be able to address, everyone in the group. Nevertheless, when it came down to real, true kinship, he, too, believed it was a matter of sex, blood, and biology. But since that was considered natural it was not of much interest to sociocultural anthropologists. That is, not until Bronislaw Malinowski's study among the Trobriand Islanders.

2.2   Bronislaw Malinowski

In 1914, Malinowski, a Polish anthropologist who studied in England, went to New Guinea to begin ethnographic work. But when World War I broke out he was unable to return to England due to his citizenship. Fortunately, the Australian government permitted him to remain and pro-ceed with his work. He chose to go to the Trobriand Islands in Melanesia and settled on the island of Kiriwina where he set about learning the local culture. The most remarkable thing, for which he became famous, was his claim that the Trobrianders were ignorant of paternity (1927). Instead, according to the people, a woman became pregnant when a spirit (*baloma*), from the woman's ancestors (her *dala*), tired of his or her exist-ence on Tuma – an island where the spirits dwelt – and decided to re-enter the substantial world to live again among the people. The *baloma* first had to regress from its aged spirit-body to that of a tiny spirit-fetus, small and light enough to float on the foam of the waves or driftwood to arrive at the shores of Kiriwina. There it would enter the woman who was bathing at sea, or be carried in a bucket of water to the home of the woman, or possibly be carried by another *baloma* spirit and deposited with the woman. Sometimes the *baloma* would enter vaginally, but more often via the head where it would descend on a tide of blood into the womb. The rising of the blood would make the woman feel dizzy and nauseous and was a sign that she was pregnant.[2] For the Trobrianders, sex had little to do with it, and the people could not understand Malinowski's and other Europeans' insistence on this relation.

   As they tirelessly noted, the young people engaged in sexual activity often, even with different partners, yet rarely did a girl become preg-nant. They challenged Malinowski to "account for the discrepancy why the cause which was repeated daily, or almost so, produced effects so rarely" (1954: 236). Just so! Malinowski, unlike others before him, did wonder why European officials and missionaries focused so doggedly on their ignorance of paternity rather than on so many other possibilities – disease, anatomy, health – and came to the conclusion that it had to do with Europeans' religious beliefs.

The whole Christian morality (he wrote) ... is strongly associated with the institution of a patrilineal and patriarchal family, with the father as *progenitor* and master of the household (and that) a religion whose dogmatic essence is based on the sacredness of the father to son relationship, and whose morals stand or fall by a strong patriarchal family, must obviously proceed by confirming the paternal relation, by showing that it has a *natural* foundation.

(1932: 159, my emphasis)

When the natives asked Malinowski about his and, by association, the beliefs of his countrymen, he replied: "The facts of procreation could be represented by the simile of a seed being planted in the soil and the plant growing out of that seed" (1954: 223). That is, he repeated the age-old biblically based theory. Ironically, it is just as erroneous as that of the Trobrianders!

The genetic theory of procreation as applied to humans was unknown at the time. In the late nineteenth century Gregor Mendel, who founded the science of genetics, studied the genetics of pea plants, and others in the early twentieth century worked with fruit flies. It was not until the 1940s and 1950s that it was explored in terms of sperm and egg. And the dis*semination* of the genetic theory to the wider society took much longer. People today are unaware how relatively recent is the genetic theory of procreation. Fortunately, Malinowski demonstrated that the old folk theory was alive and well during his time.

The Trobrianders did have a reasonable explanation for the male ejaculate: they said it was a kind of food to feed the growing fetus. In other words, a man was a partner in nurturing a developing child and, later, also in caretaking after its birth. Regarding social structure, the primary bond was not husband and wife but brother and sister. Land as well as people were affiliated through the female line (*dala*); brothers worked their sister's land and protected her rights, and their own benefits came, not from the wife's land but from their sister's lands. Similar notions surfaced among some other groups, see for example, M. F. Ashley Montague's *Coming into Being among the Australian Aborigines* (1937 [1974]).

The issue of so-called "ignorance" of paternity sparked a big debate that became known as "The Virgin Birth Debate," initiated by the 1967 paper by Edmund Leach entitled simply, "Virgin Birth." This is an ironic and misleading title, however, for none of the Trobriand women were virgins! But there is a more important reason it is misnamed. In the Christian notion of the Virgin Birth it is the male-imaged God whose son lodges in the virgin womb of Mary. Medieval paintings show a fully formed baby Jesus descending on beams of light to Mary's ear. She does not create, nor is she co-creator; she only contributes a supposedly immaculate womb that nurtures the already created child. The Father's seed is the son, Father and son are one – it is all about creative paternity.

Although Trobriand notions of "coming into being" were very much integrated with notions of gender, kinship, and their religious views, and Malinowski clearly saw that Europeans' notions were integrated with their religion, no one seemed to pick up on this. Instead, kinship continued to be investigated in terms of marriage, blood, kinship terminology, and their relation to social structure.

2.3 David Schneider

And that was true even with David Schneider, though he radically changed our way of thinking about these terms. Stressing that kinship is a cultural, rather than a natural, system, he said that it is a system of symbols and thus cannot be analyzed separately from the rest of culture. The task for the anthropologist, thus, is to learn what those cultural symbols are, but did he really do that? While he did focus on kinship and relate it to some other cultural units, he neglected to relate it to one of the most important: religion.

Regarding American kinship, he learned first, that a relative is different from a friend or colleague: informants told him that a relative is someone related by blood or marriage or, in a more restrictive sense, only by blood since one does not usually marry a blood relative.[3] While blood might seem to be a natural, in the sense of biological, category, that is not actually the case regarding kinship. Schneider made his point in an oft quoted statement, where he noted how difficult it is "at times to convince an American that blood as a fluid has nothing in it which *causes* ties to be deep and strong" (1972: 48). Instead, blood does not constitute but *symbolizes* certain types of relations. Continuing, Schneider claims that in American kinship, sexual intercourse between a married pair of male and female is the major symbol that makes a family. No doubt that is a belief held by many, but then, to me, he goes astray.

Symbolically, he implies that "marriage" is a union between equals, usually illustrated by the equal sign in kinship charts, but it has not been an equal relationship. In other words, he did not really explore the symbolic meanings of gender. Schneider believed that language was an important indicator of the cultural units; thus it is surprising he did not really look at the way procreation was talked about colloquially or consider the symbolic implications of traditional wedding ceremonies. First, the woman's father is asked to "give away" his daughter, a transaction between men; second, the woman had to promise to "obey" the husband, whereas he did not have to agree to obey his wife; third, the union was solidified by a priest or minister reciting some version of the following: "I now pronounce you man and wife," not "husband and wife." Finally, addressing the man, told him: "You may now kiss your wife." Later, this couple would be introduced as Mr. and Mrs., followed by the husband's first and last name. Some of these traditions have been changing, but slowly.

Schneider also ignored the fact that etymologically, the word "family" has meant all those dependent on a male head including, in the past, even servants. But more to the point, he seems to have assumed that all Americans know the modern, medical, scientific theory in which

> both mother and father give substantially the same kinds and amounts of material to the child, and that the child's whole biogenetic identity or any part of it comes half from the mother, half from the father. It is not believed that the father provides the bone, the mother the flesh, for instance.
>
> *(1968: 23)*

That may be the case if informants were directly confronted (something he discouraged) but at the cultural level, I suggest, the age-old folk theory persists not just in the Bible but in words such as "seminal," to characterize a creative work, and in metaphor, imagery, literature, poetry, and song. Yet, even in his biogenetic definition, the woman provides much more than just half the genetic endowment of a child. She also provides the nurture in the womb, and often also at the breast – the only aspects that have defined her role for millennia. Indeed, in 2014 a Virginia senator said that women are merely incubators! No doubt he is not alone.

Had Schneider explored the ways in which the culture has symbolized procreation, he might have quickly encountered what I have called the monogenetic, "seed-soil" theory in which it is men who plant the seed and women provide the nurture. It is the seed that provides the identity, and typically children take their father's not their mother's name, further solidifying that identity.

But he might also have thought in terms of origins and that might have taken him to another major cultural unit: religion and origin stories. All cultures have stories about "coming into being," whether about the world, the people, or a baby. And, not surprisingly, as in the case of the Trobrianders, there is often a relationship between them. The origin story of the Abrahamic religions presents a male-imaged God who is Creator, par excellence. Not only did He create the natural material world – generally imaged as female, even as "mother earth" – but also created a man, Adam, from whose body, He took a woman, Eve, in a complete reversal of what actually happens, namely that male and female babies come out of the body of a woman. As an anthropologist who advocated a symbolic approach, Schneider might have asked what this reversal symbolized.

He also paid no attention to the fact that the sign of the covenant between God and Abraham – circumcision – was (and is) inscribed on the male procreative organ! The biblical (and Qur'anic) origin story *is* all about gender, sex, procreation, and kinship.[4] He might, then, have paid more attention to gender and the notion of *seed*, all the *begats*, and the patrilineages. He might have realized how the "monogenetic" notion of procreation is intertwined with and perpetuated by the monotheistic religions of Judaism, Christianity, and Islam. The Gospel according to St. John opens with: "In the beginning was the Word and the Word was with God … And the Word was made flesh and dwelt among us … the only begotten of the Father" (John 1: 14), that is: Jesus. That the Word was imagined as God's seed was made clear to me from the inscription on the pulpit of the Basilica of the National Shrine of the Immaculate Conception in Washington DC, "The Word is the Seed of God." And the role of priests is to spread the word – the symbolic seed – rather than physical ones.

***

Because I was convinced that the symbolic approach in anthropology espoused by the University of Chicago was most productive, I applied to and was accepted to their doctoral program and David Schneider became the chair of my dissertation committee. At first, when I proposed to study the theory of procreation among Turkish villagers, he, like the other professors, was dismissive: "That is just about nature, not culture!" Nevertheless, he was supportive and when I returned from the field and presented my dissertation, he came around.[5]

2.4 More Recent Trends

While the study of kinship continues to be an important part of the anthropological enterprise, the focus has shifted in recent years, as is attested by some of the other articles in this volume. Feminist anthropologists have pointed out that conventional kinship studies were based on assumptions about gender. Even though anthropologists were aware that *male* and *female* were defined differently in other cultures and also that their roles differed, they did not follow through to use that as a mirror to their own society. It took feminist anthropologists like Jane Collier and Sylvia Yanagisako to

> argue that gender and kinship have been defined as fields of study by our folk conception of the same thing, namely the biological facts of sexual reproduction. Consequently, what have been conceptualized as two discrete fields of study constitute a single field that has not succeeded in freeing itself from notions about natural differences between people.
>
> *(1989: 15)*

They continued:

> men and women are different, just as individuals differ, generations differ, races differ, and so forth. Rather, we question whether the

particular biological difference in reproductive function that our culture defines as the basis of difference between males and females, and so treats as the basis of their relationship, is used by other societies to constitute the cultural categories of male and female.

(1989: 48)

Perhaps somewhere gender differences are defined by the differential distribution of hair on the body or by breasts or the lack of them. But even if procreation is a salient area, it is clear from the foregoing that different cultures, including our own, have understood the process very differently. It matters whether the male is seen as *the progenitor* or the woman, or whether it is a process that takes place when a particular sperm and an egg are joined; or whether it is imagined to be the project of ancestral spirits rather than that of the two people intimately involved.

Other recent voices working on kinship have begun to be heard: (1) gays and lesbians have questioned the heterosexual basis/bias of kinship and gender studies (e.g. Weston 1990); (2) people who feel a kinship bond because they or their children share the same genetic disease (e.g. Rapp, Heath and Taussig 2001); (3) those with adopted children who argue that kinship is about care and nurture not sex and blood (e.g. Howell 2001); and (4) others who have used new reproductive technologies which fragment the roles, e.g. sperm donor, egg donor, and the splitting of the role of mother into biological, surrogate, and birth mother (e.g. Franklin 1995, 2001).[6] All of these people have been challenging the taken-for-granted notions of kinship and forging new definitions, the implications of which we are only beginning to understand and accommodate socially and culturally. Still, none of them have used their insights to challenge the theology and religious institutions that hold such sway over sex, marriage, and procreation. But one thing is clear: kinship is not something given "in the nature of things," but is constructed in particular cultures in particular ways around particular notions of persons and the cosmos.[7]

2.5   Conclusion

If our own cultural theory of gender and procreation has been intertwined with religious (biblical) conceptions, one wonders whether or how the modern, scientific theory will affect religion. Or will the spiritual and the natural continue to be kept in separate spheres? It is interesting to note how, in recent times, issues of gender and procreation have become prominent within the Abrahamic religious traditions, for example, birth control and abortion, test-tube babies and genetic engineering,[8] attempts to define and control marriage (who can marry whom), and divorce, and whether a divorced person can remarry or still be included in the fellowship.

Concomitantly, there has been an upsurge of religiously inspired violence between the three religions. To me, these sibling religions seem like three brothers fighting over the patrimony, who will inherit the "kingdom" and who has the right interpretation of the "father's" will? The fallout, however, tends to land on the heads, often literally, of girls and women: keeping them from school, discouraging them from pursuing careers, restricting them to the domestic realm, head coverings, forbidding them to drive, kidnapping them for the sexual gratification of soldiers, honor killings, and stoning them for adultery.[9] In our secular society, I believe that the increase of rape in the armed forces and on college campuses, while seemingly unrelated to religion, is nevertheless related to the age-old gender definitions inscribed there. Is male power dependent on keeping women in their supposedly divinely ordered place?

Some changes have occurred, of course. For example, changes in the language of religious texts such as from "seed" to "progeny" (but I find this problematic, see above), some women have become rabbis and ministers, but not imams, cardinals, or the pope, and the image of God is still male. What does it mean for more women to enter into these patriarchal traditions and institutions? How much will they be able to change the underlying structure or challenge the theology? Perhaps the time has come to consider whether it was God who created man in his image or whether, millennia ago, acting on their thoughts about procreation,[10] a group of men in the Near East created God in *their* image, and thereby launched the most powerful myth and institutions the world has ever seen, including definitions of gender, family, and kinship.

Notes

1. Many of the ideas discussed in this article have been published previously; in this case from Delaney (2004: 192–200).
2. Taken from my "The Meaning of Paternity and the Virgin Birth Debate" (1986: 506).
3. Yet Morgan married his first cousin and the practice was common in Boston – referred to as a "Boston marriage," and in a number of other places. In the Turkish village where I worked, it was an esteemed marriage but not the only kind. See also *Cousin Marriage: Between Tradition, Genetic Risk and Cultural Change* (Shaw and Raz 2015).
4. Perhaps, as a secular Jew he felt these were just ancient stories that had no relevance for contemporary life.
5. I had the last laugh when I won the prize for the best dissertation in the social sciences, 1984.
6. *The New York Times* (February 4, 2015, page A4) reported that Britain would allow "the in vitro creation of babies using the DNA of three people" as a way to prevent genetically transmitted diseases. But this

would mean "altering a human egg or embryo before transferring it to the womb." Naturally, the Catholic Church and the Church of England weighed in, decrying the procedure.

7. One might also imagine whether the monotheistic religious view of Creation also has subliminally affected scientific cosmologists who have been searching for the original "singularity" often described as a "single *seed* smaller than an atom (yet) so potent it blossomed into everything there is" via the "big bang." Quotation is from a TV film, *Creation of the Universe*, first shown on November 20, 1985.

8. See note 6.

9. "Schoolgirls Are Facing More Threats, UN Report," *The New York Times*, February 10, 2015, also article and letters about the Pope's position on birth control.

10. Many anthropologists believe that women were responsible for domesticating plants and thus understood the relationship between sowing seeds and the plants that developed. Men were off hunting and eventually domesticated certain animals. But the early Israelites, unlike the people in Mesopotamia, were pastoralists, not agriculturalists. Watching their animals produce offspring, perhaps it was but a short step to make an inference or analogy, using the seed metaphor to apply both to their animals and themselves.

References

Collier, Jane and Sylvia Yanagisako. 1989. *Gender and Kinship: Toward a Unified Analysis*. Stanford, CA: Stanford University Press.

Delaney, Carol. 1986. "The Meaning of Paternity and the Virgin Birth Debate." *Man* 21(3): 494–513.

1991. *The Seed and the Soil: Gender and Cosmology in Turkish Village Society*. Berkeley, CA: University of California Press.

1998. *Abraham on Trial: The Social Legacy of Biblical Myth*. Princeton, NJ: Princeton University Press.

2004. *Investigating Culture: An Experiential Introduction to Anthropology*. Malden, MA: Blackwell.

Franklin, Sarah. 1995. "Postmodern Procreation: A Cultural Account of Assisted Conception." In *Conceiving the New World Order: The Global Politics of Reproduction*, ed. Faye D. Ginsburg and Rayna Rapp, 323–345. Berkeley, CA: University of California Press.

2001. "Biologization Revisited: Kinship Theory in the Context of New Biologies." In *Relative Values: Reconfiguring Kinship Studies*, ed. Sarah Franklin and Susan McKinnon, 302–326. Durham, NC: Duke University Press.

Howell, Signe. 2001. "Self-Conscious Kinship: Some Contested Values in Norwegian Transnational Adoption." In *Relative Values: Reconfiguring*

Kinship Studies, ed. Sarah Franklin and Susan McKinnon, 203–223. Durham, NC: Duke University Press.

Leach, Edmund. 1967. "Virgin Birth." *Proceedings of the Royal Anthropological Institute*, 39–49.

McLennan, J. F. 1896. *Studies in Ancient History*. London: Macmillan and Company.

Malinowski, Bronislaw. [1916]. 1954. "Baloma: Spirits of the Dead in the Trobriand Islands." In *Magic, Science and Religion*. New York: Doubleday Anchor Books.

1927. *The Father in Primitive Society*. London: Kegan, Paul, Trench and Trubner.

[1929]. 1932. *The Sexual Life of Savages in North-Western Melanesia*. London: George Routledge and Sons.

Meeker, Michael. 1970. The Black Sea Turks: A Study of Honor, Descent and Marriage. Ph.D. dissertation, University of Chicago.

Montague, M. F. Ashley. 1937 [1974]. *Coming into Being among the Australian Aborigines*. London: Routledge & Kegan Paul.

Morgan, Lewis Henry. 1871. *Systems of Consanguinity and Affinity in the Human Family*. Smithsonian Contributions to Knowledge, 17. Washington DC: Smithsonian Institution.

Rapp, Rayna, Deborah Heath and Karen-Sue Taussig. 2001. "Genealogical Dis-Ease: Where Hereditary Abnormality, Biomedical Explanation and Family Responsibility Meet." In *Relative Values: Reconfiguring Kinship Studies*, ed. Sarah Franklin and Susan McKinnon, 384–410. Durham, NC: Duke University Press.

Schneider, David. 1968. *American Kinship: A Cultural Account*. Englewood Cliffs, NJ: Prentice-Hall.

1972. "What Is Kinship All About?" In *Kinship Studies in the Morgan Centennial Year*, ed. P. Reining, 3-63. Washington DC: The Anthropological Society.

Shaw, Alison and Aviad Raz. 2015. *Cousin Marriage: Between Tradition, Genetic Risk and Cultural Change*. New York: Berghahn Books.

Weston, Kath. 1990. *Families We Choose: Lesbians, Gays, Kinship*. New York: Columbia University Press.

3

Descent in Retrospect and Prospect

Gillian Feeley-Harnik

Descent is the basis of anthropology: the study of human similarities and differences that developed in Europe and North America in the 1700s became a profession there in the 1800s, and spread in the process. The multiple fields of anthropology – social-cultural, linguistic, archaeological, and biological – emerged from intense debates over how best to understand the diversity and unity of human beings through space and time, and whether they constituted one kind of creature or many. Anthropology today is based on the assumption that we are one in *Homo sapiens*, one species sharing common descent, and as *Homo sapiens*, we are related to all other kinds of organic beings on earth alive and extinct. This hard-won claim is not a consensus even in its heartland. Nor has it resolved all outstanding questions about our humanity by folding them under the one wing of our physiology. We still seek a common understanding of the *relations among our many ways of unifying and differentiating ourselves* – social-cultural, linguistic, physiological, and ecological – that inspired our comparative historical inquiries in the first place, and thus the term *descent* still shared among them.

"What is the pattern which connects all the living creatures?" asked the social anthropologist Gregory Bateson (1979: 8). No one pattern of relations has emerged from the data anthropologists have amassed so far. Decades of ethnographic and historical research document the diversity of people's conceptions of humanity and their vulnerability to challenge by reason or force. Understanding the complexities of descent – its inclusions and exclusions – is as critical now as ever in our history. Yet divisions persist even among anthropologists. The biblical trees of "Jesse begat David" (Isaiah 11: 1, Matthew 1: 6) contributed to the history of family trees as analytical tools in social and biological anthropology alike (Bouquet 1996; Klapisch-Zuber 1991; Pietsch 2012), but the study of descent in these increasingly specialized sub-fields has taken different paths.

Nonhuman primates are highly social, but owing to debates over the extent and nature of their sociality, "Most primatologists have defined kinship exclusively in terms of genetic relatedness: kin are individuals who share genes inherited from a recent common ancestor" (Trautmann, Feeley-Harnik and Mitani 2011: 165). In social-cultural anthropology: "Kinship theorists are agreed that genealogical relations are not relations of biological or genetic connection. They define them as relations deriving from the engendering and bearing of children as this process of human reproduction is known or understood in any given society and not as it may be known or understood by biologists or geneticists" (Holý 1996: 15; see Sahlins 2013).

The social basis of kinship is an insight hard-won against concurrent developments in so-called scientific racism. Anthropologists have won the argument in part by documenting the social-cultural dimensions of descent, alliance, kinship terminologies, inheritance practices, and the like, while bracketing off "biological" processes as defined by race scientists drawing on the life sciences of biology and genetics that developed alongside anthropology in Europe and North America in the nineteenth and twentieth centuries. In documenting the social basis of descent, social-cultural anthropologists have also documented ideas and practices concerning such matters as birth, death, fertility, barrenness, generation, illness, and healing in humans, animals, plants, lands, in short: alternative theories of life and death processes associated with their own forms of inclusion and exclusion. From the perspective of these alternatives, we must consider the possibility that so-called scientific racism did not emerge as the perverse child of orthodox parents in the professionalizing fields of biology and social anthropology. On the contrary, kinship practices everywhere may have an ugly underside explaining and justifying, for example, who counts as a forebear, a spouse, a child, and who does not. A holistic view is essential to understand the power of kinship relations to forge ties of amity and enmity alike and the capacities of kinship theorists to comprehend them in the same analytical framework.

Comparative and historical research shows that ideas and practices of descent, kinship, and racism – forms of discrimination based on assumptions about inborn attributes of people transmitted from forebears to descendants (Beasley 2010: 1) – are all variable, and they are constantly being reinvented. Ideas and practices of descent in greater Europe and North America have changed over time, especially since the mid-1700s. A key factor seems to have been the intensification of domestication, which involved substantial geographic transfers of animals and plants associated with European imperial expansion, but ultimately closer confinement in space to achieve tighter controls over generative processes in time, including the destruction of those unwanted. These changes had complex roots, but the data shows that human manipulation of the generational relations of animals, plants, and themselves are closely related owing to their common ground in cultural theories of life and death processes.

Ideas and practices of descent, kinship, us and not-us are variable and multiple. They coexist with other such clusters of ideas and practices. Scholars' theories of kinship coexist with their personal theories of how kinship works in their everyday lives, and these in turn with the kinship theories of other social groups however they may be defined. These clusters are relationally defined in part because they are ranked in relation to one another. Thus, past and present, we are dealing with plural systems of descent, in which one of the most basic analytical questions is whose theories of thriving and dying are prevailing, how, why, and with what consequences? This chapter on descent is based on the premise that to understand both the animating and decimating dimensions of kinship systems, we must incorporate the life sciences into the analysis of cultural ideas and practices of life and death processes worldwide on the same footing.

In this chapter the observers and observed occupy the same social-historical fields. I examine the insights anthropologists achieved in analyzing *descent* in others' social systems, while using those insights to illuminate *descent* as it emerged as an important focus of inquiry in anthropologists' own works (and lives at least briefly). The dangers of tautology in this approach are compounded by the fact that *descent*, together with every other key term in the study of kinship in which we are all experts, were and are so intensely debated that they invariably remain "half … in other people's mouths" in Bakhtin's (1981 [1934–1935]: 293–294) terms, despite our attempts to make them "one's own."

Some social-cultural anthropologists have argued that competing definitions of the biological or social basis of (for example) *descent* and *genealogy* in anthropologists' everyday lives, persisting in their adoption of these words as analytical terms in their ethnographic research, have vitiated the study of genealogies in the work of Morgan (1871) and virtually all his successors up to around 1970 (Schneider 1972, 1984) and perhaps much longer (Ingold 2011 [2000]); vitiated the "'lineage theory' or 'descent theory'" of British social anthropologists in Africa in the 1940s–1960s (Kuper 1982: 71); and obscured, if not obstructed the understanding of kinship outside Africa (e.g., Barnes 1962; Pina-Cabral 1989; Rivière 1993; Bamford and Leach 2009). Such concerns derive from the growing, if not universal dominance of biological, or genetic, genealogies over competing alternatives evident not simply in the growing popularity of DNA-genealogies in the United States and elsewhere, but also in debates over what kinds of genealogies – a question inseparable from *whose* genealogies – should be considered proof of property rights in court cases, for example, in Australia (Patterson 2005: 9), Vanuatu (Kolshus 2011), the Solomon Islands (Berg 2014), and Romania (Chelcea 2016). The historical development of such competing systems and their contemporary significance in plural, relationally defined, competing systems of kinship all warrant close analysis.

Some social-cultural anthropologists now identify *genealogy* with *biological* theories of *descent*, seeming to accept the would-be cultural domination of biological definitions of descent in our own time. In this chapter, I insist that neutral definitions of descent and genealogy are essential to analyze social fields in which genealogy and descent are never neutral. I define *descent* as ideas and practices of intergenerational relations between antecedents and descendants, or ancestries and posterities, however understood, and *genealogy* as the record thereof, whatever its form.[1]

In my view, descent and genealogy are intensely debated because of their enormous social value: *descent*, expressed in genealogies and other forms, is the crossroads between kinship – ideally "mutuality of being" (Sahlins 2013) – *and* discrimination. Mutuality is as much about who's out as who's in. These relations may be expressed metaphorically, but those metaphors (whatever they may be) owe their clout to their roots in real lives and deaths, however they happen. To assume *genealogy* is ultimately biological is to assume that people cannot be nurtured, sickened, or killed by, for example, common words, social acts, structures of privilege and prejudice, divine imprecations, or environmental injustice. In short, our theories of life and death processes require an integrated comparative historical understanding of physiological, political-economic, linguistic, phenomenological, and ecological processes, just to list some of the main contenders going way beyond simplistic binaries like "biology" and "society."

I cannot hope to present such a fully integrated analysis here. But through this retrospective on *descent*, as it emerged historically in the heartlands of *anthropology* in its early forms and was, and is, tested repeatedly in comparative ethnographic research throughout the rest of the world, I hope to illuminate some of the reasons why we must continue to deepen our understanding of the paradoxical unity of amity *and* enmity, respect *and* contempt, inclusion *and* exclusion at the heart of *kinship*, in which – as decades of feminist research has shown – our most intimate familial relationships are inextricable from political-economic relations on the widest scale, and our workplaces likely to be the most crucial forcing-houses of our intimate-civic relations.

"Look ... to the hole of the pit whence ye are digged" (Morgan 1871: xxiii, citing Isaiah 51: 1). So Morgan advised the reader about to plunge into the deep history of the Human Family from its primal origin to its present diversity outlined in *Systems of Consanguinity and Affinity of the Human Family*, which founded the comparative study of kinship. Our ancestral trials and errors, "instead of revolting the mind," will reveal "with sensible clearness" how we got to our current state. Drawing on the ethnographic and historical research inspired by Morgan and his successors, we can apply Morgan's maxim to the study of descent in the lives and works of anthropologists' subjects and selves alike, thereby clarifying the multiple understandings of descent that all parties brought to their encounters and the consequences of their relations for our present views and ways forward.

3.1 "So Familiar Are These Ancient Household Words": Descent, Mother, Earth, Blood, Child …

"So familiar are these ancient household words, and the relationships which they indicate," so deeply embedded in our closest relationships over our lifetimes, that they might seem "simple … contain[ing] nothing of interest" (Morgan 1871: 11). If we suppose others' words are similar to ours, we might disregard their words or not even hear them (Rivers 1914a: 3–4). Had Morgan been raised by the Seneca or Ojibwe Indians with whom he later did research, or had he or Rivers grown up in New Guinea, or West Africa, or the Amazon, then they might have been multilingual from infancy, familiar with many kinds of relationship terms, and – depending on their relationships – they might have learned to shift easily among them.

Morgan trained as a lawyer, so he was aware of the antiquity of these words. His analysis drew on legal, religious, political, and medical terminologies that had dominated professional and popular practices of kinship in Europe for at least two millennia. "The Human Family" was a common phrase in Protestant periodicals since at least the mid-1700s based on biblical conceptions of the unity of humankind descended from Adam and Eve. While Morgan considered "blood ties" to be primordial, his assumptions about blood in life-and-death processes must be seen in the context of the debates over religion, medicine, and the environment in his lifetime (Feeley-Harnik 1999). *Consanguinity* and *affinity* derive from Roman law, the basis of law codes throughout Europe and its dominions abroad; Morgan adopted them from William Blackstone's *Commentaries of the Laws of England* (Trautmann 2008 [1987]: 51). Blackstone himself recognized the gaps between jurists' Latin and the vernacular languages of kinship in his lifetime (1723–1780).

The changing meanings of *blood*, *Blut*, *sang*, and comparable terms in Europe over the past thousand years are still wide-open fields of inquiry.[2] Despite the prominence of *consanguinitas* in discussions of inheritance in Roman law, and in the European law codes it influenced, *blood* was not prominent in vernacular expressions of kinship, descent, or generation in medieval Europe (Sabean and Teuscher 2013). According to Guerreau-Jalabert (2013) and Teuscher (2013) Christians in medieval Europe were concerned not with *blood* relations, but relations of *flesh*, and not *flesh* in isolation but in relation to *spirit* – *caro et spiritus* in Latin. These must be analyzed together as a relationally defined pair. Blood began to figure into vernacular theories of descent in Europe only in the 1500s, beginning in Spain. Nirenberg's (2009: 248–249) observations are especially valuable.

Spanish ideologies of blood, drawn from vernacular theories of animal breeding, spread to their plantation-colonies in the New World as a way of solving labor problems (Hill 2015). Nelson (2010: 1376, see pp. 1370–1373, 1378–1380) documents comparable ideas in the French colony of Saint-Domingue (later Haiti) in the 1750s–1780s about the relevance of *improving* and *perfecting* kinds of animals – *améliorer, perfectionner les espèces* – to achieving these goals in humans. Ideas and practices of descent in animals and humans were inseparable from far broader political-economic goals called *improvement* in Great Britain, *amélioration* in France, *mejoramiento* in Spain, and in their colonies.

More detailed historical data on ideas and practices of descent in humans and in animals – including particular species of animals – is essential because ultimately Merino sheep became the focus of experimental animal breeding in northern Europe, leading to new ideas about descent and generation in human beings. The Spanish royal embargo on the export of Merinos was broken in 1723 with a secret shipment to Sweden in 1723. Merinos were imported into Germany by 1765, France by 1767–1786, Austria by 1775, and Great Britain by 1787 (Ryder 1983: 427), raising questions about descent and inheritance in animals that resulted in a gradual shift from elements of places, especially *soil, ground, Boden*, and *climate* or *Klima*, considered as *outer/Äussere*, to reproductive processes expressed generically as *blood/Blut/sang*, increasingly seen as *inner/Innere*.

3.2 From Soils-Airs-Waters ... to Blood-based Theories of Descent

The breeding experiments of farmer Robert Bakewell (1725–1795) at Dishley Grange, Leicestershire, were crucial to these transformations in two respects. First, Bakewell soon discovered that breeding for mutton degraded the quality and quantity of sheep's wool (Orel 2009: 421). So breeders in Great Britain became mutton producers while breeders in Moravia (in the Austro-Hungarian Empire, now in the Czech Republic) became Europe's leading producers of fine wool, and central Europe a leader in the manufacture of fine woolen textiles, from the 1700s to the 1830s–1840s, when the British established Merino sheep in Australia (Orel and Wood 1998: 81–82), using their colonial subjects from nearby islands in the Torres Strait as laborers, a point to which we will return. During that period, "nothing compared with wool as a generator of wealth" (Wood and Orel 2001: vi).

Second, Bakewell's experiments resulted in a shift in emphasis from *soil* (also *pasture* or *ground*) to *blood*. William Marshall (1745–1818), the son of yeoman farmers from North Yorkshire writing on Britain's rural economy in the late 1700s, explained the distinction by comparing the *management* of farms in Lincolnshire to those in neighboring Norfolk, where the connection of *soil* to *stock* (also called *breed* or *blood*) still prevailed (1787, 2: 136, his emphasis; see 1790, 1: 462, 464). By contrast Bakewell put the emphasis on "BREED, or what is technically termed BLOOD, namely, on the specific quality of the parents." Bakewell's "means of improvement" was based on breeding "not from the same line only, but the same family," a practice so long established that it was known by its own "technical phrase" called "BREEDING INANDIN." By "letting male stock" to other breeders in the district, "the blood, in a short time, circulates through every part, and every man of spirit partakes of the advantage" (Marshall 1790, 1: 298–300, 305, his emphasis).

In the 1820s, Moravian sheep breeders began to shift from "generation" (*Zeugung*) to "heredity" (*Vererbung*) in discussing the transmission of traits from parents to children (Orel and Wood 1998: 79, 81), with a corresponding shift from outer to inner processes. Franz Cyril Napp, abbot of the St. Thomas Monastery at Brno (whom Mendel succeeded in 1867), argued in a Sheep Breeders Society meeting in 1836 that heredity involved the animals' *inner* physiology affecting their *outer* forms, and therefore required a focus on the inner physiology of animals not the *Boden* and *Klima* in which they were raised.

Historical links between the animal-breeders in Moravia and Great Britain in the 1760s–1830s to the new field of blood chemistry and morphology, which emerged in the 1770s (Coley 2001), remain to be explored. A British pioneer in this field in the 1840s was George Gulliver, a physiologist and anatomist at London's Royal College of Surgeons, whom Darwin consulted in 1855–1856 when he extended his morphological studies of fancy pigeons to their blood corpuscles, the selective breeding of fancy pigeons being his model for "natural selection" in *Origin of Species* (1859: 4–5, 7–43).

3.3 Material Structures of Descent in Animals and Humans: Breeding under Confinement

Charles Darwin (1809–1882) and Lewis Henry Morgan (1818–1881) incorporated the breeders' shift from soil to blood into the foundations of anthropological theory, but in very different ways. The shift from soil to blood took different forms in different regional and political settings (see for example, Frémont 1992). Further research may show these to be related to, for example, new ways of conceptualizing nationality in place and time and citizenship in terms of *jus soli* (right of soil, or birthplace) and *jus sanguinis* (right of blood, or descent), as well as local ideas and practices of belonging. More research on these complexities is essential for a deeper understanding of the social and political implications of shifts from locally understood *soils*, *airs*, *waters*, and the like, to *bloods*, and in understanding their transfer – as I will argue here – from understanding descent in animals considered other-than-human to humans, and for transforming would-be sciences of descent into social ideologies of us and not-us. A key issue must be a deeper understanding of the material dimensions of descent practices.

Breeders' ideas and practices of descent worked through material structures, the most important of which for participants and observers alike involved *breeding under confinement*. The shift from outer to inner, from soil to blood, was associated with a shift from many different methods of manipulating reproductive relations among free-ranging animals to a focus on breeding under confinement, enabling the selective process determining, as Darwin (1859: 467) stated, "which individual shall live and which shall die, – which variety or species shall increase in number, and which shall decrease, or finally become extinct" (1859: 467).

Practitioners conceptualized the shift in terms of *improvements* in breeding based on greater understanding of processes of reproduction in animals and plants. Yet breeding animals under confinement was clearly intended to give breeders greater control over the animals' lives and deaths absolutely. Confinement is a spatial-temporal process: fixing the animal in space, restricting its freedom of movement, in order to control its reproduction over time and focus on forms of generation – documented in the animals' genealogies or pedigrees – that appear to be temporal because they have been abstracted from their spatial framework. The old and new sciences of reproduction and selection must be understood in an inherently political context based on the ultimate inequality of breeder and bred.

What does this imply for anthropologists' studies of descent in human kinship? Their subjects were not confined like animals, but most of them over the next century were restricted in low-wage labor at the bottom of political-economic hierarchies worldwide. A rough analogy to the labor relations that Rivers later encountered in Melanesia – rough in part because men were the main labor migrants, leaving kinswomen and children behind – would be rural to urban migration in England concurrent with the shift from soil- to blood-based ideas/practices of descent and free-range to confined breeding and selecting. In Thompson's (1967) classic study of "Time, Work-Discipline, and Industrial Capitalism," the workers' spatial confinement is already invisible. The value of this pioneering study was to point to the significance of clock-timed work discipline in the formation of industrial and governmental labor regulations alike. But time-discipline depended upon the confinement of workers – *working families* – in *places* as Engels (1887 [1845]) documented in the case of Manchester based on research in 1842–1844.

Yet there is little research on how these workers conceptualized their kinship relations in these surroundings. Given the bits of countryside – from pigs to auriculas to pigeons – they famously bred into art forms in London, Birmingham, and Manchester, workers' understandings of thriving and dying are likely to have been complex. One possible hint of that complexity might be evident in the term *make-up* among people "born and bred" in Bacup (Edwards 2000, 2005), who might include descendants of Midlands-farmers. In the Midland counties of Marshall's day, *make-up* was the process of "making up rams for showing," that is, "the ART OF MAKING UP." Making up was an art because it required the careful selection of lambs on the basis of "blood, or parentage," then carefully feeding and sheltering them so they would become well-formed and fat, "fat [being] the best evidence ... of their fatting quality, – their natural propensity to a state of fatness" that rams let to breed will transmit to their progeny (1790, 1: 418–419, his emphasis).

In cultivating flowers and birds, factory workers in the heart of Great Britain's industrial cities might have retained some of the highest ideals of earth-based practices of descent, even while the cultivation of fancy animals and plants was increasingly governed by ideas about blood-based descent, and the workers themselves subject to what, in domesticated animals, would be called *confinement*. Whence a last caution about the need for further research. Earth-based ideas and practices of descent must have been associated with their own forms of exclusion as well as inclusion in the past, fully as draconian as blood-based forms have proved to be. Furthermore they clearly persisted alongside blood-based theories in some parts of Europe and in more submerged forms elsewhere. Richard Walther Darré (1930), who coined the Nazi slogan *"Blut und Boden,"* was trained in animal breeding; his teacher Gustav Frölich was an expert on breeding Merinos and other fine-wool sheep which – in Germany – retained both soil and blood-based theories (see Frölich, Spöttel and Tänzer 1929).

3.4 Charles Darwin and Lewis Henry Morgan: Anatomical and Social-linguistic Perspectives on Descent

Darwin and Morgan were contemporaries in a trans-Atlantic field of social relations, both with a foot in farming and both with an eye to *improvement* in humans, animals, and plants. Both incorporated the breeders' shift from soil to blood into the foundations of anthropological theory, but in very different ways. *Genealogy* became the documentation and analysis of these relations of descent based on *blood* as then conceived, yet both Darwin and Morgan retained important elements of earth-based ways of conceptualizing descent in ways that cannot be discussed fully here (see Feeley-Harnik 1999, 2004, 2013, 2014). While Darwin argued in *Origin of Species* (1859) that "descent is the hidden bond of connection," linking all the earth's creatures, extinct and living, the American lawyer-ethnologist

Morgan argued in *Systems of Consanguinity and Affinity of the Human Family* (1871) that "systems of relationship" link all "the great families of mankind," showing that they constitute one human family.

Darwin got models of descent from many sources, including human pedigrees and genealogical models in historical philology, as well as the work of naturalists. Much of his data came from the geological, botanical, and zoological research he conducted as a naturalist on his round-the-world voyage on the *H.M.S. Beagle* (1831–1836) and the years thereafter. In *Origin* he also credited the insights he got from animal and plant breeders in Great Britain with whom he started working on his return to England. The breeders informed him about the methods of "picking" and "roguing" (killing those that "deviate from the proper standard") they called "selection," or more generally "improvement" (1859: 29–43). He drew on their increasingly genealogical approach to breeding, commenting in *Origin* on "the remarkable effect which confinement or cultivation has on the functions of the reproductive system; this system appearing to be far more susceptible than any other part of the organization, to the action of any change in the conditions of life" (1859: 8).

The Variation of Animals and Plants under Domestication (1868) was the first of several books in which Darwin elaborated on his concept of "natural selection": "selection [is] the paramount power, whether applied by man to the formation of domestic breeds, or by nature to the production of species" (1868 [2nd], 2: 426). The manipulation of genealogies was well known to all – farmers, heralds, and the public at large. Darwin was more concerned with rejecting breeders' claims to mold life as they chose, lest his use of "natural selection" should suggest a divine plan. In *The Descent of Man, and Selection in Relation to Sex* (1871), he analyzed the natural history of human beings as a process of domestication in which "sexual selection" – a form of natural selection by attracting mates and repelling rivals – was paramount. Yet Darwin never examined the social complexities of the selective breeding he posited among people, whereas the patterning of marriage and descent among people worldwide was Morgan's preoccupation.

Morgan was born on his family's farm in central New York state; his father's will listed some 1,200 Merino sheep among his assets at death in 1826. Morgan studied classics and became a lawyer in Rochester while doing ethnology first as a member of a men's group, then – after meeting Ely Parker, a Seneca Indian from the Tonawanda reservation near Buffalo – as a serious venture (Morgan 1851). Morgan first learned about Iroquois relationship terms through Ely Parker and his family in the 1840s, enough to recognize comparable patterns later among Algonquian-speaking Ojibwe in northern Michigan, which inspired his further inquiries worldwide. Morgan's argument in *Systems* (1871) – that people are one "human family" – was based not on comparative anatomy and related fields, but on historical philology: the study of relationship terminologies, the semantic patterns among words like "mother," "father," "sister," "brother," and the like.

Scholars had begun to show that widely varying "Semitic" languages had originated by branching descent from a common source, as had the many languages classified as "Indo-European." The outstanding question was whether these several language families had common historical roots, thus proving the common historical origins of all of humankind. As Trautmann (2001, 2008 [1987]) documents, Morgan's innovation was to show that the linguistic patterns in kinship terminologies are not simply phonological or syntactic. They are semantic, articulating a limited number of patterns in sets of relationship terminologies, which Morgan broadly distinguished as "descriptive" or "classificatory," depending on the extent to which their terms separated or merged lineal and collateral lines (e.g., M and MZ, which in Morgan's American practice would have been distinct). Subsequent linguistic and historical evidence has confirmed Morgan's claims for the existence of such patterns and their persistence over centuries, if not his particular assumptions about how they related to patterns of marriage and descent.

Darwin articulated a new consensus about the nature of descent in animals and humans that had been roughly a century in the making. Morgan's discovery of patterns of relationship terms among humans worldwide was unprecedented. What was the immediate effect on anthropology of their almost simultaneously published major works? Darwin's bio-genealogical model provided the very basis of the new Anthropological Institute of Great Britain and Ireland formed in 1871 (Royal from 1907). Darwin's cousin Francis Galton, who assisted in its creation with colleagues including Thomas Huxley, John Lubbock, and E. B. Tylor, dominated its activities, including publications in its *Journal* before, during, and well after his four-year presidency of the AI in 1886–1889. Morgan's work was attacked immediately by Lubbock, in an address to the Anthropological Institute in London in 1871, printed as the lead article in their inaugural journal (Lubbock 1872), McLennan (1876), and later by Kroeber (1909), and generally ignored in Great Britain, Europe, and North America (but not in the Pacific) until Rivers (1914a) revived it.

3.5   Genealogical Methods and "the Genealogical Method": W. H. R. Rivers

W. H. R. Rivers (1864–1922), physician turned anthropologist, transformed the complex legacies of both Darwin and Morgan into "the genealogical method" (Rivers 1900, 1910). Ethnographic fieldwork in the Torres Strait Islands, South India, Melanesia, and the Pacific in 1898–1908 was the crucial factor.

Rivers trained as a medical doctor and worked in general medicine in London, Chichester, and at sea, as a ship's surgeon, before returning to St. Bartholomew's Hospital, London, in 1889–1890. In 1890, he began to focus on neurology, getting additional training in London, Jena (summer 1892), and Heidelberg (summer 1893), where he studied experimental psychology with Emil Kraepelin, chair of psychiatry at the University of Heidelberg, preparing for his lectureship on the physiology of the senses at Cambridge University starting in the fall of 1893 (Haddon 1922 and Head 1922). In 1897, Rivers was appointed university lecturer in physiological and experimental psychology at Cambridge (Haddon 1922: 786), whence Haddon's invitation to join Cambridge University's anthropological expedition to the Torres Strait Islands to do research in comparative psychology.

Rivers did not "consult" the eugenicist Francis Galton in 1897 before leaving England in April 1898, as historian George Stocking (1995: 112, 452n51) stated. Rivers' one letter to Galton in January 1897 and four letters to Galton's acolyte Karl Pearson in 1896–1897 (on various administrative matters) show that Rivers was already a member of the Anthropometric Committee of the Cambridge Philosophical Society that Galton initiated around the same time the members of the Anthropological Institute of Great Britain and Ireland elected him to be their president for four years.[3] Rivers knew Galton's genealogical methods, and he would have learned Kraepelin's methods when they worked together in 1893.

Rivers' first paper (1899a), presented to the Anthropological Section of the British Association for the Advancement of Science, described his work in "comparative psychology": physiological tests of sensory acuity, color vision, writing, and drawing. The first of the two "new departures" announced in his second paper (1899b) was also physiological: a new method of measuring skin color. The second departure – "genealogies" – was the *unanticipated* result of his following conventional practice in experimental psychology. The genealogies intended to provide data on what he called "real" or "blood" ties (1900: 76–77, 81; 1904: 144; 1907: 322–323; 1908: 65) revealed instead a new world of *social, historical,* and *geographical* data on interpersonal and interfamilial *relationships* across the islands and beyond.

As he explained in his third paper (1900), now entitled "A Genealogical Method of Collecting Social and Vital Statistics," he did genealogies to

> study ... as exactly as possible the relationship to one another of the individuals on whom we were making psychological tests. I soon found that the knowledge possessed by the natives of their families was so extensive, and apparently so accurate, that a complete collection of the genealogies as far back as they could be traced would be interesting and might enable one to study many sociological problems more exactly than would be otherwise possible.
>
> *(1900: 74)*

Studying genealogical relations with local people provided "social and vital statistics" in "native terms" with "concrete instances" of relations undistorted by English-language abstractions (1899b: 879). In addition he learned "*the names of relationships* which given individuals apply to other members of their community" (1900: 78, my emphasis), which are tied to the social "functions" of particular kin, like the "maternal uncle" and "son-in-law" and "brother-in-law," the subjects of his fourth and fifth papers (1901a, 1901b).

"On the Functions of the Maternal Uncle in Torres Strait" (1901a) and "On the Functions of the Son-in-Law and Brother-in-Law in Torres Strait" (1901b) in *Man* might seem now to exemplify the arcane preoccupations of the old guard, but they were revolutionary in their time. The author of the lead article in this issue of *Man* 1 was Francis Galton, the Anthropological Institute's erstwhile president, and now the Institute's first Huxley Memorial Lecturer (after an inaugural biography of Thomas Huxley). His subject, summarized as "Race Improvement" by editor John Linton Myres, was his Huxley Lecture: "The Possible Improvement of the Human Breed under Existing Conditions of Law and Sentiment" (Galton 1901). Rivers' revival of Morgan's conception of classificatory kinship systems was a direct rejection of racializing eugenical approaches to kinship and descent not limited to Galton. Note that Rivers' contemporary Durkheim (1898a: 318) made his more radical claim, that kinship "is a social tie or it is nothing," in the midst of the Dreyfus Affair in France. Durkheim never said he emphasized the sociality of relationships to counter the biometrics of Galton's counterpart in France, Alphonse Bertillon (who, as a self-described hand-writing expert gave false testimony at Dreyfus' trial that contributed to prolonging his incarceration). Yet Durkheim's "L'individualisme et les intellectuels" (1898b), supporting Dreyfus and arguing in the face of rampant anti-Semitism for a new religion of humanitarianism, appeared the same year.

Rivers' field notes preserved in the Haddon Papers at Cambridge University Library show that Rivers collected many more genealogies in far more detail than any of his publications suggest: some 67 three-to-five generation groups he called "families" or "clans" in the Torres Strait Islands in 1898 to 300 or more such clusters in the New Georgia Islands, western Solomons, in 1908.[4] But the big surprise, given Rivers' background, is to find that he made lists of *names of relationships* beginning already in his earliest research in 1898, the names, like the genealogies, neatly summarized on 6 × 8-inch cards in the form: X [name] called Y [name] Z [relationship term in local language] = A [English-language equivalent in X's immediate lineal kin].

How did Rivers learn about "names of relationships" associated with "classificatory systems" of kinship (Rivers 1900: 78)? Morgan's *Systems* died at birth in Great Britain, when McLennan (1876: 249–315) claimed his relationship terms were merely terms of address, as Rivers (1914a: 6–8) later explained. But Morgan's work lived on in the Pacific through the efforts of the missionary-ethnologist Lorimer Fison, who responded to his questionnaire with data from Fiji and continued corresponding with Morgan until his death, while spreading Morgan's methods among his colleagues, including Codrington in the Solomons and Howitt in Australia, whence they came to anthropologists like Haddon, and to Codrington's students and their descendants, like John Patteson Pantutun with whom Rivers worked in 1908 (see Gardner 2008, 2009; Kolshus 2014: 161–164, Stocking 1995: 23, 46). Based on his fieldwork in Vella Lavella, where Rivers worked in 1908, Berg (2014: 110) suggests that "Genealogical charts in Rivers's published and unpublished materials may in fact well represent what were people's own depictions of their own kinship systems." Rivers (1914a: 1, 4–5) celebrated Morgan's singular discovery of classificatory systems of relationships, and his insistence on their social significance, together with his own genealogical method. Praising Rivers in the wake of his early death, Mauss (1923: 2–3) too celebrated his "méthode généalogique" together with Morgan's "méthode de nomenclatures" as landmarks in the comparative historical study of social forms.

Rivers did try to assimilate native "relationship terms" into the biogenealogical methods of experimental psychologists in Germany and Great Britain. In his account of "Kinship" in the western Torres Strait Islands (1904: 129) he acknowledged the disparity between his genealogies (and English relationship terms implicit therein) and Islanders' relationship terms: "The system of kinship is of the kind known as 'classificatory', and none of the terms have exact English equivalents." But he still provided "a genealogy of an ideal family" marked with relationship terms, followed by a list of the terms "with their approximate meanings" in English, both limited to the positions – (great) (grand) parents, siblings, and (grand) child – that would make sense to his English readers (1904: 129, Table 18).

Yet he kept recording the discrepancies between "classificatory" terms and their seeming counterparts in English. In 1898, he encountered Murray [Mer] Islanders' insistence on the social reality of "very secret" adoptions over "real parentage," the subject of recent land disputes in courts decided for the adoptee (1904: 151). Murray Islanders also introduced Rivers to "the relationship of *tukoiab* ['brothers'] ... this artificial relationship ... apparently regarded as equivalent to the real relationship so far as those individuals were concerned" (1904: 131). And here too he encountered *lu giz* (described below), which he did not pursue, but did not forget either. In *Reports ... VI* (1908: 92), the list of relationship terms and their "approximate translations" are followed by "more complete accounts of their meanings." *Lu giz*, at the head of the list is defined approximately as: "great-grandfather or great-grandmother, their brothers and sisters and older ancestors." Rivers then adds: "This term, which means the founders of things or the foundation of things, is used for all ancestors and collateral relatives of generations earlier than that of the grandparents," to which he appends this footnote: "*Lu giz* is also the name for the swollen base of a tree trunk, such as that of the coco-nut palm" (1908: 93 and n2), a hint of links between humans and plants (especially cultivars), that have since proven basic to cultural theories of the generation, growth, and death of organisms in the region more broadly (e.g., Bamford 2007; Fox 1971; Leach 2003; Mosko 2009; Peluso 1996).

Reaching for approximations to build bridges to his English-speaking colleagues, Rivers laid the foundations for what Hocart (1937: 545) later denounced as the fallacy of "kinship extensions," in which the English model – "descriptive," as Morgan called it – was not approximate but presumed universal, and the kin deemed immediate in that model (or later counterparts like "nuclear family") were claimed to be ontologically, historically, developmentally, or evolutionarily primary, all others being secondary derivations. Thus, as Hocart (1937: 545–546) observed: "A great many investigators never get beyond the first use of a word that happens to come their way … Upon this muddled lexicography has been built up a whole edifice" of fantastical social life.

Writing in the midst of the soon to be "World War," Rivers (1917: 308) began to think differently about the "language which is used between a subject people and its rulers [which] usually differs in pronunciation, vocabulary, and grammar from that which the people use in their intercourse with one another" (1917: 308). He argued that inequality fosters incomprehension, beginning with the "distorted language" that arises when a person from the dominant group "does not learn from the natives but from those of his own race … [t]he incorrect usages are thus passed on and perpetuated … produc[ing] a systematized form of language … which is adopted by the rulers and becomes the accepted means of intercourse between them and the people they govern." The "whole range of [local] culture" may thus be distorted, leading to "injustice and misunderstanding … hypocrisy and double-dealing" (1917: 308–310).

Following his work with shell-shocked soldiers in the war, Rivers seems to have become more aware of the political-economic dimensions of social-psychological processes of death, regeneration, and regrowth. In his several discussions of the value of his genealogical method for gathering "social and vital statistics," he always put the social before the vital – such measures as "the average size of families, the proportion of the sexes, the proportion of children who grow up and marry to the total number born, the proportion of the sexes who grow up to adult life, etc." (1900: 80–81). When he returned to these issues in "Depopulation in Melanesia" (Rivers 1922), he was concerned about the effects of political-economic factors like forced labor recruitment and long-term labor migration on what he saw as social-psychological matters of fertility, morbidity, and mortality. Scholars have since argued that introduced diseases were sufficient to account for the drastic population declines that Rivers and his colleagues attributed to abuses in labor relations in Melanesia in the late nineteenth and early twentieth centuries (Bayliss-Smith 2014;

Bennett 2014). Akin's ethnographic and historical research in Malaita, southeast Solomons, shows that local men, who had been involved in the colonial government's repopulation project before World War II, initiated the *Maasina Rule* movement in the mid-1940s in the focal area of the project, with local concerns about repopulation among their main concerns (2013: 120–127, 166–167; see 234–235, 393n10). A full-scale historical restudy of depopulation in Melanesia from the perspectives of local people has yet to be done.

3.6   From Rivers' "Genealogical Method" to "Descent Theory"

With Rivers, the "genealogical method" he had announced in English and French became widespread in anthropology. His words have kept echoing, but his legacy following his early death in 1922 was complex, as Langham (1981: 159) notes. Our understanding would benefit from "alternative histories of British social anthropology" (Kuper 2005) and worldwide. To my mind these alternatives should include what cannot be done in this short chapter: consider the possible relevance to intellectual transformations in kinship studies of the second "world war" in which genealogy and descent were to become central to ideologies in Europe and North America defining who should live and die and related matters like who counted as an acceptable citizen or refugee. The most striking development in the anthropological study of descent in the decades from the 1920s into the 1960s was a shift to focus on the politics of *lineages*, separated from *kinship*, exemplified in the Africanist ethnography of the 1930s, 1940s, and 1950s into the early 1960s when most European colonies in Africa became independent.

Rivers' emphasis on "intensive research," especially on documenting kinship relations "in native terms," shaped how anthropologists' studies of the politics of descent developed in different regions. Rivers would have acknowledged that he did not perfectly exemplify the ideal of "intensive research" he advocated for himself and his students based on his experiences (1914b: 1–2). His linguistic skills were limited. Working with people in communities, speaking mainly the pidgins he despised, he had to use interpreters to get to vernacular ideas and practices, and in his "survey work" he often fell back on single informants. Yet his emphasis on the complexities of relationship terms, and other matters of social relations more generally, promoted ideals of working closely with local people to get their understanding in their own terms – an ideal now more commonly attributed to Malinowski (but that Malinowski understood to come from Rivers, see Young 2004: 161–167), and evident already in the work of his predecessors like Morgan, Fison, and Codrington, among others. Malinowski and Firth both criticized Rivers for what he did not see or understand. But they both carried his ideals of intensive fieldwork based on vernacular understanding of kinship even further, including pioneering ethnographies of sexuality, love, and desire (Malinowski 1929; Firth 1936: 125–185, 1990). Thus they built on Rivers' study of depopulation in Melanesia even if they did not further his historical political-economic analysis. By 1930, Malinowski (1930: 22, 19) had identified Rivers' goal – which he expressed as "what kinship really means to the native" – as his own, while attributing "the bastard algebra of kinship" to contemporaries "one and all influenced by the work of Rivers" (though perhaps he meant Radcliffe-Brown in particular).

While Malinowski is recognized for his pioneering work in the pragmatics of speech (Young 2011), Firth's work with Tikopians integrating linguistic, social-cultural, material, and historical intricacies of kinship and descent in Tikopia is especially outstanding. More than any others of his contemporaries, even Hocart, he retained Tikopians' vernacular terms, or the roots of such terms, in his analytical vocabulary, for example, the use of *ramage* rather than *lineage* and his retention of the Tikopians' own term *paito* ("house") as a still more accurate expression of their views of what he called a *ramage* (Firth 1936: 344–370). Two decades later, Firth (1957: 6) – striving for a comparative perspective on kinship in Polynesia – shifted to more abstract analytic terms tied to generic social "functions," abandoning *paito*/"house" for *lineage* and limiting *ramage* to non-unilineal descent groups based on choice. Leach (1958), on the other hand, went deeper into the vernacular significance of Trobriand kin terms, arguing that the multiple meanings of *tabu*, which Malinowski claimed to be homonyms, were related aspects of one complex semantic field.

Radcliffe-Brown took Rivers' work in an altogether different direction. By his own account he was Rivers' pupil in psychology for three years and "his first pupil in social anthropology in the year 1904." Yet in 1931 – now president of the Anthropology Section (H) in the British Association for the Advancement of Science – he announced to his constituency that Rivers was a psychologist with "no training in ethnology or in archaeology [and] a partial acquaintance" at that. Rivers' integration of history and ethnology was to be set aside from "social anthropology" conceived as "Comparative Sociology" based on applying "the generalizing method of the natural sciences" to society and culture (Radcliffe-Brown 1931: 146–148).

Radcliffe-Brown's studies with Rivers and Haddon at Cambridge in 1902–1904 were followed by fieldwork in the Andaman Islands (1906–1908) – where he confessed to failing at the genealogical method – and a fellowship at Trinity College, Cambridge, in 1908–1914 (Firth 1956: 288, 291n1). In 1910–1912, he did two years of research in Australia among coastal communities of Aboriginal people displaced from their ancestral lands. He documented his research in reports culminating in "The Social Organization of Australian Tribes" (1930–1931), a reconstruction of their ancestral practices based on interviews using interpreters as he had in the Andaman Islands. In the process, he steadily drained his predecessors' approaches to living social relations, resulting in what even his supporter A. P. Elkin (1956: 246–248) regarded as the classification of cultural ideals at best, reifying "lines of descent" abstracted from the vicissitudes of everyday life.

The counterpart to Radcliffe-Brown's "social organization" in Australia in 1930–1931 is *African Political Systems* (1940), a collection of papers edited by Fortes and Evans-Pritchard with a preface by Radcliffe-Brown. But there is a crucial difference between them: in the African context, lines of descent – *lineages* – have been redefined as *political* structures *divorced from kinship*. How did that happen? Fortes (1955: 22) and Eggan (1963: 121) cite different papers by Radcliffe-Brown in the1920s and 1930s as his stepping stones. Thus Africa became the *locus classicus* of what became known as " 'lineage theory' or 'descent theory' " (Kuper 1982: 71): the place where it was born, lived, and proclaimed dead of its own excesses.

Descent and *lineage*, like *genealogy*, are ancient household words, and like genealogy, they have been commonly – but variously – embroiled in political significance – and insignificance – among peoples throughout the world for millennia. So how did anthropologists come to see *lineages* as *political* independently from kinship – and in what senses political – in working with these people in these parts of the world (at least from the Pacific to Africa) in these decades from the 1920s–1960s, where they were not in fact self-governing, but European subjects striving for political independence achieved in national terms mainly in the early 1960s? And how might these anthropological inquiries about descent have been related to scholarly and popular debates about descent in intra- and inter-national struggles, culminating in World War II and its aftermath, in which Europeans and North Americans (and many of their colonial subjects) were ultimately involved?

Evans-Pritchard's *The Nuer* (1940) is so celebrated and criticized in part because Evans-Pritchard so clearly elucidated Radcliffe-Brownian principles of *descent* – and now *social structure* rather than Rivers' *social organization* – in relation to ethnographic particulars of Nuer life that seemed at first, or at least partially, to affirm them. So how did Evans-Pritchard come to his understanding of *lineages* as *political* structures distinct from *kinship*, which he restricted to a *domestic* domain? As he put it: "We thus formally distinguish between the lineage system, which is a system of agnatic groups, and the kinship system, which is a system of categories of relationship to any individual" (1940: 194). An immediate answer might help in exploring broader questions ultimately.

Evans-Pritchard began working in the Sudan in 1926, first among the Azande, then other groups in the region, then in 1930–1936 with the Nuer (Beidelman 1974). In August 1931 – as he and Fortes, who was present, later reported – Evans-Pritchard was discussing Nuer descent groups with Radcliffe-Brown who suggested that he should use "lineage" to describe their "kind of agnatic groups" (Evans-Pritchard 1946: 908), or in Fortes' recollection: "'My dear Evans-Pritchard, it's perfectly simple, that's a segmentary lineage system, and you'll find a very good account of it by a man called Gifford'. Thereupon Radcliffe-Brown gave us a lecture on Gifford's analysis of the Tonga system" (Fortes 1979: viii; see Fortes 1978: 2). Still later Evans-Pritchard (1973: 12n2) recalled that he and Max Gluckman agreed Robert Lowie's *Primitive Society* (1920) was the one book he should bring into his fieldwork with the Nuer: "It was a very good choice" (Evans-Pritchard 1973: 12n2). Lowie's *Primitive Society* was the book that Radcliffe-Brown and Malinowski recommended to their students in the 1920s and 1930s – after Rivers' death and before their own general treatises (Matthey 1996: 23, citing observations by Isaac Schapera and Hortense Powdermaker as well).

Lowie's subjects, ranging from "marriage" to "government" and "justice" (in that order), draw on ethnography from all over the world, including Gifford's earlier research with Miwok Indians in California focusing on *moieties*. In "Government," Lowie (1920: 391) accepts Maine's (1861) and Morgan's (1877) "sharp distinction between kinship (tribal) and territorial (political) organization," questioning only "to what extent it is coterminous with the distinction between rude and advanced cultures." Lowie kept the question open, imagining that emergent governments might be based on either, both, or some other principle altogether (1920: 396).

Perhaps Gifford was keeping these questions open too. But in 1920–1921 he did research with Tongans – they seem to have been from the governing class – who explained the *haa* – the basis of government called "tribe, class, family" in English: "Each consists of a nucleus of related chiefs about whom are grouped inferior relatives, the lowest and most remote of whom are commoners." They gave Gifford manuscripts documenting their historical antiquity (some dating to the early 1600s), otherwise proclaimed publically in genealogical recitations preceding important speeches (Gifford 1929: 29–30, see pp. 29–47). Gifford's talks with Tongans seem to have persuaded him to talk again with Miwok in California. Gifford (1944: 376) later recalled his awakening in these terms: "At the time I wrote 'Miwok Moieties' [1916, based on research in 1913–1915] I knew nothing about lineages among the Miwok. The presence of lineages [as 'autonomous political units'] obtruded itself in 1923."

As he had in Tonga, Gifford discussed with the Miwok the relationship of persons to places. *Nena* proved to have a "two-fold meaning [as] a male lineage or patrilineal joint family [*and as*] the ancestral home in which the lineage is supposed to have arisen" (my emphasis). Tongan rulers retained sovereignty over their country throughout the colonial period. In California, the Miwok had been pressured since 1848 to move from their ancestral places and resettle in villages where they had no sovereignty. Even so: "Yet in spite of one hundred years of … pressure we find that every person today remembers the putative place of origin of his paternal ancestors" (Gifford 1926: 391–392). *Nena* – people *and places* – could still have been critical to Miwok ideas and practices of descent as later studies suggest (e.g., Basso 1996; Thornton 2008). But in California in the early 1920s the status of *nena* as a *lineage* in political terms, which *excluded* the dimensions of *place* that Miwok might still have considered crucial, was the very outcome of the territorial expansion of the US government in which they were now politically encapsulated.

Perhaps in 1931, or in 1932–1934 when he was teaching sociology at Fuad University in Cairo, Evans-Pritchard also read William Robertson Smith's analysis of the political relations of *kindred* groups (or *local groups* or *septs*, never *lineages*) in ancient Arabia as discussed by Arab genealogists of the time. Writing about "tribe and clan" among the Nuer for *Sudan Notes and Records* in 1933–1935, Evans-Pritchard (1935: 79n1) noted: "I have constantly found myself comparing the Nuer system of lineages and tribes with those of Arabia in olden times. These words of Robertson Smith fit Nuer conditions exactly." Dresch (1988) argues that Smith's work was critical in moving Evans-Pritchard from the historical study of the formation and dissolution of lineages based on ideologies of agnatic descent he presented in these essays to his structuralist focus on "time and space" at the heart of *The Nuer* (1940: Chapter 3). In fact, these essays – now little read – are fascinating for their fine detail on the vicissitudes of Nuer social relations west and east of Bahr el-Jebel River (the "White Nile," which had been the major ivory- and slave-trading route in the nineteenth century, persisting into the twentieth, see Johnson 1989, 1994: 114–115, 130). They also include a much fuller account of the *Kuaar Muon*, "land experts" with "ritual powers over the earth … and its productiveness and by extension over mankind which lives on and by the earth" (1934: 43), discussed in far narrower terms as a "leopard-skin chief" in *The Nuer* (1940: 172; see Hutchinson 1996: 131–132 on their fate in the political consolidation of the Anglo-Egyptian Sudan).

In positing for the Nuer a form of political organization considered historically and evolutionarily prior to the current "territorial" colonial system in which they were contained; in positing their lineage system to be *the* political form among people otherwise imagined as having no formal government; in describing that system by the oxymoron "ordered anarchy" anchored to an abstract model of time and space; and in following Radcliffe-Brown in separating the political domain of *lineages* from the domestic domain of *kinship*, thereby making the place of kin – conceived narrowly as *residence* – secondary to *descent*, Evans-Pritchard (1940: 3–7) set his analysis of Nuer politics into a cultural, social, geopolitical, and historical limbo replete with contradictions. Evans-Pritchard himself had to conclude his summary of "Kinship and the Local Community among the Nuer" by suggesting that "the clear, consistent, and deeply rooted lineage structure of the Nuer … the agnatic principle … unchallenged" explained why "the tracing of descent through women is so prominent and matri-locality so prevalent" (1950: 391). The work was controversial from the start. Many anthropologists have since returned to what Marshall Sahlins (1965: 105) called "the E.-P. paradox." Kuper (1982) and Holý (1996) offer full discussions of the literature within and beyond Africa. My brief comments will focus on issues more overlooked.

The complexities of lineage relations on the ground, over generations, in a steadily expanding social, political-economic, and historical frame-work – this was the focus of the studies that Evans-Pritchard's provoca-tive study inspired. The reassessment of *The Nuer* began with Audrey Richards' (1941) review calling for much closer attention to the variability of "lineages or 'segments'" and "their liability to change owing to his-toric factors," as well as the influence of individuals and groups organized by alternative principles that could reinforce or conflict with lineages. Noting that "[t]he very existence of so many principles of ranking makes for varied status of the individuals within the segment concerned," she concluded: "I therefore cannot see the distinction between domestic and political systems of segments sharply defined as Dr. Evans-Pritchard has described it. The two systems seem to me to grow out of one another and in the dynamics of a social situation constantly to overlap" (1941: 51). Feminist scholars have since followed up on all these issues in detail, showing that descent traced through women, and communi-ties organized around them, were crucial elements of Nuer-Dinka polit-ical life in the precolonial and colonial periods; multiple perspectives on kinship relations coexisted, including multiple systems of marriage and other partnerships, ranked hierarchically (e.g., Gough 1971; McKinnon 1999). Hutchinson's (1996, 2000) research among the Nuer in 1980–1983 (with brief visits in the early 1990s) documents the wide-ranging debates among Nuer and Dinka on these issues.

Meyer Fortes (1953) argued that unilineal descent groups could act as corporate bodies under certain conditions, but his main focus was on how lineages were transformed over time through developmental and histor-ical processes. In "The Significance of Descent in Tale Social Structure" (1944: 363), he argued that the major contribution of Tale ethnography was to illuminate "the time factor in social structure ... [the] relationship between the component parts of a social system *in time* as well as *at a given time*" (his emphasis). His analysis of "Time and Social Structure" based on Ashanti ethnography – part of a collection dedicated to Radcliffe-Brown – inspired many later studies of "developmental cycles" in domestic groups set in the context of broader political-economic processes (Fortes 1949; see e.g., Chelcea 2003; Nave 2016).

Evans-Pritchard's student, Emrys Peters, returned to the Cyrenaica Bedouin (where he had been stationed with the R.A.F. during World War II), to do fieldwork in 1948–1950. He had intended his research to supplement Evans-Pritchard's (1949) study of the Sanusi Brotherhood of the Cyrenaica Bedouin done during the war and thus based mainly on texts but drawing on his model in *The Nuer*, despite significant differences in social-cultural, historical, and ecological circumstances. The research outlined in meticulous case studies published years later caused Peters to question models of so-called segmentary lineage organizations: "agnation is not one thing but many" (Peters 1960: 49); "Once contingencies are permitted to enter in, the lineage model ceases to be of use" (1967: 271).

John Middleton (1960), based on fieldwork with Lugbara in north-western Uganda and guided more by Fortes than by his advisor Evans-Pritchard (Beidelman 2010: 147), analyzed how demographic and ecological pressures could lead to the breakup of patrilineal kin groups over time. He focused on the deeply ambiguous position of elder men, heads of patrilineages, expected to act on behalf of their descendants in relation to their ancestors, but perennially suspected of acting in their own self-interest. T. O. Beidelman (1986), based on fieldwork among the Kaguru of Tanzania, wrote extensively on Kaguru views of the complex-ities and conflicts at the heart of matrilineal relations, epitomized in tales of Hyena and Rabbit, mother's brother and sister's son. Beidelman is unique in having written extensively – based on his own field notes – about the broader social and political fields of interaction between local people and the European and African officials with whom they interacted, uncommonly as kin (Beidelman 1982, 2012).

Carsten's (1995) and Graeber's (1995) analyses of the manipulation of genealogies in Malaysia and in Madagascar picked up on the processes of forgetting people's names that Evans-Pritchard documented in *The Nuer*, but never analyzed in case studies that might have revealed the ambiguities in ancestor–descendant relations, the blessings and curses, mutuality and violence, involved in making kin forgotten. Carsten (1995, 1997) set these processes in the historical context of migration in island Southeast Asia, and related the "forcible incorporation" of newcomers in cognatic kin groups to patterns of marriage and childbearing through which differences in people are remade into similarities, later contrib-uting to the study of remembering and forgetting to kin–state relations in Europe, Asia, and North America (Carsten 2007).

Irvine (1978), based on fieldwork among the Wolof, showed how the his-torical accuracy of genealogies was enforced among the Wolof in Senegal by low-born *grewal*, "praise-singers, genealogists, musicians – a kind of *griot*, or speech specialist" (Irvine 1978: 653). Setting their recitations into a "comparative political-economy of compliments and praise," Irvine argued that "*any* system of prestations and counter-prestations – that is, an economy (in a broad sense) – will necessarily include authori-tative statements as part of the exchange system" (1989: 258). In short: "Utterances, and indeed various aspects of linguistic form and its production, *can* be viewed as presentations, and thus as part of a political economy, not just a vehicle for thinking about one" (Irvine 1989: 262, her emphasis). Irvine's insights are especially relevant to scholars whose work on the invocation of kin terms in genealogies and in reciprocal terms of reference and address is already set in the context of political-economic relations. Three important examples would be Shryock's (1997) study of struggles over the authority of *isnad* – "chains of transmission" – of genealogies, oral and written – among Bedouin in contemporary Jordan; McGovern's (2012) study of claims and counter-claims to be "mother's brothers" and "sister's sons" among war refugees and locals in the forests at the boundaries of Guinea, Liberia, Sierra Leone, and Côte d'Ivoire; and Marques' (2013) study, based in Brazil's Pernambuco *sertão*, focusing on genealogical narratives of past and present conflicts, fraught with racializing tensions, as a means to reassess their kin relations in time *and in space*, including the settlements to which they aspire, which are key "centre[s] of socio-political gravity" (2013: 727).

Evans-Pritchard (1940: 192–195, 222, 247) was aware that what he called "agnation," the Nuer with whom he worked called *buth* ("to share"). What he called "lineage," the Nuer most often called *thok dwiel* (' "the entrance to the hut', the mother's hut"), also *thok mac* ("the hearth"), and sometimes *kar* ("a branch"). They also diagrammed "a lineage system" differently, not in bifurcating branches, but as "a number of lines running at angles from a common point" (1940: 202). Myhre (2014: 522n1), noting many studies of East African peoples documenting the presence of house-words among kin terms, has documented their significance among Chagga-speaking people in northeastern Tanzania in conveying the movement of *horu* ("bodily power") through humans, animals, and crops. Johnson's (1989, 1994) historical studies of the Upper Nile region since the early 1800s help to set patterns of kinship, descent, and prophecy among Nuer, Dinka, and others in this region into a broader political-ecological framework.

Scholars have yet to examine the links that might exist between (1) Nuer and Dinka terms of kinship and descent based on dwellings (of people, prophets, and others, living and ancestral), (2) the social geography of the particular places that could be involved – for example, houses, cattle pens, graves, spirit-sticks, waterholes, trees, mounds, dry and wet season settlements, shrines, and (3) the political-ecology of the region throughout the past two centuries to the present, including the soils, airs, and waters that might be relevant to local ideas and practices of the life, growth, and death of humans, animals, and plants alike. But Salas Carreño (2016), like Marques (2013), links the temporal and spatial dimensions of genealogical relations, and he incorporates the analysis of places as kin. Metcalf's (2010) analysis of the space–time dimensions of longhouses in Borneo is set in a deep historical analysis of political-economic and ecological transformations in the region, albeit one that sees "kinship organization to be largely irrelevant to longhouse communities … that grew up around enterprising men" (2010: 23). Shryock's (forthcoming) study of the "name/space" of the house, and hospitality within, as "an effective means to historicize patterns [of competing visions of sovereignty] that outlast events" is set in the context of two centuries of political-economic transformations in "the Adwan country" now mainly in Jordan. Cannell (2011) and the contributors to *New Directions in Spiritual Kinship* (Malik, Thomas and Wellman 2017) set these relations of person and place into cosmic realms encompassing spiritual beings.

3.7 Descent and Discrimination

I have argued that Darwin's and Morgan's works marked a shift from soil to blood in ideas and practices of descent. Yet both Darwin and Morgan retained important elements of earth-based ways of conceptualizing descent, and this is wholly likely to have been the case more broadly. What might be called the geography of descent, or better, the political economy and ecology of descent, may be inferred from Darwin's work with breeders in the mid-nineteenth century and his study of worms at the end of his life (Darwin 1881). In Morgan it is evident in his work on human migrations, his beaver research (1868), and his study of *Houses and Houselife* (1881) at the end of his life, which he'd hoped to include as part of *Systems*. Even so, one clear result of the shift in emphasis from soil to blood in later work was a focus primarily on the *temporal* dimensions of descent, to the relative neglect of its spatiotemporal dimensions, ranging from lands, their soils and airs, to the no less chronotopic, and thus mnemonic and historical, dimensions of dwellings and related structures, their disruption akin to forgetting. *Residence* in a narrow sense became subordinate to *kinship* in many Anglophone and Francophone ethnographies of the 1930s–40s–50s–60s. (Audrey Richards' work with the Bemba is one striking exception.) The secondary status, or even invisibility, of the spatial dimensions of descent may have been compounded by the loss of sovereignty resulting from colonialism, persisting in postcolonial forms in and beyond the independence movements throughout the world in the early 1960s.

Social anthropologists' renewed attention to houses seems to have emerged in the late 1950s and early 1960s, but not from Morgan's *Houses and Houselife* (1881), obscured in the focus on *Systems of Consanguinity and Affinity* (1871). It is noteworthy that at least two among the earliest signs of renewed interest – Littlejohn's "The Temne House" (1960) and Bourdieu's attention to *la maysou* of his natal region of Béarn in "Célibat et condition paysanne" (1962: 37, 49, 53, 83–84, 106–107, Fig. 2, Photos 2, 5, 6) were by scholars who had done research in and outside their natal countries, and seen the impoverished agrarian communities in both, and military resettlement camps in the case of Algeria, tied into a common geopolitical-economic system riven with growing class differences within and across national and colonial borders. But the literature on "house societies" that emerged in the 1970s, largely associated with Lévi-Strauss, did not pick up on the political-economic or ecological dimensions of housing.

Sahlins (1965: 106) noted that the complex relationships between ideologies and the social organization of groups required examination from within and from without, "from the vantage of larger ecological circumstances, including relations to other groups." Later studies of descent got entangled in debates about actors' and analysts' models (see Holý 1979). Schneider's (1972, 1984) critiques of "the genealogical method" derived from those debates. Schneider was right to insist that we scrutinize terms like "blood relations" for cultural bias. But he ignored the arguably deeper issue, namely, the exclusionary dimensions of kinship theory and ethnographic practice still rooted in assumptions about "Civilized" middle-class families a century after Morgan's old dichotomy between Primitive Promiscuity and Monogamy had broken down, but not his distinction between descriptive and classificatory systems and the divide it marked among the world's peoples. The descriptive systems, those most distinguishing lineal from collateral lines, were those of the "Semitic, Aryan, and Uralian Nations" in the northern hemisphere, cirum-Mediterranean region, and European settlements abroad; the classificatory systems, grouping lineals and collaterals in various unfamiliar ways, were those of the rest of the world (1871: 73–75).

Rivers rejected Galton's scientific racism, but he retained the difference between peoples with "classificatory" systems and those with "descriptive" systems, as Morgan had defined them. He didn't go the next step to argue that relationship systems worldwide are *all classificatory*, all composed of complex semantic fields of significance. Rivers inspired a renewed interest in "classificatory" systems of relations, which eventually expanded to encompass the study of society-wide systems of symbolic classification. There was no corresponding study of so-called descriptive systems. On the contrary, Evans-Pritchard (1940: 194) separated the lineal dimension, *lineage*, from the "system of categories of relationship," which he identified with *kinship*. As generic political forms, *lineages* were devoid of semantic significance. Evans-Pritchard (1940: 205, 211, 212, 228, 236) refers to a "lineage idiom," or "lineage value," or "a system of values … providing the idiom in which their [lineage] relations can be expressed and directed"; later scholars speak of ideologies. Feminist scholars insisting on the mutual formation of kinship and political economy have examined particular categories like *mother* and *father* in cultural terms, especially with reference to gender relations. Actors and analysts alike may invoke *blood* relations to explain what gives these ideologies their political clout (Carsten 2011, 2013). Now we might inquire how they are tied into larger *classificatory systems* of kinship and discrimination, and how these might be grounded in broader ideas and practices of life and death.

Why systems? Barnes' (1967: 101–102) how-to on "Genealogies" makes two important points at the outset: "In kinship there are … always two parties to be considered," for people are never sons, daughters, or aunts on their own but always the son, daughter, or aunt of particular people. "Furthermore, in kinship there are no logically privileged positions," because everyone is someone's grandchild and potentially the grandparent of someone else. To these I would add a third point: however logically privileged or unprivileged they may be, or be culturally asserted to be, these positions, their relations, are never neutral. There are always depths, heights, nears, fars, thens, nows, befores, afters, first- and last-borns and dieds, articulated in these webs of relations. In short, these equivalences and unequivalences are the very stuff of which social similarities and differences are made and remade within and across generations, honed, at least in some cases, on the grindstone of human–animal relations.

These logical relations, which seem to be universal to kinship systems around the world, are the basis of social anthropologists' comparative perspective on kinship, including descent, and not any one culturally particular definition of the physiological processes involved in generation. This is a significant but not unique factor in kinship relations. Our "biology" of today is not the "biology" of a century ago, nor even the "biology" of a decade ago. As ideas and practices of descent shifted in greater Europe over some three centuries (if variably and inconsistently) from soil to blood, first in animals, then in people, and then to particles of blood in "genetics," so too genetics is being radically transformed by new techniques like precision breeding, and new discoveries like lateral gene transfer and epigenetics (that might seem to bring blood back to soil but now in radically changed political-economic and ecological conditions). And our physiologies – those of humans and the countless multitudes of organisms in which we are involved – are changing, and being changed, in the process. All biologies are "local" – to use Margaret Lock's (1993) term; geneticists in some parts of the world would make them individual. No one has yet become so Argus-eyed as to see our entwined lives and deaths in their entirety. Therefore the diverse perspectives of people all over the world, however they trace the pathways of life and death, are an invaluable resource, and the "biologies" of the erstwhile descriptivists must be incorporated into that comparative historical framework of analysis, set in relation to the multiple ways in which we unify and diversify ourselves, grounded in attention to political economy and ecology.

My ongoing hypothesis is that kinship systems articulate people's ongoing understandings of, and efforts to control, life and death processes. Kinship relations are where people first, last and ultimately, deal with such matters as the creation of life, gestation, birth, growth, death, decay, and transformation. Life and death are large and vague, whence the sharp learning curves of our close encounters.

Descent is a touchstone for these matters because descent, perhaps more than any other aspect of kin relations, is where kinship, its inclusions and exclusions, mutualities and discriminations, meet in the births and deaths of generational relations. Descent is where we all – kinship experts in our everyday lives – sort out again and again who counts as human now and for our past and future.

Acknowledgments

Many thanks to Sandra Bamford for inviting me to participate in this collection; to the staffs in Archives and Manuscripts at the Wellcome Library, University College, London, and at Cambridge University Library; to David Akin, Andrew Shryock, and Thomas Trautmann for their very helpful comments on a would-be ultimate draft, and to Alan Harnik for countless readings before and after.

Notes

1. Thus a genetic genealogy is a record of descent based on genetics, coined in England in 1906 to refer to the then emerging science of heredity and variation now commonly called genetics. Physiology is my term for ideas and practices of bodily processes involved in living and dying; biology (*biologie*, *Biologie*, etc.) – terms coined in the late 1700s–early 1800s, are the sciences of life and death processes (later including genetics) that developed in Europe and North America alongside various anthropologies (see above). Local biologies (Lock 1993: xxi, 39, 373–374) I take to be local physiologies shaped by and shaping vernacular ideas and practices of bodily processes. I follow Needham's approach to comparison based on polythetic classifications in which we may find "serial likenesses" among categories, without assuming "any one property … common to all of them" (1971a: cvii; 1971b: 13, 29–32; see 1975, a position valuable in the analysis of "folk-classifications, especially [in] the biological domain" (Ellen 1977: 177). Our understanding of these provisional comparisons requires ongoing analysis of the social-historical relations that formed them.
2. These are merely a sample of words that are not synonyms, but keywords with complex semantic fields; they mark significant differences in conceptions of peoples, persons, humans, nations, and their study, all requiring further research as exemplified in Carsten (2011, 2013) and Strathern (2014).
3. See University College London, Wellcome Library, Archives and Manuscripts: for Rivers to Galton, January 4, 1897 (Galton Papers,

PP/ESS/B.54/15) and Rivers to Pearson on May 2, 1896, May 21, 1896, January 11, 1897 and March 2 [1897] (PEARSON/11/1/17/47).
4. See Haddon Papers, Cambridge University Library, Rivers Papers, envelopes 12009, 12082, and 12084.

References

Akin, David W. 2013. *Colonialism, Maasina Rule, and the Origins of Malaitan Kastom*. Honolulu, HI: University of Hawai'i Press.

Bakhtin, M. M. 1981 [1934–1935]. Discourse in the Novel. In *The Dialogic Imagination: Four Essays by M.M. Bakhtin*, ed. Michael Holquist, 259–422. Translated by Caryl Emerson and Michael Holquist. Austin, TX: University of Texas Press.

Bamford, Sandra. 2007. *Biology Unmoored: Melanesian Reflections on Life and Biotechnology*. Berkeley, CA: University of California Press.

Bamford, Sandra and James Leach, eds. 2009. *Kinship and Beyond: The Genealogical Model Reconsidered*. New York: Berghahn.

Barnes, J. A. 1962. "African Models in the New Guinea Highlands." *Man* 62 (Jan.): 5–9.

——— 1967. "Genealogies." In *The Craft of Social Anthropology*, ed. A. L. Epstein, 101–127. London: Tavistock.

Basso, Keith. 1996. *Wisdom Sits in Places: Landscape and Language among the Western Apache*. Albuquerque, NM: University of New Mexico Press.

Bateson, Gregory. 1979. *Mind and Nature: A Necessary Unity*. New York: Dutton.

Bayliss-Smith, Tim. 2014. "Colonialism As Shell-Shock: W. H. R. Rivers's Explanations for Depopulation in Melanesia." In *The Ethnographic Experiment: A. M. Hocart and W. H. R. Rivers in Island Melanesia, 1908*, ed. Edvard Hviding and Cato Berg, 179–213. New York: Berghahn.

Beasley, Edward. 2010. *The Victorian Reinvention of Race: New Racisms and the Problem of Grouping in the Human Sciences*. New York/Abingdon: Routledge.

Beidelman, Thomas O. 1974. "Sir Edward Evan Evans-Pritchard (1902–1973): An Appreciation." *Anthropos* 69(3/4): 553–567.

——— 1982. *Colonial Evangelism: A Socio-historical Study of an East African Mission at the Grassroots*. Bloomington, IN: Indiana University Press.

——— 1986. *Moral Imagination in Kaguru Modes of Thought*. Bloomington, IN: Indiana University Press.

——— 2010. "John Middleton (1921–2009)." *Africa* 80(1): 147–151.

——— 2012. *The Culture of Colonialism the Cultural Subjection of Ukaguru*. Bloomington, IN: Indiana University Press.

Bennett, Judith A. 2014. "A Vanishing People or a Vanishing Discourse? W. H. R. Rivers's 'Psychological Factor' and Depopulation in the Solomon Islands and the New Hebrides." In *The Ethnographic Experiment: A. M. Hocart and W. H. R. Rivers in Island Melanesia, 1908*, ed. Edvard Hviding and Cato Berg, 214–251. New York: Berghahn.

Berg, Cato. 2014. "The Genealogical Method: Vella Lavella Reconsidered." In *The Ethnographic Experiment: A. M. Hocart and W. H. R. Rivers in Island Melanesia, 1908*, ed. Edvard Hviding and Cato Berg, 108–131. New York: Berghahn.

Bouquet, Mary. 1996. "Family Trees and Their Affinities: The Visual Imperative of the Genealogical Method." *Man* (n.s.) 2(1): 43–66.

Bourdieu, Pierre. 1962. "Célibat et condition paysanne." *Études rurales* 5–6 (April–Sept.): 32–135.

Cannell, Fenella. 2011. "English Ancestors: The Moral Possibilities of Popular Genealogy." *Journal of the Royal Anthropological Institute* 17(3): 462–480.

Carsten, Janet. 1995. "The Politics of Forgetting: Migration, Kinship and Memory on the Periphery of the Southeast Asian State." *Journal of the Royal Anthropological Institute* (n.s.) 1: 317–335.

1997. *The Heat of the Hearth: The Process of Kinship in a Malay Fishing Community*. Oxford: Clarendon Press.

ed. 2007. *Ghosts of Memory: Essays on Remembrance and Relatedness*. Oxford: Blackwell.

2011. "Substance and Relationality: Blood in Contexts." *Annual Review of Anthropology* 40: 19–35.

2013. "Introduction: Blood Will Out." *Journal of the Royal Anthropological Institute* 19, Issue Supplement: S1–S23.

Chelcea, Liviu. 2003. "Ancestors, Domestic Groups, and the Socialist State: Housing Nationalization and Restitution in Romania." *Comparative Studies in Society and History* 45: 714–740.

2016. "Kinship of Paper: Genealogical Charts As Bureaucratic Documents." *Po-LAR: Political and Legal Anthropology Review* 39(2): 79–90.

Coley, Noel G. 2001. "Early Blood Chemistry in Britain and France." *Clinical Chemistry* 47(12): 2166–2178.

Darré, Richard Walther. 1930. *Neuadel aus Blut und Boden*. Munich: Lehmanns.

Darwin, Charles. (1859) 1964. *On the Origin of Species by Means of Natural Selection, or the Preservation of Favoured Races in the Struggle for Life*. Facsimile of the first edition, with an introduction by Ernst Mayr. Cambridge, MA: Harvard University Press.

1868. *The Variation of Animals and Plants under Domestication*. 2 v. London: John Murray.

1871. *The Descent of Man, and Selection in Relation to Sex*. 2v. London: John Murray.

1881. *The Formation of Vegetable Mould through the Action of Worms: With Observations on Their Habits*. London: John Murray.

Dresch, Paul. 1988. "Segmentation: Its Roots in Arabia and Its Flowering Elsewhere." *Cultural Anthropology* 3(1): 50–67.

Durkheim, Émile. 1898a. "III. La Famille. [Review of] Prof. J. Kohler. *Zur Urgeschichte der Ehe. Totemismus, Gruppenehe, Mutterrecht*. (Contribution à l'histoire primitive du mariage. Totémisme, mariage collectif, droit maternel.) Stuttgart, Entke, 1 vol. in-8vo." *L'année sociologique* 1(1896–1897): 306–319.

    1898b. "L'individualisme et les intellectuels." *Revue bleue*, 4e série, 10: 7–13.

Edwards, Jeanette. 2000. *Born and Bred: Idioms of Kinship and New Reproductive Technologies in England*. Oxford: Oxford University Press.

    2005. "'Make-up': Bringing Out Persons in New Reproductive and Genetic Technologies." *Ethnos* 70(3): 413–431.

Eggan, Fred. 1963. "The Hopi and the Lineage Principle." In *Social Structure: Studies Presented to A. R. Radcliffe-Brown*, ed. Meyer Fortes, 121–144. New York: Russell and Russell.

Elkin, A. P. [Adolphus Peter]. 1956. "A. R. Radcliffe-Brown, 1880–1955." *Oceania* 26(4): 239–251.

Ellen, Roy F. 1977. "Polythetic Classification." *Man* (n.s.) 12(1): 177.

Engels, Friedrich. 1887 [1845]. *The Condition of the Working Class in England in 1844*. Translated by Florence Kelley Wischnewetsky. New York: J. W. Lovell.

Evans-Pritchard, Edward E. 1933–1935. "The Nuer: Tribe and Clan." *Sudan Notes and Records* 16(1) [1933]: 1–53; 17(1) [1934]: 1–57; 18(1) [1935]: 37–87.

    1940. *The Nuer: A Description of the Modes of Livelihood and Political Institutions of a Nilotic People*. Oxford: Clarendon Press.

    1946. "[Review of] *The Dynamics of Clanship among the Tallensi*." *Bulletin of the School of Oriental and African Studies* [University of London] 11(4): 906–908.

    1949. *The Sanusi of Cyrenaica*. London/Oxford: Oxford University Press.

    1950. "Kinship and the Local Community among the Nuer." In *African Systems of Kinship and Marriage*, ed. A. R. Radcliffe-Brown and D. Forde, 360–391. London: Oxford University Press for the International African Institute.

    1973. "Some Reminiscences and Reflections on Fieldwork." *Journal of the Anthropological Society of Oxford* 4: 1–2.

Feeley-Harnik, Gillian. 1999. "'Communities of Blood': The Natural History of Kinship in Nineteenth-century America." *Comparative Studies in Society and History* 41(2): 215–262.

    2004. "The Geography of Descent." *Proceedings of the British Academy* 125: 311–364.

    2013. "Placing the Dead: The Kinship of Free Men in Pre- and Post-Civil War America." In *Vital Relations: Kinship and the Critique of Modernity*, ed. Fenella Cannell and Susan McKinnon, 179–216. Santa Fe, NM: School for Advanced Research Press.

    2014. "Bodies, Words, and Works: Charles Darwin and Lewis Henry Morgan on Human–Animal Relations." In *America's Darwin: Darwinian Theory and U.S. Culture, 1859–Present*, ed. Tina Gianquitto and Lydia Fisher, 265–301. Athens, GA: University of Georgia Press.

Firth, Raymond. 1936. *We the Tikopia*. London: George Allen and Unwin.

1956. "Alfred Reginald Radcliffe-Brown, 1881–1955." *Proceedings of the British Academy* 42: 286–302.

1957. "A Note on Descent Groups in Polynesia." *Man* 57(Jan.): 4–8.

1990. "Sex and Slander in Tikopia Song: Public Antagonism and Private Intrigue." *Oral Tradition* 5(2–3): 219–240.

Fortes, Meyer. 1944. "The Significance of Descent in Tale Social Structure." *Africa* 14(7): 362–385.

1949. "Time and Social Structure: An Ashanti Case Study." In *Social Structure: Studies Presented to A. R. Radcliffe-Brown*, ed. M. Fortes, 54–84. Oxford: Clarendon Press.

1953. "The Structure of Unilineal Descent Groups." *American Anthropologist* 55(1): 17–41.

1955. "Radcliffe-Brown's Contributions to the Study of Social Organization." *British Journal of Sociology* 6(1): 16–30.

1978. "An Anthropologist's Apprenticeship." *Annual Review of Anthropology* 7: 1–30.

1979. "Preface." In *Segmentary Lineage Systems Reconsidered*, ed. Ladislav Holý, vii–xii. The Queen's University Papers in Social Anthropology, 4. Belfast: The Queen's University.

Fortes, Meyer and E. E. Evans-Pritchard, eds. 1940. *African Political Systems*. London/New York: Oxford University Press for the International African Institute.

Fox, James J. 1971. "Sister's Child as Plant: Metaphors in an Idiom of Consanguinity." In *Rethinking Kinship and Marriage*, ed. Rodney Needham, 219–252. London: Tavistock.

Frémont, Armand. 1992. "La terre." In *Les lieux de mémoire, III. Les Frances, 2. Traditions*, ed. Pierre Nora, 18–55. Paris: Gallimard.

Frölich, Gustav, Walter Spöttel and Ernst Tänzer. 1929. *Wollkunde: Bildung und Eigenschaften der Wolle*. Berlin: J. Springer.

Galton, Francis. 1901. "The Possible Improvement of the Human Breed under the Existing Conditions of Law and Sentiment." *Man* 1: 161–164.

Gardner, Helen. 2008. "The Origin of Kinship in Oceania: Lewis Henry Morgan and Lorimer Fison." *Oceania* 78(2): 137–150.

2009. "'By the Facts We Add to Our Store': Lorimer Fison, Lewis Henry Morgan and the Spread of Kinship Studies in Australia." *Oceania* 79(3): 280–292.

Gifford, Edward Winslow. 1926. "Miwok Lineages and the Political Unit in Aboriginal California." *American Anthropologist* (n.s.) 28(2): 389–401.

1929. *Tongan Society*. Bernice P. Bishop Museum Bulletin, 61. Honolulu, HI: The Museum.

1944. "Miwok Lineages." *American Anthropologist* 46(3): 376–381.

Gough, Kathleen. 1971. "Nuer Kinship: A Re-examination." In *The Translation of Culture: Essays to E. E. Evans Pritchard*, ed. T. O. Beidelman, 79–121. London: Tavistock.

Graeber, David. 1995. "Dancing with Corpses Reconsidered: An Interpretation of *Famadihana* (in Arivonimamo, Madagascar)." *American Ethnologist* 22(2): 258–278.

Guerreau-Jalabert, Anita. 2013. "Flesh and Blood in Medieval Language about Kinship." In *Blood and Kinship: Matter for Metaphor from Ancient Rome to the Present*, ed. Christopher H. Johnson, Bernhard Jussen, David Warren Sabean and Simon Teuscher, 61–82. New York/Oxford: Berghahn.

Haddon, A. C. 1922. "Dr. W. H. R. Rivers, F.R.S." *Nature* 109(2746) [June 17]: 786–787.

Head, Henry. 1922. "W. H. R. Rivers, M.D., D.Sc., F.R.S.: An Appreciation." *The British Medical Journal*, June 17: 977–978.

Hill, Ruth. 2015. "The Blood of Others: Breeding Plants, Animals, and White People in the Spanish Atlantic." In *The Cultural Politics of Blood, 1500–1900*, ed. Kimberly Anne Coles, Ralph Bauer, Zita Nunes and Carla L. Peterson, 45–64. London: Palgrave Macmillan.

Hocart, Arthur M. 1937. "Kinship Systems." *Anthropos* 32 (3/4): 545–551.

Holý, Ladislav, ed. 1979. *Segmentary Lineage Systems Reconsidered*. Queen's University Papers in Social Anthropology, 4. Belfast: Queen's University.

1996. *Anthropological Perspectives on Kinship*. London: Pluto Press.

Hutchinson, Sharon E. 1996. *Nuer Dilemmas: Coping with Money, War, and the State*. Berkeley, CA: University of California Press.

2000. "Identity and Substance: The Broadening Base of Relatedness among the Nuer of Southern Sudan." In *Cultures of Relatedness*, ed. Janet Carsten, 55–72. Cambridge: Cambridge University Press.

Ingold, Tim. 2000. "Ancestry, Generation, Substance, Memory, Land." In *The Perception of the Environment: Essays in Livelihood, Dwelling and Skill*, 132–51. London/New York: Routledge.

Irvine, Judith. 1978. "When Is Genealogy History? Wolof Genealogies in Comparative Perspective." *American Ethnologist* 5(4): 651–674.

1989. "When Talk Isn't Cheap: Language and Political Economy." *American Ethnologist* 16(2): 248–267.

Johnson, Douglas H. 1989. "Political Ecology in the Upper Nile: The Twentieth Century Expansion of the Pastoral 'Common Economy'." *Journal of African History* 30(3): 463–486.

1994. *Nuer Prophets: A History of Prophecy from the Upper Nile in the Nineteenth and Twentieth Centuries*. Oxford: Clarendon Press.

Klapisch-Zuber, Christiane. 1991. "The Genesis of the Family Tree." *I Tatti Studies: Essays in the Renaissance* 4(1): 105–129.

Kolshus, Thorgeir S. 2011. "The Technology of Ethnography: An Empirical Argument against the Repatriation of Historical Accounts." *Journal de la Société des Océanistes* 133(2): 299–308.

2014. "A House upon Pacific Sand: W. H. R. Rivers and His 1908 Ethnographic Survey Work." In *The Ethnographic Experiment: A.*

M. Hocart and W. H. R. Rivers in Island Melanesia, 1908, ed. Edvard Hviding and Cato Berg, 155–178. New York: Berghahn.

Kroeber, Alfred. 1909. "Classificatory Systems of Relationship." *Journal of the Royal Anthropological Institute of Great Britain and Ireland* 39(January–June): 77–84.

Kuper, Adam. 1982. "Lineage Theory: A Critical Retrospect." *Annual Review of Anthropology* 11: 71–95.

——— 2005. "Alternative Histories of British Social Anthropology." *Social Anthropology* 13(1): 47–64.

Langham, Ian. 1981. *The Building of British Social Anthropology: W. H. R. Rivers and His Cambridge Disciples in the Development of Kinship Studies, 1898–1931*. Dordrecht: D. Reidel.

Leach, Edmund R. 1958. "Concerning Trobriand Clans and the Kinship Category 'Tabu'." In *The Developmental Cycle in Domestic Groups*, ed. Jack Goody, 120–145. Cambridge: Cambridge University Press.

Leach, James. 2003. *Creative Land: Place and Procreation on the Rai Coast of Papua New Guinea*. New York/Oxford: Berghahn.

Littlejohn, James. 1960. "The Temne House." *Sierra Leone Studies* (n.s.) 14(December): 63–79.

Lock, Margaret. 1993. *Encounters with Aging: Mythologies of Menopause in Japan and North America*. Berkeley, CA: University of California Press.

Lowie, Robert H. 1920. *Primitive Society*. New York: Boni and Liveright.

Lubbock, John. 1872. "On the Development of Relationships." *Journal of the Anthropological Institute of Great Britain and Ireland* 1: 1–29.

McGovern, Mike. 2012. "Life during Wartime: Aspirational Kinship and the Management of Insecurity." *Journal of the Royal Anthropological Institute* 18(4): 735–752.

McKinnon, Susan. 1999. "Domestic Exceptions: Evans-Pritchard and the Creation of Nuer Patrilineality and Equality." *Cultural Anthropology* 15: 35–83.

McLennan, John Ferguson. 1876. *Studies in Ancient History*. London: B. Quaritch.

Maine, Henry Sumner. 1861. *Ancient Law: Its Connection with the Early History of Society, and Its Relation to Modern Ideas*. London: John Murray.

Malik, Asiya, Todne Thomas and Rose Wellman, eds. 2017. *New Directions in Spiritual Kinship: Sacred Ties across the Abrahamic Religions*. New York: Palgrave Macmillan.

Malinowski, Bronislaw. 1929. *The Sexual Life of Savages in North-Western Melanesia*. London: G. Routledge.

——— 1930. "Kinship." *Man* 30(February): 19–29.

Marques, Ana Claudia. 2013. "Founders, Ancestors, and Enemies: Memory, Family, Time, and Space in the Pernambuco *Sertão*." *Journal of the Royal Anthropological Institute* 19(4): 716–733.

Marshall, William. 1787. *The Rural Economy of Norfolk*. 2 v. London: T. Cadell.

——— 1790. *The Rural Economy of the Midland Counties*. 2 v. London: G. Nicol.

Matthey, Piero [introduction and selection]. 1996. "A Glimpse of Evans-Pritchard through His Correspondence with Lowie and Kroeber." *Journal of the Anthropological Society of Oxford* 27(1): 21–45.

Mauss, Marcel. 1923. "W.R.H. Rivers." *Revue d'ethnographie et des traditions populaires* 4(13): 1–7.

Metcalf, Peter. 2010. *The Life of the Longhouse: An Archaeology of Ethnicity.* Cambridge/New York: Cambridge University Press.

Middleton, John. 1960. *Lugbara Religion: Ritual and Authority among an East African People.* London/New York: Oxford University Press for the International African Institute.

Morgan, Lewis Henry. 1851. *League of the Ho-dé-no-sau-nee, or Iroquois.* Rochester, NY: Sage & Brother.

1868. *The American Beaver and His Works.* Philadelphia, PA: J. B. Lippincott.

1871. *Systems of Consanguinity and Affinity of the Human Family.* Smithsonian Contributions to Knowledge, 17. Washington DC: Smithsonian Institution.

1877. *Ancient Society, or Researches in the Lines of Human Progress from Savagery through Barbarism to Civilization.* New York: Henry Holt.

1881. *Houses and House-life of the American Aborigines.* U.S. Geological Survey, Contributions to North American Ethnology, 4. Washington DC: Government Printing Office.

Mosko, Mark S. 2009. "The Fractal Yam: Botanical Imagery and Human Agency in the Trobriands." *The Journal of the Royal Anthropological Institute* 15(4): 679–700.

Myhre, Knut Christian. 2014. "The Multiple Meanings of *Moongo*: On the Conceptual Character of Doorways and Backbones in Kilimanjaro." *Journal of the Royal Anthropological Institute* (n.s.) 20(3): 505–525.

Nave, Carmen. 2016. "One Family: Defining Kinship in the Neighbourhoods of Kumasi, Ghana." *Journal of the Royal Anthropological Institute* 22(4): 826–863.

Needham, Rodney. 1971a. "Introduction." In *Rethinking Kinship and Marriage*, ed. Rodney Needham, xiii–cxvii. London: Routledge.

1971b. "Remarks on the Analysis of Kinship and Marriage." In *Rethinking Kinship and Marriage*, ed. Rodney Needham, 1–34. London: Routledge.

1975. "Polythetic Classification: Convergence and Consequences." *Man* (n.s.) 10(3): 349–369.

Nelson, William Max. 2010. "Making Men: Enlightenment Ideas of Racial Engineering." *American Historical Review* 115(5): 1364–1394.

Nirenberg, David. 2009. "Was There Race before Modernity? The Example of 'Jewish' Blood in Late Medieval Spain." In *The Origins of Racism in the West*, ed. Miriam Eliav-Feldon, Benjamin Isaac and Joseph Ziegler, 232–264. New York: Cambridge University Press.

Orel, Vítězslav. 2009. "The 'Useful Questions of Heredity' before Mendel." *Journal of Heredity* 100(4): 421–423.

Orel, V. and R. J. Wood. 1998. "Empirical Genetic Laws Published in Brno before Mendel Was Born." *Journal of Heredity* 89: 79–82.

Patterson, Mary. 2005. "Introduction: Reclaiming Paradigms Lost." *Australian Journal of Anthropology* 16(1): 1–17.

Peluso, Nancy Lee. 1996. "Fruit Trees and Family Trees in an Anthropogenic Rainforest: Property Rights, Ethics of Access, and Environmental Change in Indonesia." *Comparative Studies in Society and History* 38(3): 510–548.

Peters, Emrys L. 1960. "The Proliferation of Segments in the Lineage of the Bedouin of Cyrenaica." *Journal of the Royal Anthropological Institute* 90(1): 29–53.

1967. "Some Structural Aspects of the Feud among the Camel-Herding Bedouin of Cyrenaica." *Africa* 37(3): 261–282.

Pietsch, Theodore W. 2012. *Trees of Life: A Visual History of Evolution.* Baltimore, MD: The Johns Hopkins University Press.

Pina-Cabral, João de. 1989. "L'héritage de Maine: Repenser les catégories descriptives dans l'étude de la famille en Europe." *Ethnologie française* 19: 329–340.

Radcliffe-Brown, Alfred R. 1930–1931. "The Social Organization of Australian Tribes." *Oceania* 1(1[1930]): 34–63; 1(2[1930]): 206–246; 1(3[1930]): 322–341; 1(4[1931]): 426–456.

1931. "The Present Position of Anthropological Studies." *British Association for the Advancement of Science Report of the Centenary Meeting, London, September 23–30, 1931.* London: Office of the British Association.

Richards, Audrey I. 1941. "A Problem of Anthropological Approach." *Bantu Studies* 15(March): 45–52.

Rivers, W. H. R. 1899a. "Contributions to Comparative Psychology [from] Torres Straits: General Account and Observations on Vision, etc." *Journal of the Anthropological Institute* 29(1/2): 219–221.

1899b. Two New Departures in Anthropological Method." *Report of the 69th Meeting of the British Association for the Advancement of Science*, 879–880. London: John Murray.

1900. "A Genealogical Method of Collecting Social and Vital Statistics." *Journal of the Anthropological Institute* 30: 74–82.

1901a. "On the Functions of the Maternal Uncle in Torres Strait." *Man* 1: 171–172.

1901b. "On the Functions of the Son-in-Law and Brother-in-Law in Torres Strait." *Man* 1: 172.

1904. *Reports of the Cambridge Anthropological Expedition to Torres Straits, IV: Sociology, Magic, and Religion of the Western Islanders.* Cambridge: Cambridge University Press.

1907. "On the Origin of the Classificatory System of Relationships." In *Anthropological Essays Presented to Edward Burnett Tylor in Honour of His 75th Birthday Oct. 2, 1907*, ed. H. Balfour, 309–323. Oxford: Clarendon Press.

1908. *Reports of the Cambridge Anthropological Expedition to Torres Straits, VI: Sociology, Magic, and Religion of the Eastern Islanders.* Cambridge: Cambridge University Press.

1910. "The Genealogical Method of Anthropological Inquiry." *The Sociological Review* 3: 1–12. (Republished the same year as: "La méthode généalogique dans les enquêtes anthropologiques." *Revue d'ethnographie et de sociologie* 1(8–10): 201–209.)

1914a. *Kinship and Social Organisation.* London: Constable.

1914b. *The History of Melanesian Society.* 2v. Cambridge: Cambridge University Press.

1917. "The Government of Subject Peoples." In *Science and the Nation: Essays by Cambridge Graduates*, ed. Albert C. Seward, 302–328. Cambridge: Cambridge University Press.

1922. "The Psychology of Depopulation." In *Essays on the Depopulation of Melanesia*, ed. W. H. R. Rivers, 84–113. Cambridge: Cambridge University Press.

Rivière, Peter. 1993. "The Amerindianization of Descent and Affinity." *L'Homme* 33(126–128): 507–516.

Ryder, Michael L. 1983. *Sheep and Man.* London: Duckworth.

Sabean, David Warren and Simon Teuscher. 2013. "Introduction." In *Blood and Kinship: Matter for Metaphor from Ancient Rome to the Present*, ed. Christopher H. Johnson, Bernhard Jussen, David Warren Sabean and Simon Teuscher, 1–17. New York/Oxford: Berghahn.

Sahlins, Marshall D. 1965. "On the Ideology and Composition of Descent Groups." *Man* 65(Jul.–Aug.): 104–107.

2013. *What Kinship Is – and Is Not.* Chicago, IL: University of Chicago Press.

Salas Carreño, Guillermo. 2016. "Places Are Kin: Food, Cohabitation, and Sociality in the Southern Peruvian Andes." *Anthropological Quarterly* 89(3): 813–840.

Schneider, David M. 1972. "What Is Kinship All About?" In *Kinship Studies in the Morgan Centennial Year*, ed. Priscilla Reining, 32–63. Washington DC: The Anthropological Society of Washington.

1984. *A Critique of the Study of Kinship.* Ann Arbor, MI: University of Michigan Press.

Shryock, Andrew. 1997. *Nationalism and the Genealogical Imagination: Oral History and Textual Authority in Tribal Jordan.* Berkeley, CA: University of California Press.

forthcoming. "Dialogues of Three: Making Sense of Patterns That Outlast Events." In *The Scandal of Continuity: Form, Duration and Difference*, ed. Judith Scheele and Andrew Shryock. Bloomington, IN: Indiana University Press.

Stocking, George W., Jr. 1995. *After Tylor: British Social Anthropology, 1888–1951.* Madison, WI: University of Wisconsin Press.

Strathern, Marilyn. 2014. "Reading Relations Backwards." *Journal of the Royal Anthropological Institute* 20(1): 3–19.

Teuscher, Simon. 2013. "Flesh and Blood in the Treatises on the Arbor Consanguinitatis (Thirteenth to Sixteenth Centuries)." In *Blood and Kinship: Matter for Metaphor from Ancient Rome to the Present*, ed. Christopher H. Johnson, Bernhard Jussen, David Warren Sabean and Simon Teuscher, 83–104. New York/Oxford: Berghahn.

Thompson, Edward P. 1967. "Time, Work-Discipline, and Industrial Capitalism." *Past and Present* 38(1): 56–97.

Thornton, Thomas F. 2008. *Being and Place among the Tlingit*. Seattle, WA: University of Washington Press.

Trautmann, Thomas R. 2001. "The Whole History of Kinship Terminology in Three Chapters: Before Morgan, Morgan, and after Morgan." *Anthropological Theory* 1(2): 268–287. (See Trautmann 2008: Appendix 3.)

2008 [1987]. *Lewis Henry Morgan and the Invention of Kinship*. With a new introduction and appendices by the author. Lincoln, NB: University of Nebraska Press.

Trautmann, Thomas R., Gillian Feeley-Harnik and John Mitani. 2011. "Deep Kinship." In *Deep History: The Architecture of Past and Present*, ed. Andrew Shryock and Daniel Lord Smail, 160–188. Berkeley, CA: University of California Press.

Wood, Roger J. and Vítězslav Orel. 2001. *Genetic Prehistory in Selective Breeding: A Prelude to Mendel*. Oxford: Oxford University Press.

Young, Michael W. 2004. *Malinowski: Odyssey of an Anthropologist*. New Haven, CT: Yale University Press.

2011. "Malinowski's Last Word on the Anthropological Approach to Language." *Pragmatics* 21(1): 1–22.

4

The Alliance Theory of Kinship in South Indian Ethnography

Isabelle Clark-Decès

This chapter traces the formation of the French alliance theory of kinship and its application to the South Indian context in the early 1950s. The first part provides enough background for the reader to understand how this theory once contributed to the anthropological study of kinship, in general, and that of South Indian kinship, in particular. The second part of the chapter shows how current ethnography (including my own work) in the South Indian state of Tamil Nadu does not support the forms of sociality ("exchange," "reciprocity," women's passive roles, and so on) privileged by the French scholars of kinship. To ask why South Indian kinship remained a showcase for the alliance theory for over half a century is beyond the scope of this chapter. A full answer would entail taking into account a whole range of factors that cannot be examined here. But the list would have to include David Schneider's demolition of kinship studies around the mid-1980s.[1] While his *Critique* (1984) opened a vibrant new theoretical vein for discussing the realities of nature and culture, it is fair to say that it inhibited the ethnographic study of kinship. In the context of South India, for example, the repositioning of kinship studies has raised new questions about the social construction of emotion most notably but it has not produced original ethnographic facts (Trawick 1990). This chapter attempts to do the reverse. Rather than re-ordering longstanding ethnographic data in a new, meaningful, i.e., theoretically relevant, way, I present new observations with the aim of continuing the anthropological conversation about South Indian kinship.

The alliance theory took its root in the French school of anthropology, specifically in Marcel Mauss' classic essay, *The Gift* (1990 [1925]). Mauss' comparative study of "archaic" societies led him to suggest that the act of giving is at its core an obligation that entails two others: namely the obligation to receive and return the gift be it an object, or service, and so on. It is compulsive reciprocity, he argued, that maintains and strengthens social relations (cooperative, competitive, or antagonistic) in primitive societies. Mauss further discerned that "the archaic forms of exchange" are not confined to economic transactions; they permeate all spheres of social life. The gift is political, kinship-oriented, legal, mythological, religious, magical, practical, personal, and social so that when it moves through the social landscape it creates the fabric of sociality. Mauss' influence on the development of the alliance theory is evident in the fact that its founder Claude Lévi-Strauss (1969 [1949]) shares his understanding of the nature of social life.

For Lévi-Strauss, the true place where kinship originates is not in the nuclear family, nor in the lineal/ancestral or filial relations within the group, as was the case for contemporary British social anthropologists such as Meyer Fortes and E. E. Evans-Pritchard. Kinship means marriage, particularly the systematic relations of exchange that link affinal groups. Lévi-Strauss further noted that in every human society certain categories of relations are regarded as too close for marriage, hence the universal "negative" or proscribing rules of marriage known to us as incest taboos. It follows that everywhere men are required to give up their sisters and daughters as potential marriage partners and obtain other women in return. This exchange of women comes in two different structural modes. Either the women are offered by means of "explicitly defined" social institutions, these are the "elementary structures of kinship." Or the group of possible spouses for the women is "indetermined and always open," to the exclusion, of course, of the tabooed kin-people (siblings, children, parents, and so on) as is the case in Western societies. As the title of Lévi-Strauss' book (*The Elementary Structures of Kinship*), suggests, it is the first or "elementary structures" which interested him. In them he discerned "positive marriage rules," which "*prescribe* marriage with a certain type of relative" (1969: ix).

The rules, Lévi-Strauss explained, varied in form, content, and intricacy. They may involve just two groups of men exchanging women in a form of reciprocity that is direct, immediate, and restricted: men of group A have to marry women of group B, while men of group B have to marry women of group A. According to Lévi-Strauss, this sets up a distinction between "wife givers" and "wife takers" that produces the first kinship categories. Much more complex are "generalized" forms of exchange that involve three or more groups exchanging women in one direction (from group A to group B to group C and back to A). Here exchange is delayed and indirect but holds the potential to integrate indefinite numbers of groups. Whether "restricted" or "generalized," the exchange of women can only function if men who give their sisters (or daughters) away in marriage can in turn receive the sisters (or daughters) of other men. Reciprocity – the trademark of Mauss' sociology – is all the more critical in this exchange that women's fecundity is vital to the reproduction of the group. Clearly if a group does not play by the obligation to give back, it will sooner or later be dropped out as a trading partner, thereby facing isolation and extinction.

In Lévi-Strauss' general theory of kinship, then, affinal (that is marital and reciprocal) relations formed among individuals and groups are fundamental to social cohesion. These relations also frame the most basic and irreducible unit of kinship – what he called the "atom of kinship" (1983). Whereas British descent theorists defined a set of parents and children as the core of kinship relations, Lévi-Strauss defined it as a husband and wife, their son, and the wife's brother. The inclusion of the wife's brother indicates the importance of marriage as a relation of exchange between men who are related as in-laws.

In the 1970s and 1990s, the questioning of kinship studies by David Schneider (1984) cast a significant blow to both the descent and alliance theory of kinship. Schneider and then Marilyn Strathern (1988) contested the universalism of Lévi-Strauss' structuralist approach, and explored kinship systems, models, and relations that do not conform to the alliance model. The key theoretical idea was that kinship is a kind of *doing*, which does not reflect a prior structure of relations, and can only be understood as enacted practice (Schneider 1984). For feminist anthropologists, Schneider's critique freed kinship from the limitations of biology, providing a context for establishing gender as a cultural construct (Collier and Yanagisako 1987; di Leonardo 1979). Hence these scholars did not simply charge that Lévi-Strauss was reducing women to objects (or means) of exchange between men. They argued that women's oppression is not the source of social organization but the product of it as kinship systems often deny women's right to choose their own destiny (Rubin 1975). Despite these criticisms, Lévi-Strauss left a clear and enduring mark on kinship studies. The fundamental importance of treating marriage as an exchange between groups eventually became a more or less accepted tenet within anthropology, particularly in New Guinea, Indonesia, and South America – areas where it was difficult to discern corporate groups operating in the manner described by the classic British models of descent. The next section turns to Louis Dumont's adaptation of the alliance theory to the South Indian context.

4.1 Louis Dumont and Dravidian Kinship

It is customary to link Dumont's analysis of South Indian kinship to the ideas developed by Claude Lévi-Strauss in *The Elementary Structures of Kinship*. There are grounds for this, as Dumont himself stressed, "the remarkable convergence between Lévi-Strauss' theory of marriage alliance and the emphasis put by [his own] Tamil informants on analogous themes" (1986: 4). The "convergence" in question, however, is uneven. As the noted sociologist Patricia Uberoi suggests, Dumont did not merely apply the structural approach to the South Indian data; he modified the structural vision of kinship in the process (2006: 161).

By the time Dumont turned to the study of South Indian kinship, anthropologists had long analyzed the key features of what was called then the "Dravidian kinship terminology" (Rivers 1907, 1968 [1914]).[2] This has to be understood in light of the argument made by the inventor of kinship studies, the American anthropologist Lewis Henry Morgan (1871), that terminological systems contain principles that organize social relationships in human societies. Although Morgan's contemporaries and successors eventually discarded the grand evolutionary story he derived from his data, the notion that kinship terminologies encode critical information regarding past and present marriage arrangements and natural facts of procreation profoundly shaped the anthropology of South Indian kinship. Again and again scholars emphatically made the case that Dravidian kinship "classificatory" terminologies reflected marriage preferences, in particular, the custom, which the anthropologist Edward B. Tylor first labeled "cross-cousin marriage" (1889: 263). W. H. R. Rivers (1907) explained how among the Todas of South India:

> the same term is applied to the father of the wife as to the mother's brother, while the wife's mother and the mother's brother's wife also receive the same name. To these people the orthodox marriage regulation is that the children of brother and sister should marry, so that the mother's brother and the wife's father are one and the same person, and we have therefore a correspondence between a marriage regulation and the designations applied to certain kin.
>
> *(1907: 619–620)*

Since Tamil and Telugu languages made the same classification, Rivers was sure that there was an obvious and precise correlation between South Indian terminologies and marriage practices on the ground (see also 1914: 47–48; Emeneau 1953).

Dumont also focused on terminology if only to show that the stated relationships were theoretical constructs used to model social life rather than real or even directly observable (1953). He objected to Rivers' understanding that the main feature of the Dravidian kinship system was the distinction between parallel cousins (children of same-sex siblings) who were classified as siblings to whom marriage (and sexual relationship) was forbidden, and cross cousins (children of opposite sex siblings) who were assimilated with husbands and wives and expected to marry. To Dumont, the key distinction lay somewhere else (1953: 12). "In the father's generation," he wrote, "there are two kinds, and two kinds only of male relatives … the father and the mother's brother respectively" (1953: 35) who are linked by a "principle of opposition" that neither "lie[s] in the relation with the Ego" (the child) nor in the relation with (the child's) mother (1953: 35). Here we note Dumont's elimination of relationships (and emotions) between consanguineous relatives, in preference to the structural differentiation of two classes: kin and affines. Even the relation between mother and child is conspicuously absent from his model for he postulated that the mother's brother is related to the child *not* through mother (a genealogical relation) but through father (a classificatory relation). As he stated it, in Dravidian kinship, "my mother's brother is essentially my father's affine" (1953: 39).[3]

Dumont's method of analysis was structural in that it consisted in identifying sets of relations between abstract terms, kinship terms so as to establish how their interaction – or rather opposition – determined the appearance and functioning of a phenomenon such as cross-cousin marriage. His conception of kinship was also structural in that for him, as for Lévi-Strauss, the true place where kinship originates is not in the nuclear family, nor in relations among individuals, but rather in the systematic relations of exchange that link social groups that stand in affinal relationships to one another. Finally, both Lévi-Strauss and Dumont took their notion of exchange from Marcel Mauss but they focused on different elements of matrimonial reciprocity.

In keeping with earlier analysis of Dravidian kinship Dumont gave priority not to the logic of marriage rules (as Lévi-Strauss had done) but, as we have seen, to kinship terminology. Moreover, he stressed the "vertical dimension" (1953: 38) of the relationship between "kin" and "affines" rather than its socially integrative power (or its lack) as Lévi-Strauss did. To him, affinal roles and concomitant ceremonial obligations were inherited from parent (father in particular) to child (son) without being transformed into blood relations. It was the function of the cross-cousin marriage and associated gift-giving relationships – Dumont took this much from Marcel Mauss – to perpetuate the alliance relationship, which he found in the nomenclature and he suggested it was reaffirmed generation after generation. In a nutshell, then, his theory was an account of the inheritance of affinal alliance, and his theoretical model came to define Dravidian kinship up until the early 1990s despite the fact that newer ethnography challenged it on many fronts.

In 1980, the British anthropologist Anthony Good stated loud and clear what others had said for some time: namely, that among many South Indian castes a man's most "preferential" marriage partner was *not* his "cross cousin" but his elder sister's daughter.[4] That uncle–niece marriage was not merely an upper-caste phenomenon, as Dumont believed,[5] was later borne out by Katherine Hann's (1985) tabulation of the incidence of close-relation marriage, as reported for various South Indian communities in the four southern states (Andhra Pradesh, Karnataka, Kerala, and Tamil Nadu). Her results showed, "that about 10 per cent of the marriages are between an uncle and his niece" (1985: 62). A decade later Good himself updated Hann's chart and the "striking" statistics on uncle–niece marriage (1996: 6) led him to boldly state that, "There is *no* such thing as the Dravidian kinship system" (1996: 1, his emphasis). Yet the British anthropologist somehow shied away from making the obvious point that if there is no Dravidian kinship, the structuralist theory of Dravidian kinship cannot hold. For one thing, when a Tamil man marries his own sister's daughter, genealogical relations (niece, sister) merge with affinal relations (wife, mother-in-law) so that there cannot be any sharp or stable "opposition between kin and affine," the opposition promoted by Dumont as fundamental to Dravidian kinship in general (1983: 103). Moreover, the relations of exchange here clearly originate from within a very tight group of kin; so tight, in fact, that the category "exchange" cannot function in the broad sense of "alliance" as defined by the French theory of kinship.

My own ethnographic work in Tamil Nadu suggests that the many castes that practice uncle–niece marriage praise it for the very reason that Lévi-Strauss and Dumont object to it – it restricts the circle of exchanges. I was told that this marriage allows daughters to stay close by – a formulation often put to me like this: "We don't want our girls to marry far." "We don't want to let go (*pōhaviṭa*) of our love (*pōcam*) for them." Sometimes people expressed this wish – to preserve the relation (*contam*) with daughters – in economic terms. "We don't want to lose the money and jewels." This last comment has to be understood in light of the fact that when this marriage is repeated, jewels, gold, money, land – the usual valuables gifted to daughters at marriage – keep coming back at the very next generation. Everyone agreed that no one likes "to share or divide property (*cottu*) with outsiders." I elicited other points of view, too. "We know the daughter-in-law, she obeys us and takes good care of us when we get old; an outsider has less affection." "An unrelated wife tries to divide her husband and his sister but not a sister's daughter." I was also told that these marriages were more stable. Since the mother-in-law is the girl's grandmother, problems in the family do not escalate. The wife and husband cannot make that all-too-common accusation in Tamil Nadu, "You don't respect my parents." Finally, the couple is less likely to separate. As one male informant put it to me: "When they fight, the wife can't go back to her mother's house. What is the woman to do? Keep her daughter away from her brother?" He underscored that the fight would not last anyway: "If the husband raises his voice, his wife forgives him. She tells herself, 'He's my mother's brother; he has the right to grumble.'" "An outsider," the same man reasoned, "wouldn't be that understanding, she'd complain and leave."

In sum, these marriages are best because they prevent the family and the couple from breaking up. Mothers and daughters (note that there are no fathers and sons in the exegeses reported so far), brothers and sisters, maternal uncles and nieces are to remain *cērntu* – from *cēr*: "be near," that is "together," "united" – forever. For the many castes that favor marriage with elder sister's daughter, the "optimal" or "preferential" society is one in which there is no flow of signs, no institutionalized exchange of women between families, no general circulation of goods and therefore no transversal social networks. The social cosmology evoked here is one that lends itself in an especially powerful way to self-segregation, sameness, repetition – in short, to the complete negation of the regime of reciprocity celebrated by alliance theory. Thus it becomes clear that uncle-niece marriage forces us to rethink the nature of the social relationships involved in Tamil marriage patterns and to revise their anthropological description and theory – just as this particular marriage, I have shown elsewhere, is on the verge of disappearing forever (Clark-Decès 2014).

4.2   A Kinship of Rights

Neither the French theory of alliance nor the formal studies of Dravidian kinship terminology factored in the general kinship vocabulary used by South Indian people or their explanations of their own matrimonial arrangements. This is too bad, at the least, for in these very terms and local exegeses there is also a theory of what marriage and kinship mean for them. Consider the Tamil Lexicon's entry for *contam*, the general Tamil equivalent for the English word "kinship": "one's own peculiar right, exclusive property, that which belongs to oneself" (2007: 1651). Thus Indira Arumugam is onto something when she writes: "it is only when we turn to kinship that we can discern indigenous notions of individual rights" (2011: 7). In my field experience, however, it is not merely members of the patrilineage who are "individuated in terms of … inalienable rights" (Arumugam 2011: 7). Each and every Tamil kinship relation comes with rights (*urimai*) that are quasi-legal. That the category *urimai* is pervasive across the entire field of Tamil kinship, including relations with same-sex siblings, parents, and children became evident when I asked mostly mature women to define this word. "I've *urimai* in my husband," they would say or, "I've *urimai* to ask anything from my mother or father. I've *urimai* to their property." One of these respondents volunteered that: "after moving with her in-laws, a newly married girl has *urimai* to proclaim: 'This is my house.'"

Notice that the Tamil gloss of kinship makes reference neither to relations of biological or genetic connection nor to genealogical ties arising from procreation. It does not even mention consubstantiality. *Contam* may be mutually related because they share blood[6] or suckle the same milk. But such notions do not come out in conversation. What is said instead is that what my kin have is mine. I can help myself to their food, utensils, tools, grooming products, and so on. I don't even have to ask, for my claim goes without saying. The reverse is also true, and what I have is theirs. Arumugam is correct to state that this particularly applies to the patrilineage (*paṅkali*), for each member of this kinship group has a "share" (*paṅku*) in descent from a common male ancestor and in the ritual cult of a tutelary deity. This means that with *paṅkali*, these "shareholders," one is at home, somewhat free from the elaborate codes of conduct regarding appropriate media and appropriate contexts of gift-giving activities and commensality (Appadurai 1981, 1985).

This is not the case with in-laws, which in Tamil Nadu the reader will recall include the mother's brothers, their wives and children, and the father's sisters, their husbands, and children. With in-laws the Tamils enter in straight relations of gift giving as Dumont rightly pointed out (1986). And yet in-laws also count as kin (*contam*), and as such they too have rights: the right to receive assistance and new cloth at funerals, for example, the right to be invited when a marriage takes place. In addition, in-laws have major matrimonial rights. In this respect, as in others, however, some have more privileges than others.

We have seen how the priority given to Dravidian kinship terminology gave the impression that the Tamils systematically and indiscriminately marry cross cousins. But in point of fact, many castes have (or at least used to have) a marriage rule (*kalyōnam muṟai*) – or at least a preference – for marrying on one "side" (*pakkam*), as the Tamils put it, rather than the other. Among many families, a boy's "right girl" (*muṟai poṇṇu*) is *either* his mother's brother's daughter *or* his father's sister's daughter. For a girl, the "right boy" (*muṟai paiyaṉ*) is *either* her mother's brother's son *or* her father's sister's son. Thus, in general, one and only one set of so-called "cross cousins" (either on the mother's or the father's side) is right or preferential, or at least more so than the other. Moreover, among the Kaḷḷars with whom I worked, the marriage rule or preference does not apply to all boys and girls. Let me make this more concrete by taking the hypothetical case of four married siblings born in the following order: brother, sister, brother, sister. As I proceed, the reader should keep in mind that we must look at Tamil marriages from the point of view of the senior generation. The first brother does the "right thing" with the first sister by marrying his (preferably) first daughter to her (preferably) first son. The second brother does the same thing with the second sister. Now, let us consider the case of three elder brothers and their younger sister. Here only the first brother is required to do *muṟai* with the sister. If he does not have a daughter, the second brother must offer to do it for him (and so on). But if the elder brother does *muṟai* with the sister, his younger brothers are free to marry their children however they wish.[7]

So far I have conveyed the sense that the "right" partners are required to marry in accordance with particular caste rules. But it is important to note that such an obligation is also a prerogative. The right spouses have rights of ownership (*urimai*) and as such are entitled to marry the person whom from their point of view is theirs. Here we see how the category "exchange" fails to gloss the meanings embedded in Tamil "right" marriages. The families with rights do not exactly give and take women (or men for that matter). The "right" spouse *already belongs* to them. Moreover, a logic of elitism is encoded in the law (*muṟai*) itself, which works to advantage a particular "side" (mother's or father's) and/or those who are firstborn. Those who do not meet the "right" qualifications (the folks on the other side, for example, or those born last) also get to marry kin, including cross cousins, but they cannot make ownership claims. Since they have no legal claims, they have to ask and negotiate. This clarifies that Tamil "right" marriages provide the context for displaying and maintaining distinctions of rank among kin (*contam*). Dumont discerned that much when he noted that Kaḷḷar sons of "senior" wives did not intermarry with those of "junior" wives or of illegitimate unions (1983: 44). But the priority he (and just about all scholars of Dravidian kinship) gave to the system of categories generated by the terminology prevented him from pushing his insights into the selective and discriminatory aspect of Dravidian marriage. Quite simply the Tamil marriage law does not so much sanction "the opposition between kin and affines" (Dumont 1953: 39) as the distinction between those who have the right to intermarry and those who do not.

4.3   The Mother's Brother

What about the mother's younger brother? Among the castes who practice uncle–niece marriage, I have already suggested, the man comes before any "right" boy: be he the bride's father's sister's son or the bride's mother's elder brother's son. The full extent of his privilege was vividly conveyed by one consultant: "the mother's younger brother has the freedom to come to his sister's house whenever he wishes, ransack the place, elope with her girl and joke about it, if it pleases him. The girl is his." We note that the hierarchical principle of birth order governing the "right" marriages discussed in the previous section is reversed here. It is because he comes *after* his sister that the maternal uncle has the license to marry his niece, and a Tamil man should not marry his younger sister's daughter.[8] It is therefore obvious that in examining this form of marriage, we are entering the cosmology of matrimony from a different vantage: one in which a junior (and therefore substandard) status and relationship to a senior woman are the major matrimonial qualifications.

We have seen how for the French structuralists the avuncular figure is not, in sociological fact, a mother's brother – someone tied to the child through its mother – but a wife-giver or a wife taker. As Dumont put it in the context of Tamil society: the man is "an affine pure and simple" (1983: 77). The problem, as Thomas Trautmann points out, is that Dumont gives no evidence that the Tamils themselves conceptualize what we call in English "the mother's brother" as the father's brother-in-law (1981: 175). In fact, in my experience the Tamils seem to think of this man as indeed just what they say: he is the mother's brother (*tōymōmō*). This is evidenced by the fact that the word *tōy* means "mother." The Kaḷḷar term "ammōṉ" is even more indicative of his relationship to mother, since it is undoubtedly related to "ammō" ("mother"). Moreover, in a small survey I conducted, four out of ten respondents defined *tōymōmō* as "the one who was born with mother." Two answered, "*tōymōmō* is another mother."

A strong indication that the mother's brother is coupled with mother is that both personify the emotion of love (*pōcam*), as many women said in answer to a survey I instigated: "*Ammō* has a lot of love for her daughter. The first love of her first love is for her daughter" (Padmini age 40). "*Ammō* is like a God. She protects her child from the world until her death. She never loses her love" (Sridevi age 25). "*Ammō* is the first eye to her children. Until she dies her love remains the same" (Thangal age 61). "*Ammō* is everything to me. If I don't eat, my mother won't eat either. *Ammō* is the only one who can feel her daughter's feelings" (Indira age 28). "Without *Ammō*, we wouldn't be in this world. We wouldn't exist" (Minakshi age 33). "*Ammō* is the bridge of the family. She has the first place. Without mother, there's no family" (Celvi age 44). "*Ammō* loves her children until she dies. Mother's affection (*pōcam*) is the best in the world. Nothing compares to her love" (Arulmori age 55).

Of course, these are idealized statements made in order to "inform" the anthropologist of positive cultural stereotypes. They are not necessarily representative of personal experience. In fact, over the many years I have worked in Tamil Nadu I met women and men who did not think that their *own* mother was particularly loving. But in general, "*ammō* is a wonderful relation," as one of the surveyed women put it. I should say "ammōs" because mother's "big" and "little" sisters are mothers as well. These *periyammōs* and *ciṉṉammōs* love their sister's children the way they love their own. The same holds true for the mother's brother; he too has, "immense affection (*pōcam*) for his sister's children," as Kirin Kapadia also notes (1995: 20).

Thus, from the perspective of a Tamil child the mother's brother is associated not with affinity but with kinship, particularly filiation, and is related not through father but mother. Born with her, he loves her sons and daughters in the way she does. What characterizes motherly "love" in Tamil society (I suspect in other societies as well) is that it transcends the field of mutual exchange. In anthropological terms we might say that this love falls outside the Maussian paradigm of obligatory reciprocity. "You don't return a gift to mother," the women quoted above pointed out. It is much the same with the mother's brother: he is a one-sided giver, and a very generous one at that. When his sister's family needs money to help defray the cost of a life-cycle ritual, the mother's brother makes a donation that no matter how substantial – and it is likely to be very substantial – remains unspecified and unreciprocated. Among the Kaḷḷars, I was told, "the mother's brother doesn't have the right to ask for his money back."

As for the maternal uncle who marries his niece, he takes less. This is evident by the fact that the sister "doesn't have to spend much on the marriage of her daughter to her brother." Again and again my consultants would say, "the younger brother is not as demanding. He takes less." Less than whom? Less than an outsider (*anniyam*) – who nowadays asks for a sizeable dowry – but also less than the "right" boy: either the mother's brother's son or the father's sister's son. As one man told me, "the brother isn't expecting grand things. He understands that his *akkō* [elder sister] can't afford to give more." For her part, this sister takes a lot. She visits the couple whenever and for however long she wants, helping herself to whatever they own. This is not a likely scenario if the brother is married to an outsider (*anniyam*). Even with a "right" girl, the *akkō* is prone to curb her acquisitive tendencies. But with her daughter in charge of her brother's household, she feels free and at home. Better yet, if the young couple lives with the brother's parents and male married siblings in a joint-family situation, this woman *is* at home, not in her capacity as estranged guest or in-law but as daughter.

The full generosity of the man who marries his older sister's daughter comes to light when we consider two other things. The first has to do with sexuality. Usually (but not always) the couple has no, or has little, "sexual interest" in one another (see Clark-Decès 2014: 84–87). This is especially the case if they grew up together in the same house or the same neighborhood. The men I interviewed, in particular, grumbled that the trouble with marrying a niece who lives nearby is that "there isn't mystery," and a few admitted, "I had no desire for her. I knew everything about her." The second thing has to do with power. After the marriage the man is likely to live with his mother for a Tamil woman is entitled to live with her married son. His older sister (his wife's mother) visits for long periods of time and may even move in altogether for she likes being with her mother, younger brother, and daughter, "more so," I was often told, "than with her own husband and/or her own married son(s)." Needless to say, in the day-to-day functioning of the household the two "mothers" (the husband's mother and the wife's mother) do not stand on ceremony with regard to each other. They certainly do not behave as if they were in-laws, and they help themselves to whatever they want without being specifically invited to do so. They act like the mothers and daughters that they are. In the household I am describing here the younger brother is encompassed by senior women who occupy the "central position," as Brenda Beck noted of women in general in her analysis of kinship in Tamil folklore (1974: 7; see also Fuller 1995).

The brother who marries his elder sister's daughter, I am suggesting, performs a kind of sacrifice. In effect, the man relinquishes his sexual desire (he is not exactly attracted by his niece), his autonomy and rank (he is dominated by his elder sister and mother), his "right" to enter more profitable matrimonial transactions (he "takes less"), his political role in public life (his ability to form "alliances" with other men), as well as his own independent line of descent (which merges with that of sister/mother) in order to reclaim the family women (which is, the reader will recall, the common explanation for marrying a sister's daughter).

My interpretation is not as far-fetched, even psychologically, as it may seem. Scholars have long documented the close association of marriage and sacrifice in the Tamil religious tradition (Harman 1989; Hudson 1977). David Shulman (1980), in particular, has shown how Tamil myths of the marriage of Siva to the goddess promote sacrifice as the central metaphor for divine matrimony, devotion, and regeneration. The god offers his life in the form of a gift, with which he is identified, to his consort. The consort here is no submissive Sanskrit goddess, but a dangerous, often malevolent, feminine power, who entices "her husband to a violent, self-sacrificing death" (1980: 212), or slays him as he attempts to unite with her (1980: 224). The Tamil goddess, Shulman proposes, is the source first of death, then of a new flow of vitality as she rewards her victim, here the god, with rebirth from her womb (1980: 297).

What is the reward or pay off of the younger brother's sacrifice? In exchange for his devotion, the man – much like the god of Shulman's study – totally merges with the deity of Tamil kinship, mother: he gets to reproduce in her direct line of descent with her daughter's daughter. That this is conceived as a privilege is evidenced by the fact that the man has exclusive right over his elder sister's daughter. I will say it again: the young maternal uncle is entitled to come "first" in marriage, even before the "lawful" partners (the so-called "cross cousins" of anthropological jargon). Notice what is happening here: the sphere of activity predominantly associated with men – ranking first in public life – derives from a sacrificial relationship to mother and her daughter. At the very least, the source of a man's kinship and ritual primacy lies in his surrendering to the mother's "side."

4.4 Conclusion

It is not surprising that there is little convergence between the alliance theory and my ethnography of Tamil kinship. This theory, we have seen, was developed without any input on the part of the Tamils – without their explanations and understandings of kinship relations and kinship terms. Why should my informants, then, conform to a model that was constructed from a distant, detached position of theoretical reflection, like Dumont's? Their very term for kinship, I have suggested, does not point to structuralist notions of alliance, exchange, and associated consequences for social solidarity. Instead it is conceptually linked with rights of ownership. *Contam* points to meanings of legitimate possessiveness. My kin are mine, I can help myself to what they have. Such a privilege, for that is what it is, is a major reason why the Tamils preferred, and still prefer, marrying kin. If we were to transpose the meanings of *contam* into the language of alliance theory it would amount to something like this: the Tamils prefer marrying (that is "exchange") with people (kin) who already own what they have and vice versa. With *contam* (that is with one's own) one does not have to worry about being placed in the types of awkward and socially risky, or even humiliating, situations that are only too common in the public sphere of exchange where one has no right of ownership; quite simply, with kin one has leverage and power.

We have also seen, however, that the field of *contam* is not equal. When it comes to marriage, at least, not all kin are equivalent, some are "righter" or/and have exclusive marital "rights." In the priority given to one side (for example, mother's) rather than the other (father's), and to firstborn daughters and sons, we discern the association of marriage (and its potential for procreating life, for generating continuity, and so on) with asymmetry, and hierarchy. There is even a critical notion of hereditary aristocracy. The kin who are on the "right" "side" (mother's or father's) and firstborn are expected, among some castes required, to intermarry. It is moral and legal for them to do so. Tamil "right" marriages legitimize a concept and practice of endogamy that sanctions not interdependence of various families and lineages as the French theory of alliance would have it, but the very institutionalized hierarchy that Dumont himself found in the Indian caste system (1980).

The uncle–niece marriage is of a different sort from the "right" unions with "cousins." Its main orientation – women-centered, consanguineous, inward, and sacrificial – is unique. This marriage certainly does not support the notion that marriage is a relation of exchange between men who are related as in-laws. In fact, in the attributes that the people like and seek in this union, or at least idealize for the benefit of the anthropologist, we see an absolute rejection of the so-called "exchange of women." With this marriage, "girls do not marry far." They stay at home or come back. The family does not have to divide property or even transact with outsiders. They remain "together." We even see a condemnation of marriage – the cornerstone of the alliance theory. For to say, as my informants did, that you marry daughters close by so that they do not leave is in effect to work against the very meaning of marriage, which, throughout India and Tamil Nadu, is to send women away to another family. Whether in theory or in practice there is nothing to indicate that "the commonest form of close inter-marriage" (Good 1996: 6) works in favor of marriage itself.

Moreover, women, the very gender group ignored by French structuralists, prevail in this union. The maternal uncle's mother and the niece's mother – who happen to be in the relationship of mother-daughter are most likely to arrange it. In effect the first mother has the right[9] to wed her son to her daughter's daughter and vice versa. This fact leads me to suggest that the most critical bond of the Tamil most preferential marriage is not that between a man and his brother-in-law (as Dumont contends of Dravidian marriage on the whole) nor between a brother and his sister (as Margaret Trawick [1990] generalizes about Tamil kinship) but between a mother and a daughter. Their relation has all the elements eliminated by French structuralists: it is one of filiation, emotion, and "love" as the women of the survey quoted above told me. Since the older woman has wedded her son to the younger woman's daughter they are simultaneously kin and affines. In the household formed by this marriage, all the usual boundaries between "in-laws" and "kin" are blurred: son-in-law is brother, mother-in-law either mother or sister, daughter-in-law granddaughter, and so on. Notice what is happening here: consanguinal identities encompass affinal relations. And the "vertical dimension" of Dravidian kinship stressed by Dumont (1953: 38) is preserved by the conflation – not the differentiation – of kin and in-laws. It is also protected by minimal gift giving: the "younger brother takes less," the girl is already his.

Finally, the women who arrange this marriage live in a household headed by a man who is de facto junior to, and therefore lower, than them for the younger brother comes *after* his mother and elder sister. To appreciate his weak position in the household is to grasp the full dimension of his sacrificial marriage to his niece. The maternal uncle steps in not merely to keep women at home, which is (to repeat myself) the common explanation for marrying a sister's daughter, but to put them (in particular, mothers and elder sisters) before men (fathers and older brothers). In essence, the *tampi* sacrifices his masculinity, autonomy, and higher rank in the household in order to give women first place in the world of kinship, which for many Tamils may very well be the only world that matters. At the very least, the uncle–niece marriage removes the paternal "side," thereby championing the other side which represents "the best love," likeness, and one-sided generosity – everything unaccounted by the alliance theory of kinship.

Notes

1. After a lifetime working on the subject, Schneider (1984) came to believe that his discipline's obsession with "kinship," "the idiom of kinship," and "the kin-based society" was a serious ethnocentric mistake brought on by biologism.
2. It was Bishop Robert Caldwell (1856), an Evangelist missionary based in the Tinnevelly district of Tamil Nadu, who first adopted the term *Dravidian* to distinguish a family of languages (Tamil, Telugu, Malayalam, Kannada, Tulu, and so on) spoken mainly in South India from the family of Indo-Aryan languages (Hindi, in particular) spoken in North India.

3. For scholarly debates about Dumont's analysis of South Indian kinship see Good 1981; Parkin 1996a, 1996b; Rudner 1990; Scheffler 1977, 1984; Trautmann 1981; Trawick 1990; and Yalman 1962.

4. At the Congrès International des Sciences Anthropologiques et Éthnologiques held in London in 1934, A. Aiyyappan presented a paper that aimed to "invite attention to a form of enjoined marriage less known outside India than cross-cousin marriage, and, therefore, very little studied – the marrying of one's own sister's daughter" (1934: 281). In 1972, Brenda Beck reported that in the Koṅku area of Tamil Nadu, "marriage with the ZD [sister's daughter] is generally warmly approved … [and] is, in fact, a more frequent marriage statistically than a match with a [cross cousin]" (1972: 249). Her data shows that 5.9 percent of the 525 marriages she recorded were with actual mother's brother's daughter, 5 percent with actual father's sister's daughter and 6.5 percent with actual elder sister's daughter. She concludes that, "of the three types of marriages considered, ZD [sister's daughter] is clearly the most popular, while MBD [mother's brother's daughter] runs second, and FZD [father's sister's daughter] unions are generally the least frequent of the three" (1972: 253). Good's own data is somewhat consistent: of the 194 marriages he recorded in Tirunelveli, 5.6 percent were with mother's brother's daughter, 6.3 percent with father's sister's daughter, and 8.2 percent with elder sister's daughter (1980: 484). But the Indian anthropologist, Govinda Reddy's statistics on this last union are even more striking: of the 979 marriages he recorded among three communities residing in the Nellore district of Andhra Pradesh State, 18.88 percent (or 185 marriages) were of the uncle–niece type (1993: 36). See also Annoussamy 2003; Kapadia 1995; McCormack 1958; Rao 1973.

5. Dumont's ethnographic focus on the Kaḷḷars (1986) led him to overlook what used to be the most common and most valued marriage in South India.

6. Anthony Good, however, notes that: "the empirical evidence for Indian and Sri Lankan Tamils … is that most people do not habitually speak about kinship in terms of blood … and may even, as I found, deny its relevance when the question is explicitly put to them" (2000: 326).

7. My information here contradicts that of Dumont, who noted that among the Kaḷḷars: "In principle the obligation is to provide a partner for each *eldest* son of sisters and for each *eldest* daughter of brothers" (1986: 207, his emphasis). As he explained: "Suppose, for example, that three sisters are born in T and marry respectively into A, B, C. One son of each, and only one, must receive a wife from T. More specifically, he must receive a daughter of one of the three sisters' brothers in T. If there are three brothers, they will provide wives in their own birth order to A, B, and C respectively. If there is only one brother, however, and he has three daughters, he will be obliged to give them in marriage

to his sisters' sons in A, B, and C respectively. If there are five brothers and all have daughters, in principle, the last two will have a right to marry their daughters to one of the extra sons of A, B, and C. Not only are other children (brothers' sons, sisters' daughters) involved in other alliances, but once the obligations have been fulfilled, even children of the relevant sex may be married freely" (1986: 207). Dumont further repeats, "While eldest children's marriages are strictly regulated, younger children's marriages seem free, as a sort of irrelevant addition" (1986: 207). Similarly from the area of Konku Brenda Beck notes, "Once one brother has married a girl of the correct genealogical specification, then the other brothers have no further claim upon other girls in the same category. Some informants say it should be the eldest brother who makes such a marriage and the younger ones who are 'free' to marry elsewhere, but no one would argue over this fine point as long as one of several brothers will consent to take the urimai [mu*ṟ*ai] girl" (1972: 238). The men and women I worked with were categorical: only pairs of cross siblings, especially the first pair (and not all firstborn children of sisters and brothers) are required (or rather entitled) to practice a higher degree of endogamy, and the following unmatched siblings can marry however they want.

8. The common explanation is that the age disparity between a man and his younger sister's daughter would be too great.

9. In the area of Konku Brenda Beck noted, "people say ... 'a man has a very strong right,' implying that the woman's claim is less" (1972: 238). But in my field experience, sisters, mothers, and daughters have *urimais* as well, and the elder the woman is, the stronger her right, for we recall that in the Tamil world seniority always establishes priorities.

References

Aiyyappan, A. 1934. "Cross-Cousin and Uncle–Niece Marriages in South India." In *Congrès International des Sciences Anthropologiques et Ethnosociologiques*. Compte-rendu de la Première Session. London: Institut Royal d'Anthropologie.

Annoussamy, David. 2003. "Le mariage entre oncle et nièce dans le sud de l'Inde." In *Etudes en hommage à Eugène Schaeffer*, ed. Gauthier Bourdeaux and Susy Berthier, 63–75. Paris: Emile Bruylant.

Appadurai, Arjun. 1981. "Gastro-Politics in Hindu South Asia." *American Ethnologist* 8(3): 494–511.

1985. "Gratitude As a Social Mode in South India." *Ethos* 13(3): 236–245.

Arumugam, Indira. 2011. Kinship as Citizenship: State Formation, Sovereignty and Political Ethics among the Kallars in Central Tamil Nadu. Ph.D. Thesis. Department of Anthropology of the London School of Economics.

Beck, E. F. Brenda. 1972. *Peasant Society in Koṅku: A Study of Right and Left Subcastes in South India*. Vancouver: University of British Columbia Press.

1974. "The Kin Nucleus in Tamil Folklore." In B. Beck, Issue 7 of *Michigan Papers on South and Southeast Asia*, 1–27, Center for South and Southeast Asia Studies, University of Michigan.

Caldwell, Robert. 1856. *A Comparative Grammar of the Dravidian or South Indian Family of Languages*. London: Harrison.

Clark-Decès. 2014. *The Right Spouse: Preferential Marriages in Tamil Nadu*. Stanford, CA: Stanford University Press.

Collier, Jane F. and Sylvia J. Yanagisako. 1987. "Toward a Unified Analysis of Gender and Kinship." In *Gender and Kinship: Essays toward a Unified Analysis*, ed. Jane F. Collier and Sylvia J. Yanagisako, 14–50. Stanford, CA: Stanford University Press.

di Leonardo, Micaela. 1979. "Methodology and Misinterpretation of Women's Status in Kinship Studies: A Case Study of Goodenough and the Definition of Marriage." *American Ethnologist* 6(4): 627–637.

Dumont, Louis. 1953. "The Dravidian Kinship Terminology As an Expression of Marriage." *Man* 53: 34–39.

1980. *Homo Hierarchicus: The Caste System and Its Implications*. Chicago, IL: University of Chicago Press.

1983. *Affinity As a Value: Marriage Alliance in South India, with Comparative Essays on Australia*. Chicago, IL: University of Chicago Press.

1986 [1957]. *A South Indian Subcaste: Social Organization and Religion of the Pramalai Kallar*. Delhi: Oxford University Press.

Emeneau, B. Murray. 1953. Dravidian Kinship Terms. *Language* 29(3): 339–353.

Fuller, C. J. 1995. "The 'Holy Family' of Shiva in a South Indian Temple." *Social Anthropology* 3(3): 205–217.

Good, Anthony. 1980. "Elder Sister's Daughter Marriage in South Asia." *Journal of Anthropological Research* 36(4): 474–500.

1981. "Prescription, Preference and Practice: Marriage Patterns among the Kondaiyankottai Maravar of South India." *Man* (n.s.) 16: 108–129.

1996. "On the Non-existence of 'Dravidian Kinship.'" *Edinburgh Papers in South Asian Studies* 6: 1–12.

2000. "Power and Fertility: Divine Kinship in South India." In *Culture, Creation and Procreation*, ed. Monika Bock and Aparna Rao, 323–356. New York: Berghahn.

Hann, Katherine. 1985. "The Incidence of Relation Marriage in Karnataka, South India." *South Asia Research* 5(1): 59–72.

Harman, William P. 1989. *The Sacred Marriage of a Hindu Goddess*. Bloomington, IN: Indiana University Press.

Hudson, Dennis. 1977. "Siva, Minaksi, Visnu: Reflections on a Popular Myth in Madurai." *The Indian Economic and Social History Review* 14(1): 107–119.

Kapadia, Karin. 1995. *Siva and Her Sisters: Gender, Caste, and Class in Rural South India*. Boulder, CO: Westview Press.

Lévi-Strauss, Claude. 1969. *The Elementary Structures of Kinship*. Translated from the French by James Harle Bell, John Richard von Sturmer and Rodney Needham. Boston, MA: Beacon Press.

———. 1983. "Reflections on the Atom of Kinship." In *Structural Anthropology* 2: 82–112. Translated by Monique Layton. Chicago, IL: University of Chicago Press.

McCormack, William. 1958. "Sister's Daughter Marriage in a Mysore Village." *Man in India* 38(1): 34–48.

Mauss, Marcel. 1990. *The Gift (The Form and Reason for Exchange in Archaic Societies)*. Translated by W. D. Halls. Foreword by Mary Douglas. New York: W. W. Norton.

Morgan, Henry Lewis. 1871. *Systems of Consanguinity and Affinity of the Human Family*. Smithsonian Contributions to Knowledge, 17. Washington DC: Smithsonian Institution.

Parkin, J. Robert. 1996a. "On Dumont's 'Affinal Terms': Comment on Rudner." *Contributions to Indian Sociology* 30: 289–297.

———. 1996b. "Genealogy and Category: An Operational View." *L'Homme* 139: 87–108.

Rao, Kodanda M. 1973. "Rank Difference and Marriage Reciprocity in South India. An Aspect of the Implications of Elder Sister's Daughter Marriage in a Fishing Village in Andhra." In *Contributions to Indian Sociology* (n.s) 7: 16–35.

Reddy, Govinda. P. 1993. *Marriage Practices in South India: Social and Biological Aspects of Consanguineous Unions*. Madras: Department of Anthropology, University of Madras.

Rivers, W. H. R. 1907. "The Marriage of Cousins in India." *Journal of the Royal Asiatic Society*, July, 611–640.

———. 1968 [1914]. *Kinship and Organization*. London: The Athlone Press.

Rubin, Gayle. 1975. "The Traffic in Women: Notes on the 'Political Economy' of Sex." In *Toward an Anthropology of Women*, ed. Rayna R. Reiter, 157–210. New York: Monthly Review Press.

Rudner, David West. 1990. "Inquest on Dravidian Kinship: Louis Dumont and the Essence of Marriage Alliance." *Contributions to Indian Sociology* 24(2): 153–174.

Scheffler, Harold. 1977. "Kinship and Alliance in South India and Australia." *American Anthropologist* 79: 869–882.

———. 1984. "Markedness and Extensions: The Tamil Case." *Man* (n.s.) 19: 557–574.

Schneider, David M. 1984. *A Critique of the Study of Kinship*. Ann Arbor, MI: University of Michigan Press.

Shulman, David Dean. 1980. *Tamil Temple Myths: Sacrifice and Divine Marriage in the South Indian Saiva Tradition*. Princeton, NJ: Princeton University Press.

Strathern, Marilyn. 1988. *The Gender of the Gift: Problems with Women and Problems with Society in Melanesia*. Berkeley, CA: University of California Press.

Tamil Lexicon. 2007. *Tamil Lexicon*. University of Madras, 1924–1936. At http://dsal.uchicago.edu/dictionaries/tamil-lex/.

Trautmann, Thomas R. 1981. *Dravidian Kinship*. Cambridge: Cambridge University Press.

Trawick, Margaret. 1990. *Notes on Love in a Tamil Family*. Berkeley, CA: University of California Press.

Tylor, Edward B. 1889. "On a Method of Investigating the Development of Institutions: Applied to Laws of Marriage and Descent." *The Journal of the Anthropological Institute of Great Britain and Ireland* 18: 245–272.

Uberoi, Patricia. 2006. "Hierarchy and Marriage: Alliance in Indian Kinship." In *Caste, Hierarchy and Individualism: Indian Critiques of Louis Dumont's Contributions*, ed. R. S. Khare, 159–163. New Delhi: Oxford University Press.

Yalman, Nur. 1962. "The Structure of the Sinhalese Kindred: A Re-Examination of the Dravidian Terminology." *American Anthropologist* (n.s.) 64(3): 548–575.

5

The Anthropology of Biology: A Lesson from the New Kinship Studies

Sarah Franklin

A combination of influences over the past few decades has steadily raised the profile of the anthropology of bioscience and biomedicine, and this field has now become a well-established subdiscipline.[1] This new field has several antecedents. The move within the discipline towards greater reflexivity and the critiques of various kinds of ethnocentrism contributed to the emergence of bioscience as a subject of anthropological study in the 1990s – a transition that was aided by the emergence of the human genome project as a source of both ethical uncertainty and funding for research into its ethical, social, and legal implications (Franklin 1995). Anthropological interest in new reproductive technologies in this same period further encouraged a more critical engagement with biological models of "natural facts" (Strathern 1992a, 1992b), and Sandra Bamford's (2007) pioneering account of a society in which physiological explanations of conception play only a minimal role in understandings of both reproduction and kinship has offered a distinctive foil against which to contrast a Euro-American emphasis on biology that has increasingly come to be seen as extreme. At the same time it has remained unclear precisely how biological and physiological explanations function in contemporary society, since they are at once apparently literal and yet are often employed in ways that are self-evidently figurative (Franklin 2003; Nelkin and Lindee 1995). The dual quality of biological explanations also appears as a difference between what people say and what they do (many couples emphasize the importance of having a biological child of their own but will use a variety of means to achieve this end, including other people's eggs and sperm, Thompson 2005). Another striking and well-documented distinction is the considerable difference between how

DNA is interpreted in a lab and how those technical meanings change as they travel across different contexts (Fulwiley 2011; M'charek 2005; Rapp 1999). Likewise, the meaning of a biological fact to a specialist scientist may be considerably more vague and uncertain than it might appear to be in an article about that same biological fact in a magazine or newspaper (Franklin 2013).

These polysemic qualities of the biological are hardly surprising given that, like ideas of the natural, biology serves a wide variety of functions in many systems of both formal and informal knowledge – from ideas about kinship and gender to models of plant and animal life. Furthermore, it is clear that ideas about biology are changing rapidly. And the addition of new terms to refer to biology, such as cis-gender, or synthetic DNA, seem at once to reify the emperor's clothes that were never there and to camouflage still further the question of how many different forms "biology" can take simultaneously. Consequently, biology remains an unresolved lesson in hermeneutical practice within anthropology, and ethnographers have responded creatively to this challenge – through multispecies models of environment (Kirksey 2014), studies of oceanography and symbiosis (Helmreich 2009), ethnographies of the metabonome (Levin 2013), and new contributions to the field of epigenetics (Landecker 2011), to name but a few contributions to this rapidly expanding field.

This chapter attempts to offer a singular perspective on the ways in which anthropologists continue to struggle with the question of how to study biology by revisiting one of the key anthropological debates about biological facts in the 1980s, namely the now famous crucible of gender and kinship studies that has continued to generate so many new avenues of enquiry for the discipline. While offering a reinterpretation of the origin story of the new kinship studies, and in particular the place of the "biological facts of sexual reproduction" in many accounts of its emergence, the primary aim of this chapter is to revisit some of the ways biology has been theorized by feminist scholars at a time when the anthropology of biology is expanding more rapidly than ever.[2] By this means, we can forge new agendas for an anthropology of biology – both in terms of what anthropology can contribute, and how anthropological approaches overlap with those from other disciplines. Although a scholarly argument, the aim here is also political: if biology is often politics by other means, it's all the more important to continue to keep track of their shape-shifting variegations with all the clarity we can muster.

5.1   Paternal Paradigms?

Standard accounts of the emergence of the field of new kinship studies in anthropology have accurately and consistently emphasized the foundational influence of David Schneider, and in particular his analysis of the role of biological facts and biological science in the study of kinship. While rightly acknowledging Schneider's influence, however, this now canonical narrative also has its shortcomings. In particular, it commonly obscures both some of the key confusions in Schneider's models of biology and science, and more importantly the very different source of influence on the new kinship studies that came from feminist critiques of reproductive biology. Significantly, and also curiously, Schneider's many arguments against the biologization of kinship never engaged with any of the similar arguments being made by several generations of feminist writers from the 1940s onwards about the overemphasis on biology in both normative and professional accounts of gender, and this disconnection may be more revealing than previously assumed. Since critical interrogations of how the biological facts of sexual reproduction are represented, and a sustained challenge to the exaggerated gender binarism that is so often legitimated in their name have been core strands of feminist scholarship for at least three-quarters of a century (or longer, depending how this history is reckoned), it is crucial to distinguish the feminist critique of biology-as-politics from Schneider's account of biology-as-culture – and to critically examine the significant gap between the two. Interestingly, the lessons here are not only about how biological arguments have been variously used within anthropology, but how the histories of such intellectual "genealogies" have themselves been biologized.

Intellectual genealogies, after all, provide crucial resources in the formation of disciplinary identities: they are literally canon fodder. Highly gendered and unmistakably racialized canonical histories are further biologized through idioms such as the "founding fathers" of disciplines, leading to fierce ongoing criticism of established canonical histories as lineages of occlusion and mystification – as well as histories of colonization and subjugation which position the white male intellect, or "genius," as the origin of canonical thought with no regard to the circularity of a system that constantly conflates the hegemonic privilege of white male intellectuals with their own individual talent.

Consequently, the discipline of anthropology is no exception to the new expectation that canonical thought be taught both as a received history of conceptual development, and as a case study in the forced exclusions and histories of violent appropriation the canon at once reproduces and conceals within itself.

The canonical status of David Schneider's work on American kinship is a productive example to engage with, not least because he would happily have volunteered to be a founding father "straw man" for a text book case of anthropological decanonization (a pursuit he avidly practiced himself). Schneider's positioning as the "father" of the new kinship studies ironically recapitulates some of the very same structural dynamics and cultural codes he engaged with as a kinship theorist, not least in his most highly cited textbook, *American Kinship* (1968). The very fact that this publication has been cited more than 15,000 times (according to Google) raises another question that Schneider might himself have posed about gender, genealogy, and academic reproduction – namely what might be called the naturalization of scholarly citation. The lessons here are not only canonical: they point directly to the much wider role of naturalizing and biologizing discourses, concepts, and idioms – indeed they point to exactly the same problem of biology as consciousness that feminists have been critiquing since feminism first began.

Genealogizing, in anthropology as elsewhere, has form – and its form has a content that the familiar and familial idiom of Schneider's intellectual paternity tellingly reveals. The irony of his "fatherly" role in begetting the new kinship studies wasn't lost on Schneider, much as he might have engaged with it more explicitly, for example in his conversations with Richard Handler (1995). Schneider had been an early supporter of feminist scholars at a time when not many established senior male anthropologists stepped forward to show solidarity, and he actively sought to promote the work of feminist theorists such as Gayle Rubin, Ellen Lewin, Kath Weston, and Sylvia Yanagisako who brought the relation of gender and sexuality to kinship to prominence in the 1980s and 1990s. The complicated questions that surround the overlapping idioms of intellectual and biological paternity are the true conceptual heirs to anthropology's famous "virgin birth" debates, in which Schneider played a central role as a critic of the obviousness of biological paternity in the 1960s – perhaps fittingly in the journal *Man*.

Part of the problem then, as now, is the lack of an adequate critical language with which to discuss "biology" or "the biological," which in turn makes it hard to specify, exactly, what "biologizing" or "biologization" mean. "Biology" refers both to a discipline and its object of study: "the biology of the human female" is what you might read about in a textbook on "reproductive biology." Traditionally, "biological" refers to the phenomena studied by the "life sciences" – as opposed to the "hard sciences" that study things like stars. However, stars are "born" and "die": they have "life cycles," as do hurricanes and volcanoes. These overlaps become even more complex in everyday and popular culture where, for example, it is now common to refer to a corporation's "DNA" or the "male" and "female" parts of electrical devices. However, the borders between scientific and idiomatic, or expert and popular, uses of biological terms matter for more than technical reasons. Indeed, given the oddly vast range of uses of the biological, it is somewhat surprising an anthropology of biology is not itself a core subject within the discipline already.

But like Gayle Rubin's (1975) account of psychoanalysis as a feminist theory *manqué*, the non-existence of an anthropology of biology is a case of *enfin presque*. It's not that anthropologists haven't noticed the proximities between languages of gender, genealogy, and generation, and it is to David Schneider's credit that he not only noticed but foregrounded the ubiquitous biologisms that saturate everyday American parlance. Like many feminists before and after him, Schneider demonstrated how biology is more than an influential branch of the life sciences, because it is even more influential far beyond the lab as a source of cultural ideologies, assumptions, "common sense," or everyday mythologies that are used to justify, legitimate, or "explain" social roles and norms, many of which are directly responsible for gender stereotypes, such as the idea that women are weaker at math and scientific abstraction. There is, furthermore, an obvious overlap between Schneider's critique of biology in the context of anthropological research on kinship and critical feminist analyses of how "the facts of life" are often used to justify restrictive and hierarchical gender norms. Indeed garden-variety biological determinism has long been viewed as one of the most politically important targets of modern feminism, and has been used as a prime example of patriarchal oppression by scores of influential feminist authors and theorists – from de Beauvoir (2014 [1949]), Firestone (1970), and Butler (1990) to Haraway (1978a, 1978b, 1989, 1991, 2007, etc.), Martin (1987, 1991), and Keller (1983, 1995). According to many feminist critiques, biology and evolution are two of the most insidious and pervasive legitimating metanarratives of male dominance. Moreover, as feminist activists such as the Boston Women's Health Collective (1976) have long argued, biological explanations of women's reproductive capacity has long been used as one of the chief mechanisms to ensure subordination of the female sex. Probably one of the best known anthropology of biology articles (although not commonly referred to as such) is Emily Martin's (1991) "The Egg and the Sperm," which both humorously and tragically illustrates the ways in which both popular and "textbook" biology exacerbate masculinist hegemony, reshaping even cellular and molecular life in the image of heroic male agency to the detriment of women's health, agency, equality, and sanity.

Although the irony of positioning Schneider as the "father" of the new kinship studies has not been lost on many commentators, less attention has been paid to what this version of intellectual paternity both obscures and distorts. Morgan Clarke, for example, argues in his account of kinship's "overt comeback" as a form of gender studies that feminists were inspired by Schneider's work "questioning as it did [the] 'natural facts' of 'biological' reproduction that were held to ground Euro-American conceptions of gender relations" (2008: 156). While not technically false, such accounts are also not entirely accurate. Not only had feminist anthropologists been critiquing the natural basis of gender (and even the idea of there being a natural basis for anything) long before Schneider examined the cultural role of biology in American kinship systems, but they had also done so in far more depth. Above all, they had identified what Ruth Hubbard would call "the politics of biology" much earlier on, and had made it a prime target of feminist critique. In contrast to the neutral and detached accounts of the male breadwinner in *American Kinship*, feminists have tended to view everyday biological sexism as oppressive and immoral. To say they found Schneider's work "inspirational" is true, but not for his critique of gender inequality (which was muted), nor his critique of "nature" – which feminists had already developed much further than Schneider ever would. As we shall see further below, feminists such as Marilyn Strathern (1992a, 1992b, 2016) (one of the architects of what has come to be known as the new kinship studies), were inspired by Schneider's *model of culture*. In particular, Strathern valued his support (and she dedicated her 1992 book *After Nature* to him), but as her recently published early work on gender demonstrates (2016), Strathern had been theorizing gender, kinship, nature, and biology in unison since the 1970s. It is thus an interestingly complicated claim that it was Schneider's critique of natural facts that links him as a founder figure to the new kinship studies: this makes sense looking backwards only if you leave out most of the rest of what was going on (which in general is what lineages do ...).

In relating a tale of two biologies – how biology is analyzed within anthropology, and how discipline formation is itself biologized – it is helpful to reconsider the question of how Schneider's analysis of biology came to be seen as a template, or ancestor, for the feminist contribution to the new kinship studies. Schneider was supportive of feminist scholarship and the aim here is not to dismiss his contributions to feminist – and later queer – anthropology. His work also served as a model for feminist anthropological work on gender through his turn to culture as a mechanism of social action, and his attempt to morph a Parsonian concern with social institutions into a structuralist account of culture-as-code. But there is less of a connection between the feminist attempt to analyze gender in the 1970s and Schneider's cultural account of kinship than might appear from the vantage point of their presumed shared origins in the 1990s. Given the now established narrative about the diffuse enduring solidarity that links *American Kinship* to the new kinship studies, what is telling is instead the historical distance between them. This specific historical disconnect is worth revisiting precisely because it sheds light on a more general problem, namely what it is an anthropology of biology should be addressed to, exactly. The historical disconnect between the "biology" feminist anthropologists were analyzing in the 1970s and the "biology" David Schneider had in mind suggests that neither project recognized much kinship with the other. It is as telling that Gayle Rubin does not cite David Schneider or Clifford Geertz in her analysis of "the sex/gender system" as it is revealing that Schneider never cites any feminist scholars in any of his works. The reason for the disconnect is that they had very different political as well as analytical aims. For Schneider, the anthropological critique of biology needed to be brought closer to how anthropology views religion. Religion isn't taught in anthropology in terms of a dual focus on the actual or "real" underlying facts of divinity as opposed to the various cultural interpretations of this undeniable empirical certainty. Schneider's point was that kinship *is* taught in this way, and the question he very helpfully started asking is whether anthropologists could study biology the way they study religion, ritual, exchange, magic, or mythology (Boon and Schneider 1974). The question feminist scholars had been attempting to address for decades, but from a very different standpoint, was how arguments that posit biology as a basis for gender and kinship are reproducing inequalities.

5.2   Myths of Biology

Much feminist research on biology, for example, is premised on the argument that biology functions as a form of social mythology. This is at once a claim that has been made by innumerable feminist authors and activists, and one that has been associated with both revolutionary political change and heavy social penalties. To question the biological basis of sex, Shulamith Firestone claimed on the first page of *The Dialectic of Sex*, is to risk being declared insane: "the reaction of the common man, woman and child … to changing such a fundamental biological condition," she writes, is that "You must be out of your mind!" (Firestone 1970: 1).

> This gut reaction [to] so profound a change … is an honest one. That so profound a change cannot be easily fit into traditional categories of thought, e.g., "political," is not because these categories do not apply but because they are not big enough: radical feminism bursts through them. If there were another word more all-embracing than revolution we would use it.
>
> *(Firestone 1970: 1)*

Even in the early 1970s, Firestone was treading a well-worn path to the bonfire of biological excuses for sexist society. It is now more than 60 years since Ruth Herschberger forcefully set out one of the earliest feminist critiques of what she called "patriarchal myths of biology" in *Adam's Rib*, the pioneering feminist text she wrote between 1941 and 1946. Herschberger claimed that the extreme male bias in biological narratives about sex and reproduction is a primary source of sexist imagery and female subordination in the first iteration of an influential argument that became foundational to twentieth-century feminism. Her comprehensive critique of sexist biological bias includes a lengthy satire of how the egg and sperm are depicted in standard reference texts through familiar gender clichés.

> [T]he male sperm is by all odds the central character. We watch his actions with breathless suspense. He is an independent little creature,

single-minded, manly, full of charm, resourcefulness and enterprise, who will make his own minute decision to swim toward the egg. The female egg is portrayed as the blushing bride, ignorant but desirable, who awaits arousal by the gallant male cell. The egg, like the human female, is receptive ... The sperm is the purposeful agent in reproduction; the egg learns direction and purpose only after union with the sperm.

(Herschberger 1970: 72)

In Herschberger's far-reaching review spanning sexology, primatology, genetics, physiology, psychology, behaviorism, evolution, gynecology, anatomy, and embryology, the biological and medical sciences are repeatedly identified as the source of unhelpful fictions concerning sexual difference and "innate" male and female traits. Keenly attentive to the prescriptive slippage between "normal" and "natural," Herschberger repeatedly returns to the biological facts of sexual reproduction, which she claims play a critical role in perpetuating and legitimating both sexual difference and sexual inequality. The "marked difference" between women and men – that the former have babies – has been heavily overplayed, she argues. Most of the time, she notes, women are not having babies, and for most of their lives they are not even fertile. Reproduction, she proposes, is a weak excuse for dichotomizing humanity.

The history of mankind has been the search for some difference between individuals and groups of individuals – color, geographical location, sex – that would really count for something, a difference on the basis of which society could get organised, once and for all, and settle down to peaceful senility ... The marked difference that distinguishes women from men is one of the most palpable differences to be found. It is women who have babies, men who cannot. Among legislative groups, in fact, women are sometimes regarded simply as the pregnant species. While only women can have babies, it must be remembered that they are not always having them. Women, during the childbearing period between adolescence and menopause, are not even fertile much of the time.

(Herschberger 1970: 171)

The problem with biology, according to Herschberger, is not only the insistence on binary sexual types, or even the hierarchical way in which such differences are ordered, but the silencing effect of such authoritative scientific claims, which give the appearance of placing the natural facts of sexual hierarchy beyond question – as established, objective truth. The problem with biology, she is suggesting, is its effects on consciousness. In a context of such pervasive and sexist biologism, the mere mention of menstruation, motherhood, or childbirth, she argues, brings with it such an "overwhelming" determinism of women's character, psychology, instincts, and capacities that they have "silenced the tendency on the part of women to question [their] uniformity" (1970: 174) – thus rendering women complicit with their own devaluation. "Must a woman cultivate only that uniqueness which distinguished her from man (and links her with the animals), or is she to be allowed to exhibit some purely human characteristics as well?" (1970: 177)

Writing almost simultaneously in the 1940s, on the other side of the Atlantic, Simone de Beauvoir notably opened her account of "Destiny" in *The Second Sex* with a chapter entitled "The Data of Biology."[3] Like Herschberger before her, de Beauvoir condemns biological science as a foundational source of sexist mythology, and points her finger in particular at the representation of reproductive roles: "Woman? ... she is a womb, she is an ovary"(1974: xv), de Beauvoir sarcastically proclaims at the outset of her influential mid-century feminist primer. The primacy of reproductive roles in defining maleness and femaleness, de Beauvoir repeatedly claims, rigidly confines each sex to a narrow path, while perpetually stratifying them in unequal complementarity. Famously de Beauvoir analyzes allegorical accounts of the egg and sperm as figurations of immanence and transcendence, asking why such philosophical principles have been so fundamentally confused with biological form.

Despite the fact that the biological facts of sexual reproduction were already an established target of feminist critique by the mid-1960s, when an unprecedented outpouring of feminist literature began to saturate popular media and public debate, the feminist critique of biology – and in particular reproductive biology – showed no signs of waning in the following decade. To the contrary, the dissection of biological mythology became even more elaborate, and politically central, to a vast range of feminist critiques including the classic accounts of Firestone (1970), Greer (1970), Evelyn Reed (1970), Kate Millett (1970), Anne Koedt (1970), and Robin Morgan (1970) at the outset of a decade that would conclude with pivotal and far-reaching critiques of biology from Donna Haraway (1978a, 1978b) and Adrienne Rich (1976). A parallel feminist revolution was of course well under way within anthropology in this same period, to which a critique of the role of biology was central, leading to an interrogation of not only sex and gender but the very basis of scientific investigation itself (Strathern [1974] 2016).

5.3 Cultural Anthropology

When he began his project on American kinship in the 1950s, David Schneider had recently moved to the University of Chicago, where he took charge of The Kinship Project – a research initiative that would lead to many publications, and ultimately to his influential 1968 monograph *American Kinship: A Cultural Account*. Schneider's kinship project was a mid-century hybrid, combining a Parsonian approach to social structure and action with an early version of symbolic anthropology, partly based on the work of Lévi-Strauss, but also inspired by Ruth Benedict's model of cultural pattern. Like Clifford Geertz, who was also Parson's student, Schneider sought to establish a cultural approach to American kinship, modeling his efforts in part on the ethnographic studies of British anthropologists Raymond Firth (1956) and Michael Young and Peter Willmott (1957) of kinship among urban households in London. However, although he had a substantial interest in kinship systems, the American kinship project was explicitly intended as an effort to develop new ways to model cultural systems. As so often in the past, kinship analysis in Schneider's case exemplified a new methodology – one that would ultimately come to be known as "interpretive," "symbolic" – or simply "cultural" anthropology.

Parsons had outlined a sociological model of American kinship in the early 1940s, distinguishing between the "procreative family" and the "family of orientation." To Parsons, the interesting feature of the American family was the high level of independence of the conjugal unit from the wider family network – a fact which led him to differentiate American from European kinship, and to refer to "conjugal families" (1943: 184). In her study of urban kinship in London in the mid-1950s, the British sociologist Elizabeth Bott (1957) developed the related observation that conjugal independence was cultivated in inverse proportion to social network density. This finding allowed her to contrast conjugal roles, and to emphasize the wide range of their variation according to different circumstances. A similar contrast was explored in Young and Willmott's studies of Bethnal Green (inner London) families who moved out to the suburbs, isolating them from wider kin networks, and often increasing the isolation of wives who previously might have spent more time with siblings or parents than their husband or in-laws.

This was not the analytical path Schneider chose to follow in his attempt to isolate a new and different set of systemic elements unifying American kinship – namely its core cultural symbols. As Schneider himself later described his aim, it was "to beat the culture drum," and thus to show how culture was itself a kind of institutional force (Schneider in Handler 1995: 203). He sought to identify, isolate, and elucidate the cultural and symbolic basis of American kinship, and thus to establish a "cultural" version of Parsonian structuralism, with its emphasis on roles, functions, sanctions, norms, and corresponding types of social system. But in his elaboration of the relation between the symbols of "love," "diffuse enduring solidarity," "nature," "blood," and "family," variation in social practice was sacrificed to consistency of cultural pattern in the name of identifying the underlying symbolic logics organizing the meanings of kin relatedness, and giving the kinship system its grammar or "code." In order to depict American kinship as a unified cultural system, the pieces had to neatly interlock in the same way Parsonian roles, structures, and institutions had in order to demonstrate and explain the social forces holding them together.

Schneider was not unaware of feminism, and he had undoubtedly read Simone de Beauvoir as well as other feminist works – possibly including Herschberger. His argument that biology performs a symbolic role in American kinship complemented the feminist claim that biology has many functions above and beyond its role as a form of scientific description or analysis (and even that biology has a mythical function in social life). The arguments of Herschberger, Firestone and de Beauvoir anticipate those of Haraway (1989, 1991, 1997), Martin (1987, 1991), Keller (1983, 1995), and many other later feminist scholars who analyzed biological discourse in much greater depth to demonstrate how biological facts are used to script normative and appropriate gender behavior. Dozens of feminists in the 1980s including Ruth Bleier (1984, 1986), Anne Fausto Sterling (1985, 1987, 1989), Ruth Hubbard (1988a, 1988b, 1990), and Lynda Birke (1980, 1982, 1986), among others, showed how biology and genetics serve as the source of deterministic arguments about innate capacities that have a substantial influence on the definitions of social roles, institutions, and identities. Schneider's argument about the role of biology in American kinship had arrived, by a different route, at the same conclusion: biology provided a code or grammar for the cultural systems on which social roles were based.

Albeit for reasons that had nothing to do with feminism, Schneider could easily have been seen, at least superficially, to be nailing his colors to the same mast as contemporaneous feminist authors such as Germaine Greer, who dismissively referred to "the secret ministry of biology" and its doctrinal ordinations (1970). Indeed Schneider did not need to spell out the implications of his arguments about biology as a source of social rules, since feminists already had. Schneider's most substantial affinity with feminism came from his use of structuralism to demonstrate the capacity for cultural systems to have institutional effects. For example, in its combination of structuralist analysis with quasi-feminist content, *American Kinship* clearly anticipates the logic of Sherry Ortner's "Is Female to Male as Nature Is to Culture?" published shortly afterwards in 1972. In Schneider's account, as in Ortner's, the biological facts of sexual reproduction – and the "marked difference" that women have babies – are analyzed as a cultural code, or structural fiction, guiding social action. However, whereas Ortner's article, first published in *Feminist Studies* in 1972, and later reprinted in the pioneering feminist anthology *Woman, Culture and Society* edited by Lamphere and Rosaldo (1974), was an explicit critique of female subordination, and denounced "the universal devaluation of women," Schneider's project had no such aim, and makes no mention of sexual inequality, feminism, or what was coming to be known as "sexual politics" (Millett 1970).

This omission is important since a lack of attention to feminism and sexual politics had significant and limiting consequences for Schneider's argument about both culture and kinship. For example Schneider's argument about the importance of sexual difference to the "codes" of American kinship could not be extended to other "codes" – such as those of American nationalism. It also became impossible to historicize these cultural codes. As Carol MacCormack and Marilyn Strathern would later argue in their landmark 1980 anthology *Nature, Culture and Gender*, the symbolic systems of nature, culture, and sexual difference are distinctively intertwined in the Eurocentric imagination in a way that is neither universally shared nor even consistent with earlier periods of European history (1980). Their deconstructive effort to challenge the intransigent binarisms of much anthropological analysis was also aimed at feminist anthropology, and Strathern's banner headline "No Nature, No Culture" (1980) anticipated some of the most important later works in gender and queer theory, including Judith Butler's *Gender Trouble* (1990). Apart from the moral reasons, a concern with women's subordination might have been more fully acknowledged in *American Kinship*, the omission of a critical concern with sexual politics and sexual inequality in Schneider's work significantly limited and impeded his project initially to deconstruct the kinship category, and later to reject it altogether.

As notable as the lack of any reference to gender inequality or feminism may be from *American Kinship*, published in 1968, an even more striking absence is the lack of any reference to feminist anthropology, or feminist scholarship in general, from Schneider's later, final, and most radical, book, *A Critique of the Study of Kinship*, published in 1984. Here, in a continuation of his heated and longstanding argument with Rodney Needham over structuralist accounts of kinship, Schneider substantially extends his signature claim that kinship is a figment of the Eurocentric imagination. His *Critique* is centrally concerned with the "biological mechanisms" on which kinship is supposedly based, as well as the role of natural science as an authoritative belief system, and he returns repeatedly to the status of biological science and "the facts of life." As in much of his earlier work, Schneider was centrally concerned both with the language and imagery of the life sciences, and their relationship to idioms such as the blood tie. More than any other source of imagery, however, he is concerned with sexual intercourse and the corresponding model of the biological facts of sexual reproduction. These are the tools he wishes to employ to demonstrate that kinship is a cultural system made up of core symbolic units, and it is an argument he first sets out in full in what is still his most popular, influential, and best known book.

5.4 Sexual Intercourse

American Kinship was written for the influential Prentice Hall "Anthropology of Modern Societies" series, and it was intended to mark a shift toward the anthropological study of contemporary Western culture as well as to demonstrate the application of "one particular kind of cultural analysis" (1968: iv). In his Editorial Foreword to the book, Schneider further emphasizes the value of this approach for the reader who will be familiar with the examples being presented, so that "the student is provided with a particularly clear example of how this theory of culture works, since the data are American data and as such are familiar to every American reader" (1968: iv). He then begins his exegesis by emphasizing the isolation – or "differentiation" – of the domain of kinship in American kinship. Unlike premodern societies in which "whatever a man does ... he does as a kinsman of one kind or another," in the United States "all of these institutions are quite clearly differentiated from each other" and "one owns property in one's own right and enters into economic relations where one chooses and according to rules which are supposed to be quite free from the constraints of kinship, religion or politics" (1968: v–vi). Religion, employment, and politics are similarly differentiated from kinship, and for Schneider this has a major analytic advantage, because it enables analysis of a kinship system "as close to its 'pure form' as possible" and thus promises to reveal "the question of 'the nature of kinship' in the sense of establishing just what the distinguishing features of kinship consist of" (1968: vi).

Schneider's concern is thus both to demonstrate a method of cultural analysis and to perform an exegesis on a specific cultural system, and his core method is through the interpretation of the elementary symbolic units – or what he calls cultural constructs – of the American kinship system. A cultural system is made up of basic cultural elements and core ideas which have a grammar and a syntax defining their relations to each other. But culture is also more than a language, and cultural symbols are more than words, because in addition to the rules governing how words are used, and the multiple meanings of words that correspond to different contexts, "the cultural construct has a reality of its own" (1968: 5), and it is this distinct property of cultural meaning Schneider is at pains to reveal. His debt to Lévi-Strauss, to semiotics, and to structuralist anthropology is clear in his methodological ambition to isolate and examine the "core symbols" of American kinship that are "formulated as a part of the cultural system" and thus to show how "meaning is systematically elaborated ... throughout its differentiated parts; and how the parts are differentiated and articulated as cultural units" (1968: 8). *American Kinship*, Schneider clarifies, is not about how Americans do, or think, or talk about kinship – although it is based on data drawn from all three of these activities. It is instead, he clarifies, "about symbols, the symbols which are American kinship" (1968: 18).

Schneider begins his analysis with the two kinds of relative that can exist in American kinship, namely those that are defined by blood and those who are established through marriage.

The blood relationship, as it is defined in American kinship, is formulated in concrete, biogenetic terms. Conception follows a single act of sexual intercourse between a man, as genitor, and a woman, as genetrix. At conception, one half of the biogenetic substance of which the child is made is contributed by the genetrix, and one-half by the genitor.

(1968: 23)

Americans do not believe the man contributes the bone and the woman the flesh, and they don't believe the male seed is the primary cause of the establishment of pregnancy. Americans believe in nature, biology, and science: "In American cultural conception, kinship is defined as biogenetic. This definition says that kinship is whatever the biogenetic relationship is. If science discovers new facts about biogenetic relationship, then that is what kinship is and was all along, although it may not have been known at the time" (1968: 23).

In American kinship blood establishes a bond "which is 'real' or 'true' [and] 'by birth' [so it] can never be severed, whatever its legal position" (1968: 24). Based on the real, true, and scientifically verifiable facts of nature, "nothing can terminate or change the biological relationship" that exists between a parent and child, or siblings, who are permanently related as blood kin regardless of how they behave toward each other (1968: 24). Even if people deny the scientific authority by which biological facts are determined to be real, true, and objective facts of nature, the point remains that "the cultural definition is that kinship is the biogenetic facts of nature" (1968: 24, fn). Blood is a substance, a material thing, and divisible: people can trace their blood, and they have differing proportions of genetic substance from different sides, lines, or relations, which are part of their unalterable nature as individuals. Blood is thus a core symbol defining both a category of relation, and an essential element of individual kin identity.

Whereas the blood relation is natural, material, unalterable, and cannot be terminated in American kinship, relationships by marriage in this same system are none of these things – indeed they are the opposite. Whereas the blood relation is part of "the natural order of things" corresponding to "the way things are in nature" and " 'the facts of life' as they really exist" (1968: 26), marriage is an artifice defined solely by convention, or in Schneider's term it is "a special instance of ... the order of law" manifest as both a "pattern for behaviour" and a "code for conduct." This purely social order – the order of law – consists of "rules and regulations, customs and traditions" which are in turn derived from "the government of action by morality, and the self-restraint of human reason" (1968: 27). These two classes of relatives – those that derive from the order of nature and the order of law – yield the three main categories of relatives in American kinship: those who are related by blood, those who are related by marriage, and those who are related by both – who include the parents and offspring in the nuclear family unit.

It is from the latter point that Schneider extends his initial exegesis of nature, science, and biology beyond the American cultural construct of blood relation to include the nuclear family, and he does so via "the act of procreation." Sexual intercourse "is the symbol in terms of which members of the family as relatives and the family as a cultural unit are defined and differentiated in American kinship," he writes: "Male and female, the opposites, are united in sexual intercourse as husband and wife" (1968: 39). In his attempt to provide an "ethnographic account of the cultural unit, 'the family,' in American kinship" (1968: 32–33), Schneider first returns to ideas of what is natural: "the family is formed according to the laws of nature and it lives by rules that are regarded by Americans as self-evidently natural" (1968: 34). So too is the sexual division of labor "only natural, in the American view":

> Women bear children, nurse them, and care for them. This, according to the definition of American culture, is part of women's nature. They can do these things by virtue of their natural endowment ... men do not bear children, nor can they nurse them from their own bodies. The cultural premise is that they are not naturally endowed with ways of sensing infants' needs ... It is in this sense that the distinctive features or defining elements of the family posit the mated pair who rear their young in a place of their own.
>
> *(1968: 35–36)*

He adds that the family is also more than merely a natural entity, being the outcome of human reason "added to" the facts of nature, so that ultimately the cultural construct of the family in American kinship selectively combines elements of the order of nature on the one hand and the order of law, or rule of reason, on the other. The nuclear family, in this view, is not so much a partial whole, as a single unit in which different cultural logics are combined to create a distinctive hybrid entity.

This ability of the family not only to combine, but to resolve, the differences between the order of nature and the rule of reason, is repeated, Schneider argues, by the role of the family unit as a mediator between relations of blood and relations of law. This is why, he argues, the act of sexual intercourse is the core of the American kinship system: it is the "figure [which] provides all of the central symbols of American kinship" (1968: 37).

> Sexual intercourse as an act of procreation creates the blood relationship of parent and child and makes genitor and genetrix out of husband and wife. But it is an act which is exclusive to and distinctive of the husband–wife relationship: sexual intercourse is legitimate and proper only between husband and wife and each has the

exclusive right to the sexual activity of the other. These are the tenets of American culture ... All of the significant symbols of American kinship are contained within the figure of sexual intercourse, itself a symbol, of course. The figure is formulated in American culture as a biological entity and a natural act.

(1968: 38–40, passim)

Sexual intercourse is furthermore "a symbol of love," and occupies a uniquely central symbolic position as the sole unifying act mediating between, and conjoining, conjugal and parental, or cognatic, types of love. The act of procreation is "a symbol of unity, or oneness" uniting the "flesh of opposites, male and female, man and woman [and] also in the outcome of that union, the unity of blood, the child ... The child thus affirms the oneness or unity of blood with each of his parents and with his siblings by those parents. At the same time, that unity or identity, of flesh and blood, that oneness of material, stands for the unity of cognatic love" (1968: 39).

In her recently published manuscript on sex and gender, originally written in the early 1970s for a series that folded, we can now see that Marilyn Strathern would have been among the very first authors to turn to Schneider's work as a useful resource for feminist anthropology, and her use of his work is instructive. Like many other feminists writing in the early 1970s, Strathern was centrally concerned both with the role of biology in the reproduction of gender hierarchies, and with its status as a symbol or myth. Central to her analysis of both the sexual division of labor and gender conflict was the use of sexual relations and sexual difference as "seductive symbols."

Myths frequently contain within them symbols. A symbol is an item, often a concrete, material object, which stands for something else, often an abstract notion, a value, an aspect of a relationship. It describes one thing in terms of another. Like myths, symbols make statements which put certain values on the thing being symbolized. They express emotions people have (or should have) toward these things. Whether we call something a myth or a symbol is largely a matter of analysis. Take the dogma of Mae Enga men: "females can harm males." In so far as it purports to be a statement about the physical capacities of females, in which Mae Enga men believe, an outsider could call it a myth. It is a fact Mae Enga men hold about women but one which does not correspond to physical reality. We can dismiss it as a lie; or we can say that Mae Enga men are afraid of something and this is how they express their fear. But supposing the anthropologist suggests that one of the origins of this fear is the fact that the women with whom men most often come into contact come from enemy groups, and enemy men certainly have to be feared because they (in reality) kill men of one's own group. Then we can look on the phrase "females can harm males" as a symbol – it stands for something else. It stands for: "men can be harmed by the groups from which women come." Wives originate in enemy clans, and wives are enemies too.

(Strathern [1974] 2016: 20)

As we can see from Strathern's analysis, she was at once describing what men and women do, and how these actions are represented and interpreted. Her exemplification of symbolic representation cut two ways: she described the kinds of statements people make about each other in a specific community, and then she described how these might be interpreted, and indeed how an anthropologist might hypothetically have challenged those interpretations by giving the statements a different meaning. Her book, she explained, was "concerned with both kinds of symbols" – meaning what symbols mean to people consciously or unconsciously when they use them in their native context, and what they mean to outsiders.

Characteristically, Strathern went on to significantly complicate her argument by pointing out that symbols are not only made out of objects, or people, but may also use relationships as their currency. And when relationships are used as symbols, she pointed out, their meaning becomes especially ambiguous. It was here that she drew on Schneider's account of sexual intercourse and biology to make a cultural point about symbols.

> David Schneider, in his account of American kinship, makes just this point. He is concerned with the place of sexual intercourse (a "fact of nature") in the thinking of Americans, as a symbol "in terms of which members of the family are defined and differentiated and in terms of which each member of the family's proper mode of conduct is defined."
>
> *(Schneider 1968: 33, cited in Strathern 2016: 23)*

She went on to quote from *American Kinship*:

> It will be helpful to begin with a few simple distinctions. First, sexual intercourse can be seen as a set of *biological facts*. These are part of the world. They exist, and they have effects. Second, there are certain cultural notions and constructs *about* biological facts. The example *par excellence* in American culture is the life-sciences – biology, zoology, biochemistry, and so on. This is a cultural system explicitly attuned to those biological facts as such. It discovers them, studies them, organizes what it regards as facts into a system. But it remains a system of cultural constructs which should not be confused with the biological facts themselves.
>
> *(Schneider 1968: 114, cited in Strathern 2016: 23)*

Later in the book Strathern returned to Schneider's description of sexual intercourse, quoting it at length in the context of analyzing Euro-American understandings of sexual mythology (extracts from pp. 33–52 and 116–117 of Schneider's book are quoted over three pages of Strathern's book, from pp. 239 to 242). But her immediate interpretation of his example added another dimension to it: "Schneider takes sexual intercourse as ultimately providing a model for commitment," she noted, agreeing that this was indeed "one of the uses" to which it could be put. "But," she added,

> [It] may also stand for the opposite: for exploitation, not solidarity ... Males dominate women through sex ... [T]there is more [at stake] here than vagaries in conjugal arrangements ... Over the last hundred years, a very explicit equation has been made between female bondage and (first) woman's deprived marital status, and (then) her mutilated sexuality.
>
> *(Strathern 2016: 242–243)*

This was not a point Schneider chose to pursue, and as Strathern noted, the fact of female subordination complicated his argument. She agreed with him that sexual intercourse was a *model*, but she added that *so is sexual difference*. By this insistence, moreover, she was not simply adding that nature and biology are *also* symbols for sex difference. Strathern's addition to Schneider was to complicate his interpretation of both symbols and sexuality. "Sex is an extremely powerful source of symbolism," she argued, "so powerful it can symbolize quite contrary notions and still lend weight to each."

Although he had not criticized gender models as sources of inequality, and nor had he analyzed the overlapping-but-contrary uses of biological "symbols" in the contexts of gender and kinship, these had nonetheless featured quite prominently in Schneider's account of American kinship, where, to a feminist eye, they also stood out. "In American culture, the definition of what makes a person male or female is the kind of sexual organs he has," Schneider noted, adding that "[A] male or female is established at birth by its genitals" (1968: 41). It is a little unclear in his account how biology is functioning as an explanation system when he describes what might otherwise have been called sexual stereotypes:

> Temperamental differences are held to correlate with the differences in sexual organs. Men have an active, women a passive quality, it is said. Men have greater physical strength and stamina than women. Men are said to have mechanical aptitudes that women lack. Men tend toward an aggressive disposition said to be absent in women.
>
> *(1968: 41)*

It is similarly unclear how exactly the cultural logic of American kinship explained the sexual division of labor, except that in the context of the nuclear family there were clear roles for men and women corresponding to perceived differences between maleness and femaleness:

> The different qualities of maleness and femaleness are said by informants to fit men and women for different kinds of activities

and occupations. Men's active, aggressive qualities, their strength and stamina, are said to make them particularly good hunters and soldiers and to fit them for positions of authority, especially where women and children are concerned. Women are presumed to be nurturant and passive in ways that make them particularly good at teaching school, nursing, food preparation, and homemaking. Men's mechanical aptitudes are said to make them good at working with machines – at designing, building and repairing them – in ways which women cannot match.

(1968: 41)

Reverting to a more Parsonian mode, Schneider's account of the fit between sex roles, the sexual division of labor, and the nuclear family was a neat one. Indeed they made up a nearly seamless whole. Thus,

In American culture, sex role occurs in a context which further selects, modifies, or emphasizes some of its special aspects. A man is a policeman, a repairman, a clerk or a soldier. A woman may be a nurse, a school teacher, a cook, or a chambermaid. The attributes of the sex-role have different values in each of these cases. Not only is the policeman a man, but he is a man relying on his strength and fortitude in a context of maintaining law and order and preventing crime. The same qualities of maleness in a soldier are not matters of law and order at all, but are defined by the nature of war. And the repairman using the qualities of his masculinity to tend machines finds his sex-role spelled out in a context of machinery and mechanical aptitudes which may or may not have anything to do with law and order or war, but which focus instead on the efficient operation of machinery ... The same is true for the family. Wife, mother, daughter and sister are female; husband, father, son, and brother are male. It is often said that wives and mothers are the proper members of the family to cook, keep house, and care for children, and husbands and fathers are the proper members of the family to go out to work, earn a living, be in charge of the family, and have authority.

(1968: 41–42)

Informants offered "a very fundamental and important piece of evidence," Schneider added, when they stipulated the clarification that:

[I]f wives and mothers are the proper members of the family to cook and keep house, this is *not* because they are wives and mothers but because they are *women*. And if husbands and fathers are the members of the family who should go out and earn a living, who should be in charge of the family, this is because they are *men* and *not* because they are husbands and fathers.

(1968: 42, original emphasis)

However, his account of the means by which especially good informants distinguished between orders of cultural logic – between, in his words, a "defining element," such as being a man or a woman, and a "role definition," such as cleaning the house (1968: 43) – did not explain how biological sex difference came to be a defining element to begin with.

5.5   Circulating Conundrums?

The task of asking whether the displacement of one binary opposition onto another could serve as an "explanation" – even of a symbolic system – was not only undertaken by feminists in the 1970s and 1980s. Other critics of both structuralism and structural functionalism made similar points about the somewhat circular arguments that resulted from what Carol MacCormack described as "stark categories standing in wooden opposition" (1980). However, feminist anthropologists working on sex and gender in this period (and there were a lot of them) repeatedly pushed their boats quite far out into the uncharted territory described by Yanagisako and Collier in the effort to question the relationship of "biological" reproduction to the perceived differences between women and men.

This task required a conversion of Schneider's observation that biology serves as a core symbol for the nuclear family into a question about how sex comes to be seen as biological to begin with?

> Having recognised our model of biological difference as a particular mode of thinking about relations between people, we should be able to question "the biological facts" of sex themselves. We expect that our questioning of the presumably biological core of gender will eventually lead to the rejection of any dichotomy between sex and gender as biological and cultural facts and will open up the way for an analysis of the symbolic and social processes by which both are constructed in relation to each other.
>
> *(Yanagisako and Collier 1987: 42)*

Wisely, Yanagisako and Collier placed the analysis of the cultural habit of "continually rediscovering gendered categories" (1987: 49) central to their prescription for the reinvention of both kinship and gender studies. Their call to reject the cycle of presuming a binary form of gender, and then rediscovering gender in every binary form, advocated a form of analytical prophylaxis that required a cull of established interpretive devices, including Schneider's neat divisions and alignments.

> Both gender and kinship studies, we suggest, have foundered on the unquestioned assumption that the biologically given difference in the roles of men and women in sexual reproduction lies at the

core of the cultural organization of gender even as it constitutes the genealogical grid at the core of kinship studies. Only by calling this assumption into question can we begin to ask how other cultures might understand the difference between women and men, and simultaneously make possible studies of how our own culture comes to focus on coitus and parturition as the moments constituting masculinity and femininity.

(Yanagisako and Collier 1987: 49)

Increasingly in the decades since Collier and Yanagisako, among many others, called for a questioning of the binary form of sexual difference, and the focus on heterosexual intercourse as the defining element of kinship and gender, all of these elements have begun to disaggregate. In a kind of reverse proof of how tightly bound together it is possible for kinship, gender, sexuality, and parenting to be, the formerly presumed unities and dependencies among them have been exposed as forced contingencies. Schneider was prescient in arguing that sexual intercourse is the core symbol of American kinship because it offers a folk model of human reproduction. History has shown him to have been very accurate on this point. But it is feminist anthropology, and feminist scholarship more widely, that has revealed why sexual difference is inextricable from what Kate Millett famously named sexual politics – and why this connection matters.

5.6   Conclusion

As anthropology moves forward in what has been called the "Century of Biology" it will be important to remember that both the politics of sexuality and gender and the politics of biology continue to diversify in both their content and their form. And while many of the post-Foucauldian projects dedicated to the changing life of biopower will become even more important in the context of increasing biological surveillance, complex biosocialities, and new molecular identities, there will also be the not-so-new bio-logics of racism, sexism, and xenophobia to contend with. So much is already clear from the undisguised Malthusianism of current debates about migration, the intractable hold of a highly iniquitous sexual division of labor, and the flight from the STEM subjects of young women and girls. The complicated politics of fertility remain dominated by "the biological facts of sexual reproduction" in the new form of the ticking biological clock, and women continue to be blamed for "postponing" pregnancies, when they pursue higher education and for having too many children too early when they don't.

It is ironically a symptom of these same sexist reproductive patterns that within the academy much of the important feminist literature from the 1970s and 1980s is no longer taught, and no longer appears on syllabi. Despite having been one of the most intellectually powerful influences on twentieth-century anthropology, the feminist debates over gender, reproduction, and kinship are rarely brought into conversations about, for example, egg freezing or IVF. Both the anthropology of reproduction and the new kinship studies have fortunately continued to thrive, alongside queer anthropology and the anthropology of the biosciences. These are crucial resources in the effort to address climate change, migration, and the food supply as the century progresses. And if an anthropology of biology is to take its place alongside these closely related subdisciplines, it will be as well if it remembers its origins in the feminist writings where the politics of biology have received one of their most thorough critical assessments to date.

Acknowledgments

I am very grateful to the editor, Sandra Bamford, for her considerable patience in the production of this chapter, and for the invitation to contribute to this volume. I'm also deeply indebted to Marilyn Strathern and Susan McKinnon for their characteristically generous, encouraging, forensic, tactful, and insightful suggestions.

Notes

1. See Franklin and Lock 2003; Gibbon and Novas 2007; Good 1995, 2001; and Lock and Nguyen 2010.
2. Although the anthropology of biology is overdue for a synthetic assessment and meta-review, this chapter takes a different approach, by moving back in time to examine some of the important origins of this field. I am grateful to Sandra Bamford for the invitation to contribute to this volume with a chapter linking the new kinship studies to feminist anthropology and the politics of biology and it is my hope this intersectional genealogy will continue to inspire critical scholarship interrogating the complex role of biological knowledges and idioms in contemporary society.
3. Herschberger's text was written between 1941 and 1946, while de Beauvoir's account was written slightly later, and published in 1949. These two mid-century feminist texts significantly preceded, and presciently anticipated, the period of widespread feminist activism that took hold in the 1960s. They thus form a bridge of sorts between the popular and successful feminist movements of the early and late twentieth century, and what is notable about these two key transitional texts is their primary emphasis on reproductive biology.

References

Bamford, Sandra. 2007. *Biology Unmoored: Melanesian Reflections on Life and Biotechnology*. Berkeley, CA: University of California Press.

Birke, L., ed. 1980. *Alice through the Microscope: The Power of Science over Women's Lives*. London: Virago.

1982. "Cleaving the Mind: Speculations on Conceptual Dichotomies." In *Against Biological Determinism*, ed. The Dialectics of Biology Group, 60–78. London: Allison & Busby.

1986. *Women, Feminism and Biology: The Feminist Challenge*. New York: Methuen.

Bleier, Ruth. 1984. *Science and Gender: A Critique of Biology and Its Theories on Women*. Oxford: Pergamon Press.

1986. *Feminist Approaches to Science*. The Athene Series. New York: Pergamon Press.

Boon, J. A. and D. M. Schneider. 1974. "Kinship vis-à-vis Myth Contrasts in Lévi-Strauss' Approaches to Cross-Cultural Comparison." *American Anthropologist* 76(4): 799–817.

Boston Women's Health Collective. 1976. *Our Bodies Ourselves*. Harmondsworth: Penguin.

Bott, E. 1957. *Family and Social Network: Roles, Norms, and External Relationships in Ordinary Urban Families*. London: Tavistock.

Butler, J. P. 1990. *Gender Trouble: Feminism and the Subversion of Identity*. New York: Routledge.

Clarke, M. 2008. "New Kinship, Islam, and the Liberal Tradition: Sexual Morality and New Reproductive Technology in Lebanon." *Journal of the Royal Anthropological Institute* 14(1): 153–169.

Collier, J. F. and S. J. Yanagisako, eds. 1987. *Gender and Kinship: Essays Toward a Unified Analysis*. Stanford, CA: Stanford University Press.

De Beauvoir, S. 2014 [1949]. *The Second Sex*. Translated by Constance Borde and Sheila Malovany-Chevallier. London: Vintage [1974. Translated by H. M. Parshley. New York: Vintage].

Fausto-Sterling, A. 1985. *Myths of Gender: Biological Theories about Women and Men*. New York: Basic Books.

1987. "Society Writes Biology: Biology Constructs Gender." *Daedalus* 61: 62–69.

1989. "Life in the XY Corral." *Women's Studies International Forum* 12(3): 319–331.

Firestone, Shulamith. 1970. *The Dialectic of Sex*. New York: William Morrow.

Firth, Raymond. 1956. *Two Studies of Kinship in London*. London: The Athlone Press.

Franklin, Sarah. 1995. "Science As Culture, Cultures of Science." *Annual Review of Anthropology* 24: 163–184.

2003. "Re-thinking Nature-Culture: Anthropology and the New Genetics." *Anthropological Theory* 3(1): 65–85.

Franklin, Sarah. 2013. *Biological Relatives: IVF, Stem Cells and the Future of Kinship*. Durham, NC: Duke University Press.

Franklin, S. and M. Lock. 2003. *Remaking Life and Death: Toward an Anthropology of the Biosciences*. Santa Fe, NM: School of American Research Press.

Fulwiley, Duana. 2011. *The Encultured Gene: Sickle Cell Health Politics and Biological Difference in West Africa*. Princeton, NJ: Princeton University Press.

Gibbon, S. and C. Novas, eds. 2007. *Biosocialities, Genetics and the Social Sciences: Making Biologies and Identities*. Abingdon: Routledge.

Good, M. J. D. 1995. "Cultural Studies of Biomedicine: An Agenda for Research." *Social Science & Medicine* 41(4): 461–473.

2001. "The Biotechnical Embrace." *Culture, Medicine and Psychiatry* 25(4): 395–410.

Greer, Germaine. 1970. *The Female Eunuch*. London: MacGibbon & Kee.

Handler, Richard. 1995. *Schneider on Schneider: The Conversion of the Jews and Other Anthropological Stories*. Durham, NC: Duke University Press.

Haraway, Donna. 1978a. "Animal Sociology and a Natural Economy of the Body Politic, Part I: A Political Physiology of Dominance." *Signs* 4(1): 21–36.

1978b. "Animal Sociology and a Natural Economy of the Body Politic, Part II: The Past Is the Contested Zone: Human Nature and Theories of Production and Reproduction in Primate Behavior Studies." *Signs* 4(1): 37–60.

1989. *Primate Visions: Gender, Race, and Nature in the World of Modern Science*. New York: Routledge.

1991. *Simians, Cyborgs, and Women: The Reinvention of Nature*. London: Free Association Books.

1997. *Modest_Witness@Second_Millennium. FemaleMan_Meets_OncoMouse: Feminism and Technoscience*. New York: Routledge.

2007. *The Companion Species Manifesto: Dogs, People and Significant Otherness*. Chicago, IL: Prickly Paradigm Press.

Helmreich, Stefan. 2009. *Alien Ocean: Anthropological Voyages in Microbial Seas*. Berkeley, CA: University of California Press.

Herschberger, Ruth. 1970. *Adam's Rib*. New York: Harper & Row.

Hubbard, Ruth. 1988a. "Some Thoughts about the Masculinity of the Natural Sciences." In *Feminist Thought and the Structure of Knowledge*, ed. M. Gergen, 1–15. New York: New York University Press.

1988b. "Science, Facts, and Feminism." *Hypatia*. Special Issue: *Feminism and Science* 3(1): 5–17.

1990. *The Politics of Women's Biology*. New Brunswick, NJ: Rutgers University Press.

Keller, Evelyn Fox. 1983. *A Feeling for the Organism: The Life and Work of Barbara McClintock*. New York: Freeman.

1995. *Reflections on Gender and Science*. New Haven, CT: Yale University Press.

Kirksey, Eben, ed. 2014. *The Multispecies Salon*. Durham, NC: Duke University Press.

Koedt, Anne. 2000 [1970]. "The Myth of the Vaginal Orgasm." In *Radical Feminism: A Documentary Reader*, ed. Barbara A. Crow, 371–377. New York: New York University Press.

Lamphere, Louise and Michelle Z. Rosaldo, eds. 1974. *Woman, Culture, and Society*. Palo Alto, CA: Stanford University Press.

Landecker, Hannah. 2011. "Food As Exposure: Nutritional Epigenetics and the New Metabolism." *BioSocieties* 6(2): 167–194.

Levin, Nadine. 2013. Enacting Molecular Complexity: Data and Health in the Metabonomics Laboratory. Ph.D. Dissertation, Department of Anthropology, University of Oxford.

Lock, M. and V. K. Nguyen. 2010. *An Anthropology of Biomedicine*. Chichester: John Wiley & Sons.

MacCormack, Carole P. and Marilyn Strathern, eds. 1980. *Nature, Culture and Gender*. Cambridge: Cambridge University Press.

Martin, Emily. 1987. *The Woman in the Body: A Cultural Analysis of Reproduction*. Boston, MA: Beacon Press.

1991. "The Egg and the Sperm: How Science Has Constructed a Romance Based on Stereotypical Male–Female Roles." *Signs* 16(3): 485–501.

M'charek, Amade. 2005. *The Human Genome Project: An Ethnography of Scientific Practice*. Cambridge: Cambridge University Press.

Millett, Kate. 1970. *Sexual Politics*. New York: Doubleday.

Morgan, Robin, ed. 1970. *Sisterhood Is Powerful: An Anthology of Writings from the Women's Liberation Movement*. New York: Vintage Books.

Nelkin, Dorothy and Susan Lindee. 1995. *The DNA Mystique: The Gene As Cultural Icon*. New York: Freeman.

Ortner, Sherry B. 1972. "Is Female to Male As Nature Is to Culture?" *Feminist Studies* 1(2): 5–31.

Parsons, Talcott. 1943. "The Kinship System of the Contemporary United States." *American Anthropologist* 45(1): 22–38.

Rapp, Rayna. 1999. *Testing Women, Testing the Fetus: The Social Impact of Amniocentesis in America*. New York: Routledge.

Reed, Evelyn. 1970. *Problems of Women's Liberation: A Marxist Approach*. New York: Pathfinder Press.

Rich, Adrienne. 1976. *Of Woman Born: Motherhood As Institution and Experience*. New York: W. W. Norton.

Rubin, Gayle. 1975. "The Traffic in Women: Notes on the 'Political Economy' of Sex." In *Toward an Anthropology of Women*, ed. Rayna Reiter, 157–210. New York: Monthly Review Press.

Schneider, David Murray. [1968] 1980. *American Kinship: A Cultural Account*. Chicago, IL: University of Chicago Press.

1984. *A Critique of the Study of Kinship*. Ann Arbor, MI: University of Michigan Press.

Strathern, Marilyn. 1980. "No Nature, No Culture: The Hagen Case." In *Nature, Culture and Gender*, ed. C. MacCormack and M. Strathern, 194–222. Cambridge: Cambridge University Press.

1992a *Reproducing the Future: Essays on Anthropology, Kinship and the New Reproductive Technologies*. Manchester: Manchester University Press.

1992b *After Nature: English Kinship in the Late Twentieth Century*. Cambridge: Cambridge University Press.

[1974] 2016. *Before and After Gender: Sexual Mythologies of Everyday Life*. Chicago, IL: Hau Books.

Thompson, Charis. 2005. *Making Parents: The Ontological Choreography of Reproductive Technologies*. Cambridge, MA: The MIT Press.

Yanagisako, Sylvia J. and Jane F. Collier. 1987. "Toward a Unified Analysis of Gender and Kinship." In *Gender and Kinship: Essays toward a Unified Analysis*, ed. J. F. Collier and S. J. Yanagisako, 14–52. Stanford, CA: Stanford University Press.

Young, Michael D. and Peter Willmott. 1957. *Family and Kinship in East London*. London: Routledge and Kegan Paul.

6

The Stuff of Kinship

Janet Carsten

This chapter is a reflection on the ways kinship is made and dissolved through time, and on the materials through which these processes occur. I consider gradations of kinship, and the different substances and metaphors in which accretions and diminutions of kinship are enfolded. The emotions and morality of kinship have powerful resonances that echo in personal and familial contexts but also across wider political terrains. These effects are achieved at least in part through the material stuff to which ideas about kinship are attached. Drawing on recent fieldwork on blood, as well as previous research, I enlarge on the ways in which temporality and substance are mutually entwined, suggesting that they are inextricably embedded in kinship and in the capacities it evokes.[1]

I take as my starting point Marshall Sahlins' recent account of *What Kinship Is ... and Is Not* (2013). Rather than focusing on definitional issues, however, I sidestep these and the now well-worn discussion of what is "biological" and what is "social" in kinship to focus instead on the *effects* of kinship. Sahlins' discussion evocatively captures something immediately recognizable about kinship. Across cultures, eras, and social backgrounds, he argues, kin "participate intrinsically in each other's existence"; they share "a mutuality of being," and are "members of one another" (2013: ix). This is intuitively graspable – not as an analytic abstraction, as many definitions of kinship seem to be, but in a way that palpably makes sense of a whole range of human experience as described in the ethnographic record, but etched too in the personal memories of ethnographers. This immediately recognizable quality of kinship is captured in the striking epigraphs to Sahlins' book. One, by E. B. Tylor, concerns "South American tribes" who believe "there is such a physical connexion between father and son, that the diet of one affects the health of the other" (Tylor 1865); the other, from an article on "What Baseball Does to the Soul" from *The New York Times* in 2012, describes how "We become the children of our children, the sons of our sons. We take on the burden of their victories and defeats. It is our privilege, our curse too. We get older and younger at the same time" (McCann 2012).

Sahlins' focus on kinship's inclusive tendencies illuminates its seemingly endless capacities to shape-shift, appearing in different guises with different effects: food, land, procreation, memory, emotion, and experience – to mention just a few – can be effortlessly encompassed by the idea of "mutuality of being." Taking Sahlins' definition of kinship as "mutuality of being" as my starting point is then partly a way to avoid an extended discussion of the significance of ties deriving from sexual procreation. But procreation and birth have of course a particular significance in Euro-American understandings of kinship, and also, as David Schneider (1984) underlined, in anthropological accounts. Here I take a cue from Michael Lambek's (2011) argument where he underlines how recent kinship studies have tended to focus on procreation and birth rather than other moments or processes, such as marriage, death, or succession. While he makes an argument in this context for the importance of *ritual* as opposed to *everyday* practices of kinship, I prefer simply to reiterate his suggestion that we continue to hold all of the life course in view rather than allowing birth to overshadow other significant processes.

Sahlins is the latest in a long line of scholars to frame his discussion of kinship around the dichotomy between culture and biology, social ties and birth ones. This symbolic opposition provides one deep-running axis in a rich repertoire of idioms for participants in Euro-American cultures to reduce or undercut but also to thicken their own potentially infinite universe of kinship ties (Edwards and Strathern 2000). Thus idioms of social ties may be mobilized to reduce, replace, or reinforce biological ones – sisters or mothers and daughters may be so close that they are "best friends," but friends, in the absence of kinship ties – or sometimes in contrast to them – can also be "like sisters." Mostly, in English kinship reckoning, as Edwards and Strathern point out, the reduction or cutting of kinship ties proceeds implicitly and gradually, without paying it undue attention.

It is perhaps because the opposition between culture and biology, social ties and birth ones, is so deeply etched in Western cultural history that it is sometimes difficult to keep all its effects in view. Sahlins synthesizes a wealth of ethnographic evidence around this theme to demonstrate that the intersubjective relations of kinship are "the *a priori* of birth rather than the sequitur" (2013: 68), or "relations of procreation are patterned by the kinship order in which they are embedded" (2013: 76), not the other way around. In spite of his chapter titles then ("What Kinship Is – Culture" and "What Kinship Is Not – Biology"), he concludes:

> It is probably better not to speak of "biology" at all, folk or otherwise, since few or no peoples other than Euro-Americans understand

themselves to be constructed upon – or in fundamental ways, against – some biological-corporeal substratum. For many their kinship is already given in their flesh.

(2013: 77)

Or as he puts it, commenting on Meggitt's ethnography of the Mae Enga of the New Guinea Highlands, "The larger structures and values of society are realized in the microcosm of human reproduction" (2013: 84).

The attempt to shift the definition of kinship away from the enframing division between the "biological" and the "social" while simultaneously placing it under scrutiny echoes earlier discussions – for example, the use of the term "relatedness" as a way to sidestep the biological/social dichotomy and the particular baggage that "kinship" carries as an analytic term (Carsten 2000a; see also Carsten 1995, 1997). A broad and inclusive definition of kinship runs counter to a long tradition in kinship studies that is the product of Western history and philosophy in which "what kinship is" is precisely defined against what it is not, and in which biology has a defining role. And so, the more one tries to dispense with the dichotomy, the more one seems to end up reiterating it. Feeding and sex are obvious examples here. Although anthropologists of the cultural persuasion are prone to ascribing feeding relations to the "social" category, and sexual procreation to the "biological," this has always been a strangely arbitrary assignment (Carsten 1995; Sahlins 2013). For human beings, feeding and sex are surely both physical and social processes. In the end, as Sahlins notes, this too-pervasive distinction disappears up its own tail – in the sense that, if kinship is intrinsic to human nature/culture, then it is also biologically given.

There is a sense then in which Sahlins' intervention in the end seems to reach a familiar intellectual impasse. But here I want to draw attention to another feature of his discussion. Following many scholars who write on kinship, Sahlins concentrates on the positive aspects of kinship rather more than the negative ones. "Mutuality of being," on the whole, emanates a warm, fuzzy glow rather than a cold shiver (see also Shryock 2013). Kinship, however, as Veena Das (1995), Michael Lambek (2011), Michael Peletz (2000), and others have noted, often carries ambivalent or negative qualities, which anthropologists dwell on rather less. Indeed, Jeanette Edwards and Marilyn Strathern (2000) have commented on the "sentimentalised view of sociality as sociability and of kinship ('family') as community that pervades much Euro-American commentary of an *academic* kind" (2000: 152, original emphasis), and that this is a reflection of the positive, generative ideological force of ideas about connection, belonging, and kinship in Euro-American cultures.

In connection with this, Sahlins has a suggestive comparison of kinship and magic, the latter "a technique for the transpersonal imposition of being into other subjects" (2013: 58).[2] But he argues that "the intersubjectivity of magic may be coercively introjected, in which respects it is not the same as the mutuality of kinship" (2013: 59). Commenting on Achuar magic, he continues, "by harming or consuming the other, sorcery ('black magic') and witchcraft are quite analogous to failures of kinship, and in such regard they can be included in the same animist ontology, if on the darker side thereof" (2013: 59). One might suggest, however, that it is not the coercive quality of the intersubjectivity that distinguishes witchcraft from kinship – kinship itself often has a coercive edge (see, for example, Carsten 1997; Foster 1990). This can be particularly evident in feeding relations, which as Bloch (2005) notes, are often fraught with danger. Poisoning is of course a classic form of witchcraft (see da Col 2012 for a recent discussion of this association), and Sahlins concludes this passage by stating that "as the consumption or penetration of the body of the other with the intent to harm, witchcraft and sorcery are rather, by definition, negative kinship" (2013: 59). Thus it is the "intent to harm," he argues, that distinguishes the positive from the negative. But rather than making a sharp opposition, it is worth pausing over the more subtle gradations in qualities and intent between kinship as positive, and witchcraft as negative force.

This point about gradations of kinship (which of course does not necessarily correlate with genealogical closeness) also highlights that a focus on what kinship is or is not, and on definitions of kinship, necessarily pays less attention to the ways that kinship accumulates or dissolves over time – processes of "thickening" or "thinning" of relatedness. Here one might want to look at the way that certain vectors or registers of "mutuality of being," which Sahlins brings together, such as feeding, procreation, living together, memory, or land, complement or counteract each other in particular contexts. Thus, for example, residence rules – particularly following marriage – may, without dissolving ties of birth, lead to a "thinning" of those ties where adult children move away from the natal home, and this effect will tend to be compounded if distances are great and visits are rare. Paradoxically, moving away may also intensify nostalgic ties of memory to a natal home as, for example, Joelle Bahloul (1996) documents in her wonderful ethnography of memories of a Jewish-Muslim home in colonial Algeria. Here temporality becomes significant, and not just in relation to a remembered past. While most studies of kinship are necessarily synchronic – though sometimes encompassing different kinds of evidence about the past – kinship futures remain unknowable. In the study of reunions between adult adoptees and their birth kin that I carried out in the late 1990s, I was struck by the way that seemingly trivial avenues of communication, Christmas cards, for example, might have left small openings for the potential reestablishment or strengthening of bonds in the future (Carsten 2000b). Slight in themselves, such channels of communication might offer generative possibilities when relations seemed unable to proceed in the present, too heavily encumbered by the weight of the past. Whether such potential was in fact ever activated is unknown to me, but it underlines that our interpretations of kinship are severely hampered by the limitations of our methods.

Sometimes, however, a long familiarity with a particular field site and its people may surmount these constraints. Michael Lambek's evocation of "Kinship as Gift and Theft" (2011) illuminates how knowledge of a particular family over many decades can shed light on the ways in which death brings about a rearrangement of relations among the living – involving a thickening in some cases but a dissolution or rupture in others. The gift of succession from parents to children in Mayotte can also involve illicit acts of theft when one sibling claims ownership of spirits that might have been thought to rightfully transfer to another. Kinship, as Lambek memorably puts it, "entails promises and breaches of promise, acts and violations of intimacy, and acts of forgiveness and revenge" (2011: 4). In the case he examines, when one adult offspring successfully lays claim to the spirits raised by her mother, she simultaneously excludes the claims of her older sister. And Lambek lays out how this act is in fact the culmination of a long process of exclusion experienced by the older sister whose life he is able to document. In European contexts, trivial acts of exclusion (the forgotten birthday, the missing wedding invitation) are often the subject of family tensions that have the potential to grow into more serious rifts. These are familiar narratives; tellingly, they may resurface and take on an expanded significance after a death or when dealing with inheritance and succession. However strong the tendency we face as participants in our own cultures of relatedness to focus on kinship as a positive force, it is important as analysts of kinship to grasp that acts and processes of exclusion are an integral part of kinship and its multiple temporalities – rather than an occasional or accidental byproduct.

Rather than reiterate debates about the social and biological, I turn to temporality as a means of grasping the gradations and accumulations of kinship as well as its ruptures and dissolution. Temporality encompasses abuses of kinship as well as its mutuality. In earlier work I have considered absences and memories of kinship through such themes as houses, adoption, and ghosts (Carsten 2007). In what follows I attempt to put together these ideas with another theme from recent work in kinship studies: that of substance. If "mutuality of being" captures something important and recognizable about how kinship is experienced, we also need to understand the media or vectors of that mutuality and its reversals, how they may operate, and how time might be sedimented into these processes.

6.1   Substance Revisited: The "Stuff of Kinship"

In an earlier discussion of how ideas about substance have been used in anthropological discussions I suggested that the usefulness of the term for the study of kinship arises precisely from the problems in defining it analytically (Carsten 2004, Chapter 5). Because "substance" conveys many meanings in English (some of them mutually contradictory), it can be used in different ways, and especially to lend flexibility to anthropological definitions, and to highlight the importance of bodily processes to understandings and practices of kinship. Sexual fluids, gametes, blood, bones, and maternal milk can be described as "bodily substance"; ideas about their mixing and separation in and between bodies, or the transformation of food into blood or other bodily matter may be conveyed using the same term. So, substance seems to offer a way to describe and analyze how the production and decay of bodies over time is implicated in kinship. Crucially, "substance" implies flow and exchange as well as essence or content, and this ambiguity can be put to work to tease apart what kinship involves. Likewise, it can be used to convey the contrastive physical properties of liquidity or solidity, which seem apt in connection with bodily processes.

More loosely, substance may be extended from "bodily stuff" to other kinds of stuff. I have mentioned food already, and we might want to include other vectors of kinship that are linked to food, land, for example, or houses. And then there are the less material – but arguably no less important – vectors or "substance" of kinship: the spirits inherited by Lambek's informants are just one of many possible kinds of ghostly presence that indicate the lingering presence of kinship after death. Other intangible forms are memories, such as those described by Bahloul, or the sometimes startling instances of convergent thoughts and emotions that can occur between close kin or friends who have known each other for a long time. These less solid presences come into play when we describe kinship as mutuality of being. Between the seemingly ethereal and the obviously physical "stuff of kinship," we might also want to include other more papery kinds of materials: photographs, letters, certain kinds of documents, genealogies, or the Christmas cards to which I alluded earlier. Family photographs, notoriously, are frequently cited when people are asked what they would rescue from their burning homes. And all of these – in paper and more virtual forms – may convey qualities and attributes of kinship.

Putting all of these different kinds of stuff into the same frame is not just another way of pointing out the diverse attributes and means of expressing kinship – although it is that. It also highlights two other important points to which we can link Sahlins' definition of kinship as mutuality of being. The first is the multiple temporalities – and sometimes geographies – called forth by these different kinds of substance. They apparently have the capacity to build and extend kinship beyond the here and now, and to evoke or summon up relationships in the past as well as those in the future, those that have moved elsewhere as well as those that are close at hand. To say this also means that these substances are also integral to what I referred to earlier as the "thinning" and "thickening" of kinship.

Although the experiential sensation of "mutuality of being," which Sahlins emphasizes and which seems intrinsic to kinship, is apparently an affective quality, it actually seems to have a strong tendency to attach itself to *stuff*. We might therefore want to examine more closely the way that kinship seems to adhere to particular kinds of material. Procreative substances are of course the most obvious example here but, as Sahlins notes, blood, bones, land, and food occur with great frequency in the ethnographic record of what makes kinship. In a review of "Substance and Relationality" (Carsten 2011), I suggested that we might look at the transfers of different kinds of bodily substance as being on a rough continuum in terms of their apparent power to evoke a sense of kinship in different cultural contexts. Procreative material and blood would probably score quite highly on such a continuum, skin, hair, or nails rather lower. Interestingly though, some of these "more peripheral" bodily substances are widely used for nefarious purposes in witchcraft. The Malay villagers I got to know in the 1980s spoke vividly about how hair left in a comb or nail parings obtained surreptitiously from a victim could be used in witchcraft for their entrapment.

I am not of course suggesting that one could construct a cross-culturally valid numerical score-sheet for correlating substance and relationality – merely that we consider the apparently greater power of some kinds of substance compared to that of others to evoke or create kinship. I would also not attribute a necessary priority to procreative substances or to ties of filiation in kinship (see Bamford 2004, 2007, 2009; Carsten 2011). But I am interested in how, in particular ethnographic contexts, these may or may not complement, take their place beside, or undercut other kinds of connections – for example, those articulated in terms of siblingship, land, food, or sentiment. Could we then draw any links between the various materials to which kinship seems prone to be attached, the temporality that may be enfolded in these materials, and the "symbolic density" of kinship – its power to evoke "mutuality of being," or feelings of participation in each other's lives, as well as the more negative counterparts of these? And if so, what argument could we make about such links? Bearing in mind the methodological difficulties of elucidating the temporality of kinship to which I have alluded, but also the way that time is made material as it is lived, substances might perhaps offer a way to think through these issues. I draw on recent research on blood to speculate on these issues.

6.2   Blood, Space, and Time

It was partly blood's apparently unusual capacity for symbolization as well as the central role it often has in articulations of kinship that drew me to the idea of carrying out research on what happens when blood moves between different domains of social life. If the symbolic dimensions of blood are readily observable in religious, political, and kinship idioms across many cultural contexts, I was interested in how it travels between these domains, and the consequences of this "symbolic flow." How is blood transformed from one kind of substance into another? What is the source of its extraordinary range and plasticity of meanings? And what can the anthropological analysis of its symbolic power tell us about the nature of symbolism? At once bodily substance, biomedical resource, diagnostic tool, as well as an unusually potent metaphor with a heightened propensity to flow between different social domains, blood seems to be a paradoxical kind of object. The remarkably plural meanings of blood in a given cultural and historical location might, I hazarded, reveal previously unexplored properties of kinship, as well as of politics, ethnicity, science, and wider sociality.

This research, which began in clinical pathology labs in Penang, Malaysia, ended up drawing in a wide range of topics and sites – from political rhetoric to matters of health or kinship, and from the hospital clinical pathology labs to eating stalls and temples in Penang. The labs themselves were of interest partly because their working practices seemed to rest on assumptions that they existed as a bounded space, set off and separated from the diverse interests of politics, religion, or kinship. Showing that this was far from being the case, and the ways in which aspects of daily life that originate outside the labs could become problematic for those who worked, there was one theme to emerge in this work. If the boundaries of the lab seemed necessarily to be permeable – in spite of efforts to keep them secure – this could carry both risks and benefits for the staff and for the work processes. While, for example, the scientific objectivity of the work might potentially be compromised, it was also evident that the interest of staff in expediting a diagnosis, which could be heightened through ethical, religious, or kinship concerns, also ensured their continued engagement in routine work, and thence the high quality of results. Stepping beyond the labs, other themes emerged through listening to blood donors, and discovering how the reasons they ascribed to giving blood enfolded their own memories of relations with kin, as well as family histories of illness, and ideas about health, illness, and life more generally. When I conducted comparative research among blood donors in Edinburgh, I was interested to find quite similar articulations there concerning the reasons for giving blood. Here too familial memories, and the illnesses of close relatives and friends, were often spoken of as motivating donors to give blood.

On a wider stage, public discourses in Malaysia about blood donation in which politicians were simultaneously reported as exhorting the public to give blood and drawing lessons about political harmony in a multiethnic political context were a frequent feature of media news items. But in

July 2008 another kind of rhetoric erupted in the Malaysian press, which featured blood in a quite different and highly contested register. A series of political events following elections in March 2008 culminated in the surprise arrest of the leader of the Malaysian opposition coalition, Dr. Anwar Ibrahim (see Carsten 2013a). Following his arrest, Anwar was asked to give a blood sample for DNA testing, which he refused to do. Significantly, however, the exact purpose of the tests and what they were supposed to reveal was never made explicit. The charge against Anwar Ibrahim, however, was clear; it concerned an allegation of sodomy made by one of his political aides. HIV status, a possible crime scene, political intimidation, and most centrally, Anwar's moral status were thus potentially imputed.

The issue of Anwar's blood sample assumed an iconic significance in these events, and also illuminated the myriad connections between blood as biomedical object and blood as a substance replete with kinship, ethnic, religious, and moral significance. The blood sample was used to undermine not only his moral status but also the legitimacy of political opposition to the government. But this usage also had the unforeseen potential to be turned back on itself, and to undermine the legitimacy of the government that had set these tactics in play. The "uncontainability" of the different meanings of blood, its propensity to exceed the limits of any particular domain in which it occurs here illuminates particularly clearly the connections between such disparate fields as morality, kinship, the body, political legitimacy, and scientific testing.

I have mentioned briefly just a few highlights from this research in Malaysia in order to suggest how meanings of blood deriving from particular social settings could be implicitly alluded to, or carried over, from one context to another. While it was the uncontainability of the different meanings that I found striking in the Malaysian case, when this research was put in a wider and more comparative frame, other aspects of its significance have emerged more clearly. A recent collaborative volume (Carsten 2013b) juxtaposes depictions of the symbolic propensities of blood in widely disparate cultural and historical contexts: the history of blood donation, banking, and transfusion regimes in twentieth-century North America, and in wartime London; sacrificial idioms of replenishment of bodily fluids by peasants in Northeast Brazil; an exhibition of portraits painted in blood of Indian martyrs of Independence held in twenty-first-century Delhi; Medieval medical and religious texts from Germany concerning the maintenance of blood inside and outside the body; contemporary Mormon ideas in North America about the inheritance of blood; discourses surrounding the latest images of brain scanning in which blood seems strangely absent; and sanguinary metaphors of blood which permeate descriptions of the contemporary global financial crisis. There is a cumulative and comparative force to considering these very different contexts together – without of course assuming that blood is necessarily the same across them.

Rethinking these depictions of the material and symbolic significance of blood through the lens of kinship highlights the wider importance of temporality, which emerged, somewhat unexpectedly, as a linking thread between them. For example, probing the extraordinary polyvalence of blood, Kath Weston (2013) lays out how the metaphors of blood that occur in depictions of the financial system enfold different somatic models with different historicities. Images of "lifeblood," "circulation," "flow," "liquidity," "hemorrhaging," "stagnation," or the necessity of "blood-letting" in the financial system occur alongside each other. While the circulatory model discovered by William Harvey in the early seventeenth century is predominant here, Weston elucidates how older notions that pre-date Harvey's model are also present.

In fact, when we considered the different depictions of blood imagery in the cases discussed, it seemed that in almost all of them the deployment of blood as a metaphor implicitly invoked quite different temporalities. The Brazilian peasants described by Maya Mayblin (2013) use a modern technique of intravenous rehydration to replenish the fluid in their body when they feel unwell, but in so doing they evoke a Catholic imagery of Christ's sacrifice in which blood, sweat, tears, and water can be seen as transformations of each other, and have a particular local ecological and religious salience. In a quite different setting, Jacob Copeman (2013) shows how the importance of the literal use of blood to paint the portraits of Indian martyrs of Independence is intended to evoke both the past sacrifice of those martyrs, and also vividly reminds the viewers of these paintings that their own blood may be called upon in further acts of political sacrifice in the future. Shifting to a radically different context, Emily Martin (2013) uncovers how contemporary medical discourses surrounding MRI scans of the brain, from which blood has mysteriously been purged, in fact reveal a deeper archaeology in which different kinds of blood, referring to somatic models with a different historicity, occur in a gendered hierarchy in the body.

In all of these cases, the imagery of which blood partakes evokes understandings that originate in different historical epochs. The "uncontainability" that occurred in terms of the spaces and domains in which blood participates in the Malaysian contexts that I observed, thus also has this multiple temporal (or atemporal) dimension. This leads me back to my earlier suggestions about the temporalities of other kinship substances. If kinship necessarily involves relationships that can be envisaged as potentially stretching forwards and backwards in time (though not necessarily with equal emphasis on past, present, or future), might this also be a quality with which the substances to which kinship adheres are invested? Could we then understand the symbolic power of blood, and that of other more or less corporeal substances, in terms of the connection they afford between physical "stuff" and more abstract qualities of kinship?

Here I am particularly concerned with the idea that kinship is a "mutuality of being" – and simultaneously a process of exclusion – that allows relatedness and sociality to be imagined beyond the temporally present, reaching into the past and towards the future. As Andrew Shryock observes in the context of what he calls the "spatio-temporal declines" that kinship may help to offset, "kinship, in this sense, becomes a special mode of travel, a way to engineer secure social landscapes and reliable histories" (2013: 278). Shryock here builds on an essay on "Deep Kinship" by Thomas B. Trautmann, Gillian Feeley-Harnik, and John C. Mitani (2011), which attempts to overcome the divide between "social" and "biological" kinship in a quite different way from Sahlins – through the use of primatology and archaeology in combination with the anthropology of kinship to probe the long-term evolutionary significance of human kinship. The insights of these authors concerning the "mnemonic properties of artifacts deliberately intended to bind relations over time and space" (2011: 185) are highly pertinent. Their discussion focuses particularly on the importance of houses and food that evoke memories and emotional responses through their association with the sensory patterns of childhood. But it also includes other kinds of artifacts and mnemonic forms, including jewelry, pots, clothing, kinship terminologies, and genealogies, which are part of "the heavy memory work" that operates through kinship (2011: 186). While blood symbolism may work in a somewhat different way from the artifacts on which Trautmann, Feeley-Harnik, and Mitani focus, their discussion of the importance of memory work to kinship is highly relevant to my attempt to elucidate the connections between temporality and substance.

6.3   Temporality, Materiality, and Naturalization

Mayblin (2013) observes that, for her informants, the transubstantiation of wine into the blood of Jesus in the Eucharist is a literal truth, and essential to their sense of the beauty of, and aesthetic pleasure in, the Catholic Mass. She notes that a crucial quality of blood is that it can function as both metaphor and metonym – and this is central to theological debates about the Christian Eucharist (see Bynum 2007). In this sense, the link between Christ's sacrifice and the daily sacrifice of labor is made tangible. Metaphorical and material understandings of blood are in constant play with each other, and this is part of blood's heightened capacity for naturalization, and its symbolic power. Drawing attention to this interplay of signification in multiple directions, Weston emphasizes "the generative possibilities of blood, as well as its ability to pre-empt debate as it naturalizes social processes, and perfuses multiple domains" (2013: 33). She uses the term "meta-materiality" (2013: 35) to convey that what is invoked goes beyond both metaphor and the material – but also, and simultaneously, relies on both the material and the metaphorical to generate further resonances and further naturalizations.

Thinking further about these qualities, I turn to Webb Keane's suggestive discussion of Peircian semiotics and the analysis of material artifacts. In his attempt to "situate material things within a dynamic social analysis" (2003: 410), Keane, drawing on Peirce, notes how sign/object relations become increasingly arbitrary in shifting from the iconic (a relation of "resemblance"), to the indexical (a relation of "causal or proximal linkages"), to the symbolic (an "arbitrary" relation deriving from social convention) (2003: 413). He argues, following Peirce, that different historicities are embedded in these different sign/object relations. Iconicity invokes past experience; indexicality refers to the present; symbols are oriented towards the future and because of this they have a crucial capacity to act (2003: 419). Extending Michael Silverstein's work, he suggests that "the social power of naturalisation" comes from reading indexicals "as if they were merely expressing something … that already exists" (2003: 417). Thus a past entailment of the indexical is read into the present.

Keane's exposition of the historicity of semiotics, which explicitly rejects a totalizing logic, can be put to work here. It is significant that blood seems to lend itself to operating in all three ways – iconically, indexically, and symbolically. If blood's symbolic power is partly derived from its naturalizing capacities, then this might suggest that this connects to its ability to convey multiple historicities separately and simultaneously as it acts as icon, index, and symbol. In other words, the potential blood has for naturalization – and by implication that of other substances too – is linked to this particular capacity to convey different historicities. And although I have left out some crucial parts of his argument (particularly, the importance of ritual speech in historical transformation), if I have paraphrased Keane correctly, we can also see how these different semiotic modalities allow us to grasp how blood might both have an unusually open and transformative power and also, simultaneously, carry meanings and qualities that seem paradoxically over-determined.

In this light – and bearing in mind blood's vivid material qualities of liquidity and flow, and of clotting and stoppage – we can also begin to understand blood's association in many cultures with notions of descent. I am struck by the resonances between evocations of blood drawn from widely different epochs and cultural locations. Here is Lewis Henry Morgan writing in 1871 about the broad history of human kinship in the preface to *Systems of Consanguinity and Affinity of the Human Family*:

> In the systems of relationship of the great families of mankind some of the oldest memorials of human thought and experience

are deposited and preserved. They have been handed down as transmitted systems, through the channels of the blood, from the earliest ages of man's existence upon the earth.

(1871: xxii)

And here is Webb Keane writing in 1997 specifically about the society of Anakalang in Sumba, Eastern Indonesia:

People say it is blood that joins them to others in inherent relations of empathy. Blood-based identity is situated in bodies, local memories, and emotions and lacks public, objectified forms.

(1997: 50)

Transmission is clearly central to kinship – as Shryock (2013: 278) notes, citing with approval another definition of kinship from Sahlins: "the transmission of life-capacities among persons" (Sahlins 2013: 29). The aptness of blood as metaphor for transmission and descent is worth pausing over, as are the other meanings it may encompass.

Partly because of the way memories, thoughts, and experiences may be folded into understandings of blood, and through the way blood may be endowed with agentive force, it seems to offer a potent idiom for political ideologies. Such ideologies come, as it were, "already naturalized," and freighted with implicit meanings that defy questioning. This naturalization effect seems particularly marked in the case of blood, and is likely connected to blood's association with animation (see Carsten 2011; Fontein and Harries 2013). This in turn may partly explain blood's widespread occurrence as a symbol of kinship in quite different historical and cultural contexts. But it should also alert us to the way other materials and artifacts to which I have alluded, from bodily stuff to houses, land, or food, may be endowed with qualities that evoke kinship. These "vectors of kinship" have a similarly heightened potential to carry associations linked to different temporalities; their emotional resonances are, as it were, sedimented within them like so many archaeological layers (see also Verdery 1999). But crucially, these are, to echo Mary Douglas' famous phrase, "implicit meanings" (1975) – they do not require articulation, and their implicitness means that such associations and the emotions they evoke are already naturalized. The apparently benign resonances of kinship conveyed by these vectors simultaneously have the capacity silently to encode hierarchies of birth, gender, or age. In other words, they are inextricably entwined with political distinctions and processes of exclusion. The fact that they may operate without explicit articulation – by moving through a house, partaking in a family meal, growing crops – means that as analysts of kinship we need to be particularly alert not just to the positive effects of kinship as "mutuality of being" but to its long-term political potentialities.

6.4   Conclusion: What Kinship Does – and How

In pushing at our understandings of substance, and thinking further about the semiotics of blood, I have focused particularly on historicity, temporality, and naturalization. Returning these insights to the discussion of kinship, I have argued for the productivity of concentrating less on its definition and more on how it works, why it matters, and what makes it powerful. There are of course many ways to go about answering these questions. Kinship is a practical realm of action; it is also, as Meyer Fortes (1969), James Faubion (2001), Michael Lambek (2011), and others have shown, an ethical resource, "a philosophy" as Robert McKinley (2001: 152) puts it, "concerned with human obligation." Precisely because the ethical obligations of kinship tend to be already invested with positive moral associations, it may be difficult to discern or articulate the possibilities they afford for cooption in exclusionary or hierarchical processes – whether intentionally or not. This is all the more the case when such processes occur through material such as blood or land that encapsulates highly condensed layers of symbolic meaning. In these ways naturalization is central to the power of kinship, both in its capacity to evoke strong and unquestioning responses in intimate familial contexts and its potential to evoke emotion in political discourses.

Kinship also, crucially, provides an imaginative realm for thinking, partly in ethical terms, but also more speculatively, about who we are, and how we might be in the future; about our connections in the present as well as to past generations, and to the unborn. "We become the children of our children, the sons of our sons ... We get older and younger at the same time," as Sahlins' epigraph has it. In this way, temporality is a crucial part of the imaginative potentiality of kinship. I have also suggested that temporality and other abstract or ineffable qualities of kinship may be rendered more immediate and thinkable through their adherence to less abstract, and more material, stuff, what I have called substance here. Such material substances, in other words, help to enable the imaginative leaps that "mutuality of being" encompasses, and they allow us to think about the "thickening" and "thinning" of kinship over time and space. The connections substances allow between bodily processes and persons, on the one hand, and different temporalities on the other, are vital to the embedding and threading of kinship in everyday life. Sexual fluids and blood are thus not the only, or even necessarily the most privileged, sites of such symbolic work. And we might want to think more about the different emotional registers and valences evoked by different kinds of bodily materials. Contrasts between the imagery and metaphorical extension of bone and blood, for example, may be connected to the solidity and liquidity of these media, while nail fragments and hair offer possibilities for illicit removal that can render their owners vulnerable to the will of others. We can understand why sexual fluids and blood seem to occur very commonly as media for the transmission of kinship. But these take their place beside other corporeal matter, and also beside food, living space, photographs, letters, clothing, relics, and other "substances" that are good for transmitting the essences of people and relationships over time.[3]

In focusing on what kinship *does* and *how*, I have argued that we should take a closer look at the importance of temporality in kinship, and how it is possible to imagine kinship relations as enduring over time and distance. This has also involved thinking about the place of material stuff in mutuality of being, and the way essences of people and relations adhere to materials, or may be metaphorically assigned to them, and how these materials evoke temporal qualities. Partly because of its unique and striking material qualities, its association with the body and with life, and its apparent aptness for metaphoricization, blood offers a potentially rich avenue for such kinds of speculation. Temporality invites us to see how kinship is an inherently graduated process; to think about time and kinship is also to think in terms of more or less, and of allowing for the way kinship relations may accumulate or dissolve over time. Analytically, it means taking seriously the place of experience, intuition, emotion, and memory in kinship, and of how they may be invested with particular qualities and resonances. And it means being attentive to the ways in which the particularities and hierarchies of gender, birth order, and age rest in larger and smaller histories. This returns us to the insight that, for many people, time and history are largely understood through idioms of kinship, and that historicity is a fundamental property of kinship (see Carsten 1997: 12–17). As Peter Gow has written of the native people of the Bajo Urubamba river of the Peruvian Amazon, "Kinship relations are created and dissolved in historical time, and historical time draws its meaning and power for native people by being structured by kinship relations" (Gow 1991: 3). Kinship is in this way part of the creation of larger as well as more personal histories. When time is erased and memory occluded, many people find themselves in danger of losing not only their connections to the past, but also their sense of who they are in the present, and the possibility of creating kinship in the future.

The experience that makes aspects of kinship mutually comprehensible across different cultures and historical epochs, which is Sahlins' starting point, is worth reemphasizing. And this is because such experience, however culturally variable, is part of what is immediately recognizable and translatable about kinship across cultures, and also because of the implicit meanings it carries. These meanings not only convey hierarchies of gender, age, and generation, they carry with them possibilities for exclusion, which both explicitly and implicitly are readily enfolded into political discourse. I have tried to keep in mind that kinship can be a force for harm as well as for good because the assumption that kinship is intrinsically ethical is itself part of its political and ideological capacity that requires investigation. This seems particularly salient in the long history and multiple temporalities of European ideas of blood, race, and kinship, and in the hierarchies and exclusions that are part of what kinship enables.

Notes

1. This chapter is a much-expanded and rewritten version of a contribution to a book symposium on Marshall Sahlins' *What Kinship Is ... and Is Not* (2013): "What Kinship Does – and How." *HAU: Journal of Ethnographic Theory* 3(2): 245–251 (2013). An earlier version was delivered at a colloquium in the Department of Anthropology at the University of Michigan in 2013. I am grateful to the audience there, and especially to Gillian Feeley-Harnik, for their comments and the inspiration of their work.
2. See also Robert McKinley on the "elective affinity between the pervading values of the philosophy of kinship and witchcraft beliefs" (2001: 154). McKinley too highlights kinship as a "positive doctrine" (2001: 154).
3. These observations could be read as extending in various ways Robert McKinley's argument that "kinship has been about the embodiment of relational qualities right from the start" (2001: 158).

References

Bahloul, Joelle. 1996. *The Architecture of Memory: A Jewish-Muslim Household in Colonial Algeria, 1937–1962*. Cambridge: Cambridge University Press.

Bamford, Sandra. 2004. "Conceiving Relatedness: Non-Substantial Relations among the Kamea of Papua New Guinea." *Journal of the Royal Anthropological Institute* 10(2): 287–306.

——— 2007. *Biology Unmoored: Melanesian Reflections on Life and Biotechnology*. Berkeley, CA: University of California Press.

——— 2009. "'Family Trees' among the Kamea of Papua New Guinea: A Non-Genealogical Approach to Imagining Relatedness." In *Kinship and Beyond: A Genealogical Model Reconsidered*, ed. S. Bamford and J. Leach, 159–174. New York/Oxford: Berghahn Books.

Bloch, Maurice. 2005. "Commensality and Poisoning." In *Essays on Cultural Transmission*, 45–59. Oxford: Berg.

Bynum, Caroline Walker. 2007. *Wonderful Blood: Theology and Practice in Late Medieval Northern Germany and Beyond*. Philadelphia, PA: University of Pennsylvania Press.

Carsten, Janet. 1995. "The Substance of Kinship and the Heat of the Hearth: Feeding, Personhood and Relatedness among Malays of Pulau Langkawi." *American Ethnologist* 22(2): 223–241.

1997. *The Heat of the Hearth: the Process of Kinship in a Malay Fishing Community*. Oxford: Clarendon Press.

2000a. "Introduction: Cultures of Relatedness." In *Cultures of Relatedness: New Approaches to the Study of Kinship*, ed. Janet Carsten, 1–36. Cambridge: Cambridge University Press.

2000b. "Knowing Where You've Come From: Ruptures and Continuities of Time and Kinship in Narratives of Adoption Reunions." *Journal of the Royal Anthropological Institute* (n.s.) 6: 637–653.

2004. *After Kinship*. Cambridge: Cambridge University Press.

ed. 2007. *Ghosts of Memory: Essays on Remembrance and Relatedness*. Malden, MA: Blackwell.

2011. "Substance and Relationality: Blood in Contexts." *Annual Review of Anthropology* 40: 19–35.

2013a. "'Searching for the Truth': Tracing the Moral Properties of Blood in Malaysian Clinical Pathology Labs." In *Blood Will Out: Essays on Liquid Transfers and Flows*, ed. Janet Carsten, 130–148. Malden, MA: Wiley.

ed. 2013b. *Blood Will Out: Essays on Liquid Transfers and Flows*. Malden, MA: Wiley. Also published as *Journal of the Royal Anthropological Institute*. Special Issue 19, May 2013.

Copeman, Jacob. 2013. "The Art of Bleeding: Memory, Martyrdom, and Portraits in Blood." In *Blood Will Out: Essays on Liquid Transfers and Flows*, ed. Janet Carsten, 149–171. Malden, MA: Wiley.

da Col, Giovanni. 2012. "The Poisoner and the Parasite: Cosmoeconomics, Fear, and Hospitality among Dechen Tibetans." *Journal of the Royal Anthropological Institute* (n.s.) 18: S175–S195.

Das, Veena. 1995. "National Honour and Practical Kinship: Unwanted Women and Children." In *Conceiving the New World Order: The Global Politics of Reproduction*, ed. Faye D. Ginsburg and Rayna Rapp, 212–233. Berkeley, CA: University of California Press.

Douglas, Mary. 1975. *Implicit Meanings: Essays in Anthropology*. London: Routledge & Kegan Paul.

Edwards, Jeanette and Marilyn Strathern. 2000. "Including Our Own." In *Cultures of Relatedness: New Approaches to the Study of Kinship*, ed. Janet Carsten, 149–166. Cambridge: Cambridge University Press.

Faubion, James, ed. 2001. *The Ethics of Kinship: Ethnographic Enquiries*. Lanham, MD: Rowman & Littlefield.

Fontein, Joost and John Harries. 2013. "Editorial. The Vitality and Efficacy of Human Substances." *Critical African Studies* 5(3): 115–126.

Fortes, Meyer. 1969. *Kinship and the Social Order*. London: Routledge & Kegan Paul.

Foster, Robert J. 1990. "Nurture and Force-Feeding: Mortuary Feasting and the Construction of Collective Individuals in a New Ireland Society." *American Ethnologist* 17(3): 431–448.

Gow, Peter. 1991. *Of Mixed Blood: Kinship and History in Peruvian Amazonia*. Oxford: Oxford University Press.

Keane, Webb. 1997. *Signs of Recognition: Powers and Hazards of Representation in an Indonesian Society.* Berkeley, CA: University of California Press.

2003. "Semiotics and the Social Analysis of Material Things." *Language & Communication* 23: 409–425.

Lambek, Michael. 2011. "Kinship As Gift and Theft: Acts of Succession in Mayotte and Ancient Israel." *American Ethnologist* 38: 2–16.

McCann, Colin. April 1, 2012. "What Baseball Does to the Soul." *The New York Times.*

McKinley, Robert. 2001. "The Philosophy of Kinship: A Reply to Schneider's *Critique of the Study of Kinship.*" In *The Cultural Analysis of Kinship: The Legacy of David M. Schneider,* ed. Richard Feinberg and Martin Ottenheimer, 131–167. Urbana and Chicago, IL: University of Illinois Press.

Martin, Emily. 2013. "Blood and the Brain." In *Blood Will Out: Essays on Liquid Transfers and Flows,* ed. Janet Carsten, 172–184. Malden, MA: Wiley.

Mayblin, Maya. 2013. "The Way Blood Flows: The Sacrificial Value of Intravenous Drip Use in Northeast Brazil." In *Blood Will Out: Essays on Liquid Transfers and Flows,* ed. Janet Carsten, 42–56. Malden, MA: Wiley.

Morgan, Lewis Henry. 1871. *Systems of Consanguinity and Affinity of the Human Family.* Washington DC: Smithsonian Institution Press.

Peletz, Michael. 2000. "Ambivalence in Kinship since the 1940s." In *Relative Values: Reconfiguring Kinship Studies,* ed. Sarah Franklin and Susan McKinnon, 413–444. Durham, NC: Duke University Press.

Sahlins, Marshall. 2013. *What Kinship Is ... and Is Not.* Chicago, IL: University of Chicago Press.

Schneider, David M. 1984. *A Critique of the Study of Kinship.* Ann Arbor, MI: University of Michigan Press.

Shryock, Andrew. 2013. "It's This, Not That: How Marshall Sahlins Solves Kinship." *HAU: Journal of Ethnographic Theory* 3(2): 271–279.

Trautmann, Thomas, Gillian Feeley-Harnik and John C. Mitani. 2011. "Deep Kinship." In *Deep History: The Architecture of Past and Present,* ed. Andrew Shryock and Daniel Lord Smail, 160–188. Berkeley, CA: University of California Press.

Tylor, Edward B. 1865. *Researches into the Early History of Mankind and the Development of Civilization.* London: J. Murray.

Verdery, Katharine. 1999. *The Political Lives of Dead Bodies: Reburial and Postsocialist Change.* New York: Columbia University Press.

Weston, Kath. 2013. "Lifeblood, Liquidity, and Cash Transfusions: Beyond Metaphor in the Cultural Study of Finance." In *Blood Will Out: Essays on Liquid Transfers and Flows,* ed. Janet Carsten, 24–41. Malden, MA: Wiley.

Part II

The (Non)Biological Basis of Relatedness

7

Embodied Relationality Beyond "Nature" vs "Nurture": Materializing Absent Kinships in Japanese Child Welfare

Kathryn E. Goldfarb

It was lunchtime at Chestnut House,[1] the child welfare institution ("children's home" or "orphanage") outside Tokyo where I conducted ethnographic fieldwork.[2] I was cross-legged on the floor next to the child-sized table while the youngest children – ages two and three – ate lunch, each seated in diminutive chairs. A staff member sat down beside me and, with a thoughtful smile, watched as one of the boys devoured his rice ball. "You know," she said, "I've often noticed that there is a disproportionate number of kids in child welfare institutions who are left-handed. Just as they were when they were born (*umareta mama*)." Her phrase, *umareta mama*, emphasizes that these children remain as they were at the time of birth because no caregiver intervened to teach the child to use the right hand instead of the left, as many parents do in Japan. Some staff members saw the children of Chestnut House as having remained unchanged by caring intervention: their bodies reflected a type of state-sanctioned neglect. While maltreatment is often understood to have concrete bodily effects, my interlocutors saw the *absence* of contact as having equally bodily, and perhaps more durable, impact on children.

Is being left- or right-handed biological? Is it cultural? Or is it an emblematic case of "local biologies," the result of dynamics across both domains (Lock 1993)?[3] This opening example exemplifies the slipperiness of posing something like handedness as either one or the other, and highlights the ways that observations and judgments about embodied practices can be highly normative, pointing to the ways a child "should" be socialized.[4] With this in mind, I take this Part's provocation – to consider the "(non)biological basis of relatedness" – by suggesting that we as scholars of kinship move concertedly away from discussing the question of whether kinship "is" biological or cultural (cf. Sahlins 2013). Even posing kinship as something biological *and* cultural supposes that these categories are separable, a proposition that we should interrogate rather than presume (Keller 2010). We might also see the "nature vs. nurture," "biology vs. culture" polarity as a Western conceptual pre-occupation that, as such, may be a misleading and ultimately unhelpful framework for understanding kinship across cultures (McKinnon and Silverman 2005). Within kinship studies (and indeed more broadly in popular discourse), "nature" or "biology" is often tacitly under-stood to mean only processes surrounding heterosexual reproductive relationships, including genetic heritage, and tends to focus on the moment of birth as the dividing line between that which is "innate" and that which develops during life. Many commentators have pointed out the oddness of reducing kinship to conception, gestation, and birth, with little attention to what follows (including death). Other scholars have conducted beautiful work exploring kinship as processually emer-gent throughout life. For instance, taking an affirmative stance that bio-genetic ties themselves do not determine kinship ties, anthropologists of the "new kinships" have illustrated how kinship emerges over time, in both embodied and non-embodied ways (for example, Bamford 2009; Carsten 2004; Counts and Counts 1983; Goldfarb 2016a; Howell 2006; Leinaweaver 2008; Stasch 2009; Weismantel 1995). These scholars have illuminated how bodily similarity is understood to emerge through caregiving relationships and particularly the sharing of food, such that parent and child bodies come to "share the same flesh" (Weismantel 1995: 695) or "their blood becomes progressively more similar" (Carsten 2004: 40), regardless of whether Western academics would understand these families to be "biologically" related.

However, even as processual arguments regarding the cultural construc-tion of kinship do often attend to embodiment, these aspects of kinship generally remain conceptually situated within the "cultural" domain of "nurture," rather than "nature." Embodiment, then, is generally a subject treated by anthropologists as essentially cultural, even though the material body is inherently implicated in these theorizations. This is because, I argue, cultural anthropologists in general and scholars of the new kinships more particularly understand kinship and relationality as open to cultural meaning making and contestation, rather than as "determined" by biological reproduction. And this, in turn, is because references to biology are all too often reductive or deterministic, what McKinnon and Silverman call the "recurrent claim that 'biology is des-tiny'" (2005: 2). The content of "biology" remains either black-boxed or (in kinship theory) assumed to mean something specifically related to heterosexual reproduction. I suggest that this is an oddly limited understanding of biology, which further shapes a limited theorization of embodiment.[5]

In this chapter, I argue for greater attention to the ways that relatedness itself has biological materiality, and I propose a model of embodied relationality that troubles any easy separation between nature and nurture, biology and culture. In what follows, I destabilize conventional ways of treating embodiment by showing that a fruitful way to explore kinship ties is through their absences, and specifically, the ways that these absences are often perceived and experienced through the body. While kinship ideals in many ways align with David Schneider's old notion of "diffuse, enduring solidarity" (1968) or Marshall Sahlins' recent articulation of kinship as "mutuality of being" (2011, 2013), otherness and difference, hierarchy, and violence are also very often at the heart of how kinship is known and experienced, if not idealized (Goldfarb and Schuster 2016; Stasch 2009; Yanagisako and Collier 1987). Even as kinship ideals may contain and even imply the possibility of their failure (Sahlins 2013: 24; Stasch 2009: 136), the lived meanings of kinship – the nitty-gritty aspects of kinship that sometimes hew far from cultural concepts of kinship as "mutuality," for example – are sometimes best understood through exploring the absence of locally meaningful kinship ties. I explore how kinship's absences are understood discursively and experienced materially as embodied evidence of social relationships. I highlight the often very normative and normalizing ways that locally relevant epistemologies, specifically conventional and specialized knowledge about child development, inform how my interlocutors identify and interpret material signs of caregiving relationships in a context where parental ties are lacking. These cases prompt us to consider the materiality of human social interactions – including the biology of the body – in the holistic ways we have long considered culture. Thus, I explore how kinship's absence is expressed bodily, and how my interlocutors take these biologies not as deterministic – which is how biology is often viewed by (non-biologist) academics – but as open-ended and expansive.

The accounts I discuss here emerge from long-term ethnographic fieldwork from 2008 to 2010 in Japan, and include continuing research in the United States, Canada, and Japan through 2018.[6] My ethnographic research explores how "non-normative" kinship practices articulate with family ideologies in Japan, and I particularly attend to the ways social relationships and their absences are materialized and embodied, with very real stakes for well-being. One of my long-term field sites is a child welfare institution outside Tokyo, which I call Chestnut House, introduced above. I have also conducted extensive research with foster and adoptive parents and families, workers within child welfare institutions, people who themselves were raised in institutional and foster care, and more recently, psychotherapists and specialists in child development and interpersonal trauma. My orientation to kinship studies is thus motivated by my empirical findings that show kinship to be contingent, fragile, and sometimes a source of violence and harm, but also creative and potentially transformative, particularly in the case of chosen or emergent families (Weston 1991).

In the service of developing a concept of embodiment – and embodied social relationships – that richly brings together both "nature" and "nurture," I make use of two rather distinct sets of ethnographic data. First, I show how child welfare caregivers interpret children's bodily signs to guide their own understandings of the quality of care a child is seen to have received in the past, and these discursive figurations shape their interpretive practices, thus co-producing a particular bodily semiotics (Goldfarb 2016a; Jasanoff 2004; Stasch 2009). I then explore how contemporary understandings of attachment, neuroscience, and trauma might influence kinship theory within anthropology, directing cultural anthropologists to take "biology" as seriously as our interlocutors do in their efforts to understand the material ways social ties shape lived experience.

7.1   Context: State Care in Japan

Japan differs from many other industrialized nations in that the backbone of its child welfare system is a vast network of institutions caring for newborns, children, and young adults. The dominant reasons children are placed into Japanese state care are maltreatment, parental mental health problems and hospitalization, parental poverty or work-related reasons, neglect, abandonment, and parental divorce (parental death is a relatively rare cause, documented as the reason for state care placement in only 2.5 percent of cases in 2008) (MHLW 2014).[7] While in many families, these problems might be addressed through informal practices, such as a grandparent or aunt caring for a child, the fact that a child is placed in state care often indicates that for these particular families, kinship resources may not be available.

The average length of state care placement is 4.6 years, and almost 90 percent of these placements are institutional, not foster family-based. Almost 28 percent of children spend between four and eight years in state care, 14 percent spend between eight and 12 years, and 5.2 percent spend over 12 years in state care (MHLW 2014). These figures likely underreport years in care, because they track only unique placements rather than the common situation in which children move in and out of care. A significant percentage of children who come into the state care system spend a large portion of their childhoods in care. If they do not go on to high school, state wards age out of the system as early as 15 years at the end of their compulsory education; otherwise they age out at 18 years, before they become legal adults at age 20. (If they have special needs or are in higher education, young people might receive extensions in order to stay in the state care system until age 20.) Critics of this system note the need for more in-depth social work intervention for both parents and children. Most parents do not receive targeted assistance to remedy the problems that required separation from their children in the first place, and while many people with mental health problems in Japan receive psycho-pharmaceuticals, psychotherapy, and behavior-oriented treatments are often not covered by medical insurance and are expensive (Kitanaka 2011).[8] Young people who leave the state care system are impacted by the general inaccessibility of mental health care as well as the lack of government-mandated after-care services (CVV 2015; Hinata Bokko 2009).

There are many reasons why institutions are prioritized over family-based care, like foster care, which comprises only around 10 percent of all Japanese state care placements. One significant reason is that child welfare institutions were developed post-World War II to care for war orphans and eventually evolved into durable and often family-run organizations with deep ties to local government (Goodman 2000). Another reason is a perception, among the public in general, child welfare practitioners, and family court officers, that biological parental rights to decide a child's living arrangement and retain custody should guide child welfare placements (Goldfarb 2013; Tsuzaki 2009). The adoption of unrelated and unknown children is not a common practice in contemporary Japan, and has only been taken up by small numbers of activists as a compelling child welfare intervention for children whose parents cannot care for them (Hayes and Habu 2006). Child welfare placement workers carry immense caseloads (according to one statistic, the average is 107 cases at a time [JaSPCAN 2010]).[9] There is little systemic support for foster families, so many workers find it easier to place children in already established institutions (Goodman 2000; King 2012). Reformers working to increase the priority placed on family-based care cite data on child development, neuroscience, attachment theory, and trauma theory to motivate claims that institutional care can be harmful to children, most particularly newborns and infants (Browne 2009; Browne et al. 2006; Goldfarb 2015; Tsuzaki 2011; Zeanah et al. 2005). Firsthand accounts of the troubles formerly institutionalized youth face when they leave state care and must make their own way, often without family or other social ties on which to depend, highlight the mundane ways that disconnection from biological or created kinship networks in Japan often takes a significant toll on well-being (CVV 2015; Goldfarb 2016b; Hinata Bokko 2009). These experiences are situated within a system that normatively prioritizes care and support from biological kin, a structural instantiation of the ways "nature" and "nurture" play out in child welfare policy and practice.

7.2 Embodied Signs of Care and Neglect: Perspectives from Institutional Caregivers

Caregivers in Japan are highly attuned to physical and embodied signs of care and its absence. Foster parents and staff members in child welfare institutions often understand children's bodies to express accumulated histories of both nurturance and neglect: absent kinship bonds constitute a recognizable embodied presence that is visible materially and knowable through observation of children's behaviors. Caregivers understand these signs as indicators of pasts not clearly known or knowable, and as suggestions of children's current development. While I focus on child welfare workers' perspectives in this section, I note that this attention to physical manifestations of a child's past was a characteristic of observations made by non-specialists, as well: for instance, a Japanese woman who grew up near a child welfare institution once asserted to me that the community members could tell which children were from the institution. "Their bodies were smaller than normal," she said. "You know, because they were neglected or abused, and that affects physical development."[10] Staff members, too, paid close attention to a child's bodily size, noting sudden growth when a child became more secure or calm (Goldfarb 2015; Rutter and ERA 1998). Theories of child development constituted a semiotic and epistemological framework through which people interpreted the embodied signs of state wards, drawing attention to these children's bodies as visually marked expressions of neglect and trauma. In this section, I focus on institutional staff members' understandings of signs pertaining directly to food and its consumption, not because caregivers perceive institutionalized children as undernourished but because food-related practices are often at the center of staff members' efforts to re-socialize the children in their care. A focus on eating allows caregivers to intervene into and shape a child's embodied habitus, and further help children conform more closely to valued behavioral norms (Bourdieu 1977).

While the accounts in this section seem to sit on the borderline between "biology" and "culture," they all make explicit the ways social relationships are experienced and expressed in the body, which is constantly open to new environmental and social stimuli. Although some might assume that the human body is always animated by internal progressions of growth that fluctuate little across cultures and across populations,[11] many of the foster and institutional caregivers I knew in Japan had experiences that threw into relief the fact that "normal" development is not always a useful heuristic. These findings recall Margaret Lock's theory of local biologies, in which biological processes are "products of an ongoing dialectic between biology and culture in which both are contingent" (Lock 1993: xxi; 2001).[12] Lock and Nguyen call this "'biosocial differentiation' to refer to the continual interactions of biological and social processes across time and space that eventually sediment into local biologies" (Lock and Nguyen 2010: 90). The concept of "local biologies" helps explain diverse phenomena: different physiological and phenomenological experiences of menopause in different cultures, neurological, and genotypical changes caused by endocannibalism among the Fore people of Papua New Guinea, and disproportionately low birth weights among African American populations (Lock and Nguyen 2010). Epidemiological studies correlating the experience of racism with the birth of low-birth-weight infants is a classic example of "how people, as both biological organisms and social beings, literally embody … the dynamic social, material, and ecological contexts into which we are born, develop, interact, and endeavor to live meaningful lives" (Krieger 2006). These examples from medical anthropology and clinical epidemiology bring together lived, situated life experiences with phenomena that might seem more or less rooted in "biological" causation. But the lines between biological and social factors are ever blurry, as illustrated by historical approaches to eugenics in Japan, where eugenic scientists focused on socialization and habits of women of reproductive age rather than sterilization (Robertson 2002).

So is left- or right-handedness biological? Cultural? The following examples of biosocial and embodied engagements with the world are certainly cultural and they are explicitly bodily, and they are also not *not* biological. The ways children in Japanese state care engaged with their bodies – particularly at meal times – told caregivers a lot about a child's former caregivers, the child's present state of being, and clarified these caregivers' goals to re-socialize a child through caring interventions.

For instance, the way a person holds chopsticks in Japan is often understood as a key index of personal histories of care and neglect. A child welfare officer, who I call Tanabe Nobuko, once explained to me that she had received important information about a new client at the child guidance center where she worked.[13] The client, Tanabe said, held her chopsticks improperly: "Like this," Nobuko told me, crossing her fingers in the shape of an X. She looked at me significantly. After a pause, she explained: "It means, you know, this woman wasn't raised well (*daiji ni sodaterarenakatta*). And now she's having trouble raising her own children." The way a person holds his or her chopsticks emerged many times in conversations as a marker of past and present social relationships, a salient piece of information for many of my interlocutors. Although people in Japan sometimes cite improper chopstick use as a sign of the failures of the contemporary family, individual cases, like the one Nobuko mentioned, often are interpreted as significant markers of social class and family (in)stability. The staff at Chestnut House, the child welfare institution where I conducted fieldwork, also commented on how skilled the children had become with chopsticks in the time since they moved in. Almost all of the children in the youngest cohort were between two and three years of age, and had come to Chestnut House directly from baby homes.[14] None of these children could use chopsticks when they arrived, but within a few weeks they had all become adept. Staff members had been careful to teach the children correct usage, and overtly praised the children for their skills.

At meals, adult research subjects who had spent time in child welfare institutions themselves sometimes commented on their own improper way of holding chopsticks, bemoaning the fact that they had never been taught to use chopsticks properly. I recalled the concern with which this particular task was undertaken at Chestnut House, which highlights the variations among institutional practices in Japan. In these moments I was also aware of my own embodied presence, with a slightly vertiginous sense that I, although not Japanese, *do* hold my chopsticks properly because a series of host parents cared to teach me.[15] Both my and my research subjects' embodied habits traced out histories of care. By correcting their chopstick use, the Chestnut House staff gave the children in their charge two distinct inheritances. One was the ability to inhabit a set of unmarked embodied practices: proper chopstick use would never mark them visibly as having lowly origins, a non-middle-class upbringing, or parents who did not properly care for them. Their way of eating would never be cause for concern or comment from a caseworker like Nobuko. Further, the Chestnut House staff shaped the children's embodied practices so that these indelible forms of care would be present always, reminders to the children themselves that they had been cared for in the past.

The children who arrived at Chestnut House directly from baby homes had another problem that I often heard discussed regarding baby homes in general. Many of these children did not know how to chew. Baby homes care for both infants and toddlers, and most of these institutions provide the same food for all children who were no longer drinking formula: rice gruel and very soft pastas and vegetables. According to staff members, the children did not develop jaw strength or the ability to chew and swallow harder foods. A Chestnut House staff member described how one of the little girls put food in her mouth and, uncertain how to chew and swallow, sometimes choked. Those critical of institutions for infants point out that the failure to meet this developmental milestone indicates durable, but less visible, signs of developmental delay caused by insufficient stimulation inherent in the institutional care of infants (Browne et al. 2006; Goldfarb 2015). In this sense, staff members understood that bodily capacities opaquely indicated the possibility for (neuro)biological developmental shifts that were perceived as abnormal and potentially long-lasting. As one of my interlocutors repeatedly claimed, "Baby homes are institutions that create developmental disabilities."

Recall that children in institutions are disproportionately left-handed compared to the general Japanese population, because no one corrected them to use the right hand as is typical in Japan. Similarly, the staff members at Chestnut House observed that the toddlers who came from one particular institution for babies sucked their fingers, a practice that was marked as unusual. The staff at this home apparently did not remove children's fingers from their mouths as they slept, a lack of intervention with embodied consequences, parallel to the staff member's observation about left-handed children. These examples highlight forcefully normalizing elements of "proper" care. Further, certain types of institutional care give rise to their own "local biologies" that are, in turn, deeply related to kinship disconnections and the fault lines within family networks that would necessitate a child's institutionalization.

While the caregivers directly responsible for the children's daily nourishment provided a pragmatic and commonsense perspective on the children's bodily signs, Chestnut House's director, Kitahara Shinobu, elaborated a comprehensive normative philosophy that brought together the biology of nourishment, the welfare goal of re-socializing children with troubled pasts, and the psychosocial lacks that contributed toward children's material food practices. Kitahara made clear that eating together went a long way toward producing a home for the children. Kitahara and many of his staff viewed food practices as central to the child welfare institution's goal to produce community and a kin-like network for children who had none, and to re-socialize the children as "normal" or "ordinary" (*atari mae*) members of Japanese society.

Kitahara provided a concrete example of how he perceived the pasts of many of the children at Chestnut House, and the reasons (as he saw it) that the children must be re-socialized – reasons directly connected to bodily orientations toward food. A common social problem with children in state care is shoplifting (*manbiki*), Kitahara told me. Kitahara explained that because the children who were now living at Chestnut House were not cherished or raised well in the past (*daiji ni sodateraretekonakatta*),[16] shoplifting became a bad habit (*kuse*) that the staff must now address in order to give the children a firm sense of values. If a child got into trouble, Kitahara explained, a staff member went with the child to apologize: they bowed their heads in apology together. It is through this process that a sense of right and wrong becomes part of the body, Kitahara told me. This perception of discipline, or *shitsuke* in Japanese, echoes Joy Hendry's canonical analysis:

> In a literal translation of a widely used definition of *shitsuke*, from a dictionary of folklore, the meaning is said to be "the putting into the body of a child the arts of living and good manners in order to create one grown-up person," (literally, one portion of a social person – *ichininmae no shakaijin*). Another such definition, quoted by Hara and Wagatsuma, is similar: "the putting into the body of a child the patterns of living, ways of conduct of daily life and a mastery of manners and correct behaviour."
>
> *(1986: 11)*

For Kitahara, then, past parent–child relationships are indicated by children's present behavior and are only remediable through the body: through collective ways in which staff and children apologized together, embodying values through what will eventually become habit.[17]

Kitahara well understood the socioeconomic privations faced by most of the families whose children end up in state care, but in his mind, these socioeconomic difficulties were often related to failures in the ways care was given and received between parent and child. Kitahara explained, expressing highly normative perspectives on correct and incorrect parenting:

> In the end, stealing ... If daily life is tough, the parent can't give the child an allowance. Some parents might cut back on smoking or drinking to give their child an allowance, but if daily life is tough, the parent doesn't do it. But this is the thing. If the parent and child have a secure relationship, for example, if the kid says "I want to drink juice," and the parent says, "Be content with water," the kid is content with water.

However, Kitahara continued, if the relationship between the parent and the child isn't secure, if the child hasn't learned morals and ethics from the parent, and if that parent gambles and there is not enough money in the household, the dissatisfactions and deficiencies in the children's lives become the basis for shoplifting habits. Parents may lack the income to put food on the table at all, or they drink or gamble money away. Mothers often work in *mizu shobai*, or "night work," and children are home alone. Because parents cannot give their children allowances, it is natural, Kitahara explained, that a child will begin to steal food from supermarkets and convenience stores. These perspectives harken to older eugenic beliefs in Japan that population "quality" is improved by improving the embodied habits of parents, and connects parenting habits to heritable, embodied characteristics of children (Robertson 2002).

Stealing, Kitahara told me, is a way for these children to satisfy a basic lack within their lives: they have to eat. Thus it all starts with stealing food. However, in Kitahara's account this material lack of nourishment bleeds into other forms of deprivation. Kitahara told me,

> They shoplift in order to satisfy the discontent they feel at home. And it's of course also about eating. They steal other things, DVDs and such, but the majority is food. It begins with food. They take it, they eat it. It's because their lips are lonely (*kuchi biru ga sabishii*).[18] When children's needs aren't met, they steal and put these stolen things into their mouths.

In Kitahara's formulation, these children's lack of kinship ties was embodied as anti-social, intensely material behavior.

Kitahara thus understood these parents to have failed in creating proper, normative caregiving relationships with their children. Through a child's food practices, staff members were able to deduce a parent's inability to give a child affection, time, and money. Kitahara evoked a process by which these lacks produce a poorly socialized child without a good sense of values or ethics: the nourishment these children put into their bodies was stolen, an embodied practice that reflected lack, loneliness, and unsatisfied desire. Extending his analysis of shoplifting practices, Kitahara summoned a complex set of claims regarding the interactions of biological nourishment, the habituated embodiment of family and social norms, and the ways children's eating practices made knowable long-lasting relationships between parents and children.

Institutional caregivers evaluated the embodied signs of their charges (and these children's parents) in a manner that traverses domains which might be understood as eminently "cultural" – the ways a child uses chopsticks, or whether a child shoplifts – but I return to my claim that it is not useful to define these expressions of embodied relationality as divorced from the biological. Body size, the ability to chew, habituated patterns of chopstick use, left-handedness, the addictive predilections of the child's parents expressed by children's behavior, and the loneliness of a child's lips – the desire for sustenance that is both relational and physical – are indexes of absent relationships that span biological and cultural fields. Here, children's bodies were "embedded" bodies, in Jörg Niewöhner's felicitous turn of phrase. An "embedded body," Niewöhner writes, is "heavily impregnated by its own past and by the social and material environment within which it dwells. It is a body that is imprinted by evolutionary and transgenerational time, by 'early-life' and a body that is highly susceptible to changes in its social and material environment" (2011: 289–290).[19] Interpersonal histories perdure in these embedded bodies, producing "somatic memory effects" (2011: 290) that remind both caregivers and children of these pasts. They are traces of these children's "lifelines" (Rose 1998). The experiences of caregivers and children receiving care within the Japanese child welfare system belie the stability of the concept of standard child development across populations, and draw into relief the diversity of ways biological processes occur, signify, and are experienced.

7.3 Embodied Absence: The Space a Parent Should Have Filled

In this section, I focus not on the ways caregivers interpret children's bodily signs as indications of past kinship relationships, but on one man's exploration of his own bodily experience of kinship's absence. His account has made me consider the diversities of ways that kinship and its absence can be embodied and theorized on the ground, the complexity of which leaves biology vs. culture debates behind and blurs material and immaterial categories of experience. His narrative epitomizes the ways phenomenological theorizations of the body – which highlight the body as both subject and object to itself – can also incorporate scientific knowledge and intersubjective context (Csordas 1990; Hacking 1996; Merleau-Ponty 1968). My analysis is guided by this man's own exegesis of past and present events.

In March of 2015, I presented a research paper in Japanese to an audience composed of Japanese child welfare researchers, foster and adoptive parents, child welfare institution caregivers, and people who had grown up within Japan's child welfare system. My argument, in short, was that although people in Japan often describe "Japanese people" as such as valorizing blood ties within family (and thus stigmatizing families in which parents and children lack a biogenetic bond), the very concept of "blood tie" is itself culturally and historically specific and has transformed substantially over time within Japan (Goldfarb 2018). I asked my audience to consider blood ties as a cultural concept, and to reflect on the ways that the meaning of blood ties has shifted with different understandings of intimacy within Japanese families.[20] One of my motivations was to give my interlocutors some social science fuel with which to counter ubiquitous claims regarding "normal" families that naturalize and dehistoricize Japanese family practices.

During the question and answer period, the first person to raise his hand was a man I know well, who I will call Hanashima Shinichi. Hanashima, who is now in his mid-fifties, had lived his entire infancy and childhood in Japanese child welfare institutions. He had never been raised by his parents and he had experienced sexual and physical abuse in the child welfare institution where he grew up. Although his current life was successful and rich, by most measures – with a stable job, a companionate marriage, one biological child and one foster child – his experiences in state care continued to indelibly mark his life, and he still sometimes experienced traumatic flashbacks. He worked tirelessly to campaign for the placement of infants in foster and adoptive homes, rather than in institutions, and he was deeply involved with an organization whose goal was to eliminate abuse within child welfare institutions.

In his question after my presentation, Hanashima said that he understood my argument, that "blood ties" are a cultural concept and that the cultural meanings of blood are in many ways more important than biogenetic parent–child relationships. But from the perspective of the people who grew up without parents – for them, was there some sort of inherent, indwelling, internal (naizaika) sense of "parent" that exists inside them? Hanashima had begun with my argument about culture and taken it to a place that sounded universal, psychological, and in some way biological – in the ways that Japanese people often merge a cultural concept of "blood ties" with genetics or biological substance – or even perhaps neurological.

I stumbled through an inadequate reply. At the same time, I was not surprised that he had asked this question. Eighteen months previously, I had attended the International Foster Care Organization's biennial congress, which had been hosted in Osaka, Japan, and over the course of the multi-day event, Hanashima had come to articulate a version of this question that he asked, in different ways, of many different people. For instance, after an international panel of youth presented accounts of their experiences in foster and institutional care, Hanashima had asked them whether they themselves had a parent who resides in their hearts or spirits (*kokoro ni omou oya ga imasu ka?*). Surely surprised by both the frankness and somewhat abstract nature of the question, which is hard to pin down both in Japanese and in English, none of the panelists had answered in a way that satisfied Hanashima. I realized he had been experimenting with this question since I'd last seen him.

In what follows, I will focus on Hanashima's experiences as he has described them to me in hours of interviews, more recently in 2013 and also from conversations in 2010. For the purposes of this chapter, I am interested in how he articulates the absence of kinship connections in an exceptionally physical way, making use of his own embodied perceptions as he thinks alongside child development scholars like John Bowlby and Mary Ainsworth. In line with his question to me, I hope to linger with Hanashima not on the culturally specific elements of kinship, but rather those that he perceives as intensely material and psycho-biological.

In response to his own question about an "indwelling" parent, Hanashima had noted, "I personally don't have a parent that resides in my heart." In posing his question to the foster care conference panelists, he was trying to figure out whether other people who had never experienced care from biological parents did, nonetheless, possess an internal parent figure. As Hanashima and I discussed the panelists' confused reception of his question, Hanashima said, his voice catching:

> But this is the thing. I've *always* – to put it frankly – it's like I've always had this feeling of a hole open in my chest (*mune ni ana ga aiteiru*). It's anguishing. Probably, by all rights, there has always been this place left open in my heart for the parent that should have filled that space (*watashi no kokoro no naka ni hairu beki oya*), a parent or someone who would have raised me. But I have lived this entire time without someone filling that space.

Hanashima explained that he had read accounts of institutional care and foster families from other countries, and he noticed that the expression "a hole in the heart" appeared often. "I've had that feeling my entire life," he told me.[21]

"That sounds like it hurts."

"It does, it hurts so much! There are times when it *physically* hurts," he replied. He hypothesized that his own Christianity (he was raised in a Catholic institution) might have filled some of the space long left open. Hanashima's belief that everyone has a space within that should be filled by a parent figure indicates a visceral sense of a universal need *to be* parented, to be cared for by someone whose existence would dwell within their own throughout their entire life. Notably, Hanashima did not focus on kinship based on "blood ties" but rather the persistent role of a caring someone.

Hanashima's own embodied sensibility hews quite closely to attachment theorists, whom he has read.[22] He referenced Mary Ainsworth's canonical experiments, the Strange Situation Procedure. The Strange Situation experiments were designed to evaluate a child's attachment type by examining the child's proximity-seeking behavior to the parent, after the parent leaves the child alone or with a stranger and then later returns.[23] Ainsworth's research was based on John Bowlby's (1953) attachment theory, which posited that "attachment behaviors observed in infancy are evidence of the development of an internal working model of social relations" (Gaskins 2013: 33): in other words, key relationships with important caregivers are understood to shape the way the child thinks of him- or herself, which will in turn shape the child's expectations for relationships with other people. Bowlby developed the concept of the "secure base," in which (in its ideal-typical form) an infant is able to check in with a parent while exploring new surroundings. If the child has a secure base, so the theory goes, the child will be able to encounter novel situations and also know that his or her needs will be met. Children without this sense of security, attachment scholars argue, live with the internalized expectation that their needs will only be met sporadically and unpredictably, or that their needs will cause in the parent a sense of alarm or panic, or that their needs will not be met and the child cannot depend on anyone (other than the child's own self) to fulfill basic needs (Bowlby 1982 [1969]; Levy and Orlans 2014). A third important scholar of whom Hanashima is likely aware, but did not mention, is Allan Schore, who posited that a major parental role is to help an infant regulate and organize his or her own affect and emotions. Sebern Fisher, a psychotherapist and trauma specialist, notes that a child need not be actually abandoned or abused "to be in trouble: he needs *only* to experience himself as abandoned" (2014: 4, italics in original).

Both Hanashima and Fisher's explanatory models provide compelling grounds for thinking the ways that kinship's absences might be materially, psychologically, and neurologically embodied. Fisher is an interesting figure, a psychotherapist with her own history of trauma and attachment problems, who is now a leading expert on the use of neurofeedback (a type of biofeedback) in the treatment of childhood trauma. Her use of neuroscience, as she explains key tenets of her treatment modality, is sometimes impressionistic and poetic, and she often focuses more on the reported lived experience of her patients than clinical nosologies that, she argues, hinder therapeutic intersubjectivity and understanding of patient experience (2014: 6). Reading Fisher, who is not a scholar Hanashima has likely read, I was struck by the similarities in how she explained the felt experience of an absent parent, and Hanashima's own language. (I use the word "parent" in my own descriptions even though Fisher consistently uses "mother"; Bowlby himself focused on "one special type of social relationship, that of attachment to a caregiver," not necessarily a "mother" (Bowlby 1982 [1969]: 376).[24]) Fisher writes, "Children not held in the minds of their mothers are lost, forgotten. Being held in the mind of the mother is the original holding environment" (2014: 8). Fisher later writes,

> Many of my patients report no remembered or felt experience of being held or rocked – maternal activities that promote cerebellum development. Some have even told me that they feel an absence at the back of their heads where a loving hand should have cradled them. This is probably the first place in the brain that encodes the mother's presence. If she were there, we would never forget her. Her presence is held in procedural memory. And so is her absence.
>
> *(2014: 22)*

Hanashima's own visceral sensibility of an experienced absence, that he feels in his body and that *should* have been filled but never was, resonates poignantly with Fisher's description, which she uses to make arguments about brain development, affect regulation, and possibilities for therapeutic intervention.

Hanashima developed his own notion of the parent that inheres in one's heart or spirit by thinking alongside attachment scholars about his own experiences. "If a parent leaves the room, the ['securely attached'] child will cry, right? When I thought about those [Strange Situation] studies, I thought, 'Ah, what about myself – do I have an internalized parent?'" Hanashima seemed to be wondering whether he himself had a "secure base." But it wasn't just himself he was thinking about: he was also considering his foster child, who a social worker had identified as attachment disordered. He explained that his idea of the internalized parent also meant a person's awareness and memory of the parent's way of thinking, the things the parent said, and parental discipline. (This would presumably be the case whether or not the parent was a "good" caregiver, per Kitahara's definition in the previous section.) If the parent has been internalized, Hanashima posited, this internalized parent should exist within a child, over a child's whole life. Without an internalized parent to act as the child's moral compass, that child is extremely difficult to discipline. A child with an internalized parent can live and act independently,

Hanashima explained, but a child without will be dependent and unable to inhabit social rules and expectations. He argued that he himself had no internalized moral compass – it was simply logic that told him that if he did something bad, he would lose his job. He conceded, however, that his religiosity might play a substitute role as well. Perhaps God was Hanashima's internalized parent, we speculated.

Motivated by both his own embodied experience and by his reading of child development literature, Hanashima had developed a firm model for child welfare. For him, it boiled down to "not creating people who have no one (*dare mo inai hito wo tsukuranai*)." People with no one are those most likely to commit crimes, he said, and those people were also the most difficult to socially rehabilitate. His personal goal to place infants and very young children in family-based settings rather than institutions was, then, a wide-reaching goal to place a parent *inside* that child. This parent would live inside the child's heart (*sono kodomo no kokoro ni sumu*). Hanashima pointed out that in his own activities, he never wavers: he insists without exception that babies should be placed in households, not institutions. "It's because for me, inside me – I understand. I understand the cause of my own suffering, the cause of my own difficulty in living (*ikizurasa*)."[25]

Even as Hanashima makes use of attachment theory, trauma theory, and neuroscience in his appeals to Japan's Ministry of Health, Labor, and Welfare, and in the homemade pamphlets he distributes at events in which he advocates for the elimination of infant institutionalization, I find Hanashima's most compelling evidence to rest on his personal, and highly visceral, experiences of lack.[26] In a 2010 interview, he described his first visit to an institutional baby home in Japan, the cribs like small cages or pens (*ori no yō*) lined up one after another with solitary babies lying behind tall railings in each one.

> When I saw those, it was – agonizing – those babies had been abandoned, thrown away, and I saw that my former self – of course I have no memory of that time, but as one would expect, there were no adults there, just children all lined up alone, and I saw them and it was myself, too, it somehow overlapped, it was agony. I felt I had to somehow help these children, but it was also connected to a need to help my former self.

Hanashima said that despite recurrent flashbacks from which he still suffers, he has mostly managed to process his experiences of abuse in the institution where he grew up. Those memories, he said, are now "sepia-colored," and while scars remain, they are old scars. But the one topic that remains an ever present source of suffering, a topic he speculates he will be forced to deal with for his entire life, is the fact that as a child he had always been alone, there was never anyone there for him (*dare mo inakatta*).

At the same time, it is Hanashima's sense of internal emptiness that provides him energy for his activist work. He had always enjoyed physics, and if he had had the financial resources to go to university, that is what he would have studied. He said, "It's like the physics concept of the Dirac Sea[27] – the idea of limitless energy that is also a space of nothingness. Within myself, from that place of total nothingness, from that completely empty part, that's where I draw energy to continue my activism." In the process, he said, and despite the long perception of himself acting totally alone, he has also discovered that he is surrounded by people who support him. Hanashima's embodied sensibilities are exquisitely attuned to relationality, and particularly to the absence that he experiences as a productive but painful presence.

7.4 Conclusion

The accounts I have told here suggest that kinship relationships can be explored through their embodied absences. Rather than focusing exclusively (if productively) on the ways that relatedness can emerge over time and through caregiving, I have shown that temporally extended absences leave their own material traces. Institutional caregivers at Chestnut House understand children's bodies to reflect absent social ties, conveying the degree to which children have been left "just as they were when they were born": caring interventions and neglect inscribe indelible presences through embodied practices and bodily memory. These materializations may also be experienced subjectively as a visceral absence. A combination of attachment theory and everyday understandings of child development provides caregivers an interpretive and epistemological framework with which they connect their own experiences of giving care with their observations of children's behavior and bodies. Similarly, Hanashima himself understands his condition holistically, making use of international expert knowledge on child development, attachment theory, trauma theory, and neuroscience to give texture to his own culturally and historically specific – and very bodily – experiences.

This chapter has offered a model of embodiment that provides an expansive vision of the embeddedness of bodies and selves in relationships, with the objective of destabilizing reductive claims about kinship as a product of "nature" or "nurture," "biology" or "culture." Cultural anthropology's aversion to engagement with biology has a long history – a history in which biological evidence has been (mis)used to rank human "races" in a "great chain of being," a history of eugenic policy making, a history in which biological sex difference has been used to justify the subjugation of women, a history of explaining present-day inequalities by reference to supposedly inherent genetic predilections (Ehrenreich and McIntosh 1997; Gould 1977; Graves 2015; Oyama 2000; Rose 1998).[28] It is no wonder that anthropology in the service of progressive social change would embrace "culture" as a better explanation for human differences and social inequalities. And yet, most scholars who take biology seriously understand both the constant interplay of biology and culture, and the inherent malleability of biology itself – which was one of Darwin's central insights. The cases presented in this chapter thus illustrate that "biology is more naturally eccentric, more intrinsically preternatural than we usually allow" (Wilson 2004: 12), and they invite cultural analysis that takes "the social life of persons as an aspect of organic life in general" (Ingold 1990: 208).

I suggest that cultural anthropologists should pay serious attention to all sorts of embodied processes in order to better understand the interactions between bodies, interpersonal relationships, minds, nonhuman entities, sociality, culture, genetics, neurology, affect, technology, emotion … as these shape us as social beings. For instance, research on the field of epigenetics leads one to wonder what it can possibly mean to discuss "nature" (understood as genetic predispositions) as separate from "nurture" (understood as the input of cultural surroundings, parenting, food, etc.), when gene expression changes over time and is indeed heritable, based on factors like stress, exercise, drug use, and early life adversity (Lock 2015; Niewöhner 2011).[29] Scholars of genetics point out both the historical contingency (Müller-Wille and Rheinberger 2012) and the conceptual incoherence of imagining that "nature" and "nurture" could be held as discrete objects, where nature is understood as "prenatal" while nurture takes over as "postnatal" (Ingold 1990; 2004; Keller 2010: 74). Tim Ingold points out that this opposition "effectively reduces the biological to the innate … thus excluding from 'biology' the entire gamut of ontogenetic or developmental processes by which humans and other animals become skilled in the conduct of particular forms of life" (2013: 4). Scholars of kinship – trained as we are to think carefully and broadly about surprising forms of relatedness – should thus welcome material, embodied, and biological processes as interlocutors, and work toward theorizing relational embodiments beyond the nature/nurture divide.

Acknowledgments

I am ever grateful to my research interlocutors in Japan. I received helpful comments on earlier versions of this chapter from Sandra Bamford, Elayne Oliphant, Alex Blanchette, Alison Cool, Kristen Drybread, Carly Schuster, Tatiana Chudakova, Hisako Omori, the students in my kinship seminar at the University of Colorado at Boulder, and Junko Kitanaka and her advanced seminar students at Keio University in Tokyo. Particular thanks to my research assistants, Kelly Graves Zepelin and Matt Zepelin.

Notes

1. All personal and institutional names are pseudonyms.
2. Chestnut House is a small-scale "household-style" child welfare institution in the Tokyo metropolitan area and was opened in 2009 in response to a shortage of accommodation for children in state care. I attended trainings for the staff members before the institution's opening, beginning in October 2008, and conducted participant-observation fieldwork at the institution from July 2009 to December 2010.
3. I avoid referring to "interactions" between biology and culture, a term that implies the separability of these domains. Karen Barad's concept of intra-action, in which these categories "do not precede, but rather emerge" relationally through "mutual entanglement" (Barad 2010: 267), is apropos.
4. Handedness itself has been explored by anthropologists as exemplifying symbolic classification practices and normative social views (Hertz 1973 [1909]; Needham 1960).
5. For instance, in Marshall Sahlins' recent sharp treatise on what kinship "is" and "is not," if we take biology to narrowly mean heterosexual reproductive processes, I wholly agree with his argument that kinship "is" culture. But biology is not only heterosexual reproductive processes, and holding apart the terms "culture" and "biology" suggest what Steven Rose might call a "spurious dichotomy" (1998: 142), a "nothing but" framework in which kinship must be *either* cultural *or* biological (1998: 295).
6. I gratefully acknowledge research support from Fulbright IIE, the Wenner-Gren Foundation, a Social Science Division Small Research Grant from the University of Chicago, a Postdoctoral Award for Professional Development from Harvard University, a grant from the McMaster University Arts Research Board, and a grant from the University of Colorado at Boulder's Center to Advance Research in the Social Sciences.
7. For more detail on why children end up in Japanese state care, see Goldfarb 2013 and Goodman 2000. Children are very rarely forcibly removed from parental care in Japan – there tend to be only a few cases each year of court-ordered parental rights termination in Japan (Tsuzaki 2009). In the case of parental mental health problems, children would be placed into state care because parents were themselves institutionalized or hospitalized. In the case of divorce, Japan does not have a dual custody law, and a single parent often struggles to care for children alone.
8. This welfare structure, aligning with neoliberal trends focusing on the "responsible" subject, psychologizes and pathologizes the individual rather than interrogating problematic social structures.

9. A "typical" number of cases mentioned by social work interlocutors from other countries hovers around 30.

10. While this woman did not explicitly mention scientific studies on child development, her perspective is substantiated by the literature (Rutter and ERA 1998; Vorria et al. 2006).

11. For example, Tim Ingold has pointed out that in popular discourse, "Whatever humans have in common is [commonly] attributed to biology, whereas their differences are attributed to culture" (1990: 210).

12. Lock (2001) writes, of "local biologies," "This concept does not refer to the idea that the categories of the biological sciences are historically and culturally constructed (although this is indeed the case) nor to measurable biological difference across human populations. Rather, *local biologies* refers to the way in which the embodied experience of physical sensations, including those of well-being, health, illness, and so on, is in part informed by the material body, itself contingent on evolutionary, environmental, and individual variables. Embodiment is also constituted by the way in which self and others represent the body, drawing on local categories of knowledge and experience ... The material and the social are *both* contingent – both local" (483–484).

13. Japanese child guidance centers are government-run offices charged to address social issues involving children: truancy, disability, child maltreatment, parenting issues.

14. Baby homes are child welfare institutions for newborns and infants. There are approximately 3,000 infants in 131 baby homes in Japan (MHLW 2014). Around the age of two or three, these babies are either transferred to a child welfare institution, or their caseworkers attempt to reunite them with their family of origin. Less frequently, babies are sent to foster or adoptive care, as long as the legal parent has given official permission for home placement.

15. Chopstick use might seem essentially cultural, but some Japanese people interpret correct use as an innate, racially charged perspective on biological Japaneseness, while incorrect use points to foreignness.

16. The Japanese here replicates almost exactly the language Tanabe Nobuko used in describing the same concept of having not been raised well (*daiji ni sodaterarenakatta*). However, Kitahara's use of the longer form *sodateraretekonakatta* evokes time passing, and a process of becoming. The children were not only not raised well, they have arrived at this present state having experienced a period of time in which they were not raised well.

17. While the notion of *shitsuke* has historically implied physical discipline (*taibatsu*), I emphasize that this was not Kitahara's use of the term. The habits he spoke of can be understood as "techniques of the body" that are learned over time and are culturally specific (Mauss 1973), or

a "habitus" that associates the individual with socially normative and valorized qualities (Bourdieu 1977).

18. Kitahara's words echo an idiomatic phrase, "*kuchi ga sabishii*," "the mouth is lonely." A person might say this if she is trying to stop smoking and wants to have something in her mouth. "*Kuchi biru ga sabishii*" is not, in my understanding, an idiomatic phrase.

19. Ingold would point out that these bodily effects are indeed explicitly biological: "those specific ways of acting, perceiving and knowing that we have been accustomed to call cultural are enfolded, in the course of ontogenetic development, into the constitution of the human organism, then they are equally facts of biology" (2004: 215).

20. This symposium was organized by Shirai Chiaki, and its English title was, "Foster Care and Adoption: Japan in the World." It took place at Japan Women's University in Tokyo on March 8, 2015.

21. I don't know if Hanashima picked up this phrasing for the first time after seeing it written in overseas contexts, or if it was a phrase that had come to him independently. Regardless, it powerfully resonated with him.

22. These conceptual alliances may be illustrations of the "looping effect" in practice – the ways scientific knowledge is taken up, influences people's perceptions of themselves, and in turn impacts the evolution of scientific concepts (Hacking 1996); another way to think about this process might be a recognition that scientific and embodied self-knowledge are themselves co-produced (Jasanoff 2004).

23. Naomi Quinn and Jeannette Mageo's edited volume, *Attachment Reconsidered: Cultural Perspectives on a Western Theory* (2013), provides a smart and incisive analysis of attachment theory, which has been criticized for assuming a fixed number of normative, optimal attachment "types," regardless of culture, and for conducting evaluations in clinical environments out of context from a child's normal social sphere. Studies of attachment patterns in Japan specifically have labeled Japanese children as "insecure-ambivalent," and critiques (focusing, among other things, on the fact that it is odd to imagine an entire population as essentially insecurely attached to their parents) might lead one to believe that attachment theory is not relevant in Japan (Quinn and Mageo 2013: 14–16). However, knowledge of attachment theory has been revolutionary for many of my research interlocutors in Japan, including Hanashima. For foster and adoptive parents struggling to parent their children, the understanding that early childhood relationships with caregivers can impact a child's behavior and development is often an enormous relief. In Japan, these parents are often negatively viewed in light of poorly behaved or unmanageable children, as either using inappropriate childrearing techniques or as not "loving enough" to make a child behave.

24. Scholars of attachment often discuss "the mother" as the single most important figure in an infant's life; other scholars explicitly recognize that it need not be the mother rather than the father, or the biological mother, or even a single caregiver, as long as there are a small number of important caregivers who can meet the child's needs. Other scholars seem to use "the mother" as a placeholder to describe this role without explicitly discussing whether they view this position as inhabitable by someone other than a single biological mother.

25. While Hanashima was raised Catholic and speaks openly about his own religiosity, he has never intimated that his child welfare activism is rooted in Christian orientations toward welfare. In fact, while he might understand Catholicism to have helped fill the hole a parent should have filled for him personally, it is clear that to him, religion is but a pale substitute for the parent he should have had.

26. The history of attachment theory has been one inflected with activism, and Hanashima's work is part of this lineage. Bowlby authored his initial study on attachment for the World Bank in 1953, and attachment theory since then has been "infused with Bowlby's ideological fervor for more humane child care … In its assertion that humans could develop only in the context of a tender, sensitive one-to-one bond, attachment theory militated against the dehumanizing tendencies of institutional care in industrial society … In the wake of Bowlby's writings, as a result, attachment theory became a blend of academic school and political movement" (Quinn and Mageo 2013: 26).

27. Wikipedia describes the Dirac sea as "a theoretical model of the vacuum as an infinite sea of particles with negative energy." An online blog in Japanese (http://oshiete.goo.ne.jp/qa/621393.html, accessed August 12, 2015) points out that while a vacuum is conventionally understood as entirely empty, the Dirac sea model argues instead that a vacuum contains positive and negative energy in equal measure and only appears to contain nothingness.

28. Anthropologists who might devalue the explanatory capacity of "nature" while unilaterally celebrating "culture" as the measure of humanity, may be unwittingly falling into the trap that Sherry Ortner diagnosed in 1972, with her article "Is Female to Male as Nature Is to Culture?"

29. Epigenetics "is a process in which the body, understood as coalesced inseparably with environmental forces (macro and micro) from the moment of conception on throughout life, is ceaselessly modulated" through mechanisms that control gene expression (in part through DNA methylation) but "do not involve DNA modifications" (Lock 2015: 151).

References

Bamford, Sandra. 2009. "'Family Trees' among the Kamea of Papua New Guinea: A Non-Genealogical Approach to Imagining Relatedness." In *Kinship and Beyond: The Genealogical Model Reconsidered*, ed. Sandra Bamford and James Leach, 159–174. New York: Berghahn Books.

Barad, Karen. 2010. "Quantum Entanglements and Hauntological Relations of Inheritance: Dis/continuities, Spacetime Enfoldings, and Justice-to-Come." *Derrida Today* 3(2): 240–268.

Bourdieu, Pierre. 1977. *Outline of a Theory of Practice*. Cambridge: Cambridge University Press.

Bowlby, John. 1951. *Maternal Care and Mental Health*. Geneva: World Health Organization.

   1982 [1969]. *Attachment and Loss, I*. New York: Basic Books.

Browne, Kevin. 2009. *The Risk of Harm to Young Children in Institutional Care*. London: Save the Children.

Browne, Kevin, C. Hamilton-Giachritsis, R. Johnson and M. Ostergren. 2006. "Overuse of Institutional Care for Children in Europe." *British Medical Journal* 332: 485–487.

Carsten, Janet. 2004. *After Kinship*. Cambridge: Cambridge University Press.

Children's Views and Voices (CVV) and Masako Nagase. 2015. *Shyakaiteki yōgo no tōjishya shien gaido bukku [A guidebook for the support of child welfare tōjishya]*. Osaka: Children's Views and Voices.

Counts, Dorothy Ayers and David Counts. 1983. "Father's Water Equals Mother's Milk: The Conception of Parentage in Kaliai, West New Britain." *Mankind* 14(1): 46–56.

Csordas, Thomas J. 1990. "Embodiment As a Paradigm for Anthropology." *Ethos* 18(1): 5–47.

Ehrenreich, Barbara and Janet McIntosh. 9 June 1997. "The New Creationism: Biology Under Attack." *The Nation*.

Fisher, Sebern F. 2014. *Neurofeedback in the Treatment of Developmental Trauma: Calming the Fear-Driven Brain*. New York: W. W. Norton & Company.

Gaskins, Suzanne. 2013. "The Puzzle of Attachment: Unscrambling Maturational and Cultural Contributions to the Development of Early Emotional Bonds." In *Attachment Reconsidered: Cultural Perspectives on a Western Theory*, ed. Naomi Quinn and Jeannette Marie Mageo, 33–64. New York: Palgrave Macmillan.

Goldfarb, Kathryn. 2013. "Japan." In *Child Protection and Child Welfare: A Global Appraisal of Cultures, Policy and Practice*, ed. Penelope Welbourne and John Dixon, 144–169. London: Jessica Kingsley Publishers.

   2015. "Developmental Logics: Brain Science, Child Welfare, and the Ethics of Engagement in Japan." *Social Science & Medicine* 143: 271–278.

   2016a. "'Coming to Look Alike': Materializing Affinity in Japanese Foster and Adoptive Care." *Social Analysis* 60(2): 47–64.

2016b. "'Self-Responsibility' and the Politics of Chance: Theorizing the Experience of Japanese Child Welfare." *Japanese Studies* 36(2): 173–189.

2018. "Beyond Blood Ties: Intimate Kinships in Japanese Foster and Adoptive Care." In *Intimate Japan*, ed. A. Alexy and E. Cook, 181–198. Honolulu, HI: University of Hawai'i Press.

Goldfarb, Kathryn and Caroline Schuster. 2016. "Editor's Introduction: (De) materializing Kinship: Holding Together Mutuality and Difference." *Social Analysis* 60(2): 1–12.

Goodman, Roger. 2000. *Children of the Japanese State: The Changing Role of Child Protection Institutions in Contemporary Japan.* New York: Oxford University Press.

Gould, Stephen Jay. 1977. *Ever since Darwin: Reflections in Natural History.* New York: W. W. Norton & Company.

Graves, Joseph L. 2015. "Great Is Their Sin: Biological Determinism in the Age of Genomics." *The ANNALS of the American Academy of Political and Social Science* 661(1): 24–50.

Hacking, Ian. 1996. "The Looping Effects of Human Kinds." In *Causal Cognition: A Multidisciplinary Approach*, ed. D. Sperber, D. Premack and A. J. Premack, 351–383. Oxford: Clarendon Press.

Hayes, P. and T. Habu. 2006. *Adoption in Japan: Comparing Policies for Children in Need.* New York: Routledge.

Hendry, Joy. 1986. *Becoming Japanese: The World of the Pre-School Child.* Manchester: Manchester University Press.

Hertz, Robert. 1973 [1909]. "The Pre-eminence of the Right Hand." In *Right and Left: Essays on Dual Symbolic Classification.* Translated by Rodney Needham and Claudia Needham, ed. Rodney Needham, 3–31. Chicago, IL: University of Chicago Press.

Hinata Bokko. 2009. *Shisetsu de sodatta kodomotachi no ibasyo "Hinata Bokko" to shyakaiteki yōgo [A place to belong for children who were raised in institutional care: Hinata Bokko and social protective care].* Tokyo: Akashi shyoten.

Howell, Signe. 2006. *The Kinning of Foreigners: Transnational Adoption in a Global Perspective.* New York: Berghahn Books.

Ingold, Tim. 1990. "An Anthropologist Looks at Biology." *Man* 25(2): 208–229.

2004. "Beyond Biology and Culture: The Meaning of Evolution in a Relational World." *Social Anthropology* 12(2): 209–221.

2013. "Prospect." In *Biosocial Becomings: Integrating Social and Biological Anthropology*, ed. Tim Ingold and Gisli Palsson, 1–21. Cambridge: Cambridge University Press.

Japanese Society for the Prevention of Child Abuse and Neglect (JaSPCAN). 2010. *Nihon kodomo gyakutai boshi gakkai [Japanese Society for the Prevention of Child Abuse and Neglect].* Materials distributed at 16th annual meeting, Nov. 27–28, 2010.

Jasanoff, Sheila. 2004. "The Idiom of Co-Production." In *States of Knowledge: The Co-Production of Science and Social Order*, ed. S. Jasanoff, 1–12. New York: Routledge.

Keller, Evelyn Fox. 2010. *The Mirage of a Space between Nature and Nurture*. Durham, NC: Duke University Press.

King, Michael Maher. 2012. "Who Cares? Exploring the Disparity in Contemporary Japanese Rates of Tertiary Education Progression between Children from Child Welfare Institutions and the General Population." Master's Thesis, University of Oxford.

Kitanaka, Junko. 2011. *Depression in Japan: Psychiatric Cures for a Society in Distress*. Princeton, NJ: Princeton University Press.

Krieger, Nancy. 2006. "*If 'Race' Is the Answer, What Is the Question? On 'Race,' Racism, and Health: A Social Epidemiologist's Perspective*." http://raceandge nomics.ssrc.org/Krieger/, accessed October 28, 2016.

Levy, Terry M. and Michael Orlans. 2014. *Attachment, Trauma, and Healing: Understanding and Treating Attachment Disorder in Children, Families and Adults*. London: Jessica Kingsley Publishers.

Leinaweaver, Jessaca. 2008. *The Circulation of Children: Kinship, Adoption, and Morality in Andean Peru*. Durham, NC: Duke University Press.

Lock, Margaret. 1993. *Encounters with Aging: Mythologies of Menopause in Japan and North America*. Berkeley, CA: University of California Press.

    2001. "The Tempering of Medical Anthropology: Troubling Natural Categories." *Medical Anthropology Quarterly* 15(4): 478–492.

    2015. "Comprehending the Body in the Era of the Epigenome." *Current Anthropology* 56(2): 151–177.

Lock, Margaret and Vinh-Kim Nguyen. 2010. *An Anthropology of Biomedicine*. Malden, MA: Wiley-Blackwell.

McKinnon, Susan and Sydel Silverman. 2005. "Introduction." In *Complexities: Beyond Nature and Nurture*, ed. Susan McKinnon and Sydel Silverman, 1–20. Chicago, IL: University of Chicago Press.

Mauss, Marcel. 1973. "Techniques of the Body." *Economy and Society* 2(1): 70–88.

Merleau-Ponty, Maurice. 1968. *The Visible and the Invisible*. Translated by Alphonso Lingis. Evanston, IL: Northwestern University Press.

Ministry of Health, Labor, and Welfare (MHLW). 2014. *Shyakaiteki yōgo no genjyō ni tsuite [Present conditions in social protective care]*. March. (Japanese). www.mhlw.go.jp/bunya/kodomo/syakaiteki_yougo/dl/yougo_genjou_01.pdf, accessed August 13, 2015.

Müller-Wille, Staffan and Hans-Jörg Rheinberger. 2012. *A Cultural History of Heredity*. Chicago, IL: University of Chicago Press.

Needham, Rodney. 1960. "The Left Hand of the Mugwe: An Analytical Note on the Structure of Meru Symbolism." *Africa* 30(1): 20–33.

Niewöhner, Jörg. 2011. "Epigenetics: Embedded Bodies and the Molecularisation of Biography and Milieu." *BioSocieties* 6(3): 279–298.

Ortner, Sherry B. 1972. "Is Female to Male As Nature Is to Culture?" *Feminist Studies* 1(2): 5–31.

Oyama, S. 2000. *The Ontogeny of Information: Developmental Systems and Evolution*. Durham, NC: Duke University Press.

Quinn, Naomi and Jeannette Marie Mageo. 2013. "Attachment and Culture: An Introduction." In *Attachment Reconsidered: Cultural Perspectives on a Western Theory*, ed. Naomi Quinn and Jeannette Marie Mageo, 3–32. New York: Palgrave Macmillan.

Robertson, Jennifer. 2002. "Blood Talks: Eugenic Modernity and the Creation of New Japanese." *History and Anthropology* 13(3): 191–216.

Rose, Steven. 1998. *Lifelines: Biology beyond Determinism*. Oxford: Oxford University Press.

Rutter, M. and the English and Romanian Adoptees (ERA) study team. (1998). Developmental Catch-up, and Deficit, Following Adoption after Severe Global Early Privation. *Journal of Child Psychology and Psychiatry* 39(4): 465–476.

Sahlins, Marshall D. 2011. "What Kinship Is," Parts I and II. *Journal of the Royal Anthropological Institute* (n.s.) 17: 2–19, 227–242.

———. 2013. *What Kinship Is – and Is Not*. Chicago, IL: University of Chicago Press.

Schneider, David. 1968. *American Kinship*. Chicago, IL: University of Chicago Press.

Stasch, Rupert. 2009. *Society of Others: Kinship and Mourning in a West Papuan Place*. Berkeley, CA: University of California Press.

Tsuzaki, Tetsuo. 2011. "Minpō kaisei to higyakutaiji no shyakaiteki yōgo: Jidō fukushi no shiten kara" ["Revisions to the civil code and social care for abused children: from a child welfare perspective"]. *Hōritsu Jihō* 83(7): 72–77.

Tsuzaki, Tsuzaki. 2009. *Kono Kuni no Kodomotachi: Yōhogo Jidō Shyakai-teki Yōgo no Nihon-teki Kōchiku; Otona no Kitoku Keneki to Kodomo no Fukushi [This country's children: constructing social care for children in need of care; the vested interests of adults and children's welfare]*. Tokyo: Nihon Kajyo Syuppan.

Vorria, P., Z. Papaligoura, J. Sarafidou, M. Kopakaki, J. Dunn, M. H. van Ijzendoorn and A. Kontopoulou. 2006. "The Development of Adopted Children after Institutional Care: A Follow-Up Study." *Journal of Child Psychology and Psychiatry* 47(12): 1246–1253.

Weismantel, Mary. 1995. "Making Kin: Kinship Theory and Zumbagua Adoptions." *American Ethnologist* 22(4): 685–709.

Weston, Kath. 1991. *Families We Choose: Lesbians, Gays, Kinship*. New York: Columbia University Press.

Wilson, Elizabeth. 2004. *Psychosomatic: Feminism and the Neurological Body*. Durham, NC: Duke University Press.

Yanagisako, Sylvia and Jane Collier. 1987. "Toward a Unified Analysis of Gender and Kinship." In *Gender and Kinship: Essays Toward a Unified Analysis*, ed. Sylvia Yanagisako and Jane Collier, 14–50. Stanford, CA: Stanford University Press.

Zeanah, Charles H., Anna T. Smyke, Sebastian F. Koga and Elizabeth Carlson. 2005. "Attachment in Institutionalized and Community Children in Romania." *Child Development* 76(5): 1015–1028.

8

Kinship in the Andes

Mary Weismantel and Mary Elena Wilhoit

A 2010 webpage on Christian parenting describes what families look like in unequivocal terms: "The ideal, established at the beginning of humanity, is for one man and one woman to join in a ... committed union for a lifetime, conceiving and rearing children."[1]

Anthropologists, of course, have long rebutted statements like this, plucking examples from elsewhere in the world to show how very different peoples' notions of a "traditional family," the "ideal" number of spouses, or the durability of a marriage can be. Except, perhaps, in the Andes. At first glance, twentieth-century anthropological descriptions of kinship in the Andean nations of Ecuador, Peru, and Bolivia[2] almost seem written to order to match an idealized picture of premodern rural life as imagined by US conservatives. This literature describes no plural marriages, female husbands, matrilineages – nothing to disrupt Euro-American ideas about the family. Instead, books like Mayer and Bolton's landmark edited volume on kinship (Bolton and Mayer 1977) depict a familiar-sounding landscape of small houses surrounded by fields, each inhabited by a husband, wife, and children (and perhaps an elderly grand-parent). The bonds between adults appear to be heteropatriarchal and based in marriage, and those between adults and children to be biological and based in birth. These autonomous households are the basic units of a community that appears to be homogeneous and tightly knit, consisting of small family farms with strong links to one another but relatively few to the outside world: the classic Latin American closed corporate community (Harris 1980; Isbell 1977a; Lambert 1977; Wolf 1955, 1957).

Our own work in the Ecuadorian and Peruvian Andes in the late twentieth and early twenty-first centuries, however, has consistently undermined some of the premises built into this picture (Weismantel 1988, 1995, 2001; Wilhoit 2017b). So, too, does other recent research in the region, which has documented a very different kind of social landscape, shaped by, among other things, increased rural landlessness, state and guerilla violence leading to massive upheavals and population shifts (Degregori 1991; Starn 1995a, 1995b; Theidon 2004), transnational outmigration (Miles 2004; Pribilsky 2004, 2007), international adoptions (Anderson 2009; Leinaweaver 2007, 2008), and new reproductive technologies (Roberts 2012).

But how different is this newer picture, really? A closer look at the classic kinship studies from the mid- to late twentieth century reveals that in the Andes, just as in metropolitan centers of the global North, the stability and homogeneity of families was always something of a fiction. Instead of timeless stability, individuals and communities continually responded to the challenges of colonialism, modernity, and globalization with creativity and flexibility. And as in the urban United States, the social fabric of the rural Andes is more heterogeneous than homogeneous, shaped by female agency as well as patriarchy, held together through social ties that are as much socially constructed as biological, and through links that reach between, across, and outside households, families, communities, and nations. In addition to heterosexual households, there are female-headed households – now and in the past. In fact, if we look for comparisons to kinship ideals from the contemporary United States, we find Kath Weston's concept of "chosen families" (1991) to be a closer match than more conservative notions of the heterosexual, nuclear family. However, households in the Andes do differ from Euro-American norms – old and new. There are cultural differences (like the use of four gendered terms to refer to siblings rather than two), but the biggest differences have to do with gender and economics.

Where gender is concerned, Andean literature provides ample evidence to support conservative claims such as James Dobson's assertion that "The primary responsibility for the provision of authority in the home has been assigned to men."[3] In fact, a dissertation about family structure in Ecuador was titled *Es el que manda* [He's the one who gives the orders] (Weiss 1985). That was an urban mestizo case study, however, and the picture looks very different in Quechua and Aymara communities, where most kinship work has been done. There, contradictions between gender equity and inequality have long been the subject of debate among scholars and among indigenous people themselves (Burman 2011).

The most radical difference, though, is economic. In the United States, families are conceptualized primarily as units of consumption (although women's unpaid household labor has been a consistent feminist issue), and anthropologists like Weston describe the links between members of chosen families in primarily affective terms (1997). In contrast, Andean ethnographers old and new describe households as units of production and exchange, not just consumption, in which each member has specific roles and responsibilities. These activities link kin groups to the outside world: in the older literature, through links between humans and nonhumans within an agrarian economy; in newer studies, through participation in local and global markets, including markets in people. The gender dynamics of this participation are unlike those in the United States, where economists can still say, "By traditional family, I mean a husband that works for wages while the wife and children stay home."[4] In the "traditional" Andean family, women and children are full-fledged economic actors.

Just as we conceive of the Andean household as an open system engaged in exchange with other, dissimilar systems, we also look at the anthropological study of kinship as something that is always in dialogue with other systems of thought. Andean ethnographers have been influenced by important trends outside anthropology, especially the indigenista and indigenous movements. Scholars have documented female agency in particular by working with women activists and by taking alternative approaches to literature such as *testimonio*, a popular form of literature in Latin American Studies for some decades (most famously resulting in the publication of "I, Rigoberta Menchu").[5] Like Menchu, many subjects of *testimonio* have been women, and many have used the form as a platform for political influence.

In turn, anthropological publications have influenced activists; they are also widely read within religious missions, NGOs, and state agencies, where they may influence policy in ways we neither intend nor foresee. In evaluating the kinship literature, then, we try to look at its role outside the academy as well as within it.[6]

8.1 Early Twentieth-Century Studies and *"lo Andino"*: The Heyday of Andean Kinship Studies

Ethnographers in the 1960s and 1970s went to the Andes eager to compare their own data to two important schools of research. One was the British school of structural-functional anthropology, with its heavy emphasis on African systems of kinship, marriage, and descent (Evans-Pritchard 1950a, 1950b; Radcliffe-Brown and Forde 1950). The other was new scholarship on the Inka Empire, which suggested that the Andes had its own distinctive model of social organization. Ethnohistorian John Murra used Marx, Mauss, and especially Polanyi in his innovative analysis of Inka political economy (Murra 1975); anthropologist R. T. Zuidema wrote from a Lévi-Straussian structuralist perspective about kinship, religion, myth, and ritual as the symbolic underpinnings of the Inka state (1964). Both scholars sent students into the field to discover whether contemporary communities still structured aspects of their lives according to these principles.

The result was a rich body of publications documenting kinship systems that differed from Africa or Western Europe. Murra's students, like their professor, conceptualized kinship primarily in economic terms (Brush 1977; Mayer 1977a, 1977b, 1980), while Zuidema's emphasized ritual and symbolism (Allen 1988; Isbell 1977a). These studies were often complementary; in contrast, fierce disputes raged between Zuidema and American scholar John Rowe, whose strict empiricism and literal reading of the archive differed markedly from Zuidema's attention to myth and metaphor (Rowe 1979). Aspects of this schism were carried forward by their respective students and echo today.

8.1.1   Kinship and Exchange

As its title suggests, Mayer and Bolton's *Andean Kinship and Marriage* is a South American response to Evans-Pritchard's *African Systems of Kinship and Marriage* (1950a) (as was Maybury-Lewis' 1979 volume on Amazonian social structure). The studies it contained documented novel kinship institutions such as the *sirvanakuy* or "trial marriage" (Carter 1977), as well as South American versions of the Latin American/Mediterranean institution of *compadrazco* or ritual co-parenthood, already documented extensively in Mesoamerica (del Castillo 1989; Gudeman 1971; Mintz and Wolf 1950; Nutini and Bell 1980; Spedding 1998; Van den Berghe and Van den Berghe 1966). The innovative aspect of this work was its emphasis on lateral, synchronic connections between adults of the same generation – siblings, affines, and "fictive kin" – rather than the vertical, diachronic lines of descent emphasized in African kinship studies. Two Quechua terms, *ayni* and *minka*, were seen as indigenous expressions of Polanyi's concepts of reciprocity and redistribution, and as the backbone of social and economic relations in the agrarian community (see also Alberti and Mayer 1974).

This work made three significant contributions. First, it shifted emphasis from an abstract political and legal definition of kinship, as seen for example in Meyer Fortes' (1969) emphasis on the distinction between the legal father or pater and the merely biological "natural" father or genitor, to a picture of kinship as a set of active social and economic links enacted in real life – an emphasis that prefigured Bourdieu's theory of practice. For economic anthropologists such as Mayer, Stephen Brush, and Benjamin Orlove, exchange reinforced social ties between kin, established fictive kinship with non-kin, and created webs of relations between households. Gifts of labor – reciprocal between siblings, unilateral from affines – were foundational for the twentieth-century peasant economy, especially during planting and harvesting. In this description, Andean kinship resembled neither the large co-resident corporate kin groups of Africa and Asia, nor the isolated nuclear families of modern Europe and Euro-America. It constituted a third model.

A second theme is the downplaying of biology. The equal importance given to siblings, compadres, and affines put kin relations initiated as adults on a par with relationships inherited at birth. Although not articulated as such, we can see here the nascent emphasis in the field more broadly on identities as socially constructed rather than biologically determined – a trend that began with Lévi-Strauss and reached its apogee in 1980s feminism with Judith Butler (1990, 2002).

Weismantel's 1980s work on kinship in the Ecuadorian Andes developed this theme. Rather than seeing *compadrazco* as a "fictive" imitation of blood relations between siblings, she reversed the terms, arguing that relations between adult siblings were modeled on chosen relations with compadres. In practice, the "fictive" relationship was the ideal (1988, 1995; see also Collins 1988). Adults did not passively accept kinship ties inherited at birth and then add to them; instead, they actively created all their economic and social relationships over the life course. Kin formation was not static or fixed but flexible and dynamic. Within an extended family of married adult siblings, some dyads were actively developed while others atrophied or turned hostile, with family members choosing to invest instead in relations with non-biological kin.[7] The latter were then turned into kin over time through marriage, *compadrazco* or godparenting, fostering, and adoption.

Third, these studies were innovative for their attention to ecology. This can be attributed directly to Murra's concept of "Andean verticality," which proposed a unique political economy based in the ecological particularity of western South America (1975). In this mountainous geography, changing altitude creates multiple micro- and macro-ecozones that provide richly various resources, from the maritime coasts to high altitude landscapes to the tropical eastern slopes. Murra argued that indigenous people had created a distinctive social geography in response to this environment. Unlike influential models such as Wissler's culture areas (Kroeber 1931; Wissler 1927), Andean households, corporate kin groups, ethnic groups, and polities dispersed themselves across as many different ecological zones as possible, often stretching out into long, narrow strips or even non-contiguous "vertical archipelagos" rather than occupying a single niche. This strategy enabled groups to obtain diverse resources through internal, non-market exchange, rather than through trade with non-kin, ethnic others, or political aliens. The Inka Empire provided its member polities with access to distant resources through mechanisms of gift exchange writ large, using the same principles of *ayni* and *minka* that operated between kin.

Ethnographers found this concept invaluable: it let them see how kin groups and communities used formal exchanges based in biological and fictive ties of consanguinity and affinity to exploit multiple ecosystems. They argued that this system was not only ideally suited to the vertical ecology of the Andes, but allowed indigenous people to protect themselves from a hostile and racist national society, providing a means to gain access to resources through internal, non-monetized, reciprocal exchange between allies, rather than through trade with strangers on unequal terms.

We can see here a tension between depicting the rural Andes as a refuge from modernity or as intrinsically enmeshed with it – a tension that pervades Andean studies, and is often referred to as the debate over "*lo andino*," or what it means to be Andean or an Andeanist (Mayer 1992; Starn 1992). For some authors, *lo andino* is something intrinsically non-Western, non-capitalist, and non-modern; for others, it is indigenous but fully engaged with modernity. Thus while some studies (Brush 1977; Flores Ochoa 1977) emphasized the retention of economic and kinship forms seen as pre-capitalist, others, such as Mayer's classic article on communal land tenure (1977b) or Orlove's study of alpaca farmers (1998) dealt with the articulation of non-capitalist, kin-based exchange systems with national and international capitalist markets.

We belong to the latter camp, and would like to bring this orientation forward in considering twenty-first-century kinship formations. Demographic dynamics are radically changed, but could still be described in Murra's terms, as an even more expansive vertical archipelago. This concept would describe the way that the flood of migrants from the highlands into the cities flows along kinship networks that connect the rural hinterlands and the urban slums, and even the still larger-scale expansion of these networks to encompass the enormous outmigration from South America to the United States and Europe (Miles 2004; Pribilsky 2004, 2007). At the same time, we honor the capacity of indigenous cultural forms to provide a defense or refuge from colonial, postcolonial, racist, and capitalist assaults on indigenous communities – a position held by many indigenous activists.

8.1.2 Kinship and the Sacred

For R. T. Zuidema's students and other researchers interested in religion, it was the ritual aspects of *ayni* and *minka* that were most compelling: the formalities observed in sharing meals, chewing coca, and exchanging toasts of the traditional Andean beer known as *chicha* in Spanish or *aswa* in Quechua (see Allen 1988; Jennings and Bowser's 2009 volume). They documented rituals celebrating life crises, especially funerals (Allen 1988) and first haircutting (Hickman and Stuart 1977; Mayer 1977a). And they described a cycle of fiesta sponsorship with clear parallels to Mesoamerica (Isbell 1977a, 1977b). Consanguineal, affinal, and fictive kin bonds formed the heart of this system, both in the selection of the male–female pairs of sponsors – typically a husband and wife or mother and son – and in the redistributive labor system through which sponsors called upon their social networks to help stage the fiesta: men as performers, women as cooks (Abercrombie 1998). Ethnographers detailed intertwined relations of reciprocity and obligation, asymmetrical and symmetrical bonds, and elaborate rituals of asking for and acknowledging help. Some scholars directly linked *ayni* values to kinship beliefs and practices (Leinaweaver 2005; Mannheim 1991; Van Vleet 2002; Wilhoit 2017b) – they described reciprocity as the "glue" keeping kinship and social hierarchy intact – a comprehensive value ordering social life (Isbell 1977a: 3).

In these studies, too, ecology mattered. These ethnographies knitted together religious thought, kinship structures, and ecosystems in a cosmovision that linked humans and the nonhuman world, especially mountains and bodies of water. Mountains were described as living personages with human-like bodies, linked to one another through kin relations such as husband and wife, parent, and child, or siblings (Allen 1988; Bastien 1985; Harris, Platt and Cereceda 1987). Human relations with these beings were also conceptualized in kin terms, creating a single system that embraced human and geomorphological entities, as seen in two classic and much-cited ethnographies, Catherine Allen's *The Hold Life Has* and Joseph Bastien's *Mountain of the Condor*. These authors suggested continuities between the twentieth century and ethnohistoric kin systems, which blurred the lines between human ancestors and local geological formations.[8]

These relationships were enacted through rituals, especially libations to the *Pacha Mama* or feminine earth deity, mountain peaks, and sacred places (Allen 1988; Isbell 1977b). Allen evocatively depicted everyday rituals that continually reinstated human and nonhuman kinship hierarchies and relationships. We can see Lévi-Strauss' influence here: this is a socially constructed system of material metaphors rather than of biological ties. Symbolic and economic systems overlap in the relationship between ecological zones, which were conceptualized – and actualized – in terms of gender and generation. Unmarried young adults were sent to herd animals in the high grasslands, an arrangement that gave them great freedom to explore their sexuality away from parental eyes; this zone was thus associated with the untamed sexual energy of youth, while the lower cultivated fields were the realm of settled households and social reproduction (Abercrombie 1998; Salomon and Urioste 1991; Weismantel 1988). Dyadic relationships took a more aggressive turn in high-altitude *tinkuy* rituals, in which males from two different communities engaged in ritual battles that could end in injuries and even death (Abercrombie 1998; Harris 1994; Orlove 1994; Urton 1993; Van Vleet 2010). The *tinkuy* concept can be seen broadly as an expression of affinity: sexual tension, hostility, and violence that lead to new life (Harvey 1998; Urton 1993).

Discrepant views of *lo andino* show up here too: some authors depict indigenous communities as egalitarian enclaves of pre-capitalist life, others enmeshment with modernity and active responses to exploitation and external threat. Allen portrayed the indigenous ecological/social system as a fragile whole that could not withstand outside intervention; the outmigration of the young to urban areas, in her eyes, sounded its death knell. In contrast, *Mountain of the Condor* (Bastien 1985), while certainly one of the more romantic and idealized descriptions of verticality as a deeply spiritual system, presented it as a robust defense against outside forces that wanted to "dismember" the mountain's body by dismantling the archipelago of agricultural fields and pasturelands occupied by far-flung kin groups. Although they did not address kinship per se, Nash's ethnography of the tin mines (1979) and Taussig's study of indigenous perceptions of the capitalist economy (1980) deserve mention for further developing this view of *lo andino* as resistance and critique.

In the twenty-first century, indigenous and environmental activism has given new life to these ontologies. Quechua and Aymara beliefs about living mountains have become part of a new "earth politics" that has given them new salience (de la Cadena 2010). We also note their ubiquity in the ever-more-popular indigenous performances of shamanic ritual for tourists; few foreigners leave Bolivia or Peru without learning to make offerings to the Pacha Mama and so absorbing a small part of the ancient belief in kinship with nonhuman entities.

Another contribution to kinship studies was Zuidema's innovative – and controversial – theory of double descent, in which women were descended from women and men from men (1964). His focus was the Inka, but his student Billie Jean Isbell argued that the system was still operating in the Ayacucho region in historic times, based on the evidence of baptismal records in which children inherited their family name from their same-sex parent (1977b). It is possible that contemporary inheritance patterns, in which males and females inherit equally from parents and women and men continue to both hold property independently of one another after marriage, are a legacy of an earlier system of gendered inheritance derived from double descent.

However, John Rowe (1979) strenuously rejected Zuidema's proposition, insisting instead on a somewhat bilateral but strongly patrilateral system not unlike the dominant modern kin systems of Western Europe and Euro-America. Other scholars proposed that the Aymara, in particular, had a more patrilineal system of inheritance. British scholar Denise Arnold rejected these interpretations, arguing that outsiders overlooked equally strong matrilateral tendencies in Aymara kin reckoning (1988). There has also been disagreement over the nature of the *ayllu*, a Quechua word for "family," "kin group," or "descent group" that seems to vary widely in its usage across the region (a debate that took on new life in archaeological circles in 2010 with a controversial definition of "*ayllu*" made by Zuidema student William Isbell).

From the perspective of 2015, we can find some undisputed themes among the controversies. One is that the uncertainty in definition arises from the flexibility and variability of the institution itself: efforts to define the *ayllu* too rigidly may violate its very essence. Nevertheless, patterns stand out. The most significant is that women usually inherit property equally with male siblings. (Birth order inflects this pattern: older children receive substantial gifts of property upon marriage, while the youngest child inherits the house in which they cared for aging parents.) In practice this gender-egalitarian principle can negatively affect women (Weismantel 1988); nevertheless, this structural equity is striking when compared to other agricultural regions of the world such as East Asia and North Africa.

8.2   Later Kinship Studies and Inequality

In kinship studies from the later twentieth and twenty-first centuries, several themes remain salient. Specifically, issues that have long been quintessential in kinship studies including birth order, residence patterns, and questions of affinity versus consanguinity are still paramount in recent literature. At the same time, Andean kinship studies have increasingly incorporated examinations of inequality, violence, migration, transnationalism, and race and gender relations. It is to this variety of issues that we will now turn.

8.2.1   Inequality

Although we have focused thus far on the roles of reciprocity and exchange in kinship relations, kinship is also the site of many complex, hierarchical distinctions and even intrapersonal abuse and violence (see also Carsten, Chapter 6, and Goldfarb, Chapter 7, this volume). Scholars working in the Andes have coupled study of the intricacies of kinship with attention to hierarchies therein, asking how power relations within the home impact relationships outside and vice versa (Harris 1994; Harvey 1994; Van Vleet 2002), and documenting hierarchy or inequality in many kinds of kinship relations, from parent–child, sibling, and affinal relationships to marriage partnerships. The latter, however, have received by far the most scholarly attention largely due to the work of numerous feminist scholars in the region and to interest in the question of "Andean gender complementarity," to be discussed in detail in Part III, as well as to encroaching NGOs' concern with domestic violence.

8.2.2   Violence

Although intrapersonal violence among kin is seen around the Andes and both women and men are observed to commit acts of violence against one another, anthropologists have focused on the physical and verbal violence that women experience at the hands of male partners and in-laws as the most common (Harris 1994; Harvey 1994). Marriage in the Andes is often described as based on practices that may not entail love or easy companionship (Van Vleet 2002: 569), and scholars have noted that respected men are ideally both authoritative in the community *and* in the home; marriage can therefore entail a semi-accepted right to commit physical acts of aggression (Harvey 1994).

In some highland communities, gendered violence among couples is rendered symbolically acceptable even before marriage, in the traditional act of proposition in which the groom's family "attacks" the bride's parents' home, "stealing" the bride (Lambert 1977). Marriage and even sexual lust among couples are thus somewhat symbolically linked to men's violence against women before a bond is community-sanctioned (Harvey 1994). For Penelope Harvey (1994), true gendered "complementarity" may therefore be illustrated most evocatively in the relationship "between spouses who both feed and beat each other" (referencing women and men's roles, respectively) (1994: 73).

Harvey, Olivia Harris, Krista Van Vleet, Marisol de la Cadena, and others have questioned an imposition of Western values in attempts to understand this kind of violence, however. Firstly, this is because wives often stay with husbands who hit them and expect or even condone violence, particularly in times of fiesta or drinking (the same periods in which sexual activity is most prevalent). Additionally, Harvey and de la Cadena have suggested that affinity, rather than gender, is the primary source of permissible violence (de la Cadena 1995; Harvey 1994), highlighting the need to consider the intersection of kinship *and* gender in understanding violence, rather than evaluating it as an affect of gender politics on their own.[9]

Affinal relationships between brothers and sisters-in-law and parents-in-law with daughters/sons-in-law are often described in terms of difficulty or outright brutality, and the burden of these complex relations rests on women as those traditionally moving to live with husbands' families. The relationship between daughters-in-law and mothers-in-law has been described as particularly fraught, and violence between *swiras* (mothers-in-law or *suegras*) and *qhachunis* (daughters-in-law) has long been observed around the Andes, with daughters-in-law subordinate and sometimes denigrated and abused (de la Cadena 1995, 1997; Harvey 1994, 1998; Rens 2003; Van Vleet 2002; Weismantel 1988).

As in regards to inheritance, birth order becomes important in determining responsibility to parents and in-laws, and can affect exposure to affinal control and/or abuse. The obligations of parental care fall generally on the youngest son, whose wife in turn assumes those responsibilities and whose burden may become particularly intense if he migrates for wage labor (Van Vleet 2002). This, in turn, bolsters preference for male children, who will bring new members and help into the house, while females may leave it. Similar such findings led Harvey (1994) to propose that while parents and children, and siblings, are kin, husbands and wives are never truly "kin" in the Andes but remain affines who *create kin* together (in the form of children). A wife can at best hope to have children herself and move out, starting her own kin group and amassing her own power and independence therein (Harvey 1994: 77).

Numerous studies have linked these kinds of subordination within the home with a more systemic exclusion and silencing of Andean women, particularly middle-aged and/or childrearing women, from public and community affairs. Since the 1970s and 1980s traditional divisions of labor in Andean peasant communities, inextricably tied to kinship roles and responsibilities, have been found to exclude women from political arenas while giving them greater responsibility for family and household reproduction (Burman 2011; Bourque and Warren 1981), limiting their authority while over-burdening them with responsibilities for family and community survival. More recently, I. S. R. Pape (2008) noted that the idea that such divisions are "complementary" allows men to claim women influence decision making *at home*, impacting community issues indirectly and through culturally appropriate channels. As she demonstrated, however, women were often not consulted; instead, the positing of "separate but equal" gender relations served to interpret women's exclusion as integral to harmony.

8.2.3 Divisions of Labor

In these studies, harmonious household and community relations depend, then, upon recognition and acceptance of the responsibilities involved in any member's particular position. When women's work relates primarily to family propagation and certain productive/agricultural tasks, however, they become disproportionately responsible for literally creating kin by nourishing and caring for bodies; this becomes, in turn, the site at which women experience judgment and critique.

Famously, de la Cadena (1995) found that their relegation to domestic labor led indigenous women's interrelated gendered and racialized positions to become salient, excusing affinal violence toward them. In "Women are More Indian," she documented women's racial subordination within families they married into as a factor of the ability to work, and in what specific capacity/context. The latter essentially determined race, and as the former was itself determined by gender, women were doomed to remain "more indian" and therefore more subject to control, denigration, and abuse, because of their limited ability to integrate themselves into capitalist modes of production.[10]

Such discussions of women's silencing have influenced broad, negative conceptualizations of a contemporary Latin American gender culture dominated by a sort of inescapable machismo; the idea that cultural tradition and family survival in such areas are anchored in women's subordination (Baud 1997; Jelin 1990). These divisions of labor are *changing*, however, due in part to the growing number of female-headed households around the Andes. Female-headed households have increased in response to a number of factors, including shifting, gendered migration patterns and agricultural transitions following political and economic restructuring, as well as, in Andean Peru, the dramatic and gendered warfare of the 1980s and 1990s. Concomitantly with this, many women have been taking on labors outside the home and fields (Deere and de Leon 2001; 2002; Wilhoit 2017a, 2017b).

As Deere and de Leon (2001, 2002; Deere 2009) among others have described, women are increasingly dominating rural spaces in Latin America and taking over subsistence agricultural work. Critically, however, responsibilities for household reproduction do not seem to be evolving as quickly as gendered workplaces and income strategies. While inheritance remains bilateral in some areas, in practice sons tend to obtain slightly larger and better parcels than daughters (Bolton 1974). And as caps on landownership are increasingly done away with and free trade agreements increase the need to produce cash crops or export goods, land is often consolidated under one child (and/or eventually sold to wealthier families or corporations). This has meant that fewer children can remain on farms or in rural communities and has factored into the growing inequalities seen between urban and rural areas. Women remaining in rural areas, even those with access to farmland, have been forced to diversify their sources of income in order to keep families together.

In many areas of the Andes, therefore, poverty rates have been rising in rural areas and particularly among female-headed households, and women are increasingly represented among temporary, part-time, and low-wage workers, facing the difficulties of balancing work and household needs while, as development scholars have noted, *also* taking responsibility for social services abandoned by the state (Alvarez 1996, 1999; Hays-Mitchell 2002; Moser 2004). Increasingly providing household income while still responsible for family reproduction and domestic labor, women are still forced, in other words, to juggle an astonishing number of roles. In the meantime, studies crossing the past several decades have found that men seem often able to shirk childcare and financial responsibility for family, migrating for long periods of time or spending money earned on other things (Harvey 1994; Wilhoit 2017b). As some women continue to house and feed such partners, Alison Spedding's (1997) contention that Andean men obtain more benefits from marriage than women is very convincing (1997a: 337). The increasing prevalence of women's joint families, as documented by Wilhoit (2017b), suggests growing reluctance to "subsidize" such partners.[11]

8.2.4 Alternative Households

Wilhoit (2017a) worked with single mothers in the Ayacucho region who were primarily landless and who constructed joint households with sisters, mothers, nieces, and aunts but also friends and boarders, creating uniquely supportive situations with biological and non-biological kin. They were more able to engage in horizontal kinds of aid with others who had similar responsibilities, and their choosing to create fluid, non-nuclear families with one another strengthened lasting connections between them, providing them the means, as Wilhoit found, to take on local jobs in development and sometimes even government.

Although these women lacked a specific, occupational community for support, they expressed a reproductive autonomy reminiscent of the market women in many earlier studies, from Florence Babb (1989) to the Buechlers (1996), Weismantel (2001), and Linda Seligmann's (2004) studies. Strenuously diversifying, striving to be "both mother and father" and to provide better futures for their children, single and landless women worked and lived together in rural Ayacucho. Previously, Babb, the Buechlers, Weismantel, and Seligmann had described the unique power that female market vendors have wielded, with Weismantel in particular noting the reproductive authority and even masculinity Andean market women amassed. Women in her study described being self-sufficient mothers, feeding, supporting, and defending children and playing both parental roles. They considered themselves self-sufficient even in reproductive terms (Weismantel 2001: 36, 238, 253). These women's power depended to some extent on a control of the market itself, where they formed bonds that were both economic and affective, of mutual dependency, and fictive or practical kinship (2001: 236).

Despite the difficulty of rural life for women in the Andes, these shifts in kinship and household formation were described in potentially empowering terms, highlighting women's agency, autonomy, and authority. This kind of depiction is incredibly valuable, because in spite of the impact that queer theorists including Weston have had on kinship studies in the *West*, much recent work in the global South, particularly studies focusing on economic development, has tended to postulate (if inadvertently) that alternative households and/or women's changing household strategies must be simply adaptation to hardship. Single mothers have been demonized simply for being single or failing to fit conventional gender roles, and studies of organizing among them are rarely celebratory or positive; this is doubly or triply the case when subjects are poor (Baud 1997; Chant 1985, 2002; Lind 2003). Some development scholars have noted that single mothers in "extended" households are less vulnerable to poverty than those living alone (see Trent and Harlan 1994), but these have generally assumed the importance of biological kin. Andean anthropologists have long provided important correctives to this.

Critically, such fluidity between households had been discussed as both economic and affective practice in what Leinaweaver (2007, 2008) called the "circulation of children." In keeping with studies on women's work, this phenomenon, consisting of informal adoption practices among families and/or between friends and compadres, was also a site at which unequal social relations became apparent.

8.2.5 Adoption and *Compadrazco*

The circulation of children has been common in many areas of the Andes, with practices therein varying from permanent incorporation of a child into another family to temporary care arrangements, to "patron–clientelism," in which children provide labor in exchange for providing resources such as education (Leinaweaver 2007, 2008; Seligmann 2004: 122; Van Vleet 2002, 2008). Children in such arrangements are generally moved from poorer households to wealthier ones, whether these are the homes of parents' siblings, compadres, neighbors, or virtual strangers (as in the many stories of women actively giving up babies they could not care for see Van Vleet 2009). For Leinaweaver, therefore, adoption can be viewed in terms of "improving oneself": that becomes the primary reason for sending children to live with wealthier or urban relatives. Conversely, sending children to poorer or rural families may allow parents to achieve that goal.

Ties of *compadrazco* have also been assessed in terms of desire to improve one's own lot in life. *Compadrazco* is a vastly important social tie between households in many areas of the Andes, superseding even sibling and marriage ties. In *compadrazco* relations, a sponsoring person or couple assumes the spiritual aspect of parenting a child or a married couple, creating kinship with the individual(s) and his or her parents. This relationship, both part of Catholic practice around the world and also something documented in the Andes pre-conquest, is a special relationship demanding respect and formality on the part of children, and placing god-parents or compadres in the role of providing for god-children, disciplining when necessary and mediating disputes between god-children and spouses, in-laws, and sometimes siblings (Gudeman 1971; Mayer 1974). Given that compadres can be called upon to provide aid in times of need, many families seek wealthier compadres or compadres with access to greater social capital. Compadres are a sort of kin-as-resource, and white anthropologists working in the Andes, arriving with trappings and racial signifiers of wealth or power, have sometimes found themselves becoming comadres or compadres to a large number of local children (Isbell 1977b; Weismantel 1988).

While both *compadrazco* and informal adoption practices can foster closeness across social groups, they may also exacerbate inequality. In the rural Andes, wealth and success are associated with having many children – both as a measure of one's ability to support dependents, and because dependents produce wealth through their labor. As has often been noted, the word for orphan is also the word for poor person: poverty of kin is poverty in all regards. Similarly, people desire children, but because giving birth does not define motherhood there is a tendency for younger and poorer women and men to lose children to those who are older, better established, and more well-to-do (Weismantel 1995). While this is often understood as good and necessary for children who are raised in households where there is enough to eat instead of going hungry, or may go to live with a relative who can send them to school, it also results in a loss of reproductive rights for poor women.

Official adoption processes can also highlight racial, class-based, and gendered inequalities. In formal adoption processes, of course, children are often adopted into wealthier families, and in transnational adoptions, children are generally taken from poorer homes or homes in the global South into wealthier (whiter) homes in the North (Cardarello 2009; Fonseca 2009; Leifsen 2009; Leinaweaver and Seligmann 2009). These shifts are symbolically seen as "moral hierarchies" as Jeannine Anderson (2009) has summarized; children are assumed to be moving from abandonment and institutional care to families with presumed stability, capital, and "values" (i.e., wealthier, white families) (Anderson 2009; Leifsen 2009; Leinaweaver and Seligmann 2009). Such processes highlight and can exacerbate extant inequalities.

8.2.6 Race and Kinship

Clearly then, questions of racial subordination, *mestizaje*, and the post-colonial power of whiteness are important in Andean kinship studies, and many scholars working in the Andes have discussed the open and more subliminal forms of racism plaguing social life both inside and outside the home (Canessa 2005, 2012; Orlove 1998; Poole 1997; Wade 2008; Weismantel 1997, 2001; Weismantel and Eisenman 1998; Whitten 2008). Weismantel (2001) has repeatedly analyzed the interrelated ways in which race and gender together inform Andean positionalities and described the ways in which indigenous women's bodies, in particular, become sites for racial subordination. And as she and Canessa (2005) among others have explained, race is not an issue exclusively of pigment, but involves myriad markers – size, wealth, hairiness, accessories, technologies, and gender. Things such as food, clothing, and language reveal or bestow race, separating "Indians" and "non-Indians."

Literal skin color is also an important marker of positionality within and outside kinship groups, however (Anderson 2009: 191; de la Cadena 1995; Roberts 2012). Roberts (2012), for example, in a wide-ranging and theoretically insightful study of assisted reproduction in Ecuador, found that the desire for multiple, overlapping kin ties and racial preference influenced the decisions made by urban women. Defying the advice of medical professionals who advised anonymous, unrelated egg donors because they assumed that every child should have only one mother and father, these women preferred to ask close kin to donate eggs – expressly because they hoped to share maternity with female kin (Roberts 2012); they were also encouraged, however, to seek lighter offspring when having in vitro fertilization or surrogate children with an egg donor. In keeping with this, nicknaming children after gradations in skin color (i.e., "*negra/negro, gringa/gringo*") is a long-accepted practice. While this is sometimes described as entailing a kind of affection, children in Wilhoit's study expressed discomfort with such labels. In Ayacucho, where race and poverty became key predictors of victimization during the terrible warfare between the Shining Path and the Peruvian military, people do not, today, particularly like to identify with a specific race in many contexts. Both militarized groups' brutal exploitation, torture, and massacre of local peasant communities and families clarified most forcefully the stakes of racial and class-based inequality there.

8.2.7 Migration

During and following the warfare in Peru, rural to urban and also transnational migration increased significantly. Migration is not at all a new phenomenon in Andean areas, however, and studies of migration in Andean regions have long highlighted experiences with racialization as well as affects on kinship strategies. Migration patterns have greatly impacted contemporary family relationships (Pribilsky 2007; Radcliffe 1990) and served as an important impetus for scholars beginning to study the "household" as fluid (Buechler and Buechler 1971).[12] Historically, both seasonal/local and transnational migration has often been assumed carried out in the interest of family, rather broadly conceived, as remittances have been a primary reason for labor migration from the South to West. Examining migration patterns, however, scholars have also noted its role in heightening a kind of perception of unequal access to capital at local, national, and international levels, and its role in perpetuating inequalities in racial and gendered as well as class-based terms.

Miles (2000) and Pribilsky (2007) described the former phenomenon. While family members in sending communities may benefit materially from remittances and gifts, they can also have an exaggerated perception of migrants' financial success, demanding more than those returning can easily afford. Pribilsky also explained that migration affects parent–child dynamics in powerful ways, describing international migrants' work in maintaining family ties with wives and children back in Ecuador as difficult and critical to their well-being. As he documented in an excellent ethnography on binational Ecuadorian marriages, kin ties between males are the conduit for migration, while affinal ties between women and men keep kinship structures intact despite years and even decades of separation.

While Pribilsky described the tactics employed by separated families to stay in touch across continents, Miles (2000) examined families who had migrated together, finding that relations therein could also become difficult in new settings. Children who migrated from rural areas and were living in poverty in the city experienced stress at observing the experiences of the wealthy, leading to family conflicts. Gendered dynamics within the family also became stressful as parents in urban settings guarded daughters' chastity more carefully. The latter was seen as reflective of a father's control and authority (and a source of pride or shame); Miles suggested such control appeared more important for families that migrated to the city from a rural area. When peasant men living in urban areas were seen as rural/ traditional or indigenous, they particularly needed respect from others in similar social positions (2000: 63). This resulted in daughters' frustrations; young women in Miles' study described open anger at their own poverty, gendered subordination, and the unattainability of wealth and Western ideals of beauty that they encountered (2000: 69–71).

The forms that migration patterns take, and the gendered effects of migration, vary considerably across studies, however. Sarah Radcliffe (1990) described the role of gendered divisions of labor within the household as impacting women's responsibilities for labor migration, while Canessa (1997) found that gendered differences in labor migration gave men a greater burden or obligation to leave the community (see also Pribilsky 2007). Wilhoit (2017b) found, conversely, that women's lesser ability to migrate for work, something they sought as local wage labor was scarce, was to their detriment; men could make far more money leaving families behind, while women with children had a perceived responsibility to stay put and care for children. Men's increasing mobility did not always mean more resources for families.

8.3   Continuities

As should be clear, there is vast complexity, diversity, and also continuity throughout decades of social sciences research on Andean kinship. Among the continuities are the production of kin through substance including food and earth as well as biological input, the interdependence of race, gender, and labor relations, and ongoing debates over the nature of gender equality, as we will briefly elaborate here.

To explain the complexity and diversity in findings, some research we have not yet touched on suggested alternative, specifically Andean conceptualizations of reproduction itself that do not (and have never) replicate the nature/culture duality of Western thought. Instead, such conceptualizations might be more readily described using feminist theories of "social reproduction" or "natureculture."

8.3.1   Social Reproduction and Natureculture

Weismantel's work on this topic developed out of observing seeming contradictions in her interlocutors' attitudes towards race. They adamantly insisted that racial differences between bodies could be seen, felt, and even smelled, rather than being socially constructed; at the same time, they talked about people changing their race during their lives (Weismantel and Eisenman 1998). The solution to this seeming conundrum lies in notions of the physical body that depend less on genetics or qualities fixed at birth, and more in the constitution of the body through ingestion and other daily bodily practices. Eating together, living in the same immediate environment, and interacting with others feed, shape, and alter the body. This way of thinking affects not only race, but kinship: adoption and fostering can be a means to create kin who literally become "flesh of their flesh" through ingesting the same foods, air, water, and sensory experiences over an extended period (Leinaweaver 2008; Weismantel 1995).

Ethnohistoric data suggests an ecological component to this sharing, through eating plants and animals raised on a family's own lands, which may be seen as eating or drinking a personified or deified mountain or spring or consuming products that originate in *ayllu* ancestors. Social reproduction also takes literal form in the knowledge that agricultural products are the products of collective family and community labor, which literally sustains, feeds, and grows children. A nature-cultural understanding of the person as the product of collective or social reproduction, with a corresponding de-emphasis on genitor and birth mother as the only parents has also been described more recently (Weismantel 1995; Weismantel and Eisenman 1998). The contributions of sperm, egg, birthing, and breastfeeding are all recognized as necessary aspects of reproduction, but so too are growing food, providing water, healing injuries and illnesses, and teaching language, song, and skills.

There are several implications to these findings. One is that people actively create complex, overlapping webs of kin, and are comfortable with ambiguous kin relationships. For example, in the 1980s, Weismantel found that adults often described having had more than one mother or father at different points in their lives, all of whom they considered parents to different degrees. It was also the case that grandmothers often assumed the role of mother because true motherhood was associated with maturity, whereas young birth mothers were considered too immature to fully parent their children. As a result, and highly resonant with the later work of Leinaweaver and Wilhoit, a child might grow up thinking of her birth mother as an older sister and her grandmother as her mother – while recognizing the other set of relations as secondary (Weismantel 1995). Like other aspects of "traditional" Andean kinship, then, these concepts have taken on new form in the twenty-first century rather than disappearing.

Along the same lines, questions of gender equality have characterized kinship studies across eras and have shifted in response to changing political and social climates. There is ample evidence throughout the corpus discussed here to demonstrate that women in indigenous Andean communities suffer from gender inequality. Gendered violence, female poverty, and restricted roles in the public sphere and formal sector have been described. But on the other hand, historical studies as well as more recent work have described dual inheritance and uniquely gender-sensitive structural principles of gender complementarity known as *chachawarmi*.

8.3.2 Gender Complementarity

The notion of gender complementarity has a long history in Andean studies, but was formally articulated by several scholars in the 1970s and 1980s, especially British anthropologist Olivia Harris (1980), and Billie Jean Isbell (1977a) as gender became a focus of research. Harris described relationships between men and women as complementary as well as combative. These scholars argued that gender was different in the Andes than in the Western tradition, where the full-fledged, ideal human being was conceptualized as male, while female was incomplete and dependent. In Andean culture, they said, the full-fledged adult human being ("*jaq*" in Aymara) was conceptualized as a married person, half of a male–female pair. Neither male nor female was complete without the other: the basic unit of humanity was not an individual, but rather the "*chachawarmi*," the male–female unit (Burman 2011; Harris 1980, 1994).

The Aymara term *chachawarmi* or its Quechua variant, *jariwarmi* (orthography may vary, i.e., *qariwarmi*, *khariwarmi*), joins words that are usually translated as "man" and "woman." It may refer to two humans, one male and one female: a married couple, or a pair of fiesta sponsors or *padrinos*, for example. But this is a limited and, some would argue, a distorted sense of a word that is better conceptualized as the joining of two opposed but symbiotic principles, rather than a literal description of two sexes. It can apply to two people of the same gender who are linked together, notably the dual leaders who ruled indigenous polities from the Inka down to local Aymara communities today, whose relationship could be described variously as: spatially "upper" and "lower," "older" and "younger" siblings, "male" and "female," or "husband" and "wife" to one another.[13] Despite the apparent inequality between the two terms, they are nevertheless supposed to be equal in rank and power, although the "upper" leader can represent both. It can also apply to one individual, in which case it refers to the joining of masculine and feminine properties within a single body and person.

Scholars have seen the implications of this concept very differently. One of the most sympathetic discussions is by Catherine Allen (1988). In her understanding, the fact that any individual of any sex or gender is seen as containing both principles allows Andean people to inhabit a cultural system with separate and interdependent gender roles and expectations, while allowing individuals to deviate from expectations according to necessity or inclination. In her fieldwork, she saw that while farmers insisted on the gender complementarity of certain tasks (most famously in plowing, when men vigorously plunge the phallic-shaped *chaquitaclla* or foot-plow into the earth while women follow behind, taking round potatoes out of bags slung over their bellies and placing them in the holes), in fact everyone did both kinds of work. Allen similarly recounted a moment when two male interlocutors congratulated her for learning to spin wool – one of the most feminine of tasks – with the words, "You're a real *warmi* (woman) now!" As they spoke, both men were themselves spinning (1988: 59).

A transgender lens can be applied to this concept as well. Although understudied, there is evidence that rural Andean society allows for individuals to adopt the clothing and working lives of a gender different from the one they were assigned at birth, and even to enter into marriages based on their chosen gender (i.e., an individual who transitions socially from male to female might then marry a cisgender male [Paulson 2003]). However, at least one Aymara intellectual has used the concept to argue that lesbianism is a deviant Western practice with no place in Andean society (Rivera Cusicanqui 1996).

When first introduced, this conceptualization of complementarity and unity resonated with liberal feminist goals in the United States and UK. It undermined conservative notions of male supremacy as universal, especially in "traditional" societies, while reinforcing the gender binary and heteronormativity. It placed woman at man's side within marriage as his equal partner, and emphasized interdependence between the sexes rather than female autonomy.

In the intervening years, two distinct readings of the principle emerged. Some looked closely at the conceptual underpinnings of *chachawarmi* and found it to be a more radical conceptualization than it even initially appeared, serving, in part, as a criticism of colonialism, racism, sexism, Eurocentric imperialism, and the inferiorization of indigenous tradition of thought. But on the other hand, researchers and activists who looked critically at the workings of Andean marriage and social life often found that the reality was far less ideal for women; many found that women were silenced or subordinated in ways facilitated by the very divisions of space and labor accompanying *chachawarmi* (Bourque and Warren 1981; Harris 1980; Luykx 1999; Pape 2008). As Burman (2011) has summarized, "complementarity" could, therefore, really imply something other than *harmony*, perhaps even a continual cycle of contestation and reconstructed coherence.

One easy solution to these contradictions appeared, at least to some activists, to be the imposition of a timeline. Some argued that inequality was introduced into an egalitarian society by modernity, European colonialism, or the Inkas (Silverblatt 1987). Others assumed that issues like domestic abuse and increasing female-headed households were recent phenomena caused by social upheavals that undermined traditional marriage. Decolonial philosopher María Lugones has asserted, for example, that it is simply erroneous to use the Western concept of gender to understand Aymara culture. Like some Bolivian activists, she sees gender itself as an entirely *colonial* imposition – one that will no longer have relevance in a decolonized world (Lugones 2007, 2011).

Many Aymara intellectuals are currently engaged in fierce debate on this point. Most, including women fighting to have a larger political role, reject feminism as a Western imposition and see the concept of *chachawarmi* as evidence that the precolonial Andes were free of patriarchy, misogyny, or machismo. As scholars like Burman (2011) have described, indigenous activists have used the term as emblematic of a notion of precolonial equality, when women and men completed one another and were equally respected and valued. The term thus forms part of a "decolonization project" and rejection of the forms of subjugation inherent in colonialism. Other writers and activists, notably Julieta Paredes, disagree with such an orientation (2008).

We find it prudent, in light of the fact that these debates reflect and affect real women and men's lives, yet are being articulated here at a removed, international, and scholarly level, to remind readers that variability and even contradiction are always part of social life, so that the coexistence of these seemingly incompatible gender patterns may not be so surprising after all. This is especially true in a region as large and varied as the Andes. We also take this opportunity to direct the readers' attention to *testimonio*, a final and key site at which the complex and contradictory ideals and practices of complementarity and power struggles within families can be observed throughout Andean studies.

As a form of literature that attempts to allow interlocutors to speak almost completely for themselves, *testimonio* has been revelatory of Andean experience for many decades and has both reflected clear and disturbing gender inequalities *and* important, sometimes overlooked examples of women's and men's collaborative agency in their dealings with family and society. The *testimonio* of Gregorio Condori Mamani and Asunta Condori, for example, recorded in the mid-1970s by Peruvian anthropologists Ricardo Valderrama Fernández and Carmen Escalante Gutierrez (1996), seems to highlight gender subordination and violence as well as agency. While Asunta's narrative is much shorter than Gregorio's and recounts repeated incidences of domestic abuse, she highlights the fact that women pick the *padrinos* for a couple's marriage, asserting that this is a powerful decision given that *padrinos* will serve as the mediators of marital disputes.[14]

Another famous example, *The World of Sofia Velazquez*, recounted considerable female autonomy and economic independence as well as the importance of family (Buechler and Buechler 1996). Velazquez remained a single mother, describing marriage as a barrier or distraction, and was highly financially independent. While she enjoyed keeping lovers at times, she saw them as secondary or disposable, utilizing kin ties with other women to facilitate economic success and valuing her relationship with her daughter above all. Divergently and yet similarly, famous labor organizer Domitilia de Chungara, the subject of a 1978 *testimonio* by Moema Vizzier, wielded a great deal of authority in rallying others working in the Bolivian tin mines, all the while promoting the idea that Bolivian women's struggle was one for economic, not gendered, equality and one that must be fought at their husbands' sides.

Given these present *and* past complexities and continuities, we clearly advise against reification of any particular gender relations and against reification of the male–female-headed, nuclear household in places like the rural Andes. It would be a mistake to write the complementarity concept off as a romantic misunderstanding of indigenous culture by white outsiders – as we write, indigenous activists in Bolivia are actively championing, and debating the meaning and implications of, *chachawarmi* and using it to design new social systems. We also advise against the (US-derived) idea that female-headed households mean poverty, despair, and unhappy children. Families in the Andes have been innovative and tireless in their political, economic, and social strategies in spite of difficult circumstances, recently and in the past. Ultimately, this may be a time when we need to sit on the sidelines and watch while twenty-first-century Andean women and men decide the future of family and of gender – as ideals and as everyday practices.

8.4   By Way of Conclusion

A long-held image of Andean kinship as consisting of nuclear families as autonomous, homogeneous social units based on a heteropatriarchal sexual bond between man and woman and descent based in blood is, clearly, complete neither for past scholars and/or populations nor for contemporary ones. Instead, as we have endeavored to explain, ties between households may be as strong or stronger than within. Relations between friends and coworkers may *become* kin ties; and substances other than blood, such as food, may be equally constitutive of kin in the form of adoption, fostering, and non-reproductive technologies.

Both households and communities in the Andes are highly heterogeneous, and issues of inequality, racial divisions, intersectionality, and transnational ties are paramount in the decisions that individuals make regarding their kinship strategies. The great strength of Andean kinship studies lies in the ability of old and new studies to (1) show-case an alternative indigenous system, not as a vanishing relic, but as a resilient response to changing historical circumstances; (2) cast new light on taken-for-granted premises in Euro-American and European kinship studies, including the definition of what is "old" and "new."

Andean subjects have consistently responded to the challenges of colonialism and neo-colonialism, of global capitalism, and of religious and other social shifts with creativity and flexibility. Non-nuclear, non-patriarchal, and non-heteronormative forms have long existed in Andean kinship systems, as have more traditionally expected structures. The kinship arrangements we see in the Andes today are heteroge-neous, built through social ties that are as much socially constructed as biological, and rife with ties between households, towns, and even nations. As much as Andeanists can learn from ongoing and innova-tive approaches to kinship theory in anthropology and across the social sciences, kinship studies has much to learn from Andeanists and from Andean people.

Notes

1. www.insight.org/resources/articles/parenting/what-is-a-christian-family.html#sthash.1XysnNaA.dpuf, accessed September 1, 2018.
2. For reasons of space, we omit discussion of the Andean regions of Colombia, Argentina, and Chile.
3. From "Straight Talk to Men," http://drjamesdobson.org/Solid-Answers/Answers?a=c4b8312e-8ab5-4c90-877d-28c4aba0a225, accessed September 1, 2018.
4. http://rdwolff.com/content/what-exactly-traditional-american-family-and-how-it-modeled-feudal-economic-system, accessed September 1, 2018.
5. *Testimonio* is essentially one or more individuals' life story, recorded and published by an ethnographer or social scientist. John Beverley and Mary Louise Pratt have called it a kind of "autoethnography" (see Beverley 2004); an attempt to get closer to a particular kind of "truth" by allowing subjects to truly speak for themselves and have their life narratives transcribed word for word. The most famous *testimonio* subject, Rigoberta Menchu, has spoken explicitly about the function many anthropologists have seen in the form, that of representing the lived realities of a larger group of community through retelling one's own story, using one's own experiences to make broader claims about societal patterns, gender relations, and kinship strategies as well as political issues.
6. Regretfully, this article makes only passing mention of some important work on kinship in the Andes: the study of Inkaic

kinship systems, most closely associated with Dutch scholar R. T. Zuidema (1964). Our focus here is the twentieth and twenty-first centuries.

7. Weismantel's article was published together with a challenge by South Asianist Susan McKinnon, a student of Schneider, who found its emphasis on economic factors too deterministic. The article, McKinnon's critique, and Weismantel's rebuttal can all be found in Volume 22 of *American Ethnologist* (1995).

8. One widely republished ethnohistoric document, a sketch by the Inka prince Pachacuti Yamqui, shows human females and males as descended respectively from natural and celestial features: the moon and sun, morning and evening star, ocean and earth.

9. Supporting this, Weismantel (1988) discussed witnessing a *man* being beaten by his wife and daughter. The man was in the rare, subordinate situation of residing with his landowning wife and her kin.

10. Labor has also been a reason for preferring male offspring. Sons are seen as working more, more useful for the family, and less likely to leave after marriage (see Rens 2003 among others).

11. Van Vleet (2002) found similarly that while marriage in the Sullk'ata region of Bolivia was based on idealized gender complementarity, Sullk'atas recognized that women, even married women, contributed more labor to the household than men (569–570).

12. The Buechlers found it difficult to pin down family parameters in 1970s La Paz, seeking a flexible way of describing family ties as related to income and migratory strategies (see also Buechler and Buechler 1993).

13. For an interesting West African comparison, see Amadiume (1987).

14. Rens' (2003) dissertation, focusing on the life stories of a few interlocutors in a *testimonio*-like style interspersed with commentary, similarly describes women's strategic uses of *compadrazco* ties. Her interlocutors take abusive husbands to be admonished by *padrinos*, thereby achieving peace. While she also discusses general preference for male children, women in her study also control the important decision of whether their daughters will attend school.

References

Abercrombie, Thomas. 1998. *Pathways of Memory and Power*. Madison, WI: University of Wisconsin Press.

Alberti, Giorgio and Enrique Mayer. 1974. "Reciprocidad Andina: Ayer y Hoy." In *Reciprocidad e intercambio en los Andes peruanos*, ed. Giorgio Alberti and Enrique Mayer, 13–36. Lima: Instituto de Estudios Peruanos.

Allen, Catherine. 1988. *The Hold Life Has: Coca and Cultural Identity in an Andean Community*. Washington DC: Smithsonian Institution.

Alvarez, Sonia. 1996. "Concluding Reflections: Redrawing the Parameters of Gender Struggle." In *Emergences: Women's Struggles for Livelihood in Latin America*, ed. John Friedmann, R. Abers and L. Autler, 153–184. Los Angeles, CA: University of California Press.

1999. "Advocating Feminism: The Latin American Feminist NGO 'Boom.'" *International Feminist Journal of Politics* 1(2): 181–209.

Amadiume, Ifi. 1987. *Male Daughters, Female Husbands: Gender and Sex in an African Society*. London: Palgrave Macmillan.

Anderson, Jeanine. 2009. "Assembling and Disassembling Families." *The Journal of Latin American and Caribbean Anthropology* 14(1): 185–198.

Arnold, Denise. 1988. Matrilineal Practice in a Patrilineal Setting: Rituals and Metaphors of Kinship in an Andean Ayllu. Dissertation, University College London.

Babb, Florence. 1989. *Between Field and Cooking Pot: The Political Economy of Market Women in Peru*. Austin, TX: University of Texas Press.

Bastien, Joseph. 1985. *Mountain of the Condor: Metaphor and Ritual in an Andean Ayllu*. Long Grove, IL: Waveland Press.

Baud, Michiel. 1997. "Patriarchy and Changing Family Strategies: Class and Gender in the Dominican Republic." *History of the Family* 2(4): 355–378.

Beverley, John. 2004. *Testimonio: On the Politics of Truth*. Minneapolis, MN: University of Minnesota Press.

Bolton, Ralph. 1974. "Tawanku: Vínculos intermaritales." In *Reciprocidad e intercambio en los Andes peruanos*, ed. Giorgio Alberti and Enrique Mayer, 153–170. Lima: Instituto de Estudios Peruanos

Bolton, Ralph and Enrique Mayer, eds. 1977. *Andean Kinship and Marriage*. Washington DC: American Anthropological Association.

Bourque, Susan and Kay Warren. 1981. *Women of the Andes: Patriarchy and Social Change in Two Peruvian Towns*. Ann Arbor, MI: University of Michigan Press.

Brush, Stephen B. 1977. *Mountain, Field, and Family: The Economy and Human Ecology of an Andean Valley*. Philadelphia, PA: University of Pennsylvania Press.

Buechler, Hans and Judith-Maria. 1971. *The Bolivian Aymara*. Foreword by George and Louise Spindler. Case Studies in Cultural Anthropology. New York: Holt, Rinehart & Winston.

1993. "Networks Domesticated: Work and Household Economies among Producers and Vendors in La Paz, Bolivia." *Anthropology of Work Review* 13(4–1): 3–5.

1996. *The World of Sofia Velasquez: The Autobiography of a Bolivian Market Vendor*. New York: Columbia University Press.

Burman, Anders. 2011. "Chachawarmi: Silence and Rival Voices on Decolonisation and Gender Politics in Andean Bolivia." *Journal of Latin American Studies* 43(1): 65–91.

Butler, Judith. 1990. *Gender Trouble: Gender and the Subversion of Identity*. New York: Routledge.

2002. "Is Kinship Always Already Heterosexual?" *Differences: A Journal of Feminist Cultural Studies* 13(1): 14–44.

Canessa, Andrew. 1997. "Género, lenguaje y variación en Pocobaya, Bolivia." In *Más allá del silencio: las fronteras de género en los Andes*, ed. Denise Y. Arnold, 233–250. La Paz: ILCA/CIASE.

2005. "Introduction: Making the Nation on the Margins." In *Natives Making Nation: Gender, Indigeneity and the State in the Andes*, ed. A. Canessa, 3–31. Tucson, AZ: University of Arizona Press.

2012. *Intimate Indigeneities: Race, Sex, and History in the Small Spaces of Andean Life*. Durham, NC: Duke University Press.

Cardarello, Andréa. 2009. "The Movement of the Mothers of the Courthouse Square: 'Legal Child Trafficking,' Adoption and Poverty in Brazil." *The Journal of Latin American and Caribbean Anthropology* 14(1): 140–161.

Carter, William E. 1977. "Trial Marriage in the Andes." In *Andean Kinship and Marriage*, ed. Ralph Bolton and Erique Mayer, 177–216. Washington DC: American Anthropological Association.

Chant, Sylvia. 1985. "Single-Parent Families: Choice or Constraint?" *Development and Change* 16(4): 635–656.

2002. "Researching Gender, Families and Households in Latin America: From the 20th into the 21st Century." *Bulletin of Latin American Research* 21(4): 545–575.

Collins, Jane. 1988. *Unseasonal Migrations: The Effects of Rural Labor Scarcity in Peru*. Princeton, NJ: Princeton University Press.

de la Cadena, Marisol. 1995. "'Women Are More Indian': Ethnicity and Gender in a Community Near Cuzco." In *Ethnicity, Markets and Migration in the Andes: At the Crossroads of History and Anthropology*, ed. Brooke Larson and Olivia Harris with Enrique Tandetter, 329–348. Durham, NC: Duke University Press.

1997. "Matrimonio y etnicidad en comunidades Andinas (Chitipampa, Cusco)." In *Más allá del silencio: las fronteras de género en los Andes*, ed. Denise Arnold, 123–150. La Paz: ILCA/CIASE.

2010. "Indigenous Cosmopolitics in the Andes: Conceptual Reflections beyond 'Politics.'" *Cultural Anthropology* 25(2): 334–370.

Deere, Carmen Diana. 2009. "The Feminization of Agriculture?: The Impact of Economic Restructuring in Rural Latin America." In *The Gendered Impacts of Liberalization: Towards "Embedded Liberalism"?* ed. S. Razavi, 99–130. New York: Routledge.

Deere, Carmen Diana and Magdalena de Leon. 2001. *Empowering Women: Land and Property Rights in Latin America*. Pittsburgh, PA: University of Pittsburgh Press.

2002. "Who Owns the Land? Gender and Land-Titling Programmes in Latin America." *Journal of Agrarian Change* 1(3): 440–467.

Degregori, Carlos Ivan. 1991. "Por que aparecio Sendero Luminoso en Ayacucho? El desarrollo de la educacion y la generacion del 69 en

Ayacucho y Huanta." In *Historizar el pasado vivo en America Latina*, 1–108. www.historizarelpasadovivo.cl/es_contenido.php, accessed October 23, 2018.

Del Castillo, Angel Montes. 1989. *Simbolismo y poder: un estudio antropológico sobre compadrazco y priostazgo en una comunidad andina, 21*. Barcelona: Anthropos Editorial.

Evans-Pritchard, Edward E. 1950a. "Kinship and the Local Community among the Nuer." In *African Systems of Kinship and Marriage*, ed. A. R. Radcliffe-Brown, 360–391. London: Oxford University Press.

   1950b. "Marriage Customs of the Luo of Kenya." *Africa: Journal of the International African Institute* 20(2): 132–142.

Flores Ochoa, J. A. 1977. *Pastores de Puna*. Lima: Instituto de Estudios Peruanos.

Fonseca, Claudia. 2009. "Transnational Connections and Dissenting Views." In *International Adoption: Global Inequalities and the Circulation of Children*, ed. Diana Marre and Laura Briggs, 154–173. New York: New York University Press.

Fortes, Meyer. 1969. *Kinship and the Social Order: The Legacy of Lewis Henry Morgan*. Chicago, IL: Aldine Publishing Company.

Gudeman, Stephen. 1971. "The Compadrazco As a Reflection of the Natural and Spiritual Person." *Proceedings of the Royal Anthropological Institute of Great Britain and Ireland* 1971: 4–71.

Harris, Olivia. 1980. "The Power of Signs: Gender, Culture and the Wild in the Bolivian Andes." In *Nature, Culture and Gender*, ed. Carol MacCormack and Marilyn Strathern, 70–94. Cambridge: Cambridge University Press.

   1994. "Condor and Bull: The Ambiguities of Masculinity in Northern Potosí." In *Sex and Violence: Issues in Representation and Experience*, ed. Penelope Harvey and Peter Gow, 40–65. London: Routledge.

Harris, Olivia, Tristan Platt and Verónica Cereceda. 1987. *Tres reflexiones sobre el pensamiento andino*. La Paz: Hisbol.

Harvey, Penelope. 1994. "Domestic Violence in the Peruvian Andes." In *Sex and Violence: Issues in Representation and Experience*, ed. Penelope Harvey and Peter Gow, 66–89. New York: Routledge.

   1998. "Los 'hechos naturales' de parentesco y género en un contexto andino." In *Gente de carne y hueso: las tramas de parentesco en los Andes*, ed. Denise Y. Arnold, 69–82. La Paz: ICLA/CIASE.

Hays-Mitchell, Maureen. 2002. "Resisting Austerity: A Gendered Perspective on Neo-Liberal Restructuring in Peru." *Gender and Development* 10(3): 71–81.

Hickman, John M. and William T. Stuart. 1977. "Descent, Alliance, and Moiety in Chucuito, Peru: An Explanatory Sketch of Aymara Social Organization." In *Andean Kinship and Marriage*, ed. Ralph Bolton and Enrique Mayer, 43–59. Washington DC: American Anthropological Association.

Isbell, Billie Jean. 1977a. *To Defend Ourselves, Ecology and Ritual in an Andean Village*. Long Grove, IL: Waveland Press.

1977b. "Those Who Love Me: An Analysis of Andean Kinship and Reciprocity in a Ritual Context." In *Andean Kinship and Marriage*, ed. Ralph Bolton and Enrique Mayer, 81–105. Arlington, TX: American Anthropological Association.

Isbell, William H. 2010. *Mummies and Mortuary Monuments: A Postprocessual Prehistory of Central Andean Social Organization*. Austin, TX: University of Texas Press.

Jelin, Elizabeth. 1990. "Introduction." In *Women and Social Change in Latin America*, ed. E. Jelin, 1–11. London: Zed Books.

Jennings, Justin and Brenda J. Bowser, eds. 2009. *Drink, Power, and Society in the Andes*. Gainesville, FL: University Press of Florida.

Kroeber, Alfred L. 1931. "The Cultural Area and Age Area Concepts of Clark Wissler." In *Methods in Social Science*, ed. Stuart A. Rice, 248–265. Chicago, IL: University of Chicago Press.

Lambert, Berndt. 1977. "Bilaterality in the Andes." In *Andean Kinship and Marriage*, ed. Ralph Bolton and Enrique Mayer, 1–27. Washington DC: American Anthropological Association.

Leifsen, Esben. 2009. "Adoption and the Governing of Child Welfare in 20th Century Quito." *The Journal of Latin American and Caribbean Anthropology* 14(1): 68–91.

Leinaweaver, Jessaca. 2005. "Accompanying and Overcoming: Subsistence and Sustenance in an Andean City." *Michigan Discussions in Anthropology* 15(1): 150–182.

2007. "On Moving Children: The Social Implications of Andean Child Circulation." *American Ethnologist* 34(1): 163–180.

2008. *The Circulation of Children: Kinship, Adoption and Morality in Andean Peru*. Durham, NC: Duke University Press.

Leinaweaver, Jessaca B. and Linda J. Seligmann. 2009. "Introduction: Cultural and Political Economies of Adoption in Latin America." *The Journal of Latin American and Caribbean Anthropology* 14(1): 1–19.

Lind, Amy. 2003. "Feminist Post-Development Thought: 'Women in Development' and the Gendered Paradoxes of Survival in Bolivia." *Women's Studies Quarterly* 31(3/4): 227–246.

Lugones, María. 2007. "Heterosexualism and the Colonial/Modern Gender System." *Hypatia* 22(1): 186–209.

2011. "Toward a Decolonial Feminism." *Hypatia* 25(4): 742–759.

Luykx, Aurolyn. 1999. *The Citizen Factory: Schooling and Cultural Production in Bolivia*. Albany, NY: State University of New York Press.

Mannheim, Bruce. 1991. *The Language of the Inka since the European Invasion*. Austin, TX: University of Texas Press.

Maybury-Lewis, David. 1979. *Dialectical Societies: The Ge and Bororo of Central Brazil*. Cambridge, MA: Harvard University Press.

Mayer, Enrique. 1974. *Reciprocity, Self Sufficiency and Market Relations in a Contemporary Community in the Central Andes of Peru*. Ithaca, NY: Cornell University.

　　1977a. "Beyond the Nuclear Family." In *Andean Kinship and Marriage*, ed. Ralph Bolton and Enrique Mayer, 60–80. Washington DC: American Anthropological Association.

　　1977b. "Tenencia y control comunal de la tierra: caso de Laraos (Yauyos)." *Cuadernos* 24: 59–72.

　　1980. "Repensando 'Más allá de la familia nuclear.'" In *Parentesco y matrimonio en los Andes*, ed. Ralph Bolton and Enrique Mayer, 427–462. Lima: Pontificia Universidad Católica del Perú.

　　1992. "Peru in Deep Trouble: Mario Vargas Llosa's 'Inquest in the Andes' Reexamined." In *Rereading Cultural Anthropology*, ed. G. Marcus, 181–219. Durham, NC: Duke University Press.

Miles, Ann. 2000. "Poor Adolescent Girls and Social Transformations in Cuenca, Ecuador." *Ethos* 28(1): 54–74.

　　2004. *From Cuenca to Queens: An Anthropological Story of Transnational Migration*. Austin, TX: University of Texas Press.

Mintz, Sidney W. and Eric R. Wolf. 1950. "An Analysis of Ritual Co-Parenthood (Compadrazco)." *Southwestern Journal of Anthropology* 6(4): 341–368.

Moser, Annalise. 2004. "Happy Heterogeneity? Feminism, Development, and the Grassroots Women's Movement in Peru." *Feminist Studies* 30(1): 211–238.

Murra, John. 1975. *Formaciones económicas y políticas del mundo andino*. Lima: Instituto de Estudios Peruanos.

Nash, June. 1979. *We Eat the Mines and the Mines Eat Us: Dependency and Exploitation in Bolivian Tin Mines*. New York: Columbia University Press.

Nutini, Hugo Gino and Betty Bell. 1980. *Ritual Kinship: The Structure and Historical Development of the Compadrazco System in Rural Tlaxcala, 1*. Princeton, NJ: Princeton University Press.

Orlove, Benjamin. 1994. "Sticks and Stones: Ritual Battles and Play in the Southern Peruvian Andes." In *Unruly Order: Violence, Power, and Cultural Identity in the High Provinces of Southern Peru*, ed. Deborah A. Pool, 133–164. Boulder, CO: Westview Press.

　　1998. "Down to Earth: Race and Substance in the Andes." *Bulletin of Latin American Research* 17(2): 207–222.

Pape, I. S. R. 2008. "'This Is Not a Meeting for Women': The Sociocultural Dynamics of Rural Women's Political Participation in the Bolivian Andes." *Latin American Perspectives* 35(6): 41–62.

Paredes, Julieta. 2008. *Hilando Fino: Desde el feminismo comunitario*. Quito: CEDEC.

Paulson, S. 2003. "Gendered Practices and Landscapes in the Andes: The Shape of Asymmetrical Exchanges." *Human Organization* 62(3): 242–254.

Poole, Deborah. 1997. *Vision, Race, and Modernity: A Visual Economy of the Andean Image World*. Princeton, NJ: Princeton University Press.

Pribilsky, Jason. 2004. "'Aprendemos a convivir': Conjugal Relations, Co-parenting, and Family Life among Ecuadorian Transnational Migrants in New York and the Ecuadorian Andes." *Global Networks* 4(3): 313–334.

2007. *La Chulla Vida: Gender, Migration, and the Family in Andean Ecuador and New York City*. Syracuse, NY: Syracuse University Press.

Radcliffe, Sarah A. 1990. "Between Hearth and Labor Market: The Recruitment of Peasant Women in the Andes." *International Migration Review* 24(2): 229–249.

Radcliffe-Brown, Alfred Reginald and Cyril Daryll Forde. 1950. *African Systems of Kinship and Marriage*. Oxford: Oxford University Press.

Rens, Marjan. 2003. *Es él que manda*. Quito: Abya Yala Fundación Marjan Rens.

Rivera Cusicanqui, Silvia. 1996. "Los desafíos para una democracia étnica y genérica en los albores del tercer milenio." In *Ser mujer indígena, chola o birlocha en la Bolivia postcolonial de los años 90*, ed. Silvia Rivera Cusicanqui. La Paz: Ministerio de Desarrollo Humano.

Roberts, Elizabeth F. S. 2012. *God's Laboratory: Assisted Reproduction in the Andes*. Oakland, CA: University of California Press.

Rowe, John Howland. 1979. "Archaeoastronomy in Meso America and Peru." *Latin American Research Review* 14(2): 227–233.

Salomon, Frank and G. L. Urioste. 1991. *The Huarochiri Manuscript: A Testament of Ancient and Colonial Andean Religion*. Austin, TX: University of Texas Press.

Seligmann, Linda. 2004. *Peruvian Street Lives: Culture, Power and Economy among Market Women of Cusco*. Urbana and Champaign, IL: University of Illinois Press.

Silverblatt, Irene Marsha. 1987. *Moon, Sun, and Witches: Gender Ideologies and Class in Inca and Colonial Peru*. Princeton, NJ: Princeton University Press.

Spedding, Alison. 1997. "'Esa mujer no necesita hombre': En contra de la 'dualidad andina.' Imágenes de género en los yungas de La Paz." In *Más allá del silencio: las fronteras de género en los Andes*, ed. Denise Y. Arnold, 325–343. La Paz: ILCA/CIASE.

1998. "Contra-afinidad: algunos comentarios sobre el compadrazco andino." In *Gente de carne y hueso: las tramas de parentesco en los Andes*, ed. Denise Y. Arnold, 115–137. La Paz: ICLA/CIASE.

Starn, Orin. 1992. "Missing the Revolution: Anthropologists and the War in Peru." In *Rereading Cultural Anthropology*, ed. G. Marcus, 152–180. Durham, NC: Duke University Press.

1995a. "Maoism in the Andes: The Communist Party of Peru-Shining Path and the Refusal of History." *Journal of Latin American Studies* 27(2): 399–421.

1995b. "To Revolt against the Revolution: War and Resistance in Peru's Andes." *Cultural Anthropology* 10(4): 547–580.

Taussig, Michael. 1980. *The Devil and Commodity Fetishism in South America*. Chapel Hill, NC: The University of North Carolina Press.

Theidon, Kimberly. 2004. *Entre projimos: el conflicto armado interno y la politica de la reconciliacion*. Lima: Instituto de Estudios Peruanos.

Trent, Katherine and Sharon Harlan. 1994. "Teenage Mothers in Nuclear and Extended Households Differences by Marital Status and Race/Ethnicity." *Journal of Family Issues* 15(2): 309–337.

Urton, Gary. 1993. "Moieties and Ceremonialism in the Andes: The Ritual Battles of the Carnival Season in Southern Peru." *Senri Ethnological Studies* 37: 117–142.

Valderrama, Ricardo Fernandez and Carmen Escalante Gutierrez, with Paul Gelles and Gabriela Escobar. 1996. *Andean Lives: Gregorio Condori Mamani and Asunta Quispe Huaman*. Austin, TX: University of Texas Press.

Van den Berghe, Gwendoline and Pierre L. van Den Berghe. 1966. "Compadrazco and Class in Southeastern Mexico." *American Anthropologist* (n.s.) 65(5): 1236–1244.

Van Vleet, Krista. 2002. "The Intimacies of Power: Rethinking Violence and Affinity in the Bolivian Andes." *American Ethnologist* 29(3): 567–601.

2008. *Performing Kinship: Narrative, Gender, and the Intimacies of Power in the Andes*. Austin, TX: University of Texas Press.

2009. "'We Had Already Come to Love Her': Adoption at the Margins of the Bolivian State." *The Journal of Latin American and Caribbean Anthropology* 14(1): 20–43.

2010. "Narrating Violence and Negotiating Belonging: The Politics of (Self-) Representation in an Andean Tinkuy Story." *The Journal of Latin American and Caribbean Anthropology* 15(1): 195–221.

Wade, Peter. 2008. "Race in Latin America." In *A Companion to Latin American Anthropology*, ed. D. Poole. Malden, MA/Oxford: Blackwell.

Weismantel, Mary. 1988. *Food, Gender and Poverty in the Ecuadorian Andes*. Philadelphia, PA: University of Pennsylvania Press.

1995. "Making Kin: Kinship Theory and Zumbagua Adoptions." *American Ethnologist* 22(4): 685–704.

1997. "White Cannibals: Fantasies of Racial Violence in the Andes." *Identities: Global Studies in Culture and Power* 4(1): 9–43.

2001. *Cholas and Pishtacos: Stories of Race and Sex in the Andes*. Chicago, IL: University of Chicago Press.

Weismantel, Mary and Stephen F. Eisenman. 1998. "Race in the Andes: Global Movements and Popular Ontologies." *Bulletin of Latin American Research* 17(2): 121–142.

Weiss, Wendy. 1985. Es él que manda: Sexual Inequality and Its Relationship to Economic Development in the Ecuadorian Sierra. Ph.D. Dissertation, Bryn Mawr College.

Weston, Kath. 1991. *Families We Choose: Gay and Lesbian Kinship*. New York: Columbia University Press.

Weston, Kath. 1997. *Families We Choose: Lesbians, Gays, Kinship*. New York: Columbia University Press.

Whitten Jr, Norman E. 2008. "Blackness in Latin America." In *Encyclopedia of Race and Racism*, ed. John Moore, 1: 217–222. Detroit, MI: Macmillan Reference/Thomson Gale.

Wilhoit, Mary Elena. 2017a. "EnGendering the State: Women's Work and Peru's 2012 Agrarian Census." *Anthropology of Work Review* 38(2): 67–80.

2017b. "Un Favorzote … : Gender and Reciprocity in the Andes." *Journal of Latin American and Caribbean Studies* (JLACA) 22(3): 438–458.

Wissler, Clark. 1927. "The Culture-Area Concept in Social Anthropology." *American Journal of Sociology* 32(6): 881–891.

Wolf, Eric R. 1955. "Types of Latin American Peasantry: A Preliminary Discussion." *American Anthropologist* 57(3): 452–471.

1957. "Closed Corporate Peasant Communities in Mesoamerica and Central Java." *Southwestern Journal of Anthropology* 13(1): 1–18.

Zuidema, Reiner Tom. 1964. *The Ceque System of Cuzco: The Social Organization of the Capital of the Inca*. Leiden: Brill Archive.

9

Kinship and Place: The Existential and Moral Process of Landscape Formation on the Rai Coast of Papua New Guinea

James Leach

There are myriad ways in which people are connected to places (Feld and Basso 1996). For most, these connections are practical, the foundation of livelihood and economy. Some are ideological. Many are political (e.g., Bender 1998; Rowlands 2008). There are less conventionally familiar, but sometimes more experience proximate emotive connections of affection, awe, (dis)comfort, succor (e.g., Brody 1983; Shephard 2008). Narratives of individual or collective history combine experiences of being in particular places with memories of events (Basso 1988). Places are not only *where* things happen, they are part of what happens. More than merely traces of past activities, places often enter into relations between people affording common or divergent activities in fundamental and vital ways (Ingold 2000).

This is a chapter about a particular place and people, and about the existential connection between them. I will be clear about the scope from the outset. It is not a survey chapter collecting together different archaeological, historical, geographical, and anthropological perspectives on places and kinship in human history (see e.g., Tilley 2006). Neither is it a history of the way place has been understood in anthropology (see e.g., Hirsch and O'Hanlon 1995; Ingold 2000: 190–193). Rather, the aim of the chapter is *suggestive*. Suggestive, that is, of an open investigation into the creative aspects of kinship, of self and other formation, and ultimately, of the process of making human life in particular ways *with* particular places. This will be through the prism of one group of people's connections with land and place.

The location is the Rai Coast of Papua New Guinea; an out of the way, little known area of the otherwise densely investigated island (see Sillitoe 1998). Melanesia, and New Guinea in particular, has provided a wealth of opportunity for the anthropological study of kinship, and especially the role and scope of kinship in providing principles for the organization of economy, exchange, warfare, and ritual. It has also been seminal in understanding peoples' connection to place (Weiner 1991) and of the relation between land and kinship (Strathern 1973). Here, I draw on my own ethnography from the region to offer a description of how people are connected to places and how kinship itself enfolds (Wagner 2001), makes alive, and is given its reason, by these connections.

People do not arise *sui generis* from places. They work with others to grow each other and in that process the differences between places come to have value and meaning. Imagine for a moment that everything you are, your very flesh and blood, your body and all you know, come from specific other people. (Is this so far-fetched?) It is those other people who have labored to produce you, who have dedicated their capacities and efforts towards the production of your body. The substance with which that body is made and sustained, the foods that give it solidity and have grown it, the knowledge that allows you to do anything at all, this is what connects you to those others and to the place in which you have grown. It is in them in which you have your origin. And your status as a human being is dependent upon the recognition of this reality. You are a transformation of the potential of a place through others' labor and nurture into a specific product of this work. In turn, what you do with your body, what motivates "you" to create or make or choose is not only influenced by the ongoing history of your emergence *in relation* to other people and powers of the place, it is actually *only possible* because of these relations. They are always placed.

The differentiation of places is the difference between people that make marriage and procreation possible. Close family take different roles in constituting the very body you operate. More distant kin provide other elements appropriate to their relation and interest in you. Your body is always their interest, and whatever you can produce has to be thought about in terms of what and how you can acknowledge and reciprocate. In this situation, knowing and acting around the potential of places and lands to grow people is what it *is* to be a human being. And just as you are grown by others, all those whom you yourself – in your extended form of already being many other people – nurture, feed, advise, offer company or land or labor to, are parts of you.

Focusing on how people are connected to places is necessarily a focus on how they figure in each other's lives, how human worlds grow out of human activities and efforts. In what follows, I draw attention to how people from the hamlets of Reite on the Rai Coast of Papua New Guinea take responsibility for making a human world in their actions. Their endeavors are practical in the sense of being existential. They make the Reite world and Reite persons with and from places.

Children take the place of a generative nexus in Reite. Being the focus of growth action, they simultaneously are the reason for actions that draw forth the potential of places and kin groups and a pivot point in relations between places. Their position constitutes the relations that give places existence. The birth and growth of children is the reason for different people and groups working together in a common but distinct set of interests. In pursuing these interests, landscape (that is, what is known about land and its places, its human potential and meaning, its history and form) is created.

9.1   Relations

Recently, Marilyn Strathern has re-formalized some of her earlier conceptualizations of types of relation (2012). One type that she calls "mode 1 relation," or "relation1," takes as given the entities that are related. That is to say, while putting things into relation reveals new aspects of them, provides different uses, or potential combinations, the entity itself is prior to the relation. It exists as potential for relation. Relations in turn draw out different aspects of its qualities or potentials. This mode 1 relation is the familiar mode of Western science and sociality. Entities are given. The classification of entities reveals their inherent similarity to or differences from other entities. The discovery of further properties or elements through new organization, knowledge, or equipment, reveal further aspects and connections. "Relations1 bring into new positions of stability the properties of the (pre-existing) terms they conjoin, the combinations they create, demarcating (old or new) categories of existence" (Strathern 2012: 10).

Mode 2 relations, or relation2 is of a different order. In this case, the entities themselves are given form by the relation. The terms come to have their properties as an element of the relation itself. The relation takes precedence and forms its terms. The difference is perhaps difficult to grasp, but illuminating. Relations2 are not between pre-given entities with potential properties internally, waiting to be drawn out by specific relations1 (approaches, combinations, perspectives, etc.) but rather are brought into being in relation2. "Relations2 are indeterminate as to the pre-existence of the terms … the terms (their qualities and capacities) are evident less as categories of existence than as functions or effects of a relational facility" (Strathern 2012: 10).

Relation2 is another way of expressing one of the core insights of Strathern's approach to Melanesian ethnographic materials (see 1988).

The distinction is one that (has already) informed many analyses of Melanesian ethnography (Wagner 1975), and is worth recalling in the context of kinship rites as ways of being in landscape. The point here is about the difficulty we tend to have, conditioned to relations1, to keep indeterminacy in mind. That as anthropological observers we are likely to view the development of the child as the stage-by-stage transformation of a unitary self, a body with internal properties and capacities for growth that *put into the right relation* (relation1 mode of thinking) has different aspects highlighted or focused upon during its inevitable development. There is no formative relation to land, as land is just the place growth happens to occur. This amounts to a dualist view: a naturally given and specified entity (the natural human body) is socialized into different roles and identities in parallel with their ontogenetic development (and see Ingold 2009: 194). Landscape formation is merely a side effect of human subsistence activity.

But what if growth itself were at issue? What are the "contours of a non-dualistic world where mutual embeddedness rather than separation characterizes human–environment relations" (Bamford 1998: 30)? What if achieving the desired form for bodies and kinship were not about moments of reclassification (boys reclassified as men, for example, as their physical maturity demands social recognition) but is about achieving that growth and transformation itself? And what if that growth were also the constitution of a world of distinct places in a particular form? This is to be my contention in the case of Reite people.

9.2 The Life Cycle and the Landscape: Growing Human Worlds

I will set out an argument that suggests life-cycle rites in Reite hamlets are existential in this strong sense. That is, they are world creating. The focus on growth and transformation through the life cycle is the mode in which the world is made and remade in human form in each generation. Places come into being as the outcomes of this human effort to sustain the human world. These life-cycle payments are the core constitutive moments of marriage and affinity. They thus also invoke the responsibility for moral behavior. The emergence of places is not a byproduct of other practical subsistence activity, but a moral injunction at the core of human kinship.

Many life-cycle rites in Reite involve the "consumption" of substitutions for the child or person. It is in these substitutions that materials, the things that give specific form to the relation, are deployed. I briefly interrogate the qualities of the substances utilized, exchanged, and consumed in each case. My purpose is to demonstrate how life-cycle rites give a distinct form to the terms, that is the entities, involved. These are not pre-given, and work is required to achieve the correct form of growth and transformation in each case. The process has its culmination in marriage exchanges in which a full effigy of the body is constructed by one side, and dismantled and consumed by the other.

Reite people live by horticulture and hunting in rainforest near the north coast of the island. They reside in small hamlets that are based around a meeting house and a cult house. The residential group is named the *palem*, a word that also refers to a platform adjacent to the meeting house on which ceremonial payments to affinal kin are placed. The cult house contains the paraphernalia of different spirits (*kaapu*) that are called upon by men. *Kaapu* are musical, known by their "voices," which are the melodies of sacred songs. They reside in specific places in the landscape and are called to the hamlet for specific purposes: life-cycle events involving exchanges and ceremonial performances.

Palem are the focus of a generative system. Persons become related to one another through living together in a *palem*. All second-generation residents of a *palem* are siblings in Nekgini reckoning. The hamlets are recognized as whole units (*palem konaki*) at the point where they collectively produce a payment to another residential group. These payments are made in recognition of work and input from people from other places.

In Reite, one looks for marriage partners among one's cross cousins. Categorically, people living in other *palem* are not siblings, and therefore are potentially marriageable. Women move to their husband's *palem* on marriage. Previous marriages between *palem* mean other *palem* are categorically and actually the places of affines, and thus of cross cousins. As we will see below, there are numerous payments made to affines (other *palem*) during the life cycle.

The archetypal or key payments are those given in return for "bodies." That is, for women who arrive in marriage, and for firstborn children who are acknowledged to belong to the wife's originating *palem*. These major payments take the form of an effigy, made up of garden produce, wealth items, and a live pig. These items are explicitly named as body parts. The *kaapu* (spirits) animate this body, giving it voice and calling for the recipients to come. *Palem* as kinship groupings are named after the site of their cult and meeting house, and the effigy is constructed "at their door," born from their collective work. Places then are combinations of people related as siblings, parents and children, and their land-based spirits. They come to have their social identity, their name, and political recognition through the recognition they gain in producing payments for their affines in life-cycle rituals. Places are explicitly recognized as producers of bodies. The lands in which these bodies arise provide the identifiable materials with which different bodies are made. They thus are also the substance with which human kinship, the morality of affinal inter-responsibility, and inter-group politics, are generated. In this complex, mother's brothers (MBs) come to represent the affinal *palem*'s input and work.

9.3   Life-Cycle Rites: The Making and Remaking of Human Relations

There are at least ten life-cycle rites for boys and girls before marriage in Reite (Leach 2003: 129).[1] It is important to note, as I do elsewhere, that these rites are for firstborn children (2003: 130). This is in keeping with Nekgini speaker's emphasis on the emergence of a *place* (2003: 211–215), that is, a situated nexus of human and spirit/land-based powers. This *place* emerges when a sibling set (2003: 130–131), defined by their differentiation from affinal kin through geographical and thus categorical separation (2003: 84), achieves recognition of their productivity. This recognition always takes the form of producing a body (of one sort or another) for others to see and thus possess. Achieving this effect is to become a named place, a *palem* in Reite terminology, in the regard of those who receive wealth from it.

The recognition of the firstborn child of a hamlet group as the visible aspect of engagement with categorical others (maternal kin) (2003: 151–156) is demonstration of the emergent *palem*'s motivation of land and people in productive creation. The emergence of the child is simultaneously the emergence of a place *that is also* the possibility for others to act in regard of that place. As I said above, children are the nexus of activity that re-enacts the separation of places. Maternal kin expect and demand their role in recognizing them. Mother's brothers are made by the actions of the father and mother as much as they make the child grow in specific ways. Far from being unwelcome obligations, these obligations are claimed and guarded because they are vital for all sides.

Why firstborn? Firstborn children lead and carry their siblings (Leach 2012: 35). They do so by being the reason for, and the manifestation of, a transformative relation to affinal/maternal kin.[2] Subsequent children can and do make payments and strengthen the *palem* image. For them to do so before their elder siblings is to "step over" these siblings and relegate them to an inferior position within the *palem* hierarchy. It is the image of productive unity that is important externally, and thus the firstborn child is the focus of life-cycle payments because they are the first manifestation of that productivity.

9.4   The Rites

A glance at the list of life-cycle rites as a whole gives an overview of the progression of growth. Two things are obvious. First, the role of the maternal kin, and second the extensive and sustained attention that the rites demand. It is clear that people take responsibility for the growth and emergence of the child. It is not left to chance. More accurately still, particular people take responsibility for the growth of specific others. Let us

Table 9.1 *Reite life-cycle rites*

Name of payment	Procedure and wealth to be given	Boy	Girl
Eemung uret	"Face them." Woman's brothers come, give decorated spear and coconut to newly pregnant girl. Return of betel nut and coconuts.	×	×
Nek sulitikung	"Washing the child." Mother's brother receives the child from back wall of house. Palieng to MBs.	×	×
Yungyung	"Heavy foods." F and M of child cook post-partum taboo foods and give to MB.	×	×
Unamau pusiraeo	"Not to be carried." Opossum (*pununung*) draped over shoulders, MB removes and eats.	×	×
Maal rongairni	"Fasten loincloth." Eel tied around child's waist, MB removes and cooks.	×	×
Ming kupiret, tari talang'yenda	"First haircutting, rubbing dye into skin." Pig, rawirawi and palieng – to mother's brother.	×	×
Po asumiket	"Spitting [cooking juices of] a pig." Cooked pig with wealth given to MBs. Child spits out juices spooned by MB into his/her mouth.	×	×
Kalawung	"Present." Child cooks a pig for his/her M and F and their same-sex siblings. Small items (household goods) exchanged.	×	×
Yaan utae	"Inside the house." First menses, girl secluded. MB receives tabooed foods to finish her seclusion – as in *yungyung*. Pig and meat – MB.	–	×
Matopo katiret yuna'wae	"Tie-up [your] body and give them." Pig tied up and given with rawirawi and palieng to MB.	–	×
Kaap wangiret, matopo katiret yuna'wae	"First view of tambaran, tie-up [your] body and give them." Pig, rawirawi and palieng given to MB.	×	–
Yong utae	"Hide in the shade." First view of tambaran of the sea. Pig and palieng to MB who performed initiation.	×	–

Source: reproduced from Leach (2003: 129).

look at them in turn, some more briefly than others, to get a sense[3] of the way the form of the relation is carefully managed to turn indeterminacy into recognizable human forms and relations.

In the pregnancy rite "Face them," a spear and a decorated coconut are passed from the maternal kin to the expectant mother (M) and father (F). Conventional hospitality is returned. This one-sided action mirrors the one-sided redefinition of the relation by the M and F in producing a potential child. Their return here (of hospitality) is a passive acceptance of the items given. In a simple sense that Reite people would assert, this is a polite way to tell maternal kin of the change in status of their sister/daughter. However, the presentation of the spear (marking hostility), and the decorated coconut (a person's head, a possibly growing person[4]), instantiates a dual claim over the entity now in the belly of the woman. It is not an entity that will be ignored. The child is already recognized as a potential for the maternal kin's own growth and transformation. A strong claim is made over the possibility, and their interest in it. The following rites make this power clear by taking responsibility for the growth of the child at crucial moments.

The first substantial rite is that of "washing" the child for the first time. Once the umbilical cord is dry and the baby's "skin is strong," maternal kinsmen are called upon to come and receive the baby from a newly made opening in the rear wall of the natal house. In a clear image of birth, one that I have argued elsewhere asserts an image of the mother and father (that is, the *palem* body) as jointly responsible for the child (Leach 2003: 147), the first *appearance* of the baby is limited to his/her maternal kin. They (not the M and F) become responsible for showing the child publically, as the rear of the house is not a public space, and not the usual "door" at which valuable entities are offered. The mode of presentation is particular. The child is placed upon a wooden plate (mirroring how ceremonial food is served) and surrounded by dogs-teeth valuables. Taking the wealth and plate, the maternal kin remove the baby to a nearby stream, and wash it for the first time. Only after this washing do they move into a public space. Reite people emphasize coming back to a frequented and open area by a path, where the maternal kin begin a pantomime of adult life. They cut small trees and clear scrub bush as if for a garden. They climb small trees, mimicking adults climbing huge forest trees when hunting birds.

Two aspects merit particular attention. First, the alimentary image. The maternal kin receive, as from a birthing body, a baby. But they do so on a food plate, surrounded by teeth. Instead of actually consuming the child[5] they consume the wealth, and facilitate the first appearance of the child by cleaning it, and then very publically demonstrating their expectation that this is an entity that will become capable of human activities.

Second, the materials and actions including the house give a particular form to the transaction. They make real the emergence as a planned, elicited act by maternal kin. The parents place the child in the position, quite literally, of an item to be consumed by those others. The child is taken in seclusion away to the water, just as game animals would be, to be cleaned and prepared. But what returns to the house is a potential human child, made so by the actions of the maternal kin.

I suggest that mother and father can anticipate this result for their firstborn, but the responsibility for making it happen is ceded, as it must be, to those who are in a position to give a human form to the emergent body. That form is of one who has maternal kin who do not consume it, but will support its emergence. By their actions they make it human, not game. Their categorical otherness as *affines* and MBs is not there prior to the rite. It is achieved by *not* consuming the child, by accepting their difference from it, by taking the substitution for it. The differentiation of MB from M and F is made real by placing the child in a public space. Public space has to be *made*. It is not a stable geography, but somewhere that emerges because of the presence of the child. "Public" means not hidden in, or consumed by, one or another *palem*, but as something in between them. The child becomes the object of their common concern.

It is clear that the seclusion in the house is an enactment of the state of pre-partum integration of the child. The relationship established is between the mother/father as a unit, and mother's kinsmen, prior to the emergence of a first child. Mother and father take the role of the *palem* unit itself, producing something "at their door," thus demonstrating their powers of productivity. But the child emerges from a "new" door at the rear of the house associated with menstruation. Unlike menstruation, when women are secluded and nothing emerges, in this case the host *palem* ask for witnesses to their productivity.[6] One could suggest here the transformation achieved by the form and materials is from a hostile claim to possess and consume a product of another's actions (in "*eemung uret*"/ face them) into a nurturing role, activating the potential human possibilities of both themselves, and their sister's child in the action. Their role is already different from the M and F, and thus a future trajectory is sketched out.

Analyzing Highlands material, Marilyn Strathern writes,

> [a] Hagen child is created through a metonymic transaction between parents, each contributing a part of their substance while retaining their distinctiveness. The *relationship is reified in the child who substitutes for it*, and who duplicates the identity of neither parent but combines them both within itself. Its androgyny symbolizes a completed transaction. As an inert objectification of a relation it cannot be further reproductive but it can be added to a male or female person/ collectivity.
>
> *(1988: 262 my emphasis)*

She goes on to state the conceptualization of the child as wealth "holds only to a limited extent," and then to liken the propagation of children in Hagen to the propagation of food (1988: 262).

This perception of the child as *added* to a person or collectivity may be accurate for the lineal system of Mt Hagen. There, recruitment to group is given, as it were, and children are added to the lineage. They are "visible as increments to others with whom they are related" in "agnatic regimes of the Hagen kind" (1988: 260).

Reite, with their emphasis on place, and incorporation of persons into productive units as places, rely on a different mechanism of value recognition. *Palem* units come into being as such based on their members' ability to produce from a place. (Firstborn) children are not increments (of an existing "clan," as Strathern tells us they are in Hagen), they are the manifestations of a newly productive combination in/of a place. Each *palem* generation regenerates the form of the human world through these activities. But they cannot, in themselves, constitute the world as human. For that they need others, and those others are engaged exactly by the production of things from that place that are not consumed by their producers.

"As long as a product is encompassed within its source it grows; but evidence of it having grown can only be given when it separately embodies the growth in an independent form. It is such visible evidence of separation and growth which both ceremonial exchange and initiation cults seek to display" (Strathern 1988: 266). What seems different in Reite is that the increment can only be recognized as *between* the *palem* groups. It is valuable as and when it is recognized by both sides. And its value seems to be that its existence allows the two sides to see each other at the same time as see the product of their combination.

In the Reite case, the image of the rebirth of the child from the house likens it to the production of other items of value, other items of *palem* labor. That is, in particular, food items: tubers from a garden. These everyday food items are *also* mythic transformations of ancestral persons (see Fortune 1932; Gudeman 1986; Malinowski 2002 [1935]). And these grown things constitute the persons who consume them, weaving complex relations of kin dependency and obligation in their movements. But the myths make the tubers inert, as it were. They go from ancestor to tuber, from active person to item appropriate for consumption. That is, made to be consumed by others as elements of existing relationships. They do not *make relations* in themselves. They are appropriate food items because they are grown for consumption.

So, to make the child an entity born of a place, and to demonstrate that its appearance is the outcome of a combined labor by mother and father that is *of* the place it is grown in, the mother/father unit produce it as an entity that could be consumed by others. The hope is that the wealth and bowl will be taken as substitute for the child. The child then can be returned with an addition, from the external gaze as it were. That addition is to recognize its potential for human development in the future. But the offer is made for the MB to consume the child. The offer challenges them to act towards the child, and thus to the M and F, as affinal kin, as human kin who make the human world again in their action of accepting the substitution. It is a key moment. It "stimulates a flow of messages about the calibre of the relationships in question, through what appears to be the vehicle of mediated items" (Strathern 1988: 264).

The next rite is to release the mother and father from their post-partum taboos on foods deemed "heavy." These are the foods that were given to Reite people by powerful ancestors and mythic characters. Their revelation allowed the world of yam and taro gardening, which in turn was the inception of the male spirit cult, and thus of human existence as an emplaced mode of being. These foods are cooked by the M and F (along with hunted game[7]) and given to the maternal kin, who "carry the weight" of these foods for them, releasing them from their taboo.

We might interpret this as follows. These are moments where the simple, everyday staples of life become unstable, dangerous, and uncertain. Real foods are grown with, and in the image of the powerful first beings to be human. Moreover, human foods always come from somewhere, and from someone. They connect kin and kin bodies, and they connect those bodies to a mode of existence that implies knowledge and obligation. Their manifestation is a moral matter. To eat them without acknowledging their generative role at the nexus of human life is to act amorally, and to risk reverting to an inhuman state of being. The "uncertainty" surrounding relations2 is palpable in such moments. Because the mother and father have entered a different phase of their development in relation to the maternal kin on the birth and acceptance of the child, their constitution is ambiguous. As parents of a child to be human, they require their own constitutive relations to others to be remade. That is, for others who are human to take responsibility for their re-emergence into the moral human world of taro gardening.

To just eat is to be nobody. To eat taro and other ancestrally revealed foods, and to eat game animals, is always to be in relation to those other people. That, in turn, amounts to a remaking of both parties, with MB as much as M and F transformed into the particular human forms of their association through the emergent child. The MB carries, that is, gives back to the M and F their state of human consumption, which is to be in relation to others, to be exchanging real foods with them. To eat of oneself is to collapse these relations of humanness and become monster, other than human. The danger post-partum is a sense of autonomy ("we can produce for ourselves and our consumption") that must be counterbalanced.

It is said that in the (mythic) past, the firstborn child of some Reite people was consumed by their mother's brother. In grief and anger, the child turned into a pig, and pigs became an acceptable substitute for human children. A fundamental item in affinal exchange (the pig) is what humans use in order not to revert to the nonhuman world of myth in which beings ate their nephews and nieces. This is mirrored in the Reite myth of yams, for example, in which a man was being eaten by his children until he made the transformation into a yam, and thus transformed the mythic world where people ate each other into the human world where people eat tubers.

The next two rites are focused on carrying and clothing the child for the first time. Before a child can be carried on the shoulders of its parents, M and F must hunt a large marsupial (a cuscus). Maternal kin are then asked to attend the child, who is presented to them with this marsupial draped over their shoulders. The MB takes the marsupial and returns the child to the parents, who may then carry the child in a similar fashion. The transformation is quite clear. The child is recognized as a human child, but this recognition comes in the form of substituting them for a game animal that carries it's young in its body, against its chest. Now the child carries the marsupial. They are not carried as a marsupial, held against the breast of the parents. Here the "terms" of the relation remain MB and M+F. However, now in addition there is a child and MB relation, which is mediated through a game animal. This animal also substitutes for the possibility of consuming the child as marsupial prey. The object here becomes the transformative element between both M and F and MB, and MB and child.

The child's emergence has commenced once this complex is established. The child reifies the affinal relation. Marsupials or other objects (see below), transform the MB/ZS relation. The object substitutes the child, allowing them to stand forth from the relation of M and F and MB as a distinct entity. As such, a new aspect of equivalence and exchange is introduced. The F and M prepare a small bracelet of dog's teeth and small shells that the child will wear during the rite. The MB removes this bracelet and replaces it with an identical one that he has prepared himself. This wealth does not go back to the M and F, but remains on the child's skin. This type of exchange (where things are replaced like for like and remain on the child's body) becomes a part of each of the subsequent rites, up until the final payment to the MB.

To take stock: each stage of growth and development is made to happen as an aspect of the relation with the MB. This involves a dual differentiation. Differentiation of the child from the item to be consumed by the maternal kin is also the differentiation of the maternal kin from the child itself. And that process of substitution and differentiation remakes the maternal kin in regard of the child as much as the child in regard of the maternal kin. This dual aspect, of substitution that creates the child as a party to the relation, and of the exchange between MB and M and F, is very clear again in two subsequent rites that further the emergence of the child as a growing human child. The exchange of wealth and of substitutes for the child in each case generates and sustains exactly the tension of the human world *in the specific instance* of this child. Because *at this moment* the two groups take responsibility. The exchanges are necessary, they are *moral*, because they create the human world as such.

The first time the child eats pork is understandably an important moment. To be able to eat pork meat, the father must cook a pig, and present the cooked meat on a plate with taro and yam to the maternal kinsmen. The MB uses a shell valuable to spoon the cooking juices from this plate into the child's mouth. The MBs now take the cooked pork and consume it themselves, freeing the child to eat pork in the future.

Cooked pork is not just taken as substitute for the child, but is also used to make possible their future consumption of *that which stands for them*. The significance of the MB giving soup to the child is that as an emergent person, it is affines who will be the source of pork in the future. (People do not eat their own pigs, just as they do not marry their own children.) Places stand apart. But pigs and children are different entities. The one can substitute the other, but the equivalence is not two-way. By feeding the child with pork, the MB acknowledges it is not a pig. The child is not a pig because of the relationship with them, one in which humanity on both sides is actively being constituted. (They give pigs, we return them.)

Consumption in this form is a version of obligation. Eating is to be in relationship to other powers and people. What you choose to consume shows what the relationship generates. The complexity of these rites is complexity around this emergent obligation. To be a human, not a monster, to be a mother's brother, not a father. One eats what one eats in order that other humans can come into being and provide the necessary other for the self. Responsibility is to keep the world as a human world. And that leads us to particularity. Particular mother's brother, particular emergent child. Place is unique. There is no generic place, only the existent ones that people have taken responsibility for bringing into being as emergent human possibilities. Hence the appearance of newly created places in each generation that is so characteristic of Reite sociality.

We have seen that it is the child who becomes the pivot for the relation between MB and M and F. The transformation manifest in the body of the child is a transformation not of his relation to his MB, but of the transformed relation between MB and M and F. The child's body, their growth, is the evidence of this transformation. And that is why it makes sense to say the rites are only partly "about" transforming the child. They are generally "about" the relation between affines. And that in turn makes the position of the child, and its substitutes, interesting. Once the child has grown to the stage of having the first hair cut, and putting paint on the skin for the first time; once grown to the point at which there is a real reason for a full substitution, that is, once the child can emerge as a person who causes effects in others through displaying their strength and wealth on their skin, a body payment is made.

Let us look now at the archetypal "body payment," the *palem* itself. *Palem* is (also) the name for a presentation of garden food, accompanied by a live pig and substantial wealth. It is made from a pile of taro (grown especially for the purpose) that is supported at the center by a bamboo tube. This tube is placed there by the male cult, with ceremony. The taro pile is called the viscera. It is surrounded by a wooden frame, upon which large yams are hung. These yams make the ribs. They are further fleshed out with ancestral bananas and sugar cane. The whole construction, as I have said, is thought of as an effigy, a substitute body for the person who presents it. The *palem* is accompanied by a live pig, given "with a rope." That is, with a series of other items of wealth that make up the "body pay" for the person.

The *palem* is the form that affinal exchange takes in Reite. The first *palem* was made by the characters of a central Reite myth about the origins of kinship and exchange. It is the archetypal substitution that keeps the world as a human world of kinship and exchange. *Palem* construction was a direct result in the first separation of gender, the resultant separation of siblings into cross cousins living in different places, and the subsequent appearance of exchange as the result of these two differentiations.

Palem construction begins with producing a large garden of taro. From the very outset in the garden, it is a man's knowledge of local names, myths, and animating spirits that allows him to grow the elements that are finally given away. Reite people plant taro with much skill: they have garden magic involving the names of taro deities (*pel-patuki*), and secret procedures for ensuring that the taro grows correctly, replenishes itself in the garden, tastes sweet, and so on. These procedures are vital, as the first responsibility of a man and wife who need to produce an affinal payment in the form of a *palem* is to produce abundantly from garden land. In addition in these presentations, there ought to be dried marsupials and other wild meat caught through hunting on a man's land, as well as some left over to feed spirits when they are first called to the hamlet. Hunting successfully involves the knowledge of names of places and events in the land on which a man hunts. Growing pigs likewise is accomplished speedily when a man has knowledge of esoteric names, procedures and specific mythic places from which to draw substance for the pigs' growth (Leach 2008).

When his garden is ready to be harvested, a man enlists the support of the *kaapu* (spirits), which reside in pools formed by springs in the limestone hills. These *kaapu* are summoned from their different pools on land owned by close kin. They are brought to the hamlet's men's house, where they are kept out of the sight of women. Spirits actively contribute to the preparations for the *palem* from there.

At the time when the child is decorated with paint and has their hair cut for the first time, they are decorated with wealth items by their F and his kin. These items are substituted like for like, by wealth items supplied by the maternal kin, before the child appears in public. The *palem* is then pulled apart by the maternal kin, and distributed among themselves. The pig is taken back to their hamlet where it is killed and distributed.

The *palem* is explicitly a substitute body. It is consumed. It is appropriate to be consumed. In that guise the appearance of the *palem* is the culmination of the efforts at moral action by the two sides in the growth of the child.

From this time on, the child may wear paint on their skin, and participate in ceremonial occasions. Another result of the payment is that the affinal kin do not claim the bride payment of the child on her marriage if she is a girl, or that they will assist gathering the required marriage payment if he is a boy. In other words, the payment is for a body, which then can stand on its own as part of the place of its emergence. Again, note the replacement of wealth items by the MB, balancing those put there by the F.

Each payment made as a *palem* constitutes the work of the *palem* as the work of producing its children. Such children are siblings because they embody elements from the same place. They are differentiated from one another, just as *palem* themselves are, through the relationships they have external to the *palem*. It is in these relationships that the particularity of the person/*palem* emerges because of its unique position (name) and unique set of constitutive relations to other places, affines, or maternal kinsmen. This is a system that generates new *palem*, new named social groups, and new spirits (and designs to accompany them) through the work of growing crops, growing animals, and entering into complexly structured exchanges that are ultimately focused upon the becoming of subsequent generations.

Sandra Bamford points to the fact that in many Melanesian societies, sociality and landscapes are a "becoming" (after Wagner 1974) in which distinctions are actively sought and created through (ritual) and everyday action. She demonstrates that for the Kamea of the Eastern Highlands of Papua New Guinea,

> the resources upon which they depend for a living – the land and the different species of flora and fauna which they utilise – are not simply appropriated via pre-existing social ties, but instead furnish an important venue through which social distinctions are created in the first place. Gender and different categories of social relationship *sediment out* of the different uses to which the non human environment is put.
>
> *(Bamford 1998: 29)*

Bamford describes how Kamea operate in their lands to generate the key differences that make human life possible. Children are gendered – that is, go from an undifferentiated and ungendered state (see 2007: 66) to being girls and boys – through different life trajectories that are centered in the social and geographical origin of the foods they consume. Girls are actively fed and thus grown by food provided by their future in-laws, foods that their male siblings are prohibited from eating. In this way, affines grow reproductive difference (capacity) into the bodies of their future spouses through moving foods and game from their lands into her body. Boys on the other hand gain their reproductive potential from feeding on particular foods (restricted from their female siblings) from their own lands. The landscape, dotted with different resources and shaped by the activities geared towards making gender appear, to making kinship possible, is thus actively present in the core processes of social life. Kamea, unlike Reite people, do not consider that they share substance by being fed from the same places, but they do consider that land and its produce are pivotal in shaping and making the human world of kinship possible.

9.5 Conclusion

Bamford's work builds on and extends other studies of Melanesian sociality that demonstrate the impossibility of thinking about kinship without reference to connections between people and land, and to the active constitution of human moral worlds that make the emergence of places a part of that moral endeavor. The two parts of my exposition here, that pertaining to relations2, and the emphasis on generating a human landscape, feed into this endeavor. The world is not existent until made human by human activity. If entities are emergent from relations, then so, too, are the worlds that those entities populate. This is the focus of the work of Reite kinship, the reason for taking responsibility for the form and growth of specifically human entities.

Four more points emerge. First, the life cycle in Reite is not a series of spontaneous developments in the body of the child or person, that then gain social recognition as an overlay or addition of meaning. The series of developments in the body of the child are things that are caused to happen by other people. Second, that these deliberate moments of transformation are established on the premise that the transformation of the body is also and always the transformation of the relations that constitute it. The processes engender recognition because they are actions that are always for, directed towards, or instigated by, those who will acknowledge the transformation. Third, the "relations" we are discussing here are those Strathern called "mode 2 relations." That is, they are relations that dynamically transform the entities *in their constitution*. That in turn results from the fact that the actions of life-cycle rites are always *in regard* of someone else. What is done, demonstrated, made present is not a generic form but a particular form that already highlights certain connections and attributes that are of interest to, and are already part of, we might say, those who receive them. Fourth, this means something important logically. That is, the process of life-cycle change for one person is also the transformation of those persons who grow and recognize the growth of the child. If the relations constitute the entities, and the purpose of rites and actions is to advance the innovative differentiation of entities, reinventing, as it were, the meaning of being human in each turn (because each appearance of the human is a deliberate act of some in regard to particular others), then the transformation is of both terms to the engagement.

In my analysis of this Reite material I have previously called this visibility. That to be visible, or make visible, is an act that both requires and demands things of other parties. What we have seen here is that those others are party to the emergent entity in a way that is explicitly dealt with through mechanisms that keep separate, as it were, the entities and the emergent object. It follows that these rites are not "about" the initiate or child development. That is to think in mode 1 relational terms. These rites are about maintaining the world. They are "about" ensuring the continued production of places as the moral mode of human being.

Growth and nurture, and the labor involved in nurture is always focused on the elicitation of power and substance from the land. This is the basis of kinship, but the work is not just laboring to make others, it is laboring in places to elicit kinship as a form of the world that is human and appropriate. Ceremony then becomes the crucial and life-generating endeavor. Cycles of life and work are centrally organized around these moments of place-based generation. Relations are remade and regenerated as life giving in each generation. This is an endeavor in land and with land that culminates in a human world.

We often imagine that people are attached to places or connected to them through familiarity or sentiment. But here people are attached to places because they share something substantial with them. An anthropological approach to kinship that takes account of place must take account of the very many instances in the world where people and places are connected *bodily*.[8] That is to say, that people are from places, not in the sense of departing from or originating in them, but in the sense of being them, their very bodies made from, grown out of, or being, land in another form.

In some Melanesian modes of life (as elsewhere), places "figure ... significantly in the ongoing elicitation of social identities and relationships" (Bamford 1998: 30). In this part of the world, engagement with land and place is literally vital (Leach 2009). Melanesian people's relational and existential attachments to land are how human life is known and experienced (Telban, 2019). Paths, movements, and places are also the engagement of others in a coming into being for all.

Notes

1. Rather than go through the list in full, I will examine three of them in depth. I will then compare their form to the form of a marriage payment: another act of substitution and consumption that acknowledges transformation while cementing it.

2. See Leach (2003: 145) on the "affinal" nature of the role of the mother's brother.

3. And a different sense to my analysis in *Creative Land*, which was focused on an argument about lineality and payments for substance in this cognatic, place-based kinship system.

4. There are at least two senses in which coconuts are associated with people in Reite. The *palem*-effigy is decorated with a mast of piled coconuts, alluding to a myth in which a man became a coconut. Heads are piled up. A shooting coconut is one of the items that passes from the wife's family to the husband's on marriage, indicating its growth will be mirrored by the growth of children.

5. Which was perhaps anticipated by the pregnancy rite, where knowledge of the entity in their sister's belly, and an indication they will use force to claim it, is demonstrated.

6. The production is not actually "at their door," as the body-payments for incoming wives are, but from the very body of the house, as it were, into a private space where the maternal kin are also hidden. They maintain this hidden state until the child has been washed, at which point, it is no longer received/carried as food, but as a potential human child.

7. In many Reite myths game animals are kinds of person, or transformed persons, or live in parallel nonhuman worlds into which people sometimes descend through amoral behavior. Game animals are valued as protein (of course), but have special significance as entities not unlike people but available for consumption.

8. There is, of course, often a political aspect to this assertion, and sometimes a disturbing or exclusive claim attached. The ways that different ideologies invoke or rely upon connections between substance, race, and place is not within the scope of this chapter. Suffice it to say that my description of Rai Coast practices is intended to demonstrate the very real interweaving of person and place in this instance, and that far from being exclusionary, given, or essentialized, Rai Coast people practice connection to place as inclusive, achieved, and mutable.

References

Bamford, Sandra. 1998. "Humanized Landscapes, Embodied Worlds: Land and the Construction of Intergenerational Continuity among the Kamea of Papua New Guinea." *Social Analysis* 42(3): 28–54.

———. 2007. *Biology Unmoored: Melanesian Reflections on Life and Biotechnology*. Berkeley and Los Angeles, CA: University of California Press.

Basso, Keith H. 1988. "Speaking with Names: Language and Landscape among the Western Apache." *Cultural Anthropology* 3(2): 99–130.

Bender, Barbara. 1998. *Stonehenge: Making Place*. London: Bloomsbury Academic.

Brody, Hugh. 1983. *Maps and Dreams: Indians and the British Columbia Frontier*. Harmondsworth: Penguin.

Feld, Steven and Keith H. Basso. 1996. *Senses of Place*. Santa Fe, NM: SAR Press.

Fortune, R. 1932. *Sorcerers of Dobu*. New York: E. P. Dutton.

Gudeman, S. 1986 *Economics As Culture: Metaphors and Models of Livelihood*. London: Routledge & Kegan Paul.

Hirsch, Eric and Michael O'Hanlon. 1995. *The Anthropology of Landscape*. Oxford: Oxford University Press.

Ingold, Tim. 2000. *The Perception of the Environment*. London: Routledge.

2009. "Stories against Classification." In *Kinship and Beyond: The Genealogical Model Reconsidered*, ed. Sandra Bamford and James Leach, 193–213. Oxford: Berghahn Books.

Leach, James. 2003. *Creative Land: Place and Procreation on the Rai Coast of Papua New Guinea*. Oxford: Berghahn Books.

2008. "An Anthropological Approach to Transactions Involving Names and Marks, Drawing on Melanesia." In *Trademarks and Brands: An Interdisciplinary Critique*, ed. Lionel Bently, Jennifer Davis and Jane Ginsburg, 319–342. Cambridge: Cambridge University Press.

2009. "Knowledge As Kinship." In *Kinship and Beyond: The Genealogical Model Reconsidered*, ed. Sandra Bamford and James Leach, 175–192. Oxford: Berghahn Books.

2012. "Leaving the Magic Out: Knowledge and Effect in Different Places." *Anthropological Forum: A Journal of Social Anthropology and Comparative Sociology* 22(3): 251–270.

Malinowski, B. 2002 [1935]. *Coral Gardens and Their Magic, II: The Language and Magic of Gardening*. London: Routledge.

Rowlands, Mike. 2008. "Postconflict Heritage." *Journal of Material Culture*. Special Issue 13(2): 131–134.

Shephard, Nan. 2008. *The Living Mountain: A Celebration of the Cairngorm Mountains of Scotland*. Edinburgh: Cannongate.

Sillitoe, Paul. 1998. *An Introduction to the Anthropology of Melanesia: Culture and Tradition*. Cambridge: Cambridge University Press.

Strathern, Andrew. 1973. "Kinship, Descent, and Locality: Some New Guinea Examples." In *The Character of Kinship*, ed. Jack Goody, 21–33. Cambridge: Cambridge University Press.

Strathern, Marilyn. 1988. *The Gender of the Gift: Problems with Women and Problems with Society in Melanesia*. Berkeley, CA: University of California Press.

2012. "Remaking Knowledge: Relations and 'Relations.'" Presented at Tribute to *La Pensée Sauvage*. Nature, Relationships and Contributions to Indigenous Knowledge. Collège de France, May 14–15, 2012, Convenor Manuela Carneiro da Cunha.

Telban, Borut. 2019. "Places and Paths in Melanesian Landscapes." In *The Melanesian World*, ed. Eric Hirsch and Will Rollason. London: Routledge.

Tilley, C. 2006. "Identity, Place, Landscape and Heritage." *Journal of Material Culture*. Special Issue 11(1–2): 7–32.

Wagner, Roy. 1974. "Are There Social Groups in the New Guinea Highlands?" In *Frontiers of Anthropology*, ed. M Leaf, 95–122. New York: D. Van Nordstron Co.

1975. *The Invention of Culture*. Chicago, IL: University of Chicago Press.

2001. "Condensed Mapping: Myth and the Folding of Space/Space and the Folding of Myth." In *Emplaced Myth: Space, Narrative and Knowledge in Aboriginal Australia and Papua New Guinea*, ed. James F. Weiner and Aland Rumsey, 71–78. Honolulu, HI: University of Hawai'i Press.

Weiner, James F. 1991. *The Empty Place: Poetry, Space and Being among the Foi of Papua New Guinea*. Bloomington, IN: Indiana University Press.

10

Adoption

Christine Ward Gailey

Adoption refers to the inclusion of a previously unaffiliated person into an ongoing kin group, generally as a child of a designated adult or adults, or as an heir. Historically and across cultures the meanings of adoption have varied widely along lines of rights and obligations, expectations regarding affect or emotional attachment, whether the new connection severs or strengthens prior affiliations, and whether people previously connected to the adoptee are included in the expanded kin group. Adoption may be formalized in law, informal, or customary; it may be normalized culturally or seen as a different kind of kin connection than birth-related associations. The adoptee may be viewed socially as disadvantaged or privileged, unfortunate or lucky, or simply as arriving into a kin group in an acceptable non-birth manner.

These variations are embedded intricately in a sociopolitical and economic web of kinship ideologies and, where they exist, hierarchies of class, race, gender, ethnicity, nationality, sexualities, and often religion. There are patterns to adoption across societies and cultures, but these require framing by the above factors. In all cases, however, adoption practices provide a lens through which we can discern how people create kinship in particular contexts and, therefore, how genetic connections do not predict forms of affect and attachment unless ideologies stress genetic similarity as the bedrock on which kinship is constructed.

10.1 Motivations to Adopt

Reasons for adoption are myriad in class-based societies, viewed comparatively and historically, but they tend to be intimately connected to the needs for children as validations of adult or gender status, the need for children as family workers or future caregivers to aging parents, and retention or inheritance of property. Today in capitalist countries the most common motivations in order of magnitude are marking inclusion of a stepchild, infertility, and the desire to expand a family without giving birth.

In the slave-based and patrilineal Roman Empire, for instance, wealthy Roman men – particularly if they were politically prominent – could adopt a chosen heir whether or not they had birth sons. Usually these adoptive heirs were adults or nearly adults at the time of adoption (Lindsay 2009). Pressure on women in some other patrilineal and patriarchal state settings, such as Tudor-era Britain, to bear male heirs could lead to clandestine adoptions at birth by a high-ranking woman who bore a daughter or stillborn son and another woman giving birth, arranged at times with haste through trusted servants with the collusion of others whose interests were served by there being a male heir. In such politically sensitive settings, secrecy was crucial, for all parties could forfeit their lives if discovered.

In pre-revolutionary, pre-capitalist China, patrilineal patriarchal structures demanded male heirs for use-rights or property transmission at all levels. Impoverished families could ill afford the cost of dowries for their daughter or daughters. This could result in selling daughters into slavery or concubinage, or adopting an even poorer son-in-law. A tenant farming family with a son, who stood to inherit nothing, could seek a marginally landed family with a daughter and negotiate an adoption of the son with the promise of inheriting the father-in-law's land as a dowry. Adopting a son-in-law was a recognized practice and persisted until the mid-twentieth century in areas of China that had widespread tenancy coupled with small holdings.

Reported in some non-state and state societies, adoption also can serve, much as marriage can, as a means of alliance, extending trade or other relationships, resolving conflict between enemy groups, or constituting restitution for an admitted infraction. The adopted child or adult is a token of the relationship of the two groups. If the purpose of the adoption is to ensure peace, or to signify an end of hostilities, the literature often refers to the adoptees as hostages, although as they mature, they generally marry as a person in the adopter group would. Among non-state societies, the precolonial Igbo of southeastern Nigeria had this practice, as did a number of Native American peoples. The health and well-being of the adoptee mattered to both communities. In some cases, if the hostage died, the relationship between communities would be compromised. In other cases, a hostage/adoptee could be sacrificed to maintain peace disrupted by other hostile acts or in a few cases, the adoptee could be sacrificed in the event of catastrophe. In most cases, the adoptee maintained a profile as a symbolic liaison between communities, even as he or she would not be treated differently outside the intercommunity context.

Among the matrilineal nations comprising the Iroquois Confederacy, generally children were spared in warfare and raids. These children were adopted into the local group, often as symbolic compensation for lost children or those taken by other groups. White colonists sometimes tried to steal the child back or offer compensation for them, but to consider the children being held for ransom is not accurate. These children were reared as members of the adoptive/captor matrilineage. Birth relatives sometimes sought to reclaim adoptees or attempts were made to "free" them: but Mary Jemison, captured by the Seneca after a raiding party killed most of her relatives, and reared as Seneca, rejected such an attempt (Seaver [1824] 2015).

Adoption, thus, may be marked positively or negatively. In the contemporary United States, where prevailing ideologies stress genetic connection as a bedrock of kinship, adoption is widely viewed as a "second-best" way to create family, most often undertaken in the event of infertility; this varies, however, with class and other dimensions of social hierarchy (Gailey 2010). Adoption may convey a special status, be viewed as a decided advantage to a child, or be seen as involving children suspected of having problems. Let us consider some of the contours of contemporary adoption in the context of social hierarchies, state policies, and geopolitical dynamics.

10.2 Adoption as an Arena of Kinship, Gender, Class, and Race

Contemporary adoption in Euro-American contexts is a terrain heavily marked by gender, race, and class ideologies. It is gendered as a women's domain, associated as it is with kinship, but also because sociologically the principal players are women. Birth mothers are forefronted, although if named, birth fathers must also relinquish parental rights for an adoption to be legal. The vast majority of adoptions are initiated by women; the literature is clear that prospective adopter men are persuaded by their spouses to adopt. The exception is, of course, gay men adopting, but this is a small minority of adoptions today. The third marking of women in adoption are the adoption professionals, especially social workers, the vast majority of whom are women. Beyond the personnel of adoption, the arena is a charged playing field for ideologies of motherhood (Gailey 2000b). The idea of giving up one's child conjures images of abandonment and bad mothering, but this negative stereotype is often paired with an ambivalent narrative. This encompasses widespread beliefs that birth mothers who give their children up for adoption are not bad, but too poor, uneducated, incompetent, and/or sexually promiscuous or victims of partner abandonment or rape. They are portrayed as "trying to do what's best for the child": this belief ranges from not having an abortion, to seeking prenatal care, to seeking treatment for any addiction issues and living a healthy lifestyle during pregnancy. The mark of altruism or at least being practical about a predicament is their relinquishing the child as close to birth as possible. In fact, in the United States white women are proportionately more likely to give children up for adoption than women of color, and better educated women are more likely to place children for adoption.

Racial ideologies loom large in both domestic and international adoption. The belief in a "white baby shortage" is the rationale often given in the United States for state agencies seeking to place children of color with white adopters. The legalization of abortion after 1973 did reduce the number of children born outside marriage, but the decline in such births over the years is more a result of the widespread availability of effective contraceptives and the growing acceptability of unmarried women keeping their babies. These shifts are true as well for women of color, but black women in particular are at risk for reasons of class and hyper-surveillance that accompanies systemic racism, of losing children to foster care and involuntary termination of parental rights. Today there are few white infants available for public adoption, but religious organizations – above all conservative Christian groups – have become a source of both infants and targeted clients through private religious agencies or private independent adoption.

Public agencies place children voluntarily relinquished by birth parents or taken for reasons of abuse or neglect by state Child Protective Services (or similar moniker) into foster care. What varies through time and policy shifts is the period the child may remain in foster care without what is called "permanency planning" – either return to the birth family or termination of parental rights. This makes it rare for children in public care to be infants, unless they have significant developmental disabilities or compromised health. Because the United States has time limits on the receipt of social welfare and accompanying childcare supplements for indigent mothers and because women of color and women in poverty have fewer opportunities for employment and less employment security, their children are at greater risk of being placed in foster care because of neglect after they reach the maximum length of time they are eligible for welfare. Working mothers at the minimum wage level or part-time workers cannot afford childcare outside the home. Nevertheless it is the case that black women and women of color in general are only half as likely to voluntarily terminate parental rights as white women.

The new reproductive technologies of the late twentieth and twenty-first centuries have deep implications for adoption. Wealthier couples and individuals tend to avoid seeking children through public agencies, either because the available white children tend to be older or have significant health or cognitive problems, or have traumatic histories. These by and large heterosexual married couples have sought children considered white through international adoption, white infants through private agencies or private "adoption facilitators" and lawyers, or through the husband providing sperm in surrogacy arrangements or one or both parties (or sometimes other donors) providing gametes through gestational surrogacy. Surrogacy and gestational surrogacy, thus, are heavily classed and raced phenomena.

Almost all surrogacy involves working-class women contracting with professional-class child seekers. Race is also a major consideration. In the vast majority of known cases, the clients are a heterosexual married couple. Where the husband is the sperm donor, the aim of most couples is to find a birth mother with similarities of race and often other phenotypical features as one or both members of the contracting couple. In gestational surrogacy, where the birth mother does not provide the egg, the aim is to contract with a healthy but phenotypically different birth mother (Ragoné 2000). In the United States these differences reflect both racialized child preferences on the part of the adopter couple and legal cases where birth mothers have claimed prenatal bonding to break surrogacy contracts. Because of the primacy of largely class-rooted beliefs that genetic connection grounds kinship, courts have generally not supported gestational surrogate claims. In terms of adoption, several of the class issues are clear: (1) the contracting couple is generally much better off than the birth mother; (2) contractual decisions about what happens in the event of multiple births or medical problems with the infant(s) favor the party with the better lawyer, i.e., the potential adopters; and (3) those who are more apt to pursue such lawyer-mediated private arrangements are also concerned with notions of exclusive possession of the child.

Class ideologies predict that there would be a paucity of studies of abuse in adoptive families. Mandatory pre-adoptive home studies (regardless of how expedited the privatized ones may be), create an assumption that adopters are prepared to be effective, nonviolent parents. If we note that professional class people have resources to avoid legal scrutiny in cases of domestic violence in general, we have no way, except in episodic scandals, to assess how prevalent or rare child abuse is in adoptive families.

The forms of adoption (informal vs. formal, public vs. private, domestic and international) reflect the intersection of these hierarchies of class, gender, race, and sexualities. The particular contours and tensions will differ with legal codes, policies regarding discrimination, and the extent of social safety nets for women with children.

10.3 Formal and Informal Adoption

Informal adoption can be found in all societies, although some communities may be more likely to practice it than others. Legal transfer of affiliation may be impossible, complicated, or unaffordable. In other cases relationships among the affected adults may be fractious and fragile (as where drug or alcohol addiction is involved) and informal intervention to transfer effective parental roles the only feasible way to navigate familial dynamics while ensuring comparative stability or safety for the child or children. While some might consider this arrangement as foster care, it usually is long-lasting and the effective transformation of kin roles is from, for instance, grandmother or aunt, to mother.

Among informal adoptions, affiliation may involve exclusive transfer of kin obligations and rights, or an extension of these to the adoptive parent(s) or group. The adoption of children by market women in Baulé society in the Côte d'Ivoire strengthens and extends the connections among adult women, notably the birth and adoptive mothers, expressed through the adoptee (Etienne 1979). Baulé consider adoption advantageous to all parties, most often expanding opportunities for the adoptee, while linking the birth and adoptive mothers through the child, facilitating rural–urban transfers of other kinds as well. Adoption is both an expression of an existing relationship among the adult women, and a way to make the connection even closer. The openness of the adoption may include the child visiting the birth mother.

Formal adoption varies with the basis of the legal codes of the country or countries involved. Plenary adoption characterizes the form of legal adoption in most contemporary state societies, particularly those that have ratified the so-called Hague Conventions discussed below. Plenary adoption permanently severs the adoptee's natal connections and reassigns them to the adopter(s). Internationally, this is the most common type of formal adoption today. The exceptions derive either from customary practices – especially in indigenous, non-state communities – and countries where the national legal structure descends from the Napoleonic Code: primarily countries that were French colonies, such as Haiti. In Napoleonic Code-based settings, natal ties of an adoptee cannot be legally erased, although new obligations and rights can be augmented by inclusion in the adoptive group. Birth children cannot lose their right to inherit from natal kin, nor can they evade their legal obligation to help support their birth parent(s) in old age.

Following a series of international scandals regarding the health of adoptees from particular countries, the omnipresent shadow of baby markets, and a labyrinth of inconsistent policies and regulations regarding international adoption, donor and adopter countries have sought to make the process more uniform and less prone to trafficking, abuse, and forms of corruption. The Hague Conventions on international adoption were drafted by a number of countries, to regularize transfers of affiliation, granting of visas, coordinating Napoleonic and plenary legal frameworks for adoption, and to address issues arising from scandals that erupted regularly, including deception by sending countries, graft by adoption agents and lawyers, what is and is not informed consent in the termination of birth parent rights, and outright marketing of infants and children. The signatory countries have had to show compliance with the new provisions and ratify the agreement; this process can take many years and some of the major sending and receiving countries remain out of compliance.

10.4   Public Adoption

Formal adoption is done through the state, whether this is conducted through state agencies or whether it merely finalizes placements by private agencies or lawyers and adoption facilitators. Public adoption draws on children legally freed for adoption from foster care or, in many countries, a state-run orphanage system. Typically, this form of adoption mandates involvement by licensed social workers.

In the United States and Europe, the clients in public adoption are the children. Potential adopters must undergo a series of screenings, training sessions, and other requirements before a child can be placed with them. Often there is a "foster to adopt" status that permits state agencies to scrutinize the well-being of the child after placement, before the adoption can be finalized. The relative rigor of pre-adoptive screening varies markedly by country and between provinces or states. Typically there is a home study examining the family and personal histories of each prospective parent and including a criminal background check, a series of parenting and adoption classes and workshops to prepare the adopters, and site inspections with child safety preparation. The degree to which there can be social worker visitations or well-child checks after the adoption is legalized varies.

The degree to which public domestic adoptions are "open" or "closed" – permitting contact of some sort between birth parent(s) and adoptee – has become more common over the past 25 years in the United States (Grotevant and McCoy 1998), but so-called open adoption has been in place in many European countries since the end of World War II (Wegar 1997). Child development and adoption social workers concur that some form of open adoption – anything from an annual exchange of photographs, to social media contact, to monitored and unmonitored visitation, to the rare but reported informal adoption of the birth mother by the adopters – is best for the child's sense of identity and belonging. The exceptions are when the birth parent is alcoholic or drug-addicted, or suffers from certain forms of mental illness.

One variant of public adoption is *kin adoption*, formalizing what has been an informal practice for centuries: adoption of a child from a dysfunctional relative or relatives to provide a more stable and supportive environment. While fostering by relatives has been acceptable social work practice in the United States since the late 1950s, it was not until the 1980s that state agencies routinely permitted formal adoption by relatives. National adoption reforms in the name of "family preservation" during the last quarter of the twentieth century (and the first expanded federal acknowledgment of a widespread addictive drug use, especially in urban areas) sought to ensure child safety, reducing time in foster care, and minimizing disruption to children whose parent or parents had addiction problems. This initiative has proven successful in the main, but problems have arisen when the extended family is itself riddled with violence, addiction, or mental health issues. The immediate adopter(s) may be parenting effectively, but may be unable due to familial pressure to prevent demands by dysfunctional birth parents for unmonitored access to the child. Proponents argue that day-to-day stability and guidance are the focus for most foster placements, and kin adoption should involve no more scrutiny for kin adopters than foster parents might expect.

Financial barriers to public adoption in the United States have crumbled in large part due to militation by the National Association of Black Social Workers' efforts since the early 1970s to stimulate formal adoption of black children by black parents; indeed kin adoption and adoption by foster parents accelerated after this effort gained traction in the states (Gailey 2000a). The effect has been greater adoption by working-class people in general.

10.5   Private Adoption

Adoptions that are not arranged through state agencies are called private adoption. Private agencies, either secular or religiously affiliated, may focus on domestic or international adoption. Unlike public agencies, the clients are potential adopters, not the children. The non-profit agencies operate using licensed social workers that may be on staff or contracted, and networks that may include religious orphanages in other countries, networks of subcontracting organizations or individuals that locate pregnant women or available children that "match" the potential adopters' desires, or the adoption resource lists of legally freed children currently in state care. Home studies must be approved by the state, but in general private agency home studies are not as long or as detailed as those through public agencies. In practice in the United States there is little regulation of the quality of home studies conducted by private agencies and in general, there is little or no mandatory follow-up after the adoption is complete.

Adoptions through individual contracting parties, mediated by lawyers and licensed operators called "adoption facilitators," are called private adoptions or independent adoptions in the United States. They are illegal in most of Europe because of a perceived danger of child trafficking. In the United States an adoption facilitator is a licensed businessperson that is not required to be a social worker: for a fee this entrepreneur identifies a child or a pregnant woman willing to relinquish her rights to her child for a client person or couple. The contract is drawn up by lawyers. Legally, there can be no direct payment for a child, since that would be trafficking, but the clients pay the facilitator's professional fees, costs incurred by the pregnant woman, and sometimes a donation to the denomination if the pregnant woman or the facilitator is religiously affiliated. An approved home study has to be produced for any adoption in the United States, but the facilitator generally arranges this through subcontracted social workers.

Banning independent adoption in Europe prevents a clandestine market for children. There are indications that this is emerging in the United States, namely, informal transfers (sometimes involving payment) of children adopted privately to other parties if the adoption is not working. These pass-along transactions that often involve social media contacts generally operate within religious communities, usually fundamentalist Christian sects. The practice has been reported by responsible journalists, but as yet there has been no national investigation or crack-down on the parties or sects involved. The fate and mental health of children "passed along" is simply unknown.

10.6 Stepparent Adoption

Next to private infant or young child adoption, stepparent adoption is the most prevalent form of domestic adoption in the United States today. The in-marrying spouse seeks to adopt the child or children of the spouse, who is the birth mother or birth father of the children. Legally, the parental rights of the other birth parent must end for this to occur. In practice, stepparents may adopt the children soon after the marriage, but more typical is to wait until bonding and attachment occur, or a complicated divorce custody arrangement resolves. In situations where courts have awarded child support to the custodial parent, adoption may not be financially advantageous. Applying to the ex-spouse for termination of parental rights may trigger another round of custody hearings. As a result, adoption of stepchildren may be the intention long before it becomes possible. It is far from unusual for a stepparent that has been the effective mother or father to children in the family to delay formal adoption until the children are adolescents.

10.7 International Adoption

International adoption generally means countries of the global South becoming child providers for adopters from prosperous sectors of wealthier countries. In the United States, international adopters are in the main white professionals, most of whom do not have ongoing links with the country from which the child came. In seeking children, international adopters differ from domestic ones in not being receptive to "open adoption." Many express a desire to adopt internationally precisely to avoid any presence or claims by birth relatives associated with "open adoption" (Gailey 2010). These professionals rely on the private agencies or legal agencies specializing in international adoption to ensure that the child is one suitable to their desires. Often they accept without much questioning a core legal definition that verges on a myth, namely, that the children they are seeking are "orphans." In the Hague Conventions, "orphan" means a child whose birth mother and birth father have relinquished parental rights or had them terminated by the state. People adopting from China are aware that the available children are usually not orphans in the sense of having no living birth parents because international media coverage of the One-Child population policy has made abandonment a widely accepted explanation for the numbers of female infants and young girls in state orphanages.

Most do not return to the countries of their children's birth or conduct searches for living relatives. There are exceptions, enough to spawn a small travel industry in European and American countries. These so-called Heritage Tours for older adoptees and/or their adoptive families often include as part of the cultural exposure travel, a trip to the adoptee's orphanage, access to birth records if they exist, a meeting with the caregiver if she still works there, or actual contact with birth relatives. Reunions can result in a second rejection, or when the adoptee is welcomed, involve considerable cultural misunderstanding about kinship and expectations of an adult adoptee who is the de facto wealthy relative in an overseas country. "Daughter of Danang" is a documentary film that tracks conflict over remittance expectations that a biracial woman reared in the United States experiences after she meets and spends time with her Vietnamese birth family in Vietnam.

Scandinavian and some other European countries subsidize the cost of international adoptions for people of more modest means, as in some European countries. The United States has become a sending country as well as a receiving country: children of color awaiting adoptive placement in foster care in several of the southern states have become targets for adopters in the United Kingdom. Per capita, Norway, is the largest importer of adopted children in the world.

The People's Republic of China leads in sheer numbers of children (mostly female) placed with adopters from other countries. China's position is due to two factors: the One-Child (now Two-Child) population policy in a context of patriarchal practices that pressure daughters-in-law to abandon female infants, and policy making domestic adoption difficult if adopters are fertile or unmarried (Dorow 2002; Johnson, Banghan and Liyao 1998). Scholars have focused on the ways adopters of Chinese girls address the circumstances through which their children came to be adopted, and, like other international adopters, how to integrate cultural heritage issues into familial dynamics. Parental commitment to helping adoptees from other countries varies greatly, from books on the society, to integrating foods and holidays into family rituals, to seeking degrees of integration into transnational or immigrant communities from that country, to what Dorow calls "full immersion" – learning and teaching the language, visiting the country periodically, developing peer relationships with people from that country, joining adoptive support groups for families with children from that country, and conducting searches for birth relatives if an older child or young adult wishes (Dorow 2002).

Controversies in international adoption surround the power differences between sending and receiving countries, the ways in which children come into adoptive status, the adoption process in the sending country, and identity issues for adoptees in their new families and societies (Triseliotis 1999). Class issues loom large in international adoption, as does race. For example, as soon as the Soviet Bloc crumbled, Romania became a sending country for adopters from Western Europe and the United States. The wretched conditions in Romanian orphanages, coupled with the prospect of white "orphans" readily adopted, was a magnet at first. After a year or so of a virtual "run" on Romanian children, beyond unusually high rates of HIV infection due to reuse of needles for vitamin injections, a range of attachment, fetal alcohol syndrome, and developmental problems typical of post-institutionalized children became an international scandal (Johnson and Groze 1993). In addition, the chase for hard currency led to what became a baby market, reported cases of forced pregnancies for baby sales by in-laws, unscrupulous brokers, and pawning off unrelated children as sibling pairs. The problems led to international pressure to close down Romanian exports of children until the government could address the scope and scale of irregularities. Similar scandals followed as the "search for Baby White," as I have termed it, came to involve orphanage systems in the Ukraine, Russia, and Georgia (Gailey 2000a). Some of the international adopters, faced with children having traumatic histories or unreported developmental problems, sought to return the children or sue the private agencies. Media coverage of these cases was uniformly sympathetic to the adopters and little was said about the potential effect on the child of being returned (Gailey 2010).

In Brazil, how children come to be adopted internationally has become a recurrent national controversy and source of an inflammatory urban legend of adoption for organ donation. The problem centers on a structural collision between the state orphanage system and the need for poverty-stricken mothers to find temporary placements for their children (Fonseca 1986). While the system of child-sharing in poor urban neighborhoods constitutes a kind of informal adoption practice, repeated or extended usage of state orphanages while women arrange ways to support children can result in the state severing parental rights and moving the child to international adoption. Compounding this horror for birth mothers are the actions of paramilitary death squads, where street children that usually do have families disappear from the streets where they work (Bolton 2012). In addition, there have been kidnappings of adults for kidney transplants. The lack of reliable information or sympathetic guidance regarding relinquishment for largely illiterate mothers or grandmothers, the scouring of *favelas* by local "adoption facilitators"/ baby brokers, and the brief stays of international adopters in the country, coupled with death squads and kidnapping of children and youth (Fonseca 1986), have led to the widespread belief that international adopters are absconding with children to use as organ donors in the adopters' home countries. While this is not true, the layering of brutal conditions and opaque policies make the widespread belief understandable (Gailey 2010).

International adoption across race and color lines varies with countries. Adoption of Chinese and Korean "orphans" is widespread. Once in the adopters' country, adoptees may face racial discrimination for which their families are ill-equipped to negotiate (Yngvesson 1998). In some countries, such as Sweden, adoptees also must navigate a cultural script that views them as superior and privileged vis-à-vis Swedish birth children (Yngvesson 2010). Their own experiences of being uprooted and experiencing prejudice that may be socially denied makes this a distressing situation.

As adoptees adopted internationally become adults, social media sites are problematizing such dilemmas and challenging the social scripts and expected identities (Volkman 2005). Adult Korean adoptees have led the way in the United States for this discussion of complex identities, belonging in a society that views them as different and not fitting stereotypes of the "model minority" immigrant, and rejection by the society into which they were born because of their birth mothers' marital status or being of mixed race (Kim 2010).

10.8   Contemporary Debates in Adoption

Bridging public and private, domestic and international adoption are debates regarding the extent to which group or community rights and identities should be factors in adoptive placement. Other debates surround who should or should not be allowed to adopt, and what information about adoptees and their birth families should be available to adopters and adult adoptees.

10.9   Transracial Adoption

Adoption across socially constructed and sometimes politically ordained racial lines is termed interracial adoption in the United Kingdom and transracial adoption in the United States. While a range of contextually racialized adoptees fall into this category, the lines of debate have focused in an enduring manner on the adoption of black children by whites. In the United States and Canada, the debates also center on adoption of First Nations or Native American children by Anglos.

Native American communities in the United States have struggled to gain control over the disposition of the children born to the group on reservations and off reservations. The Indian Child Welfare Act is supposed to facilitate tribal control over what had been virtually unregulated access to Native children by Anglo adopters, but the loopholes and differences in infrastructure and sovereignty status have made efforts at exercising group rights over children extremely uneven (Strong 2002). In legal cases and in opposition to adoption reforms that would truncate tribal rights over children, Native communities have deployed the sovereignty clauses of various treaties with the national government. At stake is what First Nations activists call cultural genocide, creating identity crises for the adoptees and threatening the social reproduction and cultural health of Native communities weakened by centuries of colonization, suppression of language and cultural practices, and theft of children for the infamously harsh assimilationist boarding school system that operated well into the twentieth century. Today, some tribes with social service agencies built into their tribal governments have been able to reduce the rate of Anglo adoption, but children living off reservations are most at risk of state termination of parental rights and placement without recourse by tribal agencies.

For African American communities, no claims of sovereignty are possible legally. In the early 1970s the National Association of Black Social Workers moved to encourage formal adoption of black children by African American families, kin adoption, low-fee public adoption, and much more careful scrutiny and training of non-African American families before black children were placed with them. This highly controversial initiative dramatically increased formal adoption within African American communities, often through church programs, and revision in many states of home study protocols and training workshops. In the mid-1990s, however, a series of adoption reforms by the US Congress made consideration of race in foster care or adoptive placement grounds for losing federal funding for state programs. These reforms were praised by most white would-be public adopters as "race-blind" and moving foster children more quickly into permanency placement. But a range of interracial adopters sided with critics (see Gaber and Aldridge 1994; McRoy and Hall 1995), arguing that children pay the price for "race-blind" policies, as they face discrimination, violence, and attacks on their sense of worth through racism whether the proponents want race to be a factor or not. Authors urging that, because of abiding racism in the country, race should be one of the considerations in placement (see Patton 2000), explored the experiences of the participants in transracial adoption. Longitudinal studies of black children placed in white adoptive homes stressed the overall positive outcomes of such adoptions (Simon and Altstein 2000). Studies of adoptees or parents of transracially placed older children report the crucial importance of making race matter in familial discussions, living in well-integrated neighborhoods, having peer relationships across color lines, developing mentoring relations for the children through inclusive kin formation (aunties and uncles, "othermothers"), and developing strategies for well-being despite structural and interpersonal racism (Gailey 2010; Patton 2000). The experiences of adult adoptees who are black and reared by white parents and of white parents of black children report similar difficulties surrounding the development of a positive self-image and formation in adolescence, prejudice, and negative perceptions of them by both white and black individuals in the process (Hall and Steinberg 2000; Simon and Roorda 2000).

10.10   Who Can Adopt?

In countries around the world, debates have emerged surrounding who can adopt. Most countries have formal or informal barriers to adoption by people over a certain age, meant to ensure that children could expect to grow up with one set of adoptive parents. Exceptions to this exist, but typically these are in so-called private adoption, especially adoptions arranged without adopters seeking placement through an agency. In general challenges to age restrictions have emphasized the extension of life expectancy in recent decades. Categories of adopters that are banned in some countries but permitted in others include: single mothers, single fathers, and gay and lesbian couples.

10.11   Single Parent Adoption

Historically in the United States, adoption of orphan children – often simply homeless or poverty-stricken – by wealthy individuals was acceptable, viewed as an act of charity and generosity on the part of the adopter, and a stroke of luck for the adoptee. In the early decades of the twentieth century, this practice was wide enough as to become a theme in movies (as in Shirley Temple's "Curly Top"). The adopter was either male or female, and their morality was presumed from their social status. Orphanages did little or no investigation of the motives or life style of the adopter. Little is known about the scale or outcomes of these adoptions.

Barriers to single mother adoptions have been breached in many countries, although in some, single women can be seen as inappropriate mothers. In the United States, many public agencies view single women as less desirable adopters and so tend to "match" them with less desirable (often older or traumatized) children (Gailey 1998). Like other public adopters, in most states single women are apt to receive a modest monthly subsidy post-adoption, renewable to age 18. This helps to cover the financial handicap that not having gender equity in pay and having a single-income household poses for a child who often has what are called "special needs." The prohibitive costs of mental health care in the United States can result for these families in bankruptcy or a lower standard of living post-adoption than before the woman became an adoptive mother. It is remarkable under these circumstances that the failure rate of such adoptions is no greater than for other kinds of public adoption (Gailey 2006). The resilience of these adoptive families is a testament to the resourcefulness of the mother in developing support networks (Gailey 1998).

Single women with the financial means to do so can pursue private agency adoptions although they are even less desirable as adopters in this sector than in the public sector. It is rare for "adoption facilitators" with religious networks of young white pregnant women to agree to help single women adopt. Often the birth mothers themselves stress their desire for religious, heterosexual, married couples as preferred adopters for their children.

10.12   Gay and Lesbian Adoption

While adoption by homosexuals generally lumps gay men and lesbian women, the situation for adoption is quite different in terms of practices in many countries. Historically, it has been easier for homosexual women to adopt than homosexual men, due to ideologies even within homophobic societies that view the desire to have and rear children as either natural for women or at least much stronger in women than men. Coupled with this "passing" for homosexual women is the myth that children, especially boys, would be at risk of molestation by homosexual men – despite reams of sociological studies to the contrary (Barrett and Tasker 2002; Jenny, Roesler and Poyer 1994). But until same-sex marriage was legalized, adoption was restricted to only one partner.

Until inroads by lesbian and gay activists, homosexuals faced heavy discrimination when seeking to adopt. Even though ideologies of maternal instinct favored lesbians over gay men, lesbian women faced agency bias against single parent adoption, but at the same time, could not present as a stable couple – more desirable for agencies – because of their being same-sex. Some public and private agencies, especially those in large urban areas, permitted lesbian and gay adoptions as an "open secret" even before same-sex marriages were legitimated. Indeed, because of the dearth of foster parents for adolescent children, a number of public agencies had for years permitted fostering by same-sex couples, and sometimes singles. But until the legalization of same-sex marriage, the foster parent(s) or adopter(s) had to keep their sexual orientations officially "in the closet" and one partner had to be the foster parent of record.

Adoption of the partner's birth child by a same-sex partner became legal in parts of the United States beginning in the 1990s, that is, decades before same-sex marriage was legalized. In keeping with gendered kinship ideologies, adoption by same-sex partners was legalized first for lesbians and only later for gay men.

For homosexuals rejected for adoption by policy or de facto agency bias, the routes to parenthood have involved international private agencies or so-called independent (private party) adoption. The emphasis on international adoption is a reflection of the domination of private agencies by religious denominations that tend (not exclusively) to discriminate against homosexuals. Many countries also ban homosexual adoption, but some state and private orphanage systems are strapped for operating funds and rely on hard currency donations from international adopters to support their operations. The result, as for single parent adoptions, is a revolving open-and-closed-door for prospective adopters as countries loosen restrictions or clamp down on single parent adoptions that can cloak a homosexual couple.

The other route to parenthood involving adoption for gay men is designated guardianship by a dying friend, or surrogacy. Here, the dynamics of surrogacy differ markedly from those for heterosexual couples. Research is sparse to date, but it appears that in US urban areas, gay men tend to arrange for surrogates within their own social class, community, and sometimes friendship network, with an intention of having an open adoption with the birth mother.

10.13   Sealed Records and Searches

Countries vary in whether or not adoptive parents and/or adult adoptees can have access to their birth and pre-adoptive records. In all but a few states in the United States, for instance, records are "sealed," although legislative and media lobbying by adoption advocacy groups has softened this in some places to permit access to information that pertains to medical conditions of the birth parents and their families to the extent this is known. In other countries, such as Finland (Wegar 1997), records are unsealed and adoptees have access to the names and contact information of their birth parent(s). The arguments for unsealing records center on the belief that adoptees have a right to know their histories. The arguments against unsealing records focus on the privacy rights of the birth parent(s). There are concerns about birth mothers in particular needing to keep adoption a secret if they are in unaccepting environments, but other birth mothers are forthright about their histories with partners and subsequent children. Proponents of sealed records point to the potential danger for birth mothers in some domestic circumstances if the adoption is revealed. Attempting to discover medical and social histories places adopters and adoptees in the position of doing searches, while trying to maintain respect for the birth parents' lives.

Circumventing remaining sealed-record jurisdictions, social media have become an informal clearing house for adoptees and birth parents seeking information or to make contact. There are search sites where birth relatives and adoptees can register. Parties can exchange information and the contact may lead to a reunion. The consequences of reunions are variable, ranging from "a second rejection" to creating an extended family. Disturbing are reported instances of reunions between birth mothers and adult sons that become sexual relationships. Some researchers have seen this as one possible fruition of what they call a "birthbond" (Gediman and Brown 1989), others reject this notion and have considered it an attraction based on the adult son being about the same age as the birth father when the child was conceived (Gailey 2010). Anthropologists probably would not consider this kind of liaison as incest, since the two parties are sociologically strangers, but the reports are that these are short-lived relationships and emotionally volatile for both. Most reunions are an exploration of an ideology of "blood ties" where one or both parties has an expectation of closeness, while as the connection plays out, the realities of non-kinship or of kin-making as a process come to the fore (Modell 1997).

10.14   Embryo "Adoption"

In recent years, the ongoing controversy over reproductive rights and, specifically, legalized abortion and what constitutes a person has permeated adoption issues in some Christian religious circles in the United States. An organization called "Snowflake Adoption" developed in concert with the growing infertility industry, notably with in vitro fertilization. Fertilized ova that are not implanted can be disposed in accordance with the clients' wishes: frozen for future implantation, donation for medical research, or destruction. Snowflake Adoption lobbies for the "adoption" of fertilized ova from fertility clinics by unrelated, Christian married couples, for future implantation in the wife (Cromer 2018). This movement drew the tacit support of the Bush administration. It only constitutes adoption if one assumes that a fertilized ovum is a legal person. No legal adoption proceedings accompany the claims, and no home studies or other regulatory processes associated with legal adoption are involved. As long as there are no monetary transfers, it is considered a private donation and not subject to the ban on the sale of fertilized human eggs.

10.15   Kinship Formation in Adoption

Adoption provides a way of viewing kinship formation in a particular society. Unhampered as it is by ideologies of natural relationship (blood, genetics), it frees us to see how people actually construct kinship. Researchers have explored how adoption transforms strangers into kin (Modell 1993). It should not surprise us that where there are social hierarchies, their cross-cutting and reinforcing character will produce variations on what constitutes kinship in that particular "intersection" historically (Gailey 2000a). Class, race, gender, sexualities, immigration status, religion, and nationality would create inflections of what it means to belong, what family is, and how people enter and exit circuits of relationship (Seligmann 2013). Since adoption necessarily forces people to confront the degree to which their relationship to each other involved unshared histories, and how children are not replicants of their sociological parent(s), it is especially good as a way of gauging the power of naturalized ideologies of kinship. In short, adoptive kinship renders kin formation transparent. Issues unique to adoption – being a minority form of family, identity formation as an adoptee, ideologies of "unnatural" motherhood of both the adopter and birth mother, marking of sameness and difference in the family, discrimination against adoptees in the wider society, issues of abandonment and foster care treatment, unknowable histories – enter into kinship formation as a process within the framework of race, class, gender, and other vectors of social stratification.

In studies of how adopters speak of their children, class appears as a major consideration in how children are claimed conditionally or included wholly in families. Language used, such as "We love him like our own" versus "She's one of us," mark partial or full inclusion. The former phrase crops up especially in extended family discussions among wealthier adopters, the latter found primarily in single-mother and working-class adopters. In all fairness, this difference may be characteristic of kinship in general in these sectors: performance-based, parent-centered, conditional, and implicitly measured against genetic relationship in wealthier sectors; inclusive, decentered, and without implicit reference to genetic connection in working-class settings (Gailey 2010). The images of single motherhood and women giving up children in adoption, whether negative or sympathetic, tend to be from a distance in wealthier sectors. In working-class arenas, the woman who relinquishes her child may be judged by the adoptive relatives, but it is from a sociological proximity – it could have or did happen to one of the relatives. The effect is to make the child feel more or less different in origin from more prosperous adopters, and more recognizably similar to working-class adopters (Gailey 2000b).

Race enters into adoptive kin formation in similar ways as it does through birth kinship in societies with racial hierarchies. It is more common to encounter "race-blind" attitudes among white adopters (Yngvesson 1998): "We don't care what color she is" or "We don't see color when we see him," although those involved in race issues tend to problematize race in parenting, schooling, and the like. Among black adopters, race is a common topic of familial discussion; it also tends to be problematized in single-mother transracial adoptions and for similar reasons: the adopters recognize that the safety and well-being of children depends on preparing them for navigating racism throughout life. It is more common in single-mother transracial adoptions for the mother to seek out support persons, mentors, and role models from the racialized communities of the child's perceived, not always known heritage (Gailey 2006).

Kinship in general involved claiming one another, understood obligations and expectations, sharing of material resources, generalized reciprocity (giving and sharing without expectation of immediate or comparable return), contributing work along lines of gender and age category as well as acquired skills, emotional support, shared and newly created rituals – for adoptive families this can include celebrating the anniversary of the day the child came home or the day the adoption was finalized – and, in short, developing a sense of group identity materialized through pooled resources and practiced through caregiving. Each of these dimensions is modulated in relation to social hierarchies and shared and unshared histories. In adoption some of these dimensions can be materialized in an accentuated fashion, such as scrapbooking, photography, social media postings and communication, and gifted valuable objects that are historically meaningful or personalized. Others remain non-material, such as family stories, adoption origin myths of foresight and claiming ("I dreamed you before we met," "I fell in love with you the minute I saw you,") shared positive and negative experiences.

In sum adoption creates kinship in ways similarly inflected by race, class, gender, and other stratification dimensions as birth families. Where it appears different is in conditions prior to when the children "come home" – foster care, abuse or neglect, early relinquishment – how the adopters' communities and surrounding institutions integrate or discriminate against the child as an adoptee, and the ways adoptive families cannot depend on the powerful myth of genetic connection or birth as a foundation of kinship.

References

Barrett, Helen and Fiona Tasker. 2002. "Gay Fathers and Their Children: What We Know and What We Need to Know." *Lesbian and Gay Psychology Review* 3: 3–10.

Bolton, Alicia. 2012. A rua é nossa (The Street Is Ours): In Search of Childhood and Rights on the Street of Guarulhos, Brazil. Ph.D. Dissertation, University of California, Riverside.

Cromer, Rita. 2018. "Waiting: The Redemption of Frozen Embryos through Embryo Adoption and Stem Cell Research in the United States." In *The Anthropology of the Fetus: Biology, Culture, and Society*, ed. Sallie Han, Tracy Betsinger and Amy Scott, 171-199. New York: Berghahn Press.

Dorow, Sara. 2002. "'China R Us'?: Care, Consumption, and Transnationally Adopted Children." In *Symbolic Childhood*, ed. Daniel Thomas Cook. New York: Peter Lang Publishing.

Etienne, Mona. 1979. "The Case for Social Maternity: Adoption of Children by Urban Baulé Women." *Dialectical Anthropology* 4(1): 237-242.

Fonseca, Claudia. 1986. "Orphanages, Foundlings, and Foster Mothers: The System of Child Circulation in a Brazilian Squatter Settlement." *Anthropological Quarterly* 59(1): 15-27.

Gaber, Ivor and Jane Aldridge, eds. 1994. *In the Best Interests of the Child: Culture, Identity, and Transracial Adoption*. London: Free Association Books.

Gailey, Christine Ward. 1998. "Making Kinship in the Wake of History: Gendered Violence in Older Child Adoption." *Identities* 5(2): 249-292.

2000a. "Race, Class, and Gender in Intercountry Adoption in the USA." In *Intercountry Adoption: Developments, Trends, and Perspectives*, ed. Peter Selman, 315-345. London: British Agencies for Adoption and Fostering.

2000b. "Ideologies of Motherhood in Adoption." In *Ideologies and Technologies of Motherhood: Race, Class, Sexuality, Nationalism*, ed. Heléna Ragoné and France Winddance Twine, 11-55. New York: Routledge.

2006. "'Whatever They Think of Us, We're a Family': Single Mother Adopters." In *Adoptive Families in a Diverse Society*, ed. Katarina Wegar, 162-174. New Brunswick, NJ: Rutgers University Press.

2010. *Blue Ribbon Babies and Labors of Love: Race, Class, and Gender in U.S. Adoption*. Austin, TX: University of Texas Press.

Gediman, Judith and Linda Brown. 1989. *Birthbond: Reunions between Birthparents and Adoptees – What Happens After ....* Far Hills, NJ: New Horizon Press.

Grotevant, Harold and Ruth McRoy. 1998. *Openness in Adoption: Exploring Family Connections*. Thousand Oaks, CA: Sage Publications.

Hall, Beth and Gail Steinberg. 2000. *Inside Transracial Adoption*. London: Jessica Kingsley Publishers.

Jenny, Carole, Thomas A. Roesler and Kimberly L. Poyer. 1994. "Are Children at Risk for Sexual Abuse by Homosexuals?" *Pediatrics* 94(1): 41-44.

Johnson, A. and Victor Groze. 1993. "The Orphaned and Institutionalized Children of Romania." *Journal of Emotional and Behavioral Problems* 2(4): 49-52.

Johnson, Kay, Huang Banghan and Wang Liyao. 1998. "Infant Abandonment and Adoption in China." *Population and Development Review* 24(3): 469–510.

Kim, Eleana. 2010. *Adopted Territory: Transnational Korean Adoptees and the Politics of Belonging.* Durham, NC: Duke University Press.

Lindsay, Hugh. 2009. *Adoption in the Roman World.* Cambridge: Cambridge University Press.

McRoy, Ruth and C. Hall. 1995. "Transracial Adoptions: In Whose Best Interest?" In *Multiracial People in the New Millennium*, ed. M. Root, 63–78. Newbury Park, CA: Sage Publications.

Modell, Judith Schachter. 1993. *Kinship with Strangers: Adoption and Interpretations of Kinship in American Culture.* Berkeley, CA: University of California Press.

1997. "Where Do We Go Next? Long Term Reunion Relationships between Adoptees and Birth Parents." *Marriage and Family Review* 25(1, 2): 43–67.

Patton, Sandra Lee. 2000. *BirthMarks: Transracial Adoption in Contemporary America.* New York: New York University Press.

Ragoné, Helena. 2000. "Of Likeness and Difference: How Race Is Being Transfigured by Gestational Surrogacy." In *Ideologies and Technologies of Motherhood: Race, Class, Sexuality, Nationalism*, ed. Helena Ragoné and France Winddance Twine, 56–75. New York: Routledge.

Seaver, James. [1824] 2015. *A Narrative of the Life of Mary Jemison: White Woman of the Genesee.* London: Forgotten Books.

Seligmann, Linda. 2013. *Broken Links, Enduring Ties: American Adoption across Race, Class, and Nation.* Stanford, CA: Stanford University Press.

Simon, Rita and Howard Altstein. 2000. *Adoption across Borders: Serving the Children in Transracial and Intercountry Adoptions.* Lanham, MD: Rowman and Littlefield.

Simon, Rita James and Rhonda Roorda. 2000. *In Their Own Voices: Transracial Adoptees Tell Their Stories.* New York: Columbia University Press.

Strong, Pauline Turner. 2002. "To Forget Their Tongue, Their Name, and Their Whole Relation: Captivity, Extra-Tribal Adoption, and the American Indian Welfare Act." In *Relative Values: Reconfiguring Kinship Studies*, ed. Sarah Franklin and Susan McKinnon, 468–493. Durham, NC: Duke University Press.

Triseliotis, John. 1999. "Inter-Country Adoption: Global Trade or Global Gift?" In *Mine – Yours – Ours and Theirs: Adoption, Changing Kinship and Family Patterns*, ed. Anne-Lise Rygvold, Monica Dalen and Barbro Saetersdal, 14–31. Oslo: University of Oslo/GCS.

Volkman, Toby, ed. 2005. *Cultures of Transnational Adoption.* Durham, NC: Duke University Press.

Wegar, Katarina. 1997. *Adoption, Identity, and Kinship: The Debate over Sealed Birth Records.* New Haven, CT: Yale University Press.

Yngvesson, Barbara. 1998. "'Un niño de cualquier color': Race and Nation in Intercountry Adoption." In *Globalizing Institutions: Case Studies in Regulation and Innovation*, ed. Jane Jenson and Boaventura de Sousa Santos. Burlington, VT: Ashgate.

2010. *Belonging in an Adopted World: Race, Identity, and Transnational Adoption*. Chicago, IL: University of Chicago Press.

11

"Natural" Achievements: How Lesbian and Gay Families in North America Make Claims to Kinship

Ellen Lewin

Lesbian and gay (hereafter LGBT) kinship studies represent a tiny area of research, deeply divided into two fundamentally different ways of thinking about issues of family formation. Some scholars have focused on the idea that kinship and family are domains from which LGBT people have either been banished or that they have affirmatively rejected. Proponents of this perspective have produced impeccable descriptions of the alternative forms of family and kinship that LGBT people have crafted – or perhaps into which they have been forced. Contrasting with what we might call the "alternative families" approach is work that shows how LGBT people have embraced so-called mainstream kinship ideologies and family forms, locating themselves firmly at the heart of the wider culture. This approach emphasizes what the alternative families folks might consider accommodation to "straight" values, at odds with what many have lauded as "queer" (understood as inherently subversive) kinship formulations. In other words, one approach emphasizes (and celebrates) the existence of autonomous LGBT cultures, while the other situates LGBT people decisively in the larger culture.

In this chapter, I will show that the apparent conflicts between these two approaches reflect the particular LGBT populations scholars have worked with even as they seem to represent inflexible ideological contrasts. Both ways of understanding LGBT kinship are descriptive of explicit times and circumstances, and attending to the specificity of these distinctive kinship systems allows us to better appreciate how varied LGBT lives and cultures actually are. The differences between these approaches lie in part in the extent to which their authors understand LGBT people as possessing a culture of their own that can be readily recognized. Is being LGBT akin to belonging to an ethnic group that possesses a distinctive cultural repertoire? Or is LGBT identity a feature that is negotiated along with other cultural attachments, sometimes very salient and sometimes nearly irrelevant within the cultural context in which they live?

11.1   Some Background

When I first started research on lesbian mothers in 1977, my colleagues in anthropology were baffled. Where did I expect to find people who fit such an oxymoronic category? Didn't I know the "facts of life" – where babies come from? This was the era when lesbian mothers who had had their children in the course of heterosexual marriages were beginning to make it into the news, typically fighting their ex-husbands for custody, so my colleagues' questions gradually subsided as these stories reached the mainstream media.[1] And as I continued my research, I moved from looking only at formerly married lesbian mothers to talking with women who had decided to have children after they had defined themselves as lesbians, women associated with what was being called the "gayby boom."[2]

These were women who made an affirmative choice to be mothers, under conditions where achieving pregnancy would take some ingenuity. They seemed to be doing something that confounded ordinary understandings of kinship (if not biology), in some cases becoming sole parents when they used anonymous, and usually socially insignificant, sperm donors, and in other cases, taking conception out of ordinary (domestic) locations and into medical settings. Remember, this was a time before ARTs (assisted reproductive technologies) became a reasonable option for engendering a child. These women were also challenging prevailing assumptions that lesbians lacked the requisite moral foundation to be mothers. If being a lesbian was all about gratifying unconventional, morally ambiguous sexual urges, as popular stereotypes asserted, then how could such a person muster the altruism necessary to successfully care for a child's needs (Lewin 1993)?

The work I did with lesbian mothers eventually led me to research with gay fathers, whose hold on "natural" reproduction seemed even more tenuous than that of women (Lewin 2009). In US cultures, men in general are typically understood to be less committed to parenthood than women, and overcoming infertility among heterosexual couples is conventionally thought to be a woman's problem, no matter how urgently a man may wish to become a father (Greil 1991). For gay men, these cultural obstacles are amplified by assumptions that they are too debauched to be appropriate material for parenthood. Nor are such concerns limited to homophobic opponents of gay rights; many gay and lesbian people share an uneasiness about lesbian and gay parents, either viewing "family" as an intrinsically straight domain (Newton 1993), or representing the desire of some lesbian and gay people to gain access to marriage and family as expressions of craven assimilationism (Halberstam 2013; Warner 1999; West et al. 2013). Still, like lesbians, some gay men resist or refute such approbation and seek out parenthood even when the time and expense of becoming and being parents entail burdensome costs and dramatic changes to the way they live their lives.

My research also included work on same-sex commitment ceremonies or "weddings," ritual occasions that served to communicate the significance of a partnership or marriage to an audience carefully selected to leap over the boundaries of the gay community – family, friends, neighbors, coworkers (Lewin 1998). I carried out this project before there was anywhere in the world where same-sex couples could be legally married – that right was first won in the Netherlands in 2001 – so I was eager to understand what motivated couples to stage these ceremonies in the absence of any sort of legal benefits that would accrue from their new status. While many couples I interviewed insisted on legal correctness and hesitated to call their unions "marriages" or these rituals "weddings," many others were less reticent and most couples carefully reproduced culturally recognizable weddings in crafting their ceremonies.

These days lesbian and gay families have become the stuff of ordinary experience, even being portrayed sympathetically in the US mass media ("Modern Family," "The Kids Are Alright," etc.), and, far from being invisible, the children of lesbians and gay men have become central to battles over marriage equality currently ongoing in the courts. Rather than assuming that lesbians and gay men can't (or shouldn't) have children, those adjudicating demands for marriage equality often use the status of children to justify ruling in favor of legalizing same-sex marriage. For example, in his majority opinion striking down most provisions of the Defense of Marriage Act (DOMA) in *United States v. Windsor* (2013), Supreme Court Justice Anthony Kennedy said that DOMA "humiliates tens of thousands of children now being raised by same-sex couples. The law in question makes it even more difficult for the children to understand the integrity and closeness of their own family and its concord with other families in their community and in their daily lives." The presence of children in these families was not a source of controversy for Justice Kennedy; he simply took their existence for granted and thus was inclined to raise their well-being as an issue that the Court needed to address.

Despite the rapid changes taking place on the legal front, anthropology has been less than energetic as a field in documenting the forms lesbian and gay families take;[3] most work on these topics has been produced by sociologists, psychologists, and legal scholars. But I can draw on the growing field of lesbian and gay/queer anthropology and on a small body of literature that focuses on lesbian and gay reproduction, and then will use my own work to argue that lesbians and gay men who are parents, as well as those who enter into formal unions or marriages, largely find ways to adhere to what might be considered "conservative" or "traditional" constructions of family. I found that these socially constructed families emphasize the salience of biological connections they understand to be grounded in "nature," and take pains to naturalize even the most carefully crafted family-forming strategies within recognized kinship categories. Many readers will recognize the reliance on constructions of nature that are also typical of heterosexuals who make use of assisted reproductive technologies as well as the discourses of adoptive parents (see, for example, Modell 1994; Sandelowski 1993; Thompson 2005).

On the other hand, distinctive kinship forms have arisen among some LGBT people who have been rejected by their family of orientation or other key community institutions. They thus aim to organize some sort of solidary, reliable units that can step up to do the traditional work of kinship under adverse conditions. In the cases I've reviewed, such alternative strategies appear among LGBT people who are neither parents nor married; parenthood and marriage seem to produce kinship ideologies that more closely resemble those of the wider, "mainstream," society.

11.2   Anthropology's Bifurcated View of LGBT Family and Kinship

11.2.1   Alternative Kinship/Families

Kath Weston's important work (1991) in many ways set the agenda for future studies of LGBT kinship. In *Families We Choose*, Weston documented how lesbians and gay men responded to rejection by their biological (straight) families by forming and elaborating a parallel universe of kinship they often called "chosen" family. Chosen families, a term that is so apt that it has entered the LGBT lexicon, were constituted from (mostly gay and lesbian) friends, a category elsewhere called "fictive kin," and were understood to be more resilient and reliable than "straight" families. Indeed, the formation and continuity of these families stood as a direct challenge to the conventional assumption that "blood is thicker than water," or that one's kin are the most steadfast source of truly solidary support, while friendships are ephemeral and unreliable. Weston's gay and lesbian interlocutors explicitly compared their "chosen" families, which rarely included children, with their "straight" families, likening the depth and strength of their chosen relationships with the characteristics assumed to be associated with blood kinship, and finding the latter wanting. As Weston explains, "I have situated chosen families in the specific context of an ideological opposition between families defined as straight and gay – families identified with biology and choice, respectively" (Weston 1991: 108). She notes that these gay families have "fluid boundaries," thus resembling "kinship organization among sectors of African-American, American Indian, and white working class" populations (Weston 1991: 108; see also Schneider and Smith 1978).

Weston's narrators were mostly relatively young lesbians and gay men in San Francisco who did not have their own children. Many had migrated to the San Francisco Bay Area from elsewhere in the United States to find a supportive gay or lesbian community, so their presence in this particular location reflected their purposefully separating themselves from the communities where they had been raised, either because they had come to see them as alien, or because they had suffered painful rejection by their kin. Still, these LGBT people didn't jettison the category of kinship, but rather re-populated it to make it operate as they imagined it ideally should. Weston showed, as well, that many lesbians and gay men continued relationships with their "straight" families, sustaining both kinds of kinship alongside one another.[4]

More recent ethnographic work by Marlon Bailey has also highlighted patterns of alternative kinship that stand in stark contrast to conventional notions of family. In *Butch Queens Up in Pumps* (Bailey 2013), we learn about the world of black Ballroom culture in Detroit and in some other urban centers around the US. Bailey characterizes collectivities where black drag performers connect as "queer families," though he carefully distinguishes between the terms the queens use to describe themselves (a wide range of terms that denote sex, gender, and sexuality), and his understanding of the cultural work that Ballroom families accomplish. Bailey explains,

> I use the term *queer* to refer to the practices of identity, kinship, and community making in which the members of Ballroom culture are engaged. I do not claim, however, that members of this community use the term as a way to identify themselves … Ultimately, I deploy queer theory to examine what members of the Ballroom culture *do* as opposed to who they are.
>
> *(Bailey 2013: 23)*

Ballroom families, usually called "Houses" that take their names from fashion icons such as Galliano, Givenchy, or Chanel, take on a labor of care that would traditionally be the province of biological families – if they accepted their LGBT offspring. That the House becomes the real family of the LGBT people who populate the pages of Bailey's book is a telling indictment of the failure of biological families to do the care work for their LGBT offspring that is supposed to be their job. Each House has a "mother" and "father," who dispense various kinds of material and moral support to their "children" (who need not be chronologically younger than the parents). They are institutions that offer the love, acceptance, and sense of belonging that families are supposed to provide. They also are a site of socialization for their members, training them in the art of competing at balls. Social relationships in Houses are based on complicated gender categories that underlie Ballroom performance. They are headed by mothers who can be any of the feminine categories (butch queens, femme queens, or women) and fathers who can represent any of the masculine categories (butch queens, butches, or men).[5] In all cases they "provide parental guidance to numerous black LGBT people who have been devalued and rejected by their blood families, religious institutions of their childhood, and society at large" (Bailey 2013: 92–93). As Bailey explains, these family structures help black LGBT people survive the hostile environment with which they must contend outside the House system.

Both Weston and Bailey offer an account of kinship and family that parallels the expectations of queer scholars and political commentators who are invested in the understanding of queer life as a form of resistance to conventional, heteronormative social forms. Other anthropological approaches to lesbian and gay kinship that emphasize difference have focused on the reproductive strategies needed to form non-heterosexual families in the West. Corinne P. Hayden examined lesbian family formation in terms of the challenge it posed to conventional notions of "biology" (Hayden 1995). Drawing on Marilyn Strathern's consideration of the effects of new technologies on Western kinship (Strathern 1992), Hayden focused on the elasticity of the symbolic systems that constitute kinship to absorb new configurations of reproduction. Certainly, some elements of gender performance in families are altered by the presence of two mothers (and the typically peripheral role of the sperm donor), as is our understanding of biology when careful strategies must be employed to effect conceptions. Still, such manifestations of intention are hardly novel in a world where the use of ARTs, both low-tech and high-tech, are increasingly normative for all kinds of couples throughout the world who face "infertility" and are firmly ensconced in a web of consumption (Taylor, Layne and Wozniak 2004). Hayden argues convincingly that "lesbian mothers simultaneously affirm the importance of blood as a symbol and challenge the American cultural assumption that biology is a self-evident, singular fact and *the* natural baseline on which kinship is built" (Hayden 1995: 56, emphasis in original).

Inspired by Hayden's approach, Jacquelyne Luce's Canadian research (Luce 2010) specified the ways that the women she studied navigated the practical challenges of forming families, including choosing donors and various kinds of medical intervention. Mirroring what other scholarship in anthropology and sociology has focused on, a number of studies centered in the West and largely concerned with the ramifications of novel forms of conception on kinship systems follow this lead (see, for example Agigian 2004; Franklin 1997; Sullivan 2004; Thompson 2005; Thompson 2002).

Strathern, Hayden, and Luce focused their attention on the conceptive projects undertaken by lesbians (or others who cannot reproduce biologically without some sort of technological intervention) and how such forms of reproduction challenge – or do not challenge – biology as the symbolic core of American (or Western) kinship (Schneider 1968). In these analyses, we see approaches very similar both to the work of feminist medical anthropologists on ARTs in their various guises (see for example, Franklin 1997; Franklin and Ragoné 1998; Mitchell 2001; Rapp 1999; Sandelowski 1993; Taylor, Layne and Wozniak 2004) and to examinations of adoption that have documented the ways that ideas about "nature" make their way into the understandings of definitions of kinship embraced by adoptive parents (Modell 1994; Volkman 2005). Still, the notion that conceptive technologies dramatically alter the foundations of LGBT families, as compared with heterosexual families that use the same technical processes, fails to take into account the way these families function once their existence has been established.

11.3   Creating Lesbian and Gay Families

My work on lesbian mothers, which was conducted a decade earlier than Weston's, revealed a rather different pattern from her findings. While the lesbian mothers I studied had to contend with rejection by their biological families and other challenges that at times marginalized them from mainstream society, I found that motherhood enhanced their involvement with biological kin and tended to distance them from LGBT culture. But this was not an interpretation that I originally expected to make. Indeed, when I began to study lesbian mothers, I assumed that they would organize alternative kinds of support networks to compensate for the unreliability of blood kin and that their strategies would thus diverge markedly from those pursued by the heterosexual single mothers I also studied. This assumption was based on what Weston would call "street theory" (Weston 1998), that is, locally accepted notions about gay and lesbian communities and how they are constituted.

But when one moves beyond a focus on reproductive technologies and the ways lesbians and gay men go about constituting themselves as parents and establishing their families, the apparent differences between lesbian/gay and heterosexual families recede in importance. While there were many areas of overlap between my findings and Kath Weston's, the parents I spoke with tended to be preoccupied with maintaining the centrality of their "biological" families and were thus inclined to minimize the attention they gave to the kinds of "chosen" families Weston had so famously documented. That is, as it does in heterosexual families, parenthood seemed to make the biological family more salient in the lives of both lesbians and gay men, who often found (like heterosexual parents) that they had less and less in common with their gay and lesbian friends who didn't have children and felt they could more fully rely on their blood relatives for various kinds of support. Along the same lines, the friendships they pursued were increasingly defined by the shared experience of parenthood, so that gay and lesbian parents saw other people with children as those with whom they shared experience, regardless of whether these people were also gay or lesbian. Most notably, they saw these changes as being a *natural* outgrowth of being parents, even when maintaining kin ties required considerable effort and diplomacy. In this calculus, parenthood is such an enormous and life-altering responsibility that it effectively "trumps" other aspects of identity. While lesbian and gay parents don't stop being lesbian and gay, they tend to see their relationship to those designations changing dramatically. When I asked one gay father how having children had affected his and his partner's lives as gay men, he responded, "Oh, we're not gay anymore. We pick our friends by what time their kids take their naps." Though this response was offered in a playful vein, it clearly signaled these fathers' move away from activities and networks that are exclusively gay, and identified having children as *not* gay.

The work I present here is largely based on lengthy interviews with lesbian mothers, gay fathers, and couples who staged commitment ceremonies (Lewin 1993, 1998, 2009). Since my work focused on gay and lesbian people who *are* parents, and on those who *did* solemnize their relationships, it omits discussion of those who didn't do these things: for example, those who may have considered becoming parents but were unable to accomplish any of the various forms of reproduction available today to non-heterosexuals, either because of the challenges of biological procreation, difficulties navigating the world of adoption – public and private, domestic and international – or because of the financial obstacles that surround use of these technologies. Nor did I work systematically with lesbians and gay men who simply never considered parenthood or solemnizing their unions, whether they found either intrinsically undesirable or simply assumed that it was beyond the boundaries of what could be considered possible for non-heterosexuals.[6]

My work is further limited by the particular historical moments in which each research project was carried out. As mentioned above, I studied lesbian mothers in the San Francisco Bay Area between 1977 and 1981, though my book on the subject did not appear until more than a decade later (Lewin 1993). Subsequent to that time, important developments have shaped both the experience of lesbian motherhood and its public image, and a number of other scholars have documented the ways that the challenges facing lesbian mothers have changed over the decades (Mamo 2007; Moore 2011; Sullivan 2004). My work on gay fathers was carried out between 2001 and 2003, primarily in the Chicago metropolitan area (though I also conducted interviews in California and in Iowa), and was sparked by the greater visibility gay fathers had recently attained, including some compelling personal narratives about their struggle to achieve parenthood (Green 1999; Savage 1999). My study of commitment ceremonies ran between 1993 and 1996, long before gay marriage became a legal option anywhere in the world. Though the research was separated by more than two decades, both studies of parents were done before same-sex marriage was generally available in the United States, so couples of both genders faced considerable legal complications that are now melting away as marriage equality becomes normative rather than remarkable. While the legal climate in which parenthood is achieved does not shape all its dimensions, both bureaucratic hurdles and their associated costs imposed a burden on parents when I did my research that can be less of a factor today. The same can be said of same-sex marriage.

Besides being indebted to the path-breaking work of David Schneider, which showed us a way to disconnect kinship from assumed biological moorings (Schneider 1968), and the important research in anthropology engendered by his approach, my work also takes a page from observations by such scholars as Elizabeth Povinelli and Tom Boellstorff (Povinelli 2001; Boellstorff 2005) of how *incommensurability* is managed by people in theoretically "impossible" social categories. My focus in studying gay and lesbian parents was not to assess their competence as parents or to report on the childrearing outcomes that ensued; that was a concern that I happily left to the psychologists and others who feel compelled to evaluate the performance of parents and the well-being of their children.[7] Instead, I was interested in how lesbian mothers and gay fathers understood their identities and their place in the social order even as the wider culture considered them inappropriate aspirants to and occupants of parental roles. Did they see themselves as subverting the heteronormative obstacles to family formation? Did they intend to claim access to family on the same basis as heterosexual parents? Did they understand their families to be equivalent to or different from the kinds of normative families presumably typical of the wider culture? In the case of couples who had staged ceremonies, my concerns were parallel: I wanted to know how couples understood and communicated their status in the absence of legal or social recognition, and the extent to which they viewed their decision to marry as indicative of their equivalence to heterosexual couples or a marker or subversion and resistance to mainstream culture.

Similarly, I had little concern with discovering whether holding a commitment ceremony or wedding would enhance the longevity of lesbian or gay relationships. My assumption was that some relationships will be of long duration and that others will eventually dissolve; the same is true for heterosexuals who marry and for those who don't. In other words, I didn't regard the possible functionality of ceremonies as a topic on which I could, or indeed wished to, shed light. My focus instead was on what couples wanted to convey or perform in the rituals they staged, and on what kinds of elements they believed to be necessary for the ceremony to achieve their goals. Again, perhaps confounding the hopes of queer scholars who proclaimed such weddings to be brave displays of resistance against the wider culture, I found that couples strongly preferred to have ceremonies open to a constituency wider than other gay or lesbian people. The presence of kin was thought to be essential, as was attendance across the generational spectrum. Regardless of their positions on the importance of being part of queer culture, weddings that were purely "queer" events were not as satisfying to my narrators as those that crossed the boundaries of the gay/lesbian community, and consequently they sometimes undertook heroic negotiations to draw in members of wider networks.

11.4 Imagining Parenthood

Even as a discourse that viewed lesbians as inappropriate aspirants to motherhood dominated public conversation, the lesbians I spoke to in the late 1970s and early 1980s tended to understand their desire to be mothers as incontrovertible evidence of their womanhood.[8] In this construction, wanting to be a mother and being a mother were understood to be deeply *natural* desires, grounded in femaleness and ultimately more compelling than sexual identity. As evidence of the grounding of motherhood in nature, lesbian mothers often told me how they had *always* wanted to be mothers, that motherhood was simply a desire that was deeply rooted in their sense of self. Some saw the origins of their maternal desire in the families in which they were raised, citing their mothers and grandmothers as role models. Others simply couldn't account for the yearning they experienced, other than to assert that its intensity defied explanation. "It just kind of came over me. It wasn't really conscious at first. It was just a need," explained one mother, who attributed her sudden decision to have a child to hormonal changes she thought she must have experienced in her late twenties. Still others understood motherhood as giving them access to moral rewards that could not be achieved by non-mothers, who they saw as self-centered and not committed to the "important things in life," indeed, not as fully adult.

Fathers also described their desire to be parents using a discourse of nature, though many of the men I talked to had earlier believed that being gay would put parenthood (and marriage) in the realm of the impossible. Many of the narratives I gathered from fathers embedded the desire to be a father in family history or in something they called "tradition," presenting fatherhood as a force of nature, even a biological legacy, that is deeply rooted and irresistible. Although caring for a newborn baby was a challenging task, one father explained, "Something inside me knew that it would be inherent, the ability to do it."

Given that lesbians saw motherhood as a desire rooted in nature, the obstacles to achieving it were reduced to the status of technicalities by many of my informants. Artificial (or donor) insemination, in this understanding, was nothing more than an alternative delivery path for sperm, different from, but not inherently less natural, than a penis. While in the early years of what came to be known as the "gayby boom" (Benkov 1994) lesbians often achieved pregnancy through low-tech (and low-cost) home insemination – what were dubbed "turkey baster" babies (even though the instrument used was usually a needle-less syringe). Once the AIDS epidemic emerged in the 1980s, there was a move from do-it-yourself pregnancy to the use of medical facilities where the sperm was presumably screened to prevent the transmission of HIV and possibly other diseases (Mamo 2007; Sullivan 2004). The more general expansion of the domain of medically assisted reproduction thus signaled that technical obstacles to procreation could be surmounted with medical intervention, even as that sometimes required a considerable financial investment. As sociologist Laura Mamo documents in *Queering Reproduction* (Mamo 2007), the use of more medicalized routes to motherhood quickly became both standardized and naturalized. For more technologically ambitious and affluent lesbian couples, this might mean using in vitro fertilization so that one partner could be the genetic mother (the source of the ova) and the other could be the gestational mother (the carrier of the pregnancy), thus adapting the technologies of surrogacy to make both women biological mothers who could consider themselves related to the resulting baby. Lesbian couples sometimes attributed traits found in the child to the gestational mother, despite the fact that she shared no genetic material with him/her (Pelka 2005).[9]

The obstacles to gay men becoming fathers are more daunting. If anything, their suitability for parenthood has been even less supported by the wider culture than it is for lesbians; as I mentioned above, questioning whether gay men are appropriate aspirants to parenthood has been pervasive not only outside the gay community but within it as well (Green 1999; Newton 1993). Beyond this, of course, are the practical difficulties men face since they cannot become pregnant, none of which is easily navigated. Men who intend to be fathers must be strategic in how they pursue various alternatives, evaluating them in terms of the kind of child each yields, the cost, and the likelihood that they will encounter homophobic and in some cases, racist biases that may derail their plans. Do they want a child that physically resembles them? Do they want a healthy infant; will they accept an older child, one racially different or one with disabilities of one kind or another? How much money can they dedicate to becoming fathers, even before facing the expenses of raising a child?

Gay men (and lesbians) who seek adoption enter into a marketplace in which different kinds of children are ranked in terms of assumed desirability while prospective parents are also ranked according to how closely they resemble normative white middle-class heterosexual families. Race is a critical feature of the dynamics of this marketplace in the United States, whether it be the race of the children to be adopted (white infants are most highly prized) or that of the prospective parents. For precisely these reasons, black and Latino gay men are drawn to the public adoption system, seeing such a placement as a way to combat the racism faced by children in the system. They are also matched more quickly with non-white children who meet whatever other criteria they have – age and health status, for example.

Public adoption through the foster care system might seem the most direct way to achieve fatherhood, particularly since there is a surfeit of children in the system awaiting placement and there are few associated expenses. But following this path destabilizes narratives of nature that take phenotypic resemblance as a way to perform the authenticity of kinship bonds. Since most prospective parents in the United States entering the adoption system are white, and a disproportionate number of those children awaiting placement are of color, some (white) prospective parents do not see public adoption as a feasible route to forming their families. In addition, children in the public system are unlikely to be infants, and are thought to be more likely to suffer from psychological problems or other disabilities (Pertman 2000).

Despite these obstacles, public adoption does not necessarily make impossible the goal of having a family that is "as if" natural (Modell 1994). Both lesbian mothers and gay fathers spoke to me of the mandate they felt to adopt the particular children they chose, often children whose race differed from their own and who suffered from some kind of disability – physical, developmental, or emotional. The mandate tended to be defined as sacred or mysterious, as one dictated by God, who had selected particular parents to care for particular children. Though the road to a completed adoption was arduous, many fathers described being energized by the conviction that the ability to be a father was intrinsic, a commitment arrived at without conscious purpose. Some fathers saw themselves as made to be good parents because of their "traditional values," which they felt uniquely suited them to address the problems faced by their children.

For those gay men who adopted from overseas, nearly all from Guatemala at the time of my research, international adoption potentially provided a way to avoid adopting children with the serious emotional problems they expected would typify children from the US foster care system. Among these parents were many white men who saw a child from Latin America as less racially different from themselves than a black child would have been.[10] Some also spoke of shouldering a commitment to make the world a better place, at least in part, by parenting children whose needs were great. In the case of some gay fathers, this motivation stood in stark contrast to what they regarded as the typical life of gay men, one taken up with shallow diversions that could not add up to constituting a meaningful life. The "gay world" came to represent a pattern of frivolity and meaningless consumption that one could repudiate by becoming a parent.

But not all prospective gay parents viewed their goals in terms of a service they were performing for the wider society. Many were concerned with having a family that would be recognizable as such, where a physical or racial resemblance would silence questions about legitimacy or legibility. One way to achieve this goal was to undertake a private adoption, reaching an agreement with a pregnant woman who wanted to give up her baby. This process involved choice on both sides: the mother picked the prospective parents who best met whatever criteria she had for the kind of home she wanted for her child, and the parents identified mothers who were seeking homes for children whose personal attributes were appealing. The deciding factors in finalizing such arrangements were complex, including racial and economic criteria, and they usually involved intermediaries whose networks determined what kinds of pregnant women and prospective parents would be put in contact with one another.

The "gold standard" of making a family "as if" natural is, of course, surrogacy. For gay men who decided to form families in this fashion, surrogacy allowed them to have a family based at least partially on shared genetic material. In most cases, the surrogate was "gestational," that is, not genetically related to the fetus she carried, with a separate egg donor providing the ova that made conception possible. The intended father(s) provided sperm and fertilization was achieved in vitro. Prospective fathers had to make decisions about the characteristics they sought in the egg donor, which had a great deal to do with what they imagined their family would look like. Family for these men was largely defined by physical resemblance between parent and child and between siblings. Even with the enormous expenses associated with surrogacy (typically at least $100,000 for each child, at the time of my research), the biological link being established moved the process firmly into the realm of nature, erasing the elements of consumption that underlay the practice. Even selecting an egg donor, largely based on physical appearance, intensified the link of parenthood with nature. One of my interlocutors told me about the range of donors they were offered, and how they made their final choice.

> There were some women in there, it was unbelievable – they looked like models, with IQs like you wouldn't believe. And we were looking at them, and we said, "That just isn't us. We wouldn't date them!!"

[laughing] And it wasn't even so much that, it was just that they didn't seem like nice people, and we were getting that sense, and we don't want that. And the funny thing was, it all just kind of fell into place. It was one of those things where you know that someone is watching out for us. It just fell into place.

Working with an agency that facilitates matches between potential gay and lesbian parents and donors, they made a selection based on photographs, education, and the reason given for wanting to be a donor. Both men claimed to be able to assess a person's personality from a photograph, and they selected a donor with qualities they associated with being "a good person." Their narrative revealed a cluster of ideas about what it meant to have a family, how a family should be defined, and how genetic information can be interpreted in creating a family. Appearance, or rather resemblance, played a central part in this story, with being legible as a family understood to be based on how individuals look – interpretations that would be made both within and outside the family (Becker, Butler and Nachtigall 2005). To feel that one belongs in a family was a self-attribution, but that assessment required facilitation through perceptions from the outside. If family members were "read" as related, then the reality of their kinship connection was confirmed.

"Personality" in this calculus registers as genetically mediated, but in practice was something one could assess through physical appearance, as some men did when they surveyed photographs of potential egg donors. The authenticity of the family unit created in this way was further affirmed by the choice of an egg donor who could have conceivably dated one of the two men (notwithstanding the fact that they are gay). If a donor was suspected of being too perfect, too smart, or too beautiful, then the likelihood of her coming into their lives outside a commercial transaction declined precipitously, and the authenticity of their family unit was threatened. When they said that everything went smoothly and that that was an indication that "someone is watching out for us," they located their reproductive process in the realm of nature, as something ineffable and beyond manipulation. Even after enormous expense and complex decision making, they interpreted their ability to achieve fatherhood as having happened almost of its own accord.

11.5   Building Kinship

As I questioned lesbian mothers about how they managed the practical challenges of raising children either as single mothers or as part of a lesbian couple, patterns began to emerge. Lesbian mothers resembled heterosexual single mothers I also interviewed in reporting their reliance on support from their biological families to meet pressing financial obligations – emergency loans, making the down-payment on a house, financial advice, money for home and car repairs, a low-cost place to live, funds to support "extras" like music lessons and summer camp – and as the people on whom they relied for babysitting and other needs that came up in caring for their children.

These were not just choices that mothers made for practical reasons. Mothers spoke at length about their preference for intensifying bonds with kin as a solid "family" context in which children can grow up with a sense of security. This meant that the instrumental ties they told me about were located in a dense intersection of affective bonds, with the assistance families provided not only in meeting immediate needs, but more important, demonstrating the vigor of the kin connection. Other lesbian mothers also spoke about their reliance on their families, particularly their mothers, as a source of emotional support even when these family members had no way to contribute financially or practically.

Mothers were motivated to make relationships with their families work even when the fact of their lesbianism created strains. In some cases, this meant that mothers put up with complicated arrangements that separated their partners from their families, or otherwise made their lesbianism a topic that was off limits. This might mean spending holidays with their families while their partners went to see their own parents, or accepting arrangements whereby their parents avoided their homes.

Still, it was more common to find that even previously intolerant parents would accept a daughter's lesbianism if a grandchild came along with it. Such acceptance might come with financial support, babysitting, and other forms of assistance. This was true even for mothers whose use of assisted reproductive technologies had initially shocked their parents. Lesbian mothers spoke of the importance of maintaining family ties not only as a source of support, but as the foundation of what they considered normal lives and normal childhoods for their children. Some regarded non-familial connections with "chosen" family as inadequate and "contrived." One mother told me, "It feels like not a family, because you don't have the other part of the family that you're supposed to have." In other words, family for lesbian mothers had a relatively normative definition, even when substantial compromises and adjustments were needed to keep it on an even keel. They understood biological relatives to offer the most reliable kinds of caring that could be obtained, largely because of the "natural" bonds that blood kin have for one another.

Some gay fathers I spoke with also situated their relationship with the larger domain of family in terms of how having a child would grant them equal status in this kinship constellation, a place central to family celebrations and a unit capable of crafting family traditions. Having a partner, even one with whom one had had a commitment ceremony, wasn't enough to make them an authentic family unit: only a child would do that. Having what they could recognize as their own family made it possible for couples to create holiday traditions and contribute to the continuity of such traditions among their relatives.

Such agendas were especially significant for African American men with whom I spoke. They felt that they could not establish a fully functioning family without being parents and they could not, therefore, carry on traditions or help to generate new traditions otherwise. What distinguished their obligations as black men to carry on tradition and extend family into the future was the urgency of the crisis facing black children in the foster care system, particularly when they are boys. In other words, their affinity for tradition and family constituted more than sentiment or nostalgia: it was about the very survival of many young people, about the weight of the knowledge that some children will have no future unless responsible community members take action. Thus, family came to encompass both the personal, domestic experience and their political obligation to take action on behalf of the larger black community.

11.6   Getting Married

While we have seen that having children is usually central to strategies of family formation for lesbians and gay men, as it is for heterosexuals, seeking public recognition for their unions – whether this took the form of a commitment ceremony or a wedding – served as a powerful indicator of couples' understandings of kinship and their place in kinship systems. Indeed, couples' accounts of their decisions to stage commitment ceremonies were steeped in kinship-related themes, particularly as they explained their ideas of whose attendance would be essential to the success of such a ritual. Lesbians and gay men who marry also deploy themes of "nature" in explaining their choices, with continuity between generations often being understood as an indication of a natural process.

It was not uncommon for couples to explain their decision to marry as located in what they characterized as traditional family formations, often looking to their parents' relationship as a model they wished to emulate. For example, one ceremony I examined placed the two brides' relationship with their families at the center of the ritual. The officiant was a minister who had pastored one bride's family for decades. She invited the parents to read comments about "abiding love" their daughter had written, and commented on the "kindness, courage, and strength" that she had learned from her parents. As the ceremony progressed, friends and family members came forward to make comments about the occasion, particularly emphasizing the shared roots of both families in the Midwest. The ceremony ended with a ritual that the two women had devised to symbolize the unification of their two families. Each of the family members who were present was holding two roses, dark pink for one family and light pink for the other. The two women moved through the rows, speaking to each person and embracing him or her, and taking roses from each of them. At the end of the process, each woman held a bouquet that combined the dark and light pink roses, now tied with purple ribbons. A new family unit had been created through this ceremony, where two had existed before.

But some couples feared that their families wouldn't respect or understand the importance of their ceremony. In order to assure that all essential family members would attend, some couples wrote elaborate pre-invitation letters that explained what was going to occur and how important each family member's presence would be at the ceremony. When key family members failed to come, many couples were devastated, though there were some who came up with plausible explanations for their absence, in an effort not to further rupture the relationship. Couples also took pleasure not only in the presence of relatives, but in having a very mixed diverse group of people at the ceremony – old and young, gay and straight, friends and family.

Some couples located symbolic expressions of inclusion in their families in the kinds of gifts they received. Family heirlooms were especially meaningful, associated with their full inclusion in the wider family constellation. One couple who received what they described as "the family china" saw themselves as having thus become "the family center," charged with hosting future holiday dinners and special occasions for the wider family, and thus affirmed as part of the future stability of the family.

Just as gifts represented the legitimacy of couples' claims to being *really* married, they also deployed ritual elements to ensure that ceremonies would be acknowledged as the "real thing." This was one reason that religious ceremonies came to stand as powerful markers of authenticity, even for couples who were not particularly religious in their ordinary lives. Religious ceremonies were instantly recognizable as "weddings," often invoking the approval of the divine for the relationship. The assembled guests also represented the social approval of the wider, not just gay, community, and the fact that same-sex couples could point to the voluntary nature of their commitment also spoke to social convention having nothing to do with their union. Voluntary behavior is seen as springing from the heart, as being pure and uncontaminated by the desire to seek approval or to gain tangible benefits from the relationship. Authenticity, in such constructions, can be demonstrated both by the inventiveness of the ceremony and by its lack of originality: each speaks to a different element of genuine feeling and each makes clear the intensity of the bond being celebrated. These elements can be further strengthened by the receipt of gifts, which attest to the recognition accorded to the couple's claims.

One couple whose wedding I attended was married by a San Francisco Baptist minister in the city's beautiful Swedenborgian Church, an outstanding example of arts-and-crafts architecture, lighted only with candles during the ceremony. The minister grounded his homily in the story of David and Jonathan, which he presented as the most perfect depiction of true love in the Bible.[11] Other than the men's gender, everything about the ceremony was "traditional," from the music, to the prayers, to the lighting of a unity candle at the end of the ritual. Although the relatives of one of the grooms failed to show up, the mother of the other attended, to the delight of others in the congregation, who fussed over her and congratulated her for having come. Ultimately, both men felt the event was shaped by its spiritual contours. Both had strong religious backgrounds and had been saddened by the idea that being gay would deny them the possibility of having a ceremony blessed by God. One of the grooms explained,

> It was a spiritual experience ... Nothing can really compare to me standing there ... I have my partner to my left [who] will be there for life. I've got my best man to my right who is a person who is very dear to me ... My pastor right in front of me, guiding me. God above me ... It was one of those moments where it was just right.

The sense of everything being "right" emanated from the spiritual content of the ceremony, as well as from its adherence to every aspect of a conventional wedding ceremony. The authenticity of the occasion, the fact that it could not be mistaken for anything other than a wedding, meant that suggestions that they were mimicking straight people were demonstrably false. They were a couple like any other, presenting their union to a diverse public in the same way that other people in the society do.

11.7   Conclusion

The understandings that lesbians and gay men who have children and solemnize their relationships attach to the families they create cannot readily be disassociated from normative notions of family that pervade the rest of the culture. In the United States, the notion that the presence of a child defines a household as constituting a family has been shown by recent research to be foundational;[12] even if a household consists of a single adult and a child, or a same-sex couple and a child, that child is the *sine qua non* that permits the attribution of family to a domestic unit (Powell et al. 2010).[13] That lesbians and gay men share this view should not be surprising; they have lived their lives in this culture as much as any other population and define good lives much as do others around them.

Lesbians and gay men, like others in the society, comprehend the process whereby children come into their lives as the realization of natural impulses, a vital part of how the world works. This can be accomplished through biological means or through adoption or other devices, but lesbians and gay men continue to see reproduction and raising new generations as enterprises that are deeply rooted in nature. They tend to see such harmony with nature as a source of goodness and virtue, as do others around them, even as they are also able to specify the ways that their families sharply diverge from societal norms. Still, as for other struggling minorities, kinship provides a flexible array of tools that can be reconfigured to meet the challenges of daily life. Rejection from blood relatives may make "chosen" families a practical source of the kind of support conventionally associated with "blood" kin. Participation in a subculture like the Ballroom scene may decisively remove LGBT individuals from their kinship constellation, making the familial support provided by their Houses essential. In other words, the use LGBT people make of idioms of convention *and* resistance both illustrates the flexibility of kinship systems to serve specific needs and speaks to the need to carefully ground our interpretations of kinship ideologies in the particular experience of the populations we study. Being "just like everyone else" and part of a deeply different queer subculture are two sides of the same system, perhaps not as distinctive as some theorists would claim.

Notes

1. The most prominent such case was that of Mary Jo Risher in Dallas, Texas, who lost custody of her younger son after her older son testified against her. Her story became a book (Gibson 1977) and then a made-for-TV movie starring Gena Rowlands as Mary Jo Risher. Around the time I was starting my work, the case of Jeanne Jullion became a major focus of protest in the San Francisco Bay Area, where I lived, when her former husband abducted their son and took him to Italy (Jullion 1985). And another lesbian couple, who were both enmeshed in custody battles, also made a documentary about themselves, highlighting their evangelical religious background (Ullis 1974). There were also a few cases in which grandparents sought to wrest custody from lesbian mothers, notably the Sharon Bottoms case in Virginia (Polikoff 2000).
2. This term has been widely used in both scholarly and popular reporting on reproduction among LGBT people, for example, Benkov (1994).
3. There is even less material available on the forms such families may take in non-Western cultures.
4. Her work also intervened in the wider field of kinship, showing that this kind of flexibility is indeed a characteristic of American kinship in general; i.e., she shows that kinship always has an element of choice and that the expectation that blood kinship ties are stronger and more resilient than those that are chosen is not empirically correct.
5. Note that butch queens can be read as either masculine or feminine, depending on context.

6. Some scholarship in this field has looked specifically at debates over same-sex marriage and at LGBT people who reject the achievement of such rights as an appropriate political or social objective. See, for example, Badgett 2009; Barker 2013; Bernstein and Taylor 2013; Heaphy, Smart and Einarsdottir 2013; Hull 2006; Polikoff 2009; Richman 2014. There doesn't seem to be a similar debate over the correctness of parenthood.

7. It should be noted, of course, that such evaluation is exactly what is called for in legal conflicts such as custody disputes, i.e., what do studies show us about the mental health, gender normativity, or school performance of the children of lesbian mothers and gay fathers? (See Regnerus 2012; Stacey 1998, 2006; Stacey and Biblarz 2001.)

8. This work predates, of course, the current questioning of binary gender categories that typifies queer theory and that often repudiates use of the term "man" and "woman" to describe persons with non-normative sexual identities.

9. It is worth noting that gestational surrogacy is used in most instances precisely for the opposite reason: the surrogate believes that the fetus isn't "hers" because it doesn't contain her genetic material and therefore doesn't question the agreement to turn the baby over to the intended parents after delivery (see Ragoné 1994, 1998; Teman 2010).

10. Christine Gailey heard such children described as "a discreet shade of off-white" (Gailey 1999).

11. See Steven Greenberg (2004), for an account of how this story of intense friendship between two men can be understood as a proto-type for same-sex love.

12. The US Census defines the population in terms of households, with an individual identified as "householder," and other individuals residing in the same household defined according to their relationship to the householder: spouse, biological son or daughter, adopted son or daughter, housemate, etc. It doesn't specifically designate any social arrangement as a "family."

13. According to Powell et al. (2010), the presence of a pet also helped classify a domestic arrangement as a family.

References

Agigian, Amy. 2004. *Baby Steps: How Lesbian Alternative Insemination Is Changing the World*. Middletown, CT: Wesleyan University Press.

Badgett, M. V. Lee. 2009. *When Gay People Get Married: What Happens When Societies Legalize Same-Sex Marriage*. New York: New York University Press.

Bailey, Marlon M. 2013. *Butch Queens Up in Pumps: Gender, Performance, and Ballroom Culture in Detroit*. Ann Arbor, MI: University of Michigan Press.

Barker, Nicola. 2013. *Not the Marrying Kind: A Feminist Critique of Same-Sex Marriage*. London: Palgrave Macmillan.

Becker, Gay, Annaliese Butler and Robert D. Nachtigall. 2005. "Resemblance Talk: A Challenge for Parents Whose Children Were Conceived with Donor Gametes in the US." *Social Science and Medicine* 61(6): 1300–1309.

Benkov, Laura. 1994. *Reinventing the Family: Lesbian and Gay Parents*. New York: Crown.

Bernstein, Mary and Verta Taylor, eds. 2013. *The Marrying Kind? Debating Same-Sex Marriage within the Lesbian and Gay Movement*. Minneapolis, MN: University of Minnesota Press.

Boellstorff, Tom. 2005. "Between Religion and Desire: Being Muslim and Gay in Indonesia." *American Anthropologist* 107(4): 575–585.

Franklin, Sarah. 1997. *Embodied Progress: A Cultural Account of Assisted Conception*. London: Routledge.

Franklin, Sarah and Helena Ragoné. 1998. *Reproducing Reproduction: Kinship, Power, and Technological Innovation*. Philadelphia, PA: University of Pennsylvania Press.

Gailey, Christine Ward. 1999. "Seeking 'Baby Right': Race, Class, and Gender in US International Adoption." In *Mine – Yours – Ours – and Theirs: Adoption, Changing Kinship and Family Patterns*, ed. A.-L. Rygvold, M. Dalen and B. Saetersdal, 52–81. Oslo: University of Oslo.

Gibson, Gifford Guy. 1977. *By Her Own Admission: A Lesbian Mother's Fight to Keep Her Son*. Garden City, NY: Doubleday.

Green, Jesse. 1999. *The Velveteen Father: An Unexpected Journey to Parenthood*. New York: Villard.

Greenberg, Steven. 2004. *Wrestling with God and Men: Homosexuality in the Jewish Tradition*. Madison, WI: University of Wisconsin Press.

Greil, Arthur L. 1991. *Not Yet Pregnant: Infertile Couples in Contemporary America*. New Brunswick, NJ: Rutgers University Press.

Halberstam, J. Jack. 2013. *Gaga Feminism: Sex, Gender, and the End of Normal*. Boston, MA: Beacon Press.

Hayden, Corinne P. 1995. "Gender, Genetics, and Generation: Reformulating Biology in Lesbian Kinship." *Cultural Anthropology* 10(1): 41–63.

Heaphy, Brian, Carol Smart and Anna Einarsdottir. 2013. *Same-Sex Marriages: New Generations, New Relationships*. London: Palgrave Macmillan.

Hull, Kathleen. 2006. *Same-Sex Marriage: The Cultural Politics of Love and Law*. Cambridge: Cambridge University Press.

Jullion, Jeanne. 1985. *Long Way Home: The Odyssey of a Lesbian Mother and Her Children*. San Francisco, CA: Cleis Press.

Lewin, Ellen. 1993. *Lesbian Mothers: Accounts of Gender in American Culture*. Ithaca, NY: Cornell University Press.

1998. *Recognizing Ourselves: Ceremonies of Lesbian and Gay Commitment*. New York: Columbia University Press.

2009. *Gay Fatherhood: Narratives of Family and Citizenship in America*. Chicago, IL: University of Chicago Press.

Luce, Jacquelyne. 2010. *Beyond Expectation: Lesbian/Bi/Queer Women and Assisted Conception*. Toronto: University of Toronto Press.

Mamo, Laura. 2007. *Queering Reproduction: Achieving Pregnancy in the Age of Technoscience*. Durham, NC: Duke University Press.

Mitchell, Lisa M. 2001. *Baby's First Picture: Ultrasound and the Politics of Fetal Subjects*. Toronto: University of Toronto Press.

Modell, Judith S. 1994. *Kinship with Strangers: Adoption and Interpretations of Kinship in America Culture*. Berkeley, CA: University of California Press.

Moore, Mignon R. 2011. *Invisible Families: Gay Identities, Relationships and Motherhood among Black Women*. Berkeley, CA: University of California Press.

Newton, Esther. 1993. *Cherry Grove, Fire Island: Sixty Years in America's First Gay and Lesbian Town*. Boston, MA: Beacon Press.

Pelka, Suzanne. 2005. *Lesbian Couples Creating Families Using in Vitro Fertilization to Co-Mother: A Cultural Study of Biological Ties*. Chicago, IL: University of Chicago Committee on Human Development.

Pertman, Adam. 2000. *Adoption Nation: How the Adoption Revolution Is Transforming America*. New York: Basic Books.

Polikoff, Nancy. 2000. "Custody Litigation." In *Lesbian Histories and Cultures*, ed. Bonnie Zimmerman, 218–220. New York: Garland Publishing.

    2009. *Beyond (Straight and Gay) Marriage: Valuing All Families under the Law*. Boston, MA: Beacon Press.

Povinelli, Elizabeth A. 2001. "Radical Worlds: The Anthropology of Incommensurability and Inconceivability." *Annual Review of Anthropology* 30: 319–334.

Powell, Brian, Catherine Bolzendahl, Claudia Geist and Lala Carr Steelman. 2010. *Counted Out: Same-Sex Relations and Americans' Definitions of Family*. New York: Russell Sage.

Ragoné, Helena. 1994. *Surrogate Motherhood: Conception in the Heart*. Boulder, CO: Westview Press.

    1998. "Incontestable Motivations." In *Reproducing Reproduction: Kinship, Power, and Technological Innovation*, ed. S. Franklin and H. Ragoné, 118–131. Philadelphia, PA: University of Pennsylvania Press.

Rapp, Rayna R. 1999. *Testing Women, Testing the Fetus: The Social Impact of Amniocentesis in America*. New York: Routledge.

Regnerus, Mark. 2012. "How Different Are the Adult Children of Parents Who Have Same-Sex Relationships? Findings from the New Family Structures Study." *Social Science Research* 41(4): 752–770.

Richman, Kimberly D. 2014. *Licensed to Wed: What Legal Marriage Means to Same-Sex Couples*. New York: New York University Press.

Sandelowski, Margarete. 1993. *With Child in Mind: Studies of the Personal Encounter with Infertility*. Philadelphia, PA: University of Pennsylvania Press.

Savage, Dan. 1999. *The Kid (What Happened after My Boyfriend and I Decided to Go Get Pregnant): An Adoption Story*. New York: Dutton.

Schneider, David M. 1968. *American Kinship: A Cultural Account.* Englewood Cliffs, NJ: Prentice-Hall.

Schneider, David M. and Raymond T. Smith. 1978. *Class Differences in American Kinship.* Ann Arbor, MI: University of Michigan Press.

Stacey, Judith. 1998. "Gay and Lesbian Families: Queer Like Us." In *All Our Families: New Policies for a New Century,* ed. M. A. Mason, A. Skolnick and S.D. Sugarman, 144–169. New York: Oxford University Press.

2006. "Gay Parenthood and the Decline of Paternity As We Knew It." *Sexualities* 9(1): 27–55.

Stacey, Judith and Timothy J. Biblarz. 2001 "(How) Does the Sexual Orientation of Parents Matter?" *American Sociological Review* 66(2): 159–183.

Strathern, Marilyn. 1992. *Reproducing the Future: Anthropology, Kinship, and the New Reproductive Technologies.* New York: Routledge.

Sullivan, Maureen. 2004. *The Family of Woman: Lesbian Mothers, Their Children, and the Undoing of Gender.* Berkeley, CA: University of California Press.

Taylor, Janelle S., Linda L. Layne and Danielle F. Wozniak. 2004. *Consuming Motherhood.* New Brunswick, NJ: Rutgers University Press.

Teman, Elly. 2010. *Birthing a Mother: The Surrogate Body and the Pregnant Self.* Berkeley, CA: University of California Press.

Thompson, Charis. 2005. *Making Parents: The Ontological Choreography of Reproductive Technologies.* Cambridge, MA: The MIT Press.

Thompson, Julie M. 2002. *Mommy Queerest: Contemporary Rhetorics of Lesbian Maternal Identity.* Amherst, MA: University of Massachusetts Press.

Ullis, Karlis C. 1974. *Sandy and Madeleine's Family.* San Francisco, CA: Multimedia Resource Center.

United States v. Windsor. 2013. Supreme Court of the United States. No. 12–307.

Volkman, Toby Alice, ed. 2005. *Cultures of Transnational Adoption.* Durham, NC: Duke University Press.

Warner, Michael. 1999. *The Trouble with Normal: Sex, Politics, and the Ethics of Queer Life.* New York: Free Press.

West, Isaac, Michaela Frischherz, Allison Panther and Richard Brophy. 2013. "Queer Worldmaking in the 'It Gets Better' Campaign." *QED* 1(1): 49–85.

Weston, Kath. 1991. *Families We Choose: Lesbians, Gays, Kinship.* New York: Columbia University Press.

1998. "Theory, Theory, Who's Got the Theory?" In *Long Slow Burn: Sexuality and Social Science,* ed. K. Weston, 143–146. New York: Routledge.

Part III

Reproducing Society: Gender, Birth, and Power

12

Kinship Knowledge and the State: The Case of Argentina's Adult "Living Disappeared"

Noa Vaisman

12.1   Introduction

This chapter explores the relationship between kinship knowledge, identity, and the state. It considers the arguments made by Strathern (1999), and developed by Carsten (2007), that information about kin-persons and about the circumstances of a person's birth is constitutive of identity and of kin relations. But given the constitutive force of this information, can it (or knowledge of it) be refused? Strathern asks this question in the context of the new and evolving scientific breakthroughs in assisted procreation. She wonders whether the tendency to open the records and share information about origins can be refused because, as she explains, "one piece of information can automatically obliterate another, taking away the status of previous information. There is no choice about it; such effects are built-in" (1999: 75). For example, information about a sperm donation that brought to one's birth implies reframing who one's father is. Carsten takes this concern with information into other realms, among them adoption narratives, and suggests that even if information is not refused, persons find different ways of handling it, thereby "creating spaces to accommodate or limit the 'constitutive force' of new information" (2007: 419). In this chapter I inquire further into the intertwining of knowledge, kinship, and persons in a context where the state plays an important role in both hiding and unveiling kinship information. My concern is with the ways in which kinship knowledge is produced and used by the state in the name of human rights and justice, and the implications of that knowledge on persons and kin relations.

The chapter examines the case of the "living disappeared," the close to 500 infants – now adults – who were abducted during the last civil-military dictatorship that ruled Argentina between 1976 and 1983. They were separated from their biological parents – some at birth and others at a few months or a few years of age – and were given, in many cases, as "war booty" to the perpetrators of the crime or their accomplices. As part of this forced disappearance, their biological identities were erased and, by changing their dates of birth, names, and kinship ties, new identities were invented for them. To this day, many of the "living disappeared" are unaware of their origins and of the ongoing searches conducted by their biological families for them. From the time of the dictatorship until today, only 128 of these individuals have been located and identified.

Locating the "living disappeared" is a complex task that involves detailed investigation of anonymous tips and the analysis of forged documents and official papers. Since 1977, this search has been carried out by the human rights organization (HRO) Grandmothers of the Plaza de Mayo (Abuelas de Plaza de Mayo, hereinafter Abuelas). Originally founded by a group of women whose children and grandchildren were abducted, today the HRO includes a number of recovered "living disappeared" among its ranks. Over the last three decades, Abuelas and their persistent search have won some support from the state. In this context, the National Commission for the Right to Identity (CONADI), a combined government and nongovernmental organization, was established and since 1992 has contributed to the search. CONADI investigates cases of disappearances and identity alterations – particularly, but not exclusively, those of the "living disappeared." Further, in 2012 a new unit within the office of the Attorney General Special Unit of Crimes against Humanity was created to advance the legal treatment of these cases and the search for them. The Special Unit for Cases of Appropriation of Children during the Period of State Terrorism coordinates and offers support for cases of appropriation that are being processed by the courts across the country, and carries out systematic and extensive investigations alongside and in coordination with Abuelas and CONADI.

Locating a possible "living disappeared" is followed by DNA identification. The DNA is collected from a blood sample or from biological material left on personal objects (mostly clothes, linen, toothbrushes, and hair brushes). In both forms of collection, the DNA of the presumed "living disappeared" is compared with all the DNA samples in the National Bank of Genetic Data (NBGD). The Bank, which was created in 1987, stores the DNA of many of the families that are looking for their abducted *living* kin. Identification is considered successful when there is a very low probability of exclusion from one of the family groups (*grupo familiar*) that are represented in the Bank. In other words, the individual in question is identified as one of the "living disappeared" with over 98 percent chance of inclusion in a particular familial group (see Vaisman 2012).

The processes of localizing and identifying a "living disappeared" are complicated by the subjects' desires, missing information, and changing social context. Here I will elaborate on two such complications. First, some individuals whose histories have been investigated and who are suspected of being "living disappeared" do not wish to undergo a DNA test to find out about their origins. To overcome this obstacle, the courts may order a house raid to collect DNA samples. This procedure for identification underscores the knotty relationship between human rights and individual rights. It also sheds light on the different ways in which kinship is made and unmade in the context of an ongoing human rights violation. I return to this latter point later in this chapter. Second, while DNA identity tests may lead to the identification of a "living disappeared," in many cases they do not. This means that the DNA of many individuals who undergo an identity test does not "match" the DNA of one of the many family groups stored in the Bank. Consequently, in Argentina today there are close to 4,200 individuals who underwent a DNA test but were not identified as "living disappeared."[1] While these individuals hold official state documents stating their kinship ties and other core aspects of their identity – e.g., their name, date of birth and place of birth – they know for a fact that these documents have been altered and that the families they were raised in are not their families of origin. Their cases, and the social and political forces that led to their search for origins in the first place, will be treated in the fourth part of this chapter.

Centering on the state's reformulation of kinship ties of adult "living disappeared," my aim in this chapter is to elucidate the thorny entanglements of law, knowledge, kinship, and the state, over 40 years after the return to democratic rule. I highlight this point because the reconstruction of kinship in adulthood is rather different from its reformulation in childhood. In the past, when a child was identified as a "living disappeared," the legal debate examined the child's best interest. The courts debated whether the child should be separated from the individuals she grew up with – whom she had known until that very moment as her parents – and moved into the home of her biological family, or whether it was in her best interest to stay with her appropriators – i.e., those individuals who raised her as their own daughter and who were sometimes involved in the torture and assassination of her biological parents. Once the "living disappeared" turned adults, controversies hinged on identity and the right to truth. The issue was no longer cohabitation with the criminals or the ideological and moral positions according to which they may educate the appropriated child. Rather, courts had to rule on such issues as whether identity can be ascertained against the wishes of an adult through the use of her DNA and whether the truth about the crimes committed against the disappeared and their children had to be uncovered at all costs.

But before offering an overview of the abduction and alteration of identity during the dictatorial rule, I want to briefly pause on the term "living disappeared" for, as I will show in this chapter, this oxymoron encapsulates the contradictory nature of the individual it refers to and his or her sociopolitical position. Forced disappearance was a key feature of the repressive regime in Argentina during the years of the civil-military dictatorship. It consisted of the secret abduction of an individual and the subsequent erasure of his or her existence. There was no information about the victim's whereabouts after the abduction and no body that could attest to his or her life or the violations suffered (Calveiro 2004: 26). The disappeared were kept in clandestine camps across the country, in which they were tortured and lived in inhumane conditions before they were, in most cases, assassinated. To this day most of their bodies have not been found and thus they inhabit a place between the dead and the living, existing in the liminal zone of the not-dead-nor-alive (Gatti 2011). Against this backdrop, the identification and restitution of the "living disappeared" is all the more striking. In this case we are confronted with individuals who are alive but have been disappeared for decades – sometimes since birth – and who, through intense investigations and a DNA test, are identified and in this way recovered. As "living disappeared" they carry the marks of their time as disappeared – their previous identities, their kinship ties, and their worldviews, among others. How to settle the contradictory and incompatible nature of these ties and identities with the newly found information about kin and corresponding political histories is the challenge that each of these adult "living disappeared" now faces.

12.2   The Disappearance of Infants under the Dictatorial Rule

In 2012, in a large trial comprising 34 cases of "living disappeared," the abduction of infants and young children was recognized as a "widespread and systematic practice" that was conducted in the "frame of a general plan of extermination that unfolded on part of the population" (Plan Sistemático).[2] Although a number of cases of child abduction were incorporated into the famous 1985 trial against the Junta leaders, it was only in 2012 that the crimes of "theft, retention and concealment of minors" were defined as a widespread practice that took place in the context of a plan to exterminate subversives. In this section I draw on the detailed works of two Argentine anthropologists, as well as my interviews with lawyers and judges, to outline the ways in which abduction, appropriation, and alteration of identity were carried out by the dictatorial rule and its civilian accomplices.

Disappearances during the dictatorial rule were carried out against every category of persons including pregnant women, children, and teenagers as well as adults of both sexes. Each category was treated differently and there are many further variations and exceptions in each of the estimated 30,000 cases. Like other abducted adults, pregnant women were taken (in many but not all cases) to clandestine camps where they were tortured, bound and hooded, and nearly starved. They were kept alive in these camps until they gave birth – frequently by cesarean section so as to keep the process under control. In the majority of the known cases, the mothers were subsequently assassinated and their children were given to members of the Security and Armed Forces or their accomplices.

Children who were found with their parents during a kidnapping had a more varied fate. Some were left at the scene of the crime or were given to neighbors or passers-by, while others were abducted along with their parents. Of this latter group, while a number were returned to their biological families, others were incorporated into the secretive repressive apparatus through the erasure of their identities and the rewriting of their histories. In this way, the dictatorial apparatus forged for them a new life in a very different social context (Arditti 1999; Regueiro 2013: 96–97, 2010, 2015; Villalta 2005, 2006, 2010b). This process was carried out through state institutions and legalized in the courts, or carried out in secrecy by forging official papers and constituting fictive kinship ties. Analyzing most of the resolved cases,[3] Sabina Regueiro (2013: 109) explains that almost all of the children who were born in the clandestine camps were registered as the natural children of their appropriators. Further, about half of the children who were abducted with their parents and were under four years of age were falsely registered as the natural children of their appropriators. The rest of the children were adopted, left under legal guardianship, or placed in institutions for minors.

The appropriation and adoption of these children was possible, on the one hand, because of existing norms, legal instruments, and socially accepted practices, and on the other hand, because of the secrecy surrounding the abduction of both adults and children or their birth in clandestine camps. These enabled a large variety of appropriation and adoption practices to take place at the same time with very little overarching control. Regueiro (2013: 75–108), in a comprehensive analysis of cases of disappearance and identification of children, shows that although there were many different methods for appropriation, the secrecy of the birth generally facilitated the process of appropriation within the clandestine camps. The birth was either not registered or the birth mother and child were registered as NN (*non nominatus*). Further, with the aid of doctors and nurses, the newborns and the young children abducted with their parents were registered as the biological children of their appropriators and, in this way, their real origins were obliterated.

Furthermore, the Argentine anthropologist Carla Villalta (2005, 2006, 2009, 2010a, 2010b) shows that the legal norms that treated children raised in poverty as "abandoned minors" were adapted to the case of these "living disappeared." Villalta carefully notes that the disappearance of children during the dictatorship was an exceptional act, both in its magnitude and its systematization. However, through an analysis of various appropriations, she demonstrates that practices such as the inscription of a child of unknown parentage with a new name and an invented date of birth, without any investigation of her possible origins, enabled the erasure of prior biological relations and the production of alternative kinship ties. Additionally, she shows how children who arrived in the courts or in state institutions for minors were treated differently according to pre-existing social ties between state agents and between these and members of the Armed Forces. Thus, for example, a judge would sign adoption papers, or speed up an adoption case in the court so that his best friend could keep a child whose grandparents were trying to recover following the disappearance of his or her biological mother.[4] In other words, social practices already in place at the time of the dictatorial rule, along with personal contacts and close ideological positions, all contributed to the machination of these infants' identity alterations.

One of the key questions raised by this systematic practice is: why were the children abducted and their identity altered? A number of explanations have emerged over the years. A key one surfaces in a statement by General Ramón Juan Camps, former police chief of the province of Buenos Aires, who explained, "Personally, I did not eliminate any child. What I did was to take some of them to charitable organizations so that they could find new parents. Subversive parents teach their children subversion. This has to be stopped" (Arditti 1999: 50). By appropriating the "subversives'" offspring, and raising them in a very different political and familial context, the Armed Forces hoped to raise very different kinds of persons.

A similar explanation is heard in the testimony of Elliot Abrams in the aforementioned trial, known as Systematic Plan. Abrams (who between 1982 and June 1985 was the United States Assistant Secretary of State for Human Rights) offered two explanations for the abduction and retention of these children:

> Yes, as I remember it there were two factors that we thought were important. One was that the families of the disappeared person were viewed by the military as not fit to raise these children because these were disloyal or communist families. The second factor was, in some cases anyway, that the families to which they were given had no children. They were unable to have children, so this would be a great blessing for them. This was a great blessing for these loyal families.
> (Testimony: January 6, 2012, http://nsarchive.gwu.edu/NSAEBB/ NSAEBB383/Testigo%20de%20Elliot%20Abrams.pdf; www.youtube.com/ watch?v=yQucNEXNRks&feature=youtu.be)

The lawyers and judges that I interviewed further explained that, in all likelihood, the religious beliefs of members of the Armed Forces did not allow them to assassinate the children (although there were pregnant women who were assassinated before giving birth). Moreover, children who were born in captivity could not be returned to their biological families because their existence would attest to the fact that their biological mothers were abducted by the regime and kept alive until they gave birth. This would contradict the repeated denial of the Armed Forces of having any knowledge about the disappeared and their final fate.

Considering the varied reasons for keeping the children and raising them in familial and political contexts very different from their origins, and in view of the fact that the abduction of children was a systematic practice but was not organized from above, it is not surprising that each of the appropriation cases is different and each raises different challenges to its solution. In the next two sections I describe a few cases, trying to highlight, on the one hand, the state's position vis-à-vis kinship ties (both those created under illegal circumstances and those produced through biological reproduction) and, on the other hand, the individuals' complex positions towards their own abduction and alteration of identity.

12.3   Refusing Information: The State, Kinship, and the Adult "Living Disappeared"

A young woman walks into a pediatrician's office with her newborn and her mother (the baby's grandmother). The pediatrician asks basic questions about the birth and the child and then asks whether there is a history of illnesses in the family. The grandmother quickly answers that there are none. The mother looks at her inquisitively and states: "But dad is diabetic." The grandmother frowns at the pediatrician and asks: "But is this significant?" The pediatrician answers: "Yes, for the child it is fundamental!" As the camera moves back to show the mother holding her baby, a voice-over reads the words that appear on the screen: "Do not leave your child the inheritance of doubt. Resolve your identity now."

This television commercial,[5] produced by Abuelas as part of their ongoing media campaign to encourage individuals who have questions about their origins to come forward and search for their identity, appeared in 2013. Its timing was not coincidental. In recent years, identified "living disappeared" often mention their children as one of the triggers for their identity search (cf. Carsten 2007, documenting the search for biological parents by adoptees). The arrival of a newborn can raise questions about genetics, heritage, and kinship, which can become pressing when the parent has doubts about her own origin. Alternatively, if a search has already been initiated – whether by the individual or Abuelas/CONADI – the birth of a child may sometimes convince a person to take the difficult step of voluntarily undergoing a DNA identity test.[6] Once the person has been identified, her children may also take part in the restitution process. This involves, for example, recognizing changes in kin relations, adjusting to new familial structures and new family members, and accepting a new surname. The restituted individuals have each dealt with these changes and the inclusion of their children in different ways; however, in broad terms the next generation has had an important place in the "normalization" of this long process of identification.

The media and artistic interventions, of which the above TV spot is a part, encourage individuals to investigate their own family ties and face up to longstanding doubts about their origins. These interventions emerged when Abuelas realized that their grandchildren – the "living disappeared" – were old enough to begin searching for their own identities, and they developed alongside changes in the legal approach to the search. In this section, I describe two Supreme Court cases that have shaped the now accepted methods for investigating and identifying the "living disappeared." I focus on these two cases in particular as they concern a key problematic in the search – the refusal of the person in question to undergo a DNA identity test. In recent decades the "fate of the right to refuse cooperation" was inconsistent – some courts ruled in favor of those who refused to provide a DNA sample, while others sanctioned the extraction of the sample despite the individual's refusal (Ferrante 2011: 144). The 2003 and the 2009 decisions and their ramifications reframed the debate and highlighted the significance of biological kinship in the case of the "living disappeared." In both rulings the arguments of the justices were slightly distinct, contributing different explanations for the majority decision (Ferrante 2011: 144). In what follows I explore the decisions as key turning points that reflect the state's changing approach to kinship.

In 2003, the Supreme Court of Argentina pronounced its verdict in the case of Evelyn Karina Vázquez Ferrá, who was a suspected "living disappeared." Unlike earlier cases that reached the Court, Evelyn was an adult by the time her case was considered by the highest legal institution in the country. The case had first erupted into public attention in 1999 when Abuelas located Evelyn and her supposed parents confessed that she was not their biological child. Policarpo Vázquez and his wife Anna María Ferrá stated in court that, in late 1977 or early 1978, a military officer had offered them the child, whom they took in and registered as their own biological daughter. After she was found, the courts ordered a DNA identity test and the confiscation of Evelyn's official identity papers (the papers were thought to be forged and could therefore be used to trace the crime and its perpetrators). Evelyn refused the DNA test and appealed the verdict to the Court of Appeal and then the Supreme Court. Evelyn claimed that the DNA test constituted an inadmissible interference by the state into her sphere of intimacy, violated her constitutional right to physical integrity, and affected her dignity by going against her decision "not to betray the intense affective ties she has with the couple that raised her and whom she still sees as her real parents" (Supreme Court case v. 356. XXXVI: 5).[7] In effect, Evelyn asserted that although she may not be the biological child of the couple that raised her – a detail she discovered only when her father was arrested and her identity papers were confiscated – her feelings towards her "parents" had not changed. She expressed her gratitude towards them for their love and nurture and asserted that she was uninterested in her possible origins.

The Court, weighing Evelyn's position against the DNA test and the grandmother's demand to know whether Evelyn is the grandchild she had been searching for, ruled against the test. The Court explained that "forcing her [Evelyn] to undergo the blood test will result in a violation of respectable feelings and, consequently, the right to privacy that is guaranteed in article 19 of the Constitution" (v. 356. XXXVI: 8). Furthermore, the Court stated that if Evelyn "… – an able adult – does not want to know her real identity the state cannot force her to investigate it nor can it generate the judicial actions that will help in establishing this identity" (v. 356. XXXVI: 8). In their separate written opinions, Justice Maqueda argued that "the construction of her own identity – on the basis or not of her biological ties – is information that concerns only [the victim] herself and is excluded from the judge's authority" (v. 356. XXXVI: 76), while Justices Petracchi and Moliné O'Connor stated that using the test results and her body against those "she still sees as if they were her true parents" would be, for her, both "degrading and humiliating" (v. 356. XXXVI: 21). Based on these arguments, the Supreme Court – Argentina's last resort Federal Tribunal – rejected the obligatory blood test and accepted Evelyn's position. The Court thereby seemed to be closing the door on future investigations of individuals who were uninterested in finding out about their biological kin and genetic origins.

The search for Evelyn's origins and the legal debate around her identification did not end there. In an attempt to clarify the "criminal liability of those who had acted in the clandestine detention center" (Inter-American Court Amicable Agreement Inocencia Luca de Pegoraro y Otros Argentina, November 1, 2010: 3) and to determine with certainty whether Evelyn was the daughter of Susana Pegoraro – the presumed mother who was disappeared in 1977 when she was five months pregnant – the judge responsible for the investigation in a lower court ordered a search in Evelyn's residence. During the search, which took place in 2008, personal objects (her toothbrush, hair brush, and used clothes) were confiscated. The biological material extracted from them was used to conduct the DNA identity test that proved beyond doubt that Evelyn was the child of Rubén Santiago Bauer and Susana Beatriz Pegoraro – both disappeared in 1977.[8]

A few years before this dramatic turn of events, and only a few months after the 2003 Supreme Court decision, Abuelas filed a petition with the Inter-American Commission on Human Rights against the State of Argentina. The petitioners (the presumed grandmothers of Evelyn, represented by the HRO Abuelas de Plaza de Mayo) claimed that the Supreme Court's decision violated a number of articles in the American

Convention on Human Rights (articles 5, 8, 17 and 25) and barred further investigations in similar cases. In September 2009, the petition was resolved in an Amicable Agreement that outlined a number of important changes in the state's approach to the investigation and identification of the "living disappeared."[9] Most significant among the changes was the resolution that formed the basis for Law 26549, that was passed in November 2009. The law, which amended the federal law of criminal procedure, stipulates that in cases where the identity of an individual is in question, or where it is important to determine the identity for the investigation of the crime, DNA material may be obtained by either extracting bodily fluids (blood and saliva) or by collecting biological material that contains DNA from the individual's personal objects. The amendment further clarifies that, although blood samples may be taken against the wishes of the individual and through the use of force, all alternative methods must first be applied (see Vaisman 2014).

The agreement also had long-term implications, including the establishment of a unit that works to normalize and legalize the records and the documents of those whose identity was altered; the creation of a protocol determining the steps that should be taken in investigating cases of suspected "living disappeared" (providing directions for all public prosecutors involved in cases of appropriation and alteration of identity); and the construction of the Special Unit for the Appropriation of Children during the Period of State Terrorism within the Attorney General Special Unit of Crimes against Humanity Office (CIDH 2014: 116).[10] These various mechanisms, which were implemented gradually since 2009, reveal the commitment of the state and the judicial apparatus to the investigation of the crimes committed.

While the Amicable Agreement led to the amendment of the federal law of criminal procedure in late November 2009, a Supreme Court decision only a few months earlier demonstrates the growing commitment not only of the executive but also of the judiciary to the search for the "living disappeared." The August 2009 Supreme Court decision marks an important turning point in the state's approach to the investigation of altered identity and kinship ties in the context of adult "living disappeared." Like Evelyn, Guillermo Gabriel Prieto was suspected of being a "living disappeared," the biological child of Maria Ester Peralta and Oscar Alfredo Salazar, who were disappeared in the early years of the dictatorial rule. Guillermo was raised with his brother Emiliano by the couple Guillermo Antonio Prieto and Emma Elidia Gualtieri de Prieto. Unlike in Evelyn Vázquez Ferrá's case, Guillermo's supposed parents maintained that they were the biological parents of both children. This did not convince the courts and the search for the brothers' origins persisted for well over two decades. In the course of this investigation Guillermo was summoned repeatedly to the courts to provide a blood sample, a request he refused time and again.

Guillermo's home was raided on June 6, 2005 and his personal effects were confiscated with the aim of obtaining DNA samples (what I term shed-DNA, see Vaisman 2014). In response to this search, Guillermo appealed to the Supreme Court to stop the testing of his shed-DNA. In its ruling, the Court maintained its position from the Vázquez Ferrá case regarding obligatory blood samples but insisted that DNA tests can be carried out on shed-DNA. The Court's ruling recognized the conflicting rights at play – Guillermo's right to his privacy, his physical integrity and his right over his genetic material, and the grandmother's and family's right to know the truth about their disappeared kin – but stated that the use of shed-DNA for the purpose of identification does not violate constitutional and other basic human rights. The biological materials "were collected without invading his body, or, for that matter, without his active participation" (G. 291.XLIII: 9).[11] The Court added that, while the DNA test should be carried out, the "eventual biological ties" that could be discovered are "reduced and limited exclusively to the private and affective spheres" and therefore are not and could not be part of the judicial decision (G. 291.XLIII: 9). This ruling is significant not only because it considered the alternative methods for obtaining DNA samples and found them reasonable – a position that later appears in the amendment to the federal law of criminal procedure – but also because of the final outcome of the investigation. Specifically, after the rejection of his extraordinary appeal in front of the Supreme Court, Guillermo Prieto's DNA was compared to the DNA of all the families included in the National Bank of Genetic Data. He was not identified as a "living disappeared."

This is an important point: unlike Evelyn, Guillermo did not find his biological family, nor did he discover his real origins. Instead, while the state revealed that his parents were not his true biological parents, it was unable to provide him with any answers regarding his origins and biological kin ties. It did, however, unsettle his world. As Guillermo states in the Supreme Court appeal, the information made him "question his own identity" (G. 291.XLIII: 22) and exposed the lie existing at the core of his existing kinship ties – i.e., that the couple claiming that he was their biological child are not his genetic parents.

The two cases described above and the Amicable Agreement allow us to see the futile attempts of these individuals to refuse information and the state's changing treatment of kinship more broadly. During the dictatorial rule, the state made use of existing norms to alter, eliminate, or ignore biological kinship – keeping all these practices and their consequences secret. For well over a decade, in contrast, and through the passing of law 26549, the state has emphasized the significance of uncovering and recovering biological kinship. It is important to point out that the recovery of biological kinship in these cases is an integral part of the legal processing of crimes against humanity – as disappearance is considered such a crime – and that in both the Vázques Ferrá and the Guillermo Prieto cases, the Court clearly states that the construction of the affective dimensions of these biological relations depends on the desires and abilities of the identified individuals and their biological kin, thus falling outside the remit of the judicial apparatus. At the same time, it is clear that the state, through its judicial system and newly created institutions, considers biological kinship important. But this is true only to an extent: Guillermo Prieto's DNA test results and the subsequent silence around his non-identification is only one example of a growing number of cases of individuals who have undergone DNA tests but have not been identified as "living disappeared." These individuals are sometimes made to undergo a DNA test by the courts, while at other times they are motivated by Abuelas' media campaigns to come forward themselves. Once they receive the results, however, the state cannot offer them any form of reparation or compensation. In effect, they are left alone to deal with the mayhem created by the state's insistence on searching for biological kinship and by the growing popular support for the search and identification of the "living disappeared."[12]

12.4   Reconstructing, Refusing, and Rearranging Kinship in Adult "Living Disappeared"

The narratives in the media about kinship and affective ties among the adult "living disappeared" have been changing in recent years.[13] The changes are subtle and the stories are complex but they reflect, as I will show in this section, a growing tendency to accept more ambiguous positions and more composite forms of kinship that do not fall neatly into the social/biological dichotomy. These narratives emerge in TV and newspaper interviews, in books and plays, as well as in documentaries and verbal-performative testimonies provided in various public appearances of the "living disappeared." The consumers of these stories are not only teenager and adult radio and TV viewers, and the (mostly) middle-class urban dwellers that attend the free shows and testimonies in the annual cycles of Theater for Identity, but also children who are exposed to the complex stories of the search and identification through educational programs, books, movies, and follow-up discussions with identified "living disappeared."[14]

Every localized and identified adult "living disappeared" is different, not only because of the context and manner in which the identification took place, but also because of his or her personal reaction to the identification. For some, the initial reaction is very different from their long-term attempts to make sense of their new situation and the complex kinship ties revealed by the DNA tests, while for others the process seems (judging from their media appearances) to continue without much change over the years. Broadly, the reactions and processing of the new information after identification can be placed along a continuum. On one end of this continuum, the identified adult rejects his biological kin and remains with his social kin ties, while on the other end, the individual rejects his social kinship ties and constructs strong bonds with his biological kin. In between lies the ambiguous position in which the individual attempts to exist within both social and biological kinship. Below are a few cases that demonstrate points on this continuum.

12.5   Refusing Biological Kinship Ties

Evelyn's refusal to undergo a DNA identity test was discussed above. She had been reluctant to meet her biological family before the identification, and following it she continued to hold similar views. Responding to various attempts to cajole her into such a meeting, and after a meeting did take place, she explained to Analia Argento, a journalist and author, that she does not understand how this biological family could care for her.

> This is not automatic, maybe a relationship can be forged but I do not push a button and say my sister is not my sister or my nephews are not my nephews. That is crazy. For them [the biological family] it is not easy either, thirty years have passed, they do not know who I am, they do not know how I drink my milk, they do not know how I drink my tea.
>
> *(Argento 2009: 179)*

Even before her identification and assuming that those who were looking for her are her real biological family, she says:

> I do not have to resolve everyone's pain. They [her biological family] always say that they suffered. I do not say that this is not a terrible pain, but I did not create it, I do not have anything to do with it. What fault do I have? I am a product of being born at the wrong moment, by mistake, I am who I am. Everyone sees the rights of others. I am a victim of what had happened, that is clear to me. I was robbed, *the State was guilty and now it is again the State that is going after me.*
>
> *(Argento 2009: 174, emphasis added)*

Evelyn evidently feels she is a victim of the state's actions – both the initial abduction and disappearance and later her identification – and she is reluctant to enter into contact with her biological family. As she declared in the ESMA[15] trial in 2014: "I do not know the day I was born. Due to a personal decision I did not seek out information from my biological family. When I found out [about my biogenetic identity and kinship], I had to cope with the detention of my father." She added that she did not talk to survivors of the ESMA, where her parents and grandfather were held captive, and that following the raid on her house she had tried to "take care of her psychological soundness" (Infojus noticias 5.6.14).[16] This testimony reveals not only her rejection of her biological family, but also her clear position regarding her social kinship ties – she still calls her appropriator her "father" rather than, for example, the "father that raised me" as some "living disappeared" tend to do.

Her statement that she did not talk to survivors who knew or saw her parents should be read against the tendency of many children of the disappeared, both "living disappeared" and those who were not abducted, to reach out to survivors of the clandestine camps and to friends and colleagues of their parents in search of information about the latter (Ros 2012). Investigating and collecting details about the biological parents' likes and dislikes, social habits, and character is one way of recreating the link between the generations. Another is examining images (photos and home videos) in an attempt to identify physical similarities (Amado 2009). To aid in this reconstruction, Abuelas has developed the Biographical Family Archive (BFA), in which information about each disappeared parent is collected and organized. A dossier is created within the BFA for each "living disappeared." It includes interviews and stories from family members, friends, and colleagues, as well as testimonies from survivors of the clandestine camps and photos of his or her parents and other family members. This information enables the restituted individual to learn of her origins. Once an individual is identified, and in accordance with her own desires and the personal processes she must undergo, she receives the dossier with all of the information about her disappeared parents.

These initiatives – the individual searches conducted by the identified living disappeared and Abuelas' BFA – stand in contrast to the position presented by Evelyn in her refusal of information about her biological kin ties. Her refusal is sustained after the fact, that is, after the state has already – and against her wishes – provided her with information about her kinship ties. But does kinship information replace and obliterate other information as Strathern (1999) claims? Again the response here varies from case to case – in some, the information reshapes kinship ties quite immediately, while in others this information and the person's decision to act upon it may take years or may never happen (cf. Carsten 2007). In broad terms, however, we can expect that the person in question has the power to determine much of these processes and once the identified "living disappeared" chooses to act upon the information, changes in kinship ties will take place.

12.6   De-kinning and Re-kinning with Biological Ties

On the other end of the spectrum are adult "living disappeared" who decide to sever all ties with their social kin and create new ties with their biological kin. The process is never simple and it is often incomplete.

For example, sometimes the "living disappeared" do not fully renounce kinship ties with members of their appropriating family (brothers and sisters, cousins and grandparents), they may also stay in touch with their appropriating mothers but chose to cut off their ties with their appropriating fathers who are seen to be primarily responsible for their disappearance and identity alterations. This is because appropriating mothers are sometimes considered passive victims of the same treatment that the appropriated children received from their appropriating fathers or because they are thought to have no direct knowledge of the appropriation. However, those who do decide to go through a process of de-kinning (cf. Fonseca 2011) from their appropriating families chose, in many cases, to clearly state that position in the media. A very emotive and clear example of de-kinning is the case of María Eugenia Sampallo Barragán, who is the first identified "living disappeared" to bring charges against her appropriators.

Sampallo Barragán's parents were abducted from their home on December 6, 1977. At the time, Mirta Mabel Barragán was six months pregnant. María Eugenia was born during her mother's captivity and, two or three months after the birth she was registered as the natural biological child of Osvaldo Rivas and Cristina Gómez Pinto. She discovered her biological identity in 2001[17] and in 2008, after an important legal debate, a federal court pronounced a ruling in her case. Shortly before the ruling, María Eugenia gave a press conference in which she explained her position regarding her own disappearance and her search for justice. Below I quote at length from the text she read aloud at the press conference, as I believe it explains in no uncertain terms her attitude regarding her appropriation and kin relations.

> Usually, when information about appropriation of minors becomes known, the following terms are erroneously used to refer to the persons who registered as their own children those who were not: they [the media] use formulas [such as] "adoptive parents," "parents of the heart" or simply "parents."
>
> What I would like to emphasize is that in my case, like in many others, [we are] not dealing with "adoptive parents," for there did not exist any adoption process. I was registered as the daughter of these persons, with a false birth date, a false place of birth, false parents, a false birth certificate. It would be unfortunate that after these clear explanations [anyone] would continue to publically sustain the mistaken term "adoptive parents."
>
> …
>
> In relation to the term "parents of the heart" [*padres del corazón*], I imagine that it [they] makes reference to a certain kinship relation [that is] based on emotions. But then we can ask ourselves if

a person that abducted an infant, that concealed from her that she was kidnapped, that perhaps abducted and tortured her parents, that separated her from them [her parents] and from her family, that always lied to her about her origins, that – more often than each [of you] would like to think – mistreated her, humiliated her, deceived her, routinely [did all this], that separated her from her family knowingly, if the person that did all that, or something of all of that, can know and feel what is filial love. My response is no[;] that the relation with this type of persons [sic] is determined by cruelty and perversion.

...

[Many may ask] what is it that I feel for my appropriators. I can say that I do not feel anything. No emotional tie unites me with them. I will only refer to a certain feeling of guilt that, I believe, is at a certain moment inevitable, since the relations that they designed places them in the role of the "savior."

(Published by Equipo Nizkor, March 31, 2008)[18]

Let me begin by attending to María Eugenia's statement about adoption. While in some cases the "living disappeared" were legally adopted, in most cases, as mentioned above, they were appropriated. The distinction between appropriation and adoption "in good faith" – as this type of kinship is considered in Argentina – is vast. It challenges a simple reading of these cases using insights developed in the study of adoption and kinship. At the same time, some comparative processes are worth considering. For example, the process of de-kinning (Fonseca 2011; Howell 2003; Mookherjee 2007) from birth mothers can be considered analogous to the process of de-kinning from appropriating parents, as the case of María Eugenia demonstrates. There are, of course, key differences between these cases: first, kinning in appropriation is with biological kin and de-kinning is from social kin, while de-kinning in adoption happens from the biological mothers followed by kinning with social mothers. In other words, the kinning and de-kinning of appropriated individuals is the reverse of those same processes in adoption. Second, in the case of adult "living disappeared," de-kinning and kinning can take place according to an adult's wish and the familial context created. In contrast, in adoption decisions about kinship ties are made when the individual is not yet an "able adult" with clear wishes (to use the terms describing Evelyn in her Court case). Third, the ethical foundations of kinship in appropriation are, as María Eugenia so clearly puts it, very different from the ethical foundations in adoption, motivated as they are by the ideological-political position of the appropriators among other factors. Another point of comparison is the search for biological kin relations among identified "living disappeared" and among adoptees (Carsten 2007; Legrand 2009). When the search is initiated by the person and not by the state (as has happened in some well-known cases of individuals who had doubts about their origins and who approached Abuelas or CONADI to begin their search) the motivation is often the individual's need to find out about herself. The assumption that kinship knowledge is constitutive of the person is, in both cases, therefore, a motivating force in the search.

12.7 Coexistence of Social and Biological Kinship

Somewhere in the middle of the spectrum are those identified adult "living disappeared" who attempt to exist between their social and biological kinship ties. This ambiguous position vis-à-vis kin ties is even more difficult than in most adoption cases, both because the alteration of kinship ties was ideological and politically motivated and because, in some cases, the appropriating parents were involved in the abduction, torture, and assassination of the biological parents. At the same time, long years of nurture and (sometimes) a happy childhood make these social kin relations hard to relinquish. There is growing exposure and openness in the Argentine media in recent years for these ambiguous and complex positions that allow for kinship knowledge not to completely dislodge the self as it was before, but to reconstitute both self and kinship in new ways. Mariana Zaffaroni Isla's explanations of her position are some of the clearest in elucidating this position. Below I quote from a long interview she gave on a Uruguay television program when she was 36 years old, but first a little about her appropriation.

Mariana was born in 1975. Her parents were political activists who fled Uruguay after the rise of the dictatorship in that country and before the coup d'état in Argentina. On September 27, 1976, the family was abducted in Argentina and was kept in the clandestine center "Automotores Orletti." Mariana was 18 months old at the time. She was appropriated by Miguel Ángel Furci and his wife Adriana María González and registered as their own child under a false name – Daniela Romina Furci – and false date of birth. In 1983, information about Mariana's possible whereabouts was first registered and, in 1985, the courts ordered a DNA test. Furci and González fled to Paraguay, taking Mariana with them. In 1992, they were found and tried and Mariana recuperated her genetic identity. She was identified as the child of María Emilia Islas Gatti and Jorge Roberto Zaffaroni Castilla. It is assumed that María, Mariana's mother, was three months pregnant with their second child at the time of her abduction.[19]

Mariana was not made to live with her biological family after her identification, as she was 17 at the time and did not want to. The judge did demand, however, that she meet with her biological family in Argentina. "I did not want to, I could not, build a relationship out of obligation," she explains.[20] But when Mariana's first child was born, everything seemed to slowly change. In an interview she gave to a French radio station, Mariana states that once her daughter was born she understood "what a mother feels towards her child. What blood ties are like. "[I] understand why my biological family searched for me all those years."[21] In a long interview on Uruguayan TV she explains her situation even more clearly:

> In reality, to a certain point in my day-to-day [life] I am still Daniela [the name given to her by her appropriators], for my husband, my children, my friends, they still call me that. It seems to me that the name – although it constitutes the person – umm Daniela also constitutes me in who I am. The person that I am.

Explaining her relationship to her appropriating parents, she says:

> It is something that is very hard to explain, and I understand that no one can understand it, in fact my husband does not understand it either. Ehh, I choose to believe that he [Furci, the appropriating father] does not have anything to do with all those things [the crimes committed], it seems more healthy for me … If tomorrow I come to the realization that he really did all those things that he is accused of, I will not see him again, but that has to be a decision that implies: with you I cannot have a relationship any more. Now I do not feel ready to do that, I care for him. It's hard for me, it hurts me to think he could have done all that. I know this position is totally irrational … but I cannot do things differently than what I feel.

The question about her relations with her appropriating parents is often posed in interviews and she repeatedly states that she continues to call them "my parents" and that she maintains a relationship with them. Moreover, she states that she is thankful to them, she had a happy childhood and was raised with love.[22]

The individuals who choose to be in the complex and ambiguous position of maintaining both social and biological ties, even when these ties contain contradictions, seem to be an extreme embodiment of Sahlins' view of kinship. For Sahlins, kinship is the "mutuality of being," that is, "people who are intrinsic to one another's existence – thus 'mutual person(s)'" (2011: 2). This view encompasses social and biological kinship. Shared existence throughout childhood and early adulthood with the appropriating couple throughout childhood and early childhood creates ties that become an integral part of the person's existence and identity. And after identification and once the biological family is recognized as part of a person's kinship world, the physical similarities and similarities in character with the biological parents become an integral part of the way a person sees herself. In this way, both the appropriating family (social kinship) and the biological parents (and biological family more broadly) can become intrinsic to a person's (new) existence. In reading this position held by some of the "living disappeared" through Sahlins' model of the "mutuality of being," we gain insight into the creation of persons through kinship. At the same time, we lose very significant dimensions of these restitutions: the political and social implications of the abduction, search and identification of the "living disappeared." Kinship as the "mutuality of being" overlooks the contradictory nature of this mutuality when it is constructed after the identification. So while it may be useful for thinking about kinship in less dichotomous ways, we must not forget the political context that led to the abduction of children and to the alteration of their identity.

12.8   The State's Treatment of Identified Adult "Living Disappeared"

Over the years, identifications of the "living disappeared" have often been reported in newspapers and on television. Abuelas has tried to respect the requests of those who have been identified and to refrain from providing names or identifying information, but in almost all cases the identification is announced in a press release with the biological family, most times, present. These press reports are one way in which the stories of the "living disappeared" are disseminated in Argentina. As mentioned earlier, Abuelas has done a tremendous job of publicizing the search and of positioning the question of identity at the center of public debate through Twitter competitions, music and theater for identity cycles, and TV and radio commercials. Their publicity efforts received a great deal of support during the administrations of the Kirchners' (2003–2015). Throughout this period, Abuelas de Plaza de Mayo, and its president Estela Barnes de Carlotto, became household names. One clear example of this was the emotive meeting between the then-president Cristina Fernández de Kirchner and Ignacio (Guido) Montoya Carlotto, the grandson of Estela, the president of the organization, very soon after his identification in 2014. The meeting, which was reported on the president's Facebook page through both text and pictures, reflected Kirchner's emotional involvement in the case but also her declared position – "Guido [Ignacio] belongs to all Argentines" (*La Nacion*, August 7, 2014).[23]

This statement reflects the extent to which the search and identification of "living disappeared" has become a national project. The stories of recovery, as well as these individuals' choices, private lives, and the changes they have undergone, has been reported in various media outlets over the years and consumed by many across the country. In nearly all media presentations, the biological kinship of the individual is mentioned and elaborated upon – names of parents, the date of the abduction and disappearance, and in which clandestine centers they were seen – and the significance of this truth is highlighted. The importance of biological kinship in these representations is undeniable. But there is a caveat.

The numerous individuals who undergo a DNA identity test without finding their biological families (i.e., without being identified as "living disappeared") are not treated in the same way as those who are identified. This difference raises questions about the limits of the national narrative that positions the recuperation of biological kinship at its core. While the numbers reflect a very real and difficult phenomenon – the many irregularities in the registration of children, the transfer or sale of children, and the old adoption laws – the State has not, to my knowledge, offered substantial help with the failed search carried out by many individuals who are not identified as "living disappeared" and the lack of available information about their possible origins. A number of different groups, such as Raiz Natal, are now working towards legislation that will enable and support the searches, and the uncovering of official information about these adoptions and pseudo-adoptions. But thus far, these groups have not managed to produce significant changes in the state's approach to the question, nor have they succeeded in inserting themselves into the public discussion that has formed around Abuelas' work. In other words, the state's presumed support for the uncovering of biological kinship ties is limited. Namely, it may be more accurate to claim that, while the state supports the uncovering of biological kinship ties, there are some biological kinship ties that are more worthy of uncovering than others. Specifically, kinship with the disappeared seems to be more significant than biological kinship with others.

At the same time, as I was told by one of the key employees of the Bank in an interview, until the change in the law (2009), the National Bank of Genetic Data provided free DNA identity tests to all individuals who had doubts about their identity. Through these tests the Bank has managed to unite not only brothers and sisters but also identical twins who, although not identified as children of disappeared, were able to find each other.

12.9   Conclusion: Using Kinship to Rebuild the State and the Status of Information Refusal

Broadly speaking, while not a linear process and certainly not all encompassing, the state in recent years has tended towards the view of kinship as biological rather than social. It has positioned genetic kinship and genetic knowledge at the forefront of the restitution of the adult "living disappeared," allowing biology to determine the truth about the historical events. In this section I want to qualify this point further, while demonstrating the consequences of this tendency towards the genetic.

During the dictatorial rule, the abduction of children and infants and their appropriation was carried out, as far as we know, as part of the process of restructuring the social body. Infants were given to families that held views close to the regime, with the aspiration that they raise the children according to Western morals, Christian values, and national traditions (see Novaro and Palermo 2003: 20). The identification and restitution of the "living disappeared" when they were still young has not been discussed in the present chapter, but I will point out here that the legal decisions throughout these years go in both directions: for the genetic identification and the restitution to the biological family in some cases and for identification with no restitution to the biological family in other cases. There were also unsolved cases where individuals (and their appropriators) refused to undergo DNA identity tests and the legal battles dragged on for years, sometimes decades, until alternative methods for identity verification were discovered and used. Through the cases I presented, we can see how the state has slowly moved towards the position, later secured through the passing of law 26549, that the genetic identity of the "living disappeared" must be unveiled.[24] This law, and the legal decisions I describe, demonstrate the significance of genetic identity and heritage. But what do they tell us about kinship relations? This seems to require a more complex answer.

On the one hand, the state uses these cases for its own interest, specifically, to strengthen and legitimize itself and the justice system. For example, in the María Eugenia Sampallo Barragán case, when the courts recognized the crimes of infant abduction and identity alteration as crimes against humanity, they also reframed the search, pointing to the state's obligation to investigate the crimes and punish the perpetrators. If the state chooses to ignore this obligation, other nation-states can take responsibility for prosecuting the criminals. With respect to the classification of the crimes as crimes against humanity, the justices in the Prieto case explained that it would be in the best interest of the Argentine state to investigate the possible abduction and alteration of identity of Guillermo Prieto, as it would allow the state to guard its sovereignty. As I have argued elsewhere (Vaisman 2014), the Court is making a conscious effort to legitimize the state's legal apparatus and to reinvigorate the country's democratic rule. Investigating cases of possible abduction and alteration of identity so many years after the event sends a clear message to the Argentine public, as well as to international critics, that the Argentine legal institutions can once again be trusted to deliver justice and produce memory. Kinship in general, and biological kinship in particular, is thereby deeply implicated in the state's project to make itself democratic, and to present itself as standing at the forefront of the struggle for human rights.

On the other hand, in many of the cases I have explored and in my interviews with justices that presided on a number of restitution cases, I frequently encountered the position that, while the identification of the individual is a matter of public and legal interest, the construction of kin relations is beyond the courts' control and is best left to the identified "living disappeared" and his or her biological family. This statement appears in both the Vázquez Ferrá and the Prieto cases discussed earlier. The justices claim that identification of a "living disappeared" using her

DNA puts an end to an ongoing crime – the theft, retention, and concealment of a minor and the altering of her identity – and allows the biological family to discover the truth about their living kin. But, "anything that is a product of the biological ties that may be determined in this case, is limited exclusively to the affective and private sphere ... its channelling or external manifestation is foreign matter to any judicial decision or interference by the courts" (G. 291. XLIII: 9). The Court sees it as its obligation to find out about the crime, but distances itself from the actual construction of kinship.

While the state legitimizes its democratic institutions through the search for and the unveiling of genetic kinship ties, it does not go as far as to determine what these kinship ties will look like in practice once the adult "living disappeared" are identified. As Carsten argues, "kinship knowledge by itself does not create kinship ... knowledge must be activated in relationships" (2007: 422). Thus, against the state's positioning of biological kinship as the model for all kin ties, in recent years the identified adult "living disappeared" are beginning to tell a more complex story. For some of them kinship is both social and biological. This narrative about kinship is more open to the vicissitudes of everyday life and to the complexity of emotional ties.

Notes

1. Victor Penchaszadeh, M.D., a professor at the University of La Matanza, president of the Latin American and Caribbean Bioethics network, UNESCO and a long-time collaborator with Abuelas, writes in a recent article that "Over the past 10 years, approximately 10,000 young adults voluntarily had their DNA compared to profiles of 311 families in the BNDG [Bank]" (2015: 210). As stated above, the number that I was quoted in April 2014 from sources within the Bank is much lower.
2. The sentence in the trial locally referred to as "Systematic Plan" (an abbreviation of "systematic plan for the appropriation of minors"), was later ratified in the Federal Court of Criminal Appeals (Cámara Federal de Casación Penal) (2014), which also affirmed that "the appropriation of children constitutes a form of forced disappearance and a crime against humanity" and that this crime "is still being committed until those appropriated children recuperate their identity" (Abuelas, press release, May 4, 2014).
3. According to Sabina Regueiro, of the 107 resolved cases of individuals who were located and identified as "living disappeared" that she analyzed, more than 40 were inscribed as the natural children of their appropriators while others were adopted or were under judicial custody (Regueiro 2013: 107).

4. In some of the cases Villalta analyzes, the economic status of the adopting/appropriating parents also played an important role. Villalta demonstrates how class affected the decision of judges, not only in cases of children living in poverty but also in cases of children who were disappeared by the dictatorial regime.

5. www.youtube.com/watch?time_continue=1&v=X4kOef-xMtU

6. This is one of the first instances where Abuelas use genetic knowledge as a framing device for their call to search for one's origins. While the search is still framed as a question of identity – the underlying issue being knowledge of one's parentage – it is recast in this commercial as also a question of genes and their possible future manifestations. That is, the issue becomes the genetic traits that the now-adult "living disappeared" passes on to his/her children without his/her knowledge, due to his/her own kinship and identity alteration.

7. Quotes in this section are taken from the Supreme Court case "Vázquez Ferrá, Evelin Karina s/incidente de apelación v. 356. XXXVI." All translations from Spanish are my own.

8. Evelyn's DNA "matched" DNA of the biological family group and, as the NBGD explained, there was a 99.93 percent probability that she is part of that biological kinship group.

9. These are a few of the agreed-upon measures detailed in the Amicable Agreement: (a) the Argentine executive committed to submitting to Congress a draft resolution for the "establishment of a procedure for obtaining DNA samples that protects the rights of those involved and effectively investigates and adjudicates the abduction of children during the military dictatorship" (p. 6); (b) the Argentine executive committed to submitting to Congress a draft resolution that will "more effectively guarantee the judicial participation of victims – understanding as such persons allegedly kidnapped and their legitimate family members – and intermediate associations set up to defend their rights in proceedings investigating the kidnapping of children" (p. 6); (c) the executive branch also agreed to work on adopting measures to optimize the power of the Attorney General's office by for example "designing and executing a 'Special Investigation Plan on kidnapping of children during the military dictatorship in order to optimize the resolution of cases'" (p. 7); and the executive agreed to submit a draft bill to Congress "to amend the legislation governing the operation of the National Bank of Genetic Data in order to adapt it to scientific advances in this area" (p. 6).

10. One of the more dramatic changes in recent years was the amendment to the operation of the National Bank of Genetic Data. While important (and probably questionable), I will not develop this point here.

11. All quotes from the Supreme Court of Argentina case G. 291.XLIII Gualtieri Rugnone de Prieto, Emma Elidia y otros s/sustracción de menores de 10 años. All translations are my own.

12. In recent years there have been a number of attempts to pass laws that were aimed at giving some answers to these individuals and many others who were appropriated or adopted before or after the period of dictatorial rule. However, so far these laws have not been derogated. The National Bank of Genetic Data and other institutions have had their work restricted so as to focus solely on cases that took place during the period of the dictatorial rule and are defined as crimes against humanity.

13. This section, as well as all other references to the direct narratives of the "living disappeared," is based on the public presentation of their cases. Although I know some of these individuals personally, and have had long conversations or casual encounters with them, I chose not to interview them for my research. I have taken this ethical position based on the fact that the individuals who have chosen to talk do so in the media and their stories are repeated in numerous outlets such as TV shows, books, and documentary movies. Those who have not done so have, in effect, chosen to keep their private lives private and I respect their choice. This research is therefore based on interviews with lawyers, judges, psychologists, and human rights activists who work with and for the identification of the "living disappeared." It is also based on my ethnographic study of Theater for Identity and many artistic, public, and academic events organized by Abuelas, particularly but not exclusively during the years 2004–2014. Theater for Identity is an initiative of theater practitioners established in 2000 that organizes cycles of plays that focus on questions of identity and appropriation. During these annual cycles, which are open and free to the public, many identified "living disappeared" give their testimonies and tell their stories.

14. I had attended a discussion between young school children and an identified "living disappeared" in 2005, but since then the number of events has grown exponentially.

15. Escuela de Mecánica de la Armada (ESMA) was one of the largest clandestine detention and torture centers in Argentina.

16. www.infojusnoticias.gov.ar/nacionales/esma-no-se-el-dia-que-naci-declaro-una-nieta-recuperada-4350.html.

17. In 2001, the DNA test showed her to be the daughter of Mirta Barragán. A few months later, in 2002, paternity was also confirmed. The gap in the identification is due to the lack of information regarding her disappeared father, who was known to survivors by a slightly different name.

18. www.derechos.org/nizkor/arg/doc/sampallo1.html.

19. The search for Mariana is documented in the film *Por Esos Ojos* (1997), directed by Gonzalo Arijón and Virginia Martínez.

20. www.bbc.com/mundo/noticias/2014/08/140806_nietos_recuperados_testimonios_como_cambia_vidach.

21. http://pcu.org.uy/noticias/item/1349-mariana-zaffaroni-cuando-tuve-a-mi-hija-fue-como-parir-la-verdad.
22. www.bbc.com/mundo/noticias/2014/08/140806_nietos_recuperados_testimonios_como_cambia_vidach.
23. www.lanacion.com.ar/1716645-cristina-kirchner-guido-es-de-todos-los-argentinos.
24. This claim goes against Gandsman's argument (2009) that Abuelas' position vis-à-vis kinship and identity is not biologically deterministic. I believe that in their celebration of identification by a DNA genetic test, the HRO, like the state, are reproducing or reinstating a genetic genealogy – i.e., a view of kinship as biological. At the same time, the emergence of the ambiguous narratives of those "living disappeared" who maintain both families, and the growing acceptance of their stories in the media, including in the TV shows produced by Abuelas, is pointing towards a more open and less conservative position towards kinship.

References

Amado, A. 2009. *La imagen justa: Cine Argentino y política (1980–2007)*. Buenos Aires: Colihue.

Arditti, R. 1999. *Searching for Life: The Grandmothers of the Plaza de Mayo and the Disappeared Children of Argentina*. Berkeley, CA: University of California Press.

Argento, A. 2009. *De vuelta a casa {Historias de hijos y nietos restituidos}*. Buenos Aires: Marea.

Calveiro, P. 2004. *Poder y desaparición: Los campos de concentración en Argentina*. Buenos Aires: Ediciones Colihue.

Carsten, J. 2007. "Constitutive Knowledge: Tracing Trajectories of Information in New Contexts of Relatedness." *Anthropological Quarterly* 80(2): 403–426.

Comisión Interamericana de Derechos Humanos (CIDH). 2014. *Informe anual 2014*. www.oas.org/es/cidh/docs/anual/2014/docs-es/Anual2014-D-seguimiento.pdf, accessed October 30, 2018.

Ferrante, M. 2011. "Proof of Identity in Criminal Prosecutions for Abduction of Children and Identity Substitution." In *Making Justice: Further Discussions on the Prosecution of Crimes against Humanity in Argentina*, ed. Center for Legal and Social Studies and International Center for Transitional Justice. (English version published online.)

Fonseca, C. 2011. "The De-Kinning of Birthmothers: Reflections on Maternity and Being Human." *Vibrant: Virtual Brazilian Anthropology* 8(2): 307–339.

Gandsman, A. 2009. "'Do You Know Who You Are?' Radical Existential Doubt and Scientific Certainty in the Search for the Kidnapped Children of the Disappeared in Argentina." *Ethos* 37(4): 441–465.

Gatti, G. 2011. *Identidades desaparecidas: Peleas por el sentido en los mundos de la desaparición forzada*. Buenos Aires: Prometeo Libros.

Howell, S. 2003. "Kinning: The Creation of Life Trajectories in Transnational Adoptive Families." *Journal of the Royal Anthropological Institute* 9(3): 465–484.

Legrand, C. 2009. "Routes to the Roots: Toward an Anthropology of Genealogical Practices." In *International Adoption: Global Inequalities and the Circulation of Children*, ed. D. Marre and L. Briggs, 244–255. New York: New York University Press.

Mookherjee, N. 2007. "Available Motherhood: Legal Technologies, 'State of Exception' and the Dekinning of 'War-Babies' in Bangladesh." *Childhood* 14: 339–354.

Novaro, M. and V. Palermo. 2003. *La dictadura militar 1976/1983: Del golpe de estado a la restauración democrática*. Buenos Aires: Paidós.

Penchaszadeh, V. 2015. "Ethical, Legal and Social Issues in Restoring Genetic Identity after Forced Disappearance and Suppression of Identity in Argentina." *Journal of Community Genetics* 6: 207–213.

Regueiro, S. 2010. Inscripciones como hijos propios en la administración publica: la consumación burocrática de la desaparición de ninos. In *Infancia, justicia y derechos humanos*, ed. C. Villalta, 245–284. Bernal: Universidad Nacional de Quilmes Editorial.

    2013. *Apropiación de niños, familias y justicia, Argentina (1976–2012)*. Rosario: Prohistoria ediciones.

    2015. " 'Subversivas': 'Malas madres' y familias 'desnaturalizadas'." *Cadernos Pagu* 44: 423–452.

Ros, A. 2012. *The Post-Dictatorship Generation in Argentina, Chile and Uruguay: Collective Memory and Cultural Production*. New York: Palgrave Macmillan.

Sahlins, M. 2011. "What Kinship Is (Part One)" and "What Kinship Is (Part Two)." *Journal of the Royal Anthropological Institute* 17: 2–19, 227–242.

Strathern, M. 1999. *Property, Substance and Effect: Anthropological Essays on Persons and Things*. London/New Brunswick, NJ: The Athlone Press.

Vaisman, N. 2012. "Identity, DNA and the State in Post-Dictatorship Argentina." In *Identity Politics and the New Genetics: Re/Creating Categories of Difference and Belonging*, ed. K. Schramm, D. Skinner and R. Rottenburg, 97–115. New York: Berghahn Books.

    2014. "Relational Human Rights: Shed-DNA and the Identification of the 'Living Disappeared' in Argentina." *Journal of Law and Society* 41(3): 391–415.

Villalta, C. 2005. "La apropiación de 'menores': Entre hechos excepcionales y normalidades admitidas." *Revista Estudios* 16: 129–147.

    2006. "Cuando la apropiación fue adopción. Sentidos, prácticas y reclamos en torno al robo de niños." *Cuadernos de Antropología Social* 24: 147–173.

2009. "De secuestros y adopciones el circuito institucional de la apropiación criminal de niños en Argentina (1976–1983)." *Historia Crítica* 38: 146–171.

2010a. "Uno de los escenarios de la *tragedia*: el campo de la minoridad y la apropiación criminal de niños." In *Infancia, justicia y derechos humanos*, ed. C. Villalta, 199–244. Bernal: Universidad Nacional de Quilmes Editorial.

2010b. "De los derechos de los adoptantes al derecho a la identidad: los procedimientos de adopción y la apropiación criminal de niños en la Argentina." *Journal of Latin American and Caribbean Anthropology* 15(2): 338–362.

13

Kinship, Affliction, Proximity, and Unfinished Healing in India

Sarah Pinto

In north India, when people speak of spirits, they often speak of wind. *Hawa ati hai*, a wind comes to me, *hawa uski upar ayi hai*, a wind has come upon her. This is especially true of the spirits that cause affliction, that *are* affliction. You might hear about someone meeting a *bhut*, a ghost, on the road, near a tree, in a wild plot of brush behind a village, or hear the epithet *churel* invoking the witchy spirits of women who die in childbirth and aim unfinished longing at the living. But in much of the colloquial ways people describe the sorrow, misfortune, illness, or madness brought by spirits, they are just as likely to speak of *hawa*.

Madness, too, can be *hawa*. The fact that the term, though denoting something atmospheric, is of a kind with the humoral wind – *vata* – that, in Ayurvedic models, causes afflictions that move about the body – seizures and syncopes, nervous afflictions, madness, and certain kinds of pain – condense etiologies and paradigms that may also, on close inspection, diverge (Filliozat 1964). So, too, its materialities make it co-present with breath, another way air moves in and out of the body, a biomoral mechanics connecting people to each other and to the world that conjoins multiple senses and stakes of contagion, as Andrew McDowell (2014) describes in relation to tuberculosis in Rajasthan. Just as in Ayurveda wind and ghosts are not the same, though they may both afflict the same body at the same time, in *hawa*, a term that owes allegiance to no single "explanatory model," there is a convergence of materialities, affects, and knowledges – ghosts can be catching, they can settle in like a miasma, they can fall from above, they can change the body. Indeed, the quality of movement of *vata*, air, *hawa*, and breath threads particular kinds of bodies into particular kinds of relations that are also convergent modes of contagion (McDowell 2014). *Hawa* thickens mere proximity into a theory of relations that exceeds the boundaries of life and death; this theory of relations is also a theory of affliction and healing.

Hawa is also a richly evocative term with semiotic density – in literature, in song, in story, in everyday speech – and it is its metaphoric capacity, its ability to contain the immaterial and material, perceptibility
and the imperceptible, and, above all, *movement*, that makes me think of
it now, as I consider the relationship of kinship to affliction and to the
ongoing, often unfinished, work of healing. There is little to this line of
thinking but the tracing of movement and an emphasis on proximity.
Ethnographic linkages of air to kinship are less metaphoric than choreo-
graphic, involving a sense of both the mechanics of affliction and the way
kinship, too, can press heavily yet invisibly, can be a pressure or pressures,
force or forces, perceptible and imperceptible, material and immaterial.
Kinship and its nodal relationships and concepts (marriage, family, etc.)
has had a tendency in the anthropology of South Asia to sculpt narratives
and channel descriptions (what might be described, alongside caste, as
an anthropological fixation). We might do just as well to invoke water, or
sand, in this way, but to think with the wind takes us toward particular
languages of affliction, which brings us back around to a particular way
of seeing people as connected to each other. This is worth thinking about.

Since the work of David Schneider in the 1960s, we have likewise
become accustomed to thinking about kinship as and through metaphor,
to parsing our own terms and tools as metaphors mistaken for realities,
signs mistaken for things in a project that has long seen relationships
as the mediation of signs (see, e.g., Schneider 1968). As what kinship
is comes undone (or is at least made over) the more we think about
how kinship is known, descriptively oriented analytics and regionally
focused conversations enfold into epistemological questions and kinship
becomes, as Marilyn Strathern has observed, not just a way of knowing,
but a way of knowing ways of knowing. Relationships help us know about
relationships, kinship can be a tool for knowing other social practices
and a model – cultural as well as analytic – for knowing science, medicine, law, accounting, and other ways of orienting to things-in-relation
(2005).

Schneider and Strathern have allowed much anthropological thinking
to go well beyond telling us what kinship looks like, here and there, to
telling us what kinship is, and from there to the ways kinship is a point
of entry into what other things are, traversing levels of metaphor and cultural baggage to ask what might be taken for granted in establishing this
thing – "kinship" – as an object of study. In many ethnographic places –
especially Melanesia, but also South Asia, kinship is a longstanding tool
of both connection (as in the figuring of Dravidian kinship as a comparative pivot in Lewis Henry Morgan's early formulations of our project
or its centering in relatively similar methods of exploring personhood;
Trautmann 1987) and critique, deploying ways of being-in-relation to
show up scholarly models as folk theory and, more complexly, as bound
historically, often, to the very spaces in which kinship and personhood

are imagined as its objects of knowledge rather than participants in long-unfolding conversations. At the core of this way of asking questions of kinship is the conviction that this diversity of forms and metaphors matters. This diversity matters not only for the sake of being a kind of array, a vocabulary, of metaphors, but in the diverse ways metaphors might be stitched to and unstitched from the world – through scholarly work, everyday reflection, and, most importantly, things that happen as people find ways to share lives. In this way, kinship is, if not unique among anthropological subjects, then in a special class in being best addressed in its own undoing. In part, this may be because the "is" of kinship fits poorly with the pressure of kinship in its multiplicities – not just multiplicities of content (kinship here, kinship there, good kinship, bad kinship) but more existentially. Even our hardiest metaphors are not immune to undoing.

But embedded in the crucial early turn in our subfield's history, from descent to affinity, genealogy to marriage, is the hunch that kinship is a verb as much as a noun, the *animation* as well as the animating force, or thing animated, the pressure of and against rules as much as the rules themselves. Beyond the sense of structure as a kind of movement, enshrined in Lévi-Strauss' deployment of Mauss' understanding of gifts as things in motion, kinship is movement in its sheer forces of assertion (Levi-Strauss 1969; Mauss 1954). Kinship asserts itself in so many ways, and the ways one encounters it, even in a single day, let alone a lifetime, exposes the crush of possibilities contained in its effects. I have found this to be especially true, at times especially confounding, in spaces dedicated to healing. Whether people enter therapeutic contexts – or make spaces over as therapeutic – as individuals or in groups, they do so with, and by way of, the presence of others.

It is a truism that Indian medicine is a family affair. In psychiatry, this means that people seek care with, for, and among kin, and that the everyday ways medicine unfolds offer insight into the active nature of kinship in fraught moments of crisis. Affliction, of course, is also a matter of kin, involving not only the entanglement of care and conflict, but also the strange ways suffering can involve bonds forged across barriers between life and death. In hospital wards, religious healing centers, and households, intimate others might include both living kin and cadres of the dead. Ancestors afflict us with genetic inheritances and dispositions, but they may linger in other ways. My field notes reveal that in the course of a single week in a small north Indian city, I met no fewer than four women who were afflicted or affronted by dead female affinal kin, that is, women from their husband's families (including former wives). In one case, a young mother of four on an inpatient unit was afflicted by the spirit of her husband's first wife, who had died of an illness before she could bear a child. The first wife had also been subject to running away, fits of sudden unconsciousness, outbursts and vague pains and exhaustion (this was not what killed her) and, as was explained to me, "shared her illness" when the second wife joined the household. In another, a neighbor told me that his wife's frequent headaches were due to the presence of his (long-dead) grandmother, who in life was a mean-spirited woman. Stories like this are scattered throughout my field notes, though they did not rise out of the weeds of detail and into my awareness until much later. Contagion is material (ghosts should not be mistaken as immaterial) and generational, transcending time and death. When ghosts of mothers-in-law, grandmothers-in-law, sisters-in-law, husbands' former wives share afflictions with women, it would be foolish not to consider the ways such contagions figure in a patrilineal, out-marrying system in which women in their conjugal homes are structurally, symbolically, and at least for a time affectively outsiders, bound primarily by progeny (and that only tenuously as women with these and other illnesses might return – or be "sent back" – to natal homes to be cared for, and all are vulnerable to losing contact with children in cases of divorce). Women who die in the thick of these structural conditions and conditions of movement might persist in embodying (or disembodying) the tension between conjugal emplacement and displacement, the outsiderness of the north Indian wife manifest as poison, illness, and threat. Spirit affliction may make vivid the vulnerability of women to kinship, paradoxically by transforming women into afflicting agents, victims of each other rather than of the larger system. But affliction may signal other kinds of connection. The 2013 Bengali film, *Goynar Baksho* (The Jewelry Box; Sen 2013), as well as the early twentieth-century Shirshendu Mukhopadhyay novel on which it was based, are elaborations on this theme, but cast the ghost as, ultimately, empowering of the young wife she haunts. The ghost is the spirit of a woman widowed in childhood, bitter over not being allowed to remarry, who troubles her natal home and its descendants, especially a newly arrived young bride. Witnessing her nephew's inept business practices, she gives the young woman jewelry from the eponymous – and closely guarded – box, which the bride invests in the family business and bolsters her family's economic stability. There is much more to the plot, but in this line of the narrative, the ghost is the medium, against patriarchal kinship, of a counter-inheritance, a counter-kinship that transcends the rules of patrilineal descent and its organization of locality and claims to property. I understand the pattern of affliction by affinal female kin similarly – a counter-kinship that binds women across the inside–outside divides that organize patriliny and virilocality. That it does so as affliction might be understood as furtherance of the frictive qualities of women's feelings about and relationships within patrilineal kinship, but that it does so not through the mediation of living kin but the arrivals of dead kin bring a different order of the materialization of relationships and their effects.

Perhaps through an affinity with wind and their ways of working upon the body, the dead find their way into a range of healing spaces – hospitals and clinics, as well as religious centers, and, of course, households. Afflictions for which spirit visitation is an etiology (often among several) figure in different ways in different spaces as the work of healing (or just enduring) is often ongoing and seldom strictly affiliated with one or another paradigm ("Western," "indigenous," etc.). As the afflicted move, so do kin – as caregivers, as backstories, and as haunting spirits. Thus, different therapeutics and therapeutic spaces bring into relief the ways kinship is movement, action, impact, and choreography. At the same time, just as certain illnesses – psychosis, spirit affliction, dissociation – undo the privileging of "experience" as a stable category and gold standard of "truth" (Desjarlais 1997), the freighted actions of therapeutic effort compile kinship choreographies upon one another, displacing any sense of kinship as a unitary thing.

Working in psychiatric settings in India has given me a strong sense that for many the most impactful quality of kinship is not its rules, orienting metaphors, or exclusions, but the sheer force of dissolution. It is the falling apart, rather than holding together, and the mediations of dissolutions that I have found to have the most bearing for women, in particular, and the dissolving quality of kinship to be the often unspoken reality underneath a much louder discourse about the "strength of Indian families" and elaborate visions of togetherness evoked in conceptualizations of Indian kinship.

In cases of spirit possession, and the madness of new brides and old wives, this may mean that even after death women remind each other – bodily and subjectively – about the stakes of their position in kinship-as-dissolution, the way relationships are at stake in relationships, and one dissolution bears the potential for others. As I have come to write increasingly of kinship as undoing and to think increasingly about the pluralistic ways kinship and other intimacies exceed death, I do so alongside anthropologists such as Lisa Stevenson (2014) and Anand Taneja (2018), who observe paradigms of post-life that exceed or evade biopolitical arrangements for managing life. This ethnographic conviction requires me to pay close attention to the spaces in which kinship's transgressions (of insiderness and outsiderness, of life and death, of materiality and immateriality) unsettle certain guiding ideas about kinship's relationship to power. First is the fixation on kinship's overlapping relationships to power – those which emphasize kinship as normative and normalizing, establishing not only cultural expectations or prescriptions for organizing love, but regimes for legal recognition, moral domains of right and wrong personhood. In India, while moral regimes associated with sexuality certainly underscore the sense of kinship as regulation (a narrative structure that left two decades of Bollywood film worrying over the moral implications of non-prescribed marriage), the specificities of *actual* structures for organizing preferential unions do more than say who a person can and cannot love. They also articulate the *kinds* of relationship a person might have with ideals; they show that at stake may be the ways emotions – like longing, entitlement, disappointment, frustration, contentment, etc. – have more to do with how choreographies of preference situate people in relation to structures and expectations than with how they delineate the kinds of relationships a person should or must have (Clark-Decès 2014). In some cases, when put together with the biopolitical demands of the state and other contemporary regimes of legibility, the right *kind of human* may indeed be implicit in kinship imagined as a guide for living (Butler 2002). But in others, it is equally important to account for the range of ways kinship is orienting, and the quiet power of our metaphors of understanding – does it make "demands," establish "preference," "normalize," establish "right"? The difference matters in ways that take us further than simply to imagine a unitary thing "kinship" as a kind of intimacy that is other to the normalizing demands of biopolitics, an alternate paradigm for intimacy and being a self (Povinelli 2006). Disappointment, the foreclosure of care, and complexes of regret are as much the result of the failed promises of preferential kinship as they are the imposition of norms and rules (Clark-Decès 2014); indeed, the idea that the primary emotional effect of kinship – kinship as structured social relations – is a gendered sense of rights of persons in each other that translates into a constraint upon freedom of choice is a particular folk logic (Strathern 1981). This brings us to the other two points of emphasis in which a sense of kinship as movement and undoing might intervene: that which emphasizes kinship as care, often against biopolitical management and the normalizing work of determining what kinship properly is; and the anthropological truism that kinship is structured relationships of exchange and affinity, which may be the lineage to which both thematics are accountable – a story about persons vis-à-vis structures and the experiences made possible in the seams.

In India, the sense of kinship as cultural rules and normalizing biopolitical management may offer a fit between feminist considerations and Foucauldian thinking, involving capillary forms of power at the intersections of intimacy and institutional systems, or modes of political recognition that pit individual women as confounding group identities (a long theme of postcolonial legal and social debate). The notion of kinship as care, cultivation, or harbor might be a rejoinder to both biopolitical management (Rouse 2009) and a sense of kinship as control, locating something other than contests between authoritative and subaltern desires in connections enacted for the sake of well-being. But while these orientations are vital to reckoning with kinship, they are also the formulas against which the multiplicity of kinship energies crush. Where life involves inhabiting – as much as is bearable – the conflicting force of those energies, each formulation may be true and insufficient, apt and incomplete, illuminating and obscuring. Each may also shape the way we envision things as falling apart, or consider the stakes of falling to pieces, think of dissolution as the failure of the system rather than what the system is and does. The dissolution of which Strathern writes (1992), and the centering of dissolution as a mode of knowing relationships and their stakes which I have discussed (Pinto 2014), should mark not just an alternative to specific interpretations (what "relations" *are*, what "selves" *are*), but also the struggles of knowing kinship *in* kinship, knowing kinship in its many avatars. If the efforts of which kinship is comprised are as much matters of undoing as shoring up, then the effort of ethnographic understanding (circularly) becomes not so much one of tracing and tracking patterns, as reading at the points of disjuncture, the spaces of metaphoric undoing, grasping for the myriad movements that can – sometimes must – take place.

Still, reasserting themselves in that effort are those insistent readings – the normalizing and fixing, the care and making well, and the ordering and holding together. There is something to them, and even amid entropy we can find asymptotic urges toward normativity, care, and structure, as much as we follow leanings in other directions. I may find this to be so because these urges are part of my cultural baggage, or because they are part of my scholarly baggage. Or because they are there. Sometimes it is hard to tell.

The question remains open.

I find this openness and abundance in my own field notes, reread after several years, where I come across ten almost unbearably dense pages of single-spaced type that start, as these entries often do, with a basic resistance: "I must write, but am absolutely exhausted, and so may not have the greatest recall or most fluid of prose …"

I began by locating myself at the edges of family, indeed, of love: "I am staying in a house I have come to know well, though it is not my own (sometimes I wish it were) and with a family about whom I feel the same – I wish I were theirs, and they mine …" I have written enough about them already and so I will say little more here, except that my notes are full of interruptions – like a screen door blown open by the wind – by a family member returned home from an extended stay in a psychiatric institution. I was writing up the details of a visit – one of a series – the day before to a *dargah*, a Sufi shrine a few hours away. I had hired a driver long known to the family. He and his car were both old and reliable and slow. The car was noisy, Verma-ji (Mr. Verma) was quiet, thoughtful, and slightly worried.

I made the same day-trip with Verma-ji months earlier. It had been our first together, an adventure of discovery we shared with my five-year-old daughter and a mattress-maker we met at a crossroads outside the city. We had asked for directions to the *dargah* – which I very mistakenly thought was just a few kilometers beyond the edge of the city. He described a much longer journey, a confusing one but he knew the way, and we invited him along. But this time, it was just me and Verma-ji, no child, no new friends, and we remembered the route. It was a relief, in some ways, to be free of the timings and concerns of my daughter, but I missed her head on my lap along the dusty, bumpy way.

Visiting *dargahs* was a side-project to my larger research, and my trips were often to places I heard about from someone at another shrine ("If you are interested in healing/like this place, you should go to …"), references that usually involved only the barest, often incorrect, information about names, locations, and histories. I was not charting north India in this way as a scholar of Sufism or even ritual healing might; I had little interest (I should have had more) in religious lineages and my pock-marked knowledge of *dargahs'* histories and institutional structures was not unlike the partial knowledge of those who came to the shrine seeking healing, caught up as I was in a project seeking the ways intimacies were forged and broken through mental illness. Since then, work by Carla Bellamy (2011) has provided insight into the religious and ritual nature of *dargah* healing, with insight into the relationship between social contexts, everyday healing, space, and ritual. Likewise, Claudia Liebeskind offers an excellent historical account of Sufi traditions in north India (1998). My recollections here are offered in the shadow of these works, and in a different spirit. What was resonant to me from these unsystematic, interlinked visits, unintentionally patterned after the travels of petitioners, was in the way they were chains of affect, links of sadness, struggle, and intensities it is hard to name, strung together by the movements of people and their kin.

People traveled, for the most part, in groups of relatives, though in no particular arrangement of kin. For many, especially those in states of mental and emotional undoing, visits were carefully paced – one might do a "forty-day-course," coming every night or staying in a lodging room, or they might visit every Thursday, or on the new moon. My own visits, by contrast, were spontaneous, disorganized and urgent, stuffed in around the edges of other work, feeling less like systematic research than careening around.

On this occasion, I had less than a full day, as the journey was long, the car slow, and Verma-ji anxious to get home before evening. We found the large *dargah* complex (which I will not name, in keeping with my habit of not identifying the places where I did my fieldwork at that time) easily and managed to visit three of the four main shrines in the prescribed order, beginning at the top of the hill, a shrine generically called Imam Sahib, which was approached via a bazaar of 20 or 30 stalls selling the usual religious goods – pictures of the shrines, shiny plaques with Qur'anic verse, roses and incense for offerings, decorated skullcaps for boys, handkerchiefs with the Indian flag on them (and the English flag, I was intrigued to notice). *Nagara* players were positioned at the base of a steep staircase, and the deep pulse of their drums, along with the tinny treble of a poorly broadcast sermon, pushed people through a large arch and up to the shrine.

At the top of the stairs, the shrine rose from a partially shaded marble square. Verma-ji and I positioned ourselves along the wall. A young man in gray was behind us, lunging up the stairs, laughing, swearing, lurching, and flapping his arms, looking out from under a lowered brow. He was led by a man in a blue silk robe and turban. I took him to be a "holy man of sorts." They were accompanied by an older and weary-looking man I later learned was his father and a younger man who turned out to be his brother. Later, the father told me the man in the blue robe was "just someone who visits the shrine," someone who, like his son, was "*man-buddhi*," mentally disabled, and took it upon himself to stay near the boy and lead him through the site, a momentary intimacy of affinity and guidance.

The young man was shackled at his ankles. The chains dragged on the ground loosely enough to let him walk. "I put them on," his father told me. The chains served the double purpose of keeping the young man from running away and locking in the *shaitan*, the afflicting demon, so that, when it – the *shaitan* – was eventually released it would not spread to others. The proper unlocking of the chains would allow the *shaitan* to relinquish his grasp on his son, dissipate it without afflicting others (months later, he phoned me early in the morning to tell me that this had happened). I thought of Lévi-Strauss, effective symbols, and the multiple ways chains can do literal and meaningful work, both in this space of affliction and healing and in the worlds of the mental health and human rights activist for whom chains were a symbol of abuse.

The year before, I had taken my daughter, then four, on a visit to an elderly friend of a friend. It was a social visit, but I also thought she might be able to help me find my way to some of the many, many small shrines around the city, side-of-the-road tombs and temples where people with various afflictions were drawn. She changed the tone of her voice to deep and quiet, and spoke in a way that signaled a code of omission. I should not take my daughter with me. The *dargahs* were too dangerous for her. "You never know what you can catch there," she said. Ever primed to be annoyed by moral advice about hygiene, I said something about being very careful about water. She clarified, though in few enough words that it did not occur to me until later exactly what she had meant, that she was talking about an entirely different kind of contagion, a different way my "innocent" daughter would be vulnerable to released spirits looking for new bodies to claim.

The father had brought his son to the shrine every new moon for several cycles at the advice of the shrine's maulana. They had been sent by a friend who told them this shrine was exceptionally good at removing tenacious demons. His son was about 21 and had had *pareshani* – troubles – for several years, attacks like this one, of wildness and fear, thrashing about, that could come at any time, in the morning or afternoon, or deep in the night. He had gotten in trouble with the police, who arrested him for behavior the man did not specify. The father was concerned that his son would not be unmarriageable.

He explained that there were two sisters-in-law living in the house, the wives of his other sons. One of them had the same affliction. Her fits began after marriage, when she came to live in their home. Her *shaitan* also had a firm grip, and so as father and father-in-law he had "filed a case" for both of them here, writing their names on separate pieces of paper and tying them with yarn to the railing around the tomb.

On the ground nearby, a slightly older man (perhaps in his mid-thirties) lay shirtless, his arms reaching up as though pulled by invisible force. Like many around him, his wrists were crossed and held together as though bound. Others held their hands tightly behind their backs, but his were above his head, and he moaned and writhed as he pushed himself around on his back, propelled by his feet, or perhaps pulled by an unseen rope, with a speed that took me by surprise. He leapt up and swung around, keeping his arms outstretched, then fell back to the ground.

His family surrounded him in a kinetic vigilance. Together they held a bed sheet taught like a canopy, following his movements with shade. Above the shifting group – sometimes three, sometimes four or five – the square of shadow seemed to contain his movements as people entered and left the circle.

"The family looked anxious and tired," I wrote, "and fully focused on him."

The two men – the younger in real chains, the older in imaginary bonds – found each other. They lunged, escaping their carers, and fell into each other as though wrestlers, yelling and moaning, erratic objects drawn into an agonistic embrace. The people around them watched but did not seem perturbed. I found the calm remarkable.

It was both Jumerat – Thursday – and *navchandi* – the new moon, the holiest day of the week coinciding with a time in the lunar cycle dense with the energy of spirits. The convergent cyclical intensities had brought throngs to the *dargah* and the place was full of people, many like these men – moaning, shrieking, rolling on the ground, banging their heads against walls, lying or slouching in a faint along the edge of the room containing the tomb. Women swung their hair in circles in *peshi*, a trance state brought about by *hawa*. Their movements intensified as the spirit inside took over their limbs (women I spoke with could never remember their time in this state) and were pulled out by the saint entombed in the shrine. It was, indeed, these strong, authoritative spirits for whom people came and the afflicting spirits roared and growled through human throats for the dead saint to leave them alone – "No, baba, no," "Let me be," "Let go of me."

Women, with loose and swinging hair, made a ragged chorus around the shrine. I wrote, "their pace was rapid and wild and their arms tense with effort and the spirits of the dead, seeming just on the brink of self control, waving and flailing, and wringing, but tense, not loose, unlike the hair."

I wrote, too, about the people attending them. "No one … seems in the least perturbed. There is a sense of single-mindedness, a sense of purpose, and also a sense of calm and peace, especially as many have also come just to come and pray. But there is not fear."

Or if there was, I did not see it in ways I could recognize.

I spoke with a young man who had come with his sister, sister-in-law, and mother. The three women were afflicted by spirits that had been enticed upon them by his brother, who bore an enmity the man did not explain, and who may have put something "magical" and dark in food he fed them.

The man's mother and sister-in-law sat at the wall, covered entirely in their *dupattas*, as were many women. One was unconscious, *behosh*, he said. Many women sat with their hands pressed up against the grate outside the tomb, pulling out a force that emanated from the Baba in the tomb inside. The man's sister was rocking, moaning, with her hair loose and her eyes rolled back. She had been sick like this for a year and a half and the family had taken her to several doctors, but they gave no "relief." Someone told them come to this place, and after that they began to see change. (A plot, indeed a refrain, I heard many, many times.)

For a year, he said, "*Hamara file ban gaya hai, case cel raha hai, mukadma cel raha hai*," Our file has been created, our case is proceeding, the court is moving. The language of cases, files, and law described the healing work at the *dargahs*, and some described this particular shrine as "the supreme court." The saints buried here would deliver their verdict, or a living maulana or caretaker would offer diagnosis. The adjudicative power of healing, vivid but seldom acknowledged in medical clinics, was made literal, whether the adjudicator was living or dead.

A woman described to me the activities of her husband, a mullah. When people come to him and explain their problems, he divines their affliction, she said, first determining whether or not it is caused by a spirit. He then tells them what they should do – whether an amulet is required, or a regular visit to the shrine, visits which often induce *peshi* as the spirit is withdrawn. I asked how he is able to make these determinations. Does he look for signs in the body? No, the woman told me, the spirits themselves tell him. He can hear them even if others cannot. They speak to him and tell him they have arrived. The reason for their arrival was not his concern. Later, when I asked him why the spirits come to one person or another, he said that some are afflicted because they have "weak blood" but then added, "God only knows," a statement that was not meant rhetorically.

The man with the sick mother and sister-in-law observed that my hands were shaking (I hadn't noticed) and asked if I was scared. I was not, but I could not deny feeling unsettled. Not with the sounds or the moving bodies but with a feeling of being surrounded by affliction, by what happens at the edges of control and human singularity, at the cusp of boundedness – of energies, winds, breath, and voices. The sense of vulnerability – not to "madness" or "sickness" – but by the ratty edges of selfness, might have been in part what people meant when they warned me about being caught by the loosened spirits.

These warnings – like the one offered by the woman at the beginning of my work – were seldom of concern for me. They were meant for my daughter, and sometimes as commentary on my ignorant mothering, my unintentional lack of care. I was scolded many times by friends and acquaintances that I should not take her to "these places," where errant spirits watched for the small and vulnerable. The mullah clarified that spirits did not work separately from the materiality of the body or the cosmos, but rather on and through it. They are drawn to those with "light" or "weak" blood, those whose blood has been sapped of strength by the stars and their configuration, by youth, or sickness, or by other spirits – spirits being drawn to well-traveled paths. The concern was pragmatic, even mechanical, a matter of moving entities, of openness, and susceptibility.

There is the kind of ephemerality that is the material contagion of spirits, and there is the kind that is the moral contagion of modern institutions, and the difference suddenly clarified for me around the figuring of fear. Fear *of* the mad, of a danger posed by them was not something I felt in any of those warnings or in the spaces themselves. Loud in the history of European medicine, fear of (and fascination for) the mad was written into the structure of asylums (Showalter 2009) and remains vividly part of the disciplinary nature of emergency psychiatry, especially in the police-mediated structures of psychiatry wards and emergency care, not to mention in the language of commitment proceedings dominated by evaluations of threat. Fear of the mad contributes to the moral status of the family in the Foucauldian formulation, part of the ways families are compelled to turn over aberrant members to institutions, places that will remove them from, but keep them enclosed within, normal society (Foucault 1965). The sense of threat that conditions the relationship of kinship to therapeutics in the United States is, arguably, largely absent in Indian psychiatry. Doctors laughed or were surprised when I told them that entries and exits from American psychiatry units are often guarded by (gun-carrying) police and marked by security checkpoints. In one Indian government hospital, the doors to the men's ward were always open; in fact, I worked there for weeks before I realized it even had doors. The place held in the West (or whatever locational imaginary best attaches to Foucault's formulations) by fear *of* the mad seemed to have been taken by concern about the effects of madness on those who are socially proximate, especially kin, who might be vulnerable to the contagions of madness, not least of which spirits and winds.

Somehow kinship's quality of proximity does not feel like *enough* – many things are proximate, and kinship must be of a more special order (a possible rebuttal may go). Surely, a theory of affliction must have to involve things more meaningful than the apparently simple materiality of nearness. Yet proximity may be one of kinship's most vital features. Through qualities of movement and the kinning of affliction and healing at the *dargah*, proximity was revealed to figure quite centrally as part of what defines kinship. In a universe of contagious airy malevolence, vulnerability holds people together as all potentially afflicted. This does not mean there are not logics of removal at work, and this is not to say that the difference between madness and sanity did not matter; it mattered very much, organizing many casual accounts that hinged on recognizing if a person was mad or sane (reflected, too, in the film trope of the doctor mistaken for a patient, or vice versa). But on that day it struck me that the familiar worrying over the potential misrecognition of madness (or sanity) may not have been organized around fear. In the words and actions of families shielding flailing bodies from the sun or walking alongside the distressed, or concerned about the ignorant foreigner who thinks it is alright to take a healthy child into a space of so many threatening winds, there was a sense of shared human vulnerability, of susceptibility blowing through proximal entities. There was a feeling too that rather than being radically different in our humanity – the mad versus the sane – we are all potentially afflicted, all riskily human. As I knew from my time in psychiatric wards, very often, the symptom and sign of affliction is the breakdown of relationships, and that kinship's undoing (or potential undoing) often drives the pulse of effort to heal. This is so even as relationships' pressure of proximity is part of what makes one person's illness another's vulnerability, indeed, the vulnerability of the web of relationships. The effort to create around this a veil of protection is no longer a singularly directed act of care. It is widely dispersed. Likewise, to protect kinship's reproducibility (the persistent concern over marriageability) is a logic of both proximity and shared humanity, not normalization or difference. The winds might settle on any of us. The efforts of care should fall to the strong, but are carried out by all in spite of such risk. They can do more than shore up connections. They can break them as well. Indeed, in certain cases they depend on severing the kinds of mutated kinship that are spirit affliction.

The work of releasing spirits from the body takes time. At Imam Sahib and the other shrines at this site, I met people who continued to visit after their affliction ended, many out of gratitude and devotion, some just out of habit, they said. In the outer veranda, I talked with a family who had been coming here for some time but had not "found full satisfaction," though they anticipated it. A woman who had been afflicted by spirits for years said she got "no relief" from medications or doctor visits. She had *vajan*, heaviness, in the body, headaches, no desire to work or do anything in the house. Her hijab was wrapped tightly, surrounding her round face, glasses, and somber expression with red-flecked cloth. Her husband and her three sons were with her, as was her husband's aunt, who explained connections between spirit affliction and the cosmos, the way stars' inauspicious orientations make a person susceptible to spirits. The husband did most of the talking, describing the family's efforts. The woman said little.

A woman in a black burqa but with her head uncovered, walked in circles nearby, speaking loudly and unintelligibly, and followed by a younger man. Another man told me he had come with his wife, who had been bothered by spirits for as long as they had been married, though before marriage she had not had this problem. She lay next to him on the marble floor, still and with eyes half open. While we talked, another woman approached and said she had once come here for 40 days. Now, she could recognize the signs of affliction and brought people from her village. She was known to be something of a specialist. "I'm not related to the people I bring," she clarified. She pointed to the husband and wife, indicating she had brought them. "I can't speak for long because I have to take care of the others. I walk them around the shrine, I help them when they fall unconscious and when they come to again."

The first man's wife began to stir, and he knelt to hold a cup of water to her lips.

A man nearby told me he only came to see the place. "In fact, I don't really believe in all this saint worship stuff, or about the curing." He described himself as a Deobandhi, a sect he described as "like Shi'as" in not thinking that devotional practice at shrines represents Islam. "But," he said, "I do think there is a special power about the place."

Verma-ji and I decided to move on. We gave our bag of sweets, roses, and incense to the father of the young man in chains to offer inside. On our way to the next shrine, we passed another man in chains coming up the stairs.

The next shrine was down the stairs and around the side of the hill. It was more open than Imam Sahib and families spread in the cool shade and ate lunch on blankets. I went inside the shrine, where I pressed the head and feet of the three tombs, and circumambulated, surrounded by people intently praying, silently crying, but not weeping or shouting or speaking with the recognizable growl of ghosts.

Leaving for the third and largest shrine, we pressed through the thickening crowd in the bazaar, got into the old Ambassador, and drove across a bridge, inching between groups of people. The complex of shrines straddled a major river that, here, ran like a canal, deep and straight, hemmed by high walls edged with *ghats*, steps that caught the river as it came onto the plains from the mountains. Beyond the bridge, the road followed a steep hill, passing a smaller shrine and a mental health clinic (empty and locked) on its way to the largest of the *mazars*.

The bazaar outside the gates was thronged with beggars, and, inside, a large courtyard surrounded by lodging rooms was busier than Imam Sahib. In a fenced-off area in the middle, around a tree hanging with petitions, a *qawwali* group sang. I found a seat in a spot that, it turned out, had been temporarily vacated by a mullah, who returned a bit later and insisted I stay.

At least four women in the audience around the *qawwali* group were in *peshi*. They all seemed young, one possibly as young as my own daughter. Their hair was loose and their *dupattas* were tied tightly around their tops, making visible the form of torsos usually hidden behind loosely draped fabric. There was moaning as they whipped their hair, making fraying ribbon aureoles in the air. Occasionally one fell down, lying still, or writhing on the ground. Another stopped her head-swinging and stumbled drunkenly through the crowd, followed closely by an older woman who seemed to be trying to hold her back, to keep her from running off, perhaps, or just to keep her wild movements in check.

The next day, I wrote in a wild burst of unfinished sentences and cluttered phrases,

> I am quite taken aback this time at how sexual, how sensual and physical, their movements and sounds are, how much it looks and sounds like orgasm, or birth, agonized pain or something like ecstasy. I am also amazed at how clearly, almost too obviously – shouldn't these things be more subtle, more findable only in close interpretation? – these women are experiencing and enacting a radical and vivid break from the norms of female embodiment and en-mindment (or something) that are being displayed around them in the unafflicted, or the less afflicted, or the pious, or the family members. Women whose hair is mostly neatly combed into a part (which itself suddenly looks sexual to me), contained under our scarves, hijab, and *dupattas*, even if, like mine, they tend to slip off the back of the head. Whose clothing may be somewhat unkempt from the journey, but is nonetheless properly worn (unlike [X] who wears layers and layers and elements of Indian and western clothing improperly matched – a sari over pants, or over a *selwar qamiz*, or with a polo shirt, or a dress over a sari petticoat with a shawl on top). Whose comportment is quiet and above all *contained*. I keep coming back as I look around, as I try to put it into language for myself then, in the car in my scratched notes, and now, to the word, the sense of containment, and to the way that the women in trance are enacting its opposite. Nonetheless, in the inappropriate grunting, moaning, sexual sounds (that seem to embarrass and shame no one – indeed the lack of shame here is remarkable – seriousness yes, and concern, but I sense little or no shame), in the loosened – and exaggeratedly so – indeed, flung about – hair, in the messy and improperly worn

clothes (no *dupatta*, for instance), and in the sheer movement of the body, there is an apparent release, one that pushes women to the edges of consciousness, where they collapse. A large, middle-aged woman whose head is uncovered, though her hair is too short to fling around, begins to moan and rises from her seated position. She turns her back to the *qawwali*, which at first I don't understand, but then realize that unlike the other women who face the *qawwals*, she is facing the *dargah*, the *pir*, and seems to be calling out to him, almost singing, as she sways, pulls at and runs her hand through her hair, reaches up to the sky, falls to her knees, reaches out toward the tomb. She is plump, and her breasts are visible without the *dupatta*, the movement, almost dancing, emphasizes them, and she reminds me of the fat women who danced at the *mehndi* ceremony before Rehana's daughter's wedding.

The small girl's trance was surprising to me. Until that point, I had never seen a child go into this state, and, on top of that, had always associated it with women of reproductive age or, at the earliest, adolescence. The start of affliction, madness, and possession at marriage is a familiar theme in north India, and speaks, among other things, to the patterns of movement and relationships instigated by marriage, the structured affect of reproduction and its tension with sexual desire. I had seen unmarried girls go into trance, but what did it mean to see one so young? I asked the mullah, and he said that this was unusual but not impossible.

The mullah's wife told me that seated behind her was a woman from Delhi who had been bringing her daughter here for a few years. The daughter wore a clean and sparkly *selwar qamiz*, and the mother wore her hijab closely around her head. The girl appeared to be in her late teens or early twenties. The mullah's wife leaned in and spoke quietly, "The girl was so possessed by spirits that they used to cut her arms terribly." When the mullah returned, he said that when the girl first came to him he could see she was possessed not by one spirit, but by four or five thousand.

"This army has come and taken over this poor girl's body."

I asked why.

"God knows." Since she has been visiting this shrine, he said, they have gone.

The woman on my other side – a young Hindu woman with small children around her – asked where I was from. She said, somewhat proudly, that she had come all the way from Delhi with her husband, children, and mother-in-law. The problem, she said, was that her husband was afflicted by some kind of spirit. Later, when she came to know that the person seated near her was a mullah, she asked if this was indeed the case. "He hasn't worked for several months and is not earning money," she said. "He is not depressed, but he is very often angry."

The mullah nodded. "Yes, definitely, a spirit has afflicted him."

Someone reached through the crowd with a small child and handed it down to her. She took the baby into her lap and said that this was her youngest daughter, and that she was one-and-a-half years old. This surprised me – the child was so tiny. She could not stand on her own and had blondish hair and pallid skin – which I read as signs of malnutrition. The woman herself looked barely 19, though she must have been older than that, because her older child was seven.

I wrote the next day, "I wonder what is going on with this family. They have spent 5000 rs, she says, on a van to come up here from Delhi and shortly after, before the next round of *qawwali* starts, she stands up and says they are headed back to Delhi."

The wind had begun to blow strongly. The day was hot, and it was a lovely breeze, whipping the warm currents around us, catching the women's hair, pulling the leaves outward from their branches as though supplicants in a mass prayer, raising their arms or bending their knees in unison. And the wind caught the words written on the papers tied to the tree. The papers, with their inscribed longings, flapped audibly. Even years later, I can hear them on the tape, and in my mind.

I wrote, "So many things in the wind here – spirits one can catch and that can catch one, words – our own, the women's shouts, words written on paper, the voices of the *qawwals*. The wind seems a necessary part of the moment."

The sense of the day was changing – lifting, easing – with the shift in air and light. Verma-ji stepped through the seated crowd. He leaned over and said we needed to head back. I was a bit frustrated but I deferred. He was an old man with old eyes and an old car. The ride was long and dusty, and though the exhaust fumes made our eyes and throat burn, it was too hot for closed windows. The atmosphere cooled and settled as we reached home.

As I wrote even that into my notes, after a meal, a bath, and then a restless night's sleep, I remembered that a few days before, a question had been posed by her daughter-in-law to the woman in the home where I was staying: "Did you miss your sons while you were in that ashram with the gate?" "The ashram" is what she had called the psychiatric hospital.

She had looked at her hands as she shook her head in a gesture that felt like no. "The wind that blew in the trees outside came inside also."

References

Bellamy, Carla. 2011. *The Powerful Ephemeral: Everyday Healing in an Ambiguously Islamic Place*. South Asia Across the Disciplines. Berkeley, CA: University of California Press.

Butler, Judith. 2002. *Antigone's Claim: Kinship between Life and Death*. New York: Columbia University Press.

Clark-Decès, Isabelle. 2014. *The Right Spouse: Preferential Marriage in Tamil Nadu*. Palo Alto, CA: Stanford University Press.

Desjarlais, Robert. 1997. *Shelter Blues: Sanity and Selfhood among the Homeless*. Philadelphia, PA: University of Pennsylvania Press.

Filliozat, Jean. 1964. *The Classical Doctrine of Indian Medicine, Its Origins and Its Greek Parallels,*1st English ed. Delhi: Munshiram Manoharlal.

Foucault, Michel. 1965. *Madness and Civilization: A History of Insanity in the Age of Reason*. New York: Pantheon Books.

Lévi-Strauss, Claude. 1969. *Elementary Structures of Kinship*. Boston, MA: Beacon Press.

Liebeskind, Claudia. 1998. *Piety on Its Knees: Three Sufi Traditions in South Asia in Modern Times*. Delhi: Oxford University Press.

McDowell, Andrew James. 2014. *Troubling Breath: Tuberculosis, Care and Subjectivity at the Margins of Rajasthan*. Cambridge, MA: Harvard University Press.

Mauss, Marcel. 1954. *The Gift: Forms and Functions of Exchange in Archaic Societies*. Glencoe, IL: Free Press.

Pinto, Sarah. 2014. *Daughters of Parvati: Women and Madness in Contemporary India*. Philadelphia, PA: University of Pennsylvania Press.

Povinelli, Elizabeth A. 2006. *The Empire of Love: Toward a Theory of Intimacy, Genealogy, and Carnality*. Durham, NC: Duke University Press.

Rouse, Carolyn Moxley. 2009. *Uncertain Suffering: Racial Health Care Disparities and Sickle Cell Disease*. Berkeley, CA: University of California Press.

Schneider, David. 1968. *American Kinship: A Cultural Account*. Chicago, IL: University of Chicago Press.

Sen, Aparna. 2013. *Goynar Baksho*. Kolkata: Eagle International.

Showalter, Elaine. 2009 [1987]. *The Female Malady: Women, Madness, and English Culture, 1830–1980*. London: Virago.

Stevenson, Lisa. 2014. *Life beside Itself: Imagining Care in the Canadian Arctic*. Berkeley, CA: University of California Press.

Strathern, Marilyn. 1981 "Self-Interest and the Social Good: Some Implications of Hagen Gender Imagery." In *Sexual Meanings: The Cultural Construction of Gender and Sexuality*, ed. S. Ortner and H. Whitehead, 166–191. Cambridge: Cambridge University Press.

1992. *Reproducing the Future: Anthropology, Kinship, and the New Reproductive Technologies*. New York: Routledge.

2005. *Kinship, Law and the Unexpected: Relatives Are Always a Surprise*. Cambridge: Cambridge University Press.

Taneja, Anand Vivek. 2018. *Jinnealogy: Time, Islam, and Ecological Thought in the Medieval Ruins of Delhi*. South Asia in Motion. Stanford, CA: Stanford University Press.

Trautmann, Thomas R. 1987. *Lewis Henry Morgan and the Invention of Kinship*. Berkeley, CA: University of California Press.

14

Reproductive Remix: Law, Kinship, and Origin Stories

Valerie Hartouni

In January 2010, an op-ed piece by Adam Cohen appeared in the *New York Times*, under a hard to miss, bold headline: "A Legal Puzzle: Can a Baby Have Three Biological Parents?" (2010: A18). As someone who had written extensively on alternative reproductive arrangements throughout the mid-1980s and 1990s – a period when new reproductive innovations, practices, and collaborative arrangements seemed at every turn to generate sordid media and legal spectacles – I was hailed by the headline, but found its provocation curiously flat (Hartouni 1997). Readers might remember at least some of the many versions of this question that were posed more or less breathlessly, anxiously, and repeatedly over the course of the last several decades when new techniques of biological reproduction appeared to some to be propelling the species toward an unknown but calamitous future. And yet, with each novel reproductive technique, feared moral precipice, or pyrotechnic legal case, a certain order was reliably restored. Judges marched out across what many of them insisted was uncharted legal terrain to nevertheless recover from whatever unusual redistribution of biological material had originally compelled them forth, the two-parent natural family – miraculously intact, foundational, and inevitable. With each novel reproductive technique and the relational instability and complexity it fostered, nature prevailed in organizing and anchoring the social, at least in the eyes of the court.

By any measure, this has been an impressive feat. And it also remains an instructive one in foregrounding not so much the fixed persistence of nature as the law's aptitude in producing it as such – whether through appeals to tradition, world history, the origin and needs of the species, the insights of science, the findings of anthropology, "God Almighty," or just plain "common sense." In other words, rather than merely rendering nature or, as the headline implies, being stymied by its apparent absence in the wake of biomedical innovations, the law has been a critical technology in ensuring its reproduction. As a particularly salient example in this regard, consider briefly *Obergefell v. Hodges*, the 2015 US Supreme Court landmark decision extending the fundamental right to marriage to same-sex citizens. Wasn't it precisely the majority's misappropriation of law as a particular instrument of reproduction that led the four dissenting justices to castigate the majority and issue dire warnings about the relational chaos that was likely to follow because, in their view, the majority's opinion worked a wedge between the natural and social orders, upended innate and vital arrangements, and asserted (willy-nilly) who gets to be and make a family? Wasn't it this misappropriation that inflamed Justice Alito and led him to insist that the majority had turned a postmodern corner and gone off the rails? Indeed, from Alito's perspective, the majority had simply made up meanings and the consequences of such recklessness on the law's authority and the institutions that depend on it, he opined, were certain to be profound (Obergefell 2015, dissent)

I will come back to the *Obergefell* ruling shortly, but for the moment let's return to Adam Cohen's op-ed piece in the *New York Times*. What precipitated Cohen's reflections were experiments that at the time of his observations in 2010 had just been completed at Oregon Health and Science University's Primate Center: researchers at the primate center had successfully replaced defective DNA in the egg of one female monkey with genetic material from the egg of another. They had then fertilized and implanted the genetically modified embryo in a simian host and this had culminated in the birth of apparently healthy twins (OHSU 2009). Researchers speculated that the procedure, called "spindle transfer," would also likely work in humans and various ventures since, primarily in the UK, but also in the United States, appear to confirm their optimism (*Center for Genetics and Society* 2015; Thompson et al. 2015; Darnovsky 2013). Although the routine, clinical use of "maternal spindle transfer" in humans remains as yet only aspirational, these new gene-editing techniques herald the possibility of breakthrough treatments for not simply combating but eradicating the cross-generational transmission of a range of inherited diseases otherwise passed from mothers to their offspring.

For Cohen, the specter of altering or editing genes is disturbing. But more troubling for him than the promiscuous exchange of genetic material upon which the therapeutic promise of the technique rests is the procedure's fracturing effect on both parenthood and individual identity: apparently, without a clear sense of whose genetic baggage one carries, individuals will have no clear sense of who they really are or what their place is in the world. Thus he asks: *Could a baby one day have 100 parents? Could anyone who contributes DNA claim visitation rights? Can a baby who is born outside the United States to foreigners but who has DNA from an American citizen claim US Citizenship?* Cohen conjures for readers the socially and relationally dystopic frontier that ethicists and, more importantly, the courts have been able thus far to keep at bay. But he suspects that once genetics and kinship are no longer clearly, or at least discursively, aligned, neither scholar nor judge will be able to determine with certainty who belongs to whom or on what basis the family – an organization that the dissenting judges in *Obergefell* maintain predates the nation and constitutes its very foundation – can then be said to rest.

To underscore the many conceptual and categorical confusions that alternative reproductive arrangements have already generated socially as well as legally, well in advance of the relational entanglements he expects mitochondrial remixes might foster, Cohen turns to what he describes as the most legally and culturally disruptive surrogacy case since Baby M: *A.G.R. v. D.R.H. & S.H.* or *Robinson v. Hollingsworth* (2009) as it has since come to be known. Although the case is relatively straightforward in terms of its findings – surrogacy contracts are not valid in New Jersey and cannot serve as a basis for terminating parental rights – Cohen finds the ruling instructive in part because it rehearses a host of competing origin stories, invoked in different cases across different jurisdictions, as a basis for determining who gets to count as (the real) mother, father, parent, and family. Although these stories currently coexist, in his view their coexistence is both legally confusing and socially corrosive. For both reasons, he argues, judges and legal thinkers must work towards a more comprehensive legal framework that might provide or enforce consensus on which story is determinative and thus which familial bonds will be officially and consistently sanctioned as such.

In the discussion that follows, I revisit the surrogacy case that Cohen marshals to lend credence to his cautionary tale about the disruptive impact of new biology-based technologies on conventional, socially foundational understandings and practices in order to highlight the ways in which this case already answers in the affirmative what the article's headline treats as speculative fiction. "Can a Baby Have Three Biological Parents?": the answer is, they can and already do although the distribution of organic material and labor in this and related cases differs from what would be entailed with human germline gene editing. Nevertheless and notwithstanding these differences, given that reproductive techniques have already rendered biological parentage a two-plus affair, how does this ostensibly threatening misalignment of the biological and social plausibly remain part of an as yet unrealized, perhaps promising, certainly identity-challenging and thus anxiety-provoking future? I argue that while the spectacle of a revolution wrought by alternative reproductive techniques or arrangements or by gene-editing, modification, and/or cell exchange with all of the imagined dangers and loss of order the metaphor invokes may colonize our collective imagination and train our cultural attention on the lab and clinic, more significant if considerably more mundane are the ever-productive and (re)constitutive legal technologies at work in maintaining (through refiguring) precisely the world we seem always on the verge of losing.

"In every opinion," writes James Boyd White, "a court not only resolves a particular dispute one way or another, it validates or authorizes one form of life or another" (1990: 101, 1984). The making of law is also the making of life or a means by which one form of life is authorized and codified against other forms; and to anchor this claim, I proffer a reading of the 2015 US Supreme Court opinion on marriage equality in the final section of this chapter. *Obergefell v. Hodges* provides an especially rich lens to assess disputes about not only the nature and place of the family – how biology and the social are or should be aligned – but how law itself works as a reproductive technology: curiously, all of the justices in *Obergefell* seem to accept that it does work as such, as a practice for reproducing selves and communities, but according to what protocols and on behalf of which forms of life they disagree fiercely.

14.1

In the 2009 New Jersey surrogacy case, *Robinson v. Hollingsworth*, a gay couple, Donald Robinson Hollingsworth and Sean Hollingsworth, sought to start a family. Registered at the time as domestic partners in New Jersey while legally married in California, the men sought genetically related progeny and to this end arranged with Donald's sister, Angelia Gail Robinson to be their surrogate. After it was determined that Angelia's eggs were of poor quality (she was 44 years old), donor eggs were obtained, fertilized with Sean Hollingsworth's sperm, and once a pre-conception contract was signed establishing who had claims to what, transferred to her uterus. This was not exactly the collaboration that the trio initially intended: originally, Angelia's role, or more specifically the role of her eggs, was meant to create a biological bond between the two men and their potential offspring – Sean, through his sperm and Donald, through his sister and presumably their shared "heritage." She was his stand-in, a genetic link by proxy. But things didn't go quite as planned. This already complicated, largely symbolic network of relatedness made somehow more coherent and cohesive for its participants by blood (ties) became even more complicated with the introduction of donor eggs. We might wonder parenthetically whose genetic baggage they were carrying or how precisely that was made not to matter, but for the moment let's bracket these questions.

The eggs were fertilized in March 2006, the embryos were transferred, and twin girls were born seven months later. Two weeks after their birth, Angelia signed "A Consent to Judgment of Adoption" in favor of her brother, Donald; and while she continued to live in a carriage house on her brother's property, as she had done throughout her pregnancy, and work at his accounting business, in the months following the birth of the twins, her contact with them was limited. In January 2007, it ceased altogether when the sibling's relationship deteriorated and Angelia was fired from his firm. In March 2007, she filed a legal complaint seeking access to the children and the court responded by directing the men to allow Angelia "significant parenting time" with them. This arrangement worked at least through September when she was spending as much as three full days a week with the girls, but it too collapsed under the weight of personal enmity and distrust. The brother and brother-in-law withdrew Angelia's access to the twins on the grounds that she was emotionally unstable and, in response, she sued, seeking to have her parental rights reestablished and her rightful relationship to the girls, as their mother, legally affirmed.

The New Jersey Superior Court issued a summary judgment in the case in December 2009 finding that the gestational agreement Angelia had signed terminating her claim to the children was void. In Judge Schultz' words, "A contract alone, even though entered into voluntarily, cannot terminate parental rights. By virtue of having given birth to the child[ren], she is the natural mother" (*A.G.R. v. D.R.H. & S.H.* 2009). Calling Angelia's lack of a genetic link to the girls "a distinction without a difference," the court further determined that the rightful, which is to say legal, parents of the twins were the birth mother and the biological father, Sean Hollingsworth. Although this ruling rendered Donald (rather than Angelia) the marginal third party in this reproductive arrangement, altogether stripped of parental rights or authority, in a subsequent custody hearing in 2011, Judge Schultz awarded Hollingsworth (and his partner) sole legal custody (*A.G.R. v. D.R.H. & S.H.* 2011). The court found that the two men were able to provide the girls with a more economically stable, emotionally healthy, culturally diverse environment; and further, that they were better equipped to raise them in a way that would ensure they would not feel stigmatized or ashamed because of their unusual origins and two-father household. This had become an issue of some concern for the Judge given that their mother, Angelia, had since returned to her Baptist faith and, for religious reasons, now denounced surrogacy as unnatural and harmful to women and families; and the men's sexual orientation as perverse, morally depraved, and sinful. While seeking to shield the children as much as possible from views that, however firmly held or well-meaning, might have a negative, potentially detrimental impact on their sense of self and self-worth, the court nevertheless acknowledged that the twins had "a right to know the non-custodial parent." It thus also put in place a detailed biweekly visitation schedule (with special accommodation for holidays) to ensure that they had contact and adequate "parenting time" with their mother.

Such is the general overview of the case. What caught Adam Cohen's attention was the basis for the Court's judgment in 2009, specifically,

Judge Schultz' close reading of two prior surrogacy cases and the distinct or conflicting origin story each advanced – the 1988 New Jersey Supreme Court ruling *In re Matter of Baby M.* and the 1993 California Supreme Court ruling in *Johnson v. Calvert.* While both of these cases successfully recuperate some notion of "natural motherhood" (as well as maternal yearning), they differ radically on what each sees as signaling and expressing this nature. Significantly, and not altogether surprisingly, this difference has legal consequences for surrogate arrangements or determining whether and how the procreative process can be broken into component parts and these parts then contractually assigned, sold, or acquired.

14.2

As readers may remember, "Baby M" was one of the first cases to reach the courts concerning alternative reproductive collaborations and involved a custody dispute between Mary Beth Whitehead and Bill Stern. Stern and Whitehead met at the Infertility Center of New York in 1982 – Stern in pursuit of biological progeny and Whitehead, at least initially, in pursuit of the promised income generated by temporarily selling her reproductive labor. Both parties assumed that Whitehead would be a relatively passive "vessel" in this arrangement and certainly a genetic stranger to the child she contracted to host; and both were disturbed to learn that this would not be the case. The form of surrogacy practiced at the time, what is today referred to as "traditional" or "complete" surrogacy, entailed the use not just of Whitehead's uterus, but of her eggs as well. In exchange for $10,000, Whitehead agreed to be artificially inseminated with Bill Stern's sperm and to relinquish the child upon its delivery to the Sterns for adoption. However, once the baby was born, Whitehead refused to surrender the child and, under cover of night, fled the state. She was tracked down some three months later and the child was seized by police before a full phalanx of network news cameras. Whitehead was then returned to New Jersey, Baby M was returned to the Sterns, and a bitter, highly sensational custody battle commenced (Hartouni 1997).

Whereas New Jersey's lower court found commercial surrogacy contracts to be enforceable – Whitehead was in its view merely "a stranger who preserved a stranger's seed" (*In re Baby M.* 1987) – the New Jersey Supreme Court unanimously rejected the notion that such contracts were valid, arguing instead that they constituted a form of baby selling. Stern had paid for a product rather than a process, "purchas[ing] a child, or at the very least, a mother's right to her child" (*In re Baby M.* 1988). With respect to such transactions, the Court insisted, the moral, legal, and historical record was absolutely clear. "In a civilized society," Justice Wilentz observed:

> there are some things ... that money cannot buy ... In America,
> we decided long ago that merely because conduct purchased by
> money was "voluntary" did not mean that it was good or beyond
> regulation and prohibition ... Employers can no longer buy labor
> at the lowest price they can bargain for, even though that labor is
> "voluntary" ... or buy women's labor for less money than is paid
> to men for the same job ... or purchase the agreement of chil-
> dren to perform oppressive labor ... or purchase the agreement of
> workers to subject themselves to unsafe or unhealthful working
> conditions ... There are, in short, values that society deems more
> important than granting to wealth whatever it can buy, be it labor,
> love, or life.
>
> *(In re Baby M. 1988: 1248, 1249)*

Invoking what it took to be a settled interpretation of New Jersey law,
the Court contended that surrender of custody and consent to present
one's offspring for adoption were only rarely irrevocable. Indeed, such
agreements could be considered binding only when they were made
"knowingly, voluntarily, and deliberately," or under terms and conditions,
Justice Wilentz maintained, that surrogacy arrangements could not
ever meet.

> Under the contract, the natural mother is irrevocably committed
> before she knows the strength of her bond with her child. She never
> makes a totally voluntary, informed decision, for quite clearly any
> decision prior to the baby's birth is, in the most important sense
> uninformed, and any decision after that, compelled by a pre-existing
> contractual commitment, the threat of a lawsuit, and the induce-
> ment of a $10,000 payment, is less than totally voluntary.
>
> *(In re Baby M. 1988: 1248)*

It is this reasoning from biological norms articulated in this 1988 surrogacy ruling that Judge Schultz brings to bear in assessing and rejecting
the validity of the reproductive pact that Angelia Robinson entered into
with her brother and his partner prior to undergoing the embryo transfer
procedure. While her attachment to the twins may not have been in the
strictest sense genetically based, what the court treats instead as immutable and equally foundational is the gestationally aroused, instinctually
sustained maternal bond: "Other than survival," Justice Wilentz asks,
"what stronger force is there?"

> We do not know of, and cannot conceive of, any other case where a
> perfectly fit mother was expected to surrender her newly born infant,
> perhaps forever, and was then told she was a bad mother because she
> did not.
>
> *(In re Baby M. 1988: 1259)*

Such is the narrative favored by Judge Schultz. But in the closing pages of his opinion, he nevertheless felt compelled to contrast this story of mother love and familial ties with a significantly different origin story advanced by the California Supreme Court to settle a 1993 surrogacy dispute, *Johnson v. Calvert*. In this case, rather than defer to what New Jersey jurists construed as "instinct," the California court opted instead to privilege "intent," thereby promoting contractual obligations over those given in and by nature and, as Judge Schultz disparagingly noted, obscuring, not to mention devaluing, the unique investments and maternal determinants that shaped women's reproductive role and gestational labors (Hartouni 1997).

In the California surrogacy case, Mark and Crispina Calvert had contracted with a coworker of Crispina's, Anna Johnson, to bring to term their in vitro fertilized embryo. In exchange for $10,000, Johnson agreed to be surgically impregnated with the Calvert zygote, bring to term an infant with whom she shared no genetic link, and relinquish her parental rights to it in favor of the Calverts. However, once the child was born, Johnson sued for custody, claiming that she had bonded with the fetus in the latter months of pregnancy and that the Calverts had, in any event, breached their contract both by defaulting on a prearranged payment schedule and by not caring adequately for her or the baby. For their part, the Calverts insisted there could be no doubt as to whose baby this baby was: the gametes that created the child were theirs: he was the result of their parental yearning and carried, exclusively, their genetic history. What the Court in this case was thus called upon to determine was: (1) whether gestational surrogacy was a form of baby selling (and therefore illegal); and (2) whether and to what extent a gestational surrogate had claims over a child to whom she had given birth but to whom she bore no genetic connection. In either case, the pivotal question was the same: Was the genetic difference a difference that made a difference?

Anna Johnson insisted that it did not. As one of her attorneys plainly put the matter in court, "Genetics means crap in determining parental rights," and his claim was not without considerable grounding in legal, medical, and popular practice. For example, while fashioned in a pretechnobaby age and concerned primarily with paternity and adoption, California's 1975 National Uniform Parenting Act presumptively regarded the "birth mother" as the "natural mother."[1] And, the policy statement on surrogacy issued by the American College of Obstetricians and Gynecologists similarly endorsed treating the birth tie as the natural tie.[2] Finally, and still by way of example, there is the ever-expanding market in and marketing of donor eggs, sperm, and increasingly embryos (both orphaned and made-to-order) whose very viability as products for unspecified end-users in pursuit of family entails their genealogical depersonalization or the erasure of one possible history and identity precisely so that they can be re-embodied and imbued (anew) with another through the gestational and birth process. Nevertheless, the lower court remained unconvinced: it held that merely giving birth was not necessarily a constitutive sign of maternal status or attachment. While acknowledging Johnson's gestational contribution – she provided "a place to carry the child" and was its "host" – the court went on to characterize her attachment as primarily social rather than biological and therefore a matter of choice rather than instinct.

> Anna's relationship to the child is analogous to that of a foster parent, providing care, protection, and nurture during the period of time that the natural mother, Crispina Calvert, was unable to care for the child … A foster parent provides care always understanding that the day may come when the mother of the child will once again be able to take the child and you have to give the child to the mother when she's met whatever conditions she has had to meet to have the child returned to her and walk away and live with it. That's the way it works. That's the way it's worked for a long time.[3]

The trial court ruled that Mark and Crispina Calvert were the child's "genetic, biological, and natural" parents and, further, that the surrogacy contract did not violate public policies and adoption statutes and thus was legal and enforceable. And while the California Supreme Court ultimately agreed with the lower court on the legality of such contracts, they framed the stakes of the case somewhat differently. As they interpreted established policies and practice, *both* women had a claim to the child, Anna Johnson as the indisputable "birth mother" and Crispina Calvert as the indisputable "genetic mother" based on blood tests performed shortly after the baby's birth. There were two women, each of whom could provide clear evidence of a natural maternal bond. The challenge then, as they articulated it, was to determine whose ostensibly legitimate, equally compelling claim would prevail: Of these two women, whose bond was the more authentic? Indeed, who of these two women was the "real mother"?

While encouraged in various amicus briefs to find that the child had two *natural* mothers, the California Supreme Court declined to accept that alternative reproductive arrangements necessarily required crafting alternative familial ones. In its view, such kinship configurations were well beyond the norm and for this reason likely to create conditions that were "ripe for crazy-making" rather than enhanced connection. Turning instead to intellectual property law for guidance in reassembling the family unit, the Court argued that the role of a commissioning couple in a reproductive pact was analogous to that of an author, inventor, or "originator" with respect to ideas, novel devices, or works of art. As such, it was the commissioning couple's intentions that distinguished their pivotal place in these collaborations and took precedence if or when they collapsed. As "conceivers," they constituted the "first cause" or were the "prime movers" of the procreative relationship; they were the "originators" of the specific and unique concept of the specific and unique child they sought to make and, moreover, the initiators of the process that would ultimately bring it and a family forth (*Johnson v. Calvert* 1993: 11–12). Here is how the Court explained it:

> Mark and Crispina are a couple who desired to have a child of their own genetic stock but are physically unable to do so without the help of reproductive technology. They affirmatively intended the birth of the child, and took the steps necessary to effect in vitro fertilization. But for their acted-upon intention, the child would not exist ... Crispina from the outset intended to be the child's mother. Although the gestative function Anna performed was necessary to bring about the child's birth, [she] would not have been given the opportunity to gestate ... had she manifested her own intent to be the child's mother. No reason appears why Anna's later change of heart should vitiate the determination that Crispina is the child's natural mother.
> (*Johnson v. Calvert 1993: 10*)

With the "intent doctrine," the California Supreme Court settled the competing claims of two separate women who under other circumstances would each have been considered the natural and thus legal parent of the same child. And clearly, use of this doctrine would also have favored Sean and Donald Hollingsworth in their dispute with Donald's sister, Angelia Robinson. Regarded through this lens, the men would have been positioned as the prime movers or intending party in the reproductive collaboration – the originators and initiators of the idea and process that eventually brought forth twins, with Angelia, like Anna Johnson, merely a contractually negotiated, gestative medium. But as we saw, it was just such a rendering or disaggregation of the reproductive process that New Jersey Judge Schultz insisted was dehumanizing and potentially disruptive as well as destructive in allowing contract and commerce to overtake and remake familial bonds and relationships – indeed, bonds and relationships that discursively at least were positioned outside of and as an antidote to the drives and desires of capital. Paraphrasing Justice Wilentz, in a "civilized society," there are supposed to be some things that money cannot buy and some forms of commodification that are and must be refused. And, significantly, in her dissent, California Supreme Court Justice Joyce Kennard agreed with the spirit of Justice Wilentz' appraisal, questioning specifically whether a rationale drawn from intellectual property law – *but for the creator there would be no product* – was appropriate or useful in resolving a conflict over parentage. As Justice Kennard argued, maintaining, as the majority in *Johnson* does, that the role of a commissioning couple in a reproductive pact is analogous to that of an author or inventor in effect produces children as particular kinds of objects, owned or possessed as the property of those who first conceived of (the idea of) them. And the obvious flaw in such reasoning, she noted, is that children are not (or are no longer considered) property. The justice elaborates:

> Unlike songs or inventions, rights in children cannot be sold for consideration, or made freely available to the general public. Our most fundamental notions of personhood tell us it is inappropriate to treat children as property. Although the law may justly recognize that the originator of the concept has certain property rights in that concept, the originator of the concept of a child can have no such rights, because children cannot be owned. Accordingly, I cannot endorse the majority's "originators of the concept" or intellectual property rationale for employing intent to break the "tie" between the genetic mother and the gestational mother of the child.
>
> (*Johnson v. Calvert* 1993: 27)

14.3

There is more we could say about *Johnson v. Calvert* as well as the other surrogacy cases we've briefly considered alongside it, but let us turn back to what prompted this chapter's discussion in the first place: our point of departure was a certain set of anxieties that gravitated to the op-ed pages of the *New York Times* about the impact that the promiscuous transfer, exchange, mixing, and/or reassignment of gametes and zygotes has had and will yet have not only on the stories we tell ourselves about who we are and where we've come from, but on the law's ability to sort out these stories and rehearse them in a coherent and consistent way. To reiterate, the problem as Adam Cohen perceived it was with the conflicting origin stories propagated by the courts and the impact of discordant narratives on the coherence and place of the family. And in the cases I have thus far summarized, we've encountered at least two accounts that are ostensibly incompatible and, in any event, land us in somewhat different counties on the legal map. On the one hand, and characteristic of the New Jersey rulings, the courts have sought to recuperate conventional familial bonds and structures (and the foundational triad of categories of mother, father, child) by drawing on discourses of instinct. These feature primarily the needs, drives, desires, and yearnings of maternal nature as matters of common sense and are densely resonant with and responsive to those circulating in medicine, popular culture, and politics. On the other hand, and reminiscent of the California ruling, the courts have sought to recuperate conventional familial bonds and structures by drawing on discourses of intent. As we have just seen, these foreground choice and feature the needs, drives, and desires of autonomous, self-possessing, self-determining individuals.

Both discourses, clearly, are highly gendered and gendering. But more to the point, one cannot easily escape noticing how instinct and intent are co-constitutive and work in tandem to capture and reinscribe not only: (1) the foundational distinction of liberal societies between public and private – a distinction that works first and foremost to sustain structurally and as a matter of natural fact sexual difference and the sexual division of labor; but also (2) the divergent values, activities, and imperatives conventionally associated with each sphere even while these values, activities, and imperatives may be refigured in the process (Brown 1995; Elshtain 1981). Illustrating the recuperation of this basic social architecture, most explicitly, would be New Jersey Supreme Court Justice Wilentz' "ode to a civilized society" cited earlier in the Baby M case. In this passage, Justice Wilentz both celebrates and (re)constructs as a matter of historical fact a bifurcated public–private world of contract and predatory market relations on the one hand and, the life-giving and -preserving domain of family on the other, bound by maternal love, loyalty, and duty and untainted by instrumental exchange and the corrosive effects of exploitation.

The California Supreme Court adopts a less conventional approach but it too recuperates liberalism's bifurcated social world. It declines the opportunity that the unusual distribution of organic material in the case presents to alter the structure of the heterosexual nuclear family by acknowledging the existence of two *natural* mothers: the natural family unit is and must remain a two-parent affair. On the other hand, and less obviously, the Court keeps this family recognizably intact, indeed restores it, by relocating nature in intent such that individual intent becomes the locus for the demonstrably *natural* element in the reproductive process, the element that both captures and facilitates the intrinsic quality of the parent–child bond (Strathern 1992: 56). The problem, however, with this approach is that, unlike donor eggs which upon transfer can be made, genealogically, to signify differently, intent – and its associative meanings including calculation, choice, agency, will, desire, and whim, among others – has a genealogy as well and one that cannot be so easily rewritten, narrowly fixed, or made to fit seamlessly within a sphere that is otherwise called upon to represent the given and immutable in human life and relationship.[4]

This sphere, or what within classical liberal political theory is referred to as the private sphere of family, is considered the original, prepolitical site of natural community. Indeed, within this classical liberal scheme, family constitutes a pre-contractual form of association, organized by need, dependency, obligation, and sacrifice; it exists primarily for the nurturing and nourishment of children but also as a temporary haven for the otherwise autonomous self-interested, acquisitive, and competitive subject of civil society whose nature and capacities are fully expressed elsewhere. Although familial association may constitute the basis of civil life, it remains and, at least discursively, must be kept distinct from it – which brings us to the heart of Judge Schultz' critique of the approach adopted by the California Supreme Court in *Johnson* as well as Justice Kennard's dissent in the case.

By situating "intent" not simply in the domain of relations and processes that are and continue to be treated as self-evidently "natural," but as the locus of the natural within this domain, the distinction between spheres (along with their imperatives) is refigured. For Judge Schultz and Justice Kennard, although they describe the matter in a somewhat more decorous fashion, this formulation introduces the possibility that relations and activities discursively positioned outside of capital will become subject to its logic. In other words, and to put this more plainly, it is one thing for women to be enlisted to gestate babies as gifts: among other things, this enables the ethos of separate spheres and the practice of maternal selflessness, sacrifice, and even fulfillment to be preserved. It is quite another thing for women to be enlisted as contract workers, leasing use of their bodies for a sub-minimum wage so that patented products can be brought to market (Petchesky 1995; Shanley 2001; Becker 2000; Ragoné 1997). Such is obviously not the world that the *Johnson* court had in mind when it positioned intent as the locus of the natural. But in reprioritizing certain "biological facts" and thus shifting how instinct and intent are discursively apportioned between spheres that are otherwise configured to express their difference, the court's effort to reproduce the basic architecture of liberalism's bifurcated social world nevertheless represents, at least for some of its critics, only the specter of its collapse.

Curiously, we see resonances of precisely these tensions and attending assumptions about the basic composition, function, and identity of what might otherwise strike readers as an antiquated, perhaps rhetorical, perhaps simply fictional division of social worlds in the 2015 US Supreme Court's five–four split in *Obergefell v. Hodges* on marriage equality. With respect specifically to this chapter's discussion, what is especially interesting and instructive about this case has less to do with the court's actual finding that same-sex marriages are constitutionally protected than the distinctly different versions of liberalism's origin story that the justices marshal to legitimate or discredit this finding. To be sure, and regardless of the positions they stake out in the case, justices on both sides of the question situate the family within liberalism's so-called "private sphere" and see this sphere of primary association as the indisputable cornerstone of social order and national community (*Obergefell* 2015: 16). Where their accounts diverge is in explaining who actually inhabits this world and to what end.

For its part, the majority produces a version of liberalism's master narrative that allows a different kind of story to be told about kinship. They argue that family and the intimate bonds that constitute it – love, fidelity, devotion, and sacrifice – are not rooted primarily in instinct or configured according to what we might call essentialized understandings of gender; nor does this site of intimate association exist for the sole purpose of procreation. Rather, in the view of the majority, familial associations and intimate arrangements are longstanding forms of sociality that are shaped by and in turn shape changing historical convention and social practice. They embody and lend expression to the most fundamentally held individual liberties, are matters of choice, desire, and commitment, and exist foremost to alleviate social estrangement, isolation, and what the court describes as the "the universal fear of calling out only to find no one there" (*Obergefell* 2015: 16).

To make their case, the majority proffers a cursory look at the history and traditions of the nation, canvassing the law and legal scholarship predominantly, but other literatures, texts, and writers as well. And they single out among these Alexis de Tocqueville's mid-nineteenth century study of the character of America's bourgeoning democracy and the particular practices he believed both animated and sustained this still novel political form. Of special interest to the justices are Tocqueville's observations about the central importance of and the reciprocal relationship between society's two spheres: the public world of political and commercial life alongside the distinctly private sphere of hearth and home. The latter's two-fold function, according to Tocqueville, is not only to provide a peaceful retreat from the tumultuous passions and discord of public life, but to inculcate and cultivate in its members the values, habits, and sensibilities of order and other-regarding-ness which he believed individuals might then in turn "carry over into affairs of state" (De Tocqueville 2004: 336–337). And for the five justices, so it apparently remains: the intimate realm of family is in their view what most humanizes individuals and expands their capacities for living an engaged and empathic public life. That this is not the entire story as Tocqueville tells it merits at least a parenthetical acknowledgment: for him, America's separate spheres represented sex segregation at its finest, a gendered division of labor that in his view "made possible the great work of society" (2004: 337). Significantly, but not surprisingly given the court's focus in this case on individual autonomy, liberty, and choice, this familiar rendering and the naturalized stratification of human activity it applauds is something the majority elected simply to ignore.

Of course, the dissenting justices in the case, Roberts, Scalia, Alito, and Thomas, take critical aim at their colleague's elision and what they claim is the impulse that informs it: the majority's desire to "remake society" by transforming the place and meaning of "a social institution that has formed [its] basis for millennia" (*Obergefell* 2015, Roberts dissent: 3). Dismissing as preposterous the notion that familial associations are organized to promote the emotional fulfillment and well-being of those who form them or that those so joined in stable and supportive fellowship are somehow made better citizens, the dissenting justices contend that marriage and family have and always have had one vital purpose: they are and always have been biologically based cultural arrangements, arising from the imperative to procreate and existing "for the good of children and society" (Obergefell 2015, Alito dissent: 3–4). By deploying the force of law to insist otherwise, by denaturalizing natural bonds and willy-nilly inventing new meanings and rights, the majority has discarded the teachings of history, ignored the basic values and customs that underlie and organize society, failed in their commission to exercise judgment and restraint, and blazed a dangerous anti-democratic path, subordinating the practices and beliefs of the many (across time and cultures) to the will of an unelected, "pretentious few" (Obergefell 2015, Scalia dissent: 7).

To ground their claims, each of the four justices turns, as the majority did, to a variety of sources, texts, and writers; and, notably invoked by three of the four to help anchor and reconstruct the story they insist the founders intended to be told about individual liberty, the ends of political society, and the nature and place of the family is seventeenth-century contract theorist John Locke. We have encountered the general plot of Locke's story elsewhere in this chapter: among early liberal thinkers, it was Locke who first imagined that marriage and family predated the formation of political institutions founded on consent and remained fundamentally distinct from them even after their creation; and it was Locke as well who held that marriage and family together constituted "the first society" in nature, a paradigmatically private domain of male prerogative and paternal right, organized for the sake of procreation – but *continued*, in Locke's rendering, *for the sake of property* (Locke 1960: 362–363; Butler 1991; Pateman 1989). The dissenting justices in *Obergefell* foreground the former function of Locke's natural association as self-evident, indeed, Chief Justice Roberts insists that it is so fundamental as to hardly require articulation (2015, dissent: 5): to ensure the survival of the species and the well-being of children and the women who care for them, heterosexual sexual relations in the context of a lasting, monogamous bond are required. But, for Locke at least, the procreative origins of society are only part of the story: it is the often ignored latter function of the conjugal arrangement, family as a site and conduit for property and wealth accumulation, that is so critical to his seemingly self-evident scheme and provides, in the end, its rationale.

The organization of reproduction that Locke tells us emerges in a state of nature and takes the form of heterosexual monogamous marriage continues unchanged with the founding of civil society. And its primary purpose, beyond "ensuring the survival of the species" – because clearly there are any number of other conjugal arrangements that could have also satisfied this imperative – is to mitigate the uncertainty of paternity in the context of a world in which the possession and preservation of property are constituted as the principle ends of both individual and collective life. In other words, the organization of reproduction, whose public face is "marriage and family" and whose institutionalization within liberalism is accomplished through the bifurcation of social life is an arrangement designed to restrict women's sexual availability in order to ensure that the progeny a woman produces, to which her husband will have an exclusive right and for which he will bear the title and obligation of Father, are his own flesh and blood.

According to Locke, this is essential for the life of property and by extension the continued legitimacy of the state whose principle purpose is to protect it. Sequestering women through the bonds of matrimony in the private sphere to engage in their "most sacred natural duties," the bearing and rearing of legitimate progeny: this safeguards paternity (so much as this is possible) which in turn secures property within families while also enabling its "orderly transfer" between generations. And for Locke this "orderly transfer" of names and possessions is, in the end, the political crux of the matter. For after the original founding, he tells us, individuals in subsequent generations must consent anew and "unite their Person to the Commonwealth." And, the principle mechanism by which free individuals register their consent to be governed is through inheritance: in Locke's words, "the Son cannot ordinarily enjoy the Possessions of his Father, but under the same terms his Father did; by becoming a member of the Society and putting himself under the Government he finds there established" (1960: 393, 391). Thus contrary to the notion that marriage and family are given in nature and remain situated at its border even after the pact that creates political community, the form and organization of both are subject to acute state management and control since they function as a critical if naturalized mechanism of political legitimacy.[5]

Suffice it to say that the dissenting justices in *Obergefell* did not take up John Locke to argue with their colleagues over why reproduction is organized in the way that it is or what this organization might have to do with establishing the conditions for political community or how it produces a bifurcated world of human activity that then makes possible the unencumbered liberty of the sovereign subject who inhabits it. For Justice Thomas and Chief Justice Roberts – and, here they understand themselves to be speaking as well for, or at least on behalf of, those who drafted and ratified the Constitution – the origin story is exactly as Locke tells it: in the original state of nature, for the sake of procreation, men and women marry and – although Justice Thomas ignores this part of Locke's story – form families governed by patriarchs for the benefit of its members. And while Justice Roberts in his rendering adds to Locke a passage he takes from Noah Webster's first dictionary of 1825, defining marriage as an arrangement "between men and women to prevent the promiscuous intercourse of the sexes" – still he fails to appreciate, even modestly, that under the sign of the naturally given, normative systems operate to organize, channel, sanction, and restrict the desires and reproductive capacities of bodies according to the shifting needs and historically changing conditions of collective life (Obergefell 2015, Roberts dissent: 6).

It is precisely these changing conditions that Justice Alito laments when he notes in his dissent that traditional understandings of marriage and family no longer appear to "ring true to all ears today." He speculates that this is because "the tie between marriage and procreation has frayed" and he marshals in support of his claim data from the Centers for Disease Control and Prevention showing that 40 percent of all children in the United States are now born to unmarried women (Obergefell 2015, Alito dissent: 4–5). For him this statistic represents both "the cause and the result of changes in society's understanding of marriage," but one wishes he or his clerks had resisted the ever-ready but now tired trope of disorderly women to account for otherwise complex demographic trends and considered instead with a more critical eye not only the presumed stability of a tie he believes has only now frayed, but what its ongoing production has entailed as the practices constituting the so tied terms – marriage and procreation – have changed. Clearly, for example, heterosexuality has long since been set free of its reproductive consequences and with the use, moreover, of reproductive technologies procreation too has been freed from its dependency on heterosexual pairings.

And yet, as we have seen, coming full circle, even with such pairings, within the context of the traditional, culturally sanctioned form of marriage, procreation has been transformed and now requires for many the efforts and contributions of a host of miscellaneous and mostly anonymous actors. Such an assemblage of parts and persons may together facilitate the creation of family. But this family is not the self-contained, biogenetically aligned or genetically coherent unit implicit in Justice Alito's appeal. And when otherwise extraneous third parties in the procreative process refuse to remain extraneous, it has often been left to the courts to establish the terms according to which the family will be constituted as such: to sort through a relationally complex arrangement and produce from an assortment of possible bonds something that has a "family resemblance" to and can stand in for one biogenetically aligned; determining who created what, with what, from whom, for whom and where precisely nature resides in the mix, at least symbolically. Indeed, it has often been left to the courts to patch back together, paraphrasing Marilyn Strathern, something that looks like a traditional system because this system has come undone in pursuit of its tradition, to restabilize the tie Justice Alito refers to and along with it both the world it makes sense of and that makes sense of it (1995: 351). But not all of the parts, bonds, or practices can be made at the moment to cohere or easily fit the stories at hand to explain their place or relation in a plausibly consistent fashion – these are new life forms and entail new forms and practices of life. And so the stories we tell ourselves about who we are have begun to change in the telling, refigured to accommodate changing practices, relations, identities, and meanings. Such shifts in the organization of reproduction, of how we conceive of and constitute ourselves and our relations to others, are both foundational and consequential. Although the two-plus, genetically mixed family may remain through legal paring a strictly two-parent only, nuclear affair, this is clearly a function of the courts aggressively reconstructing nature rather than divining and transcribing what the New Jersey Supreme Court and the dissenting justices in *Obergefell* suppose can still be rendered faithfully as its immutable imperatives.

Notes

1. The significant passage of the act upon which Johnson's lawyers depended provides that the relationship "between a child and the natural mother may be established by proof of her having given birth to the child."
2. "In the committee's view, the genetic link between the commissioning parent(s) and the resulting infant, while important is less weighty than the link between the surrogate mother and fetus or infant that is created through gestation at birth. Thus, in the analysis and recommendations that follow, no distinction will be drawn between the usual pattern of surrogate parenting and surrogate gestational motherhood" ("Ethical Issues in Surrogate Motherhood," trial exhibit, *Johnson v. Calvert*, Office of the Supreme Court, California [1990], 2).
3. Invoking the testimony of Dr. Justin David Call, a child psychiatrist and pediatrician at the University of California, Irvine, and expert witness for the Calverts, Judge Parslow went on to distinguish Johnson's gestational attachment as primarily social rather than biological or natural. Bonds of the sort she insisted had formed, true maternal bonds, were likely to occur, he argued, only within the sanctity of a proper family unit, among "married mothers with husbands whose babies they carry" (1990, Trial Transcript, *Johnson v. Calvert*, 1490).
4. As the longstanding debate over abortion and women's reproductive self-determination illustrates.
5. Historian Ludmilla Jordanova takes up similar themes and what she calls the "politics of reproduction" in the work of eighteenth-century Enlightenment thinkers in her essay "Reproduction in the Eighteenth Century": "For many writers private property was closely linked with the family as an institution, which was indeed the principal means by which assets moved from one person to another through marriage and inheritance. Accordingly, for thinkers such as Hume, what was reproduced in children were wealth, name, associations with particular pieces of land, and the transmission of these occurred through the male line. This mentality placed a burden on mothers to guarantee

the legitimacy of their children in order that property went only to those entitled to it. In this case, the legal system, political theories, and reproductive behavior were simply different aspects of a single line of thought" (1995: 376).

References

A.G.R. v. D.R.H. & S.H. (*Robinson v. Hollingsworth*). 2009. Superior Court of New Jersey, Hudson County Vicinage (# FD-09-001838-07).
      2011. N.J. Super. Ct. App. Div.
Becker, Gay. 2000. *The Elusive Embryo: How Men and Women Approach New Reproductive Technologies*. Berkeley, CA: University of California Press.
Brown, Wendy. 1995. "Liberalism's Family Values." In *States of Injury: Power and Freedom in Late Modernity*, 135–165. Princeton, NJ: Princeton University Press.
Butler, Melissa. 1991. "Early Liberal Roots of Feminism: John Locke's Attack on Patriarchy." In *Feminist Interpretations and Political Theory*, ed. Mary Lyndon Shanley and Carole Pateman, 74–94. University Park, PA: Pennsylvania State University Press.
Center for Genetics and Society. 2015. "3-Person IVF." www.geneticsandsociety.org/article.php?id=6527, accessed June 18, 2015.
Cohen, Adam. 26 Jan. 2010. "A Legal Puzzle: Can a Baby Have Three Biological Parents?" *The New York Times*.
Darnovsky, Marcey. 9 July 2013. "A Slippery Slope to Human Germline Modification." *Nature* 499: 7457. www.nature.com/news/a-slippery-slope-to-human-germline-modification-1.13358, accessed August 10, 2015.
De Tocqueville, Alexis. 2004. *Democracy in America*. Translated by Arthur Goldhammer. New York: Library of America.
Elshtain, Jean Bethke. 1981. *Public Man, Private Woman: Women in Social and Political Thought*. Princeton, NJ: Princeton University Press.
Hartouni, Valerie. 1997. *Cultural Conceptions: On Reproductive Technologies and the Remaking of Life*. Minneapolis, MN: University of Minnesota Press.
In re Baby M. 1987. 217 N.J. Super. 313 (Ch. Div). www.leagle.com/decision/1987530217NJSuper313_1495, accessed August 5, 2015.
      1988. N.J. Supreme Court, 109 N.J. 396; 537 A.2d 1227.
Johnson v. Calvert. 1993. 5 Cal.4th 84, 851 P.2d 776.
Jordanova, Ludmilla. 1995. "Reproduction in the Eighteenth Century." In *Conceiving the New World Order: The Global Politics of Reproduction*, ed. Faye D. Ginsburg and Rayna Rapp, 269–386. Berkeley, CA: University of California Press.
Locke, John. 1960. *Two Treatises of Government*, Lassett edition. New York: Cambridge University Press.

Obergefell v. Hodges. 2015. 576 U. S. __ (2015), No. 14–556. www.supremecourt. gov/opinions/14pdf/14-556_3204.pdf, accessed June 26, 2015.

OHSU. 26 Aug. 2009. "OHSU Primate Center Scientists Develop Gene Therapy Method to Prevent Some Inherited Diseases." https://news. ohsu.edu/2009/08/26/ohsu-primate-center-scientists-develop-gene-therapy-method-to-prevent-some-inherited-diseases, accessed March 3, 2015.

Pateman, Carole. 1989. *The Disorder of Women.* Palo Alto, CA: Stanford University Press.

Petchesky, Rosalind Pollack. 1995. "The Body As Property: A Feminist Re-vision." In *Conceiving the New World Order: The Global Politics of Reproduction*, ed. Faye D. Ginsburg and Rayna Rapp, 387–406. Berkeley, CA: University of California Press.

Ragoné, Helena. 1997. "Chasing the Blood Tie: Surrogate Mothers, Adoptive Mothers, and Fathers." In *Situated Lives: Gender and Culture in Everyday Life*, ed. Louise Lamphere, Helena Ragoné and Patricia Zavella, 110–127. New York: Routledge.

Shanley, Mary Lyndon. 2001. *Making Babies, Making Families.* Boston, MA: Beacon Press.

Strathern, Marilyn. 1992. *Reproducing the Future: Anthropology, Kinship, and the New Reproductive Technologies.* New York: Routledge.

    1995. "Displacing Knowledge: Technology and the Consequences for Kinship." In *Conceiving the New World Order: The Global Politics of Reproduction*, ed. Faye D. Ginsburg and Rayna Rapp, 346–364. Berkeley, CA: University of California Press.

Thompson, Charis, Ruha Benjamin, Jessica Cussins and Marcy Darnovsky. 19 May 2015. "Innovation and Equity in an Age of Gene Editing." *The Guardian.* www.theguardian.com/science/political-science/2015/may/ 19/innovation-and-equity-in-an-age-of-gene-editing, accessed July 8, 2015.

White, James Boyd. 1984. "Constituting a Culture of Argument: The Possibilities of American Law." In *When Words Lose Their Meaning: Constitutions and Reconstitutions of Language, Character, and Community*, 231–74. Chicago, IL: University of Chicago Press.

    1990. *Justice As Translation: An Essay in Cultural and Legal Criticism.* Chicago, IL: University of Chicago Press.

15

Selecting for Sons: Kinship As a Product of Desire

Tine M. Gammeltoft

> I have often had occasion to point out that emotional ambivalence in the proper sense of the term – that is, the simultaneous existence of love and hate towards the same object – lies at the root of many important cultural institutions.
>
> *(Sigmund Freud 1985 [1913]: 219)*

> Relations between human beings are really established before one gets to the domain of consciousness. It is desire which achieves the primitive structuration of the human world, desire as unconscious.
>
> *(Jacques Lacan 1988b: 224)*

Across the globe, childbearing is at the heart of the practices that people define as kinship. By bearing children, people also forge connections, build alliances, develop new communities, and define political loyalties and commitments. Margery Wolf's (1972) ethnographic account of the ways in which women in Taiwan create their own uterine families by bearing children provides a classic illustration of such child-centered connection building. A more recent example is Rupert Stasch's evocative ethnography of kinship among the West Papuan Korowai: "Children," Stasch notes, "are at the center of this story that Korowai tell about the basic shape of their lives … Parent–child relations are foundational to other bonds, children are the purpose of other bonds, and children are icons of a general existential dilemma of transience within which all human bonds unfold" (2009: 141).

Childbearing is, however, not only a site of amity and bonding, but also of disconnection, violence, and exclusion. In a given society, for instance, not all parents count equally as parents. Based on research in the United States, Shellee Colen (1995) has shown how some people's bearing and raising of children are valued and encouraged, while the parenting efforts of others are systematically devalued, and Deborah Connolly (2000) has described the marginalization of poor homeless mothers who fail to live up to dominant ideals of proper mothering. Similarly, not all children are equally embraced. Meira Weiss (1994) has described how disabled children in Israel are excluded from their families by parents who refuse to grant them full family membership; and Nancy Scheper-Hughes (1992) has offered a now classic account of the ways in which, in the 1980s, poor Brazilian mothers gave up those of their children who did not show a "knack for life."

In the twenty-first century, uncertainties and doubts regarding who are socially accepted as parents and as children seem to be intensifying. Across the globe, prenatal screening and testing are becoming routinized parts of pregnancy care, offering people new means for deciding which children should enter this world and which ones not. This selective side of parenting practices has always existed, forming a silenced precondition for culturally celebrated practices of childcare and affection (Gammeltoft and Wahlberg 2014; Wahlberg and Gammeltoft 2017). Yet the global proliferation of new technologies for selective reproduction compels us to place such subdued acts and sentiments at the center of attention, paying more concerted attention to the practices of selection, exclusion, and rejection that lie at the heart of the formation of kinship.

In this chapter I focus on the most prevalent form of reproductive selection globally: sex selection. Taking Vietnam as my ethnographic case, I explore what motivates people to undertake sex selection in favor of male children. I attend particularly to the deep ambivalence that suffuses people's attitudes to their children's sex: while insisting on the value of daughters, many couples actively select for sons. Since the Vietnamese state plays an important role in this domain, I also examine the attitudes of state officials, showing how state discourse, while condemning practices of sex selection, also tends to uphold and promote family ideologies that perpetuate a cultural preference for sons. At issue, in other words, in both state discourse and day-to-day family lives, are striking contradictions between the kinship ideals that are discursively upheld and those that manifest in practice. While explicitly insisting on the value of daughters, citizens as well as state authorities continue to enact patrilineal kinship ideals.

In anthropology, ambivalence in kinship has, of course, been addressed before. Michael Peletz (2001) has shown how classical anthropological studies on kinship, such as those conducted by E. E. Evans-Pritchard and Meyer Fortes, offered rich ethnographic illustrations of the ambivalence that suffuses kinship, yet most often without incorporating these observations into more general analytical frameworks. In contemporary anthropology, Peletz finds a similar tendency: anthropologists tend to take note of ambivalence in kinship ethnographically, while often failing to address it in more theoretical terms. This leads him to propose that more consideration should be "devoted to certain psychological perspectives that have the potential to shed additional light on the mechanisms and loci implicated in the production of various types of mixed emotions" (2001: 432). Among the factors that have hindered this from happening, Peletz notes specifically the reluctance to engage psychoanalytic literature:

> it is clear that our analytic gaze needs to be focused not simply on official structures, ideologies, exegetic idioms, and public contexts but also on suppressed, submerged, and other alternative discourses that bear on the seamier side(s) of human nature and social relations, and that are in many cases articulated primarily in relatively private contexts or with reference to personal experience.
>
> *(2001: 436)*

While there may be a certain hesitation in anthropology today to engage with psychoanalytic thought, classic anthropological studies of kinship often drew significant inspiration from psychoanalysis (cf. Gammeltoft and Buch Segal 2016). Bronislaw Malinowski, for instance, found in Freudian theory an analytical lens that allowed him to interpret his ethnographic observations in the Trobriands in novel ways. Although Malinowski was critical of many of Freud's theories, it was psychoanalysis that inspired him to place repressed sentiments and passions at the center of his understanding of kinship. Psychoanalysis has, he noted, "forced upon us the consideration of the unofficial and unacknowledged sides of human life" (2007 [1927]: vii). Also Meyer Fortes' reflections on kinship were strongly influenced by Freudian ideas (Fortes 1959); and Melford Spiro's analyses of the ways in which gender ideologies operate by tapping into unconscious fantasies and desires were, of course, theoretically indebted to psychoanalytic thought (Spiro 1997).

In this chapter, I propose a return to these psychoanalytic sources of inspiration, arguing that a more finely tuned attention to silenced and repressed sides of everyday lives can deepen and extend anthropological understandings of kinship. In more concrete terms, I suggest that in order to account for the ambivalence that characterizes Vietnamese people's attitudes to their children's sex, the role of desire in the formation of family and kinship must be taken into account. Understanding kinship requires, as P. Steven Sangren has noted in his work on families in China, "incorporating desire's role both in defining institutions and in motivating their creators" (2013: 279; see also Sangren 2009). In this chapter I understand desire in its psychoanalytic sense, as a term that refers to the processes through which subjectivity is constituted: it is through strivings for fulfillment of desires that we become who we are. Such strivings are perhaps particularly dense in the realm of kinship.

Following Jacques Lacan, psychoanalysis can be regarded as "the study of the traces left in the human psyche of individuals as a result of their conscription into systems of kinship" (Rubin 1975: 188). Engagement with psychoanalytic reflections on desire may therefore allow us to bring into analysis also *sub-practices of kinship*, helping us to rethink kinship in ways that recognize not merely overt social practices, but also more subdued aspects of what it means to be related. I shall start from the empirical problem at issue: the problem of sex selection in contemporary Asia.

15.1 Sex Selection and Family Formation in Asia: The Persistence of Son Preference

Over the past decades, many countries have seen an increasing masculinization of the population, the number of male children born significantly outnumbering females. This problem is particularly pronounced in China, parts of India, and parts of the Caucasus and Western Balkans. In China, for instance, there are now 116 boys for every 100 girls born, while the figure for India is 111 boys for every 100 girls (Greenhalgh 2014; United Nations 2017). Distorted sex ratios at birth are usually interpreted as a result of son preference, a favoring of male children rooted in male-oriented kinship norms and practices (Guilmoto 2009; Miller 2001). In many societies, prescribed norms for kinship emphasize patrilocality and patrilineality, demanding that newly married couples live with the husband's relatives and defining children as belonging to their father's linage. Such normative demands tend to render sons indispensable: without sons, it is assumed, parents face a future without old-age support and lineages risk perishing. A son, in contrast, is held to provide parents and family with safety, support, and generational continuity. In the past, people might have resorted to infanticide or selective neglect when more girl children than wished for were born to a family. Today, the increasing availability of obstetrical ultrasonography in combination with induced abortion has made it possible to reject female children before they are born.

In Vietnam, the skewed sex ratio at birth arose later than in other countries in the region. Due to the relatively late advent of ultrasound technology, sex ratio imbalances did not begin to emerge in national statistics until around the turn of the millennium. In 2003, a new Population Ordinance banned prenatal sex determination and sex-selective abortions. Nevertheless, the sex ratio at birth has been rising steadily since the turn of the century, from 106.2 in 2000 to 112 at present (United Nations 2017). Statistics indicate, moreover, that some Vietnamese parents start selecting for sons already in the first pregnancy: in 2009, the sex ratio at birth was 110.2 for the first birth, 109 for the second, and 115 for the third birth (132 if the first two children were female) (UNFPA 2014). As a

Vietnamese obstetrician put it, prospective parents want to "win at the first battle" (UNFPA 2011: 44).

In Vietnam, as in many other countries, son preference has a long history (Bélanger 2006; Gammeltoft 2016 [1999]). From my first field-work, conducted in Hanoi's Red River delta in 1993–1994, I still recall the fervor with which people strove for sons. I remember rural families living in deep poverty, the parents pained by their inability to provide for their children in the manner expected by others, embarrassed to violate family planning policies that stipulated one-to-two children only – and yet having child after child after child, desperately hoping for a son. At the time, other community members defined such strivings for sons as feudal (*phong kiến*) and backward (*lạc hậu*). Still, everyone seemed to feel with sonless couples; cadres ignoring their failure to comply with the family planning policies, neighbors sharing their disappointment when yet another daughter was born.

The sense of backwardness that clung to these strivings for sons must be seen on the background of the Vietnamese government's efforts to promote gender equality. Tying women's emancipation together with national liberation, early twentieth-century revolutionary nationalists urged women to participate actively in the anti-colonial struggle (cf. Werner 2009). Revolutionary discourses defined the traditional Confucian family – with its gender and generational hierarchies – as a remnant of a colonial past; in the socialist society, such oppressive family structures were to be replaced by modern families characterized by solidarity and egalitarianism. Since the socialist government came into power in 1954, a range of legal reforms have aimed to institute new family and gender arrangements, placing women on an equal footing with men. The 1959 Law on Marriage and the Family, for instance, outlawed child marriage, forced marriage, and polygamy, calling for equality between husbands and wives, sons and daughters. In today's Vietnam, gender equality remains a government priority; among recent legislative initiatives towards this aim are the 2006 Law on Gender Equality and the 2007 Law on the Prevention and Control of Domestic Violence. Yet despite these efforts to enhance gender equality, it seems, son preference has endured in Vietnam. Its persistence demands anthropological attention.

15.2 "We Must Address This As a Cultural Problem": The Ambivalence of State Messages

The government of Vietnam defines the country's increasingly skewed sex ratio at birth as a major development challenge. Over the past few years, this demographic problem has been intensely covered in newspapers, television programs, public meetings, and cultural events, and concerted efforts have been made to increase the public's awareness of the social and demographic consequences of an imbalanced ratio of male to female children. In cities and along rural roads, large billboards remind citizens of the value of daughters, encouraging them to "leave sex determination to nature." Newspaper articles and television programs encourage people to stop selecting for sons, presenting stories of parents – often famous and admired citizens – who are completely happy with only daughters.

At a national seminar held in November 2012, the Deputy Minister of Health, Nguyễn Viết Tiến, described the problems associated with the increasing sex ratio at birth: "This situation can have unpredictable consequences for society, security, and social order, affecting the lives of individuals and families in negative ways, with disastrous impact on the stable development of the country and the people" (Hà Thu 2012a). When government officials are asked about the underlying causes behind Vietnam's imbalanced sex ratio, they usually point to a combination of two factors: a culturally ingrained preference for sons and the availability of medical technologies – ultrasounds and induced abortions. Since the use of medical technology has proven difficult to monitor and regulate by law, officials usually point to attitudinal change as the way forward. At the above seminar, Dr. Dương Quốc Trọng, head of the Ministry of Health's population/family planning office, said: "This problem has to do with culture, customs, traditions that have existed for thousands of years ... We must address this as a cultural problem." He listed a range of possible measures to address the skewed sex ratio at birth, including benefits for parents with only daughters and stricter control within the health-care system, concluding: "Of all these measures, the most important is to change people's attitudes through communication and education" (Hà Thu 2012b).

When state officials account for the country's skewed sex ratio at birth, in other words, "traditional culture" is defined as the culprit. In other policy areas, however, government officials define the same traditional culture in intensely positive terms, representing it as a firm bulwark against too rapid social change; as the guarantor of social order and stability. Since the country's 1986 shift from a centrally planned to a market-oriented economy, Vietnam has experienced rapid social changes. Economic growth rates have been high, poverty has been remarkably reduced, and commercial and cultural contacts with the world outside Vietnam have intensified. In 1996, a nationwide campaign was launched, aiming to combat so-called "social evils" (*tệ nạn xã hội*) such as drug use, gambling, and prostitution. Foreign cultural influences, government officials warned, may erode traditional cultural values, resulting in social instability and chaos. In today's Vietnam, anxieties about national cultural degeneration continue to be vocally expressed, not least by state officials. In the current situation of rapid social change, government messages emphasize, "traditional family values" are of utmost importance; in order to ensure social stability and continued economic development, families must stay morally wholesome (*lành mạnh*), preserving traditional Vietnamese cultural traits and strengths. In late president Hồ Chí Minh's often-cited dictum: "If society is good, the family will be good; if the family is good, society will be good. The family is the cell of society."

The government's *Strategy for Development of the Vietnamese Family to the Year 2020, with a View to 2030*, issued in 2012, illustrates this. Article 1 states: "The family is the cell of society. It is an important environment in which individuals are formed, brought up, and educated. It maintains and promotes beautiful cultural traditions, resists social evils, and creates the human resources that serve to build and defend the nation." The family is, in other words, represented as the foundation for social order itself. But what is it then that defines a family that "maintains and promotes beautiful cultural traditions"? A wealth of articles in the popular press tell people how to comport themselves so as to ensure wholesome family dynamics. In these articles, particular emphasis is placed on the mutual obligations of children and parents and on the duties of women to their families. One article, titled "Preserving the Vietnamese Family in the Face of Cultural Aggression," emphasizes the moral responsibilities of parents and children:

> To Vietnamese people, the family is a sacred place of support ... Vietnamese people very much respect family ways and rules. They are aware of their debts to ancestors, grandparents, and parents. A family that knows how to maintain family ways will be like a stable fortress, no social evil will be able to enter. In contrast, if parents do not serve as good examples, if they violate the law, are disloyal and deceitful, then the children will be unruly, lazy in school, disrespectful towards teachers and parents, and soon fall into social evils ... If parents know how to maintain our people's traditional cultural values, loving their ancestors, maintaining a wholesome and elevated cultural-spiritual life, then for sure their children will also know how to respect and maintain their grandfathers' and father's tradition.
>
> *(Bùi Minh Huệ 2014)*

Another article, titled "The Family's Cultural Standards Are the Foundation for Happiness," describes women's special responsibilities for preserving traditional family ways. This article makes it clear to readers that failure to uphold family values means letting down one's country, reminding citizens of their responsibility to build a family that is a "truly happy nest," while at the same time building "a beautiful image of Vietnam and its people in the era of international integration":

> Preserving family culture contributes to preserving Vietnamese traditional culture ... Even though there are many changes in life, and fewer families include three or four generations, the good and beautiful values of the traditional Vietnamese family are still appreciated

and carried on to the next generations. "Respecting those above, yielding to those below" (*kính trên, nhường dưới*), loving, paying attention to, and caring for one another are values that members of all families still preserve … Given their heavenly mandate, women are those who skillfully organize the family's life, taking care of and bringing up the children. Women have an important role in regulating family relations. They know how to organize things in suitable ways, how to share life with their husband, how to educate the children, how to care for their parents-in-law, and how to behave tactfully with the husband's family.

(Chu Thị Bích Huệ 2011)

The social importance (and the gendered nature) of "traditional family values," such as respect, care, and loving attention, are, in other words, explicitly communicated to the public. In the ideal family that official discourse conjures, husband and wife offer complementary contributions; the husband is the main breadwinner and the stable pillar (*trù cột*) of the household, while the wife attends to everyone's needs for care and emotional support. The traditional Vietnamese family is hierarchical, but in a loving and respectful way: those "above" protecting and supporting those "below."

What is less explicitly expressed is that these moral expectations and obligations are embedded in a particular kinship system – one that, particularly in the northern parts of the country, carries strongly patrilineal and patrilocal traits (Pham Van Bich 1999; Guilmoto 2012). Hy Van Luong's reflections on kinship patterns in a northern Vietnamese village resonate with the observations I have made during recent fieldwork in villages around Hanoi: "Patrilocal residence is universally taken for granted as a fundamental part of any marital relation, and the birth of a male is widely assumed to be of vital importance for the continuity of the patrilineally structured household and lineage" (1989: 750). In public discourse, this male orientation is usually expressed in subtle terms. The first of the above articles, for instance, defines Vietnamese cultural tradition as "grandfathers' and father's"; the second underscores women's duties towards affinal, not consanguinal, kin. The officially celebrated traditional family is, in other words, based on longstanding and culturally ingrained structural principles; it is assumed that lineage continuation and residence follow male lines and that household authority rests with men. Yet most often, I have found, this male orientation is left largely implicit in official discourse. It seems to be taken for granted to an extent that brings to mind Pierre Bourdieu's concept of *doxa* – a state in which the social world seems self-evident to its members, where the social universe "*goes without saying because it comes without saying*" (Bourdieu 1977: 167; italics in original). In public discourse, the male-oriented nature of kinship arrangements seems, as

Nancy Wiegersma (1988: 242–243) has put it, "so entrenched as to be invisible."

Present-day state messages tend, in other words, to place Vietnamese citizens in a double bind: on the one hand, they tell people not to select for sons, and on the other, they urge them to hold on to the country's "beautiful cultural traditions" – traditions that, everyone knows, include male-oriented kinship and dependency on sons for lineage continuation and old-age care. In their eagerness to mobilize the traditional Vietnamese family as a moral bulwark against too rapid social change, therefore, state officials indirectly support the very sex-selective practices that they tend to condemn. A similar ambivalence regarding children's sex seems to characterize people's everyday discourses on the value and importance of sons and daughters.

15.3 "Girl Power": The Emotional Ambivalence of Child Desires

In 2011, the United Nations Population Fund in Vietnam published the results of a qualitative study aiming to better understand the rising sex ratio at birth in Vietnam (UNFPA 2011). Based on research conducted in three provinces of Vietnam, the research report investigated the motivating factors behind people's desires for children of a specific sex and the ways in which people tried to realize these reproductive desires. When the report was published, one issue in particular caught the news media's attention: many respondents claimed that to them, daughters were as valuable as – if not more valuable than – sons. The online English language daily *Thanh Niên News*, for instance, published an article titled "Girl Power" (*Thanh Niên News* 2011). Noting that the UNFPA research "injected new hopes into the battle against Vietnam's skewed sex ratio at birth," this article placed the daughter-friendly attitudes reported by research respondents at the center of attention: "Daughters are more highly valued by families than previously thought, especially by parents who have no sons. Girls are prized for their emotional closeness to parents and their ability to perform ancestor worship." This indicates, the reporter suggested, that in practice, "the male-oriented family may not be as dominant in Vietnam" as often assumed. To illustrate this point, the article presented the case of 45-year-old Lê Quang Dương who claimed to be happy with the two girls that he had: "I don't see any problem [with having two daughters]. When I die, they will do the ancestor worship for me. Back in my hometown, of course I'm facing growing pressure to have a son. But so what? For me, daughters are simply far better than sons."

Many other people in present-day Vietnam seem to share Lê Quang Dương's contentment with girl children. Both men and women often express deep appreciation of their daughters, sometimes citing the old saying, "Rich rice fields and female buffalos cannot compare to one's first-born daughter" (*Ruộng sâu trâu nái không bằng con gái đầu lòng*). During a recent stay in Hanoi, I talked to Lâm, a 31-year-old father of one daughter. "So, you will have to have a son next time?" I asked him, trying to strike the light and joking tone that people often use to talk about sensitive and potentially embarrassing topics. Lâm replied in words that underscored that in his view, son preference remained associated with a premodern and "backward" way of life:

> No. For me, two daughters will be fine. I don't need a son. You have to understand that Vietnam has changed. In the past, children wore rags and hardly went to school. Today's life is different. Vietnam is a modern nation now, our society has developed, and a girl is as good as a boy. There is no difference.

When asked directly about their preferences regarding children's sex, people will usually sidestep the question, saying: "All children are one's children, just having a child is a joy" (*Con nào cũng là con, có con là vui rồi*). Everyday conversations make it very clear, however, that people place different expectations on boys and girls. Yet sons are not unambiguously favored; daughter-friendly attitudes flourish too. One woman expressing such daughter-friendly attitudes was Cúc, a 24-year-old mother of two. When I met her in April 2015, Cúc had just given birth to her second daughter. She was very happy with both of her daughters, Cúc said, and she didn't wish for any other children. It pained her, therefore, to witness her mother-in-law's disappointment with the new child. "For your own sake, you will have to have a son next time," her mother-in-law admonished her, explaining to Cúc that if she did not give birth to a son next time, her husband might turn to other women. "She says it is for *my* sake," Cúc said, "but in reality, it's my parents-in-law who need a boy, not my husband and me. We are happy with our girls."

Like Cúc and Lâm, many people insist that they do not need sons; that daughters are just as good. If a family has no sons, people claim, then a daughter can take responsibility for ancestor worship (cf. Jellema 2007). A 59-year-old woman from Hanoi, for instance, declared that in her family, the absence of sons had never been a problem, "In my family, we all have daughters only. I live in my husband's family, but I do worship my parents and grandparents. This is no problem. Everybody is happy" (UNFPA 2011: 26). Daughters are, moreover, often considered to be more loving and attentive than sons, and they are expected to become more stable and reliable income earners when they grow up. Whereas sons are considered to be at risk of ending up in drug abuse or criminal activities, draining family resources and causing their parents worry, daughters are assumed to be more consistently loyal and trustworthy. In the words of a 40-year-old mother of two daughters: "In many cases, daughters are far better than sons. For instance, my friend is very happy since her daughter takes care of her and supports the whole family financially. She makes sure that her mother has a happy and comfortable life" (UNFPA 2011: 28).

In many Vietnamese families, then, profound ambivalence seems to suffuse childbearing practices: while expressing appreciation of daughters, parents and parents-to-be continue to select for sons. Daughters are loved and embraced, and yet daughters-to-be are often rejected before birth. In Hanoi's Đông Anh district, for instance, where Lâm and Cúc live, the ratio of newborn boys to girls was 117:100 in 2013. In the commune with the highest sex ratio at birth, 141 boys were born for every 100 girls. In this locality, in other words, approximately one in three pregnancies with female fetuses was terminated. How, then, do we account for this reproductive ambivalence? One assumption might be that when people proclaim the value of daughters, they are simply repeating official rhetoric. By expressing daughter-friendly or gender-neutral attitudes, people are aligning themselves with longstanding government efforts to enhance gender equality, thereby also defining themselves as modern and well-educated citizens of a progressive socialist nation. It is people's *true* feelings about this matter, one might then assume, that manifest in practice: practices of sex-selection show that *in reality*, beneath these rhetorical proclamations, sons continue to be considered more valuable than daughters.

The argument that I set forth in this chapter is that it is the other way around: everyday experiences tell people that a daughter can provide care and support for parents and ancestors just as well as a son can. People's awareness of this must, however, be suppressed in order for certain family fantasies to be upheld. To explain how I have come to see the situation in this way, let me present the case of Liên, a woman I met during recent fieldwork in Hanoi's Đông Anh district.

15.4   "Who Else Would Have Bought Them?": Family Imaginaries

On the morning of August 30, 2014, I traveled with a female Vietnamese colleague to a rural village situated on the outskirts of Hanoi. We had an appointment with Liên, one of the pregnant women involved in the research that we were conducting.[1] The village she lived in was located in a rapidly modernizing area where rice fields were giving way to high-rise buildings. When we arrived, Liên received us in the spacious courtyard outside the family's house. "Good you didn't arrive earlier," she exclaimed, "I've just come back from work in our fields." Still sweating from her walk back to the house, Liên looked tired. She was nine months pregnant, and her belly looked heavy. My colleague and I exchanged glances. With this advanced pregnancy, I thought perhaps Liên should have spent the morning at home resting instead of doing manual agricultural work.

We sat for a while in the family's guestroom, making small-talk with Liên and her husband's grandmother. Then, for more privacy, we moved to the kitchen to continue our talk. Separated from the rest of the house, the kitchen was dark and cool. Three bicycles were leaning against one wall, and the other walls were lined with plastic containers for foodstuffs, woven baskets with papayas and green vegetables, and sooty pots and pans. Seated on the low stools that Liên used when she prepared the family's meals, we talked. Holding her arms tightly folded around her three-year-old daughter, Liên told us that she had lived here since getting married four years earlier. Her parents' house, where her sisters still lived, was around 30 kilometers away. She missed her family intensely, but being busy with work and childcare, she rarely had time to visit.

In the epidemiological part of our research project, Liên had reported not only exposure to partner violence, but also signs of depression. During our talk on that August morning, she told us in more detail about the circumstances of her life. Daily life as a daughter-in-law, she said, was hard. Before getting married, she had not been able to imagine how hard this life would be. The family she had married into consisted, apart from herself, of her husband, their daughter, her mother-in-law, her husband's paternal grandmother, and her husband's younger sister. Within this family, Liên said, she alone was responsible for all housework. Even now that she was pregnant, her husband's relatives expected her to do all the shopping, cooking, laundry, and cleaning, while also tending the family's fields. Until recently, she had undertaken these tasks while also working in a nearby factory, generating a large share of the family's income. Liên felt overburdened, she said, and she was angry with her husband's younger sister for not helping out. She also felt that no matter how much she struggled to do everything well, her mother-in-law would always find fault with her. "Can you give us an example of this," I asked. Liên then told us about a recent episode where she had lost her temper in a way that she regretted afterwards. Apart from the interviewer on our research project, Liên said, she had not told a single person about this episode. Talking to others about it would be taken as an indication that she was the kind of woman who speaks badly about her husband's family, and she did not want to risk blemishing her own or her husband's reputation in this way.

At the center of the family's guestroom was a beautifully maintained ancestral altar, decorated with plastic flowers, incense pots, and a large photo of Liên's deceased father-in-law. It was Liên who tended the altar, replacing burnt-down incense sticks with fresh ones and sometimes offering the ancestors fresh fruit and flowers. One day one of the incense sticks broke into two. In an angry and accusatory tone, Liên's mother-in-law asked: "Now, who bought these incense sticks?" Liên replied, in a loud voice, "I bought them! Who else would have bought them?" This reply shocked her mother-in-law who scolded her for being ill-mannered and disrespectful, a useless daughter-in-law. Siding with his mother, her husband intervened in the conflict by slapping Liên, telling her to be more respectful to his mother in the future. This, he said, was not the way that he wanted his wife to behave.

Sitting in the car on our way back to Hanoi, I told my colleague that I found it quite unsettling to witness how kinship arrangements – and expectations – affected the life of a woman such as Liên. The loneliness she felt, living far from her natal kin, was dizzying. The work burdens placed on her seemed exploitative. Her husband's violence, I commented, must feel humiliating. "Oh," my colleague replied, "but that was not violence. That was filial piety (báo hiếu). Her husband had to act like this, to show his love and respect for his mother."

What was most remarkable about the incident with the incense sticks was perhaps that Liên told us about it. This was the first time that my colleague and I met her; we were, in this situation, strangers to her. By telling us this story, therefore, Liên departed from cultural convention: in most situations, I have found, people in Hanoi struggle hard to keep family conflicts within the domestic and intimate sphere, trying to maintain an image of the family as unified, harmonious, and orderly. The family I lived in during my first fieldwork in Vietnam, for instance, was suffused by conflicts – between mother-in-law and daughter-in-law; husband and wife; parents and children – and I witnessed at close hand how intently everyone strove not to reveal these domestic conflicts to the outside world. One should *not*, I was instructed, "remove the shirt so that others can see one's back" (vạch áo cho người xem lưng). When family conflicts erupted and spilled out into public space, this seemed to be intensely painful for all family members; a tormenting loss of face and public standing (Gammeltoft 2016 [1999]: 219–220). The ideals that people lived by seemed, in other words, to closely resemble the ideals set forth in state rhetoric; a good family would live in concord (hòa thuận), family members loving, respecting, and supporting one another. Over the years, I have come to see this vision of the harmonious, stable, and coherent family as *imaginary* in the psychoanalytic sense, that is, as a product of desire.

15.5 Ambivalence and Desire in Family Formation: Psychoanalytic Contributions to Kinship Studies

Emotional ambivalence lies, Sigmund Freud wrote, "at the root of many important cultural institutions" (1985 [1913]: 219). Ambivalence arises, Freud argued, when there is a conflict between a person's desire to perform a given act and his/her awareness of not being allowed to realize this desire. "The prohibition is noisily conscious, while the persistent desire … is unconscious and the subject knows nothing of it … The prohibition owes its strength and its obsessive character precisely to its unconscious opponent, the concealed and undiminished desire – that is to say, to an internal necessity inaccessible to conscious inspection" (1985 [1913]: 84). In Freud's work, ambivalence is, in other words, the product of the simultaneous existence of two conflicting forces: a desire and a prohibition. Due to the risk of imitation, he notes, prohibitions are often maintained with considerable force by social communities, and transgressions heavily sanctioned: "If the violation were not avenged by the other members they would become aware that they wanted to act in the same way as the transgressor" (1985 [1913]: 87).

In Freud's work, desires, and prohibited desires in particular, occupy a central position. In German, the term used by Freud is *Wunsch*, wish, but in French and English psychoanalysis, this term is usually given as *désir*/desire. Desires, according to Freud, can be conscious, preconscious, or unconscious. Of particular interest to Freud were unconscious desires; inclinations, wishes, and longings that we struggle to keep out of conscious awareness because our society does not allow them to exist. Such forbidden wishes could be, for instance, feelings of hate towards a person whom one also, and simultaneously, loves and cherishes or is *expected* to love and cherish; or a desire to kill someone. Striving to live up to social demands, Freud argues, we seek to suppress such socially prohibited desires, thereby pushing them into the unconscious. But if certain desires are socially forbidden, one may ask, then how do they arise? According to Freud, human desires spring from mnemic images that we carry with us from the earliest days of our lives (Laplanche and Pontalis 2006 [1973]: 482). Desire is, therefore, intimately linked to fantasy, as our desires are directed towards the fantasy-scenes that we conjure based on earlier life experiences; images of situations in which our wishes were fulfilled. For Freud, in other words, a fantasy represents the fulfillment of a wish.

Writing in the early twentieth century, Freud tended to see fantasy as illusion, setting it in contrast to real, material "reality" (1964 [1911]). Freud's successors have questioned this split between illusory fantasy and "real" reality, arguing that human realities are always and invariably suffused by fantasy; underpinned by mental images of pleasurable, comforting, or frightening events (Isaacs 2002 [1952]). Lacan, in particular, has elaborated on Freud's work in ways that acknowledge the constitutive force of language and intersubjectivity in the establishment of human realities, including psychic lives. "Desire emerges," Lacan says, "just as it becomes embodied in speech. It emerges with symbolism" (1988b: 234). In Lacan's work too, the notion of desire is centrally placed. "The largest part of what the subject takes to be a certainty after due reflection is," he writes, "for us only the superficial, rationalised, subsequently justified ordering of what his desire foments, which gives his world and his action its essential curvature" (1988b: 224). Like Freud, Lacan links desire closely to fantasy. Rather than anchoring fantasies in the subject's individual past, however, Lacan emphasizes that fantasies are emergent social products; mental images that are produced out of our ongoing symbolic and social interactions with one another.

Being oriented towards linguistically mediated fantasies, then, individual desires are inherently social, or, in Lacan's often-quoted expression, human desire is the desire of the Other: "Nowhere does it appear more clearly that man's desire finds its meaning in the other's desire, not so much because the other holds the keys to the desired object, as because his first object(ive) is to be recognized by the other" (Lacan 2006 [1966]: 222). Desire is always, Lacan maintains, a desire for recognition. Striving to achieve recognition, we direct our desires towards that which we sense that the Other desires. We are therefore always trying to identify the Other's desires: "Desire full stop is always the desire of the Other. Which basically means that we are always asking the Other what he desires" (Lacan 2008: 38). Or, as Slavoj Žižek puts it: "The original question of desire is not directly, 'What do I want?' but, 'What do others want from me? What do they see in me? What am I for the others?'" (Žižek 2005: 280).

To account for the ways in which the Other becomes integral to our very being, shaping our most intimate longings and wishes, Lacan developed his theory of the "mirror stage." This refers to the time in a child's life when it becomes aware of the difference between its own, lived body – with its unruliness, restlessness, and turbulent feelings – and the complete image that emerges in the mirror. "The mirror" can be a literal mirror or it can be other people reflecting back to the child how they see it. Striving to construct its identity in accordance with the mirror image, longing to attain this fullness and completeness, the child takes into its own identity the visions of itself that it is met with by others. In this way, according to Lacan, we are always somehow alienated from ourselves, as we unconsciously take up other people's wishes, norms, and expectations, incorporating them into our sense of who we are. It is due to other people's presence at the center of our identities that our desire is always the other's desire:

> The subject originally locates and recognises desire through the intermediary, not only of his own image, but of the body of his fellow being. It's exactly at that moment that the human being's consciousness, in the form of consciousness of self, distinguishes itself. It is in so far as he recognizes his desire in the body of the other that the exchange takes place.
>
> *(Lacan 1988a: 147)*

Our efforts to shape our lives in certain ways are, in other words, suffused by the Other's desires, by that which our society and culture tell us is desirable. Desire therefore also plays a crucial role in family formation: desire is, as Sangren points out, "not only a *product* of family dynamics, it is also a *producer* of the 'family' as it is instituted. In arranging family relations, people attempt to bring into being a world as they would wish it to be – to realize a fantasy" (2013: 284; see also Spiro 1997). Fantasy, in other words, "teaches" people how and what to desire (cf. Žižek 2005: 280).

Elaborating on Lacan's work, Žižek examines how not only individual identities but also the identities of communities are underpinned by fantasies. Communities, Žižek argues, are always supported by certain "symbolic fictions," narratives that help to keep society together. Yet in reality, society – understood as a coherent, unitary whole – is not possible. Social worlds, like individual selves, are always inherently fragmented and divided. Striving to maintain the illusion that this is not the case, Žižek says, we mobilize symbolic fictions of various kinds; fictions that help to make our social worlds appear coherent and meaningful. Violence erupts, he argues, when a symbolic fiction is threatened: " *'Real' violence is a kind of acting out that emerges when the symbolic fiction that guarantees the life of a community is in danger*" (Žižek 2005: 235; italics in original).

In a psychoanalytic perspective, daily realities are, in other words, underpinned by desire-generating fantasies. Despite our efforts to uphold these fantasies, Žižek notes, something always escapes. There is always a remainder, something that does not fit in, that disturbs the fantasy. This repressed remainder – often a social antagonism – returns to haunt us, coming back as a spectral apparition: "spectral apparitions emerge in this very gap that forever separates reality from the real, and on account of which reality has the character of a (symbolic) fiction: the spectre gives body to that which escapes (the symbolically structured) reality" (Žižek 2005: 241).

On this background, then, we may – following Freud – see ambivalence in kinship as a reflection of a conflict between a desire and a prohibition; following Lacan, we may see people's desires to build families of a certain kind as desires for recognition; and following Žižek, we may see the families that people strive to build as fantasy constructions that are haunted by unruly remainders. Together, I contend, these contributions from psychoanalysis may enhance anthropological understanding of the social and psychic forces that shape kinship practices in general and ambivalence in kinship in particular. On this background, let us return to Vietnam and the ambivalence that suffuses people's desires regarding the sex of their children.

15.6 Desires for Sons As Desires for Recognition: Upholding Family Fantasies

The second time my colleague and I met Liên, in March 2015, she looked stunningly different. Carrying herself with a new self-assurance, she greeted us with a big smile. In her arms she held her son, born seven months ago. The little boy's body was plump and sturdy in the manner that people in Hanoi consider ideal for babies, and his facial features, my colleague commented, "looked so much like a man already" (Figure 15.1). Since the birth of her son, Liên told us, her day-to-day life had changed completely. Her husband's mother and younger sister now helped her with the housework, the three of them undertaking daily tasks together. She felt accepted and respected in the family in a way that was new to her, and the loneliness that she had described at our first visit seemed to have vanished.

To a woman such as Liên, the immediate and concrete benefits of having a son were clear and unmistakable. Having produced a son seemed to provide her with an entirely new position in the household; she was now an integrated member of her husband's family, the mother of the child who would carry on the lineage. This situation is not unique: over the years, I have met numerous women who shared this experience of sudden incorporation in their husband's kin group upon the birth of a son (cf. Wolf 1972). As one 67-year-old man said, relieved when his daughter gave birth to the son that her family-in-law had hoped for: "Now they cannot neglect my child" (UNFPA 2011: 33). In contrast, other women I have met have found themselves exposed to various forms of exclusion and violence – emotional, physical, or sexual – when failing to produce a son.[2] People's desires for sons must, then, be seen in the context of this sociosymbolic structure of rewards and sanctions, a structure that reaches far beyond the domestic sphere.

To me, in fact, one of the most striking aspects of family and community life in twenty-first-century northern Vietnam is the intense harassment that failure to comply with kinship norms of patrilineality and patrilocality may expose people to. "Back in my hometown, of course I'm facing growing pressure to have a son," said Lê Quang Dương, the man who claimed to be happy with his two daughters. "Pressure" is, I find, an understatement of the reproductive intimidation that often tends to occur when a couple fails to produce a son. In tight-knit communities such as the village in which Liên and her family lived, sonlessness often seems to produce relentless gossiping, ridiculing, and mocking. In the gossip that runs within hamlets and villages, women and men without sons are chided for "not knowing how to give birth" (không biết đẻ), that is, for failing to produce the culturally and politically celebrated proper family, failing in the most important mission that a person can have (cf. Gammeltoft 2014). If a couple without sons manages to accumulate the resources required to build a new house, they risk exposing themselves to other people's ridicule: they have "built a house of affection" (xây nhà tình nghĩa), a house that has been generously built for the benefit of another kin group, that of the man who marries their daughter (UNFPA 2011: 38).

Figure 15.1 Liên's children at home

As we saw in the cases of Liên and Cúc, women without sons often find themselves in situations of intense vulnerability, denied full membership of their husband's family. Men without sons often seem to be placed in situations of vulnerability too, lacking full membership of the local community. At family and community gatherings on festive days, for instance, seating arrangements often reflect local hierarchies; the most important people – usually adult men – being placed at the "high" end (*mâm trên*) in front of the ancestral altar at the center of the room, and the least important – usually women and children – sitting at the "low" end (*mâm duới*) at the margins of the room (cf. Hy Van Luong 1989: 752). At such gatherings, people say, men without sons risk being placed in humiliating "low end" positions. Similarly, at male drinking gatherings, men without sons will often be mocked and ridiculed by their peers who will tell them, for instance, that "the wife's father gets punched" (*bố vợ phải đấm*). Lacking the respect of even their son-in-law, this expression implies, men with only daughters will never attain the social standing that fathers of sons possess; their words carry less weight, and they will constantly be reminded of their social inferiority vis-à-vis other men.

A 32-year-old father of two daughters described how he felt mocked by his peers: "When I go outside, many people tease me. They say things like, 'You are a lifetime maternal grandfather'" (UNPFA 2011: 37). Similarly, a man who deviates from kinship expectations by living uxorilocally is at high risk of being exposed to harassment; he is no better, people will say, than a dog creeping under the cupboard (*chó chui gầm chạn*). In other words, men who transgress kinship norms – by not having sons or by living with their wife's family – risk bringing their own masculinity and social standing into question, depriving themselves of the respect and recognition enjoyed by men who conform with kinship expectations.

Desires for sons, this suggests, are desires for recognition; they reflect what people sense that the Other desires. In Liên's case, the birth of her son altered the moral status of her husband and his family in the local community from one day to the next, and they rewarded her by accepting her into the family. The value of this male infant, I sensed, lay not only in his expected future contributions to the family in spiritual or material terms, but also and perhaps primarily in the immediate moral recognition that other community members granted his parents and grandparents. When people resort to sex-selective abortions this must, I believe, be seen on the background of these local dynamics of desire. These observations, however, do not explain the force and source of "the Other's" desires. How can we account for the community's intensive bullying and mocking of sonless men and women? What compels people to harass others, merely because they fail to live up to culturally defined reproductive ideals? Why this policing of reproductive norms?

Reproductive intimidation happens, I will argue, as an element in people's strivings to uphold symbolic fictions. Violence occurs, as Žižek observes, when a symbolic fiction is threatened. The idealized "traditional Vietnamese family" can be seen as a symbolic fiction in this sense, as the narrative that secures the coherence of the community. Generally, people in Hanoi are well aware that actual families differ, often quite dramatically, from the state-supported vision of a harmonious and orderly "traditional Vietnamese family." In contemporary Vietnam, norms of patrilocality are far from being consistently adhered to; often, residence depends on the couple's possibilities for employment rather than on kinship expectations. In contemporary Vietnam, the wife usually contributes significantly to the family financially, in many cases exceeding her husband's contributions; and many families are inherently conflict-ridden and anything but harmonious. Real families are, in other words, disorderly and unpredictable to a higher extent than people would generally like to admit. The cozy, reliable, stable, and harmonious family is a fantasy – and it is a fantasy that seems to hold considerable power, guiding people through everyday lives, shaping day-to-day social expectations (cf. Gammeltoft 2016).

In order to maintain this fantasized family image, then, certain things must be kept out of the picture. Women's contributions to their husbands' families must be ignored or downplayed, for instance, as must daughters' contributions to their natal parents (cf. Sangren 2013). Yet these suppressed social realities tend to re-emerge, intruding into social worlds. Describing social situations in which such concealed realities – realities that must be ignored for fantasies to be sustained – re-emerge, Žižek uses the expression, "a crack in the ontological edifice of the universe" (1997: 114). Liên's verbalization of her contributions to her husband's family constituted an ontological crack of this kind: her words drew attention to the possibility that Liên, not her husband, might be the real "pillar" of this family. It was on her labor that the entire household rested. In a similar way, the birth of Cúc's second daughter could be seen as a crack in which the hard realities beneath everyday symbolic fictions became visible. Perhaps, this infant female body suggested, sons are not so necessary. Perhaps daughters too can fulfill their parents' and ancestors' needs for sustenance, love, and support. Seen in this light, sonlessness is not only a failure but also a provocation: a family without sons is socially subversive, challenging the fantasies of family and society that people strive hard to uphold. Deviations from dominant kinship norms are, in Freud's terms, "prohibited"; and people respond swiftly to transgressions. Out of this arise conflicting desires – desires to break with and desires to adapt to kinship expectations – and, as a consequence, profound emotional ambivalence.

When Liên's husband intervened in the conflict between her and his mother, then, it was not just the family's public image that concerned him. Rather, he was trying to establish a family reality of a certain kind – one in which stability, predictability, and order prevailed. The family that Liên's husband strove to form was, therefore, of an imaginary nature, suffused by his own and others' desires. In this domestic conflict, moreover, more than the character of the family was at stake. As we have seen earlier, in Vietnamese political imaginaries, the family indexes society; in Hồ Chí Minh's dictum, "if the family is good, then society will be good." Liên's husband was, therefore, not only maintaining family order. He was also maintaining social order, and this, I assume, was the reason why my colleague found his behavior acceptable. She too felt a need for social order. In a similar manner, it seems, bearing sons helps people to maintain fantasies of social order that are vitally important to them, but that are, perhaps, increasingly difficult to sustain in today's Vietnam.

15.7 Conclusion: Sub-practices of Kinship

Over the past decades, anthropological studies of kinship have undergone significant transformations, moving from systematic accounts of kinship orders and classifications towards more practice-oriented studies of the ways in which kinship is enacted. As a part of this disciplinary move, anthropologists have drawn kinship studies out of the domains of biology (Carsten 2000) and genealogy (Bamford and Leach 2009). In this chapter, I have argued that our understanding of kinship practices can be further extended by revitalizing classic anthropological concerns with aspects of kinship that lie at the edges of consciousness. It is time, I suggest, to attend closer to *sub-practices of kinship*. If relations between human beings are, as Lacan (1988b: 224) suggests, "really established before one gets to the domain of consciousness," then there is reason to refine our analytical capacities to capture also sentiments and desires that are not fully recognized by people; to address the latent, subdued, and silenced aspects of kinship practices which often tend to fall out of analysis (cf. Gammeltoft 2018).

Psychoanalytic concepts can, I have found, contribute to the development of such a heightened attention to the subconscious and the socially suppressed. Lines between "illusion" and "reality" are, as psychoanalytic theory suggests, not as easily drawn as sometimes assumed. As Lacan notes, reality cannot be distinguished from (fantasy-driven) desire: "primordially, desire and reality are related in a seamless texture. They have no need of needlework, they have no need to be sewn together" (Lacan 2002 [1966–1967]: 6). Considering ethnographic materials through notions such as fantasy and desire, this suggests, can bring into sharper analytic focus subdued facets of human existence – hopes, wishes, fears, fantasies – that may become manifest only in tentative, hesitant ways, but that nevertheless play critical roles in the formation of daily lives and realities; attaining their force and significance, perhaps, precisely *because* of their subdued status, their existence outside of socially overt realms. Psychoanalytic approaches can, in this way, help us to recognize that which our interlocutors themselves do *not* want to recognize; the specters that people strive to ignore, suppress, and deny in their efforts to sustain selves and make lives cohere.

Taking Vietnam as my ethnographic case, in this chapter I have argued that closer scrutiny of mixed emotions in the realm of kinship may point us to the power – and the fragility – of family fantasies and the reproductive desires that such fantasies generate. In Vietnam, as we have seen, both state and everyday discourses regarding children's sex are suffused by ambivalence. Despite discursive declarations of the value of daughters, male-oriented kinship practices persist. The ambivalence that characterizes people's desires regarding their children's sex points us, I have argued, to a fundamental split between the visions of family lives that people wish to uphold and the social experiences that threaten these visions. Visions of wholesome, harmonious, and orderly families are central to both state policies and day-to-day lives, forming core points of orientation when people reflect on their own lives and when state officials ponder where the nation is headed. Although – or because – this idealized "traditional Vietnamese family" is under constant pressure from everyday conflict-ridden worlds, it is a powerful fantasy, one that both state authorities and citizens try hard to hold on to. In a rapidly changing society, it seems, fantasized families of order and coherence offer both policy makers and ordinary citizens a socially stabilizing sense of identity and secure belonging.

Seen in this perspective, then, sex-selective abortions can be considered as ways in which people strive to uphold symbolic fictions, pushing out of attention the painful fact that there *is* no harmonious family or coherent social order. By insisting on the necessity of sons, people also hold on to fantasies of kinship and family life as orderly, predictable, and conflict-free. Such desire-driven fantasies seem to be shared by state authorities and citizens alike, cutting across domestic and politico-jural domains and forming a vibrant substratum to both state policies and everyday family-building practices. When people in Vietnam continue to select for sons, this indicates, they do so in an effort to maintain a personally comforting, but socially fragile, fantasy of kinship as a stable and orderly system.

Notes

1. Combining epidemiological and ethnographic methods, the PAVE project (*The Impact of Violence on Reproductive Health in Tanzania and Vietnam*) investigates how intimate partner violence affects women's reproductive health, including perinatal mental health (http://anthropology.ku.dk/research/research-projects/current-projects/pave/).
2. The results of the epidemiological part of this research showed that pregnant women with no sons were twice as likely to be exposed to partner violence as compared to women who had at least one son (PAVE 2016a). Further, if the husband expressed a preference for a son, exposure to violence increased the woman's likelihood of depression during pregnancy or after birth by four times as compared to women who were not exposed to violence (2016b).

References

Bamford, Sandra and James Leach. 2009. *Kinship and Beyond: The Genealogical Model Reconsidered*. New York/Oxford: Berghahn Books.

Bélanger, Danièle. 2006. "Indispensable Sons: Negotiating Reproductive Desires in Rural Vietnam." *Gender, Place and Culture* 13(3): 251–265.

Bourdieu, Pierre. 1977. *Outline of a Theory of Practice*. Cambridge: Cambridge University Press.

Bùi Minh Huệ. 13 Aug. 2014. "Gìn Giữ Gia Đình Việt Trước Sự Xâm Lăng Văn Hóa" [Preserving the Vietnamese family in the face of cultural aggression]. *Gia Đình và Xã Hội* [*Family and Society*].

Carsten, Janet (ed.) 2000. *Cultures of Relatedness: New Approaches to the Study of Kinship*. Cambridge: Cambridge University Press.

Chu Thị Bích Huệ. 11 Jan. 2011. "Chuẩn Mực Văn Hóa Gia Đình Là Nền Tảng Của Hạnh Phúc" [The family's cultural standards are the foundation for happiness]. *Gia Đình và Xã Hội* [*Family and Society*].

Colen, Shellee. 1995. "'Like a Mother to Them': Stratified Reproduction and West Indian Childcare Workers and Employers in New York." In *Conceiving the New World Order: The Global Politics of Reproduction*, ed. Faye D. Ginsburg and Rayna Rapp, 78–102. Berkeley, CA: University of California Press.

Connolly, Deborah. 2000. "Mythical Mothers and Dichotomies of Good and Evil: Homeless Mothers in the United States." In *Ideologies and Technologies of Motherhood: Race, Class, Sexuality, Nationalism*, ed. Helena Ragoné and France Winddance Twine, 263–294. New York/London: Routledge.

Fortes, Meyer. 1959. *Oedipus and Job in West African Religion*. Cambridge: Cambridge University Press.

Freud, Sigmund. 1964 [1911]. "Formulations on the Two Principles of Mental Functioning." In *The Standard Edition of the Complete Psychological Works of Sigmund Freud*, XII, 213–226. Translated by James Strachey. London: The Hogarth Press.

1985 [1913] "Totem and Taboo." In *The Origins of Religion: Totem and Taboo, Moses and Monotheism and Other Works*, 43–224. Translated by James Strachey. London: Penguin Books.

Gammeltoft, Tine. 2016 [1999]. *Women's Bodies, Women's Worries: Health and Family Planning in a Vietnamese Rural Community*. London: Routledge.

2014. *Haunting Images: A Cultural Account of Selective Reproduction in Vietnam*. Berkeley, CA: University of California Press.

2016. "Silence As a Response to Everyday Violence: Understanding Domination and Distress through the Lens of Fantasy." *Ethos* 44(4): 427–447.

2018. "Domestic Moods: Maternal Mental Health in Northern Vietnam." *Medical Anthropology* 37(7): 582–596.

Gammeltoft, Tine M. and Lotte Buch Segal. 2016. "Introduction: Anthropology and Psychoanalysis: Explorations at the Edges of Culture and Consciousness." *Ethos* 44(4): 399–410.

Gammeltoft, Tine M. and Ayo Wahlberg. 2014. "Selective Reproductive Technologies." *Annual Review of Anthropology* 43: 201–216.

Greenhalgh, Susan. 2014. "'Bare Sticks' and Other Dangers to the Social Body: Assembling Fatherhood in China." In *Globalized Fatherhood*, ed. Marcia C. Inhorn, Wendy Chavkin and Jose-Alberto Navarro, 359–381. New York: Berghahn Books.

Guilmoto, Christophe. 2009. "The Sex Ratio Transition in Asia." *Population and Development Review* 35(3): 519–549.

2012. "Son Preference, Sex Selection, and Kinship in Vietnam." *Population and Development Review* 38(1): 31–54.

Hà Thu. 5 Nov. 2012a. "Giảm Thiểu Mất Cân Bằng Giới Tính Khi Sinh: 'Việt Nam Sẽ Làm Được!'" [Reducing the imbalanced sex ratio at birth: 'Vietnam will be able to do it']. *Gia Đình và Xã Hội* [*Family and Society*].

12 Nov. 2012b. "Hệ Lụy của Mất Cân Bằng Giới Tính Khi Sinh: Tai Họa cho Sự Phát Triển Bền Vững" [Implications of the imbalanced sex ratio at birth: a disaster for stable development]. *Gia Đình và Xã Hội* [*Family and Society*].

Hy Van Luong. 1989. "Vietnamese Kinship: Structural Principles and the Socialist Transformation in Northern Vietnam." *The Journal of Asian Studies* 48(4): 741–756.

Isaacs, Susan. 2002 [1952]. "The Nature and Function of Phantasy." In *Developments in Psychoanalysis*, ed. Joan Riviere, 67–121. London: Karnac.

Jellema, Kate. 2007. "Everywhere Incense Burning: Remembering Ancestors in *Đổi Mới* Vietnam." *Journal of Southeast Asian Studies* 38(3): 467–492.

Lacan, Jacques. 1988a. *The Seminar of Jacques Lacan. Book I: Freud's Papers on Technique 1953–1954*, ed. Jacques-Alain Miller, translated by Sylvana Tomaselli. Cambridge: Cambridge University Press.

1988b *The Seminar of Jacques Lacan. Book II: The Ego in Freud's Theory and in the Technique of Psychoanalysis 1954–1955*, ed. Jacques-Alain Miller, translated by Sylvana Tomaselli. Cambridge: Cambridge University Press.

2002 [1966–1967]. *The Seminar of Jacques Lacan. Book XIV: The Logic of Phantasy*. Translated by Cormac Gallagher. London: Karnac.

2006 [1966]. *Écrits*. Translated by Bruce Fink in collaboration with Héloïse Fink and Russell Grigg. New York/London: W.W. Norton & Company.

2008. *My Teaching*. Translated by David Macey. London/New York: Verso.

Laplanche, Jean and Jean-Bertrand Pontalis. 2006 [1973]. *The Language of Psycho-Analysis*. Translated by Donald Nicholson-Smith. London: Karnac.

Malinowski, Bronislaw. 2007[1927]. *Sex and Repression in Savage Society*. London/New York: Routledge.

Miller, Barbara. 2001. "Female-Selective Abortion in Asia: Patterns, Policies, and Debates." *American Anthropologist* 103(4): 1083–1095.

PAVE. 2016a. *Intimate Partner Violence among Pregnant Women*. Research Update. Hanoi.

PAVE. 2016b. *Intimate Partner Violence and Depression during Pregnancy and after Birth*. Research Update. Hanoi.

Peletz, Michael. 2001. "Ambivalence in Kinship since the 1940s." In *Relative Values: Reconfiguring Kinship Studies*, ed. Sarah Franklin and Susan McKinnon, 413–444. Durham, NC/London: Duke University Press.

Rubin, Gayle. 1975. "The Traffic in Women: Notes on the 'Political Economy' of Sex." In *Toward an Anthropology of Women*, ed. Rayna R. Reiter, 157–210. New York/London: Monthly Review Press.

Sangren, P. Steven. 2009. "'Masculine Domination': Desire and Chinese Patriliny." *Critique of Anthropology* 29(3): 255–278.

——— 2013. "The Chinese Family As Instituted Fantasy: Or, Rescuing Kinship Imaginaries from the 'Symbolic.'" *Journal of the Royal Anthropological Institute* (n.s.) 19: 279–299.

Scheper-Hughes, Nancy. 1992. *Death without Weeping: The Violence of Everyday Life in Brazil*. Berkeley, CA: University of California Press.

Spiro, Melford E. 1997. *Gender Ideology and Psychological Reality: An Essay on Cultural Reproduction*. New Haven, CT/London: Yale University Press.

Stasch, Rupert. 2009. *Society of Others: Kinship and Mourning in a West Papuan Place*. Berkeley, CA: University of California Press.

Thanh Niên News. 7 Oct. 2011. "Girl Power." *Thanh Niên News*.

UNFPA. 2011. *Son Preference in Vietnam: Ancient Desires, Advancing Technologies*. Hanoi: United Nations Population Fund (UNFPA).

UNFPA. 2014. *Policy Brief: The Imbalanced Sex Ratio at Birth in Vietnam – Connecting Research and Policy for Change*. Hanoi: United Nations Population Fund (UNFPA).

United Nations. 2017. *World Population Prospects 2017*. United Nations: Population Division of the Department of Economic and Social Affairs. https://esa.un.org/unpd/wpp/, accessed July 13, 2017.

Van Bich, Pham. 1999. *The Vietnamese Family in Change: The Case of the Red River Delta*. Richmond: Curzon Press.

Wahlberg, Ayo and Tine M. Gammeltoft. 2017. *Selective Reproduction in the 21st Century*. Basingstoke: Palgrave Macmillan.

Weiss, Meira. 1994. *Conditional Love: Parents' Attitudes towards Handicapped Children*. Westport, CT: Bergin and Garvey.

Werner, Jayne. 2009. *Gender, Household and State in Post-Revolutionary Vietnam*. London/New York: Routledge.

Wiegersma, Nancy. 1988. *Vietnam: Peasant Land, Peasant Revolution: Patriarchy and Collectivity in the Rural Economy*. London: Macmillan.

Wolf, Margery. 1972. *Women and the Family in Rural Taiwan*. Stanford, CA: Stanford University Press.

Žižek, Slavoj. 1997. *The Plague of Fantasies*. London/New York: Verso.

——— 2005. *Interrogating the Real*. London: Continuum.

Part IV

Transnational Connections

16

Maids, Mistresses, and Wives: Rethinking Kinship and the Domestic Sphere in Twenty-First Century Global Hong Kong

Nicole Constable

16.1 Introduction

In a wonderful article entitled "Wives, Concubines, and Maids: Servitude and Kinship in the Hong Kong Region, 1900–1940" (1991), Rubie S. Watson described large, multigenerational Chinese households that included men who were born or adopted into the household and who shared patrilineal kinship ties and rights to the family estate, women who married in and whose main purpose as wives was to produce the next generation of male members of the family, and daughters who were expected to marry out. Most important, she stressed that households also included non-kin, such as concubines, slaves, indentured workers, and servants of various sorts, all of whom were Chinese, some of whom were recruited through "China's market in people" (1991: 232). Watson's work highlighted both the "inequality among brothers" and the ambiguities of social positions within households and kinship groups (1985). She appreciated that "clear distinctions among people living in the same household were not always easy to make; *servants, including servile menials, were often spoken of as kin, and kin were sometimes treated as servants*" (1991: 232, emphasis added). Watson criticized the tendency among anthropologists and historians to "write about the household as if it were a social actor with its own set of unquestioned goals, interests, and survival strategies." The Chinese household was often spoken of from a single, seemingly unified voice, "a voice that is nearly always male" (1991: 231). Especially important, Watson pointed to early twentieth-century differences between male and female interests within households, and to divergent interests and positioning of different women within the household. As she demonstrated, wives, concubines, and maids are all differently "affected by gender and class stratification," resulting in different ties to the household and the family (1991: 231).

This chapter takes Watson's classic work as a point of departure, and draws from and builds on her insights about inequality, fluidity and ambiguity of household membership by applying it to a more recent – and far more transnational – period of Hong Kong history. In the late twentieth and early twenty-first centuries, patterns of global capitalism and new sorts of "markets" in people have produced or contributed to new sorts of family formations and household structures in and beyond Hong Kong. There are some critical differences between the households Watson described and those of today. To be fully appreciated and understood, these new households and families require multiple lenses – one that includes within its scope the local households that include employers and foreign domestic workers, and another that encompasses the transnational and global terrain and takes careful account of domestic workers' own kin and family members who are increasingly dispersed in some unexpected ways across and beyond the borders of Hong Kong. Such dispersed and widespread families – many of which are increasingly multiethnic and multiracial – require a rethinking, a reconceptualization, and an expansion of the concepts of family, household, kinship, and reproduction that are even more fluid and ambiguous, gendered, and stratified than in the early twentieth century. Today they reach much farther across the globe and are linked to new sorts of mobilities, privileges, precarities, and racialized class and gender inequalities.

This chapter has two main sections. In the first, I provide a brief and selective history of the transformation of Hong Kong households and the related development of the market for Southeast Asian foreign domestic workers (FDWs). The employment of FDWs, also referred to locally as "helpers" or as overseas contract workers (OCWs) is tied to socioeconomic changes that took place in mid-to-late twentieth-century Hong Kong and parts of Southeast Asia. During that time, foreign domestic workers became essential to the functioning of many newly middle-class nuclear households in Hong Kong and other parts of Asia, such as Taiwan and Singapore. In this section I also introduce some key concepts, including the notion of "global women" (Ehrenreich and Hochschild 2004); the idea of domestic workers as "like one of the family" (Childress 1986); and the concept of "reproductive labor" – all of which help us to understand the importance of low and unpaid feminized household work.

The second section moves beyond the ascribed role of domestic workers as workers, and only workers, as defined by their legal conditions of stay, and shifts the lens to include stories about migrant women's own complicated family and kinship relations in and beyond Hong Kong.

While scholars have aptly pointed to the critically important role of domestic workers within their employers' households (e.g., Constable 2007 [1997]; Lan 2006), and some have looked closely at the family members and children they leave behind, I argue that understanding domestic workers only within the conventional context of the localized households and families of their employers – those for whom and among whom they work – is inadequate. Other studies have aptly shown how domestic workers are linked to their parents, partners, and children back home (see Gamburd 2000; Parreñas 2005). What has been largely ignored, however, are the new families – the partners or husbands and children – that migrant workers create while they are working abroad. In other words, for domestic workers, Hong Kong (and other migrant worker destinations) are not and can never be only a place of work. There exists no firm divide between Hong Kong as place of work (and the employers' home and family) and Indonesia or the Philippines as home. For the women I describe, and their partners and children, the location of family is far more complicated. Some former or current domestic workers are involved in more conventional – but often inter-ethnic/racial and international – heteronormative marital relationships and reside temporarily or long term in Hong Kong; some are unmarried or involved in same-sex relationships. Many have what I call stretched or temporary family formations that cross the geographic borders of nation-states. The patterns include evermore geographically dispersed patterns involving mothers, fathers, and their children.

16.2 Domestic Workers in Shifting Hong Kong Households

Anthropologists of the 1960s and 1970s studied large clans, lineages, and "traditional" and "ideal" extended households in China, Hong Kong, and Taiwan, and the classic pattern of multigenerational households structured by male agnates and their wives and yet to be married daughters (e.g., Baker 1979; Cohen 1976; Wolf 1968, 1972). The Confucian ideal of "five generations under one roof" (Baker 1979) was much admired but relatively rare, yet often strived for. Such patterns were often reflected in the architecture of Chinese rural homes, where living spaces could be expanded to accommodate multiple generations.

Rubie Watson, as noted above, drew special attention to the array of other household members, especially temporary members, most of whom contributed household labor. In Hong Kong 1900–1940, heredi-tary male servants (whose children were passed on or "inherited" by the next generation of masters) were no longer in existence (J. Watson 1980), but there were still female bondservants known as *muijai* (Jaschok 1988; Watson 1991). These were young girls whose parents were usually too poor to support them. They were paid in exchange for giving the child away to work as a household servant, at least until she reached adulthood.[1] She was not paid, but she received food and shelter. Upon adulthood, the household for which she worked was expected to arrange her marriage, and at that point she would be "free." She might continue to work for them after marriage as a paid servant. The sale and purchase of *muijai* were prohibited by the British in 1923, but the practice continued until at least the 1960s under the guise of "adopted daughters" (Jaschok 1988: 101; R. Watson 1991: 241). When I conducted research in Hong Kong in the 1980s, the practice had ended; only a few old women who had once been *muijai* were still alive (see Jaschok 1988; Sankar 1978; and R. Watson 1991).

Other types of domestic workers that coexisted with *muijai* in Hong Kong history included the famous Chinese spinster amahs or *sohei* who were considered both "professional" and "like members of the family" in their devotion to the family (Gaw 1991; Stockard 1989). These Chinese amahs were greatly valued by Chinese, especially after the mid-twentieth century, as the supply dwindled and the demand for them grew. Wealthy families competed for Chinese amahs; they were status symbols, and shared a reputation as highly devoted to the families they worked for and were spoken of as being "like members of the family." As Hong Kong's economy grew and industrialized, and women were increasingly educated, in the 1950s and 1960s Chinese women turned away from domestic work. Those who were less educated far preferred factory work, which offered greater freedom and earned them greater authority within their own families (Salaff 1981). More educated women took up jobs in shops, banks, hotels, and other sectors of Hong Kong's booming economy.

Coinciding with Hong Kong's growing population, its expanding manufacturing industry, women's increasing education and their entry into the industrial and service economy, housing patterns also shifted. Hong Kong urbanized and semi-rural "new towns" replaced rural villages and market towns. High-rise apartments and housing estates grew, as did the number of flats housing nuclear family units. From the 1970s onward, rural villages and squatter areas were razed for new developments including roads, housing complexes and other public works. Public housing grew as did the number of nuclear households. Large houses or rural dwellings that had once easily expanded to accommodate multigenerational families, with multiple sons, daughters-in-law who shared household labor, child and elderly care, and grandparents, aunts and uncles who might help watch and entertain the children, became rare. Instead, most of Hong Kong's population – especially the growing middle class – lived in small crowded urban flats in high-rise apartment buildings, some of which included a tiny room designed as a servant's room.

16.3   Like a Member of the Family

Chinese amahs of the past are remembered or romanticized fondly by
the Chinese adult children they had cared for. It is common to hear that
they were "like members of the family." There is no reason to doubt the
firsthand accounts of fond memories and familial relations, but it is clear
that not all such relations were so positive, at least not from the perspective of the amahs. As Sankar (1978: 54–55) points out, there were
also times when such amahs were neglected when they got old or sick
and were not, under those circumstances treated or cared for like ideal
family members. Moreover, as I have noted elsewhere (Constable 2007
[1997]) the nostalgic view of amahs voiced in the 1980s and 1990s was col-
ored by two other important factors. One was the short supply of Chinese
domestic workers and the presence of new foreign domestic workers.
In the 1980s and early 1990s the FDWs were almost all women from
the Philippines. Praising amahs of old was an indirect way to criticize
or comment on the cultural differences of Filipinas. In particular, they
were not Chinese, did not speak Chinese, cook Chinese food, or behave
in ways that were considered appropriately Chinese. Praising Chinese
amahs of the past was a way to talk about encounters with foreign others
whose behavior – especially from the vantage point of intimate household spaces – was considered strange and sometimes undesirable by local
Hong Kong Chinese employers.

The second factor that shaped the romantic idealization of Chinese
amahs and other "Superior Servants" of the past (Gaw 1991) was that
many of the employers of foreign domestic helpers had not grown up in
households with servants. They were newly entering – or struggling to be
counted among Hong Kong's growing "middle class." Women's employment opportunities, and the number of nuclear households residing in
small flats without the support of extended family members, meant that
those who employed foreign domestic workers spanned the spectrum
from the newly low levels of the middle class to the very wealthy. Idealized
notions of what a servant–master relationship *should* be like might be
captured by Arjun Appadurai's notion of "nostalgia without memory"
(1996: 31–32), fantasies of how they imagine that things once were.

Employer's complaints about Filipino maids, often aired in local
newspapers in the 1980s and 1990s, reflected ideas about Chinese servants
of old who "knew their place." By contrast, Filipinas were often better
educated than their Chinese employers. This created complicated and
often uncomfortable class relations between women who were college
educated and had worked as teachers, in hotels, in banks, as nurses, or
as shopkeepers in the Philippines, but were expected to behave as sub-
servient "maids" to their employers. Their employers, moreover, were
often less educated, struggling for a middle-class lifestyle, and living in
tiny urban flats that sometimes included members of three generations.

As I heard from some Chinese employers, the monthly income that a woman employer brought in might amount to just a bit more than the monthly cost of employing a domestic worker, but the expense was considered worth it as local women considered it better to go out to work than to remain at home doing boring household work or, in some cases, living under the watchful eye of her mother-in-law. Hiring a helper allowed the family to pursue middle-class ideals and allowed the working woman to become the household manager, to escape the drudgery of housework, passing it on to a low-paid foreign helper. One of the most striking examples I encountered was of a household that opted for two incomes and a helper, although the economic difference between the cost of a helper and the woman's income was only a few hundred Hong Kong dollars a month (less than US$100). The couple lived in a tiny flat and had two children. The woman sold newspapers at a roadside stand and the man drove a delivery truck. The woman explained that almost her whole salary went to pay the domestic worker's salary, but it was worth it to have a job, and the domestic worker had been a teacher in the Philippines and was considered key to the upward mobility of their children, since she could help teach them English (see Lan 2006).

While the amahs of the past are nostalgically and retroactively praised for having been like a member of the family, the concept has a highly coercive and manipulative side as well. Supposed "family membership" masks labor exploitation. While families may be idealized as cooperative and equal, there are clearly inequalities within families, based mainly on gender, age, and generation. Moreover, familial ideologies serve to reinforce the sense of obligatory hard work for one's family. The idea of domestic workers being "like a member of the family" has received much scholarly critique. Family members are expected to voluntarily work long hours for the good of his or her family. They are made to feel obligated to their kin. Being "like a member of the family" does not imply equality, but being (like) a member of the family justifies exploitation and lack of formal worker's rights. As it was put bluntly by one Filipina domestic worker I knew, being a member of the family "means you can't ever say 'no.'"

A joke that circulated among domestic workers in the early 1990s had the punch line "Oh, so you're a member of the family too!" The punch line was a common retort to a domestic worker who would say "I can't meet you on Sunday [the most common day off for domestic workers] because my employer asked me to ... [work, babysit, clean her friend's car, run an errand, etc.]." Even staying for dinner with the family meant additional chores such as cooking and cleaning on her supposed day off. As the joke clearly reflected: being "a member of the family" might sound good on the surface, but was in essence a way of denying a worker her rights and coercing her into doing more unpaid work. Employers are thus seen as blurring the lines between Chinese family members who are expected, especially in the Hong Kong context, to feel an obligation to kin for no additional compensation, and workers who need no day off or additional compensation for giving it up. Following a Confucian logic of obedience, lower level and female family members are especially beholden to men and to their elders and superiors, and by extension, poorer members of the family are beholden to the wealthier ones and are expected to be grateful to them. In exchange they should be treated well. This relationship depends, however, on a moral economy but not on legal obligations, while a worker–employer relationship ideally depends on workers' rights and employers' contractual legal obligations.

16.4   Global Women

The book *Global Woman* was highly popular and influential, drawing attention to gendered labor migration in the global economy of the late twentieth century (Ehrenreich and Hochschild 2004). The introductory chapters highlight the growing role of women in the "new economy" in which women are the "new gold" and their labor serves as a resource for exportation and exploitation. Similar to colonial exploitation of natural resources and labor in the colonies or postcolonial states, this new economy involves the exploitation and marketing of young women as resources that are supplied from the global South to become wives, nannies, maids, and sex workers in wealthier regions of the global North.[2]

The demand for Filipino foreign domestic workers in Hong Kong that began in the 1970s when they were first hired by English-speaking expatriates is part of this wider pattern. They were especially popular at first for their English-language abilities and their high level of education. The demand grew steadily among local Chinese in the 1980s and 1990s who also saw the benefit of hiring domestic workers who could help teach children English. By the late 1990s, during the Asian Financial Crisis, the Indonesian government joined the Philippines in actively promoting the exportation of Indonesian women as domestic workers to East Asia. Recruitment agencies and training camps in Java sprang up and by 2009 there were over 130,000 Indonesian domestic workers in Hong Kong and their numbers had overtaken Filipinas for the first time. As later arrivals, with relatively less education than Filipinas, Indonesian FDWs were considered less assertive and demanding than Filipinas, whose well-developed support networks and activism helped them assert their rights. For example, Filipinas often asserted their rights to a day off each week and to the legally stipulated minimum monthly wage, while a much higher proportion of Indonesian women did not know their rights or were unwilling or unable to demand them. By 2014 there were approximately 320,000 foreign domestic helpers in

Hong Kong, over 150,000 Filipinas, and over 150,000 Indonesians, and other women mostly from other regions of Southeast or South Asia. (Hong Kong agencies are ever on the lookout for new and often less expensive sources of workers, such as Myanmar and Bangladesh most recently.) These "global women" are promoted and marketed by their home countries as a quality resource for export. They are a significant source of revenue and remittances for Indonesia and the Philippines. They fill a need among the broad spectrum of middle-class and wealthy employers. But one thing that this characterization does not adequately convey is the extent to which migrant workers (men and women) choose to work abroad for a variety of reasons, not all of them economic, and not only because they are a source of revenue for the nation-state and of remittances for their families. As I have stressed elsewhere, money is the most common reason given, and it is a critically important reason why women become migrant workers. However, as I got to know them better, it became clear that other, more subtle and less easily talked about factors emerged: failed relationships, abusive marriages or domestic situations, family conflicts, broken hearts, desire for adventure, avoiding arranged marriage, ambition for a better life, desire for freedom. These factors also play a role in complicating the idea of Hong Kong as a place of work and the Philippines or Indonesia as a place of family for domestic workers.

16.5 Reproductive Labor and Care Work

Once they come to work in Hong Kong on two-year domestic worker visas, FDWs are required to live with their employers. Their work and visa status defines them as temporary workers. They cannot bring their own family members with them to Hong Kong. They receive room and board and a salary of around US$500 per month. This salary is lower that Hong Kong's local minimum wage, but significantly more than they would earn in Indonesia or the Philippines.

They perform a wide range of duties, most of which can be considered "reproductive labor" for their employers' families, labor that is necessary for the reproduction of the employers' households. Some domestic workers provide childcare, taking children to and from school, helping them with homework, feeding and changing babies. They also look after the elderly, bathing them, dressing them, massaging them, pushing them in wheelchairs, giving them medicine, and accompanying them to doctor's visits and other outings. Most do the household work: cooking, cleaning, grocery shopping, and laundry. Some walk dogs and wash cars. Often male domestic workers (but some women too) work as chauffeurs and gardeners. Some are required or coerced into providing sexual services as well. Reproductive labor is often thought of as unpaid, often devalued, or feminized work within the household often delegated to the housewife or household servants under a female household member's management. Such labor allows more "productive" forms of paid labor to take place. Domestic workers often allow the household members to go out to work for more than the wages she receives. Within the Hong Kong context, domestic work is considered women's work, work that would most likely be the responsibility of a woman, often a wife, if there was no domestic worker.

Domestic workers provide care work or reproductive labor and intimate labor of various sorts. Their work is often intimate in the sense that it takes place within a home or a family and it involves close bodily contact: domestic workers clean blood from children's knees, they wash bodies and toilets, they change the diapers of adults and babies, and they dispose of human and animal waste, to name but a few. FDWs also perform emotional labor: comforting or reassuring their charges, patiently serving the role of listener, performing obedience and patience if they are scolded. Many of these points have been made and scholars have pointed to connections between the intimacy of domestic work and other forms of intimate labor (see Boris and Parreñas 2010; Constable 2009). Partly because of the way that domestic workers are officially and legally defined as just "workers" in Hong Kong, but also because analytic frames that locate domestic workers within (or in relation to) the homes of their employers, their own intimate lives and the family formations in and especially beyond their countries of origin have received little attention, yet they open new and important directions for study.

16.6 Migrant Mothers and Babies

Little has been written about the lives of twentieth-century amahs when they left their employers, or about twenty-first-century foreign domestic workers when they return home, although there is emerging research on this topic (Chan 2018). The work lives and intimate lives of FDWs must be understood both within and beyond the context of Hong Kong and through time. This requires multi-sited research and depends on learning about topics that are often shrouded in secrecy and shame. In the course of my research among FDWs and former FDWs who had children or were pregnant in Hong Kong, it became clear that despite the moral and social pressures and disciplining forces exerted from many sides (including employers, agencies, consulates, and families back home) aimed at preventing domestic workers from forming intimate or sexual relations in Hong Kong, some nonetheless (and not surprisingly) have partners and lovers. Most such relationships that I knew about were consensual, but in some very tragic cases they were not.

16.7   Stateless Children

When I arrived in Hong Kong in May 2015 to catch up with women I knew from my earlier research and the staff at nongovernmental organizations that support them, many people were talking about a tragic event that had taken place in Repulse Bay the previous month. A 15-year-old girl had jumped to her death from an upper floor of a Repulse Bay luxury apartment building. The girl was one of two daughters born to a Filipina who had originally come to Hong Kong as a domestic worker, and a British insurance executive who worked for an elite Hong Kong firm. The story shocked the public, received a good deal of media attention, and was the subject of much on- and offline speculation, and much discussion among migrant workers, migrant activists, and advocates.

In the aftermath of the suicide, it became clear that the two sisters had no official status in Hong Kong. They had not been registered at birth and neither had attended school, as required by law. They had received private education, and presumably private health care as well. Their mother had overstayed her domestic worker visa by about 20 years, and the couple was not married.[3] One domestic worker advocate who talked to me about the story said that the most generous interpretation she could come up with was that they were trying to keep the family together; the couple were perhaps afraid that if they registered the births, officials would become aware that the mother was an overstayer and this might lead to her expulsion from Hong Kong and to family separation. Several people noted that the mother was married in the Philippines, so she was not free to marry her Hong Kong partner.

While domestic workers are required to come to Hong Kong alone, and are not permitted to bring their children or other family members with them, this story shows how domestic workers or former domestic workers may have intimate partners and kin in Hong Kong. The story struck me as remarkable for many reasons. One is that in *Born Out of Place: Migrant Mothers and the Politics of International Labor* (Constable 2014) I wrote about many current or former FDWs who got pregnant and gave birth to children in Hong Kong, some of whom, as in the Repulse Bay case, overstayed their FDW visas. The cases I knew mainly involved women whose partners were in Hong Kong temporarily, they were not among the elite. This included some men who were asylum seekers, refugees, overstayers, or undocumented workers from parts of Africa and South Asia. Some were among Hong Kong's low-paid Chinese, Pakistani, Indian, or Nepali legal residents and a few were middle-class Chinese or Western locals or expatriates. In a few cases the women's partners, or the fathers of their children, were their former employers. I knew of several women whose partners were middle-class or well-off local residents (both Chinese and non-Chinese); some such couples were married and the women had become Hong Kong residents.

Many of the women whose partners were not Hong Kong residents faced obstacles to marriage.

One particular story I wrote about presents a striking comparison with the Repulse Bay case. "Indah" (a pseudonym) had come to Hong Kong from Indonesia to work as a domestic worker (2014: 4–8, 15, 223–224). Indah met and, as she said, "fell in love" with a Nepali man. When she got pregnant, she lost her job, overstayed her visa, moved in with her partner and eventually had two children with him. Indah overstayed for more than six years. I met her in 2012 after she spotted a notice in the local Indonesian newspaper, posted by a nongovernmental organization named PathFinders. PathFinders offered assistance to migrant women who were pregnant or had babies. Indah called PathFinders' number and I accompanied a caseworker to visit her and her children. At the time, the family of four lived in a small apartment in a building on the edge of a New Territories village. Indah described how her family had been happy but living a highly precarious existence, given her status as an overstayer and her partner's economic marginality. Over the years, her partner – whom she referred to as her husband but had never officially married – supported the family by working in various low-paid jobs, but he became addicted to drugs and gradually used his earnings to support his drug habit and lost his ability to support the family. Deeply concerned for the well-being of her children, Indah contacted PathFinders. Their case-worker accompanied her to surrender to the Immigration Department and offered her housing in a domestic shelter. Several months later she was required to attend a court hearing for overstaying. The judge was sympathetic toward her and her children – the oldest then six and the younger a toddler – and gave her a suspended sentence, on condition she return to Indonesia with her children and enroll her older child in school.

Considering these two stories side by side raises many issues and many questions. In the Repulse Bay case, the father was a well-educated, wealthy, permanent resident of Hong Kong, while in Indah's case her partner was a low-paid, low-educated migrant worker. (It was never entirely clear to Indah whether or not he had ever pursued the opportunity to become a Hong Kong permanent resident, but she believed he had entered Hong Kong legally, by virtue of his father's residency at the time, but had neglected to pursue the option of permanent residence.) Both mothers had originally come to Hong Kong as domestic workers, with two-year domestic worker visas. Both on some level passed as wives, despite not having officially recognized marriages in Hong Kong. Their living conditions could hardly have been more different.

According to news reports, the family in Repulse Bay attended church, the children were educated (though not in school), and they appeared to be physically healthy. Indah and her children in the New Territories, by contrast, had some untreated medical problems and Indah worried because her older child was not in school. Indah and her partner could not afford basic health care or education for their children, which contributed to Indah's eventual decision to leave her partner, surrender to immigration, and leave Hong Kong, despite her own professed attachment to him, her children's obvious attachment to him, and her pain at the thought of separating the children from their father.

The two cases are divided primarily by economic class and financial differences more than any other factor. In the Repulse Bay case, money may have helped to create an impression that they were like everybody else, and it seemed to compensate for many things, especially the children's health care and education. Money and the lifestyle it afforded created an impression of citizenship and belonging. Those who knew them from work, church, or the community assumed they were a "normal" family: a married couple with children and legal residence in Hong Kong. The children reputedly had friends. According to news articles, the family was regularly seen together in Repulse Bay which would suggest that they were not too worried about the possibility of being stopped or detained by immigration officers in the course of their daily activities and asked for identity cards. According to news reports, the mother did not attend many of her partner's work-related social events, but this was not considered particularly odd or surprising. As one observer speculated, perhaps she did not feel comfortable with them, having once been a domestic worker.

In Indah's case, and that of many other members of non-Western minority groups in Hong Kong, she and her partner were always on alert for immigration officers who commonly patrolled areas of the New Territories where they and other immigrant and minority populations are known to reside. Like other women I knew, Indah often felt vulnerable. She was afraid that she and the children might be stopped by immigration officers and required to show Hong Kong identification cards at the market, at exits to public transportation, or in particular residential areas. When I first met her, Indah said that she was always careful, but in the days before she contacted PathFinders she had become increasingly reclusive, afraid to go out to the market or to let the children play outside, because she had seen immigration officers walking around. Although she read to her daughter and tried to teach her at home, she was well aware that she had already passed the age by which Hong Kong children normally begin to attend school. Indah's sister worked as a domestic worker in Hong Kong as well, but Indah rarely saw her anymore and felt she could no longer ask her for help as she had her own problems and her own family to support in Indonesia.

What many observers in the migrant and migrant activist community found surprising about the Repulse Bay case was that despite the resources at their disposal, the couple apparently did not seek legal solutions to remedy the woman's lack of residential status or that of their children. The understanding of less privileged migrants is that they lack the knowledge and the resources to act "responsibly" so in the Repulse

Bay case it seems shocking that the father would have allowed his partner and his children to remain undocumented for so long. One person I spoke to noted that the couple did not marry in Hong Kong because she was already married in the Philippines. This obstacle was far from insurmountable, however, because she could easily have petitioned in Hong Kong to acquire a divorce. Despite the fact that divorce is not permitted or recognized in the Philippines, many domestic workers I knew over the years had obtained divorces in Hong Kong, allowing for the possibility of remarriage overseas (Constable 2003). The same person speculated that although the children would have the right of Hong Kong residence by virtue of their father's status, this might have brought to light the mother's status as an overstayer. Another observer said that the man should at least have hired her as a domestic worker to maintain her legal standing in Hong Kong (a situation I had heard of in several other cases). Two people I spoke to speculated that perhaps the man had "control issues" and did not want his partner and their children to have legal status in Hong Kong; being undocumented meant they could not easily leave him.

Melinda, another Filipina former domestic worker who I met in 2011 and who had a young Hong Kong-born child, had overstayed her visa for around a decade. She later surrendered to immigration and was sentenced to serve six months in Lowu correctional facility for overstaying. She subsequently obtained a divorce from her husband in the Philippines, married her partner in Hong Kong, and now lives in Hong Kong with him and their child. With advice from an immigration lawyer and an NGO they were able to navigate the many obstacles and eventually – after serving her sentence which was ultimately reduced to four months for good behavior and because she chose to surrender – to remain in Hong Kong. One of the main factors that motivated Melinda to surrender to immigration was that she had a child there and other children in the Philippines. Her Hong Kong-born child was entitled to become a Hong Kong resident, based on his father's residential status, and she did not want to deprive him of that. She also longed to see her children in the Philippines but was unable to leave without revealing the fact that her visa had expired long ago. Although surrendering meant she would have to serve time in prison, and might not be permitted to remain in Hong Kong, she took her chances.

In the Repulse Bay case, it is impossible to speculate what might have happened to the children when they became adults. At birth children with a permanent resident parent are entitled to become Hong Kong residents, but parents are legally required to register their children within a short period of time from the birth, and the children must apply for permanent residence before they reach adulthood. At what point are children born of domestic workers (or other migrant workers) who overstay required to document their citizenship? Such papers are required to attend school or to use public hospitals. The undocumented status of one teenager I knew of was revealed when the child's mother was arrested. In another case, the teenager drew the attention of neighbors who noticed the child was never in school and they reported it to authorities. In another case, the mother decided the teenager needed to go to school. It does not seem so surprising that people at the lower end of the class spectrum choose to overstay their visas, especially when they do not have children in Hong Kong, given that they often feel they have little to lose by doing so and much to lose if they do not. It is far more surprising that people with economic resources (and the accompanying social and cultural capital), who could afford good lawyers, and have the financial means to challenge the system and advocate for the well-being of their partners and children would make the same choice. The stories of Melinda, Indah, and the Repulse Bay family, however, begin to show how wives, intimate partners, mistresses, and maids are still blurred and overlapping categories in twenty-first-century Hong Kong, though the particulars – especially the nationalities and ethnic parameters and the related migratory statuses and bureaucratic processes of citizenship involved – differ greatly from those of the early twentieth century.

16.8   Stretched and Temporary Family Formations

While the above examples illustrate how families of migrant workers overstay their visas so as to remain together in Hong Kong, the following ones point to patterns through which many other current or former FDW mothers, fathers, and children become geographically separated through time. The geographic and spatial movement of (former) domestic workers and their families through time is a distinctive contemporary pattern. As I have argued, a wider frame is necessary to fully appreciate how the partners and children of (former) domestic workers become geographically dispersed, distant, and sometimes lose contact entirely. The Repulse Bay family might remain in Hong Kong together, and Melinda's family likely will. But Indah's family is already dispersed across three or more countries, and those of many other former FDWs are as well.

Sring, an Indonesian FDW in her early twenties, became pregnant by her European boyfriend who was working as a teacher in Hong Kong for just a year. Her partner was eager to distance himself from her, but Sring convinced him to marry her, not because she expected him to stay or to support her, but in the hopes that it would allow her to claim residency in Hong Kong. Unfortunately, she was unaware that his status and the one-year duration of his stay in Hong Kong would foil her plan. His job ended and he left Hong Kong to return home to Europe when the child was less than three months old. She felt she had little choice but to make plans to return home with her child, and try to find a relative who would agree to take care of the baby so she could come back to work in Hong Kong and pay the caregiver and support her child. Sring did not expect to see or hear from her husband again after he left Hong Kong.

Despite her rather unusual marital arrangement, Sring is like many other Indonesian and Filipino women whom I met during my research among migrant mothers in Hong Kong from 2010 to 2012 whose families are dispersed. Many such "single mothers" – who may or may not have been married officially or religiously but whose husbands are neither with them or sending them and the child(ren) financial support – eventually (re)enter what I have called the migratory cycle of atonement. Ara and Mia, for example, are two former FDW mothers who both returned home to East Java with the children they had after short-lived intimate relationships they had with African asylum seeker men in Hong Kong. After an initial period of reunion with their parents in Java, the initial excitement about their homecoming dwindled as village gossip and criticism of their "unwed motherhood" became unbearable. To avoid the gossip and stigma that they, their parents, and their children experienced in their home communities, both women eventually left their children with geographically distant relatives and, to their parents' great relief, went abroad again to earn money and remit it home. Sending money home to support the child and to help their families served as both a way to escape the stigma they faced, and as a way to "atone" for the shame they brought to their families.

Ara eventually remarried and had a new baby with her Indonesian husband, but her first child did not live with them and she rarely saw her first child anymore. When her new baby was over a year old, she returned abroad again to work and support her new family and her first child. Indah and most of the other women I knew went to work in Singapore, Taiwan, or if they had left in good standing (within the conditions of their FDW visa), returned to Hong Kong, leaving their children in the care of elderly grandparents, aunts, or other relatives. Many of these women, rarely, if ever, heard from their children's fathers after they left Hong Kong, though some occasionally kept in touch by Facebook. Indah had tried to contact her former partner who she heard had returned home to Nepal. A few women I knew had gone to Pakistan with the partners they met and married in Hong Kong. Others were – to my surprise and theirs – able to remain in Hong Kong with their asylum seeker partners and children – for several years. While these stays were assumed to be temporary, and involved filing torture or asylum claims that they usually did not expect to win, such methods did allow them to stretch the time they could remain in Hong Kong, often for several years, while their cases were processed or under appeal (see Constable 2014). In some cases, a child's father's residence status allowed the mother to remain in

Hong Kong with the child. In other cases, women who married local legal residents were able to become legal Hong Kong residents as well.

16.9   Employers Who Are Fathers

Watson's (1991) and Jaschok's (1988) research on early twentieth-century households, and on servants, bondmaids, and concubines in Chinese households, shows that men had sexual access to women in the household other than their wives. Maids might become mistresses or concubines, and other women might be sexual partners for the men of the household. Some such relationships no doubt resulted in children. Sexual access to women in the household at the time was likely justified by notions of ownership – *muijai* were "bought" – and notions of women's inferiority and required subordination to the interests of men. Unlike today, the dominant idea was that servants "belonged" to their employers and that their owners had rights to them, including sexual rights.

Today foreign domestic workers are defined by their legal status as migrant workers. They are assumed to be "workers" with rights. They are not "owned" by their employers, nor do their employers have sexual access to them. Employment contracts and legal rights of FDWs include many (but not all) of the labor rights shared by other Hong Kong workers. For example, they have a minimum wage, a guaranteed weekly day off, and are required to live with their employers and receive food or a food allowance. Their contracts are for two years and can be renewed. As noted, they cannot bring family members with them. Although many workers and employers are unaware of it, domestic workers have maternity rights as well and are entitled to paid maternity leave.

Given the isolation of the home as a workplace, consensual and coerced sexual relationships between employers and FDWs occur. Many domestic worker NGOs and advocates have dealt with cases of domestic workers who are expected to provide sexual services (sometimes with the approval of the woman employer who is not interested in having sex with her husband). Some FDWs are raped or become pregnant by their employers. In some cases, women run away and receive medical help and the morning after pill to prevent pregnancy. Some cases of women who tolerated sexual abuse for longer periods of time suggest that the women felt they had little choice or were too afraid or ashamed to escape the situation; added pressure comes from financial need, employment debts, and the desire to support family back home. In some cases men hire migrant workers with whom they already have a relationship to allow her to continue to return to Hong Kong. In other cases, such as the Repulse Bay couple, the woman simply overstays her visa. In many cases I knew of, men and women met outside of the immediate workplace. Some got married but many relationships are temporary and limited to the borders of Hong Kong. In most such cases women eventually lost touch with their former partners, even when children were involved.

16.10 Conclusion

This chapter has traversed some distance in time and space to show that domestic workers in their various forms – the earlier *muijai*, *sohei*, and amahs, and the more recent foreign domestic workers – play various roles within the family. They provide reproductive labor for their master or employer's family and may be considered "like a member of the family," a metaphor that conveys both coercive and affective themes. As I have argued, today's foreign domestic workers – like their predecessors – cannot simply be seen as workers who provide labor to their employer's families. To understand the wider familial situation of contemporary foreign domestic workers, however, requires a much broader lens than was necessary in the past.

Unlike earlier domestic workers who, like their masters or employers, were also Chinese and had their own families in Hong Kong or China, today's foreign domestic workers are often Filipino or Indonesian or from other parts of South and Southeast Asia and belong to a different ethnic and national group from their employers, most of whom are Chinese. Today's FDWs are "global women" in the sense that they are part of a global market in low-paid feminized reproductive labor marketed and promoted by their home countries and employed abroad. They migrate further and are subject to regulations and official controls that did not exist in the time of their earlier counterparts. FDWs, drawn from much farther afield, constitute but one part of many different but overlapping contemporary regimes of mobility, including temporary labor migrants, asylum seekers and refugees, undocumented workers, and local residents and citizens, many of whom are descendants of immigrants to Hong Kong. The intimate patterns of interaction between FDWs and others in Hong Kong require a broader research lens that reveals how mobile people's lives intersect with one another, and often create new kin and family formations that eventually cross sociocultural and physical borders in new ways.

Today, unlike in the early twentieth century, complex and shifting national and international policies, rules, and regulations pertaining to migration and labor serve a critical role in shaping and framing the multiethnic, racialized, and gendered patterns of domestic work in Hong Kong. By 2017 over 350,000 foreign domestic workers provided reproductive labor for Hong Kong's middle-class households. Despite the pressures from both sending and receiving countries to define and restrict them as solely "workers" while abroad, these worker's subjectivities are more complex and their intimate lives are not simply put on hold.

Most migrant workers maintain close contact with family members back home and remit money to them. They also, in some cases, create new permanent or semi-permanent families and kin in Hong Kong. These relationships result in many different types of new family formations. Some former FDWs settle permanently and legally in Hong Kong with local resident spouses. Other women meet documented or undocumented temporary workers or refugees and asylum seekers from many other parts of the world and remain together as couples while both are in Hong Kong. Some such couples have children and struggle to remain together as families given the restrictions of their ability to remain in Hong Kong and to work there legally. Many more couples form temporary families or informal marriages that are limited to Hong Kong in time and space. Some couples break up or lose touch before either leaves Hong Kong. Most lose touch after the father or mother leave Hong Kong. Mothers occasionally give their children for adoption (see Constable 2016), but most take their children back to their country of origin.

Mothers and children who return to Java often face the stigma of being born "out of wedlock." For mixed-race children the situation can be even more fraught. To support the child and escape the stigma, women often go back to work overseas, entering what I have called the migratory cycle of atonement. Mixed-race and foreign-born (or foreign-conceived) children are becoming increasingly visible and common in migrant-sending regions of Java and regions of the Philippines. They face unique challenges, for example gaining access to schooling. Future research is needed to fully appreciate the significance of these new patterns of transnational kinship and family that blur the lines between maids, mistresses, and wives well beyond the borders of Hong Kong.

Notes

1. This once accepted cultural practice would be labeled "human trafficking" today.
2. Many of the concepts introduced in *Global Woman* are important and provocative, but some caveats are needed. Although the recent scale of the movement of women is significant, it is important to note that there are also global men – for example, men from Asia and other regions of the global South who have been recruited to work in wealthier regions of the global North as well (e.g., in construction, the oil industry, as seamen, and also as domestic workers and caregivers). Yet "global men" are, unfortunately, rarely approached as a gendered category of migration (see Margold [1995] for a noteworthy exception). Moreover, although these male labor recruits do not participate in

"intimate labor" as often as migrant women, they face many of the same problems of labor exploitation.

3. www.scmp.com/news/hong-kong/article/1763649/hong-kong-residence-status-nick-cousins-daughter-hangs-balance; www.scmp.com/news/hong-kong/article/1761289/father-daughter-reunited-after-sisters-suicide-leap-repulse-bay-flat; www.scmp.com/news/hong-kong/article/1759835/teen-repulse-bay-death-plunge-had-no-identity-records-just-her-sister; www.scmp.com/news/hong-kong/article/1758631/girl-15-dies-after-fall-repluse-bay-building-parents-arrested. All accessed April 15, 2015.

References

Appadurai, Arjun. 1996. *Modernity at Large: Cultural Dimensions of Globalization*. Minneapolis, MN: University of Minnesota Press.

Baker, Hugh D. R. 1979. *Chinese Family and Kinship*. New York: Columbia University Press.

Boris, Eileen and Rhacel S. Parreñas. 2010. *Intimate Labors: Cultures, Technologies, and the Politics of Care*. Palo Alto, CA: Stanford University Press.

Chan, Carol Zi Lin. 2018. *In Sickness and in Wealth: Morality, Gendered Migration, and Central Java*. Bloomington, IN: Indiana University Press.

Childress, Alice. 1986. *Like One of the Family: Conversations from a Domestic's Life*. Boston, MA: Beacon Press.

Cohen, Myron. 1976. *House United, Housed Divided: The Chinese Family in Taiwan*. New York: Columbia University Press.

Constable, Nicole. 2003. "A Transnational Perspective on Divorce and Marriage: Filipina Wives and Workers." *Identities: Global Studies in Culture and Power* 10: 163–180.

2007 [1997]. *Maid to Order in Hong Kong: Stories of Migrant Workers*, 2nd ed. Ithaca, NY: Cornell University Press.

2009. "The Commodification of Intimacy: Marriage, Sex, and Reproductive Labor." *Annual Review of Anthropology* 38: 49–64.

2014. *Born Out of Place: Migrant Mothers and the Politics of International Labor*. Berkeley, CA: University of California Press.

2016. "Reproductive Labor at the Intersection of Three Intimate Industries: Domestic Work, Sex Tourism, and Adoption." *Positions: Asia Critique* 24(1): 45–69.

Ehrenreich, Barbara and Arlie R. Hochschild. 2004. *Global Woman: Nannies, Maids, and Sex Workers in the New Economy*. New York: Henry Holt and Co.

Gamburd, Michele R. 2000. *The Kitchen Spoon's Handle: Transnationalism and Sri Lanka's Migrant Housemaids*. Ithaca, NY: Cornell University Press.

Gaw, Kenneth. 1991. *Superior Servants: The Legendary Amahs of the Far East*. Singapore: Oxford University Press.

Jaschok, Maria. 1988. *Concubines and Bondservants: The Social History of a Chinese Custom*. Hong Kong: Oxford University Press.

Lan, Pei-Chia. 2006. *Global Cinderellas: Migrant Domestics and Newly Rich Employers in Taiwan*. Durham, NC: Duke University Press.

Margold, Jane. 1995. "Narratives of Masculinity and Transnational Migration." In *Bewitching Women, Pious Men: Gender and Body Politics in Southeast Asia*, ed. Aiwha Ong and Michael Peletz, 274–298. Berkeley, CA: University of California Press.

Parreñas, Rhacel Slazar. 2005. *Children of Global Migration: Transnational Migration and Gendered Woes*. Stanford, CA: Stanford University Press.

Salaff, Janet. 1981. "Ci-li: From Domestic Servant to Government Service." In *Working Daughters of Hong Kong: Filial Piety or Power in the Family*, 156–74. Cambridge: Cambridge University Press.

Sankar, Andrea. 1978. "Female Domestic Service in Hong Kong." In *Female Servants and Economic Development*, ed. Louise Tilly, Susan Berkowitz Luton and Andrea Sankar, 51–62. Michigan Occasional Papers in Women's Studies 1. Ann Arbor, MI: University of Michigan, Women's Studies Program.

Stockard, Janice. 1989. *Daughters of the Canton Delta: Marriage Patterns and Economic Strategies in South China, 1860–1930*. Stanford, CA: Stanford University Press.

Watson, James L. 1980. "Transactions in People: The Chinese Market in Slaves, Servants, and Heirs." In *Asian and African Systems of Slavery*, ed. James L. Watson, 223–250. Oxford: Basil Blackwell.

Watson, Rubie S. 1985. *Inequality among Brothers: Class and Kinship in South China*. Cambridge: Cambridge University Press.

1991. "Wives, Concubines, and Maids: Servitude and Kinship in the Hong Kong Region, 1900–1940." In *Marriage and Inequality in Chinese Society*, ed. Rubie Watson and Patricia Buckley Ebrey, 231–255. Berkeley, CA: University of California Press.

Wolf, Margery. 1968. *The House of Lim: A Study of a Chinese Farm Family*. New York: Appleton-Century-Crofts.

1972. *Women and the Family in Rural Taiwan*. Palo Alto, CA: Stanford University Press.

17

Transnational Adoption

Jessaca Leinaweaver

Transnational adoption is a kinship formation that ostensibly holds notions of the nation-state at its core. As such, it can be analyzed as comparable to other kinship phenomena that bridge national borders, including "transnational marriages" – where the spouses are from two different countries (e.g., Constable 2003; Friedman 2010; Luibhéid and Cantú 2005) – or "transnational families" – that is, the dispersal and separation of immigrant kin, particularly migrant parents and children who remain in the home country (e.g., Dreby 2010; Parreñas 2005). Scholars working on such transnational kinship processes tend to emphasize the connections between people in sending countries and receiving countries (e.g., Appadurai 1991; Glick Schiller, Basch and Szanton Blanc 1992; Hannerz 1996; Ong 1999; Tsing 2005), rather than the disjunctures highlighted in earlier migration frameworks that sought exemplars of assimilation. The fact that we call transnational adoption "transnational" suggests that we should prioritize questions about how this kind of adoption creates links between people in different countries, rather than highlighting the disjunctures it might also entail.

For *transnational* adoption to be a marked kinship formation, we must understand it to be qualitatively different from *domestic* adoption, that is, adoptions that take place within a country's borders. In other words, there is – or so some believe – something distinct about a kind of adoption that creates a new family precisely through overcoming the powerful divisive qualities of national borders (though see Wimmer and Glick Schiller 2002). But there is also another feature of this phrase that is marked – transnational *adoption* as opposed to some other form of transnational exchange, such as the marriages and labor migration already mentioned as well as tourism, child sponsorship, retirement, humanitarian development, or trade. In other words, we also must tackle the presumption that transnational adoption – if it produces transnational connections at all – makes links of a different nature than those other forms of exchange.

My argument in this chapter is that by focusing on the kind of links that transnational adoption produces (and that differentiate it, ostensibly, from other forms of exchange), we can see that the "transnationalism" within transnational adoption is unevenly distributed. By this, I mean that parties to adoption in receiving countries use the metaphor of transnationalism to make sense of the transracial and cross-class relationship they have initiated. However, parties in the sending country do not at all have the same degree of relation to the transnational aspects of such adoption. This comparison exposes the unevenness and inequalities of adoption, using evidence drawn from a transnational plane. We are already familiar with some of the inequalities implicit in adoption as an instance of parent–child relations, given that parents and children (however they came to be so) participate in the hierarchies present in kinship (Leinaweaver 2008, 2013b) and the hierarchies of generation, age, and dependence (Hirschfeld 2002). Critical adoption scholars have pointed to further layers of power differentials in adoption as it is currently practiced, emphasizing the hierarchy between deserving receiver and inadequate giver of a child (Briggs 2012; Gailey 2010; Roberts 2002; Smolin 2005; Solinger 2001). Identifying the uneven distribution of access to "transnationalism" in transnational adoption contributes to these strains of scholarship on kinship hierarchy, adultism, and critical adoption studies. It also, more broadly, exposes the inequalities of other relationships described as transnational, an argument I make in the conclusion.

My own research on transnational adoption has spanned two countries and 15 years. In my first major ethnographic study in Peru, I examined poor and working-class families' kinship practices, which included child fostering and apprenticeships that at times resembled domestic child labor. These practices were framed as helping the child or his/her family, and did not usually result in permanent relocations. I simultaneously shadowed staff in the local branch of the government adoption authority, learning how fostering a child to an unrelated neighbor might be taken as one piece of evidence that a parent had intentionally abandoned his or her child (as indicated in Peru's 2000 Code of Children and Adolescents, Law 27337, article 248.h). As I have argued elsewhere, since the same article states that authorities may not remove a child on the basis of poverty, through this legal pathway "the political economy of parental support is transmuted ... into children who are 'morally and materially abandoned' so that the act of removing a poor person's child can be normalized as moral and beneficial" (Leinaweaver 2008: 46).

It was from a position of having thoroughly plumbed the way the adoption process worked in Peru – and how it sometimes caused "friction" (Tsing 2005) with local kinship practices of longer standing – that I took up a second major research project focusing on the Spanish adoptive parents who had brought Peruvian children into their homes and nation. During the first decade of the twenty-first century, Spain had one of the highest per capita international adoption rates in the world, and at the moment of its 2004 peak, annual numbers of children arriving through international adoption were second only to the United States with the latter's far larger population (Selman 2006, 2009). This high rate of international adoption coincided with one of the lower birth rates in the world (1.32 children per woman in 2012, far below replacement; see Instituto Nacional de Estadística 2014). Through interviewing adoptive parents – sometimes along with their children – as well as psychologists, officials, and researchers who contribute to the Spanish depiction of transnational adoption, and contextualizing them in view of the high rates of transnational migration of laborers and their families from many of the same countries from which adoptees were brought, I argued that what I called "adoptive migration" was particularly revelatory of how "national identity, origin, and substance are constructed in present-day Europe" (Leinaweaver 2013a: 150). This is so because – through international adoption's focus on the national origins as the locus of difference between a child and his or her new parents – "national identity is racialized, embodied, and substantial – an ideology about how people differ" (2013a: 151).

In this chapter, I build on the findings of my ethnographic research in both Peru and Spain, taking my interpretation in a more theoretical direction, as is fitting for a volume on the contemporary forms of kinship theory in anthropology. First, I define "transnational adoption," considering the history of adoption and the kinship work it accomplishes as well as the claims it makes about children's welfare and best interests. I also consider what is implied in current law by that assumption of transnationality: whether it is the place, as national container, or whether it is the citizenship, as substantial assumption of national belonging, that carries weight in such determinations. I then discuss the recent history of transnational adoption and the process of consolidating a transnational adoption. In the remainder of the chapter, I take up the issues transnational adoption raises that are most pertinent to kinship theory. They center around a question: what is so "transnational" about transnational adoption? On one hand, I consider the circulating discourses and rhetorics that parents participate in as they cement the adoption and construct kinship – transnational adoption's analogies to adventure and tourism as well as to humanitarianism and development. On the other hand, I examine how the framing as "transnational" masks other kinds of difference, transracial and cross-class in particular, and what that framing forecloses or avoids. Finally, I argue that positioning the practice under discussion as "transnational adoption" is a linguistic choice that is thoroughly perspectival. It privileges the view of the receiving country and family, and this privileging is visible when we look at how, in sending countries, everything that happens is simply prefatory to "adoption."

I close the chapter by returning to kinship theory and showing how this analysis opens new insights for other anthropological questions – particularly those about transnational connections, global inequalities, power, and privilege.

17.1   The Transnationality of Transnational Adoption

Transnational adoption is surprisingly complicated to define. I begin by defining "adoption," which refers at its most general to one entity taking in, assuming responsibility for, or claiming another. Though I will quickly narrow this definition to emphasize adults legally becoming parents to adoptable children (minors who have been orphaned or whose original parents have lost their parental rights), it is worth remembering that the term is also fairly widely used to describe those who have begun using a new technology, those who take home new pets, those who have agreed to sponsor a stretch of highway or a valued object (Leinaweaver 2008: 171n5), those immigrants who have become naturalized (Coutin 2003: 517), and others (Katz Rothman 2006: 22). In all those cases there is an element of taking in or taking on, of claiming responsibility or authority over something which was not originally one's own.

Formal, legal adoption is traceable in many countries' legal systems to the 1804 French Civil Code, itself informed by Roman law (United Nations 2009: 11; Goody 1969: 59–61). Jack Goody's classic statement on adoption in cross-cultural perspectives suggests that for Western Europe, adoption has a dual focus: providing homes for children who require them, and providing "social progeny" and heirs to childless individuals or couples (Goody 1969: 57). Goody (1969: 59) reminds us it is crucial to distinguish between Roman-style legal adoptions, where legal connections to a first family are severed and replaced by formal ties to a new kin group, and other kinds of informal and flexible fosterage (seen in West Africa in the work of Bledsoe 1990 and Goody 1982; in Oceania as depicted by Carroll 1970 and Carsten 1991; in Latin America as shown by Fonseca 1986 and Leinaweaver 2008; and in minority communities in North America as in Stack 1974 and Strong 2001). The latter are far more widespread worldwide; what we see in North America and Western Europe is globally atypical (Keller 2013). Those legal connections, emphasizing inheritance, show us the importance of property in early Western formulations of adoption (Hann 1998). As Goody explains, "Adoption of the kind that has 'nothing to do with the welfare of children' appears to be connected with vertical as distinct from horizontal systems of inheritance; it provides a descendant, not a collateral" (Goody 1969: 70). Today the complete legal replacement of one kin group by another is referred to by the term plenary or full adoption (as opposed to "simple," which is a form of adoption where the adoptee retains some ties to the birth family – this is the most common form of adoption, although not international adoption, in France; see Perreau 2014: 8). As required by the Hague Adoption Convention of 1993, transnational adoption to Western countries is overwhelmingly plenary.

Let us look for a moment at Goody's observation that adoption can provide homes for children and progeny for the childless. This is a story that makes adoption a win-win, implying a match between the number and kind of available children with what is desired by prospective adopters. Unfortunately for the appealing tidiness of this narrative, such a match empirically does not exist in a majority of instances of international adoption (Graff 2008: 59). The ideal adoptee from the perspective of many waiting prospective parents is a healthy orphaned or abandoned infant (Leinaweaver 2013a: Chapter 1). The population that is "available for adoption" is overwhelmingly older or possessing some kind of health issue or antecedent. There is also a mismatch in the size of these populations. The image of crowded orphanages may be accurate, but it does not reflect available children but rather children who are temporarily residing in orphanages but who have not been "abandoned" (Graff 2008: 61, 63). Meanwhile, the population of "waiting" adults approved to adopt is quite large, over 20,000 per country in a number of European countries – "many of those approved will face a long wait and may never receive a child" (Selman 2009: 591).

The notion that adoption can provide homes for children and progeny for the childless also leaves unstated the reasons that children "need" homes and the reasons that adults "want" children. As described below, children become "available for adoption" because of war, poverty, and underdevelopment. A widely diffused ideology of parenting asserts that it is best for children to be in a family, as opposed to an institution (see Bohr 2010 on the presumptions from attachment theory that ground this claim; and see The Leiden Conference on the Development Care of Children without Permanent Parents 2012 on the recommendation against institutionalization), leading to pressures to find an adoptive family for them. We can see the pro-family ideology, for example, in the UN Convention on the Rights of the Child whose preamble asserts "that the child, for the full and harmonious development of his or her personality, should grow up in a family environment, in an atmosphere of happiness, love and understanding" (United Nations 1995 [1989]). In other words, children "need" homes for two reasons that can be disaggregated: first because they have become separated from their families of origin through unspecified problems, and second because of an existing and widespread ideology that the best place for a child to be reared is in a family.

Meanwhile, the reasons adults are childless and turn to adoption can often be traced to delayed childbearing and structural infertility. As

Marcia Inhorn has observed drawing on a cross-cultural comparison, the primary reasons people have or state that they want to have children are as a form of family social security, to secure gendered social power, and to ensure social perpetuity (Inhorn 2003: 78). My sense of the reasons that middle-class Western adoptive parents want children are related, and are connected to ideologies about what makes a satisfying life, how to be socially respected as an adult, and the desire to self-actualize through caring for a dependent. The reasons that they want those children through transnational adoption in particular – as well as the reasons that sending countries' child welfare programs are willing to place children through international adoption – will be considered below.

Having now defined and explained the motivations for adoption in its unmarked form, I add an additional layer by unpacking what is meant by "transnational" in this context. Let us begin by turning to the principal authority in international law on such matters, the Hague Adoption Convention of 1993 (The Hague 1993), which regulates adoptions with the aid of child protection authorities in those nations that have signed and ratified it. The Convention defines international adoptions as those "where a child habitually resident in one Contracting State ('the State of origin') has been, is being, or is to be moved to another Contracting State ('the receiving State')" (Chapter 1, article 2). In other words, the Hague Convention's focus is specifically on the international relocation of a child (or even the *displacement* of said child, since the Convention frames international adoption as the least preferable outcome following reuniting with kin and being adopted within the child's country, as I discuss below).

So in the Hague's terms, the "transnational" of transnational adoption implies that the parties to the adoption (the parent/s who will adopt and the child to be adopted) are located in different nations. Through the adoption process, the new family will take its place in one of the two countries – specifically, that of the parents' residence. Here is one of the inequalities of transnational adoption – because it intersects with hierarchies of age and dependence, the adults are the ones who determine where the family will reside. Those hierarchies are also overlaid by a global national hierarchy where "sending" countries are situated as inferior to (poorer than, more dangerous than, etc.) "receiving" countries, so that the child's relocation is given a positive spin, hinted at as progress or salvation.

It is worth noting, however, that the adoption laws of the nations that have signed on to the Hague Convention may put things just slightly differently. Having studied international adoption in Peru and Spain, I draw on those countries' laws to illustrate. Peru's Code of Children and Adolescents states, "Adoption by foreigners is subsidiary to adoption by Peruvian nationals[;] … the application of the nationals has precedence." Spain's 2007 International Adoption Law 54/2007 states that international adoption "involves a foreign element, whether the citizenship or the place of residence of either the adopters or the adoptee" (Chapter I, article 1.2). Thus, both Peruvian and Spanish law prioritize status (citizenship) over state (residence). The result is that workarounds are developed for cases when the two systems collide – for example, when Peruvian nationals living in Spain want to adopt a child from Peru, they are given precedence in Peruvian law but still must follow the procedures for international adoption as the Hague requires. And when Bolivian migrants give birth in Spain, and their newborns become under current law Bolivian (and not Spanish) citizens, if a Spanish adult were to adopt such a newborn, it could technically be treated as an international adoption because it involved a "foreign element," although it is not currently processed that way. The more interesting implication is that there is "wide acceptance of an assumption that would make the two statements congruent: that citizens reside in the state to which they belong" (Leinaweaver 2013a: 80).

17.2   A Short History of Transnational Adoptions

Having now staked out a rough definition of the terrain, I will back up to give a broader panorama of where this form of kinship came from. As Laura Briggs and Diana Marre explain succinctly, "transnational adoption emerged out of war" (Briggs and Marre 2009: 1). They point to European fostering of children caught up in the Spanish Civil War and in World War II as early antecedents of transnational adoption (Briggs and Marre 2009: 3–4). Postwar evangelical Christians in the United States began sponsoring children overseas, and one Oregon couple – Bertha and Harry Holt – took such child-sponsoring and fostering initiatives to a new level, adopting eight children from Korea and founding an agency, Holt International, that is still active internationally today (Briggs and Marre 2009: 6; see also Herman 2008; Oh 2015; Kim 2010). Subsequently, different nations "opened" to adoption – Latin American states in the throes of "dirty wars," Eastern European countries in post-Soviet violence or poverty, China as it dealt with the implications of the one-child policy instituted to slow population growth, African nations continuing to experience rampantly uneven development and poverty. Many of these one-time sending countries would close or significantly limit their adoption programs after just a short period due to the difficulties of battling internal corruption, often intense external pressures, and domestic politics (Graff 2008: 60; Kligman 1992). The demographer Peter Selman has charted the "rise and fall" of specific national programs and of the practice of transnational adoption more generally. From the postwar moment to the very recent present, he estimates nearly one million international adoptions have occurred worldwide (Selman 2012: 4).

Since its recent global peak in 2004, worldwide annual numbers of transnational adoptions have notably decreased, which Selman ascribes not to a decrease in demand but rather in shrinking "supply" of children (Selman 2009). As the historian Ellen Herman has argued, stranger (as opposed to kin) adoptions occur in relatively small numbers, but "Adoption's symbolic importance in American life far outstrips its statistical significance" (Herman 2008: 5). Although adoptions – particularly transnational adoptions nowadays – take place ever more rarely, they remain an object of fascination and as such they are an important subject of anthropological inquiry. Using kinship theory to plumb the reasons that transnational adoption fascinates, both in sending and receiving countries, reveals the assumed alignment between kinship, nation-state, and physical appearance that grounds Euro-American local kinship ideologies.

17.3   The Transnational Adoption Process

In its current form, transnational adoption refers also to a lengthy process largely narrated from the perspective of those prospective parents who initiate it. An adult or a couple must choose ("opt") to begin the process, and at the beginning they must make two central decisions that affect the contours of the process: whether to adopt domestically or internationally, and if the latter, from what country (see Jacobson 2008; Seligmann 2013 on this topic)? Historians and anthropologists of adoption have located a powerful narrative that the children available through domestic adoption are somehow less desirable (Ortiz and Briggs 2003; Briggs 2012: 6; Gailey 2010), both scarce because of the availability of birth control and the destigmatization of single parenting, and risky because of the dimension where their birth parents may retain some sense of possession. I observed this in Spain, where prospective parents offered the sense that birth parents' rights were over-emphasized (Marre 2009: 230), although in recent years it appears the pendulum is swinging back to a consideration of available Spanish-born children as candidates for adoption.

Once these decisions have been made, the prospective adopter must undergo an evaluation in order to be officially designated as "suitable" to adopt. This evaluation can take several months, and requires providing evidence of various measures of suitability (such as economic stability, a clean bill of health, and a lack of police record) as well as what many prospective parents experience as intrusive interviews with psychologists and home visits by social workers. The process appears to be more of a ratification of self-selection than a high-stakes evaluation, given evidence from Spain that at the end of this onerous process, 96 percent of applicants there are deemed "suitable" (Dirección General de Servicios para la Familia y la Infancia 2014; Leinaweaver et al 2017).

At this point, the prospective adopter joins a waiting list alongside many others who have been deemed "suitable," and waits an unpredictable length of time before authorities in the selected country identify that adopter as an appropriate parent for a particular child. The focus on the process of transnational adoption from the adopter's view excludes the process of determining how that child became designated as "adoptable" (Leinaweaver 2008: 41–47), however, and it should be noted here – and will be discussed below – that child welfare authorities make this determination independent of whether the child will be traveling internationally or not. In other words, from a sending country's perspective, the child is simply legally "abandoned" and should remain in a children's home until an appropriate adoptive parent can be found, wherever that parent may be.

It is worth restating that globally, in legal arenas, transnational adoptions are already devalued or framed as a second-best alternative. The Hague Convention explicitly states that a domestic placement is preferable to an international one, as noted above. The United Nations Convention on the Rights of the Child states that in deciding through what method a child will be placed with a caregiver, "due regard shall be paid to the desirability of continuity in a child's upbringing and to the child's ethnic, religious, cultural and linguistic background" (article 20.3) and continues that "inter-country adoption may be considered as an alternative means of child's care, if the child cannot be placed in a foster or an adoptive family or cannot in any suitable manner be cared for in the child's country of origin" (article 21.b). Peru's law puts it more simply, citing a subsidiarity principle to require that "adoption by foreigners is subsidiary to adoption by nationals" (2000 Code of Children and Adolescents, Law 27337, article 116). Nonetheless, as we can see in the statistics, transnational adoptions continue to occur, perhaps partly due to the pro-family and anti-institution pressures noted above, as well as to economic features of transnational adoption such as the income it may bring to domestic child welfare programs (see e.g., Dorow 2006: 96) and the existing infrastructure of agencies that "have financial incentives as mediators of [intercountry adoptions] and are heavily invested in obtaining children for adoptive placement" (Davis 2011: 804).

Finally, once the assignment has been made and accepted come the last days of the formal adoption process: generally, the adopter travels to the child's country, meets the child and co-resides with him or her for a determined period, visited periodically by child welfare representatives in order to have the connection be evaluated. Once authorized by the representatives, the adopter may request a new birth certificate and the child's passport so that the child may depart for the receiving country. After any required post-adoption follow-up reports are completed, the adoption process has come to an end and the business of living as a member of an internationally adoptive family takes center stage. In the remainder of this chapter, I examine the implications of this lengthy process and "post-processual" family and civic life for kinship theory, personhood, identity, and global inequality.

17.4   Transnational Adoption and Kinship

As Terrell and Modell observe, raising pressing questions about nation, ethnicity, and culture,

> At core, adoption is about who belongs and how – a subject of immense political as well as disciplinary significance. It is also, and increasingly, about power, privilege, and poverty ... A study of adoption becomes an inquiry into fundamental beliefs about the person and personal connections as these intertwine with political, economic, and historical developments. Taking the perspective of constructed kinship and making the most of the "construction" it entails, so that adoption is not assumed to be univocal or universal in meaning, can advance theories of culture creativity, human agency, and identity formation.
>
> *(Terrell and Modell 1994: 160)*

A flourishing of anthropological research on adoption has occurred in the past two decades (Bowie 2004; Fonseca 1995; Howell 2006; Kim 2010; Leinaweaver 2008, 2013a; Modell 1994; Seligmann 2013; Volkman 2005; Yngvesson 2010, among others). Anthropologists have discovered that adoption has much to teach us about kinship: how it is constructed, how families are made. These are insights that allow us to turn renewed attention on the construction of all kinds of kinship, from staging family photographs (Bouquet 2001) to mourning miscarriage (Layne 2003) to contracting the womb of a surrogate (Ragoné 1994). For example, adult adoptees do important work of identity construction and thinking through what adoption has entailed for them (see Hübinette and Tigervall 2009; Leinaweaver 2011; Trenka, Sudbury and Shin 2006; Yngvesson 2010). In Janet Carsten's interviews with domestically adopted adults who searched for their birth parents, she was told that the search was motivated by the desire " 'to know where I came from,' 'to be complete,' or 'to find out who I am' " (Carsten 2000: 689). At the same time, those who had completed their searches made statements that would "disturb that primacy [of birth ties] ... strongly assert[ing] the values of care and effort that go into the creation of kin ties" (Carsten 2000: 691). Carsten showed that these narratives of adoptive kinship actually reveal a great deal about British concepts of personhood and biography (2000: 694).

Specifically considering transnational adoption raises these same questions that Terrell and Modell developed, with a focus on the nation, the ways its essence is embodied, and what it represents (a concept I have elsewhere framed as "national substance" [Leinaweaver 2013a: 67–68]). In what follows, I consider the implications for kinship of this form of transnational adoption. How is transnational-adoptive kinship produced – largely by parents as agents but also as they interpret their children's accommodations to their new homes and as social workers, psychologists, and legislators develop and articulate interpretations of national and global connectedness? I examine three issues: first, how transnational adoption is contrasted to domestic adoption; second, how transnational adoption is also often transracial and cross-class adoption; and finally, how transnationalism is unevenly distributed within trans-national adoptions, so that the links to another nation are experienced in one direction only.

17.5 Not Domestic

First, it is worth examining the qualifier, transnational. How is trans-national adoption qualitatively different from adoption within a country's borders, i.e., domestic? As one mother who had adopted domestically explained to me in Spain, transnational adoption has "a component of solidarity, another component of adventure or exoti-cism, another component of travel, leaving and returning, all things that domestic adoption doesn't have" (Leinaweaver 2013a: 93). The soli-darity theme that the mother mentions is analogous to a much critiqued undercurrent in transnational adoption, the "rescue narrative" (Briggs 2003). As Karen Dubinsky argues, "We have inherited an adoption system premised on rescue" (Dubinsky 2010: 19). It is not surprising then that transnational adoption is sometimes represented as a philan-thropic or " 'humanitarian' action interchangeable with sending money to support an orphanage or other local development programs" (Bystrom 2012: 224). But as critics of this stance have persuasively shown, an atti-tude of "rescue" puts the adopted child in a very different position than other children and tells more about the parent's self-construction than about the child's best interests (Berástegui Pedro-Viejo 2006: 7; Dorow 2006: 62). Furthermore, as with humanitarian projects more generally, the "rescue" stance precludes engaging with the structural causes of pov-erty and inequality that in these cases produce children's adoptability (Briggs 2003: 180).

The Spanish adoptive mother I quote also highlighted the importance of parents' imaginings of another country, as Emily Noonan also notes when describing US parents of Guatemalans: "Through dialogic and shared travel stories, adoptive parents construct the nature of contact with the country where their children were born and thus produce their own imagined worlds, and senses of the 'rest of the world' " (Noonan

2007: 310). Noonan's point is that adults become parents through transnational adoption precisely in the "non-spaces" of travel (Noonan 2007: 312).

Both the notion of rescuing/humanitarianism and of travel/adventure draw on the transnationalism of transnational adoption. As Laura Briggs has argued, visualizations of waifs and ideas about adoption told "American publics how to think about what was termed the Third World" (Briggs 2003: 198). Classic studies of tourism point to the self-actualizing value of encountering difference – for example in Erik Cohen's statement that "modern tourism involves a *generalized* interest in or appreciation of that which is different, strange or novel in comparison with what the traveller is acquainted with in his cultural world" (Cohen 1979: 182). In both humanitarianism and tourism, travelers encounter difference and use it to make sense of the other as well as of themselves. When this happens in the course of legally becoming a parent, the adoption project is fused with a pleasurable encounter with "that which is different, strange or novel" as well as a lesson about what makes one's own "cultural world" valuable.

17.6 (Transracial and Cross-Class) Adoption

A second observation one can make about the "transnational" in transnational adoption is that it is not only opposed to "domestic," but also replaces other possible modifiers. In particular, I note that such adoptions are also often "transracial" and "cross-class" but that emphasizing the transnational permits those other more thorny crossings to be left unexplored. In part this is of course a function of the fact that because these adoptions unfold between child protection authorities of two nations, international conventions and law regulate their practice. But at a more symbolic level, it is also the case that "transnational" evokes international exchange, a model UN, while transracial raises the concerns that a white parent may be unprepared or unable to teach their children of color what they need to know in order to "survive in a racist society," as the "Position Statement on Trans-Racial Adoption" by the US National Association of Black Social Workers stated in 1972 (Bremner 1974: 777). Instead, parents may encode race in talk of national culture which "is arguably a mechanism for avoiding engagement ... with practices of racial discrimination that affect adopted children" (Yngvesson 2010: 202n13). So, for instance, as Katrien De Graeve has written about the adoption of black Ethiopian children in Flanders, Belgium,

> Adoptive parents state that they realize their child is prone to racialization and discrimination. They say that this inspires them to develop strategies to empower the child against it. Remarkably

enough the parents indicate that their major strategy consists of giving the child pride in [his or her] own (i.e., Ethiopian) culture. It could be argued that although meant as a strategy against stigmatization, the parents' cultural labour is at the same time stressing the impossibility of a black person's becoming Flemish.

(De Graeve 2010: 371)

And as Christine Gailey observes, "the significance of class mobility in adoption has received short shrift in the adoption literature" (Gailey 2010: 121–122). The emphasis on transnationality means that adoptive parents may "conflate [their child's background] with their child's social class or an image of underdevelopment from the child's country of origin" (Gailey 2010: 145). For example, one adoptive mother I interviewed in Spain told me that her youngest daughter, who was almost ten when she was adopted, had adapted more successfully than her other children, who were younger at the time of their adoption. The mother's interpretation was that her daughter, having known life as a Peruvian and the reality of Peru, had no desire or yearnings to return, unlike children adopted when they are younger. As the mother told me almost wryly, quite aware of the implications of what she was observing, "She knows she is better off here … she has more things!" (Leinaweaver 2013a: 43). This is an apt observation, but one that also plays up the difference between "here" and Peru while neither probing the reasons it exists nor questioning the connection between those reasons and the practice of transnational adoption.

Returning to Terrell and Modell's linkages between adoption, belonging, power, and agency (Terrell and Modell 1994: 160), the implications of the focus on transnational (instead of domestic on one hand, and trans-racial or cross-class on the other) for anthropology and kinship become clear. As parents construct adoptive kinship through drawing on tropes of travel and otherness – tourism and humanitarianism – that are not available to those who adopt domestically, they also create the possibility of downplaying their child's racialized otherness, which is potentially important in a context where kinship implies racial "matching," as is the case in Spain and elsewhere, for example Israel (Bergmann 2011; Kahn 2000). Furthermore, they can take the class difference and positively reinterpret it not so much as an index of the power and privilege disparities that underlie international adoption, but as almost a justification of the relocation of their child (Leinaweaver 2015: 92). What is not said is as important as what *is* said for constructing adoptive kinship (Frekko, Leinaweaver and Marre 2015), and this is also going to be true for other forms of kinship. Furthermore, as Terrell and Modell remind us, really probing the construction of kinship "can advance theories of culture creativity, human agency, and identity formation" (Terrell and Modell 1994: 160). We see that identity is formed dialogically with adoptive parents in particular agentively and creatively conceptualizing national culture, as a proxy for other more sensitive vectors of belonging and unbelonging.

17.7   Transnationalism As Unevenly Distributed within Adoption

My focus until now has been largely on the work that transnational adoptive parents do, supported by ideologies and representatives of social work, psychology, and law. This makes some sense, as – befitting current Western ideologies of middle-class "parenting" – much of the burden is placed on those parents to research and act in such a way that they make the best possible environment for their child to grow up in. They are the agents, whose choice (recalling, as Goody tells us, that the Latin root of "adoption" bespeaks "choice, option" – 1969: 58) has generated a child's transnational relocation. As Lovelock puts it, international adoption "is instigated and achieved by individuals who are motivated by individual concerns and needs ... within a particular domestic/international/ political context" (Lovelock 2000: 910). Without delving fully into the implications of a transnational adoption for a birth mother, or others in a "sending country," some brief observations can be appended. First is that the transnationalism of the adoption is far less relevant from her perspective. It does not mean that powerful new ties to receiving countries have been forged for her through the adoption – her parental rights have been terminated. However, poignantly, it may mean that she or other birth family members imagine there to be the possibility that a child will return after being educated abroad, as Roby and Matsamura (2002) have shown in the Marshall Islands (see also Smolin 2005). It may also mean that it is far more difficult in terms of sheer logistics for her to make any effort to reclaim a child (Briggs 2012; Posocco 2015).

Focusing briefly on the birth family members in the "sending country" reveals that from some perspectives, the transnationalism in transnational adoption may be symbolically irrelevant. It matters as part of the material out of which adoptive parents in the West construct their new kinship relations and support their child's identity development – but in the sending country, it is largely a logistical barrier, and broadly a sign of a country's poverty or low geopolitical standing. Indeed, the latter is evidenced in the sending country's relative weakness in being able to affect or control the outcome of the adoption in later years: for example, a Spanish news source quoted a Chinese diplomat who beseeched Spanish adoptive parents to "maintain the child's cultural roots, because even though it is true that the children are very happy here, sometimes they forget to learn Chinese and they forget the Chinese culture; I hope that in the future they study Chinese for their own good and for the development of Sino-Iberian relations" (Noticias EFE 2011). This diplomat's statement makes clear that the adoptive parents are the ones who may elect, or not, to allow the "transnationalism" of the adoption to seed further exchanges and positive international relations between sending and receiving country. From this perspective, we can see that the "transnational" in transnational adoption matters most primarily and initially for the adoptive parents, and we can turn to focus on what they do with it, as well as what it conceals. Globalization and geopolitical inequality have produced new possibilities for how Western individuals contemplate and produce the connections of kinship. However, it has not done the same for how those in the global South experience the loss of kinship.

17.8   Conclusion: Just Adoption

I have argued in this chapter that despite the legal structures and elements of tourism and humanitarianism that infuse it, the phrase "transnational adoption" is in some ways a misdirection of focus. As anthropologists of kinship it will benefit us to distinguish carefully between several issues. First is what "transnational" allows adoptive parents to do – the way it helps them to construct themselves as creators of kinship and as meaningfully tied to a sending country. Second and closely related is what "transnational" can do as a tool through which parents offer their children ways of constructing identity and personhood – and importantly how the children themselves, in shifting ways as they grow up (see Johnson-Hanks 2002), deploy, or cancel that tool. Third however is what "transnational" is not, or what it masks: the ways in which the *sending* side of transnational adoption is all too domestic, local, and mundane. What happens in the sending country is just that a child is deemed adoptable, with the decision over the child's ultimate destination a separate matter. Birth family members do not imagine creative links between themselves and their ex-children's new countries – or if they do, they do so mistakenly for the loss of parental rights means that their former children no longer possess any legal ties to them.

I suggest that this rethinking of what "transnational" offers and masks in such kinship practices can be usefully applied to other relationships described as transnational. Perhaps transnational marriages also are premised on and coproduce significant geopolitical inequalities, as Friedman (2010) shows in the way that Chinese brides are legally conceptualized in Taiwan, and as Yuh (2002) has proposed for the experiences of Korean military brides in the United States. Similarly, perhaps the separated families that characterize contemporary migration materialize global inequalities, with "reunified" kin subjected to limiting exceptions on their ability to work (as is the case in Spain; see

Leinaweaver 2013a: 165n11) and the motivation of providing a better life for one's children through separation from the child being questioned by children around the world (Dreby 2010; Leinaweaver 2013a: 70; Parreñas 2005; Pribilsky 2001). It is becoming evident that the optimism contained in the 1990s-era transnationalism framework, while productively locating the dense network of ties between nations that are materialized in transnational migration, understates the ways that geopolitical hierarchies and national thinking limit the possibilities for the disempowered party in a transnational relationship.

What remains then is just "adoption," which infuses new understandings of belonging, power, and agency (Terrell and Modell 1994: 160) into our models of transnationalism, inequality, and globalization. Whether occurring across national, racial, or class borders, contemporary adoption (most especially of the plenary and "closed" variety) reproduces those borders through drawing on the power of the state, and the pediatric disciplines, to designate particular children who may transgress those boundaries. Sociologist Barbara Katz Rothman points out that "we also routinely distinguish between a child 'by adoption' and a child 'of one's own'" (Katz Rothman 2006: 22), a differentiation for which it matters little that the child is from another place or class or racial context. The wide-ranging consequences of contemporary adoption are still only partially understood, but they involve unfurling a new tool for adults to conceptualize themselves and the nation; situating young people in unfamiliar contexts with which they must grapple as they mature; and framing birth family members and sending countries as unsuitable locations for children to develop and thrive. The case of adoption reveals dramatically the key position kinship theory can play in helping scholars to disentangle a range of broad and pressing questions.

References

Appadurai, Arjun. 1991. "Global Ethnoscapes: Notes and Queries for a Transnational Anthropology." In *Recapturing Anthropology*, ed. R. Fox, 191–210. Santa Fe, NM: School of American Research Press.

Berástegui Pedro-Viejo, Ana. 2006. "Adopción internacional: ¿solidaridad con la infancia o reproducción asistida?" In *I Forum Internacional de Infancia y Familias "De Filias y Fobias." Del parentesco biológico al cultural: la adopción y otras formas de construcción de familias diversas.* Barcelona.

Bergmann, Sven. 2011. "Reproductive Agency and Projects: Germans Searching for Egg Donation in Spain and the Czech Republic." *Reproductive BioMedicine Online* 23: 600–608.

Bledsoe, Caroline H. 1990. "'No Success without Struggle': Social Mobility and Hardship for Foster Children in Sierra Leone." *Man* 25(1): 70–88.

Bohr, Yvonne. 2010. "Transnational Infancy: A New Context for Attachment and the Need for Better Models." *Child Development Perspectives* 4(3): 189–196.

Bouquet, Mary. 2001. "Making Kinship, with an Old Reproductive Technology." In *Relative Values: Reconfiguring Kinship Studies*, ed. S. Franklin and S. McKinnon, 85–115. Durham, NC: Duke University Press.

Bowie, Fiona, ed. 2004. *Cross-Cultural Approaches to Adoption*. London: Routledge.

Bremner, Robert H. 1974. *Children and Youth in America: A Documentary History*, 3. Cambridge, MA: Harvard University Press.

Briggs, Laura. 2003. "Mother, Child, Race, Nation: The Visual Iconography of Rescue and the Politics of Transnational and Transracial Adoption." *Gender & History* 15(2): 179–200.

   2012. *Somebody's Children: The Politics of Transracial and Transnational Adoption*. Durham, NC: Duke University Press.

Briggs, Laura and Diana Marre. 2009. "Introduction." In *International Adoption: Global Inequalities and the Circulation of Children*, ed. D. Marre and L. Briggs. New York: New York University Press.

Bystrom, Kerry. 2012. "On 'Humanitarian' Adoption (Madonna in Malawi)." *Humanity* 2(2): 213–231.

Carroll, Vern. 1970. "Adoption on Nukuoro." In *Adoption in Eastern Oceania*, ed. V. Carroll, 121–157. Honolulu, HI: University of Hawai'i Press.

Carsten, Janet. 1991. "Children in Between: Fostering and the Process of Kinship on Pulau Langkawi, Malaysia." *Man* 26: 425–443.

   2000. "'Knowing Where You've Come From': Ruptures and Continuities of Time and Kinship in Narratives of Adoption Reunions." *Journal of the Royal Anthropological Institute* 6(4): 687–703.

Cohen, Erik. 1979. "A Phenomenology of Tourist Experiences." *Sociology* 13(2): 179–201.

Constable, Nicole. 2003. *Romance on a Global Stage: Pen Pals, Virtual Ethnography, and "Mail-Order" Marriages*. Berkeley, CA: University of California Press.

Coutin, Susan Bibler. 2003. "Cultural Logics of Belonging and Movement: Transnationalism, Naturalization, and U.S. Immigration Politics." *American Ethnologist* 30(4): 508–526.

Davis, Mary Ann. 2011. "Intercountry Adoption Flows from Africa to the U.S.: A Fifth Wave of Intercountry Adoptions?" *International Migration Review* 45(4): 784–811.

De Graeve, Katrien. 2010. "The Limits of Intimate Citizenship: Reproduction of Difference in Flemish-Ethiopian 'Adoption Cultures.'" *Bioethics* 24(7): 365–372.

Dirección General de Servicios para la Familia y la Infancia. 2014. *Boletín de datos estadísticos de medidas de protección a la infancia 2011*. Ministerio de Sanidad, Servicios Sociales e Igualdad.

Dorow, Sara K. 2006. *Transnational Adoption: A Cultural Economy of Race, Gender, and Kinship*. New York: New York University Press.

Dreby, Joanna. 2010. *Divided by Borders: Mexican Migrants and Their Children*. Berkeley, CA: University of California Press.

Dubinsky, Karen. 2010. *Babies without Borders: Adoption and Migration across the Americas*. Toronto: University of Toronto Press.

Fonseca, Claudia. 1986. "Orphanages, Foundlings, and Foster Mothers: The System of Child Circulation in a Brazilian Squatter Settlement." *Anthropological Quarterly* 59(1): 15–27.

——. 1995. *Caminhos da adoção*. São Paolo: Cortez Editora.

Frekko, Susan E., Jessaca B. Leinaweaver and Diana Marre. 2015. "How (Not) to Talk about Adoption: On Communicative Vigilance in Spain." *American Ethnologist* 42(4): 703–719.

Friedman, Sara E. 2010. "Marital Immigration and Graduated Citizenship: Post-Naturalization Restrictions on Mainland Chinese Spouses in Taiwan." *Pacific Affairs* 83(1): 73–93.

Gailey, Christine Ward. 2010. *Blue-Ribbon Babies and Labors of Love: Race, Class, and Gender in U.S. Adoption Practice*. Austin, TX: University of Texas Press.

Glick Schiller, Nina, Linda Basch and Cristina Szanton Blanc. 1992. "Transnationalism: A New Analytic Framework for Understanding Migration." In *Toward a Transnational Perspective on Migration: Race, Class, Ethnicity, and Nationalism Reconsidered*, ed. N. Glick Schiller, L. Basch and C. Szanton Blanc, 1–24. New York: New York Academy of Sciences.

Goody, Esther N. 1982. *Parenthood and Social Reproduction: Fostering and Occupational Roles in West Africa*. Cambridge: Cambridge University Press.

Goody, Jack. 1969. "Adoption in Cross-Cultural Perspective." *Comparative Studies in Society and History* 2: 55–78.

Graff, E. J. 2008. "The Lie We Love." *Foreign Policy* 169: 59–66.

Hann, C. M. 1998. *Property Relations: Renewing the Anthropological Tradition*. Cambridge: Cambridge University Press.

Hannerz, Ulf. 1996. *Transnational Connections: Culture, People, Places*. London/New York: Routledge.

Herman, Ellen. 2008. *Kinship by Design: A History of Adoption in the Modern United States*. Chicago, IL: University of Chicago Press.

Hirschfeld, Lawrence. 2002. "Why Don't Anthropologists Like Children?" *American Anthropologist* 104(2): 611–627.

Howell, Signe. 2006. *The Kinning of Foreigners: Transnational Adoption in a Global Perspective*. Oxford/New York: Berghahn Books.

Hübinette, Tobias and Carina Tigervall. 2009. "To Be Non-White in a Colour-Blind Society: Conversations with Adoptees and Adoptive Parents in Sweden on Everyday Racism." *Journal of Intercultural Studies* 30(4): 335–353.

Inhorn, Marcia C. 2003. *Local Babies, Global Science: Gender, Religion, and In Vitro Fertilization in Egypt*. New York: Routledge.

Instituto Nacional de Estadística. 2014. *Indicadores demográficos básicos*.

Jacobson, Heather. 2008. *Culture Keeping: White Mothers, International Adoption, and the Negotiation of Family Difference*. Nashville, TN: Vanderbilt University Press.

Johnson-Hanks, Jennifer. 2002. "On the Limits of Life Stages in Ethnography: Toward a Theory of Vital Conjunctures." *American Anthropologist* 104(3): 865–880.

Kahn, Susan. 2000. *Reproducing Jews: A Cultural Account of Assisted Conception in Israel*. Durham, NC: Duke University Press.

Katz Rothman, Barbara. 2006. "Adoption and the Culture of Genetic Determinism." In *Adoptive Families in a Diverse Society*, ed. K. Wegar, 19–28. New Brunswick, NJ: Rutgers University Press.

Keller, H. 2013. "Attachment and Culture." *Journal of Cross-Cultural Psychology* 44: 175–194.

Kim, Eleana Jean. 2010. *Adopted Territory: Transnational Korean Adoptees and the Politics of Belonging*. Durham, NC: Duke University Press.

Kligman, Gail. 1992. "Abortion and International Adoption in Post-Ceausescu Romania." *Feminist Studies* 18: 405–419.

Layne, Linda L. 2003. *Motherhood Lost: A Feminist Account of Pregnancy Loss in America*. New York: Routledge.

Leinaweaver, Jessaca. 2008. *The Circulation of Children: Kinship, Adoption, and Morality in Andean Peru*. Durham, NC: Duke University Press.

——— 2011. "Kinship Paths to and from the New Europe: A Unified Analysis of Peruvian Adoption and Migration." *Journal of Latin American and Caribbean Anthropology* 16(2): 380–400.

——— 2013a. *Adoptive Migration: Raising Latinos in Spain*. Durham, NC: Duke University Press.

——— 2013b. "Toward an Anthropology of Ingratitude: Notes from Andean Kinship." *Comparative Studies in Society and History* 55(3): 1–25.

——— 2015. "Transnational Fathers, Good Providers, and the Silences of Adoption." In *Globalized Fatherhood*, ed. M. C. Inhorn, W. Chavkin and J.-A. Navarro, 81–102. New York: Berghahn Books.

——— 2017. Jessaca Leinaweaver, Diana Marre, and Susan Frekko. "'Homework' and Transnational Adoption Screening in Spain: The Co-Production of Home and Family." *Journal of the Royal Anthropological Institute* 23(3): 562–579. [10.1111/1467-9655.12652]

Lovelock, Kirsten. 2000. "Intercountry Adoption As a Migratory Practice: A Comparative Analysis of Intercountry Adoption and Immigration Policy and Practice in the United States, Canada and New Zealand in the Post W.W. II Period." *The International Migration Review* 34(3): 907–949.

Luibhéid, Eithne and Lionel Cantú. 2005. *Queer Migrations: Sexuality, U.S. Citizenship, and Border Crossings*. Minneapolis, MN: University of Minnesota Press.

Marre, Diana. 2009. "'We Do Not Have Immigrant Children at This School, We Just Have Children Adopted from Abroad': Flexible Understandings of Children's 'Origins.'" In *International Adoption: Global Inequalities and the Circulation of Children*, ed. D. Marre and L. Briggs, 226–243. New York: New York University Press.

Modell, Judith S. 1994. *Kinship with Strangers: Adoption and Interpretations of Kinship in American Culture*. Berkeley, CA: University of California Press.

Noonan, Emily J. 2007. "Adoption and the Guatemalan Journey to American Parenthood." *Childhood* 14(3): 301–319.

Noticias EFE. 2 July 2011. "Caen un 80% las adopciones de niños procedentes de China." *El Norte de Castilla*.

Oh, Arissa. 2015. *To Save the Children of Korea*. Stanford, CA: Stanford University Press.

Ong, Aihwa. 1999. *Flexible Citizenship: The Cultural Logics of Transnationality*. Durham, NC: Duke University Press.

Ortiz, Ana Teresa and Laura Briggs. 2003. "Crack, Abortion, the Culture of Poverty, and Welfare Cheats: The Making of the 'Healthy White Baby Crisis.'" *Social Text* 75(September): 39–57.

Parreñas, Rhacel Salazar. 2005. *Children of Global Migration: Transnational Families and Gendered Woes*. Stanford, CA: Stanford University Press.

Perreau, Bruno. 2014. *The Politics of Adoption: Gender and the Making of French Citizenship*. London: The MIT Press.

Posocco, Silvia. 2015. "Substance, Sign, and Trace: Performative Analogies and Technologies of Enfleshment in the Transnational Adoption Archives in Guatemala." *Social & Cultural Geography* 16(5): 567–584.

Pribilsky, Jason. 2001. "'Nervios' and 'Modern' Childhood: Migration and Shifting Contexts of Child Life in the Ecuadorian Andes." *Childhood: A Journal of Global Research* 8(2): 251–273.

Ragoné, Helena. 1994. *Surrogate Motherhood: Conception in the Heart*. Boulder, CO: Westview Press.

Roberts, Dorothy E. 2002. *Shattered Bonds: The Color of Child Welfare*. New York: Basic Books.

Roby, J. L. and S. Matsumura. 2002. "If I Give You My Child, Aren't We Family?" *Adoption Quarterly* 5: 7–31.

Seligmann, Linda J. 2013. *Broken Links, Enduring Ties: American Adoption across Race, Class, and Nation*. Stanford, CA: Stanford University Press.

Selman, Peter. 2006. "Trends in Intercountry Adoption: Analysis of Data from 20 Receiving Countries, 1998–2004." *Journal of Population Research* 23(2): 183–204.

2009. "The Rise and Fall of Intercountry Adoption in the 21st Century." *International Social Work* 52: 575–594.

2012. "Global Trends in Intercountry Adoption: 2001–2010." *Adoption Advocate* 44: 1–17.

Smolin, David M. 2005. "Intercountry Adoption As Child Trafficking." *Valparaiso Law Review* 39(2): 281–325.

Solinger, Rickie. 2001. *Beggars and Choosers: How the Politics of Choice Shapes Adoption, Abortion, and Welfare in the United States*. New York: Hill and Wang.

Stack, Carol B. 1974. *All Our Kin: Strategies for Survival in a Black Community*. New York: Harper & Row.

Strong, Pauline Turner. 2001. "To Forget Their Tongue, Their Name, and Their Whole Relation: Captivity, Extra-Tribal Adoption, and the Indian Child Welfare Act." *In Relative Values: Reconfiguring Kinship Studies*, ed. S. Franklin and S. McKinnon, 468–493. Durham, NC: Duke University Press.

Terrell, John and Judith S. Modell. 1994. "Anthropology and Adoption." *American Anthropologist* 96(1): 155–161.

The Hague. 1993. Hague Convention on Intercountry Adoption.

The Leiden Conference on the Development Care of Children without Permanent Parents. 2012. "The Development and Care of Institutionally Reared Children." *Child Development Perspectives* 6(2): 174–180.

Trenka, Jane Jeong, Julia Sudbury and Sun Yung Shin. 2006. *Outsiders Within: Writing on Transracial Adoption*. Cambridge, MA: South End Press.

Tsing, Anna Lowenhaupt. 2005. *Friction: An Ethnography of Global Connection*. 1 v. Princeton, NJ: Princeton University Press.

United Nations. 1995 [1989] "The United Nations Convention on the Rights of the Child." *In Children and the Politics of Culture*, ed. S. Stephens, 335–352. Princeton, NJ: Princeton University Press.

2009. *Child Adoption: Trends and Policies*. Department of Economic and Social Affairs, Population Division.

Volkman, Toby, ed. 2005. *Cultures of Transnational Adoption*. Durham, NC: Duke University Press.

Wimmer, Andreas and Nina Glick Schiller. 2002. "Methodological Nationalism and Beyond: Nation-State Building, Migration and the Social Sciences." *Global Networks* 2(4): 301–334.

Yngvesson, Barbara. 2010. *Belonging in an Adopted World: Race, Identity, and Transnational Adoption*. Chicago, IL: The University of Chicago Press.

Yuh, Ji-Yeon. 2002. *Beyond the Shadow of Camptown: Korean Military Brides in America*. New York: New York University Press.

18

Kinship in Transnational Encounters: Filipino Migrants As "Ideal Brides" in Rural Japan

Lieba Faier

In recent years, scholars have begun to explore how kin relationships are reproduced and transformed through transnational migration flows. These approaches challenge earlier studies that assumed that cultural processes, including kinship practices, were contained by ethnic, local, or national borders. We now know that kinship transgresses national borders and that transnational migration can both reinforce and transform kinship meanings and practices. Scholars have found that kinship ties motivate transnational migration (Boehm 2012; Brennan 2004; Constable 1997, 1999; Ong 1999; Parreñas 2005; Pratt and Philippine Women Centre of B.C. 2012). Moreover, they have shown that migrants engage in diverse strategies to negotiate, cultivate, and maintain kin ties as they physically and emotionally move between social worlds (Boehm 2012; Chavez 2013; Constable 1997, 1999; Ong 1999; Parreñas 2005; Pratt Philippine Women Centre of B.C. 2012). What kinds of new kinship understandings and practices does transnational migration enable? What strategies do transmigrants engage in to maintain kin ties in their home countries and how do these practices affect formations of kinship there? How do transmigrants' everyday practices link their home and host communities while contributing to the reproduction and transformation of kinship in both locales?

In this chapter, I explore these questions by considering how Filipina migrants married to Japanese men in Nagano's rural Kiso Valley reproduce and transform what it means to be *oyomesan*, "a traditional Japanese bride and daughter-in-law," while maintaining a strong sense of Filipina identity and ties with their families in the Philippines.[1] Filipina wives of Japanese men maintain kinship ties in both Japan and the Philippines: as they perform their roles as brides and daughters-in-law in their Japanese households, they also send resources to and maintain family attachments in the Philippines. Their commitments to their families in the Philippines inform their decisions to join kin networks in Japan; and their kinship practices in Japan enable them to fulfill obligations to family members in the Philippines. Many also travel between the two countries, and thus two kin groups, on a regular basis. How is their movement between these two worlds affecting what it means to be *oyomesan* in rural Japan?

To understand how the role of the "*yome*" (the informal Japanese word for *oyomesan*) is being, at once, reproduced and transformed through transnational relationships involving Filipina migrants and rural Japanese residents, we need to consider how Filipina migrants' understandings of kinship aligned and misaligned with those of the Japanese communities. I found that although resonances existed between these Filipina women and their Japanese families' views of the women's roles in their Japanese households, "being *oyomesan*" often meant very different things to members of these groups.

Here I consider how Filipinas' performances of their roles as *oyomesan* emerge in the alignments, misunderstandings, and gaps between ideas about gender and kinship circulating in Japan and the Philippines. I consider the subtle and significant ways these women are changing meanings of kinship in rural Japan as they move between two cultural worlds. As these women participate in kin groups in both Japan and the Philippines, they bring discrepant histories, cultural practices, and forms of meaning and desire into encounter. I argue that new kinship meanings and practices emerge through the processes of cultural encounter that their transmigration enables. I show that transnational migration reshapes meanings of kinship as it brings into encounter diverse cultural understandings, stakes, and desires.

Most Filipina wives in Central Kiso were raised in Catholic households and lived, or had regular contact, with large extended families. Many viewed their decision to come to Japan as a migrant laborer as a "sacrifice" to assist their natal families, sometimes drawing on Catholic idioms to liken their experiences in Japan to their "trials." They also discussed their desire to work abroad as reflecting a feeling of *utang na loob*, literally in Tagalog "a debt of the inside," a term used to express a feeling of debt or gratitude toward one's parents or others who have cared for one.[2]

In contrast, the Japanese term *yome/oyomesan* generally refers to the position of the bride and daughter-in-law in a Japanese *ie*, a kinship formation in Japan that is usually translated as the "corporate household." Scholars have argued that as a form of kinship organization, the *ie* is based on principles of successional continuity of the group (as opposed to the continuity of the individual in, for instance, a Western family) (Bachnik 1983; Nakane 1967). The organization is based around "roles" (i.e., *yome* [bride/daughter-in-law]; *shūtome* [mother-in-law], etc.), which

people temporarily occupy during their lifetimes. The primary consideration is each member's participation in sustaining the *ie* through
their performance of this role (Bachnik 1983; Nakane 1967). Although
the Occupation-inspired Civil Code of 1947 legislated the *ie* out of existence, it still is an important cultural category in Japan (Bachnik 1983;
Kondo 1990).[3] When the *ie* was first institutionalized by the Japanese government in Japan during the late nineteenth century, it was defined in
contrast to a modern, Western nuclear family (Sand 2003). Linked to the
nationalist movement, it has come to be popularly associated with a traditional, rural, and essentially Japanese way of life.[4]

For decades, kinship scholars focused exclusively on the experiences
of people on the Japanese archipelago that identify as Japanese to understand "Japanese kinship." These studies overlooked how kinship categories in Japan are reproduced and transformed through transnational
relationships. Yet we need to understand these dynamics if we are to
grasp how meanings of kinship, culture, and identity are reproduced and
transformed in a global interconnected world. Even presumably "traditional" forms of kinship such as the "Japanese *oyomesan*" are reproduced,
and in the process transformed, through the ways that transnational
migration brings different ideas about relatedness and kinship practice
into productive relation.

In what follows, I begin by offering some historical background about
Central Kiso and Filipina–Japanese marriages so that we can understand the discrepant stakes and desires Filipina migrants and Japanese
residents brought to their relationships. I then explore some of the
ways that Filipina women's performances of their role emerged in
the resonances and gaps between their understandings of kinship and
those of the Japanese communities. I demonstrate that these women's
performances of their role as *oyomesan* was shaped by both Japanese
residents' investments in sustaining a particular way of life in the region
and Filipina migrants' ideas about what it meant to be a Filipina, a good
Catholic, and a middle-class mother and housewife in the Philippines. As
these culturally specific stakes came into alignment and misalignment,
they at once enabled the reproduction of the role of the *yome* and shifted
what this role entailed.

18.1   Marginality and International Marriage in the Kiso Valley

Japanese residents' characterization of Filipina migrants as ideal *oyomesan*
is particularly puzzling because most Filipina wives in Central Kiso had
come to the region on "entertainer visas" to work in local Filipina hostess
bars. These bars are considered part of the sex industry, and Filipina
women working in them are widely disparaged as prostitutes and

foreigners. How could a Filipina woman go from being viewed as a "prostitute" and "foreigner" to being identified as an "*ii oyomesan*," an "ideal traditional Japanese bride?" Some Japanese residents even described these women as better and more desirable *yome* than contemporary Japanese women! To understand how and why this has become possible, we need to consider the context in which Japanese residents of Central Kiso have become open to viewing and treating Filipina migrants as ideal brides and daughters-in-law.

The Kiso Valley is a mountainous river valley in southwestern Nagano Prefecture. I call the central portion of the Valley where I worked "Central Kiso." Like much of rural Japan, which has suffered ongoing trends of urbanization and industrialization, Central Kiso's economy is quite depressed. The region shares many of the socioeconomic challenges that have become pronounced throughout rural Japan. These include: an absence of viable industry and, correspondingly, jobs; depopulation caused by increasing urban migration and resulting in both shrinking tax revenues and an aging local community; and, what locals called, a "bride shortage" (*yomebusoku*), by which they meant a shortage of young Japanese women interested in marrying local men, many of whom were eldest sons who remained in the area to inherit family land and care for aging parents.

These socioeconomic problems have become especially pronounced since the late 1980s and early 1990s as many of the engines driving Japanese postwar growth stalled out and the nation's economy was incorporated into the global economy in new ways. In the years following World War II, the national government launched a campaign to reforest mountainsides denuded by war mobilization and industrialization. The Central Kiso region housed a thriving forestry industry as these campaigns, which promised modern, scientific forestry techniques that would bring a prosperous future to mountainous regions, created jobs and brought workers to Kiso region. However, the high growth economy of these decades also created lumber shortages, and in the 1960s, Japan began importing large quantities of less expensive wood from Southeast Asia, North America, and Siberia. This imported wood soon replaced more costly domestic timber and transformed rural economies in forestry regions like Kiso.

To revitalize the Kiso economy, the local government turned to domestic tourism, as many rural governments in Japan have attempted to do over the past several decades. The Kiso Valley is home to a constellation of post-towns (*shukubamachi*) that flourished along the *Kisoji* (Kiso Highway) under the Tokugawa Shogunate (1603–1867). Historical inns and other structures remain in the region, particularly in the southern Kiso Valley. During the 1970s, a historical tourism boom in Japan drew domestic tourists to the area, and the Central Kiso economy benefited from the large numbers of travelers visiting the region. However, by the mid-1980s, efforts to attract tourism to the central region of the Kiso

Valley, where most historic buildings had burned in a fire, had faltered, and the tourism boom in the southern region had leveled off so that the Central Valley no longer benefited much from it. When, in 1998, I began conducting 23 months of ethnographic research in Central Kiso, local residents still endeavored to develop historical and environmental tourism in the area; however, they also spoke with bitterness about the ways that the "Kisoji Boom" had simply been a "fad" for fickle urbanites who objectified rural areas as part of a disappearing Japanese past while disparaging and neglecting these regions.

Although Central Kiso had in some sense benefited from, and identified with, Japan's postwar national affluence, the prosperous middle-class national subject that emerged through these years was by definition an urban subject. Moreover, urban economic growth in Japan rested on definitions of Japanese modernity that situated places like Central Kiso as part of a vanishing rural past against which modern Japan was constructed (Ivy 1995; Robertson 1988; Tamanoi 1998). Local residents complained about their marginality in an urban imagination and lamented that the number of children in the region was not high enough to qualify for government funding for local schools or to reproduce a labor force for the region.

Historically, eldest sons in Japan have remained in rural areas to inherit family homes and land and to care for aging parents. However, Central Kiso residents (like many in rural Japan) complained most young Japanese women do not want to join multigenerational rural families. (Young Japanese women often describe these families as feudal and patriarchal.) These women have increasingly opted to leave rural areas and move to cities and marry white-collar workers, if they marry at all. As a result, men in Central Kiso often went to local Filipina hostess bars with the purpose of meeting a potential girlfriend or even a wife. Hostess bars had become widespread in the area in the late-1950s, when they were established to provide entertainment for workers brought in for large-scale national construction projects. These bars employed exclusively Japanese women. In the 1980s, as the Japanese economy grew, Filipina women began to replace Japanese women in, what were considered, "lower-ranking" hostess bars across the country, and new hostess bars expressly employing Filipina women also opened. Filipina hostess bars were soon found throughout urban and rural Japan.[5]

When I began my fieldwork in 1998, about 60 Japanese men in the region had married Filipina women, the overwhelming majority of whom had come to the region to work in local hostess bars.[6] Residents referred to these marriages as "*kokusai kekkon*" (international marriage). Some local residents opposed these marriages, but many others hailed them as the only hope for both local men to have wives and children and the region to have a viable future.

18.2　Filipina Migration to Central Kiso

If Japanese residents were drawn to relationships with Filipina women to broaden their options for family formation and community survival, most Filipina wives of Japanese men in Central Kiso told me that they had come to Japan to find a "better life" for themselves and their families in the Philippines. The failure of structural adjustment policies in the Philippines coupled with a national "labor export policy" beginning in the Marcos era has pushed many Filipinas/os to go abroad to look for employment opportunities (Guevarra 2010; Parreñas 2011; Rodriguez 2010). The overwhelming majority of Filipina migrants in Central Kiso, like the majority of Filipina women who went to Japan on entertainer visas, came from urban or rural poor communities in the Philippines. Few had postsecondary educations or were eligible for other kinds of work visas in Japan. These women were also not able to get jobs as domestic workers in countries like Canada or the United States, which are more desirable migration destinations than Japan but also require higher levels of education or financial resources to qualify for work visas.[7] Japan does not offer residency permits for "unskilled" laborers. "Entertainer" is considered a skilled labor category and is available for "(a)ctivities to engage in theatrical performances, arts, song, dance, musical performances, sports, or any other show business."[8] Some business establishments that hired Filipina women under these pretenses did not entirely (or at all) employ them in such capacities. Yet their business practice, including their treatment of Filipina employees, was widely unregulated and labor and visa violations were often overlooked.

Filipina migrants' experiences in hostess bars were contradictory. On the one hand, the women were ostensibly going to Japan as "cultural performers" on "entertainer visas." In this way, the migration trend was linked to a prominent tradition of cultural dance performance in the Philippines. Cultural dancers have entertained elites in the Philippines since the colonial period. In postcolonial years, they traveled around Asia, performing on military bases, tourist resorts, and cruise ships. In a practice that was encouraged by recruiters and the Philippines government, Filipina entertainers were in some arenas presented as, and treated like, glamorous performers. For instance, *The Philchime Career Manual for Overseas Performance Artists*, the standard guidebook used in training programs during the early 1990s for Filipina women applying to work in Japan, asserts, "The honor, glamour, and privilege of this profession are only for those who can be considered as talented and beautiful according to standards of show business" (Esguerra 1994: 42).[9] I found that many Filipina women in Central Kiso spoke of the glamour and pleasures they found working in these bars. They shared excitement about getting dressed up for work and the attentions they received from men, including receiving expensive gifts. They also described romantic courtships with their husbands and told stories of "love at first sight" (see Faier 2009).

On the other hand, hostess work also stigmatized Filipina women in both Japan and the Philippines (see also Suzuki 2002 and Piquero-Ballescas 1992). Large numbers of Filipina entertainers began traveling to work in Japan in the 1980s in the wake of scandals surrounding Japanese sex tourism to the Philippines. Moreover, Filipina hostesses (not all of whom entered Japan legally on "entertainer visas") initially worked in bars surrounding US military bases in Japan, where prostitution is common (Sturdevant and Stoltzfus 1992). Hostess bars are considered part of the sex industry in Japan, and some women working in them are sexually exploited or choose to have sexual relationships with customers (Parreñas 2011). As mentioned above, labor parameters in bars were left to the discretion of Japanese employers, who had varying expectations of Filipina employees and in some (although by no means all) encouraged or even forced sex work.

Consequently, Filipina women who go to Japan on entertainer visas are widely disparaged as prostitutes in both Japan and the Philippines (Faier 2009; Parreñas 2011). The women were often called "*japayuki*" (literally, "one who has traveled to Japan"), following the term "*karayuki*" (literally "one who has traveled to China"), which refers to Japanese women who were sold and sent abroad to China and Southeast Asia as prostitutes during the mid-nineteenth to early twentieth century. Some Japanese residents in Central Kiso told me that Filipina women working in hostess bars had questionable morals. The Filipino uncle and nieces of a woman living in Central Kiso explained (as one of this woman's nieces put it), "The reputation of *japayukis* here is not very good: They are thought of as prostitutes." As a result, all Filipinas I knew in Central Kiso were extremely self-conscious of the stigma attached to working as an entertainer. They also told me that, as Catholics, they were "embarrassed in front of God" to do such work. They justified bar work by explaining that they were doing it out of desperation as a sacrifice to support their families in the Philippines. As discussed below, they also endeavored to challenge the stigma and remake their identities through their roles as *oyomesan* in their Japanese households.

18.3   Central Kiso Residents' Stakes in Filipina *Oyomesan*

As mentioned above, Japanese residents of Central Kiso were concerned about the sustainability of life in the region and invested in revitalizing (or at least maintaining) the community. Men were looking for companionship and wanted families. Others spoke of a need to find caregivers for elderly and help for household maintenance and family businesses. All of these factors contributed to an openness toward Filipina wives in the community. However, this openness was qualified. Many believed that Japan was more developed and modern than, and thus superior to, the Philippines. Japanese residents sometimes likened the Philippines to a "past Japan" (before the high growth period). Because they believed that Filipina women came from a country that was "poor" and "less modern" than Japan, they viewed Filipinas as similar to, what they called, "traditional Japanese women." On this account, they expected Filipina women to be submissive and to want to assimilate to their (presumed to be) advanced ways. Most local residents were open to marriages between local men and Filipina women insofar as they believed that the women were assimilating. For many in the Japanese community, these expectations included Filipina wives fulfilling their roles as "*ii oyomesan*" (ideal traditional Japanese brides and daughters-in-law, literally "good brides and daughters-in-law") and raising their children to be "good Japanese" members of the community.

Many Japanese community members had similar expectations of Japanese *yome*. When I asked local residents what it meant to be a good *yome*, they explained that a bride (whether Japanese or Filipina) was expected to give up the ways of her natal household and community and assimilate ("*dōka*," as some put it) to those of her marital ones. Many in Central Kiso suggested that a good *yome* would manage domestic responsibilities, such as housecleaning and cooking. They told me that a good bride and daughter-in-law needed to be capable – that is, have (or acquire) the knowledge, skills, strength, and independence – to carry out these responsibilities. She also needed to be compliant and willing to adjust to new surroundings and care for those around her. Most new brides learned local and household cooking styles from their *shūtomesan*, their mothers-in-law, and the women demonstrated their respect for their in-laws and their commitment to their new household by doing so. Many residents also stressed the importance of brides maintaining community relations. For instance, a farmer who had recently become engaged to a Japanese woman he had met through a local-government-sponsored marriage introduction party told me that he expected his new wife would "manage things like, for example, housecleaning and things around the house (as well as) relations with people around the neighborhood." Other community members explained that a good bride would maintain relations between her household and neighborhood associations by passing on circulating neighborhood notices and paying monthly neighborhood association dues. Moreover, they explained that she would mind local social customs and manners of socializing with a pleasant disposition. For instance, when I asked one Filipina woman's Japanese mother-in-law what it meant to be *oyomesan*, she explained, "Well wouldn't that include, for example, being easy to get along with, and greeting people in the neighborhood …?"

However, if Filipina brides were expected to manage similar responsibilities to those expected of Japanese brides, many Japanese community members framed expectations of Filipina women not only as a matter of assimilating to their marital household and community's manner of doing things but also to, what they called, "the Japanese way" of doing things. In other words, for Filipinas, as opposed to Japanese women, being an ideal *oyomesan* carried the additional meaning of learning to do things according to the ways local residents asserted they were done in Japan, or what many referred to as "*nihon no yarikata*," the Japanese way. As the Japanese boyfriend of one Filipina woman in the region explained, "If a Filipina marries a Japanese man she is supposed to become like a Japanese. She has to become a Japanese ... She has to learn Japanese traditions. She has to learn customs from years back. She must make an effort to learn them."

Filipinas' husbands, in-laws, and neighbors instructed the women on how to prepare and serve Japanese foods, greet and interact with neighbors, and care for special features of Japanese homes, such as *shōji* (sliding wood and paper doors), *futon*, and *tatami* mats. In addition, a local government sponsored a "Mothers' Class" ostensibly to help foreign brides adjust to life in the area. Although the women found the class helpful and used it as an opportunity to connect with other Filipinas in the region, the group also reinforced pressure on the women to assimilate, meeting monthly to focus on food preparation and practical matters such as riding the train and reading and writing in Japanese.

Whether or not a Filipina woman could manage the Japanese way became a key criterion through which Japanese community members evaluated her as a bride. Japanese community members explained that acquiring the ability to do things "the Japanese way" was in part a matter of attitude, and thus of character: a question of what kind of person a Filipina woman was and thus her commitment to her household and community. In this way, they not only compared Filipina women in the community but they also evaluated them in relation to Japanese women. For instance, my Japanese landlady, Emiko, reacted to some photos I showed her of a Filipina friend working in her Japanese in-laws rice fields by stating, "She's like a traditional Japanese woman." She then explained that many young Japanese women would be unwilling to do such work. Emiko later added that this Filipina friend was an "*ii oyomesan*," an ideal traditional Japanese bride and daughter-in-law.

Discussions of Filipina women in the community and their behaviors thus provided local community members the opportunity to define what they believed doing things "the Japanese way" meant and how they desired *yome*, whether Filipina or Japanese, to behave in the community. When they did this, members of the community claimed status as arbitrators of Japaneseness. Moreover, recognizing some Filipinas – but not others – as *ii oyomesan* put pressure on all women in the area – both Japanese and Filipina – to behave in certain ways. For instance, one day when I was visiting with my friend Mika's grandmother, she began to complain about the way her (Japanese) daughter-in-law treated her, explaining, "In the Philippines they *respect* the elderly." She then began to speak of a Filipina bride in the community who treated her in-laws well. These comments not only enabled Mika's grandmother to define what she believed were desirable ways for a bride to behave, they also provided a space for criticizing Japanese women in the community. Moreover, sometimes Filipinas' ideas about gender and kinship were *more appealing* than those local residents associated with Japanese women. Thus in describing Filipinas as *ii oyomesan*, local residents incorporated these ideas into what it meant to be ideal Japanese brides in the region.

However it was not simply on account of the ways the women accommodated Japanese community members' ideas about kinship that the women came to be identified as ideal brides and daughters-in-law. They also borrowed ideas about kinship from Filipina women, introducing new standards of behavior from the Philippines into Japan. Like Mika's grandmother, many Japanese residents in Kiso described Filipinas as good *oyomesan* on account of the care and respect they demonstrated to the elderly. Some local residents recognized that caring for elderly was valued in the Philippines, and this became one of a number of points of comparison (others being Filipinas' willingness to do hard work, their patience, the value they placed on family and community relations, their deference to their husbands, and their ability to cook traditional Japanese foods) between Filipinas and contemporary Japanese women in which some Filipinas came out ahead. In this way, local residents not only maintained local traditions as "the Japanese way," they also borrowed and incorporated Filipina's behaviors that they found preferable into what it meant to be a "traditional Japanese bride and daughter-in-law."

Local residents also recognized that once Filipinas had married into their families and communities, they had little to gain by refusing to accept the women. When local residents claimed that Filipinas were more amenable brides than Japanese women – as many put it, "more Japanese than young Japanese women today" – they anticipated and challenged urban ideals in Japan that have long considered Central Kiso as a backwater. They constructed Kiso and people who lived there as just as Japanese, if not more so, than those who lived in places like Tokyo and in households and communities without Filipina brides. These residents were pleased when Filipinas contemplated taking Japanese nationality. They took this as evidence of the women's commitment to their families and lives in Kiso. In a region suffering because few young people were interested in remaining, this commitment counted for a lot. We can thus see that Japanese community members had stakes not only in sustaining the position of the *oyomesan* in their households but also in shifting understandings of this role to accommodate Filipina migrants.

18.4 Filipina Migrants Performed Their Roles As *Oyomesan* through Resonant Patriarchies

If Japanese residents identified Filipina woman as *ii oyomesan* to maintain and define Japaneseness in ways that privileged their community, Filipina migrants had very different reasons for performing this role. Some Filipina women characterized their performance of their roles as *oyomesan* as both strategic and coerced. As mentioned above, most Filipinas in Central Kiso initially came to Japan to financially help their natal families. They spoke of desires to build homes and start businesses for their families in the Philippines. Scholars have shown that transnational migration is part of the ways that migrants maintain kin ties (Boehm 2012; Constable 1997; Parreñas 2001, 2005). Because their spousal visas permitted them to work in Japan, Filipina women's performances of their roles as *oyomesan* in Central Kiso enabled them to maintain their kinship ties in the Philippines. Filipina women in Central Kiso worked a range of jobs. One woman worked in her in-laws' soba restaurant. Other women (about 30 percent) worked at local Filipina bars. Still others did janitorial work at local *pachinko* parlors or worked in ballpoint pen and *annin dofu* (a packaged Japanese dessert) factories. Several did piecework at home. These women used their salaries to send money to their families in the Philippines and also to mail them enormous boxes filled with personal and household items (pantyhose, coffee, chocolates, towels, toys, electronics, and clothing) which they hoped would enable their families in the Philippines to share some of the middle-class comforts the women enjoyed in Japan.

If their spousal visas enabled these women to support their families in the Philippines, their residency permits also depended on the sponsorship of their Japanese husbands. Their spousal visas were temporary residence visas, issued first for six months, then after a while for one year, and later for three years. If women separated from their husbands or got a divorce, they risked losing these visas. Thus the vulnerability of their residence status in Japan pressured them into accommodating their Japanese in-laws' expectations.

However, even if their vulnerable status in Japan and need to support their Filipino families were considerations in their decisions to perform their roles as *oyomesan*, it would be a mistake to wholly attribute their behavior to coercion or instrumentalist strategies. These women described complicated emotional relationships to their Japanese and Filipino households, and their performances of their roles in them were in many ways tied to how they crafted senses of self. First, because being *oyomesan* enabled these women to support their families in the Philippines, it also enabled them to maintain in their Filipino families' eyes, and their own, that they were dutiful daughters, sisters, aunties, cousins, and godmothers. Although these women were stigmatized for their migration decision, their Filipino families also recognized and appreciated the "sacrifice" they were making. In the Catholic Philippines, martyring oneself for one's family is honorable, and was sometimes discussed in terms of "pity" (Cannell 1999). The niece of one Filipina woman in Central Kiso likened Filipina migrants in Japan to Jesus, who sacrificed himself for humanity. In this light, when Filipinas in Kiso complained about the sacrifices they made to accommodate their Japanese families' demands, they were also taking pride in the lengths to which they were willing to go to care for their families in the Philippines. Their claims of sacrifice were part of how these women used their performance of their roles as *oyomesan* to craft senses of self through their fulfillment of kin obligations in the Philippines.

Second, being *oyomesan* was also part of how the women presented themselves as "good" women and Filipinas. It enabled the women to challenge negative perceptions of Filipinas in Japan and gain recognition that they were more than stigmatized bar hostesses. The women knew that they were disparaged as prostitutes in both Japan and the Philippines, and many of them felt ashamed of their employment in bars. One woman, Ana, told me that she thought it was understandable that her in-laws initially disliked her because she had worked in a bar. (She explained that in their situation she would have felt the same way.) The women used their performances as *oyomesan* to reinvent themselves as "good women" in both Japan and the Philippines. Through their performances, they also cultivated positive identities for Filipina women in the region.

In addition, some women were pleased when members of the Japanese community identified them as *ii oyomesan*. They viewed these comments as public acknowledgment of their mastery of "the Japanese way," as evidence of their proficiency in a new set of cultural skills. For instance, on account of her adept performance of her roles in her Japanese family, Ana had received permanent residency much earlier than other women. She was proud of this, explaining with a sense of accomplishment that an immigration officer had told her that receiving it was a matter of whether "a person could really manage the Japanese way of life, whether they could manage it well."

Moreover, some women saw that they could benefit from and forward their ambitions by performing their roles as *oyomesan*. For example, Ana was not only proud that she had mastered "the Japanese way of life," she also told me that she found it instructive: "*Ii benkyō ni naru … nihon no seikatsu*" (The Japanese way of life is a useful thing to learn). She shared with pride that, although her in-laws had initially protested her marriage to their son, they were now training her to manage their *soba* shop after they retired. In other words, her successful performance of her role as *oyomesan* would eventually result in her ownership of her own business. She was also flattered that her in-laws had been encouraging her to

"*Nihonjin nare!*" (Become a Japanese!) by taking Japanese citizenship. She had not yet made up her mind as to whether or not she would, she said. On one hand, she had reservations about giving up her Filipino citizenship; on the other, she would be eligible for a national pension (social security) in Japan if she did become a Japanese citizen.

Moreover, when Filipina migrants in Central Kiso cared for their families (in both Japan and the Philippines) they felt like (and presented themselves) not only as good wives and mothers, Catholics, and middle-class housewives but also as different from, or special in comparison to, other Filipina women in Japan who were having problems adjusting to life in the community. On more than a few occasions, Tessie brought up that her husband had been something of a playboy before they had gotten married. With both annoyance and pride, she relayed stories about numerous Filipinas who had wanted to marry him, and about one particularly beautiful woman whom he dated before Tessie had come to Japan. Tessie suggested that, unlike herself, he did not see these women as "marriage material," and she took pride in the fact that she had landed such a financially stable and relatively supportive and understanding spouse.

The practices through which Tessie met her Japanese family's expectations also enabled her to take pride in herself as a wife, mother, and Filipina. Tessie kept her home spotlessly clean and her family's clothes were always laundered and neatly pressed. She cooked three homemade meals every day, and she participated in the activities for parents of students at her children's school. She was also appropriately deferential and polite to neighbors and her in-laws. Tessie always helped her mother-in-law, willingly assisting in her family's fields with the rice harvest and in other capacities. Sometimes, Tessie went to her in-laws to help with other chores or holiday preparations while her mother-in-law cared for her bed-ridden father-in-law. Tessie always made an effort to be a polite and helpful daughter-in-law, going out of her way to clean up her mother-in-law's kitchen and sitting room when her mother-in-law was too busy. These were all behaviors that resonated with Japanese residents as the behavior of an ideal *oyomesan*. However, Tessie framed her treatment of her in-laws in terms of how she was raised in the Philippines to be a respectful and responsible woman. For instance, she believed that she had responsibilities toward her husband's family: "I eat the rice, so I think I should help out growing it," she once told me. And one day as she cleaned her in-laws' kitchen while her mother-in-law went out to feed her cattle, she explained, "My mother in-law is so busy. She doesn't have time to do this, so I just want to help her out."

Like Tessie, many Filipinas in Central Kiso stressed the importance of respecting and caring for elderly in the Philippines. They explained that demonstrating obedience and indebtedness to aging parents is a way of showing gratitude for "the gift of life" (Hollnsteiner 1973: 76), and they emphasized that doing so was a commitment that had been instilled as children growing up in the Philippines. As mentioned above, some women's Japanese in-laws told me that an ideal *yome* would follow her in-laws' instructions and be a work hand in their homes. Similarly, some Filipina women's husbands told me that they were attracted to their wives because the women were submissive to their husbands in ways that contemporary Japanese women were not, but that traditional Japanese women used to be. A number of Filipina women told me that they believed that they should submit to their husbands. However, they did not identify these desires as accommodations of their roles in their Japanese households; rather they linked it to their Catholic faith. Although being Catholic might seem to contradict what many local residents associated with being a good *oyomesan* because few Japanese are Christian and Christianity is often posited in contradistinction with Japaneseness, in fact, the women's Catholicism offered a discourse of gender and kinship that resonated with the expectations of their Japanese community about what it meant to be a traditional Japanese bride.[10] For example, Japanese community members often described Filipinas as similar to traditional Japanese women because they deferred to their husband's desires and judgment. Although the women's vulnerable status in Japan contributed to their willingness to accommodate their Japanese family's desires, their Catholic beliefs did so as well. Tessie circulated a book among other Filipina women in the region entitled *Secrets Revealed! Twenty Ways to Use the Power of Prayer,* that discussed Biblical passages such as, "Words to live by: Wives, submit yourselves unto your husbands as unto the Lord. For the husband is the head of the wife" (from Ephesians 5: 22–25). Tessie believed that she should ask her husband for permission before going out, and she also deferred to his opinion and often cited things that he had said in ways that one might quote a mentor or scholar. This deferential attitude is one Tessie's husband once described as characteristic of a *yamato nadeshiko*, an ideal traditional Japanese woman.

In some ways too, their lives as *oyomesan* resonated with the visions of a middle-class life they saw in films and television dramas. When I asked why they chose their Japanese husbands over their longer-term Filipino boyfriends, many women explained that their Japanese husbands had jobs and would be able to provide for a family in ways that their Filipino boyfriends could not. Such statements did not reflect a woman's desire for money so much as for a certain kind of life and family. Some women cited a passage from Genesis in which God prescribed punishment to Adam and Eve for eating the forbidden fruit. The women would explain, "The husband must work to feed the family, and the wife must be in the house to raise the children and give birth." Many criticized other Filipinas who did not care for their children or husbands in the ways they felt were acceptable (i.e., by preparing their meals and cleaning the house). They also criticized Filipina women who allowed wage labor to interfere with family responsibilities. In this light, one might say that these women's performances of their roles as ideal brides and daughters-in-law were also enabled by "resonant patriarchies": discrepant discourses of gender and kinship that circulate in Japan and the Philippines but that resonate in aspects of their patriarchal constructions of masculinity and femininity. Filipina women became ideal Japanese brides and daughters-in-law on account of the ways that their endeavors to articulate themselves as good, middle-class wives, mothers, daughters, sisters, and aunties resonated with the desires of their Japanese communities to have certain kinds of brides and daughters-in-law.

18.5 Filipina Migrants Became "Ideal *Oyomesan*" on Account of Misunderstandings and Gaps Too

Surprisingly, Filipina migrants' performances of their roles as *oyomesan* were also enabled by the misunderstandings that emerged between Filipina migrants and their Japanese communities' ideas about gender and family. Most Filipina women in Central Kiso were sensitive to, and sometimes resentful of, the constraints and forms of discipline that their Japanese families imposed upon their lives. In particular, they expressed exhaustion with the expectations that they conform to prescribed ways of doing things. When I asked one Filipina woman about her Japanese in-laws' expectations of her, she premised her response by saying, "You know, this is a very disciplinary society." Some of the women shared frustration with the ways they felt that they were infantilized. One explained, "They treat us like they would treat a child. It's like they are raising us." Filipina women in Central Kiso also described being *oyomesan* as a form of labor, and they associated the expectations placed upon them and the treatment they received with that of a domestic helper in the Philippines. As one woman explained, "It's like you're the maid." In a few cases, these and other frustrations led women to run away from their Japanese families (see Faier 2009).

Yet more often, the women found more subtle ways to resist or escape from the pressures they faced in their Japanese households. In these, we can see how Filipina women came to perform their roles as *oyomesan* through the gaps between their and their Japanese families' desires. For instance, some women described being *oyomesan* as a role that they slipped in and out of when in certain parts of the house, such as the kitchen. For example, as *oyomesan*, they were expected to prepare, serve, and consume Japanese foods; they had to cut vegetables, sit, and eat in particular "Japanese"-identified ways. As one woman explained, "It's strange. I change in the kitchen. If I'm there I'm Japanese. When I go up to my room, I'm Filipina." She clarified: "Because in the kitchen you cook, you cook Japanese foods. You don't cook Filipino foods. They won't eat them. Maybe some (people's Japanese husbands and in-laws) will eat them, but in our house, they won't eat Filipino foods. Only my children and I will eat if I don't also cook Japanese foods."

Food preparation and consumption were key sites where tensions between being *oyomesan* and being Filipina played out for these women. As Ana and Cora explained above, many women's Japanese families insisted that the women prepare and consume Japanese food in their homes. Many women also complained that their husbands, in-laws, and sometimes even their children would not eat Filipino food. Instead, Filipina women found alternative spaces where they could eat Filipino food and "be Filipina" in ways unacceptable to their Japanese families and communities. They would regularly organize prayer meetings and birthday parties that only Filipinas attended. In addition to preparing and eating Filipino foods at these events, women would speak Tagalog (a few would also converse among themselves in Bicolano); often there would be Filipino or American pop music playing on the stereo, and sometimes *karaoke* and dancing. For instance, one night, Arli and I were keeping Marivic company while her husband, who also worked construction, was at a part-time job. Arli and her husband had recently moved out of her in-laws' home. She stressed how constrained she had felt living with them. "I never ate," she exclaimed, explaining that she had been embarrassed to eat in front of her mother-in-law out of fear she might be thought a glutton. She explained that she only ate when her husband's mother was out of the house or had gone to bed. Her weight had dropped from 60 kilos to 40. Now that they had moved out, she joked, she certainly was gaining the weight back.

Like Arli, many Filipina women would also cook separately for themselves and eat their meals (or leftovers from parties and friends) with their hands or cutlery after their families had finished or when their in-laws were not around. For the women, these eating and gathering strategies were both pleasurable and means for maintaining a sense of Filipina identity and resisting the pressures of their Japanese families. Ironically, however, their Japanese in-laws viewed the women as similar to traditional Japanese women and *ii oyomesan* on account of these practices. For instance, one Filipina woman's mother-in-law described how, in her day, the *yome* would serve her in-laws and husband first, offering them the best food, and then eat alone after the rest of the family had finished. By eating Filipino foods and participating in other "Filipino" activities apart from their in-laws, Filipinas were perceived as *ii oyomesan* through "crosstalk" (Tsing 1993) or productive misunderstandings. Their resistance to the discipline imposed upon them was mistaken for their compliance. In this way, Filipinas' Japanese families' misinterpretation – or willful disregard – of the women's desires to be Filipina also was part of how the women came to be identified as "*ii oyomesan*."

18.6 Conclusion

Attention to the lives of transmigrants like Filipina wives of rural Japanese men raises questions about not only how kinship motivates transnational migration but also how transnational processes shape family dynamics in the countries where migrants settle. As transnational migrants (or "transmigrants") maintain kin ties in both their "home" and "host" communities, they at once reproduce and transform kinship relationships in both sites.

Rural Japanese residents were drawn to and supportive of marriages between local men and Filipina bar hostesses because these women's presence offered hopes for sustaining life in the region. By identifying some Filipina migrants as ideal *oyomesan* (and teaching them to behave accordingly), local residents articulated standards of behavior for both Japanese and Filipina brides in the region. At the same time, they distinguished and negotiated their own experiences of marginality within Japan and redefined meanings of Japaneseness.

Filipina women's desires and convictions regarding their performances as *oyomesan* were shaped by the dual pressures of their lives in Japan and their relationships in the Philippines. When Filipina migrants participated in their Japanese households, they negotiated ideas about gender and kinship circulating in both Japan and the Philippines. The women were vulnerable on account of their residency status in Japan and the dependence of their families in the Philippines on their financial contributions. However, the women's attitudes toward their roles in their Japanese households, their deference to their husbands, and their support of their in-laws were not simply coerced performances. Their performances of their roles as *oyomesan* were also part of how these women constructed themselves as good women and as dutiful daughters, sisters, aunties, and even mothers to family members in the Philippines. It was also part of how the women constructed themselves as Filipinas, and aspects of this identity both resonated with and strained against the terms of what it meant to be *oyomesan*.

Through their roles as *oyomesan*, Filipina migrants have, in subtle and dramatic ways, come to be active and material participants in the reproduction and transformation of meanings of Japanese kinship. These marriages thus demonstrate the recent and dramatic ways that encounters between Filipina migrants and Japanese residents are transforming meanings of Japanese kinship in rural Japan. We can see in these relationships how transnational migration enables both the reproduction and the transformation of meanings of kinship. Filipina women reproduce the category of *oyomesan* through their everyday practice. They perform roles that Japanese community members identify with that of an ideal Japanese bride, and they offer an opportunity for the Japanese community to articulate practices as "tradition" and "Japanese culture." At the same time, these relationships shift these categories in subtle ways, in part because sometimes Filipinas' behaviors were more appealing than those that had become expected of Japanese women in the region and in part because it was previously hard for local residents to imagine that a Filipina could be "more Japanese than young Japanese women today."

Filipina women's performances of their roles as *oyomesan* emerged through the contingent alignments and misalignments – the articulations, gaps, and creative and coercive misunderstandings – between discourses of gender and kinship deployed in Japan and the Philippines. Only by situating these women's stakes in being *oyomesan* in relation to those of their Japanese community members can we see how it is in the alignments and gaps between the desires and agendas of these two groups that this kinship identity is being reproduced and transformed in Central Kiso.

Notes

1. *Oyomesan* is the honorific or polite version of the word, *yome*. It is made by adding the honorific prefix "o-" and the polite suffix "-san" (literally "Ms." or "Mrs.") to the word *yome*, bride. Conventionally, the polite term is used to refer to and address brides of other households.
2. An *utang na loob* has been described as an unsettleable debt that one must nonetheless regularly acknowledge (Cannell 1999; Rafael 1988).
3. For discussions of the *ie* and its place in Japan see also Befu 1963; Hamabata 1991; Kitaoji 1971; Lebra 1984; and Nakane 1967.
4. Although often assumed to be a "traditional" and essentially Japanese cultural form, the *ie* was a modern invention. It was institutionalized throughout Japan with the promulgation of the Meiji Civil Code, which introduced *samurai* practices as the legal norm for domestic units.
5. In hostess bars, Filipina women serve drinks and entertain customers by sitting with them, chatting, flirting, and sometimes going on dates. Their residence status formally prohibits them from having sexual relationships with customers; however, they sometimes do (see Faier 2009; Parreñas 2011).
6. The first Filipina–Japanese marriage in the region was registered in the mid-1980s. During my fieldwork, the two main towns in this area had populations around 7,000 each, and Filipina women were a visible and recognized presence in the region. When I returned in the mid-2000s, more than 200 Filipina wives were living in the area.
7. This contrasts with the case of Filipina domestic helpers, for example those in Hong Kong or Canada, who often come from middle-class backgrounds and have college degrees.
8. www.us.emb-japan.go.jp/english/html/travel_and_visa/visa/work-entertainer.html, accessed October 30, 2018.

9. *Philchime* stands for Philippine Chamber of Industries in Music and Entertainment Foundation, Inc. Its "member agencies" include a range of governmental and professional (talent, entertainment, and performance) groups (Esguerra 1994).
10. Most Filipinas' families respected their religious faith, and some of my friends' husbands would drive them to church in Matsumoto, more than an hour away, so that they could attend mass on Sundays and holidays such as Easter and Christmas.

References

Bachnik, Jane. 1983. "Recruitment Strategies for Household Succession: Rethinking Japanese Household Organisation." *Man* 18: 160–182.

Befu, Harumi. 1963. "Patrilineal Descent and Personal Kindred in Japan." *American Anthropologist* 65(6): 1328–1341.

Boehm, Deborah. 2012. *Intimate Migrations: Gender, Family, and Illegality among Transnational Mexicans.* New York: New York University Press.

Brennan, Denise. 2004. *What's Love Got to Do with It?: Transnational Desires and Sex Tourism in the Dominican Republic.* Durham, NC: Duke University Press.

Cannell, Fenella. 1999. *Power and Intimacy in the Christian Philippines.* New York: Cambridge University Press.

Chavez, Leo R. 2013. *Shadowed Lives: Undocumented Immigrants in American Society.* Belmont, CA: Wadsworth, Cengage Learning.

Constable, Nicole. 1997. *Maid to Order in Hong Kong: Stories of Filipina Workers.* Ithaca, NY: Cornell University Press.

———. 1999. "At Home, But Not at Home: Filipina Narratives of Ambivalent Returns." *Cultural Anthropology* 14(2): 203–228.

Esguerra, Lawrence A., ed. 1994. *Philchime Career Manual for Overseas Performing Artists.* Manila: Philchime.

Faier, Lieba. 2009. *Intimate Encounters: Filipina Migrants and the Remaking of Rural Japan.* Berkeley, CA: University of California Press.

Guevarra, Anna Romina. 2010. *Marketing Dreams, Manufacturing Heroes: The Transnational Labor Brokering of Filipino Workers.* New Brunswick, NJ: Rutgers University Press.

Hamabata, Matthews Masayuki. 1991. *Crested Kimono: Power and Love in the Japanese Business Family.* Ithaca, NY: Cornell University Press.

Hollnsteiner, Mary R. 1973. "Reciprocity in the Lowland Philippines." In *Four Readings in Philippine Values,* ed. Frank Lynch and Alfonso De Guzman II, 69–92. Quezon City: Ateneo de Manila Press.

Ivy, Marilyn. 1995. *Discourses of the Vanishing: Modernity, Phantasm, Japan.* Chicago, IL: University of Chicago Press.

Kitaoji, Hironobu. 1971. "The Structure of the Japanese Family." *American Anthropologist* 73: 1036–1057.

Kondo, Dorinne. 1990. *Crafting Selves: Power, Gender, and Discourses of Identity in a Japanese Workplace*. Chicago, IL: University of Chicago Press.

Lebra, Takie Sugiyama. 1984. *Japanese Women: Constraint and Fulfillment*. Honolulu, HI: University of Hawai'i Press.

Nakane, Chie. 1967. *Kinship and Economic Organization in Rural Japan*. New York: Humanities Press.

Ong, Aihwa. 1999. *Flexible Citizenship: The Cultural Logics of Transnationality*. Durham, NC: Duke University Press.

Parreñas, Rhacel. 2001. *Servants of Globalization: Women, Migration, and Domestic Work*. Stanford, CA: Stanford University Press.

2005. *Children of Global Migration: Transnational Families and Gendered Woes*. Stanford, CA: Stanford University Press.

2011. *Illicit Flirtations: Labor, Migration, and Sex Trafficking in Tokyo*. Stanford, CA: Stanford University Press.

Piquero-Ballescas, Ma. Rosario. 1992. *Filipino Entertainers in Japan: An Introduction*. Quezon City: The Foundation for Nationalist Studies.

Pratt, Geraldine and Philippine Women Centre of B.C. 2012. *Families Apart: Migrant Mothers and the Conflicts of Labor and Love*. Minneapolis, MN: University of Minnesota Press.

Rafael, Vicente. 1988. *Contracting Colonialism: Translation and Christian Conversion in Tagalog Society under Early Spanish Rule*. Manila: Ateneo de Manila Press.

Robertson, Jennifer. 1988. "*Furusato* Japan: The Culture and Politics of Nostalgia." *Politics, Culture, and Society* 1(4): 494–518.

Rodriguez, Robyn Magalit. 2010. *Migrants for Export: How the Philippine State Brokers Labor to the World*. Minneapolis, MN: University of Minnesota Press.

Sand, Jordan. 2003. *House and Home in Modern Japan: Architecture, Domestic Space, and Bourgeois Culture 1880–1930*. Cambridge, MA: Harvard University Press.

Sturdevant, Saundra and Brenda Stoltzfus, eds. 1992. *Let the Good Times Roll: Prostitution and the U.S. Military in Asia*. New York: The New Press.

Suzuki, Nobue. 2002. "Women Imagined, Women Imagine: Re/presentations of Filipinas in Japan since the 1980s." In *Filipinos in Global Migrations: At Home in the World?*, ed. Filomeno V. Aguilar, 176–203. Quezon City: Philippine Migration and Research Network and Philippine Social Science Council.

Tamanoi, Mariko Asano. 1998. *Under the Shadow of Nationalism: Politics and Poetics of Rural Japanese Women*. Honolulu, HI: University of Hawai'i Press.

Tsing, Anna. 1993. *In the Realm of the Diamond Queen*. Princeton, NJ: Princeton University Press.

19

Un/making Family: Relatedness, Migration, and Displacement in a Global Age

Deborah A. Boehm

For Federico and Gaby, deportation meant packing up a home and making arrangements for a sudden departure, but it also required gathering up a life of 25 years and making choices about what would have to be left behind. Federico and his family parted with nearly everything.[1] As he described: "We lost the house, we lost many things. We gave things away. We tried to make arrangements so that we could leave, but, well … we lost a lot." Many of the family's losses were material, but, as Federico described, the less tangible losses were far more profound.

Born in a small, rural community in Zacatecas, Mexico, Federico migrated as a young man to Los Angeles, California. Several months later, his wife, Gaby, followed, and they made the United States their home, living there for decades. After spending all of his adult life in the United States as an undocumented migrant, Federico wanted desperately to "fix his papers," to change his status so that he would be authorized to live and work in the country. Federico was not comfortable living "hidden," and so he consulted with an attorney and learned that he was eligible to apply for permanent residency. He felt a deep connection – and had given much – to the nation. He worked for the same company for 16 years, had five US citizen children (ages 14–24), volunteered at prisons through his local parish, and was part of a strong network of family, friends, neighbors, coworkers, and church members.

He began the paperwork to process a change in immigration status for Gaby and himself, but after the applications were submitted, they were contacted by US Citizenship and Immigration Services (USCIS) and informed that they were not eligible to receive permanent residency. Instead, they were being deported. The couple also learned that the "attorney" who had required advance payment and submitted the applications was not an attorney at all, but a notary public. They had been the victims of fraud.

Federico immediately hired an immigration attorney. However, despite efforts to cancel or defer the removal order, Federico and Gaby were told that they had to leave the country or face imprisonment. "When the letter arrived informing us that we had to leave, it was very difficult. I thought, 'How am I going to do this? What am I going to do back in Mexico?' After so many years here, so many years that my family lived here." Federico's voice trailed off, his eyes teary. "I feel it was caused by the judge's bad decisions. I'm not saying that we were without fault, but they should consider the family."

Initially, the family went south together to Mexico: Federico and Gaby went back to their home community in rural Zacatecas, while their five children "returned" to Mexico for the first time. After the family spent a brief period in their new home, the two eldest children migrated again, this time to the United States. The 24-year-old went to work and attend school part-time; the 21-year-old, who had recently married, went back to her partner and job, and soon after celebrated the birth of her first child. And so, for a time, the family lived split in this transnational configuration: two adult children, a son-in-law, and a newborn grandson living north of the border while the parents and three of the children were in Mexico.

A year later, the geographies of family changed once more. First, their 18-year-old daughter married and she and her new husband went north, joining an uncle and several cousins in Colorado. Then, after their 17-year-old daughter graduated from high school, she joined her sister in the United States and enrolled in a local community college. The family again lived divided by the US–Mexico border, this time with most family members in the United States – four of the five children – while Federico, Gaby, and their youngest daughter stayed in Mexico.

For Federico and his family, kinship was repeatedly fragmented as everyday life was turned upside down: family ties were unmade, made, and – when possible – made again. Because of migration several decades earlier and then following deportation, Federico's family was divided by a border despite the US citizenship of most family members. Still, family relations and residences were also reconfigured in a transnational space: at different junctures, they embarked on new kin arrangements as individuals migrated north or south and/or found themselves caught in either nation.

* * *

The story of this one family – which parallels the experiences of millions of others – demonstrates an argument that has structured and continues to shape my research with transnational Mexicans: that the process of making family is both strong and precarious. Migration and deportation shape kinship, eroding and undermining strong family ties but also resulting in new configurations of family and emergent strategies that migrants engage with as they move, are forced to move, and/or are unable to move transnationally. Throughout this chapter, I argue that migrants are "making" families against a backdrop of the very potent ways that nation-states are, both indirectly and actively, "unmaking" families across borders. Within intimate spheres, the geographies of migration and return are fragmented, as individuals are forced to migrate or unable to do so, resulting in both new and familiar forms of transnational kin networks.

19.1   Making (and Unmaking) Families

In my analysis, I pay close attention to this process of making family, the aftermath of families unmade, and the almost continuous endeavor of remaking kin when faced with the challenges of global movement. Families demonstrate flexibility, constructing kin ties as they are able to – even in the most limited of circumstances. Here, I am drawing on the work of scholars such as Judith Butler and Janet Carsten who have traced the "undoing" of gender and kin (Butler 2004), but have also shown how families are "redoing kinship" (Carsten 2004: 6) across time and space. As Carsten posits: "kinship is far from being simply a realm of the 'given' as opposed to the 'made'" (Carsten 2004: 9). Similarly, my analysis focuses on "what kinship *does*" (Carsten 2004: 24) and how people *do* kinship.

Yet, above all, I am attentive to how family is undone or unmade. There is a precariousness to family relations across borders, tenuous ties put in place by state action. Despite the resilience of families as they confront barriers to forming kin as they wish to, they must do so in a context of profound insecurity. As I discuss, an unprecedented number of deportations of foreign nationals from the United States in recent years severs transnational families and erodes family ties and one's membership within a kin group in ways that are familiar but also new. Although transnational families are unmade through migration, migrants find ways to restructure or remake families across borders. Still, in the face of deportation families are unmade through emergent forms of dismantling. In the current milieu of increased government control of immigration and the growing criminalization of those who cross borders, transnational families are that much more difficult to sustain.

This argument about the contradictory experiences of transnational families first came out of work that I started in the 1990s in the United States with immigrant communities and then later developed through transnational study on both sides of the border, research that resulted in a book, *Intimate Migrations: Gender, Family, and Illegality among Transnational Mexicans* (Boehm 2012). In *Intimate Migrations*, one of the arguments I make is that a contradictory pattern structures kinship:

> Even as the U.S.–Mexico border divides couples and families, Mexican (im)migrants build relationships and construct home and family in

a manner that transcends nation-states. Significantly, however, despite the fluid movement of transnational Mexicans between the United States and Mexico, the border is a barrier with a powerful and far-reaching impact on families and the geographic and symbolic locations of kin.

(Boehm 2012: 31)

In my research about deportation, I have again seen this contradiction – of the simultaneous tenacity and fragility of families – but with a renewed intensity in its effects.

This chapter explores the impact of transnationality on family life. First, I provide background about previous and ongoing research focused on families and global movement, both migration and deportation. Next, I discuss ways that anthropological approaches to kinship might be specifically applied to transnational families. How can we draw on various theoretical approaches to understand "family" in the current moment? Presenting ethnographic material, I provide snapshots of different ways that family life is made, unmade, and remade – by families and by the state – through and in response to migration and return. Finally, I conclude with a discussion of the entanglements of state power and relatedness to speculate about im/possibilities for making family in a global age. Although my focus is on Mexico and the United States, such analysis can be extended to other migration flows around the world. Indeed, comparative study underscores how the effects of global movement are ever more a part of family life in the current moment.

19.2   Families across Time and Space

My analysis of the making, and unmaking, of families comes from longitudinal and binational ethnographic research. Fieldwork with migrants and their family members began in the 1990s in Albuquerque, New Mexico, where I first met transnational Mexicans from north central Mexico. In 2001, I spent a year based in the Mexican states of San Luis Potosí and Zacatecas studying migration and its effects, followed by research trips in the summers and during other brief periods. In 2010, I again returned to Mexico for a year of fieldwork, this time for a project that focused explicitly on deportation and return. When not in Mexico, I have conducted research in the United States, in communities where migrants from San Luis Potosí and Zacatecas are living, including Albuquerque, New Mexico; Las Vegas and Reno, Nevada; Oregon's Willamette Valley; Tucson, Arizona; and Southern California.

Multi-sited research has provided insights about mobilities and immobilities across the US–Mexico border, and my analysis includes fieldwork with people who migrate and those who do not, migrants who are forcibly "removed" through deportation, and those who accompany (or cannot accompany) family members both north and south. While the research has been place-based and the geographic locations matter – for example, Zacatecas is one of the Mexican states with the highest rates of migration to the United States – the study has been focused especially on people and their relationships, the transnational lives they build or are unable to create.

The project has focused on people of all ages, from elders in communities to infants and young children who also migrate and/or are affected by the migration of others. In addition, research participants have had divergent life experiences and represent diverse subjectivities along lines of gender, sexuality, citizenship, family position, immigrant status, and migration trajectories, among others. I have employed a range of ethnographic research methods, including participant observation; interviews and life histories; and visual methodologies, such as photography and videography, as both prompt and product. Ongoing ethnographic research has been a particularly fruitful way to study familial ties across borders, gendered relations, and the experiences of children and youth in global context.

Although my findings are based on ethnographic research and data, US immigration policies provide the backdrop to, and directly shape, transnational lives.[2] Whether or not US immigration policies include an explicit focus on gender and family, legislation and government action undoubtedly direct intimate migrations. US policies and practices – ranging from immigration quotas to "deportation regimes" (De Genova and Peutz 2010) – have resulted in many different configurations of family across and divided by the US–Mexico border. Significantly, these are most frequently gendered migrations that, while also driven by factors within communities, are rooted in historical processes and produced by political-economic forces over time.

One significant influence was the Bracero Program (1942–1964), a government effort to recruit agricultural laborers and bring them to the United States on guestworker visas. Through the Bracero Program, the US state contracted with primarily male laborers from states in the region of Mexico where I have conducted research. The Bracero Program established a pattern of primarily male or male-led migration and played a fundamental role in creating the present character of gendered kin migrations. Two later pieces of legislation – the Immigration and Nationality Act of 1965 and the Immigrant Reform and Control Act (1986), called IRCA – also influenced migrations between Mexico and the United States, especially the gendered family dynamics of such movement.

The Immigration and Nationality Act of 1965 altered US immigration policy by establishing family reunification – rather than national origin quotas – as the primary criterion for immigration and naturalization. Decades later, the Immigrant Reform and Control Act-IRCA (1986) allowed individuals who could document continuous residency in the United States to legalize their status and secure US residency and eventually seek naturalization as US citizens. IRCA included Special Agricultural Worker provisions (SAW I and II) that meant that the majority of agricultural workers – and nearly all of the individuals I have interviewed over the years – who received amnesty through IRCA were male. This intersection of the Immigration and Nationality Act and IRCA has had a powerful impact on Mexican im/migrant families: once family members were able to legalize their status, they could begin the process of petitioning for additional family members. Thus, the two laws operating together established a pattern of Mexican men petitioning for female spouses, children, and parents, and, notably, have routinized male-led migration and made migration a process that is inevitably linked to kin relations – even in the case of undocumented migrations that take place outside state processes.

Deportation, return, and much of the movement from north to south have similarly been shaped by US legislation and especially increasing immigration controls, an ever more fortified US–Mexico border, and a record number of deportations in the early twenty-first century. The Illegal Immigration Reform and Immigrant Responsibility Act of 1996, coupled with expanded immigration enforcement after 9/11, has increased the stakes for those who migrate to the United States without authorization. The practice of "governing immigration through crime" (Dowling and Inda 2013) and the expansion of those who may be marked as "criminal" (Fassin 2011; Rosas 2012) – what legal scholar Juliet P. Stumpf calls "the crimmigration crisis" (2006) – has arguably had an even more profound effect on gender relations and family ties across borders. The result is that families are increasingly "unmade" by state policies and practices.

19.3   Relatedness in a Global Age

Theoretical discussions about "family" and state action inform my research, especially emergent work from what has been called the "new" kinship studies. A focus on kinship or "family" – however it may be defined – has been an integral part of the development of the discipline of anthropology. For example, Bronislaw Malinowski understood "family" to be a universal institution across cultures, with features such as ensured affection for one another or a shared physical place where family members reside (Collier, Rosaldo and Yanagisako 1997: 72). This notion of a common experience of kinship has been challenged by anthropologists who present a much more nuanced approach to the study of family (e.g., Collier, Rosaldo and Yanagisako 1997). Anthropologists' current understandings of kinship both critique and extend earlier work in the field.

There is (at least some) utility in revisiting previous anthropological theorizing about kinship, especially for its role in documenting diversity (Collier, Rosaldo and Yanagisako 1997). Through the mapping of kin and the close study of language and kinship terms, diversity was an important emphasis in early anthropological work – a point that is often overlooked because of a much stronger focus on the universal. Yet, one of the hallmarks of foundational anthropological studies of kinship was arguably this ability to demonstrate the multiplicity of kin groupings and the meanings attached to them (Collier, Rosaldo and Yanagisako 1997). In this sense, early efforts to record family or kin relations can still be useful, but especially so when coupled with insights that have come from later or "new" kinship studies.

Early anthropological assumptions about kinship have also been challenged through the experiences of transnational families. For example, those who study kinship across international borders have shown that sharing a physical residence is in no way necessary for the formation and maintenance of strong familial bonds. Furthermore, there are few (if any) universal characteristics of what constitutes "family" in a transnational space, as new relationships are eroded and/ or strengthened, kinship takes on new meanings, and the character of one's significant relationships shifts and transforms over time and across distances (e.g., Abrego 2014; Boehm 2012; Dreby 2010, 2015; Foner 2009; Menjívar 2000; Newendorp 2008; Olwig 2007; Parreñas 2005). Thus, many of the assertions of early anthropologists are problematized through the experiences of transnational families.

So, what can the new kinship literature – work that challenges many of the arguments of anthropologists who first outlined central issues related to kinship – contribute to the study of family in a global context? Above all, this work collectively captures the flexibility and multiplicity of family, and communicates this point in a much more explicit way than Malinowski and his contemporaries did. Arguably, this turn began with David Schneider's seminal works, *American Kinship: A Cultural Account* (1968) and *A Critique of the Study of Kinship* (1984) that rightly directed our attention to "meaning" and the constructed character of family. In the 1980s and 1990s, feminist anthropologists continued this endeavor, as Jane Collier, Michelle Z. Rosaldo, and Sylvia Yanagisako did, asking "Is There [even such a thing as] a Family?" In their work, rather than understanding the family as "a concrete institution designed to fulfill universal human needs," they argue that family is "an ideological construct associated with the modern state" (Collier, Rosaldo and Yanagisako 1997: 71). This focus on the state is particularly significant in the current moment, and a point I revisit below.

Anthropologist Janet Carsten further advanced this critique of kinship studies in important ways, questioning the lines of inquiry that we as anthropologists might and should follow. One of the significant contributions Carsten makes is to bring the concept of "relatedness" to the conversation, arguing that it is broader, more open, and more relevant than the concept of "kinship" and the typically static categorization that has been associated with early kinship studies in anthropology (Carsten 2000). Carsten identifies what she calls "the process of kinship" (2000: 14) – that is, the "making" of kinship – underscoring change and fluidity. Such a frame is central to analysis of transnational families, or perhaps any form of "family," especially in the twenty-first century.

In the title of one of Carsten's books, *After Kinship*, she signals the importance of this turn away from rigid or narrow ways of thinking about family, much like Judith Butler does when she calls on the burgeoning field of "postkinship studies" (Butler 2004: 127) to help move beyond normative understandings of family that ascribe how and with whom relatedness is to occur. There is significant value in applying this postkinship turn specifically to families in transnational or crossborder contexts. This body of work encourages us to continue to consider the diversity of family formations. While much of the new kinship studies has usefully focused on kinship outside of heteronormative configurations of family and how kin relations are produced through adoption or reproductive technologies, I maintain that it can also significantly contribute to understandings of transnational families. Thus, I build on rich scholarship about both transnational families *and* "new" studies of relatedness to think through how families are made and unmade through migration and return.

19.4   Intimate Migrations: Making Family Transnationally

The experiences of Marisa and her family members show how kin can be "made" transnationally. In the 1990s, Marisa's common-law husband, Vicente, traveled to the United States with plans to send money back to Marisa and their three young children.[3] The money never came, however, and after several months Vicente called to announce that he was in love with another woman, and that he had no plans to support his children financially. Faced with this crisis, Marisa put her children under the care of her mother, the children's grandmother, and left with her older brother for Albuquerque, New Mexico. She began working and sending remittances home. As Marisa recounted her first year in the United States, she fought back tears: "It was a very difficult time … I was so far from my children. I will never allow us to be separated like that again."

But Marisa's experience took a turn – one that impacted her family significantly – that was directly shaped by state policies and US immigration laws. After ten months in the United States, she met Pedro, a Mexican national who had naturalized as a US citizen. The couple began dating and soon moved in together. After six months, Marisa and Pedro decided to marry and to bring Marisa's children to live with them in the United States. Through Marisa's marriage to Pedro, Marisa and her children were able to become US residents. As Marisa described: "Now, looking back, I am grateful that I came here. Now that I have a life with Pedro, I realize that my difficulties were worth it." The union between Marisa and Pedro altered the legal status of Marisa and her children: the marriage provided a path to documented immigration and allowed her to build a life for herself and her children in the United States. As Marisa's mother explained to me, Pedro "opened the door for the family ... by marrying Marisa and adopting the children, he took them out of the shadows."

So for Marisa, state action initially divided her family – especially through the categorization of immigrants and the statuses of "legal" and "illegal" that the state constructs. Then, again through immigration policy, Marisa and her children were reunited as they *made* family through newly configured residence and relations, including Marisa's marriage to Pedro. Theirs is a family that has been made and remade as a result of and through global movement, a kin group constituted through migration itself.

* * *

Here, families are first "unmade," and then "made" or reconstituted in response and even as a challenge to state policies. These are "intimate migrations" through which family often finds itself divided by the border, but also structuring migration precisely through family ties (Boehm 2012). Clearly, US immigration laws divide families, especially through the production of "illegality" and the categorization of individuals with different statuses vis-à-vis the state. As a result of migration, families are divided, but aiming for reunification. And, despite these divisions, new forms of residence and relatedness are created.

Some examples of emergent forms of family-making in the face of immigration include the many households in Mexico that bring groups of women together and the apartments of men that are frequently the homes of migrants in the United States. In Mexico, I repeatedly have met women who have come together to live and support one another while their partners are in *el norte*. In many cases, these are households made up of multiple generations, typically mothers-in-law and daughters-in-law or sometimes sisters or cousins. These arrangements can be especially helpful in facilitating the care of children as grandmothers or aunts share in raising their grandchildren or nieces and nephews. Mothers reciprocate by taking on added responsibilities in the collective home, such as cooking and cleaning.

In my research, I have also talked with many men who have joined with other migrants to build households in the United States. They, too, share in household chores, with men engaging in activities that had they been living with women – their wives and/or mothers – these women would be expected to complete. For men, these new arrangements of relatedness mean that family, but also friends and community members, can take on new roles in supporting one another as they migrate to new places. In a transnational space both women and men come together to share in household responsibilities, and in the process, they produce new forms of "family."

In Marisa's case, family was first "unmade" as she and her children were divided from husband and father, Vicente, in large part because no one in the family had authorization to migrate to the United States. So, as is common among migrant families, Vicente went alone as an undocumented migrant. This migration put pressures on family ties and he eventually abandoned his wife and children. Next, the family was divided again, as Marisa went to the United States while her children were under the care of their grandmother in Mexico. Then, Marisa met and married Pedro, and – specifically through US immigration policies and state-defined constructions of family – Marisa was able to change her status, petition for her children and change their statuses, and reunite family in the United States, "making" family in a new way in transnational context.

So, family *and* state actions can potentially redefine and/or "reunify" kin, and US policies can both divide and bring together family. However, although "family reunification" principles guide US immigration policy, migrants face ongoing state regulation in their everyday lives. Throughout the process of securing residency, particular family members may spend years apart and their movement can be restricted by the US state. Significantly, while im/migrants reunite their families through state processes when they are able, such options are not available to the majority of transnational Mexicans, and so migrants frequently reunite families outside the state's official procedures. The state's hold on family life is strong, pushing families to work within state bureaucracies when possible, but also to operate outside state control.

19.5 Returned: Families Unmade

For Carlos – husband, father of six, and primary wage-earner – migration, but especially deportation, profoundly disrupted family life.[4] Carlos' migrations and removal were entangled with kin ties and the trajectories of his wife and children. In the 1990s, Carlos had migrated to the United States to work and send home money. After several years apart, Carlos' wife, Lucia, and their five young children went north to "reunite" with Carlos. The family then lived together in Texas, during which time another child was born. Their lives became rooted in the United States: the children attended and graduated from school, Carlos had dependable work opportunities, Lucia made friends and started a small catering business.

Years later, when his father died, Carlos decided to go back to Mexico to be with family there. The deportation took place after being apprehended at the border, while attempting to rejoin his family in the United States. Family life was upended after the deportation, fragmented in ways similar to, but also more intense than the migrations they had experienced in earlier decades. The family experienced a kind of chain return[5] that, like chain migration, involved family members migrating "back" to Mexico in stages or steps.

First, after Carlos was released from US immigration detention, he went to his hometown and lived by himself for several months. Carlos was initially hopeful about his future in Mexico. He thought he could resume his life from before, and in some ways he did: he reconnected with family and friends, and he made plans to farm his land once more. But Carlos had gone back to a past that was no longer there: his father was gone, his mother's health was deteriorating, his siblings' families were also divided by migration. When faced with the stress of being far from his spouse and children and the economic hardship of not working for a wage, Carlos started drinking. His wife, Lucia, was extremely worried about him and so she decided to return to Mexico with their two school-aged children – the youngest, a US citizen.

Meanwhile, several family members remained in Texas: three adult children and a high school student – all of whom had been living without documents in the United States for most of their lives. Two of these adult children were married and with US citizen children of their own, so their ties to the nation, despite no formal membership there, were very strong. Then, after the teenage daughter graduated, her parents made arrangements for her to return to Mexico, leaving the three eldest children living in Dallas with their spouses and children.

Despite multiple migrations and configurations of residence, the family remained apart. For Carlos, family was split down the middle: Carlos, his wife, and their youngest children were in Mexico, while three adult children, their partners, and Carlos and Lucia's grandchildren were in the United States. While the family's migration north was forward-focused, their return was discombobulating. Carlos and Lucia went back to a place where life had moved ahead without them. For the children, return meant going to a place from the past that they had never known. Deportation launched a foreign life and an unknown future for Carlos and his family.

* * *

In this case, we see how migrants "make" family transnationally, just as Carlos and Lucia did through chain migration to the United States decades ago. But, more significantly, deportation results in families again divided – "unmade" directly as a result of the US state's removal of foreign nationals and then "remade" within a frame of narrow possibilities. Removal reaches into family life in ways that are at once similar to, an intensification of, and a divergence from the effects of migration on relatedness. When families are divided because of deportation, there are far fewer options for reunification – if any at all.

While US immigration policies are ostensibly designed to facilitate family reunification, deportation results in its inverse: a form of *family deunification* or potentially reunification in Mexico rather than in the United States as families had initially hoped.[6] Such "deunification," brought on by state action – increased deportations, deportability, and border controls – is the antithesis of family reunification, disrupting and even dismantling transnational families, separating and displacing family members throughout Mexico and the United States.

A focus on government policy and state action is one of the central contributions of the new kinship studies: as anthropologists of relatedness have shown, the state is an essential unit of analysis when considering family life. Carsten calls for a "reappraisal of … the boundary between the domestic and the political" (Carsten 2000: 18) and asks us to place "the close, intimate, and emotional work of kinship beside the larger projects of state and nation" (Carsten 2004: 9). Similarly, Butler reminds us that kinship is not a "fully autonomous sphere, proclaimed to be distinct from … the regulations of the state" (Butler 2004: 103). This is especially evident in the face of deportation.

In my research with people impacted by deportation, I have seen families that are undeniably regulated by the state – directly and in more subtle yet impactful ways. As Jaime, deported as a teen, told me: family "falls apart" after migration (Boehm 2016: 74). After he was expelled from the United States, Jaime was able to re/connect with extended family in Mexico, those he had not seen since he had migrated as a toddler and therefore did not really know, and those he had never met, including a generation of cousins living in Mexico. Still, even as Jaime tried to reconstruct or remake family after his deportation, his family's unmaking was especially pronounced. After deportation, Jaime was separated from his parents, siblings, aunts, uncles, and cousins who lived in the United States, those he had lived with throughout his childhood. And, painfully, Jaime's long-term relationship with his girlfriend dissolved under the pressures of living at a distance with no real sense of when or if reunification would be possible.

State removals are reversals in many senses: removal upsets well-being and security in nearly every sphere of daily life, reaching deeply into the intimacy of gender relations and family ties. Deportation unravels kin networks as state regimes permeate family relations and restructure kinship. As with migration, when the state upends family life through deportation, family members do all they can to build and maintain kin relations, but deportation makes the endeavor that much more challenging. The unmaking of family – that is, kinship that is directly "unmade" through state action – seems to be an inevitable part of the increase in state-enacted removals in recent years. Such is the emergent character of families that "fall apart" in the wake of deportation.

19.6   Precarity

As I visited with Emy at her home in Mexico, I was surprised to hear a conversation in English coming from the next room.[7] "Do you have visitors from the United States?" I asked. "No, those are my children!" she laughed, and called for them to join us in the living room. "My four children are here with me now. It's most difficult for the oldest ones. They all miss their father, of course, but for Cora and Joaquin it has been especially challenging." Emy described how painful it was to have the family living apart, with Emy and the children in Mexico and Emy's husband, Manuel, in the United States. Emy was not sure what would happen next, so she tried to focus on the present: getting the kids enrolled in school and helping them adjust to a new place.

Before the deportation, Emy and Manuel had lived in the United States for extended periods without documents, migrating between the two countries with relative ease for years at a time. During Emy's detention and immediately following the deportation, however, the family was in crisis. They scrambled to make a plan for how and where they would reunite, which family members would live together, and how residence across a transnational space would be structured. Emy's forced migrations, orchestrated by the state, produced a series of other forms of movement, especially the migrations of her children. Emy and Manuel first made the decision to have the children stay in the United States with Manuel; later they decided that the children should join Emy in Mexico. Still, as Emy described, even as she was reunited with the children, all felt uncertain. Emy explained that during the upcoming year they would consider what was best for the family and make plans accordingly.

As Emy talked about possible arrangements the family might make – that is, whether to have Emy "return" to the United States or to have Manuel come back to Mexico – she expressed the profound uncertainty they faced. Both Emy and Manuel were trapped on opposite sides of the US–Mexico border. Similarly, their US citizen children found themselves living in a country that was not their own, also trapped – at least until they were old enough to migrate without caregivers. Because of their US citizenship, the children can, in principle at least, migrate back to the United States, but in all practical senses, they continue to be confined to Mexico until their parents can make arrangements for an alternative form of residence.

* * *

The experiences of Federico, Marisa, Carlos, Emy, and their families illustrate the multiple ways that families are made and unmade transnationally. Through migration, but especially as a result of deportation, this dynamic signals a new order of exclusion in the twenty-first century. What can kinship theories tell us about this era of inequality? How might the "new" kinship studies direct us to further uncover how exclusion from the nation plays out specifically within families and through kin relations?

First of all, much of the social injustice that I describe stems from policies and structural barriers that prevent people from constructing "family" as they wish. As Butler posits, these "regulations" are formulated through a process of "state normalization of recognizable kinship relations" (Butler 2004: 104). Here, family and gender relations become channels of control for the state (Butler 2000; Stevens 1999, 2010). In what Elizabeth Povinelli calls an "empire of love," "individual freedom" and "social constraint" are enmeshed in the intimate spheres of relatedness (2006: 3). As the state inserts itself into intimate lives, it de facto defines who can and cannot constitute "family" for those whose lives straddle the US–Mexico border – even when policy does not directly address family relations.

Furthermore, by formally and informally linking citizenship and kin ties, the state erodes individual subjects' access to full membership.[8] Consider, for example, Emy's four US citizen children. As their experiences illustrate, individuals are always embedded in broader familial relationships. When Emy was deported, her school-aged children were also forced to leave through what legal scholar Daniel Kanstroom calls "*de facto* deportation" (2012: 135). Family members can essentially became "*alien*" by association (Boehm 2011: 168), through a process in which the unauthorized status of individual family members is extended to others, symbolically and/or in concrete ways. Building on Susan Bibler Coutin's concept of "alienation" (2000) – that is, the construction of an immigrant as "alien" – I maintain that the state's making of "illegal aliens" can happen "precisely because of one's family relations" (Boehm 2011: 168). This alienation through family ties is present during migration, but especially so in the face of deportation.

Among children and partners of deportees, categories of "legality" and "illegality" are effectively linked to that of others. This directly shapes the crossborder trajectories of family members and has a profound impact on kin relations and places of residence. Despite laws that focus on and ostensibly apply to individuals, migrants cannot be understood outside of meaningful family ties. The alienation of removal reaches far beyond the individual, devastating and unraveling families. Through relatedness, immigration but particularly deportation becomes an assault on family life and one's embeddedness in kin relations. In the end, the state's removal of some members is experienced within families by all. This is among the most damaging aspects of the fallout of deportation: as families are unmade, so, too, is membership in the nation.

So in conclusion, I want to revisit the notion that family life is both precarious and tenacious. As discussed, families are certainly flexible, continually "made" and made meaningful through relatedness. As Carsten persuasively reminds us, kinship is "an area of life in which people invest their emotions, their creative energy, and their new imaginings …

kinship involves not just rights, rules, and obligations but is also a realm of new possibilities" (Carsten 2004: 9). Butler, too, writes of both the dis-possession *and* potentiality inherent to "undoing gender" (2004) and kin. Even as family is "undone," there is at least some possibility for "doing" or "redoing" family in new ways.

But family connections are also and always precarious, "unmade" transnationally through migration but increasingly through deportation. "Remaking families" (Collier 1997) is guided by the state and also by members of kin groups themselves, but for those on the ground, "making family" can be highly constrained. Whether it is an attempt at family reunification or the assertion of new meanings attached to particular family members, efforts to make family transnationally are often blocked by the state. Such is the precarity of transnational movement, whether through migration, deportation, or return. Global migrations underscore the precariousness of families, of family ties, of membership within kin groups and nations, and increasingly of citizenship itself.

Again and again, I have seen the tenacity *and* precarity of family across international borders. This contradiction was painfully evident as Carlos' wife, Lucia, showed me an altar she had created in Mexico to protect her family, kin that was again divided by the US–Mexico border.[9] Decades of migration, followed by several difficult years after Carlos had been deported, had made family connections that much more challenging to maintain. The altar included photographs of loved ones separated by dis-tance and was created to assist Lucia and family members as they worked to maintain ties in a setting that was increasingly hostile toward building family life. As she lit daily candles in hopes of some (so far unimagin-able) solution, Lucia prayed for family to be reunited – or remade – even as their kinship was defined by the state's dismantling of it. The altar was a powerful symbol of the ways that family has been made, unmade, remade, and unmade again over decades and across geographies. This one family – like so many families – continues to be both precarious and hopeful in the face of forces that threaten it.

So, what are the possibilities and impossibilities for transnational fam-ilies in a global age? Although migrants repeatedly look to the potential for making a future and remaking family life, such agency and oppor-tunity is available only in a very limited sense. Transnational Mexicans find themselves and their families "stuck," caught between systems of membership that do not readily account for their undeniably trans-national lives. Here, global movement, relatedness, and national mem-bership are unequivocally entangled. When the state denies or "undoes" presence – and removes or de facto removes migrants and their family members – it directly "unmakes" kin and, significantly, "undoes" mem-bership and citizenship in the nation and beyond.

Despite the persistence of "family" and relatedness in the face of migra-tion and removal, the precarity of family life is felt widely as migrants move by will and by force across international boundaries. As is evident through histories of migration and return between Mexico and the United States, the US state controls individuals and family life. But the emergent forms of state power and their ability to "unmake" family is ever intensified through deportation. In fact, the deunification of kin groups is one of the most insidious and damaging aspects of deportation. The state's disciplining of family life results in a form of exceptional hardship for individuals and their families.

Migrants repeatedly experience this hardship that is "exceptional and extremely unusual" (8 US Code § 1229b) – the US government's supposed threshold for a "Cancellation of Removal" and criteria that the state assigns to very few families despite the unquestionable hardship they face. The hardship families experience is indeed "exceptional," even if it is not labeled as such by the state and although it is increasingly typical because of the state's very actions. Extending Giorgio Agamben's analysis of a "state of exception" (2005), what happens within the intimate lives of family members when the "exceptional" becomes everyday, and when crisis that is indeed "extremely unusual" becomes the norm for families attempting to connect across borders?

In the end, families are most often unmade through state action. As Jacqueline Bhabha posits, in transnational contexts, the "right to respect for family life" can quickly be displaced by its elusiveness (2014), demonstrating how the state makes disorder in family life a common, everyday experience. Global movement underscores the durability of family ties, as families repeatedly make and remake kin relations. Yet, in an age of deportation, precarity also defines family, as migrants face the state's "unmaking" of kin and a multiplication of new and emergent challenges to constructions of family across borders.

* * *

During my many conversations with Emy, it was clear that the deportation had worn her down. Even as she suggested that return migration to the United States might one day be a possibility, she felt defeated and quite tentative about what the future held for her family. Prior to the deportation, Emy had migrated multiple times between the United States and Mexico – an unusual migration history for a young woman, but one that reflected her independence and tenacity. With confidence and a keen sense of humor, Emy struck me as almost invincible. Not in this case, however. She was withdrawn and quieter than usual; she told me she cried often and felt hopeless about what was next.

One day as we talked about the implications of the deportation, Emy commented on my ability to move freely across borders and the limits to her own movement. As she told me: "You can go and come, but we can't." Indeed, as Emy so clearly asserted, rather than taking the form of an inalienable right, the freedom of movement is always determined by one's national membership and embedded within relatedness to others. As

Emy recounted the removal, she articulated the sense and reality of being trapped during detention and in her daily life following the deportation. As transnational configurations and reconfigurations of family make clear, immigration and especially deportation include both movement and barriers to it, new forms of membership but also compromised citizenship, as individuals and families find themselves making connections to others and having such ties "unmade," unpredictably migrating in unexpected directions and to new destinations, but also increasingly forced – or unable – to do so.

Notes

1. This vignette and others about Federico and Gaby are in *Returned* (Boehm 2016: 43–45, 74–75).
2. For further discussion of these policies, see *Intimate Migrations* (Boehm 2012: 15–16).
3. I first described Marisa in *Intimate Migrations* (Boehm 2012: 57–59).
4. See Boehm 2016: 40–42, 81–82, 92.
5. See discussion in Boehm 2016: 82.
6. This draws on a discussion in *Returned* (Boehm 2016: 91).
7. Throughout this chapter, Emy's experiences are taken from *Returned* (Boehm 2016: 77–81).
8. See *Returned* (Boehm 2016) for an extended discussion of compromised citizenship as a result of deportation.
9. See discussion in *Returned* (Boehm 2016: 128).

References

Abrego, Leisy J. 2014. *Sacrificing Families: Navigating Laws, Labor, and Love Across Borders*. Stanford, CA: Stanford University Press.

Agamben, Giorgio. 2005. *State of Exception*. Translated by Kevin Attell. Chicago, IL: University of Chicago Press.

Bhabha, Jacqueline. 2014. *Child Migration and Human Rights in a Global Age*. Princeton, NJ: Princeton University Press.

Boehm, Deborah A. 2011. "Here/Not Here: Contingent Citizenship and Transnational Mexican Children." In *Everyday Ruptures: Children and Migration in Global Perspective*, ed. Cati Coe, Rachel Reynolds, Deborah A. Boehm, Julia Meredith Hess and Heather Rae-Espinoza, 161–173. Nashville, TN: Vanderbilt University Press.

2012. *Intimate Migrations: Gender, Family, and Illegality among Transnational Mexicans*. New York: New York University Press.

2016. *Returned: Going and Coming in an Age of Deportation*. Series in Public Anthropology. Berkeley, CA: University of California Press.

Butler, Judith. 2000. *Antigone's Claim: Kinship Between Life and Death.* New York: Columbia University Press.

2004. *Undoing Gender.* New York: Routledge.

Carsten, Janet. 2000. "Introduction: Cultures of Relatedness." In *Cultures of Relatedness: New Approaches to the Study of Kinship,* 1–36. Cambridge: Cambridge University Press.

2004. *After Kinship.* Cambridge: Cambridge University Press.

Collier, Jane Fishburne. 1997. *From Duty to Desire: Remaking Families in a Spanish Village.* Princeton, NJ: Princeton University Press.

Collier, Jane, Michelle Z. Rosaldo and Sylvia Yanagisako. 1997. "Is There a Family? New Anthropological Views." In *The Gender/Sexuality Reader: Culture, History, Political Economy,* ed. Roger N. Lancaster and Micaela di Leonardo, 71–81. New York: Routledge.

Coutin, Susan Bibler. 2000. *Legalizing Moves: Salvadoran Immigrants' Struggle for U.S. Residency.* Ann Arbor, MI: University of Michigan Press.

De Genova, Nicholas and Nathalie Peutz, eds. 2010. *The Deportation Regime: Sovereignty, Space, and the Freedom of Movement.* Durham, NC: Duke University Press.

Dowling, Julie A. and Jonathan Xavier Inda, eds. 2013. *Governing Immigration Through Crime: A Reader.* Stanford, CA: Stanford University Press.

Dreby, Joanna. 2010. *Divided by Borders: Mexican Migrants and Their Children.* Berkeley, CA: University of California Press.

2015. *Everyday Illegal: When Policies Undermine Immigrant Families.* Berkeley, CA: University of California Press.

Fassin, Didier. 2011. "Policing Borders, Producing Boundaries: The Governmentality of Immigration in Dark Times." *Annual Review of Anthropology* 40: 213–226.

Foner, Nancy, ed. 2009. *Across Generations: Immigrant Families in America.* New York: New York University Press.

Kanstroom, Daniel. 2012. *Aftermath: Deportation Law and the New American Diaspora.* Oxford: Oxford University Press.

Menjívar, Cecilia. 2000. *Fragmented Ties: Salvadoran Immigrant Ties in America.* Berkeley, CA: University of California Press.

Newendorp, Nicole. 2008. *Uneasy Reunions: Immigration, Citizenship, and Family Life in Post-1997 Hong Kong.* Stanford, CA: Stanford University Press.

Olwig, Karen. 2007. *Caribbean Journeys: An Ethnography of Migration and Home in Three Family Networks.* Durham, NC: Duke University Press.

Parreñas, Rhacel Salazar. 2005. *Children of Global Migration: Transnational Families and Gendered Woes.* Stanford, CA: Stanford University Press.

Povinelli, Elizabeth A. *The Empire of Love: Toward a Theory of Intimacy, Genealogy, and Carnality.* Durham, NC: Duke University Press.

Rosas, Gilberto. 2012. *Barrio Libre: Criminalizing States and Delinquent Refusals of the New Frontier.* Durham, NC: Duke University Press.

Schneider, David M. 1968. *American Kinship: A Cultural Account.* Chicago, IL: The University of Chicago Press.

1984. *A Critique of the Study of Kinship.* Lansing, MI: University of Michigan Press.

Stevens, Jacqueline. 1999. *Reproducing the State.* Princeton, NJ: Princeton University Press.

2010. *States without Nations: Citizenship for Mortals.* New York: Columbia University Press.

Stumpf, Juliet. 2006. "The Crimmigration Crisis: Immigrants, Crime, and Sovereign Power." *American University Law Review* 56: 367–419.

20

My Folder Is Not a Person: Kinship Knowledge, Biopolitics, and the Adoption File

Eleana Kim

This chapter explores the role of paperwork in the production of kinship knowledge and subjectivity among Korean-born transnational adoptees. I begin with the adoptee vlogger, Peter, whose YouTube vlog provides a venue for the presentation of the self, beginning with the facts of procreation and birth: his "birth parents," birthplace, and date of birth. Adoption is clearly a defining feature of his life story, and the fact that the contents of his "folder," including items ranging from photographs, brochures, legal forms, and immigration documents, have been archived and set aside indicates that his adoptive parents and he value these artifacts for the information they provide about his early history. Yet Peter's attempted "story" quickly loses its thread, precisely because the folder's information lacks a stable relationship to his pre-adoption past. Although the documents promise to reveal the truth of his adoption and provide a coherent narrative of his origins, the names, dates, and locations that constitute his "self" open up a gap between the "facts of life" and the knowledge of kinship and identity that are characteristically "coupled" in Euro-American cultural reckonings of relatedness (Strathern 1999).

> Hi, everyone, so I realize that I've been kind of a butthead just putting up videos and talking about all this stuff and I haven't formally introduced myself or my story. My name is Peter, as you know. I was born May 10th 1989 in Ulsan city in Kyungsangnamdo [South Kyongsang Province]. And I was put up for adoption – finally given up for adoption – on May 13, and adopted on September 30, 1989. My mother was 21 when she had me, which means she's 40 now. Her name was Eunkyung, yeah, Eunkyung. She was seeing my birth father at the time; he was 34. There was a 13-year age difference between them. He's in his fifties now. I think he's 53. He was 34 at

the time. His name is Sam In, like, uhm, and he had graduated from university. He had a job, it says like salary man or whatever on the profile that I got.

So here's my travel certificate that I got from Korea. Here's me as a baby. Here's a picture of my foster mom and me – my family's been really good about keeping and containing all of the adoption documents for my sister and my brother and myself, so I have this folder with all of my adoption stuff in it, as do my siblings and there are all these documents and all of the like legal stuff that they had to go through and all of the information packets [from the Korean and American agencies].

I really don't know what to make of any of the things in here. You know they have progress reports about my health as a baby when I was at the agency, they have tips for new parents, they have a list of all the other Korean American adoptees that came on my flight, they have everything I could ever want to know about my adoption except for why. I think that in some part of the application that they send it says that I was given up because of financial hardship, which is the case for a lot of adoptees – you know, single mothers don't fare well in Korea, apparently.

But I can't help but feel and wonder if some really, really important bit of information was, I don't know, lost in translation or something. 'Cuz I read it and it says that the two dated and then they realized that they were not compatible in temper. I don't know what that means. Did he hit her? Was she annoying? Did he snore? I – I don't know and I need to know why. If they were together and had a baby, what broke them up after that?

Yeah. That's basically my story I mean it's not particularly interesting. It's probably just like every other adoptee's story. I know that there are some – I've been watching a lot of YouTube videos from Korean adoptees – and there are some of you that don't have the information that I have. And I know that I am very, very fortunate and very blessed to at least have a name. You know, have something that I can hold onto but, uhm, this is not meant to offend or make anyone upset, but I have all of this information and I can read – and I've read it through and through. There is nothing in that folder that I don't know. But the only thing I really care about is that little why. *You know, my folder is not a person. My folder will only tell me exactly what it knows and nothing more, and I need more.* So, I'm definitely, definitely going to go to the agency when I go to Korea next summer.

(YouTube vlog, "The Universe, Inc." August 5, 2008)

Like many adoptees, Peter seeks an answer to a most deeply felt question: why he was sent for adoption? The adoption documents that he relies upon to tell his "story" unfold a host of other possibilities and contingencies, and the gap in knowledge that the folder reveals, its inability to yield more than its contents, generates Peter's desire for "more." Peter articulates a desire for his folder to speak as a person, with cultural memory and embodied history, with complex knowledge rather than mute information, to grant him answers beyond its original bureaucratic function. The story that Peter begins thus fails to resolve, and instead becomes a prequel to another narrative; the search story, organized around a quest for an answer to what he calls "that little why."

The epistemological limits of the folder's contents are also related to Peter's inability to read the documents socially or historiographically. The documents initially suggest transparency of information that should lead to knowledge, yet they produce a feeling of ignorance, incompletion, and non-knowledge. As Peter states, "there is nothing in the folder that I don't know," yet he expresses confusion about the meanings contained within: "I really don't know what to make of any of the things in here." Moreover, because of the transnational nature of Peter's adoption, another gap opens up, a linguistic and cultural one: "I can't help but feel and wonder if some really, really important bit of information was … lost in translation or something."

Peter's narrative does not achieve closure, but, rather, expands onto a field of historical, social, and cultural contingencies that constitute his "self" in ways that many transnational adoptees have articulated in similar ways. The circumstantial disjunctiveness of adoptee life histories and their lack of knowledge about birth and "birth family" has become a defining feature in Korean adoptee collective articulations of their shared personhood (whether or not adoptees want to search and find their parents) in which the essentialization of contingency becomes the basis for adoptee belonging and social identity (Kim 2010). Adoptees not only wonder what might have happened had they stayed in Korea, but they also ponder the possibilities of having been raised in an elite family in France instead of a working-class family in Australia, or having access to a Korean immigrant community in Los Angeles as opposed to living in a rural, homogeneously white racial setting in Denmark. At adult Korean adoptee international conferences, regional meetings and in online fora, individual adoptees exchange their "stories," a genre of speaking that constitutes the subject as an adult Korean adoptee and that performatively instantiates membership within the "global Korean adoptee network." In the adult Korean adoptee counterpublic (Kim 2010) narrating one's origins and one's adoption history is a key social practice that establishes bonds of trust, friendship, and kinship among adoptees from disparate national, familial, social, cultural, and linguistic backgrounds. As Peter's vlog suggests, adoptee personal narratives are less driven by a biologistic presumption of authenticity and more by a historiographic desire for information about their pasts. Rather than seeking to displace their adoptive parents with a more authentic, "blood"-based relationship, adoptees are more likely to articulate their desire for information or origins as a way of "repair[ing] the broken narrative" (Tomes 1997), seeking completion and answers to provide a coherent narrative to their life stories.

Since beginning my research with Korean-born transnational adoptees who returned to Korea in 1999, I have often been asked by adoptees to help them decipher their paperwork or to provide interpretation or moral support for them when they go to their adoption agencies to "view" their files. Going to view one's file can be a highly charged emotional experience, because it threatens to open up a Pandora's box of kinship information about the adoptee's pre-adoption past, and it also runs the risk of revealing insufficient, redundant, or even no information at all. Nevertheless, like Peter, who "needed more" than his mute adoption documents could provide, many adoptees also "definitely, definitely" plan to go to their adoption agencies when they visit Korea. This intention is fueled by a common belief among adoptees (many of whom, like Peter, are part of an "imagined community" of adult Korean adoptees, and networked through vlogging, blogging, listservs, international conferences, and regional organizations) that the agency has data that might provide the information that will complete their personal identities and perhaps answer many of the questions that adoptees ask themselves about why they were adopted, who their biological parents are, and what led to their relinquishments.

It isn't clear, however, from Peter's testimony whether he intends to conduct a search for his birth parents or if he just wants more information. Some adoptees I met went to their agencies out of simple curiosity, "just to see what's in there," whereas others went with the intention of beginning "a search," with the goal of ultimately meeting their Korean birth parents. Outcomes of these consultations, however, were impossible to predict in part because adoptees often had little control over the process of seeking kinship information. Some adoptees who had made multiple visits to their agencies, orphanages, city archives, or hospitals faced dead ends at every turn. Others, such as the adoptee I describe in the vignette below, who had little or no expectations to search for Korean relatives, found themselves propelled into a reunion within a matter of days or weeks.

On a hot and humid summer afternoon in August 2004, I was with Greta, a 20-year-old Korean American adoptee, whom I had met a few days prior at the start of a government-sponsored motherland tour for which I was a volunteer. She had been adopted at five years old and had memories of her mother who worked as a hairdresser. Among the documents she had at home was a pre-adoption photo that showed her dolled up with a new hairdo, and a description of her temperament as "meticulous about her appearance" and "stubborn," which she said amused her friends at home, because it was such an uncannily accurate description of her personality. She had expressed interest in finding out information about her birth mother, but was not considering searching for her. I had been helping her to contact her adoption agency since the beginning of the tour. On this day we had broken off from the rest of the group to meet with a social worker, Ms. Lee, at the agency office. We sat for what seemed like many long minutes in a sparsely decorated meeting room with low couches and a glass coffee table. Ms. Lee came in with the file, and as she showed Greta the documents contained within it, Greta realized, with some disappointment, that there was nothing there she didn't already have in the file her adoptive parents had kept for her. In what seemed to be a superfluous gesture, Ms. Lee offered to make a copy of her medical record, and left the room. Hoping for something more, a missed detail, or a possible clue, we looked at the contents of the file again: information about herself, including the photo and the description above, her adoptive parents' home study, and the few details she already knew about her birth mother, but without any identifying information. In fact, the only surprising item was a letter from another adoptive parent that had been misfiled, and which belonged in another person's records.

Ms. Lee returned after a few minutes with the copy of the medical records. She sat down on the couch next to Greta, looked her squarely in the eyes, and asked, "Do you want to meet your birth mother?" When Greta answered that she did, the social worker asked why she would want to meet her. At this point, Greta became emotional and broke down in tears. Ms. Lee rather bluntly asked her why she was crying, and if she was angry at her birth mother, as many adoptees are angry at their birth parents. She further informed her that her birth mother might not want to come forward, since she had raised Greta for five years, and might feel guilty or fear that Greta would be angry with her. Greta collected herself, and responded without hesitation, as if she had prepared herself for this line of questioning, stating, "I just want her to know that I'm fine, that I appreciate all the opportunities I've had being adopted. I've had a good life." Over lunch, I asked Ms. Lee about the possibilities of locating Greta's mother. The social worker seemed to think that it might be possible, but refused to make any promises. A few days later, Greta received a call from Ms. Lee telling her that they had an address for her birth mother and had already sent a letter requesting a reunion. Ms. Lee asked if Greta would stay another week in Korea in case her birth mother responded. Greta ended up leaving on schedule to return to the United States, but she returned six months later with plans to stay in Korea to teach English and to reunite with her birth mother.

As mentioned above, although not typical, Greta's experience was not entirely unique either. It is more common for adoptees to report frustrating or banal meetings with social workers than it is to hear remarkable accounts of sudden and unexpected reunions, but the latter also frequently circulate in adoptee circles. As I attempt to suggest with this vignette, despite the expectation that the file would contain crucial kinship information, the contents of the file were less significant than its viewing: there was no new information in Greta's file, yet the meeting to view the file became an occasion to ask, "Do you want to meet your birth mother?" When Greta said yes, other information, which was not available to her, was mobilized to locate the mother. Because of confidentiality and privacy rules, adoption agencies do not share identifying information of the birth parents directly with adoptees; instead, social workers take charge of making contact and facilitating reunions.

In my research, I found that many Korean adoptees articulate desires for information in ways that echo those of domestic adoptees in studies by Modell (1994) and Carsten (2004, 2007), for whom kinship knowledge is necessary for the completion of the self and personal identity. As Carsten found in her study, however, adoptees are also aware that searches and reunions can be tumultuous and destabilizing experiences, and seek to contain or limit the effects of revealed kinship knowledge by holding onto information rather than activating it, delaying reunions, or refusing them altogether. Thus, kinship knowledge, while it may lead to an altered sense of self, does not necessarily lead to kinship relations (Strathern 1995). Whatever their desires or beliefs about how kinship knowledge will affect their identities and relationships, adoptees who search often fetishize their adoption documents and the adoption file held by the adoption agency, in part because of their restricted access to the file and the illegibility of the documents. The mediation of information by state institutions and adoption agencies is a crucial aspect of how adoptees assimilate kinship information and kinship knowledge into their social identities.

20.1   Legibility and Illegibility

To date, studies of transnational adoption have primarily focused on the imbrications of race, ethnicity, gender, and nation in the making of transnational adoptive family relations (Dorow 2006; Howell 2006; Volkman 2005; Yngvesson 2010; Yngvesson and Coutin 2006) and on the cultural work of adult adoptees who seek their "roots" through return trips to the "birth country" (Kim 2003; Yngvesson 2010). The ways in which adoptees identify with their "birth culture" (Volkman 2005) or nation of origin have also been examined, especially in light of multiculturalism in Western societies and a growing attention to "roots" and heritage among diasporic groups around the world. Although the structures of power and governmentality that make adoption across borders possible have been examined by Howell (2006) and Yngvesson (2010), less attention has been paid to the role of the state and biopolitical institutions in the everyday understandings of kinship, cultural citizenship, and transnational identifications of adoptees.

In my previous work (Kim 2007), I argue that studies that examine transnationalism and kinship tend to leave the definitions of kinship and kinship ties uninterrogated, and moreover, pay insufficient attention to how state power underwrites and legislates certain relationships as "kin" while disallowing others. Transnational adoption provides a unique lens through which to examine how kinship relations and kinship knowledge are shaped by legal technologies and global political-economic inequalities because it makes visible the constructed and contested nature of "kinship" in transnational migration. The relationship between transnational migrations and the legislation of kinship becomes especially salient in light of the fact that, as Caroline Blesdoe notes, family reunification is becoming "the default pathway to legitimate transnational mobility" (2006: 2).

Here, I focus on one adoptee's adoption file to explore, through an extraordinary case, the legal technologies that produce adoptable children and also set the terms for adult adoptee citizenship and personhood in a transnational context. Like Barbara Yngvesson and Susan Coutin (2006) who have explored the ways in which returns to birth country are motivated by gaps opened up between de jure and de facto lives in adoption, I am also intrigued by how an adoptee's beginnings compel her to go "back" to a country that promises plenitude, but which may, in fact, lack any grounding in a pre-adoption reality. I take this exploration in another direction, however, to argue that a closer examination of the actual paperwork and adoptees' attempts to read back through their papers reveals the powerful "state effects" (Aretxaga 2003; Trouillot 2003) of adoption documents. In the case that I discuss, I provide a close reading of adoption paperwork and its indexical relationship to the past. Rather than pointing back to the pre-adoption real, it serves as the materialized traces of mundane acts of bureaucratic proceduralism. For some adoptees, the file then transforms from a fetish embodying hidden kinship knowledge into evidence of the hidden operations of state power, recalling Veena Das' contention that "It is precisely because the documents can be forged and used out of context and because the bureaucratic-legal processes are not legible even to those responsible for implementing them, that the state can penetrate the life of the community yet remain elusive" (Das 2005: 245). South Korea's adoption program provides a particularly valuable context in which to examine these dynamics because of its long history (1953–present) and because of the coincidence of the coming of age of adult transnational adoptees and South Korea's proactive globalization projects.

In my discussion, I connect paperwork to what James Scott calls state "projects of legibility" (1998), and how bodies and populations are produced as objects of knowledge and state biopower (Foucault 1979).

I frame the adoption file as an artifact of transnational governmentality in Korean adoption practice and as a technology that renders abandoned and relinquished children legally cognizable to the sending and receiving states as "orphans" eligible for transnational adoption emigration. I show how paperwork makes children's bodies legible across national contexts through physiognomic description and medical reports, yet also renders their prior histories *illegible*, thus bringing into focus the ways in which children are made and valued in their movements across national borders. For adult adoptees who seek information about their pasts, paperwork is illegible in two specific ways – in the physical inaccessibility of the file for adoptees, and in their literal inability to read the documents contained therein due to a lack of Korean language fluency. This illegibility contributes to the illegibility of the adoption system for adoptees, and thereby extends the effects and experience of state power in their everyday lives (Sharma and Gupta 2006; Das and Poole 2005). In cases of discrepancies or mishandlings of adoption cases, adoptees find that this illegibility is compounded by a lack of authorship or accountability on the part of agencies or state institutions. I highlight in my analysis how the information in the papers promises to answer questions about kinship knowledge and identity, but failing this, begins to reveal the traces of other histories that have been concealed through constitutive erasures.

Following a historical outline of adoptions from South Korea to the West, I focus on the documents contained in one adoptee's "file" and unpack the ways in which the value of the child is produced through the work of paperwork. In conclusion, I discuss how, in the context of transnational South Korea, the restoration of Korean citizenship for adoptees raises further questions about kinship knowledge, biopolitics, and the relations adoptees have to the state's vision of a global Korean "family" (Kim 2005).

20.2 Transnational Korean Adoptions

An estimated 200,000 South Korean infants and young children have been adopted to white families in Europe, Australia, and North America since 1953. Overseas Korean adoptions first began in the aftermath of the Korean War, a direct outcome of American military intervention and Western humanitarian projects. The initial wave of children were "war orphans," many of whom were Amerasian, and the circulation of sentimental media images of war waifs and "mixed-race" orphans spurred dozens of Americans to petition congressmen, Korean diplomats, and even the president of South Korea himself for the chance to raise those children as Americans. This first wave of "orphans" set the stage for subsequent adoptions, and largely due to the work of Harry Holt, an evangelical Christian from Oregon whose adoption agency continues to be a leader in international adoptions today, South Korea (hereafter, "Korea") quickly became the main source for adoptable children in the West. Although the "crisis" in mixed-race children had first motivated the salvation projects of individuals like Holt, by the mid-1960s, the majority of children sent overseas were of full-Korean parentage who were either economic orphans or whose mothers were unmarried and incapable of raising them due to the combined effects of social stigma and poverty. The state's priorities of national security, population control, and economic development contributed to the unchecked expansion of overseas adoption as a social welfare policy solution throughout the 1970s and 1980s. Adoptions of Korean children exponentially increased with more than 100,000 sent overseas during those decades. Despite the changing contexts and circumstances of these children and their natal families, these Korean adoptees continued to be referred to as "orphans," suggesting how legal categories and humanitarian ideologies were conflated in everyday discourse.

The myth of the orphan also shaped the consciousness of adoptees, many of whom assumed that they were true orphans, and that searching for information about their pasts would be an impossible task. Furthermore, before the recent transformations in adoption policy and parenting ideologies, social workers tended to construe adoptees who desired knowledge of their origins to be "maladjusted," and adoptees, then and now, often worry that curiosity about biological origins might alienate their adoptive parents. As more adult adoptees have been networking and forming a transnational social movement, and with the medicalization of identity and molecularization of personhood (Finkler 2001; Nelkin and Lindee 1996) influencing adoption discourse and practice, the exchange of information about birth family search has proliferated in adoptee spaces both online and off. Now, many are embarking on searches, some through agencies, some independently. As narratives of irregularities in the adoption file and withholdments on the part of agency social workers circulate, suspicion and rumor have come to characterize adoptee discourses of birth family search and reunion and adoption agencies are often framed as powerful brokers of transnational governmentality.

20.3   Paper Trails and Gatekeepers

Of the roughly 100,000 transnational Korean adoptees now of majority age, an expanding cohort has been returning to live or work in Korea – the "motherland," as it is constructed for them by the Korean state, or, the "birth country," as it is commonly referred to in adoption parlance. Highly sensationalized by the Korean media, reunions with birth family are often assumed to be the main reason that adoptees return to Korea, even though many adoptees come with different motivations or degrees of interest. In spite of the diversity in attitudes towards searching, it

is undeniable that a sea change took place in the late 1990s for a critical mass of adult adoptees, who grew up believing that they were true
orphans, with no living parents, or who could not fathom undertaking
a search in a distant country and a foreign culture. As dramatic stories
of search and reunion circulated at conferences and through the media,
what was once considered to be impossible or unimaginable became
increasingly feasible and desirable.

Thousands of adoptees are now seeking information about biological
family, and their receptions by adoption agencies have been mixed. Prior
to the 1996 reform legislation, adoption agencies were simply "placement
agencies" (*ibyang alsŏn kigwan*) that focused on processing paperwork and
preparing children to be legally adopted overseas. The 1996 legislation
changed their designation to "adoption agencies" (*ibyang kigwan*), stipu-
lating that they provide "after services," or post-adoption services, which
includes oversight of the adoption placement for six months following
an adoption, as well as motherland visits (Park 2000). Birth family search,
however, was not explicitly addressed and agencies are under no legal
obligation to help adoptees with their searches. In the past few years,
however, out of necessity, given the pressure from increasing numbers of
adoptees coming to find information, the agencies have been developing
internal policies that are intended to balance the rights to privacy of the
birth families with adoptees' rights to information.

In the course of my research I heard innumerable stories about "the
adoption file," invariably referring to the files at their Korean adoption
agencies. Adoptees, in actuality, have more than one file or set of
documents – there is the adoption file held by the agencies in the country
to which they were adopted, the file held by the Korean agency, and
the file that their parents may have kept for them at home. In addition,
they may find other records of their presence at municipal offices, police
stations, hospitals, and orphanages in Korea. These multiple files and
their various locations comprise the paper trail (Yngvesson and Coutin
2006) that documents their lives as objects of state and transnational
biopolitics, and they are "dispersed among different actors who do not
pursue the same interests and are not invested with the same responsibilities" (Ouellette and Mossière 2004). Finding a way to piece together
these various bits of information and their pre-adoption pasts, often in
the hopes of locating Korean family, has become a major project for some
adoptees.[1] For many, visiting their adoption agencies to "view their file"
is a key rite of passage in their personal journeys as adopted persons,
whether or not they desire to pursue a more formal search for biological
kin. Like Greta, adoptees who participate in roots tours often visit the
"post-adoption services" department of international adoption agencies
which provides adoptees an often long-anticipated opportunity to see
their files.

Each agency has a different reputation when it comes to birth family search, and treatment by social workers can sometimes seem wholly arbitrary and their attitudes fickle. The viewing of the file is generally performed in a controlled environment at the adoption agency with a social worker in the post-adoption services department who helps the adoptee interpret the contents of the file. The formal way in which the file is retrieved, presented, viewed, and returned to its place suggests how adoption files are always on reserve, and never allowed to circulate or to transfer ownership. Very often, adoptees have been disappointed to find that the information they are given is what they already have seen in their files at home – copies of their adoptive parents' home studies or other documentation from the Western counterpart agencies – and they may not know what other sorts of documents should be expected to be included in the file. Adoptees from one particular agency have often reported that, when they go to view their adoption file, they are forced to sit a considerable distance from the social worker's desk, and that only select portions of the file are shared with the adoptee. This selective viewing may be especially noticeable if the adoptee comes with a Korean speaker or demonstrates the ability to read Korean. The high degree of restriction and control over the file and its contents was brought home to one adoptee who, despite having already been reunited with her Korean mother, was not permitted to repossess a drawing she had made as a child which was in her file. Instead, she was offered a black-and-white Xerox copy.

The subjugated position of the adoptee comes through strongly in adoptee narratives of visits to adoption agencies, in which social workers stand as unpredictable gatekeepers to valuable knowledge about the adoptee's identity, as represented by her past life and biological origins. These social workers thus come to represent "the system" and the agencies' quasi-governmental roles. The wide-ranging inconsistencies in treatment by agencies suggest to many adoptees that unethical and possibly illegal adoptions are being covered up. These suspicions have been supported by stories that have emerged from adoptees who have reunited with their birth families and learned of the circumstances that surrounded their adoptions. Many who were adopted in the 1970s and 1980s have found that they were relinquished by grandparents, jealous stepparents, or well-meaning relatives, suggesting how easily the legal and social connection between Korean parents and their children could be manipulated in a system that seemed to lack adequate oversight.[2] Children who were claimed to have been foundlings, for instance, have discovered that they were dropped off at an orphanage or adoption agency by grandparents who believed it would be impossible for their widowed daughters-in-law to raise the children alone. Mothers, especially working-class widows or abandoned women, were convinced by social workers, neighbors, relatives, or religious figures that the best they could do for their child was to send her abroad for better opportunities.

Korean family law under the patriarchal family head system (*hojujedo*) has, until very recently, granted full legal custody exclusively to fathers (even if the children live with their mothers after divorce, they are registered as co-habitants, rather than as their legal offspring).[3] As divorce rates increased throughout the 1970s and 1980s, many children of divorced parents also ended up at orphanages or adoption agencies in part due to the difficulties of single parenthood in the absence of childcare services and sometimes because the children posed an impediment to remarriage. In other cases, medical emergencies, sudden economic calamities, or an overabundance of daughters in the quest for a son were contributing factors. Because agencies were focused on efficient child placement rather than on family preservation, children were accepted on the basis of minimal background investigation and shuttled quickly through a well-oiled system to their new parents overseas. What often resulted were case files filled with misinformation and spotty or incomplete data.

It is not surprising, therefore, that conspiracy theories frequently mingled with narratives about searches among adoptees I spoke with during my fieldwork in Seoul. Korean (as well as their counterpart Western) adoption agencies were often construed as corrupt corporate institutions that are in the business of protecting their own reputations rather than in helping adoptees. Already having profited from the commodification of adoptee bodies, agencies that charge adoptees for viewing their own files, or for conducting a preliminary family search were considered to be especially contemptible. The lack of systematic protocol at agencies inevitably added more provocation to an already difficult and anxious process that held no guarantees for success or happy outcomes.

Adoption agency representatives, for their part, claimed that they were legally bound to protect the identities of biological parents, and would be subject to large government fines if they released identifying information to adoptees. Moreover, they asserted that they simply did not have the resources or personnel to help the overwhelming number of adoptees who come to their offices, often without prior appointment. When adoptees reunite with birth parents, either through adoption agency assistance or through other avenues, the discrepancy between the documentation and the stories they hear from birth parents can be cause for suspicion or distrust of the agencies. Adoption agency workers who handle these cases are especially sensitive to being blamed for these discrepancies. From their perspective, they can not be held responsible for what happened in the past, and they attribute adoptees' frustration regarding the birth family search to their ignorance of the process, not because the system is flawed. But their sympathies may also lie with the social workers in the past whose job was to record whatever relinquishing parents or relatives may have told them. If other stories emerge in the aftermath of reunion, as one social worker told me, it is more likely because of the faulty memory of the birth parent or relative, especially if he or she concocted a story to tell the adoption agency, and not because the social workers intentionally falsified records.

Janet Carsten (2007) in her study of Scottish adoptees and kinship knowledge writes, "the constitutive power of new kinship knowledge might be reinforced when such knowledge has been concealed. And this is because identity for Euro-Americans rests not just with self-knowledge, and hence kinship knowledge, but also with a sense of control over one's own life" (2007: 421–422). Korean adoptees also link identity to kinship knowledge, but the adoptees' lack of control over her own life and kinship relations becomes particularly pronounced in encounters with social workers because of cultural differences and linguistic barriers and the sense that their search trajectories are controlled by adoption agencies. For some adoptees, this lack of agency becomes further articulated with broader structures of power in which agencies and the state are viewed as engaged in a collusive biopolitical project of managing populations and commodifying children. Even though adoption agencies are private institutions, adoptee attributions of state power to adoption agencies are not entirely inapt, as those agencies have long been part of a distributed state system, in which government ministries explicitly relied upon overseas adoption agencies to outsource social welfare programs.

20.4   Almost Dutch

In this section I look closely at the adoption documents of Jane Jeong Trenka, a Korean American adoptee writer and activist. Her documents are particularly intriguing because of Jane's unique personal history – unlike other adoptees, she had intermittent contact with her Korean mother after her adoption, and was reunited with her as an adult, giving her access to information about her pre-adoption past against which to read the information contained in her adoption documents. Because of this exceptional circumstance, the incongruities between the records and past events can be discerned more clearly, and quite disarmingly in this instance. Rather than underscoring the lack of accuracy in the paperwork, however, I analyze the paperwork as a representation of the knowledge practices that produced the "orphan" as an identifiable subject of social welfare and immigration policy. Adoption paperwork, which was never meant to serve a purpose beyond the adoption placement, can thereby provide a window onto the bureaucratic practices that function to reduce the complexity of personhood and biography to expedient categories and procedures. Moreover, in paperwork's afterlife, adoptees read it against

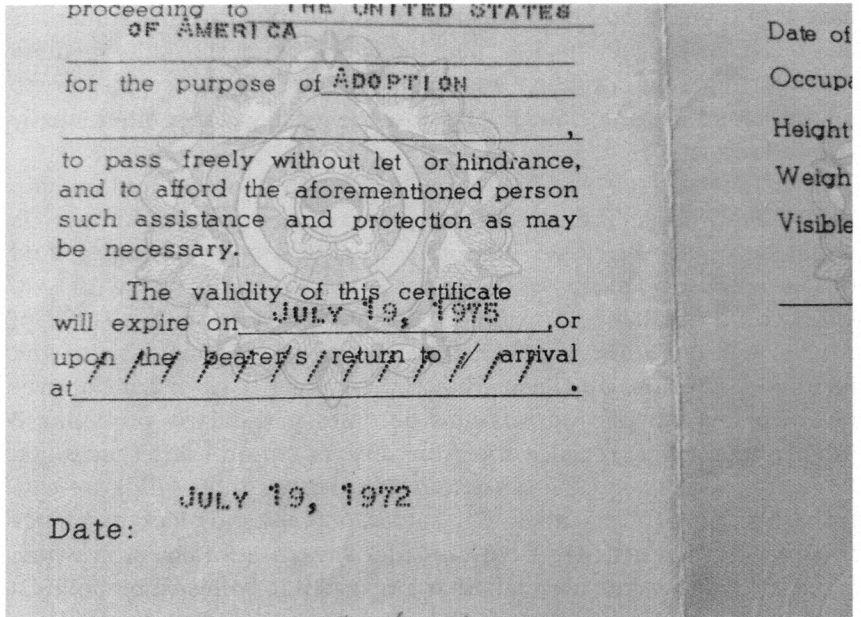

Figure 20.1 Jong Kyong Ah travel document (Jane Jeong Trenka)

the grain, interpreting it as material evidence of the biopolitical management of children's bodies and agency corruption.

"Almost Dutch" is what Jane Jeong Trenka originally named a post on her personal blog in October 2006. In it she recounted how a somewhat routine visit to the immigration office in Korea to renew her "overseas Koreans" (F-4) visa led to some unsettling discoveries. Jane was adopted in 1972 by a white family in rural Minnesota when she was five months old, accompanied by her four-year-old sister. Her Korean mother managed to maintain contact with her two daughters, and they met again in the early 1990s. For this reason, Jane has a more complete set of papers and narratives than most other adoptees.[4] The biography represented in her personal adoption file presents an unambiguous progression from Korean orphan to American citizen, a clearly documented transformation that begins with her travel document, which served as her passport on her one-way journey from Korea to the United States. The way in which the travel document (Figure 20.1)[5] was altered suggests how adoption is an exceptional type of migration – one that requires a cancellation of any return, whether required or expected – and underscores how "[p]assports and analogous documents may be used by states not to restrict but to facilitate departures and thus to rid governments of undesirable elements" (Caplan and Torpey 2001: 10).

Also among Jane's paperwork is the visa petition filed by Jane's American parents after having received the adoption agency referrals for Jane and her sister. The petition demonstrates the liminal status of the adopted child in its transfer across national borders and families, for this very same document that classifies the two sisters as "orphans" under American immigration law also permits them entry as "immediate relatives" of the adopting parents, under the clause of family reunification. This redesignation also ensures that the child will not become the first link in a chain of migration from the sending country. The notion that excess family ties will compromise the security of national and/or familial borders has also been used by adoptive parents and adoption agencies to justify the necessity of severing communication between the adopted child and existing natal relatives.[6]

Jane's other documents track the production of a new person – through baptism, adoption, (re)birth, and citizenship, attesting to and instantiating beginnings through (re)naming and naturalization (Yngvesson and Coutin 2006). The simplicity and clear legibility of these documents is predicated on the cancelation of the child's prior Korean name and family, neither of which appear on any of the American documents. Immediately following the arrival of the child "home," the orphan's former name, "Jong Kyong Ah," is wholly replaced by her baptized name as a normative American child, Jane Marie Vogler. And this name becomes her legal one upon her official adoption one year later.[7]

After her children had departed, Jane's Korean mother spent consecutive days waiting in the adoption agency office in Korea until a social worker relented and provided the address of the adopting family. With intermittent contact throughout her childhood and adolescence, Jane was able to reunite with her mother when she was an adult, an experience she rendered in her award-winning memoir, *The Language of Blood* (2003). Jane moved to Korea in 2006, and, as an adoptee, qualified for recognition as an "overseas Korean" through a special dispensation that allows adoptees to claim their extraterritorial belonging to the nation. As I describe elsewhere, the conjuncture of adoptee returns to Korea and the South Korean government's proactive globalization projects has led to a revaluation of these once excess bodies, who are now enthusiastically welcomed back as "valuable assets" and "cultural ambassadors" between Korea and the West (Kim 2005, 2010).

Any person with prior South Korean citizenship may apply for the F4, or "Overseas Koreans visa," which allows them to enter and leave the country freely and live in South Korea with most of the same benefits as nationals, but without the right to vote. The visa is good for two years, at which time, it must be renewed. Jane decided to move to South Korea in 2004 and applied for an F4 visa from a South Korean consulate before she left the United States. The application process requires proof that the applicant was once recognized as a South Korean national. Since adoption and naturalization effectively erase their Korean origins, adoptees' identification papers often serve as insufficient evidence. Proving their Korean origins thus requires additional documentation obtained from their adoption file that indicates that they were born in Korea and adopted overseas. In Jane's case, she existed on her Korean family registry (in another strange twist, her parents added her to it even after she had been sent for adoption), and was also a US citizen, two contradictory statuses that highlight the doubleness of legal personhood for adoptees. According to South Korean law, the citizenship of a child adopted to the United States is automatically nullified once it receives American citizenship. Jane entered South Korea on an F4 visa, based upon the information she provided, including her Korean family registry. Upon her attempt to renew her status, however, the immigration officer flagged a discrepancy in her date of birth between her family registry and her American passport, which led to a host of other discoveries.

As is common for adoptees, the birth date in her adoption paperwork was recorded according to the solar calendar and did not match the date of birth on the Korean family registry, which was recorded according to the lunar calendar. Given these discrepancies, she was unable to prove that she was the same person. Moreover, none of her documents from the United States or from Korea included both her legal Korean name and her legal American name. Jane was loath to reconcile her documents, which would require her to file a case in family court, in order to legally "correct" her birth date on her Korean registry with a false date. Instead, Jane requested her Korean adoption agency send her what is called the "orphan registry," which, she presumed, would have the same birth date as her American passport. For Jane, however, in the process of becoming (re)legible to the Korean state as a "Korean," she also discovered that she had almost been "Dutch."

Sometimes referred to as the "orphan hojŏk," the orphan registry inscribes the child as a legible, free-standing subject of the state (Figures 20.2 and 20.3). Modeled on the family registry (hojŏk), which, until recently, was based on a patrilineal system of successive male family heads of household, the child, in preparation for adoption and erasure as a Korean citizen, is registered as a family head of its own, single-person household and solitary lineage. The orphan hojŏk is an invention by adoption agency social workers that disembeds the child from a normative kinship structure and legally reinscribes her as a peculiar and exceptional state subject, singularizing the child as an orphan, without any extant kinship ties.[8] In the context of Korean law, she becomes a person with the barest of social identities, and in the context of Korean cultural norms, she lacks the basic requirements of social personhood – namely, family lineage and genealogical history. The spaces in the document where the names of the child's parents would have been entered, for instance, are left blank, and there is no indication that the child had a prior life or any social relations beyond that of the guardian who filed this form on her behalf. The only identifying information included is the name of the hoju, or family head, here,

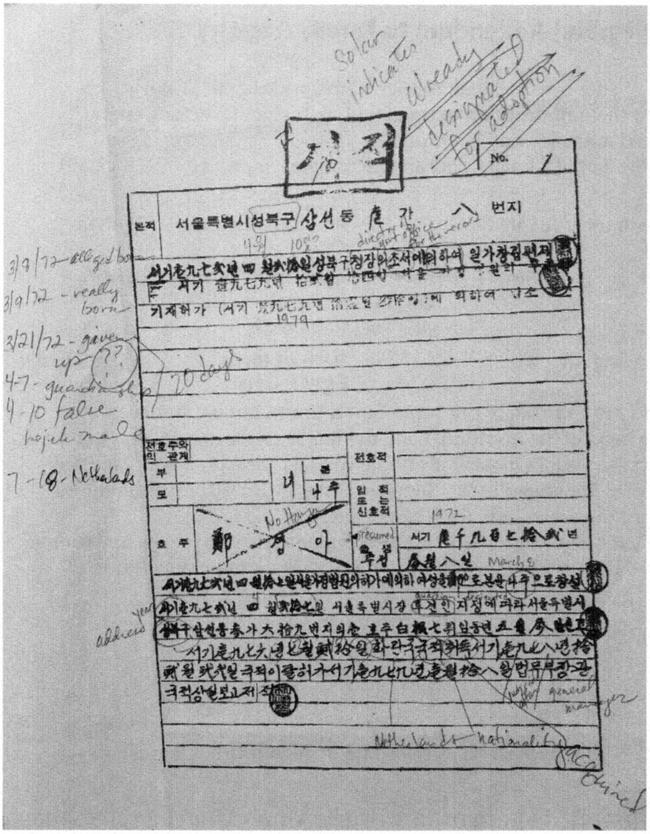
No. 1

본적 서울특별시성북구 삼선동 번지

presumed

March 8

solar indicates already designated for adoption

Netherlands nationality acquired

Figure 20.2 Orphan registry (*hojŏk*)

the "orphan," whose name is written in simple Korean (rather than the Chinese characters (*hanja*) upon which it is based), the date of birth, and the "family seat" or ancestral origins.

What first struck me upon viewing this document was its near illegibility – not only from the standpoint of the adoptee but even from the standpoint of a person fluent in Korean, and especially in contrast to her Korean family's registry. After deciphering the text (traces of Jane's attempts to work out the contents of the document appear in the margins of this copy), Jane discovered that her birthday, here, noted as "presumed," is documented as March 8, in the solar calendar, rather than lunar calendar, which is the norm for family registries.[9] Moreover, the orphan registry arbitrarily designates her "family seat" as the southern city of Naju, rather than the city of Onyang, which is where her Korean father's lineage is based. These fictions might be considered negligible, if it were not for the final and most surprising detail included in this record, which states that she was adopted to Holland and acquired Dutch citizenship in 1976.

[Illegible] Addendum to Family Registry

Address   Seoul City Söngbuk district, Samsön-dong, 1st St. #8
1972.4.20, According to the authorization of the Söngbuk District Director General
  new [illeg.] household is established [stamped]
1979.12. 14 Submitted to Seoul Family Court and record was approved (1979.12.30)

Relationship with previous head of household	[BLANK]			Previous Registry	[BLANK]
Father	[BLANK]	WOMAN	Family Origin	Entry into Family or New	[BLANK]
Mother	[BLANK]		Naju	Registry	
Head of Household	Jong Kyong Ah			Date of Birth PRESUMED	1972.3.8 [Solar Calendar]

1972. 4. 17 According to the approval of the Seoul Family Court, this woman was
  designated to be the head of the household and the family origin to be Naju. [stamped]
1972.4.27. According to the Seoul City Mayor's directive [illeg.], the guardian, Mr. Baek
  Keun Chil, of Seoul City, Söngbuk district, Samsön-dong, 3rd St., #1, recommended
  and completed record the same year, May 3 [stamped].
1976.7.20 Acquired Dutch citizenship. 1978.12.22 Permission granted to give up [Korean]
  citizenship. 1979.1.18 Reported to the Ministry of Justice and nationality forfeited
  [stamped].

Figure 20.3 Orphan registry translation

20.5   Making Orphans and Missing Persons

The inaccuracies in this document and those that other adoptees have
encountered raise important human rights concerns regarding adoptees'
rights to information about their backgrounds (Hague Convention 1993,
article 30), yet what I want to focus on here is how those mal-ascriptions
lay bare the categories and practices by which adoptees are valued
and exchanged in international adoption.[10] Whether or not this set of
fabrications was willfully made, and whether it is merely one instance
of administrative sloppiness, or else representative of a more widespread
and insidious practice (as some adoptee narratives prefer to promote),
this particular case shows how the production of legal fictions and
fictive "origins" through paperwork entails bureaucratic procedures that
objectify, singularize, and decontextualize the child for transnational
adoption. Thus, when adoptees return, they may discover that "this is all
there is" – these legal fictions, whether traceable to real people or to false
trails in Holland or Naju, are, in the end, self-referential, pointing back
only to themselves (cf. Yngvesson and Coutin 2006: 178).

For some adoptees, these falsifications serve as proof that they were
never expected to return to Korea or to be reunited with biological families, and, furthermore, that although (or because) the possibility of their
returns was anticipated, they were not only cancelled, as demonstrated
in the travel document, but preemptively thwarted. Instead of pointing

back to an imagined and longed for "authentic" kinship, then, the paper trail, in fact, leads them further into the brambles of illegibility and the arbitrary excesses of bureaucratic power. Moreover, a growing number of adoptees are beginning to identify their own subordination to state power through their inability to penetrate the illegibility of the state, and to construct a critical perspective of the "system" that produces desirable, i.e., unencumbered, children for affluent Western families. The value of the child is predicated on its alienability, effectuated through paperwork which erases prior histories and reinscribes new lives and trajectories, based on a Western bourgeois model of right families – self-contained, nuclear units of exclusive belonging. The labor of paperwork, its processing and production, is widely construed by adoption agencies as the real object of exchange in transnational adoption, to assuage some adoptive parents' discomfort with the idea of purchasing a child, rather than paying for "services rendered." Yet, as the illegibility of documents show, in adoption, the paperwork contained in the file *is* the child – for there is no prior representation of the adoptable orphan.

The labor of adoption and the work in adoption paperwork produces an "orphan," who then is free to be transformed into an exceptional immigrant and someone's as-if genealogical child. As Esben Leifsen (2004), drawing upon Marilyn Strathern's work, notes in his analysis of Ecuadorian transnational adoption practices,

> Adoption in the formalized intercountry form does not produce a person constituted of a multitude of relations. It is a much more controlled process of separation, objectification and re-constitution, one where relations are replaced and social discontinuity created. Thus the socially constitutive work going on in the adoption process is characterized *by the making of one relation*.
>
> *(Leifsen 2004: 193, emphasis in original)*

If the distinction between commodity and gift exchange is the absence of social relations in the former and the reproduction of social relations in the latter, Leifsen argues that in international adoption "the unique value of the person, which makes her or him incomparable and not exchangeable, is temporally suspended" (2004: 192).

Through the legal fiction of the "orphan," children are disembedded from prior contexts and the ground laid for the "exclusive belongings" required of plenary adoption and in American immigration law (Yngvesson 2002).[11] In a similar fashion, Barbara Yngvesson (2002) argues that the "clean break" effectuated by plenary adoptions, the making of one relation out of many, leaves behind an excess of relationships that "enchain" the child's givers and recipients and "haunt" adoptee subjectivities (see also Dorow 2006). These can be thought of as the constitutive outside, comprised of obscured or excerpted social relations. In this way paperwork not only makes children into orphans, but, over time, produces missing persons (see hers 2007), and the narrative discontinuities and gaps produced by paperwork often present challenges to adoptees' attempts to create coherent identities out of any remaining fragments.

As one can see from the marginal notes Jane made in the copy of her orphan registry, reconstructing the chronology of the first few months of her life were critical to her own history. For instance, nowhere was it indicated in her paperwork that Jane's Korean mother had retrieved her infant daughter from the orphanage to nurse her back to health, a valuable part of her biography that signified to Jane that she had not been simply abandoned. Moreover, her mother had seen her daughters off at the airport, another detail that has no appropriate place in the adoption documentation and thus has gone unrecorded. For Jane, these are proof of kinship relations and gestures of love that disprove the myth of orphanhood and the narrative of abandonment. They constitute the excess of relations that have no purchase in the process of "making one relation" and that are literally marginalized (as marginalia) in the suspension of the "unique value of the person."

Adoptees who search for kinship knowledge often hone in on the moment of suspension that Leifsen pinpoints, for this is also the point of no return, the juncture at which social relations are severed, identities are altered, and "family" reconstituted in one singular relation. That moment is represented in the adoption relinquishment document which is signed by the natal parents to permit the "overseas adoption emigration" (*haeoeibyang imin*) of the child. The document, in Korean, with a notarized English translation, notes that the child was in the custody of the mother/father/guardian "without the legal family registration." It binds the signatories to "irrevocably consent to his/her emigration and adoption ... for the child's future welfare" and requires the unconditional waiving of any rights the parent or guardian may have to the child, permitting the adoption agency to accomplish the emigration and adoption procedures. Whereas the other documents are dedicated to fixing the present identity of the child, through substitution and erasure of prior relations, here, the relinquishment form is decidedly future-oriented – for the future happiness and welfare of the child, the parents relinquish their parental authority and also vow to never change their minds about the adoption decision. The document, much like the amended travel document, at once anticipates the desire for and forecloses the possibility of reversal and return.

Paperwork is more than an indeterminate reminder and remainder of unknown origins; it has also become, for adoptees, a symbol of state power, agency corruption, child commodification, and the power and concealments of bureaucracy. Children's bodies are standardized and made legible by the category of the orphan – whether "abandoned" or "relinquished" – reducing the complexity of life choices and obscuring the ways in which states create the political and economic conditions in which adoption comes to be viewed as the "best" or only option for certain children. If, as Yngvesson and Coutin argue (2006), legal fictions compel returns to a spectral "back," the paperwork that anticipates those returns may even predetermine the course of future dead ends. In this way, documents, in their prior production of illegibility, come also to serve as present evidence of the commodity logic at the heart of transnational adoption.

Rather than the disciplinary gaze of the panopticon or the regulatory practices of population management, then, we have a kind of knowledge/power that is more akin to the legal fictions that Annelise Riles describes, which function as a "placeholder," what she calls "a technique for working with and in the meantime" (Riles 2010: 803). The as-if nature of these documents means that they have a contradictory relationship to the real – they contain traces of the truth of kinship, but not as an idealized domain of authentic intimate relations grounded in blood and biology, but as a product of governmentality and political economy. Indeed, these documents were never designed to contain the "truth" of kinship, but rather were bureaucratic tools meant to regularize a process that had no interest in origins, only in destinations. The temporality of the documents was restricted to the near future: the point at which the child was transferred and citizenship revoked was when the files were closed. Yet they continued to activate affective relations among adoptees and their imagined pasts, parents, and origins, with a politically charged valence. Because information about kinship holds constitutive force in Euro-American contexts, it collapses representation and ontology, but in law, Mariana Valverde attests, "epistemology and ontology are regarded as independent of each other," such that "no trouble arises from the fact that everyone knows that corporations are not people" (2010: 813). From the legal perspective, adoptees who read the orphan registry ontologically can be faulted for applying an inapt, positivistic epistemology to what is a provisional placeholder. The revelation of the biopolitical technologies that underwrite these practices, however, leads adoptees to transpose the non-knowledge of kinship into knowledge of a different order: an affective and politically charged one that brings political economy into the heart of kinship. Against the will to knowledge, adoption documents traffic in non-knowledge, generating unintended epistemological and emotional effects.

20.6 Making Relations

Paperwork's ability to produce legally cognizable relations also produces relations between distinct identities, contained in the same body, as Jane's final piece of paperwork illustrates. This document, specially composed for her by her adoption agency, solved the problem of reconciling her

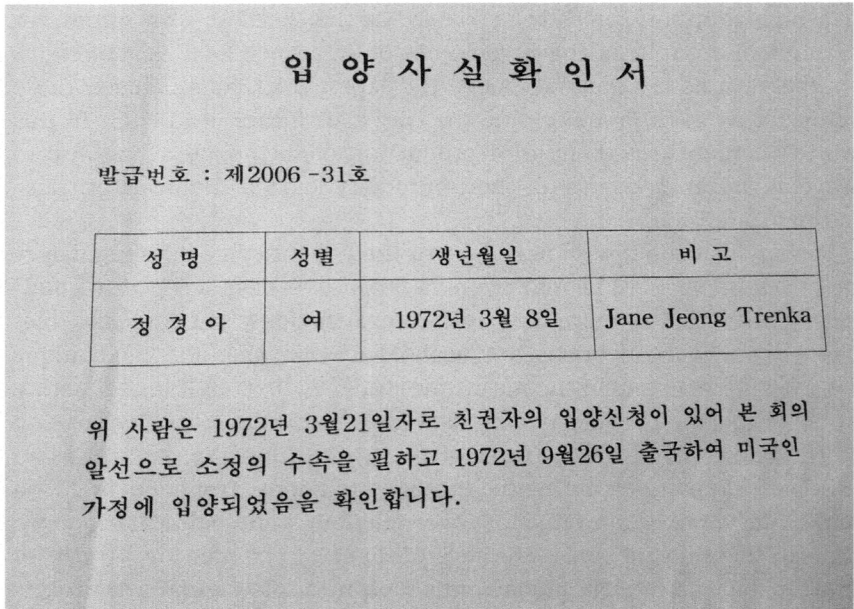

Figure 20.4 Actual adoption verification document

discrepant birth dates, names, and places of adoption. Entitled the "Actual Adoption Verification Document" (Figure 20.4), it contained a simple table that created a visual equivalence between Jane's Korean identity and her American identity.

Presenting Jane's Korean name, sex, date of birth, and, under a column titled "Notes," Jane's American name (but not her adopted family name, as she had changed her legal name upon marriage), the document reconciles Jane's paper identities (her Korean orphan *hojŏk* and her American passport) by creating an equation. In the written explanation that follows the table, it is noted that "the above person" underwent the proper adoption procedures with the approval of her Korean family, and left Korea on September 26, 1972, to be adopted into an American family. The table visually depicts in highly legible form what the orphan registry effectuated – a free-standing entity without any existing social relations – except, here, to herself. The document's purpose is to create a relation of equivalence between the Korean "Jong Kyong Ah" and the American "Jane Jeong Trenka," yet in so doing, also underscores the division between the two, highlighting at once the doubleness of identity and providing evidence of its original dislocation. Its purpose to reconcile Jane's discrepant paper biographies is attempted via the production of an absolute value between two signifiers – the Korean legal person and the American legal person – but the slippage between the two reminds us of their incommensurability and the indeterminacy of names – the multiple layers of identity and difference between (the "Korean" infant) Jong Kyong Ah, a.k.a. Jane

Jeong Trenka a.k.a. Jane Marie Vogler. Moreover, the visual and semantic equation produced out of the juxtaposition of fixed data points – sex, date of birth, and names – also suggests an erasure of time, for the very lines of the table dividing the Korean and the American identities are connected to and constituted by distinct temporalities, and were put into place through the prior labor of adoption paperwork that functioned precisely to disconnect, suspend, and disrupt the potential transnationality of the adoptee. The attempt to reconcile these incommensurable identities only makes sense in the context of contemporary global Korea, and the revaluation of adoptee bodies as "transnational," wherein reconstituting the "Korean side" of the adoptee helps to reintegrate her into the imaginary of the (deterritorialized) nation. Yet the reconciliation acknowledged by the South Korean state meets its limit at the borders of the nation-state – this document would have no force under American immigration law. Despite the complexity of recombinant family formations and diasporic identities, one can only have one identity and one family in the gaze of the US state – the tabular equivalence presented here would not compute, and Jane Jeong Trenka and Jong Kyong Ah would cease to be legible as the same "above person."

Adoption paperwork rewrites "nature" and "blood" such that there is no legitimate connection to Korean relatives – despite their genetic similarity. Whereas DNA is considered to be infallible and more than sufficient for other family reunification claims, what some Korean American adoptees, such as Jane, have discovered after reuniting with their Korean families is that the family reunification clause does not apply to them. The I-130 immigration form known as the Petition for Alien Relative specifically indicates that a petition may not be filed for "a natural parent, if the United States citizen son or daughter gained permanent residence through adoption." When Jane realized that adoptees were disallowed the same rights to family reunification as other American citizens, she launched an online petition drive to gather signatures supporting the recognition of adoptees' dual heritages, origins, and claims to full citizenship.

The overwriting of DNA's "truths" and the immediacy of consanguineous social relations by adoption paperwork suggests not only that a biologistic logic underwrites adoption law and immigration policy but also highlights paperwork's ability to authorize certain relations and to disallow others through acts of legibility and illegibility. Paperwork represents identities and produces knowledge of relations not unlike genetic knowledge/DNA does – and those relations, whether embraced or rejected, must be reckoned with in the production of personhood, understood as a position negotiated vis-à-vis dominant social categories and individual subjectivities.[12] Paperwork defamiliarizes genetic essentialism not because it textually re-presents relationships, but because, like DNA, it contains information that mediates and also *produces* relatives, animating new narratives and compelling social action, and bringing into sometimes painful focus the contingencies of belonging and the long reach of state power.

A recent development in adoptees' relations to the state has been their ability to "reactivate" their Korean citizenship. Adoptees from countries that permit dual citizenship are now able to apply for South Korean citizenship, which is legally predicated on the fact that adoptees were not granted the right to choose their nationality (to South Korea or the adoptive nation), but had their South Korean nationality involuntarily forfeited upon naturalization to their adoptive countries. Adoptees would therefore be reactivating their South Korean citizenship and would be recognized in South Korea as a citizen with all the rights and obligations accruing therewith. Whereas many adoptees find this possibility to be intriguing and a desirable way to actualize their transnationality, others find the bureaucratic procedures involved to be morally objectionable. In this instance, the paperwork necessary to substantiate the adoptee's original Korean citizenship is the very orphan *hojŏk* that had been constructed for the purposes of adoption migration.[13] This ironic recapitulation of the biopolitical logics that operated to alienate the child from Korea to now reconnect the adoptee to its birth country reproduces the erasure of kinship knowledge in the interests of bureaucratic efficiency. Making the adoptee legible to the state does not entail resuturing the kinship ties that are required to substantiate national belonging in the first place (*ius soli* and *ius sanguinis*; being born to Korean citizens in South Korea), but instead substantiates the illegitimacy of the child (under dominant social and legal norms) as the basis for national belonging.

20.7 Conclusion

Adoptees like Peter may naively believe that the documents hold some connection to the "truth," and their reading of the documents as representations of the real exemplifies their belief in the transparency of the system. Once adoptees experience their own restricted agency through encounters with social workers or bureaucrats or when they discover inaccurate or false information in their files, they begin to understand the system as opaque, rather than transparent. They also no longer view documents as a connection to the real that simply requires the right interpretation or translation to access the past. The documents, instead, undergo an epistemological shift from positivistic representations of an underlying truth to indexical traces of bureaucratic agency – material evidence of a lack of transparency and the excesses of state power.

Adoptees' understandings of "biological kinship" often conform to Euro-American kinship epistemologies that link biogenetic information, kinship relations, and personal identity such that adoptees who gain information about biogenetic origins also instantaneously discover "relatives" and a sense of completion by being connected to biogenetic facts. Modern adoptions, whether domestic or transnational, however, also add a layer of bureaucratic mediation and state power that have implications for how these kinship epistemologies unfold and how we understand the "interdigitation" of the biological and the social in contemporary forms of relatedness (Edwards and Strathern 2000). In the case of transnational Korean adoptees, the mediation of their origins, whether or not it leads to an eventual reunion, has the effect of revealing the identity of the state and its role in the production of adoptable children. The birth family search process promises to answer questions about kinship knowledge and identity, but failing this, generates state effects that have constitutive influence on adoptee subjectivities. In these instances, the *mediation* of biogenetic information and kinship knowledge through biopolitical institutions and bureaucratic paperwork, rather than the information itself, can be constitutive of adoptee subjectivity.

Acknowledgments

Thanks first and foremost to Jane Jeong Trenka for her permission to write about her personal documents, and for her assistance in clarifying the twists and turns of the bureaucratic maze. In addition to Jane, many others have helped bring this essay to fruition, including Julie Chu, Bob Foster, Tony Carter, Ayala Emmett, and Daniel Reichman. I also presented this essay at the Global Relations workshop at Brown University, and I thank organizer Jessaca Leinaweaver for including me, as well as Sherine Hamdy, Bianca Dahl, Susan McKinnon, and Sylvia Yanagisako for their engaged feedback.

Notes

1. These documents, of course, have different and competing meanings and values for people involved in the adoption process – agencies in Korea and the receiving countries hold legal ownership over the adoption files, and take as their responsibility the safeguarding of identifying information that could potentially disrupt the lives of members of the adoption triad in different ways. In Korea, birth parents may have little access to the adoption file, but may ask that letters or information be included in the file in case the child requests information at a later date. Adoptive parents may create a "memory book" out of the adoptees' documents and may be as or more curious about the biological origins of their child than the child him or herself. But there are also cases in which adoptees are denied ownership over or access to their documents by their adoptive parents who feel

threatened by the prospect of having their child reconnect with their Korean origins. Because adoption agencies have now garnered a reputation for impeding reunions rather than facilitating them and for withholding information and/or trafficking in misinformation, many adoptees seek to circumvent agencies' control over their birth family searches. The South Korean media have stepped in as a major player in what can now only be considered a veritable reunion industry.

2. Like Nancy Scheper-Hughes described the Brazilian adoption system of the 1980s, wherein poor *favela* women were tricked or coerced into sending their children for a better life in foreign families, Korean women as well may not have "easily or even fully consciously, give up their children." In ways that resonate with the Korean adoption system, Scheper-Hughes suggests that "the altruistic and religious ideology of the adoption institution masked the social process that allowed the 'rescue' of children from women, who, given the choice and material support, might have preferred to raise them themselves" (1990: 62).

3. The family registry system, initially implemented by the Japanese colonial authority, marks the boundary between the state and the household. After five decades of activism by Korean feminists, the Korean Constitutional Court determined that the family registration system was unconstitutional in 2005, and an individualized registrations system took effect in 2008.

4. She obtained documents from her adoption file from her parents, but was unable to gain access to more than a "skeleton set" due to restrictions the American adoption agency placed in the interests of protecting her adoptive parents' privacy. The tension between an adoptee's rights to information and parents' (birth or adoptive) right to privacy has been central to the struggle over access to records in the United States, and is proving to be equally as fraught in international cases.

5. The figures are reproduced and used with permission from Jane Jeong Trenka.

6. Because the paperwork functions to singularize the child, even adoptees like Jane, who were sent for adoption with biological siblings to the same adoptive families, appear to have no existing "immediate relatives."

7. Trenka wrote of her documents and their biopolitical implications in a 2007 post on her blog entitled, "Fool's Gold: International Adoption from South Korea."

8. In the case of foundlings, the orphan *hojŏk* institutes the child's legal existence, in order that it may then be nullified.

9. Jane's date of birth appears as January 24 on the lunar calendar in her actual family *hojŏk*, but here as March 8 on the solar calendar. Based on her mother's recollection, her actual birth was probably during the

early hours of March 9. The use of the solar calendar may indicate that adoptees already selected for international adoption were recorded using a "Western" calendrical system. The inconsistent use of lunar and solar dates have led to a number of adoptees discovering "new" birthdays, having spent the majority of their lives celebrating their lunar birthday on the solar calendar or vice versa. For adoptees applying for state recognition as overseas Koreans, discrepancies like this can cause further bureaucratic misunderstandings and mishandlings.

10. Article 30 provides that the information about the "child's origin, in particular information concerning the identity of his or her parents, as well as medical history, [be] preserved." It further provides for access to such information be made to the child or its proxy, "in so far as is permitted by law" of the birth country.

11. Plenary adoptions (*adoption plenière*) are those that terminate the original parent–child relationship, and in France, these are contrasted with "simple adoptions" (*adoption simple*) which are additive, i.e., they retain the validity of the original parent–child relationship and also recognize the new adoptive relation with respect to inheritance rights and parental authority. Both can be distinguished from "open adoptions" as they are practiced in the United States, in which birth parents and adoptive parents agree to maintain varying degrees of contact for the benefit of the adopted child, but no legally binding contracts are involved.

12. Certainly, some adoptees would not embrace the equation of their Korean identity with their present identity and would prefer to keep the lines of division and separation intact.

13. The restitution of citizenship contains yet another wrinkle – all Korean male adoptees under the age of 32 are required to complete mandatory military service, except for "orphans." The orphan loophole therefore permits adoptees who may still exist on their family registry, as motivation to reconnect their citizenship ties to the nation as "orphans."

References

Aretxaga, B. 2003. "Maddening States." *Annual Review of Anthropology* 32: 393–410.

Bledsoe, Caroline. 2006. *The Demography of Family Reunification: From Circulation to Substitution in Gambian Spain.* MPIDR Working Paper WP 2006-53. Max Planck Institute for Demographic Research.

Caplan, Jane and John Torpey. 2001. "Introduction." In *Documenting Individual Identity: The Development of State Practices in The Modern World*, ed. Jane Caplan and John Torpey, 1–12. Princeton, NJ: Princeton University Press.

Carsten, Janet. 2004. *After Kinship*. Cambridge: Cambridge University Press.
    2007. "Constitutive Knowledge: Tracing Trajectories of Information in New Contexts of Relatedness." *Anthropological Quarterly* 80(2): 403–426.

Das, Veena. 2005. "The Signature of the State: The Paradox of Illegibility." In *Anthropology in the Margins of the State*, ed. Veena Das and Deborah Poole, 225–252. Santa Fe, NM: School of American Research.

Das, Veena and Deborah Poole. 2005. "State and Its Margins: Comparative Ethnographies." In *Anthropology in the Margins of the State*, ed. Veena Das and Deborah Poole, 3–34. Santa Fe, NM: School of American Research.

Dorow, Sara. 2006. *Transnational Adoption: A Cultural Economy of Race, Gender, and Kinship*. New York: New York University Press.

Edwards, Jeanette and Marilyn Strathern. 2000. "Including Our Own." In *Cultures of Relatedness*, ed. Janet Carsten, 149–166. Cambridge: Cambridge University Press.

Finkler, Kaja. 2001. "The Kin in the Gene: The Medicalization of Family and Kinship in American Society." *Current Anthropology* 42(2): 251–252.

Foucault, Michel. 1979. "*Governmentality*." *Ideology and Consciousness* 6: 9–21.
    1982. *The Archaeology of Knowledge and the Discourse on Language*. New York: Pantheon.

hers, kate. 2007. *Missing*. Video. 7 minutes. Estherka Project.

Howell, Signe. 2006. *Kinning of Foreigners: Transnational Adoption in a Global Perspective*. New York: Berghahn Books.

Kim, Eleana. 2003. "Wedding Citizenship and Culture: Korean Adoptees and the Global Family of Korea." *Social Text* 21(1): 57–81.
    2005. "Wedding Citizenship and Culture: Korean Adoptees and the Global Family of Korea." In *Cultures of Transnational Adoption*, ed. T. Volkman, 49–80. Durham, NC: Duke University Press.
    2007. "Our Adoptee, Our Alien: Transnational Korean Adoptees As Specters of Foreignness and Family in South Korea." *Anthropological Quarterly* 80(2): 497–531.
    2010. *Adopted Territory: Transnational Korean Adoptees and the Politics of Belonging*. Durham, NC: Duke University Press.

Leifsen, Esben. 2004. "Person, Relation and Value: The Economy of Circulating Ecuadorian Children in International Adoption." In *Cross-cultural Approaches to Adoption*, ed. Fiona Bowie, 182–196. London and New York: Routledge.

Modell, Judith. 1994. *Kinship with Strangers: Adoption and Interpretations of Kinship in American Culture*. Berkeley, CA: University of California Press.

Nelkin, Dorothy and Susan Lindee. 1996. *The DNA Mystique: The Gene As Cultural Icon*. New York: W. H. Freeman.

Ouellette, Françoise-Romaine and G. Mossière. 2004. "La circulation des informations sur les origines des adoptés internationaux" ["The circulation of information on the origins of international adoptees"].

In *Comprendre la famille* [*Understanding the family*], ed. Gilles Pronovost, 153–172. Quebec: Presses de l'Université du Québec.

Park, In Sun. 2000. *Ppurirŭl ch'atnŭn saramdŭl* [*People who search*]. Seoul: Hana Medical Publishing.

Riles, Annelise. 2010. "Collateral Expertise: Legal Knowledge in the Global Financial Markets." *Current Anthropology* 51(6): 795–818.

Scheper-Hughes, Nancy. 1990. "Theft of Life." *Society* 27(6): 57–62.

Scott, James. 1998. *Seeing Like a State: How Certain Schemes to Improve the Human Condition Have Failed*. New Haven, CT: Yale University Press.

Sharma, A. and A. Gupta. 2006. *The Anthropology of the State: A Reader*. Oxford: Blackwell.

Strathern, Marilyn. 1995. "Displacing Knowledge: Technology and the Consequences for Kinship." In *Conceiving the New World Order: The Global Politics of Reproduction*, ed. F. Ginsburg and R. Rapp, 346–364. Berkeley, CA: University of California Press.

1999. *Property, Substance, and Effect: Anthropological Essays on Persons and Things*. London: The Athlone Press.

Tomes, Kimberly Saree. 1997. Looking for Wendy. Video. New York: Third World Newsreel.

Trenka, Jane Jeong. 2003. *The Language of Blood: A Memoir*. St. Paul, MN: Minnesota Historical Society Press.

2007. *Fool's Gold: International Adoption from South Korea*. Weblog. http://jjtrenka.wordpress.com/2007/07/10, accessed October 2, 2007.

Trouillot, M. R. 2003. *Global Transformations: Anthropology and the Modern World*. New York: Palgrave Macmillan.

Valverde, Mariana. 2010. Commentary for A. Riles, "Collateral Expertise: Legal Knowledge in the Global Financial Markets." *Current Anthropology* 51(6): 812–813.

Volkman, Toby Alice. 2005. *Cultures of Transnational Adoption*. Durham, NC: Duke University Press.

Yngvesson, Barbara. 2002. "Placing the 'Gift Child' in Transnational Adoption." *Law & Society Review* 36(2): 227–256.

2010. *Belonging in an Adopted World: Race, Identity, and Transnational Adoption*. Chicago, IL: University of Chicago Press.

Yngvesson, Barbara and Susan Coutin. 2006. "Backed by Papers: Undoing Persons, Histories, Return." *American Ethnologist* 33(2): 177–190.

Part V

Technological Conceptions

21

Surrogate Motherhood and Transforming Families

Janet Dolgin

21.1 Introduction

Since the middle of the twentieth century, assumptions about relationships among adults in US families have undergone stunning changes. Changes regarding children in families have occurred, but more slowly, and have been more discomforting to society. These changes and their implications for social understandings of personhood within families can be productively studied through consideration of responses to assisted reproduction (including surrogacy and reproductive technology), and more particularly, through consideration of legal responses to disputes occasioned by assisted reproduction. Such cases, more than most family disputes brought to court, compel judges to contemplate the reach and meaning of family and push them to challenge familiar assumptions about the parent–child relationship. The cases reveal society's ambivalence, confusion, and disagreement about the transformation of families, generally, and about the scope of childhood, more specifically.

In vitro fertilization first resulted in a successful pregnancy in 1978, with the birth of Louise Brown in Oldham, England. This represented dramatic progress in the development of reproductive technology. But it was the *Baby M.* case (*Matter of Baby M.* 1987/1988),[1] decided about a decade later, that brought the social and legal queries occasioned by assisted reproduction to national attention in the United States. The case asked courts to consider the legality and morality of significant alterations in the forms through which families are created. *Baby M.* challenged the New Jersey courts to consider the parameters of a commercial surrogacy arrangement. The case did not involve sophisticated reproductive technology. Rather, the conception of Baby M. followed the use of assisted insemination, a form of assisted reproduction used to produce a human as early as 1790. Yet the surrogacy arrangement at issue in *Baby M.*

presented some of the central challenges raised by more sophisticated forms of reproductive technology.

From the perspective of US society and its legal system, *Baby M.* framed troubling questions about the creation of the parent–child bond and, correlatively, about the implications of the arrangements through which families are created for the relationships that ensue. The case challenged the privileged position that mainstream society accorded to the nuclear family, composed ideally of two parents of opposite genders and their biological children. For almost two centuries, society had associated this so-called "traditional" family, in fact a product of late eighteenth- and nineteenth-century modernity, with virtually sacred truth. A central concern for the judges who entertained the *Baby M.* case – though one not stated so explicitly – was whether "traditional" families could be created through nontraditional processes.

The most discomforting parameters of the case at the time seem to have been the involvement of a third party (the surrogate) in a couple's reproductive effort and reliance on a commercial contract to define and cement the relationship among the parties (the surrogate, her husband, and the couple who wanted a child, as well eventually as the relationship between the child and the adults).[2] Each of these parameters conflicted with the presumptions through which mainstream society in the United States imagined families. First, the American ideal of family offered little room for anyone but parents and their biological or adopted[3] children. Second, society presumed that familial relationships were special precisely because they were understood as created through love, not commercial bargains.

This presumption has carried particular significance for understandings of the parent–child relationship. By the late 1980s, when the *Baby M.* case arose, society and the law had already begun to view adults within families as they viewed actors in the marketplace – as autonomous individuals free to design the terms of their relationships. Yet, even as enlightenment values replaced the values of the traditional family with regard to adults, society remained committed to traditional understandings of children within families. Interestingly, assumptions about children in non-domestic settings (e.g., in the criminal justice system) had begun to shift, providing for recognition of children as autonomous individuals (*In re Gault* 1967).[4] For the most part, however, this process stopped at the boundaries of family. Within families, society and the law continued to set children apart from the dictates of both the Enlightenment and the marketplace.

It has become increasingly difficult to sustain those boundaries. Both the redefinition of adults within families and of children in non-familial settings has destabilized the traditional family. It is unclear how long society can presume to safeguard traditional images of children in family settings while imaging the same children, in other settings, differently, and while reshaping relationships among adults in families away from traditional expectations. In the late 1980s, when the courts entertained *Baby M.*, society struggled to support traditional understandings of families by sustaining traditional visions of childhood. That struggle is at the center of the courts' deliberations in the case. By the second decade of the twenty-first century, it has become increasingly transparent that the effort may well flounder.

The family, understood as a hierarchical community in which participants were categorized into statuses and in which relationships operated in light of the fixed roles that each status demanded, has largely disappeared, at least with regard to adults. Attempts to preserve some parameters of that universe while abandoning others are unlikely to succeed; the traditional family was, in the nature of the case, envisioned as an integral whole to which each set of participants was essential. Society and the law have struggled to preserve a traditional vision of the parent–child relationship while abandoning traditional notions of family relationships as between adults. The struggle has not met with great success.

This chapter examines four surrogacy cases, all decided between 1987 and 2013. The cases, taken as a set, provide a wealth of information about shifts in social assumptions concerning children, families, and the parent–child bond. Three of the cases involved disputes occasioned by traditional surrogacy arrangements. One involved a dispute that arose as the result of a gestational surrogacy agreement. These cases show a slow, reluctant acceptance on the part of courts handling disputes occasioned by surrogacy to abandon traditional responses to parentage and custody cases. Each of the cases provides a context for considering the transformation of family, shifting images of childhood, and changes in the contours of the parent–child relationship.

This chapter does not presume that any of the four cases *caused* a general shift in social understandings of family. Yet, each of the cases brought extant changes to light and provided a platform for considering, disputing, and beginning to resolve disagreements about the shape of families and the scope of childhood.

Section 21.2 of this chapter examines two judges' decisions in the *Baby M.* case. Each decision (one issued by a New Jersey trial court judge, one by a judge serving on the state's highest court) assumed that its central task entailed safeguarding the best interests of the child whose parentage and custody were at stake and in that, ensuring the preservation of a traditional form of family. Section 21.3 considers a case, decided in California in the early 1990s, occasioned by a gestational surrogacy agreement (*Johnson v. Calvert* 1993). None of the three California courts that reached decisions in this case abandoned concern for protecting traditional forms of family, but in *Johnson v. Calvert* the courts focused on other matters. That may have been facilitated by the apparent biological "facts" in the gestational surrogacy case. Gestational surrogacy separates maternity into discrete parts; therefore, neither of the women claiming maternity of the child whose parentage was at issue in *Johnson* seemed clearly to be *the* biological mother. Thus, the California Supreme Court in the case resorted to a tie-breaker that predicated maternity on a combination of a biological link to the child (whether genetic or gestational) and the parties' intentions about parentage at the time that they entered into the surrogacy arrangement. Finally, in Section 21.4, the chapter examines two court decisions, both reached in 2013. Both cases involved disputes occasioned by traditional surrogacy arrangements. Neither court expressly dismantled the best-interest standard. Yet, both elided that standard and established families reflecting the terms of the surrogacy agreements.[5]

21.2 The *Baby M.* Case: Assumptions about Children and Families

Legal and social responses to the dispute at the center of the *Baby M.* case offered a set of blueprints that provided a starting point for debate as courts responded to subsequent cases (*Matter of Baby M.* 1987/1988). Although the conception of *Baby M.* involved the simplest of reproductive aids, judicial contemplation of the issues at stake and public discourse surrounding the judicial decisions encompassed many of the challenges raised by the use of more sophisticated reproductive technology during subsequent decades.

In *Baby M.*, two New Jersey courts reached contrasting positions about the legality and morality of commercial surrogacy arrangements. Yet, each court shaped its opinion around a similar effort to safeguard traditional family expectations. At the center of that effort was an assessment of the best interests of the child whose parentage and custody were at stake. The best-interest standard has been the leitmotiv of traditional responses to custody disputes in the United States for almost two centuries. The trial court's best-interest analysis, which the state supreme court applauded, presumed that the manner in which families are created need not shape the manner in which they function. More specifically, the court presumed that once formed, a family created pursuant to a commercial surrogacy agreement would not, for that reason, operate differently from other families.

21.2.1 Visions of "Traditional" Surrogacy
In June 1987, after the trial court decision in *Baby M.* and before the state's highest court overturned that decision's apparent validation of commercial surrogacy contracts, Mary Gordon (1987) published an essay in *Ms.*

Magazine in which she explained her own confusions about surrogate motherhood and about the characters central to the *Baby M.* story.

> For months, I have thought about this case, these people, and the child. Every woman I know seems obsessed by it.

> I keep changing my mind. Things that are clear to me at night grow murky the next morning. Every road I turn down opens up 10 paths overgrown with thorns and dark, engulfing brush. I will begin with some things that have seemed to stay with me over these months of thought.

> > *(1987: 25)*

Gordon pondered whether the law should permit surrogacy for money (1987: 25). Furthermore, she considered the implications of gender and class in attempting to reach solid ground from which reasonably to reach conclusions about the ethics and permissibility of surrogacy arrangements (1987: 26, 28). Focusing on the welfare of children born as a result of surrogacy, Gordon self-consciously refrained from concluding (as her musings suggested she perhaps should) that surrogacy so clearly harms children that it should be prohibited by law (1987: 28).[6] Gordon's deliberations reflected themes voiced in public discourse that surrounded the *Baby M.* case as it was being decided in the late 1980s. Many of these themes have continued to structure social debate about surrogacy.

The so-called legal "facts" of *Baby M.* encompassed presumptions about medicine, technology, family life, and one family's struggle to have a child genetically related at least to one of the intending parents (*Matter of Baby M.* 1987). The story involved William and Elizabeth Stern, the so-called intending parents. The Sterns were an upper-middle-class couple – he a scientist, she a scientist and pediatrician – anxious to have offspring but concerned that a medical condition with which Elizabeth had been diagnosed made pregnancy an unreasonable risk (1987: 1139). The Sterns thus decided to seek a surrogate to gestate and give birth to a child who would be conceived through assisted insemination using William Stern's sperm. The Infertility Center of New York connected the Sterns with Mary Beth Whitehead, then 29 years old and the mother of two children (also the children of Richard Whitehead, Mary Beth's husband).

The parties entered into a contractual arrangement, signed by Mary Beth and William and by Richard Whitehead. (Richard was a party to the contract in order to preclude his having any responsibilities for or rights to paternity.) The "surrogate parenting agreement" (1987: 1143) was not signed by Elizabeth Stern so as to limit potential claims of baby selling. Pursuant to the agreement, Mary Beth agreed to undergo assisted insemination with Stern's sperm, carry a pregnancy, if one resulted, to term, and at the child's birth yield parental rights in favor of Stern. For this, the agreement provided, Whitehead was to receive $10,000, payable at the birth of the baby, plus medical and dental expenses during the term of the contract (1987: 1143).

The child, a girl, was born to Mary Beth Whitehead in March 1986. She was named Sarah by Whitehead, Melissa by the Sterns, and was referred to as Baby M. by the courts. After the baby's birth, the Sterns agreed to allow Mary Beth, seriously depressed and threatening suicide, to take the child home with her for a week. Later, emotionally unable to give the baby to the Sterns, Whitehead traveled with the newborn child to Florida. The Sterns sought to locate Baby M. and re-gain custody of her (*Matter of Baby M.* 1988: 415–417). They hired a detective to find the Whiteheads and filed legal documents seeking enforcement of the parenting agreement. Almost three months later, the child and Mary Beth were found, and state authorities gave the baby to the Sterns.

Eventually parentage and custody were settled by the New Jersey courts. Traditionally, these have been treated quite differently in US law. Legal parentage typically follows from a person's biological relation to a child and can only be lost in the dire circumstances of abuse or neglect. Parentage can also be terminated voluntarily. For almost two centuries US courts have determined custody (with whom a child lives) through assessment of the child's "best interests."

Quite untraditionally, Judge Sorkow, who presided over the trial court that heard the *Baby M.* case, upheld the surrogacy agreement, ordered termination of Mary Beth Whitehead's maternal rights, and arranged an immediate adoption of the child by Elizabeth Stern. Yet, quite traditionally, Judge Sorkow predicated the court's decision on assurances that its conclusions about the child's parentage would serve the best interests of that child (*Matter of Baby M.* 1987: 1166). Somewhat at odds with the court's apparent approval of the surrogacy agreement, Judge Sorkow asserted that "[t]he primary issue to be determined by this litigation is what are the best interests of a child until now called 'Baby M.' All other concerns raised by counsel constitute commentary" (1987: 1132).

The New Jersey Supreme Court, which reversed the trial court's legal conclusions in almost every regard, applauded that court's best-interest determination and agreed with the trial court that Stern, not Whitehead, would be the child's custodial parent. The strength of agreement between the two courts about the child's interests and the significance of that assessment suggested, as delineated below, that both courts had a similar vision of family and of the parent–child relationship, despite their conflicting conclusions about the legality and ethics of surrogacy arrangements.

The first paragraph of the state supreme court's decision referred to Stern as the "natural" father and Mary Beth Whitehead as the "natural" mother (*Matter of Baby M.* 1988: 410–411). Use of the term "natural" in such circumstances almost always foreshadows a court's conclusions. Indeed, the state's highest court concluded that Mary Beth should remain the child's legal mother and Stern, her legal father. However, the court granted custody to William Stern and thus, as a practical, though not a legal, matter to his wife, Elizabeth Stern. More specifically, the state supreme court invalidated the surrogacy agreement, finding that it "conflict[ed] with the law and public policy of the State" (1988: 411). Further, the court "void[ed] both the termination of the surrogate mother's parental rights and the adoption of the child by the wife/step-parent" (1988: 411). The court "thus restore[d] the 'surrogate' as the mother of the child" (1988: 411). Judge Wilentz, writing for the court, further identified William Stern as the child's legal father, and opined that paternal custody would best serve the child's interests (1988: 411). In sum, the two state courts that rendered decisions in the case agreed on the dimensions of the child's best interests and shared a vision of family, even as they disagreed vehemently about the forms through which families could legitimately be created.

American lawmakers have relied on the notion of "best interests" to resolve disputes involving children since at least the early nineteenth century (*Commonwealth v. Addicks* 1815; *U.S. v. Green* 1824). Although courts' assumptions about children's best interests have shifted broadly over the centuries, the standard has been employed consistently to safeguard a traditional form of family presumed to place children and their interests at its center.

Thus, it is particularly telling that the trial court and the state supreme court in *Baby M.* reached contrasting legal conclusions but portrayed a similar vision of the terms that constituted a good home for a child. That vision is encapsulated by the criteria on which the trial court relied – criteria that the higher court praised – in assessing how adequately each of the adults seeking parentage in the case would serve Baby M. as she grew from infancy to adulthood. Comparatively neutral on their face, the best-interest criteria presume the value of – and thus they generally privilege – middle-class, mainstream (read: "traditional") homes above others. Law professor Dorothy Roberts summarized Judge Wilentz's decision – based on the trial court's best-interest determination – to grant custody to Stern. In this regard, Roberts highlighted the Sterns' "financial security" and the "expert testimony that disparaged Whitehead's fitness as a mother" (Roberts 1997: 65).

The best-interest criteria on which the trial court relied were developed by Lee Salk, a psychologist, as a tool for discerning how well a particular adult would further the child's welfare. The criteria asked courts to focus, among other matters, on the extent to which the child was "wanted and planned for"; the "emotional stability" of those in the home; "the stability, consistency and peacefulness" of the family; "attitudes towards education"; and the adults' "capacity to instill positive attitudes about matters concerning health, nutrition, and the avoidance of hazards and substance abuse" (*Matter of Baby M.* 1987: 1152).

Many people would want their child – or any child – to have stability, education, and motivation to avoid excessive alcohol and drugs. Yet, the criteria, taken as a set, will virtually always privilege prospective parents with money over those without and prospective parents with higher educational attainments over those with little education. Other societies and other sub-cultures would have framed a different set of factors in considering how best to protect children's welfare, and still other societies would have focused on matters other than children's best interests in determining parentage or custody.

21.2.2   The Background for *Baby M.*: Shifts in Society's Visions of Children, Families, and Surrogacy

Most significantly, the two New Jersey courts that rendered decisions in *Baby M.* agreed that their essential task involved preserving a traditional, mainstream family, insofar as possible, and each court justified this goal through reference to children and their welfare. In effect, the two courts shared a vision of family but disagreed about whether traditional families could be safeguarded, if families were to be created through non-traditional means. Judge Sorkow presumed that families created through the terms that govern relationships in the commercial marketplace will, once created, be unaffected by that beginning. To Justice Wilentz creating families through commercial arrangements would inevitably undermine the central social values he aimed to preserve.

By the late 1980s, when the New Jersey courts entertained the *Baby M.* case, society was openly challenging understandings of family that served the interests of the Industrial Revolution – so-called nuclear families. At that time, however, society and the law appeared far more comfortable sanctioning recognition of adults in families as autonomous individuals, free to negotiate the terms of their own relationships, than sanctioning a similar vision of children and of the parent–child relationship.

By the 1980s when the *Baby M.* case came to court, American law had validated cohabitation agreements (see, e.g., *Marvin v. Marvin* 1976: 114–116; *Morone v. Morone* 1980: 1155–1157), pre-nuptial contracts (see, e.g., *Scherer v. Scherer* 1982: 666), and no-fault divorce (Nelson 1996: 498). These developments depended on society's willingness to view adults within families as free, at least from time to time, to fashion their relationships on those of business associates and contract partners rather than those of nineteenth- and early twentieth-century kin. However, even as these changes shook the foundations of American family law, society envisioned children through the lens of the so-called traditional family. As society re-envisioned adults within families as autonomous individuals, free to design the terms of their own familial relationships, it safeguarded an understanding of children within families as treasured beings, in need of protection because they are unable safely to handle the rights and obligations of autonomy with regard to many crucial areas of life (see, e.g., *Bellotti* 1979: 633–639).

For the most part, the children to whom the law had granted rights of autonomous individuality by the 1980s had brought cases that did not directly implicate family relationships or that implicated apparently dysfunctional relationships. *In re Gault*, as noted above, has been associated with the commencement of a children's rights movement, aimed at securing for children recognition as autonomous individuals and the rights that attend that designation (Nationwide Drive for Children's Rights 1977: 207). *In re Gault* extended constitutional rights to children involved in delinquency proceedings. Although the US Supreme Court in that case did treat the children whose interests were at stake as autonomous individuals, the significance of that shift was tempered by Justice Fortas' insistence that the Court aimed primarily to protect children from the failures of the contemporaneous juvenile court system (*In re Gault* 1967: 14–19). In 1969, in *Tinker v. Des Moines Independent School District*, the US Supreme Court also recognized children's constitutional rights. *Tinker* extended First Amendment rights to children involved in conflict with their school. Interestingly, the children in the *Tinker* case were strongly supported by their parents (Tinker 1969).[7] Thus, the case did not ask the Court to interfere with traditional understandings of the parent–child relationship. In both *Gault* and *Tinker*, the Court considered how the nation's Constitution understood children in contexts that did not challenge the status of children within families. Thus, these decisions did not openly threaten traditional understandings of families, built around children and the parent–child bond.

About a decade later, the Court rendered decisions in two cases (discussed below) that *did* implicate understandings of children within family settings. But in both cases – one involving pregnant minors seeking abortions and the other involving children committed to mental institutions – the children seemed unable to rely on their parents or guardians for protection and support (*Bellotti* 1979; Parham 1979). The stories behind both cases can be read to suggest dysfunctional parent–child relationships. Moreover, the Court reached very different conclusions in the two cases. These decisions, issued by the same court in the same year, suggest the breadth of society's confusion about extending constitutional rights that assume autonomous individuality to children. Even more, each decision, read apart from the other, reflects social confusion about the scope of childhood and the capacity of children to serve as their own decision makers in contexts involving serious decisions about health care and other matters.

In one of these cases, *Bellotti v. Baird*, plaintiffs challenged a Massachusetts statute that predicated a minor girl's decision to have an abortion on parental consent.[8] The Court declared the provision invalid insofar as it precluded a girl's proceeding with an abortion without at least informing her parents. (The statute at issue provided an option for girls who sought parental consent and were refused that consent.) Thus, the decision would seem to have recognized pregnant minors as competent decision makers. Yet, at the same time, the *Bellotti* Court invoked traditional visions of children as "vulnerab[le]," unable "to make critical decisions in an informed, mature manner," and beholden to their parents for socialization (*Bellotti* 1979: 634).

In the second of the two cases, *Parham v. J.R.*, the Court gave significantly less weight to the voices of the children involved in that case than it had in *Bellotti*. *Parham* challenged a Georgia statute that allowed children to be committed to state mental hospitals as "voluntary" patients, even though only the children's parents – and not the children themselves – had sought institutionalization. The Court justified its decision by invoking the beneficence and love it assumed parents felt for their children. "Natural bonds of affection," the Court declared, "lead parents to act in the best interests of their children" (*Parham* 1979: 602 (citations omitted)).

The presumption that the Supreme Court voiced in *Parham* – that parents act on the basis of "natural bonds of affection" when they make decisions for and about their children – explains a central concern of the Supreme Court of New Jersey as it considered the legality and morality of the surrogacy arrangement at the center of the *Baby M.* case. To that court, the contract signaled illegal payment and acceptance of money for the parentage of a child (*Matter of Baby M.* 1988: 411, 423). Furthermore, the state's highest court decried the contract as "potentially degrading to women" (1988: 410–411). In contrast, the trial court in the case framed the surrogacy contract in positive terms – as an arrangement that provided a childless couple, anxious to have children, with the opportunity to become parents. Despite these determinative differences in the two courts' legal conclusions in the case, both courts viewed the "best interests" of the child (ascertained through judicial interpretation of expert testimony)[9] as the paramount issue. Each court shaped its determination of the child's fate in light of its visions of the child's welfare. And both courts viewed the child's welfare through the lens of presumptions that shaped the family in the two centuries that had passed since the start of the Industrial Revolution.

Society forged the vision of childhood underlying these cases in the early nineteenth century. An understanding of children as treasured beings – the virtual raison d'être of family – cemented and reflected family as a social order defined in sharp contrast to the dictates of the marketplace (Postman 1994: 56–64). Anthropologist David Schneider brilliantly described this family at mid-century as a unit deserving virtually sacred status, separate from work geographically and from money spiritually (Schneider 1968). In Schneider's characterization of the mid-twentieth-century American family, home stood to marketplace as love stood to money (Schneider 1968: 51–52). Schneider postulated "love," understood as "enduring, diffuse solidarity," as the central symbol of American kinship. As such, love denoted "the end to which family relations" were to be affected – "the well-being of the family as a whole and of each of its members" (1968: 50).

Children were essential to that construction. Indeed, Neil Postman identified the century between 1850 and 1950 as the "high-water mark of childhood" in America (Postman 1994: 67). This golden century for children defined them socially and legally as essentially different from adults and in that difference deserving of support and protection not assumed to be the right of adults. Children deserved, at least, the basic accoutrements of "best-interest" analyses.

The century that glorified childhood as "an ideal that transcended social and economic class" (1968: 67) ended a few decades before a surrogacy arrangement occasioned the *Baby M.* dispute. That was likely not accidental. Only after the glorification of childhood had begun to wane, though subtly and little noticed at first, was society able to entertain the possibility of creating families through surrogacy agreements and, then, through reliance on more complicated forms of reproductive technology.

21.3 Gestational Surrogacy Cases: Where Is the Child?

About a half-decade after *Baby M.*, California courts entertained a dispute that resembled the dispute at the center of the *Baby M.* case, except that the surrogate in the California case, a woman named Anna Johnson, gestated a baby conceived from the gametes of a couple who intended to become parents to the baby (the so-called "intending" parents) (*Johnson v. Calvert* 1993). Anna Johnson served as a "gestational surrogate" for a couple named Mark and Crispina Calvert. This contrasted with Mary Beth Whitehead's role as a "traditional surrogate" for the Sterns. Whitehead had a genetic link to the child she gestated. Anna Johnson did not.

Johnson v. Calvert, much like *Baby M.*, involved a couple who were anxious to become parents together. However, Mark and Crispina Calvert were unable to have a child without assistance because Crispina's uterus had been surgically removed. The surgery had not interfered with her ovarian function. The couple therefore turned to reproductive technology and a gestational surrogate for help. The Calverts entered into an agreement with Johnson, a vocational nurse who worked in the same hospital in which Crispina Calvert was employed as a registered nurse (Rothenberg 1990: 345). The parties agreed that Johnson would gestate an embryo conceived from Mark's sperm and Crispina's ovum, give birth to the baby, and at that time surrender any maternal rights she may have enjoyed in favor of the Calverts. For this, the Calverts agreed to pay Johnson $10,000 in a series of installments. Johnson became pregnant, and all seemed to go well at first. Then relationships between the Calverts and Johnson worsened (*Johnson v. Calvert* 1993: 778). In the third trimester of the pregnancy, Johnson asked for an advance on the money owed her. She wrote the Calverts, threatening to keep the baby at its birth if the Calverts refused her request for an advance. Even before the child's birth, Crispina and Mark Calvert commenced legal action, seeking a declaration of parenthood. Anna Johnson then brought a similar action in court, seeking legal maternity.

The baby, a boy named Christopher, was born in September 1990. A state court reported that "blood test result excluded Anna 'as the genetic mother' of the baby" (*Johnson v. Calvert*, sub nom. *Anna J. v. Mark C.* 1991: 373). Pursuant to a court order, the baby remained with the Calverts during the pendency of the court proceedings. Those proceedings occurred in three state courts. Taken as a set, the decisions offer a powerful illustration of social and legal confusions in responses to parentage disputes occasioned by gestational surrogacy.

Each court concluded that the Calverts were baby Christopher's parents. However, in reaching that conclusion, each court depended on a line of reasoning different from that of the other two courts. Judge Parslow for the trial court focused on the Calverts' genetic relationship to the child and thereby named them as the boy's legal parents. The judge explained: "I've got a mother and father genetically related to the child on one side of this equation. I believe he should be raised exclusively by the Calverts as natural parents" (*Johnson v. Calvert* 1990: 14). The intermediate appellate court relied on an interpretation of California statutory law (promulgated in 1975, before gestational surrogacy was possible) to name Crispina and Mark as the child's biological, and thus legal, parents (*Johnson v. Calvert*, sub nom. *Anna J. v. Mark C.* 1991: 373). Then, the California Supreme Court, certain that the trial court's reliance on biology and the intermediate appellate court's reliance on statutory rule could both be challenged by alternative interpretations, created a novel frame for reaching a decision in the case. The state's highest court concluded that in cases involving two women, each with cognizable biological claims to the same child, the law would look to "the parties' intentions as manifest in the surrogacy agreement" (*Johnson v. Calvert* 1993: 782). Thus, in California, disputes about maternity occasioned by gestational surrogacy were to be resolved by reference to the intentions of the parties when they joined together in the surrogacy arrangement. As the court explained:

> [A]lthough the Act recognizes both genetic consanguinity and giving birth as means of establishing a mother and child relationship, when the two means do not coincide in one woman, she who intended to procreate the child – that is, she who intended to bring about the

birth of a child that she intended to raise as her own – is the natural mother under California law.

(1993: 782)

The court did not assess the lives and homes of the prospective parents with the child's best interests in mind, as the New Jersey courts in *Baby M.* had done. Rather, it assumed that a "rule recognizing the intending parents as the child's legal, natural parents" would serve the child by "promot[ing] certainty and stability" (*Johnson v. Calvert* 1993: 783).

Only one judge among the many who authored decisions in this case focused on the best interests of the baby as a matter for courts to discern in every such case, and that judge did so in a dissent. Justice Kennard rejected the majority's invocation of parental intention as the determining factor in identifying the child's parents. She agreed with the majority that there was a tie to break, but she would not have relied on intentions to break that tie. She suggested that the law should rely on "the best interests of the child, rather than the intent of the genetic mother." That, she opined, "is the proper standard to apply in the absence of legislation" (*Johnson v. Calvert* (dissent) 1993: 798).[10] Justice Kennard refrained from expressing a position about whether the child would have been better served by naming Crispina Calvert or Anna Johnson as his mother (*Johnson v. Calvert* 1993: 799). (Because Justice Kennard's decision dissented from the court's majority, her conclusions about which mother was the "better" mother would not, as a matter of law, have been relied on to resolve the dispute at hand.)

Thus, with the exception of Justice Kennard's dissent, the judges who participated in the state supreme court's deliberations in *Johnson* did not frame the best interests of baby Christopher as central to the dispute's resolution. This may have followed from the novelty of the reproductive facts in the case. The concern to make sense of an entirely new form of human reproduction may have submerged traditional concerns as the judges struggled to provide order to a world of surrogacy and reproductive technology.

The position of all three California courts that wrote decisions in the *Johnson* case contrasted with the deliberations of the courts in the *Baby M.* case. Both the trial court which framed the case as one demanding an assessment of the child's best interests and the Supreme Court, which praised the trial court's best interest analysis in *Baby M.*, struggled to preserve a traditional vision of family. The decisions in *Johnson* reflected both the dimensions of and confusions generated by gestational surrogacy. The *Johnson* courts' readiness to set aside the child's best interests in resolving the dispute at the center of the case also suggests a broader disruption of traditional understandings of family and of the parent–child relationship, in particular. Far more than is the case with traditional surrogacy, gestational surrogacy unhinges familiar expectations about biological maternity and creates two biological mothers instead of one. It thus challenges society to assimilate dramatically new methods of creating families.

In fact, lawmakers have been readier to facilitate gestational surrogacy arrangements than traditional surrogacy arrangements (Hofman 2009: 460). And as the law provides for the creation of families through gestational surrogacy, lawmakers (whose assumptions generally resemble those of the society of which they are part) seem increasingly ready to elide traditional presumptions that once defined the scope of parentage.

21.3.1 Surrogacy's Disruptions

In addition to challenging understandings about parentage and custody, surrogacy challenges traditional understandings of mother and thus of woman. In Darra Hofman's phrase, it "draws down the culture's wrath" (Hofman 2009: 467). Virtually all surrogacy arrangements scramble traditional assumptions about sexuality and reproduction, and about the relation of a child's legal mother to that child's father and to the "other" mother. Two aspects of surrogacy seem especially disturbing to society and to lawmakers. One involves arrangements built around commercial agreements. The other involves the dissection of the maternal role into two or three distinct parts. Each aspect will be considered in turn.

Surrogacy arrangements, such as those at issue in *Baby M.* and in *Johnson v. Calvert*, that involve the exchange of money and contractual agreements confront traditional images of mother with a stark alternative. The woman who accepts money for her role in the reproductive process appears to conflate the roles of home and the rewards of work and to present herself, inappropriately given society's expectations, as an autonomous individual rather than as bound through sacred duty and natural process to her children and her family. Sympathy, at least among some groups, for Mary Beth Whitehead during the *Baby M.* proceedings, followed from her seemingly heartfelt connection to the child she had conceived, gestated, and to whom she had given birth. In this regard, Anna Johnson was less sympathetic. Perhaps, this was because she had no genetic relation to the baby she gestated. But, more likely, it followed from Johnson's apparent interest in money rather than in the child. Legal proceedings began in *Baby M.* after Mary Beth took the child to Florida, claiming she could not part with the baby. They began in *Johnson*, after Anna Johnson sought payments that were not yet due to her under the provisions of the contract into which she had entered with the Calverts and asserted that she would keep the child if the requested payment was not made.

Gestational surrogacy has also been discomforting to society because in addition to separating intentional maternity from biological maternity, it separates biological maternity into discrete aspects. The separation of the gestational and genetic parameters of maternity deconstructs the presumption that a child's relation to its biological mother is grounded in an unassailably integral reproductive process.

This makes it possible to contrast one type of biological mother to another type. Women who assist as third parties in achieving others' reproductive goals can be understood differently depending on whether they serve as gestators or as donors of ova. Fertility clinics have been reported to advise intending parents to rely on different women to serve in each role. In part, that advice takes account of a tendency among states to enforce gestational, but not traditional, surrogacy arrangements. Beyond this, however, it reflects a stunning notion – that the woman whom one might want as the gestator of one's baby is not the same woman one should want as one's child's genetic mother. The message is clear and terribly discomforting: good breeders and good ova donors are often different, and the ideal "mother" can be constructed only if one allocates each task to a different woman. The implications for women, families, and children are confounding.

Surrogacy's protestation against traditional visions of mother implicates traditional visions of children. The traditional family that developed alongside and served the interests of the Industrial Revolution depended on a constellation of mother and children, identified with home and health, and a contrasting vision of the marketplace, populated largely by men.[11] That vision lasted without much explicit challenge until the middle of the twentieth century. To alter understandings of women in families – and of mothers, more particularly – was inevitably to question assumptions about children. Since the last decades of the twentieth century, society has struggled to preserve traditional understandings of childhood, often with only the illusion of success.

In short, the romanticized notion of treasured children, living with doting parents (particularly mothers) who socialized and protected the children from the harsh conditions of the marketplace, cannot survive the deconstruction of mother. Understandings of mother shaped in the context of surrogacy could, in theory, remain segregated from notions of mother in other contexts, but, ultimately, various images of mother will likely merge and reshape each other. That is even more likely to happen in that images of mother had diversified long before gestational surrogacy presented a new frame within which to think about maternity. In fact, it may be that shifts in visions of mother that preceded reliance on surrogacy facilitated the development of such arrangements. That these arrangements remain controversial a quarter century after the *Baby M.* case – even as they continue to provide a reproductive option for many people – suggests the depth of society's ambivalence about reconstructing understandings of family.

In short, it is unsurprising that understandings of mother and of childhood are being transformed in several directions at once. Reproductive possibilities such as gestational surrogacy are deconstructing assumptions

about "mother." In addition, women are being redefined by their participation as autonomous individuals in the marketplace. Changing visions
of woman and of mother have consequences for social understandings of
children. As the traditional family is re-shaped, children – the presump-
tive raison d'être of that form of family – are also re-envisioned.

21.4   "Best Interests" and Surrogacy in the Early Twenty-First Century

The best-interest standard reflected and was presumed to safeguard the
traditional family. In a couple of recent cases aimed at resolving disputes
occasioned by traditional surrogacy agreements, courts have allowed contract agreements to trump best interests in determining a child's custody
and placement. These decisions are suggestive of significant change in
visions of the family. This section first summarizes the history and uses
of the best-interest standard between the early nineteenth and the late
twentieth centuries. It then discusses two recent traditional surrogacy
cases that largely abandon the best-interest standard in determining custody and placement.

21.4.1   How Far Can the Best-Interest Standard Be Stretched?

In the United States, efforts to discern the best interests of children whose
custody is up for grabs have traditionally depended, at least broadly, on
socially approved expectations about mothers, fathers, and family. The
notion that custody decisions should serve children's interests was forged
in the early years of the Industrial Revolution – more or less coincident with
the development of the traditional family. In earlier centuries, decisions
about children's custody were based on the interests of adults. Several
cases at the start of the nineteenth century predicated custody decisions
on children's interests. In one well-known case, US Supreme Court Justice
Joseph Story, writing for a Rhode Island federal court, expressly displaced
the presumption of a father's absolute right to his child with the more
flexible notion that paternal custody usually (though not always) benefits
the child involved (*U.S. v. Green* 1824).[12] Soon, courts began to examine the
possibility that maternal custody better served children than paternal custody. This preference paralleled the century's romanticization of mothers
as virtuous, compassionate, and endowed by nature with the ability to
care for children while society deemed fathers, or at least most fathers,
less competent caretakers (Mintz and Kellogg 1988: 19, 20, 108).

Indeed, the best-interest standard, shaped in the nineteenth century, flourished for so many years because of its remarkable elasticity.
As the details of the traditional family varied over time, the standard

accommodated the changes. On the whole, these changes were not funda-mental in the sense that they did not upend the traditional family. Rather, they constituted variation within a broad frame that defined family. So, for example, over time, the standard facilitated shifts from a preference for paternal custody (early nineteenth century) to one for maternal cus-tody (early twentieth century) to one for a parent of the child's gender, a "primary" caretaker, a "psychological" parent, and a variety of other options (Dolgin 1996: 5–6).

By the start of the twenty-first century, judges continued to rely on the best-interest standard in resolving custody disputes, but the standard, once freed from concrete preferences for one sort of custody or another, has provided less and less guidance to courts. Further, by the year 2000, the transformation of the traditional family had become undeniable. In that year, Justice O'Connor, in a plurality opinion for the US Supreme Court, recognized "demographic changes of the last century" that had made "it difficult to speak of an average American family" (*Troxel* 2000: 63). Courts, legislatures, and many segments of the society conceded (or exclaimed, depending on perspective) that adults within families are autonomous individuals, not beholden to traditional strictures set by fixed roles and statuses within a hierarchically organized social order. Should that view encompass children within families, as well as adults, the traditional family will have evolved into a genuinely new form of family. That form of family will likely not be regulated through reference to tools shaped to serve a different social order.

21.4.2 Moving Away from Best Interests in Surrogacy Cases

Two traditional surrogacy cases decided in 2013 – one heard by Wisconsin's highest court (*Rosecky v. Schissel*) and one by a Tennessee appellate court (*In re Baby*) – may foreshadow a move away from focusing on the best interests of the child or at any rate, an increased willing-ness to bypass best-interest assessments in response to disputes about surrogacy arrangements. In *Rosecky*, the Supreme Court of Wisconsin attempted simultaneously to preserve essential aspects of a world of status in defining family relationships and to define those relationships through reference to contractual agreements. The Tennessee court in *In re Baby* declared explicitly that a surrogacy contract obliterates the need for a best-interest determination.

Rosecky v. Schissel involved a traditional surrogacy agreement between two couples, David and Marcia Rosecky and Monica and Cory Schissel. The four adults were friends before they joined together in a surro-gacy arrangement, and the two women – Marcia, the intending mother, and Monica, the surrogate – had been friends since childhood (*Rosecky* 2013: 638–639). Marcia became infertile after treatment for leukemia (apparently successful). Monica then offered to serve as a surrogate for the Roseckys.

Both couples hired lawyers who drew up a surrogacy agreement. That agreement provided for Monica to become pregnant through assisted insemination with David's sperm and, at the birth of a child, to yield all rights to "formal custody and placement of the child." Pursuant to the agreement, Monica would not be precluded from "seeing the child through informal visits" (2013: 638). The couples, after all, were friends. David, Monica, Monica's husband, and the lawyers all signed the surrogacy agreement (2013: 638).

The child, a boy – referred to in court proceedings as F.T.R. – was born in March 2010. Before the child's birth, the relationship between the Roseckys and the Schissels deteriorated (2013: 639). Monica permitted the Roseckys to take the child home from the hospital, but then sought "increased custody and placement" in court. David and Marcia, the intending parents, argued that Monica had waived her right to the conditions she sought. They further argued that they should be granted custody and placement of the child pursuant to the contract, even if the contract provision terminating Monica's maternity was unenforceable. A trial court granted custody of the child to David and rights of visitation to Monica (2013: 641).

Justice Ziegler, writing for the Supreme Court of Wisconsin, authored a fascinating opinion that attempted to mediate between the demands of status and those of contract. The court acknowledged the importance of safeguarding the child's welfare but at the same time concluded (here echoing the trial court) that many of the 16 "factors" delineated in state law as relevant to a best-interest determination proved "difficult to apply to the facts surrounding a surrogacy" (2013: 645).

Despite nodding to the continuing relevance of the best-interest standard, the state supreme court validated the surrogacy contract. The document itself contained a severability clause (making it possible to enforce the document's terms even if various provisions were deemed unenforceable). Thus, Justice Ziegler's opinion safeguarded Monica's legal maternity but asked the lower court upon remand of the case to look to the remainder of the contractual agreement and to assume – as it did not do when it first entertained the case – the validity of the surrogacy agreement (absent the document's provision about parentage) (2013: 652–653).

The claim, at the center of the state supreme court's decision – a claim echoed by the child's guardian ad litem – that the contract was valid except to the extent that it undermined the child's best interests (2013: 647, 653) – is peculiar. That claim depends on preserving aspects of two arguably irreconcilable visions of personhood and of the parent–child bond – one framed by notions of autonomous individuality and bargained choice and the other framed by notions of community and "love" (which can here be read as protection of the child's interests despite the court's validation of the contract). As described by the court, its decision aimed to serve both goals:

> While the traditional defenses to the enforcement of a contract apply, none have [sic] been presented to render the PA [parentage agreement] unenforceable. We do not accept David's argument that the PA is wholly enforceable. In fact, the portions of the PA calling for the termination of Monica's parental rights are unenforceable. We also do not accept Monica's assertion that the PA is wholly unenforceable. The main problem with Monica's arguments is that they are based on law that was never intended to govern the various issues presented in a surrogacy.
>
> *(2013: 648–649)*

The court entertained the contract as it would entertain a contract for the exchange of material goods or services in the marketplace:

> In this case, there is no question that the PA contained the essential elements of a contract. Monica made an offer to the Roseckys that she would act as a surrogate. The Roseckys accepted Monica's offer. Consideration was provided. [Thus the essential elements of a legal contract had been satisfied.]
>
> The unique nature of this contract however, cannot be understated. Creating a child is not something that one can decide to do one day and decide not to do the next. Typical damages cannot make one whole. Nonetheless, this is a contract and we conclude that it is largely enforceable.
>
> *(2013: 649, citation omitted)*

Justice Ziegler's opinion for the Wisconsin Supreme Court aims both to preserve status and to welcome contract.[13] It is unclear whether that goal can be sustained over time.

The decision of a Tennessee appellate court in *In re Baby* abandoned status more completely and relied on a model that depends almost entirely on contract to resolve a surrogacy dispute. Judge Bennett, writing for the Court of Appeals of Tennessee, enforced a traditional surrogacy agreement involving payment of "well over $30,000" in reimbursement to the surrogate (*In re Baby* 2013: 3). Remarkably, the contract into which the parties had entered attempted to gainsay state law regarding "domestic relations" insofar as that law conflicted with the provisions of the contract (2013: 1).

Furthermore, the intending parents, the surrogate, and the surrogate's husband had sought ratification of the contract in juvenile court after the baby's conception and before the birth of the baby. That court, in an order approved by the surrogate and her husband and the intending parents, provided for termination of "any rights and responsibilities that [Surrogate and Surrogate's Husband] might theoretically claim with regard to the child," and provided that the intending parents were to be given "full legal and physical custody" of the baby after its birth (2013: 2). However, the surrogate underwent a change of mind following the birth of the baby (2013: 2).

Tennessee statutory law, unlike that of Wisconsin, contained a relevant provision. State law facilitated validation of, though it did not expressly validate, the surrogacy agreement.[14] Noting that state law did not prohibit surrogacy, the Tennessee appellate court, affirming the decision of the state trial court, decided that the contract was valid and enforceable. The court thus terminated any rights the surrogate might claim to the baby, granted legal parentage to the intending (and genetic) father, and opened the way for the intending mother to adopt the child (2013: 4). In addressing the surrogate's assertion that the trial court had failed to consider the child's best interests, the appellate court concluded that the contract, which the court considered valid, precluded the need for a best-interest determination (*In re Baby* 2013: 6). Under state law, explained the court, "there is no best interest analysis if there is a valid surrogacy contract because the surrogate has already given up her parental rights. This is not a custody dispute" (2013: 6).

In this conclusion, the Tennessee court in *In re Baby* moved further from traditional understandings of family and parentage than had the Wisconsin Supreme Court in *Rosecky v. Schissel*. The court in *In re Baby* accepted the possibility that the parent–child relationship can be grounded on contract law and facilitated the adoption of the baby by the non-biological, intending mother by rendering moot any claims that the surrogate might make to parentage. The court thereby apparently freed itself from the need to issue reassurances about the child's best interests. Contract law trumped family law, and thus assessment of the child's best interests would have been extraneous.

21.5 Conclusion

The set of surrogacy cases considered in this chapter – from *Baby M.* in the late 1980s, to *Johnson v. Calvert* a few years later, and then, finally to *Rosecky v. Schissel* and *In re Baby* in 2013 – reflect a society and a legal system that have moved from steadfast commitment to safeguarding traditional visions of family to reluctant acceptance of new approaches to family, at least in surrogacy cases. In *Baby M.* both New Jersey courts – even the trial court which seemed, though only with ambivalence, to validate a surrogacy contract – issued decisions that shared a traditional vision of family and that struggled to preserve that vision for the child whose parentage and custody were at stake.

Johnson v. Calvert brought new possibilities and new concerns. By splitting biological maternity into components, gestational surrogacy posed striking dilemmas for a society and a legal system certain that the law had the capacity to identify a child's mother (even when that child's paternity was up for grabs). The California Supreme Court in *Johnson* responded to the new biological reality and the conundrums it posed for identifying baby Christopher's legal mother by seeking an alternate to biological and statutory approaches. It looked to the intention of the parties before the conception of the child and thus relied on an essential element of the world of contract (intention), even as it attempted to assimilate parental intentions with a traditional vision of parentage. Even so, in *Johnson*, unlike in *Baby M.*, the California courts abandoned any serious effort to discern the child's "best interests."

Most recently, the *Rosecky* court forged a composite response to a surrogacy dispute. That response attempted to merge elements of a world of contract with elements of a world of status. It is possible that that response will find acceptance with regard to surrogacy arrangements, but as a general matter, it would seem unlikely to be sustainable. Finally, in *In re Baby*, a Tennessee appellate court validated the surrogacy contract into which the parties to the case had entered and concluded that that contract precluded the surrogate's maternity and in doing that also precluded the need for a best-interest determination. This case, more than any of the others, sides with contract rather than status in resolving a surrogacy dispute.

Surrogacy disputes and judicial efforts to resolve them offer the analyst a rich context for considering shifting social assumptions about the contours of family, gender, and the parent–child bond, more generally. Disputes occasioned by surrogacy arrangements compel courts to respond to difficult choices about the most essential incidents of family. And since many of these cases have garnered significant public interest, the courts' deliberations have encouraged wider social debate. That debate is not only, or even primarily, about surrogate motherhood. It is also about the meaning of family, the implications of relationships among those taken to be kin, and about the scope of personhood.

Notes

1. In the text, this case is hereinafter referred to as "*Baby M.*," rather than by the official name, "*Matter of Baby M.*".
2. In fact, the contract was signed by the intending father (William Stern), the surrogate (Mary Beth Whitehead) and the surrogate's husband, Richard Whitehead. Richard Whitehead's signature was important to preclude his paternity of a child born to his wife. Stern's wife, Elizabeth Stern, did not sign the agreement for fear that her

    participation in the contract would have led to claims of baby selling. William, but not Elizabeth, was to have a genetic relationship to the child the parties hoped would be conceived, gestated, and born.

3. Adoption provides for the creation of the parent–child tie between people without a biological connection. Massachusetts promulgated the nation's first adoption law in the mid-nineteenth century. The practice was soon accepted elsewhere and was assimilated to the model of the "traditional" (nuclear) family (Cahn 2003: 1081–1082, 1102–1103).

4. *In re Gault*, decided by the US Supreme Court in 1967, granted Due Process protection (pursuant to the Fourteenth Amendment of the United States Constitution) to children tried in juvenile courts for acts that would have been crimes had then been engaged in by adults.

5. One of the two cases invalidated an important provision of the contract, but left custody and placement of the child to be determined by the surrogacy contract (*In re Baby* 2013).

6. In fact, there is still virtually no reliable evidence that surrogacy harms children (van Zyl and van Niekerk 2000: 404).

7. In *Tinker v. Des Moines Independent Community School District*, the US Supreme Court found that high school and junior high school students and their teachers enjoyed First Amendment rights ("applied in light of the special characteristics of the school environment") (Tinker 1969: 511). More specifically, *Tinker* extended constitutional protection to students who wore black armbands in school to protest the Vietnam War.

8. The Massachusetts law at stake in the case required a minor girl to obtain parental consent to terminate a pregnancy or, if that consent were denied the girl, she could request judicial consent. Either way, the law required the girl to inform her parents that she was pregnant, and that she desired an abortion before she was able to terminate a pregnancy (*Bellotti* 1979: 625).

9. The case did not involve a jury. Thus, the trial court judge determined the "facts" as well as the law.

10. To some extent, Justice Kennard mis-read the majority decision which, in such cases, would grant legal maternity to either the genetic or the gestational mother, depending on which of them was the intending mother. Justice Kennard assumed, following the facts in the *Johnson* case, that the majority's decision would always privilege the gamete donor over the gestator. That is not what the majority said.

11. Women and, before the last part of the nineteenth century, children also worked in the marketplace but those who did so were poor and carried out burdensome tasks for little pay.

12. In *United States v. Green*, Justice Story looked to the best interests of a ten-year-old girl in deciding a custody dispute between the child's father and her maternal grandfather. As she neared her death, the

girl's mother had asked her father (the child's grandfather) to raise the girl. Justice Story concluded that the girls' father, as such, did not have "an absolute vested right" to custody of his child.

13. Justice Abrahamson, concurring with the state supreme court's decision in *Rosecky*, noted and criticized the court's elision of family law generally and of the best-interest standard, in particular, in favor of reliance on a contractual agreement (*Rosecky v. Schissel* 2013: 654–665).

14. The state's statutory law defined surrogacy and did not prohibit it. It provided, however, that the provision did not "expressly authorize the surrogate birth process" and that in Tennessee that could happen only if a court or a subsequent act of the legislature so provided (*In re Baby* 2013: 4, quoting Tenn. Code Ann. Sec. 36-1-102(48)(A)).

References

Bellotti v. Baird. 1979. 443 U.S. 622.

Cahn, N. 2003. "Perfect Substitutes or the Real Thing?" *Duke Law Journal* 52: 1077–1166.

Commonwealth v. Addicks. SC Pa. 1815. 2 Serg. & Pawle 174.

Dolgin, J. 1996. "Why Has the Best-Interest Standard Survived?: The Historic and Social Context." *Children's Legal Rights Journal* 16: 2–10.

Gordon, M. 1987. "'Baby M': New Questions about Biology and Destiny." *Ms. Magazine*, 25–28.

Hofman, D. L. 2009. "'Mama's Baby, Daddy's Maybe': A State-by-State Survey of Surrogacy Laws and Their Disparate Gender Impact." *William Mitchell Law Review* 35: 449–468.

In re Baby. (Ct of Appeals Tenn. 2013), slip opin., available at 2013 West Law 245039, appeal granted, 2013 Tenn. LEXIS 470 (S.C. Tenn. May 7, 2013).

In re Gault. 1967. 387 U.S. 1.

Johnson v. Calvert, No. X-633190, (Cal. App. Dep't Super. Ct. Oct. 22, 1990), aff'd sub nom., *Anna J. v. Mark C.*, 286 Cal. Rptr. 369 (Cal. Ct. App. 1991), aff'd 851 P.2d 776 (Cal. 1993), cert. denied, 114 S. Ct. 206 (1993).

Marvin v. Marvin, (Cal. 1976). 557 P.2d 106.

Matter of Baby M., 217 N.J. Super. 313, 525 A.2d 1128 (1987), aff'd in part and rev'd in part, 109 N.J. 396, 537 A.2d 1227 (1988).

Mintz, S. and S. Kellogg. 1988. *Domestic Revolutions: A Social History of American Family Life*. New York: The Free Press.

Morone v. Morone. (N.Y. 1980) 413 N.E.2d 1154.

Nationwide Drive for Children's Rights. 1977. "U.S. News & World Report." In *The Children's Rights Movement*, ed. B. Gross and R. Gross, 206–213. Garden City, NY: Anchor Books.

Nelson, W. E. 1996. "Patriarchy or Equality: Family Values or Individuality." *St. John's Law Review* 70: 435–537.

Parham v. J.R., 1979. 442 U.S. 584.

Postman, N. 1994. *The Disappearance of Childhood*. New York: Vintage Books.

Roberts, D. 1997. "Spiritual and Menial Housework." *Yale Journal of Law and Feminism* 9: 51–80.

Rosecky v. Schissel. 2013. 833 N.W.2d 634.

Rothenberg, K. 1990. "Gestational Surrogacy and the Health Care Provider: Put Part of the 'IVF Genie' Back into the Bottle." *Law, Medicine and Health Care* 18: 345.

Scherer v. Scherer. (Ga. 1982). 292 S.E.2d 662.

Schneider, D. M. 1968. *American Kinship: A Cultural Account*. Englewood Cliffs, NJ: Prentice Hall.

Tinker v. Des Moines Independent Community School District. 1969. 393 U.S. 503.

Troxel v. Granville. 2000. 530 U.S. 57.

United States v. Green. (Cir. Ct, D. R.I. 1824). 3 Mason 482.

van Zyl, L. and A. van Niekerk. 2000. "Interpretations, Perspectives and Intentions in Surrogate Motherhood." *Journal of Medical Ethics* 26: 404–409.

22

Kinship and Assisted Reproductive Technologies: A Middle Eastern Comparison

Marcia C. Inhorn, Daphna Birenbaum-Carmeli, Soraya Tremayne, and Zeynep B. Gürtin

22.1   Introduction

Around the world, approximately 9 percent of reproductive-aged couples suffer from infertility, or the inability to produce a child (Boivin et al. 2007). In many developing countries, the percentages of infertility are significantly higher, reaching 25 to 30 percent in some populations (Mascarenhas et al. 2012). However, the introduction of assisted reproductive technologies (ARTs) around the globe has revolutionized the treatment of infertility, turning many infertile couples' childlessness into a medical condition that can be overcome (Inhorn and Patrizio 2015). Although ART success rates are only about 33 percent per cycle even in the most technologically advanced countries (Gnoth et al. 2011), so far more than eight million "test-tube babies" have been born worldwide (De Geyter 2018), bringing great joy to their once-infertile parents (Franklin 2012).

In vitro fertilization (IVF) was the first ART to be successfully carried out in Great Britain in 1978. IVF consists of hormonal stimulation of the ovaries to produce multiple eggs, which are then surgically retrieved and placed in a laboratory petri dish, where they are fertilized with a man's ejaculated sperm. The fertilized embryos produced outside the body are then transferred into the woman's uterus. Originally developed to bypass blocked fallopian tubes, IVF is now used in the treatment of other female and unexplained infertility problems. Probably the most significant modification of IVF took place in the early 1990s, when intracytoplasmic sperm injection (ICSI) was developed in Belgium. This novel technology enables embryologists to inject a single spermatozoon into an egg under a high-powered microscope, thereby effectively "forcing" fertilization of eggs by otherwise "weak" sperm. ICSI has revolutionized the treatment of male infertility and has allowed previously "sterile" men to father genetically related offspring (Inhorn 2012). Both IVF and ICSI are used in conjunction with the freezing, storage, and subsequent thawing of sperm, eggs, and embryos, thereby enabling gametes and embryos to be preserved over time and even to be carried (in cryopreservation tanks) across national and international borders (Inhorn 2015).

ARTs have been used primarily by heterosexual married couples around the world. However, these technologies have also opened up numerous options for nontraditional kinship and family formations, including genetically related gay families, post-menopausal motherhood, and posthumous reproduction using the cryopreserved gametes (sperm or eggs) of a dead mother or father (Inhorn and Birenbaum-Carmeli 2008). As such, ARTs present epistemological and ethical challenges, creating new dilemmas for regulators and religious leaders, as well as for practitioners and persons facing infertility problems. Religious authorities have been especially assertive in some parts of the world, attempting to influence the contemporary conception and shaping of ART-created families. Even though religious rulings can be extremely deterministic, they are sometimes surprisingly adaptable as well.

In this chapter, we probe the various modes of ART application, religious intervention, and resultant kinship formations in four Middle Eastern settings: the Sunni Muslim Arab world, the Sunni Muslim but officially "secular" country of Turkey, Shia Muslim Iran, and Jewish Israel. This four-way comparison reveals significant similarities, as well as stark differences in matters of kinship and assisted reproduction in the Middle East. The permissions and restrictions on ARTs, often determined by religious decrees, may lead to counterintuitive outcomes, many of which defy prevailing stereotypes about which parts of the Middle East are more "progressive" or "conservative" (Gürtin, Inhorn and Tremayne 2015; Inhorn 2012). Indeed, as ARTs have traveled to regions such as the Middle East, local considerations – be they social, cultural, economic, ethical, or political – have shaped the ways in which these technologies are being offered to and received by infertile couples, their clinicians, and the clerics who are in dialogue with both (Inhorn 2003).

In this chapter, we begin with an outline of the major family features that are common to all of these Middle Eastern settings, as well as a description of significant local diversity. We then move on to explore how specific reproductive technologies are applied in each setting, focusing on third-party assisted reproduction (i.e., donor sperm, donor egg, donor embryo, gestational surrogacy). As we will argue, it is the use of third-party reproductive assistance – allowed in both Israel and Iran, but disallowed in the Arab countries and Turkey – that has highlighted and cemented profound regional differences in attitudes toward "biological" versus "social" parenthood and kinship. Indeed, in the Middle East, as elsewhere, ARTs have had both reinforcing and destabilizing impacts on the meanings of parenthood and family life. By means of their very existence and availability, these new reproductive technologies have expanded the limits of acceptable kinship and family formations in some parts of the Middle East, while re-entrenching and solidifying traditional family structures in others. In the Sunni Muslim world in particular, ARTs have reinscribed religious and cultural mandates regarding the primacy of biogenetic inheritance and the social sanctity of patrilineal kinship structures.

22.2 Middle Eastern Kinship: Regional Similarities and Differences

From Morocco to Iran, Middle Eastern societies can be described as family oriented, with a high value placed on marriage and childbearing (Inhorn 1996, 2012). Across the Middle East, reproduction comprises a major organizing principle, the significance of which goes well beyond individuals' emotional desires for children. Indeed, on a cultural level, reproduction within marriage is deemed a social obligation – a way to perpetuate the family lineage, as well as a vehicle for parents to receive old-age support and help with family labor. Contrary to popular stereotypes, reproduction is not the sole remit of women in the Middle East; both Muslim and Jewish Middle Eastern men often desire children and want to experience parenthood as active fathers (Birenbaum-Carmeli, Diamand and Abu Yaman 2014; Gürtin 2014; Inhorn 2012, 2014). Thus, they are often fully involved in reproductive decision making (Inhorn 2018), and later on, in childrearing. In other words, common to all of these settings is a strong social desire for children among both men and women – a desire that is first and foremost based on affection and love toward children, rather than instrumental values.

Given such strong child desire, the Middle East can be described as pronatalist: namely, aspirations for childbearing occur at the individual, social, religious, and political levels (Inhorn 1996; Kahn 2000). Yet, having said this, the number of children desired within each family has declined dramatically over the past 40 years. As shown in Table 22.1, total fertility rates in the Arab countries have plummeted since the late 1970s – from an average of more than five children per family in most countries, to an average of two children per family today (Eberstadt and Shah 2012; Inhorn 2018). Interestingly, Israel continues to have one of the highest total fertility rates in the region, with all segments of the Israeli population (i.e., Palestinians and Jews, both secular and orthodox) maintaining fertility rates well above replacement level (that is, more than two children per family).

Table 22.1 *Arab countries in the top fifteen for global fertility decline, 1975–1980 to 2005–2010*

Country	Total fertility rate		Difference	Percentage decline
	1975–1980	2005–2010		
Libya	7.94	2.67	−4.39	69.9
United Arab Emirates	5.66	1.97	−3.69	65.2
Oman	8.10	2.89	−5.21	64.3
Tunisia	5.69	2.05	−3.64	63.9
Qatar	6.11	2.21	−3.90	63.8
Lebanon	4.23	1.58	−2.66	62.8
Algeria	7.18	2.72	−4.45	62.0

Source: United Nations (2013).

In addition to positive attitudes toward childbearing, another shared feature of these Middle Eastern settings is belief in science and medicine, including the contributions of technoscience to the control and facilitation of fertility (Inhorn 2003, 2012). Both Islam and Judaism valorize scientific and medical achievements, including those that enable married heterosexual couples to have biological offspring. In this respect, both religions have taken much more positive stances toward medically assisted reproduction than either Catholicism or other Christian denominations (Inhorn, Patrizio and Serour 2010). In fact, both Islam and Judaism positively encourage biomedical treatment of infertility as a means of preserving marriage and overcoming the conjugal suffering of childlessness.

Having said this, Jewish and Muslim religious authorities have differed considerably in their attitudes toward the use of ARTs outside of marriage. Within the Middle Eastern region as a whole, Israel is the only country in which single and lesbian women are entitled to employ the same ART services that married women are able to receive. One consequence of this entitlement is that many single Israeli women, often those at the end of their reproductive lifespans, decide to conceive and raise a child although they are not married. Many of these women require technological assistance and turn to ARTs in order to conceive. In such cases, women's increasing age at conception is leading to significant age-related female infertility problems.

The same is true in the Muslim Middle Eastern countries, where age-related female infertility is a growing issue of concern (Inhorn 2015). However, in addition, in the Muslim countries, male infertility accounts for approximately 60 to 90 percent of all cases presenting to IVF clinics (Inhorn 2012). Many of these cases, furthermore, are severe, involving very low sperm count and/or poor motility (movement), as well as many cases of azoospermia (total absence of sperm in the ejaculate). Such male infertility tends to cluster in families, with multiple brothers, cousins, and other male relatives affected (Inhorn et al. 2009). Familial male infertility is probably genetic, linked to the high rates of consanguineous (cousin) marriage in the region (Inhorn 2012).

In Islam but not in Judaism, marrying one's blood relatives is condoned on religious grounds. Thus, across the Muslim Middle East, consanguineous marriage rates range from 16 to 78 percent of all marriages (Abbasi-Shavazi, McDonald and Hosseini-Chavoshi 2008; Inhorn 2012). Patrilineal parallel cousin marriage (i.e., marriage of the son and daughter of two brothers) is considered the ideal form. However, consanguineous marriages may occur between other types of first cousins, as well as more distant relatives. In general, consanguineous marriage with close relatives is considered the ideal way to achieve familial solidarity, retain the transfer of wealth and inheritance within the family, and to ensure "purity" within the patrilineage.

Because Judaism does not abide by this preference for cousin marriage, the rates of male infertility among Jews in Israel is closer to the global average of 50 percent of all cases (Farhi and Ben Haroush 2011; Sella et al. 2011). Furthermore, in the state of Israel and within Judaism more generally, when men or women are infertile, they are allowed to adopt, unlike in most Muslim countries. Although adoption receives no financial or logistical state support in Israel, it is still undertaken by some infertile Jewish couples. Adopted children are issued new birth certificates that carry the names of their adoptive parents. At the age of 18, adopted children may obtain information regarding their biological parents, if they wish. However, because healthy newborns are rarely available for adoption in Israel, international adoption is more commonly undertaken, meaning that adopted children may have no information at all regarding their biological parents.

The Islamic attitude toward adoption is quite different. Muslim couples may foster a child (through an institution of guardianship, called *kafala*). However, permanent legal adoption as it is practiced in the West is not allowed in family law in the vast majority of Muslim countries. Adoption is considered to be *haram* – or religiously illicit – for a number of reasons. Adoption is believed to blur a child's *nasab*, or biological lineage, which is considered unjust to the child and which creates concerns regarding future incest (between adoptees who do not realize that they are siblings) (Inhorn 1996, 2003, 2012; Sonbol 1995). This injunction against adoption is also upheld in Muslim inheritance laws, which require the disbursement of assets only to biological heirs (Bargach 2002). Having said this, in Shia-dominant Iran, as well as in the more secular Muslim countries of Turkey and Tunisia, adoption is legally practiced, even if it remains an unpopular and uncommon way of creating a family. In general, negative attitudes toward adoption across the Muslim Middle East, as well as the dearth of children available for adoption in Israel, mean that infertile Middle Easterners of all stripes must turn to ARTs to form their families.

22.3   ARTs in the Middle East

Given strong regional pronatalism, high rates of male and female infertility, religious and cultural prohibitions against adoption, and the valorization of science and medicine, it should come as no surprise that ARTs have been embraced with enthusiasm across the Middle Eastern region. Indeed, the Middle East hosts one of the strongest ART industries in the world, with many countries performing among the highest numbers of IVF cycles per capita (Inhorn and Patrizio 2015; Jones et al. 2010).

Israel was the first country in the region to perform IVF, with clinics opening by 1981, only three years after the birth of the first "test-tube baby" in England (Birenbaum-Carmeli 1997; Birenbaum-Carmeli, Carmeli and Cohen 2000). Since then, Israel has gone on to become the world's leading IVF "capital" – performing more cycles of IVF per capita per year than any other single country (Israel Ministry of Health 2013). Virtually all forms of ART are allowed and practiced in Israel. This welcome embrace of ARTs has allowed married couples to overcome their infertility, single and gay men and women to form families, and Israel's population to increase overall. Moreover, in Israel, IVF and ICSI are publically funded, up to the birth of two live children (with the woman's current partner). The coverage applies to all Israeli women aged 18 to 45, including single and lesbian women (Birenbaum-Carmeli 2004). The state also entitles women, and to some extent their partners, to generous paid leave and protection from being fired while undergoing IVF treatment. Not surprisingly, given this high level of state support, Israeli women have been the world's heaviest consumers of IVF and other ARTs for many years (Collins 2002; Nyboe Andersen et al. 2007; Schenker 2003).

Although Israel has always been on the forefront of Middle Eastern IVF trends, the Muslim Middle East is also home to a robust IVF industry. The Sunni-majority Arab countries of Egypt, Jordan, and Saudi Arabia were the first to open IVF clinics in 1986, following the 1980 *fatwa* endorsement of IVF for married couples by the Grand Shaykh of Egypt's famous religious university, Al Azhar. Since then, the Al Azhar *fatwa* condoning IVF has been upheld by leading clerics and religious institutions in many Middle Eastern countries. In general, Sunni authorities view IVF and related technologies as religiously permissible solutions to marital infertility, as long as these ARTs incorporate only the gametes (egg and sperm) of a wife and a husband during the course of their legal marriage. All forms of third-party assisted reproduction – including egg donation, sperm donation, embryo donation, or surrogacy (Serour 2008; Moosa 2003) – are disallowed. Thus, in the Sunni Muslim world, which includes most Arab countries, as well as Turkey, third-party reproductive assistance is never practiced, with this ban in place through various religious edicts, bioethical and professional codes of medical conduct, and legal formulations. Furthermore, in Turkey, as we shall see, a recent law has made all forms of third-party assistance, including travel to another country for such purposes, illegal (Gürtin 2011).

Indeed, like its Arab neighbors, Turkey boasts a history of IVF dating back to the late 1980s, with the first IVF baby born in 1989. As suggested above, Turkey has also closely followed the Sunni Muslim religious rulings regarding IVF, including the prohibition against any kind of third-party reproductive assistance. However, for married infertile couples who wish to use their own gametes, Turkey has been a generous supporter of IVF, introducing public insurance financing of ARTs in 2005. Since then, IVF clinics have mushroomed across the country, with Turkey now hosting more IVF clinics (>110) than any other Middle Eastern country (Gürtin 2011, 2012; Jones et al. 2010; Urman and Yakin 2010).

Whereas Turkey and the Arab countries now perform thousands of cycles of IVF without any form of donor assistance, this ban on third parties is not upheld within Shia-dominant Iran, where senior clerical sources endorsed the practices of third-party donation over the course of the 1990s, culminating in a final *fatwa* by the Supreme Leader, Ayatollah Ali Hussein Al-Khamenei, issued in 1999, which allowed both egg donation and sperm donation to be used by infertile couples (Tremayne and Inhorn 2012). Hence, in Iran, which is the demographic epicenter of Shia Islam, all forms of assisted reproduction, including egg, sperm, and embryo donation, as well as surrogacy, are now practiced. At the same time, the use of ARTs is restricted to heterosexual married couples, thereby enforcing Iran's punishable ban on homosexuality and conception outside of wedlock.

22.4   Third-Party Reproduction across the Middle East

But the question remains: Why do these Middle Eastern countries, all of which embrace ARTs, differ so considerably in attitudes toward third-party reproductive assistance? Why do Iran and Israel – usually pitted against each other as political enemies – nonetheless agree upon the use of third-party assisted reproduction? And why does Turkey – usually held up as the most "Western" and "secular" of the Middle Eastern Muslim nations – uphold an anti-donation stance that links it to the more "conservative" Arab states? These questions can be answered by turning to both religion and culture and to particular local variants of "kinship thinking." As we argue here, Sunni Islam is scripturally and legally oriented, turning to Qur'anic mandates regarding the importance of *nasab*, or known genealogy. Shia Islam, on the other hand, places a high premium on *ijtihad*, or independent reasoning, which has allowed individual clerics to permit third-party reproductive assistance among their Shia Muslim followers. In some instances, Sunni Muslims are also abiding by these Shia "permissions," leading to a private world of Shia-to-Sunni gamete donation in multisectarian settings such as Lebanon (Inhorn 2012). Finally, in Israel, the Jewish rabbinical world is diverse, leading to the same kind of independent decision making found, quite paradoxically, in Iran. This kind of "Israeli *ijtihad*" has allowed Jewish infertile couples, as well as singles and gay couples, to access a multiplicity of forms of ART within a state that is technically Jewish, but where both rabbis and secular medical forces have combined to allow virtually every form of ART-assisted kinship reckoning.

22.5   The Sunni Muslim Preservation of *Nasab*

To understand the prohibition against third-party reproductive assistance in the Arab countries as well as Turkey, it is important to examine Sunni-inspired ethical stances regarding *nasab* – usually defined as "genealogy," "kinship," "lineage," or, on an individual level, one's biological "relations" or "origins." In Sunni Islam, which is scripturally oriented, preserving *nasab* is considered a moral imperative, because the importance of knowing each person's *nasab* is described in numerous passages from the Islamic scriptures, including the Qur'an and *hadith*, or the sayings and deeds of the Prophet Muhammad. In other words, preserving *nasab* – each person's known genealogical relations – is considered not only ideal, but a moral imperative for the constitution of legitimate personhood. Because all Sunni Muslim societies are organized patrilineally – with descent and inheritance, as well as individual names and identities, figured through the father's side – knowing paternity is critical, not only for individual men as fathers, but for the patrilineal system as a whole.

Third-party reproductive assistance is thus viewed in Sunni Islam as destroying *nasab* through the "mixing" of genealogical relations. Third-party assisted conception of a donor child violates the child's rights to known parentage, which is considered not only immoral, but cruel and unjust to donor children themselves. Furthermore, donor children whose *nasab* is unknown face the threat of potential incest. Namely, if two offspring of the same anonymous donor meet and marry, they unwittingly commit incest as biological half-siblings.

Third-party reproductive assistance is also considered tantamount to *zina*, or adultery, in Sunni Islamic thinking. Although third-party donation does not involve the "touch and gaze" of adulterous relations, it is nonetheless like adultery by virtue of introducing the sperm of another man, or the egg or womb of another woman, into the marital relationship. The donor child who results from such a forbidden mode of reproduction is considered a *walad il-zina* – literally, a child of illicit sex, or an out-of-wedlock bastard. Such a donor child cannot be made legitimate through any means, including adoption by the non-biologically related parent.

In short, donor technologies, because of their association with adultery, incest, and genealogical confusion, are considered *haram* – religiously forbidden and illegal – according to Sunni Islamic jurisprudence. Accordingly, a religiously inspired ban on third-party reproductive assistance is in place in all Sunni-majority countries around the world, including the Arab states and Turkey. Couples who need donor technologies in order to conceive are told that these technologies are *haram*, going "against" the religion by "mixing" genealogical relations (Inhorn 2003). These moral concerns are taken quite seriously. IVF clinics in Sunni-dominant Muslim countries do not practice third-party assisted conception. Although some patients may be advised to travel abroad for such services (Gürtin 2011; Inhorn 2012), the majority of infertile Sunni Muslim couples agree with, and thus abide by, the religious mandates to preserve *nasab* and avoid incest and adultery (Inhorn 2003, 2012).

Even in Turkey, a country with a formal commitment to secularism, which dates back to the rule of Ataturk in the 1920s (Arda 2007), ARTs are governed by a distinctly Sunni Muslim ethos. Under the Turkish Ministry of Health, the Assisted Reproduction Treatment Centers Directorate has restricted ARTs to married heterosexual couples using their own gametes. Moreover, in 2010, Turkey banned its citizens from seeking donor technologies abroad, thereby becoming the world's first country to regulate against reproductive "tourism" (Gürtin 2011). Turkey's highest religious authority, the Presidency of Religious Affairs, has supported this sweeping prohibition against third-party reproduction, explaining that "according to the general principles of the religion of Islam, there is an imperative for a legitimate child to belong, whether by sperm or egg or womb, to a wedded husband–wife couple" (Presidency of Religious Affairs 2006, Gürtin's translation).

This approach does not apply, obviously, to every Turkish man or woman, many of whom are non-religious, or subscribe to different schools of thought other than Sunni Islam. While it is generally true that third-party reproductive assistance – especially the use of donor sperm – is highly stigmatized in Turkey, there have been reports of Turkish couples surreptitiously crossing borders to nearby Cyprus and Greece in order to access donor gametes, particularly donor eggs. Indeed, according to the director of the Ministry of Health's Treatment Services department, the 2010 legal ban on reproductive travel was introduced in response to the growing popularity of these crossborder journeys to access donor gametes (Gürtin 2011).

Given Turkey's heterogeneity – including a growing social divide between those Turks committed to secularism and those devoted to increasing Islamic piety in the public sphere (White 2002, 2014) – it is difficult to gain an accurate picture of public opinions on third-party reproductive assistance in Turkey (Baykal et al. 2008; Isikoglu et al. 2006; Kilic et al. 2009). The available evidence points to a diversity of opinions, with levels of support for egg donation varying widely (Baykal et al. 2008; Isikoglu et al. 2006; Kilic et al. 2009). Nonetheless, in one survey, sperm donation was rejected almost unanimously by Turkish respondents, in keeping with the Sunni Muslim position on the necessity of known paternity (Baykal et al. 2008). Indeed, these differential views regarding egg versus sperm donation appear to reflect the Sunni Muslim concern with patrilineal kinship reckoning and the need for "known fathers" of all children. Having said this, Turkey is one of three Middle Eastern Muslim countries (along with Iran and Tunisia) where adoption is allowed in the civil legal code. Thus, some Turks said that they would consider adoption as a way to form a family (Kilic et al. 2009).

In short, the heterogeneous views toward egg donation, sperm donation, and adoption in Turkey reveal how contemporary Turks, the vast majority of whom are Sunni Muslims, are deliberating according to their own moral stances in order to reach decisions regarding what family structure they find acceptable. The fact that at least some Turks take positions that are not aligned with official Sunni Muslim positions indicates the degree to which secularism in Turkey has also shaped moral discourses surrounding kinship and family life.

22.6   Shia Muslim *Ijtihad*: Opening the Path to Donation

The Islamic Republic of Iran, which is the demographic epicenter of Shia Islam, presents a quite different moral landscape. The leading Shia jurists, who are considered *maraji* (plural of *marja*), or sources of emulation, have also deliberated on the permissibility of third-party assisted reproduction among their Shia followers. Like their Sunni counterparts, Shia authorities have been concerned about conception outside wedlock, the impact on the lineage (*nasab*) of the resulting child, and the ensuing question of inheritance. However, the Shia tradition of Islam gives precedence to *ijtihad*, or independent moral reasoning based on the power of *'aql*, or the human intellect. Thus, through processes of *ijtihad* – or independent interpretations of the Islamic scriptures, including their relevance for contemporary social life – individual Shia jurists have reached quite dissimilar verdicts, ranging from total opposition, to conditional approval, to full acceptance of all forms of third-party reproductive assistance.

Those Shia *maraji* who are in favor of third-party donor technologies distinguish between *nasab* (biological lineage) and parenting via "consent" between the donor and the recipients. Through such consent, the donor's biological right to parenthood is effectively transferred to the recipient parents. Moreover, in order to further ensure that no birth out of wedlock is taking place, some of the Shia *maraji* who support third-party reproductive assistance generally extend the definition of marriage to include "temporary marriage" (*mut'a*), a practice that is legitimate only in Shia Islam, and which is not practiced by Sunni Muslims (Haeri 1989). Through the use of temporary marriages, egg and sperm donors can become legitimate – albeit temporary – spouses, by donating their gametes within the confines of *mut'a* marriage (Clarke 2006, 2009; Tremayne 2006, 2009). Furthermore, embryo donation has been legitimized through a law passed in Parliament, which has also allowed surrogacy to be used. As a result, Shia-dominant Iran has become more open to third-party reproductive assistance than any other Muslim country in the world, as well as many Western nations (Inhorn and Tremayne 2012).

Indeed, in Shia Islam, *ijtihad* has allowed each senior *marja* to form a valid opinion on third-party reproductive assistance, creating a truly dynamic space for the practice of ARTs in Iran. Iranian medical practitioners and infertile couples are able to choose the particular religious opinions on third-party reproduction that best meet their needs, without breaching any legal or religious rules. In fact, the final endorsement of third-party reproductive assistance by Iran's leading cleric, Ayatollah Khamenei, has given third-party reproductive assistance "official" legitimacy since the late 1990s, even though ARTs had been practiced in all their forms through the approval of other leading Shia Islamic jurists (Clarke 2009; Garmaroudi Naef 2012; Tremayne 2012).

Having said this, the high-ranking clerical approval of third-party assisted reproduction in Iran has also paved the way for some counter-intuitive outcomes. For example, in their own efforts to maintain *nasab*, or purity of the patrilineage, many infertile Iranian couples prefer to use close relatives as donors. Thus, siblings have become the major source of gamete donation in some Iranian IVF clinics (Garmaroudi Naef 2012; Tremayne 2009, 2015), creating real potential for sibling incest and genetic inbreeding. This preference for sibling donation must also be understood within the context of marital and gender relations in Iran. Relatives who are not potential marriage partners (i.e., parents, grandparents, siblings, aunts and uncles, children, and grandchildren) are considered to be *mahram*, the individuals with whom one can freely associate. *Na-mahram*, on the other hand, are those individuals of the opposite sex who are potential marriage partners and with whom sexual contact outside marriage is forbidden. Thus, choosing *mahram* relatives as gamete donors constitutes the "safer" option – basically keeping gamete donation "all in the family" – even though, in effect, it means breaching the incest and adultery taboos (Tremayne 2015).

When donors are not family members, another cultural mechanism is invoked to create kinship ties between the infertile mother and her donor-conceived child. In Islam, a woman who has breastfed a baby is considered to be its "milk mother" (*madare rezayi*) and is recognized as being equivalent to a biological mother in terms of kinship relations. Applying this system of milk kinship, Iranian women who have used donor eggs, embryos, or surrogates, but who can still breastfeed the donor child, are thereby able to form a biological bond through the nurturance of their own breastmilk. In the context of third-party assisted reproduction, this practice of milk kinship could potentially serve to mediate and enable social parenthood of donor children, establishing a biological connection based on milk, rather than "blood" or genes (Al-Torki 1980; Clarke 2009; Khatib-Chahidi 1982, 1992).

However, legitimizing sperm donation has proven more problematic (Tremayne 2012), with male infertility being stigmatized within the predominantly patriarchal Iranian culture. Regardless of the choice of sperm donor, the process leaves the infertile husband in a very passive position, external to the donor procreation of his wife. Some Iranian men seem to feel emasculated by this process, struggling to reconcile their sperm donation decisions and even harming their families in the process (Tremayne 2012). Although the acceptance of sperm donation and other forms of third-party reproductive assistance in Iran has been couched in the language of "happy families," the available evidence suggests that third-party donation has been a mixed blessing, with biological incest and family violence as the possible end results.

Having said this, most Shia Muslim clerics now accept the validity of at least egg donation, which has become a popular option for Shia Muslim couples with age-related female infertility problems. Egg donation is now available in both Iran and Lebanon, the latter of which is a multisectarian Arab country with a majority Shia population. As of this writing, Iran and Lebanon are the only two nations in the Muslim world where third-party reproductive assistance is being practiced (Inhorn 2012). As in Iran, egg donation in Lebanon is becoming a popular option, with egg donors consisting of close female relatives or friends, even though anonymous egg donors, sometimes from other countries, are also employed.

This opening of egg donation in Lebanon has facilitated so-called "reproductive tourism" within the Arab world (Inhorn 2012, 2015). Namely, both Shia and Sunni Muslims from other Arab countries are traveling to Beirut in pursuit of donor eggs. Although most Sunni Muslim couples realize that they are "going against" the tenets of their religion, they often justify this choice based on the biological connection that will be created when an infertile woman becomes pregnant and ultimately breastfeeds the donor-egg-conceived child. Furthermore, Sunni Muslim men who agree to egg donation often point out that they are allowed, via polygyny, to marry more than one wife. Egg donation is thus being construed as "like" polygyny, even if no formal temporary marriages are taking place. (Sunni Islam does not allow temporary marriage.)

Sunni Muslim couples' religious resistance to the ban on third-party reproductive assistance in the Arab countries is not surprising, given that other routes to parenthood, including gestational surrogacy and child adoption, are also banned. Thus, some Sunni Muslim couples are taking oppositional stances, accepting the benefits of donor technologies by invoking the more "permissive" Shia opinions and practices.

Indeed, the willingness of some Muslim men, both Sunni and Shia, to overcome their wives' infertility through egg donation is a powerful sign of contemporary conjugal commitments. The embrace of new forms of ARTs by *both* Muslim men and women has gone hand in hand with the emergence of the "companionate couple" – a kinship unit that challenges stereotypical images of patrilineal, patrilocal, patriarchal, and polygynous Middle Eastern marriages (Inhorn 2012). Having said this, the willingness of couples to employ donor technologies for the sake of companionate marriage stops short of sperm donation. In the Arab world, the vast majority of both Sunni and Shia men view sperm donation as a major violator of *nasab*. Sperm donation confuses paternity and destroys kinship based on patrilineal descent. Furthermore, among individual men, belief in the importance of biological fatherhood remains strong. Thus, a sperm-donor child "won't be my son," according to the vast majority of Muslim men, both Sunni and Shia (Inhorn 2006, 2012).

22.7 Israeli Jewish Kinship Accommodations

These same kinds of moral concerns about sperm and egg donation also have resonance in Israel, even though virtually all forms of ART are practiced. The application of donor technologies, which has stirred considerable moral debate in the Muslim world, has never raised serious clerical objections in Israel. Unlike Muslim religious authorities, Jewish authorities have allowed ART innovations to be smoothly incorporated within accepted Judaic law. Having been included in every significant ART-related policy discussion in Israel, rabbinical authorities have been able to introduce their requirements and modifications to the practice of ART, but invariably have demonstrated openness and flexibility toward the use of these new technologies.

The scene in Israel, however, is not trouble free. Although lineage and descent are less crucial for most Israelis than they are for Muslims, paternity is still the basis of one's family name and sense of family belonging in Israeli society. Thus, male infertility is associated with significant social stigma. Until the development of ICSI in the early 1990s, sperm donation was practiced informally by private gynecologists, under conditions of extreme secrecy (Birenbaum-Carmeli, Carmeli and Yavetz 2000; Carmeli and Birenbaum-Carmeli 2000). The parents tended never to disclose the donor conception, keeping it from the child as well, in order to create the appearance of a "natural family." This concealment of the child's origin accorded with state policy, which continues to view social paternity as inferior to genetic fatherhood. Thus, unlike IVF and ICSI cycles, donor insemination has never been publically funded in Israel. Furthermore, for years, the Ministry of Health's regulations instructed doctors to maintain permanent secrecy, and to mix the donor's sperm with the husband's sperm whenever possible, so as to create ambiguity regarding the identity of the actual biological father (Carmeli and Birenbaum-Carmeli 2000; Carmeli et al. 2001). In other words, in sharp contrast to Muslim countries where preserving *nasab* is deemed essential, Israel has actively encouraged a kind of counterfeiting of the child's lineage, by completely removing any trace of the donor father and masking social fatherhood as presumably genetic.

Having said this, ultraorthodox Jews – who are not allowed by religion to "waste" any sperm (including for the purposes of semen collection in IVF clinics) – need not abide by this dictate. In fact, ultraorthodox couples typically use the donor sperm of non-Jewish men, because use of such sperm bypasses the prohibition on sperm wasting (via masturbation in semen collection), which does not apply to non-Jewish men. Additionally, using "foreign sperm" removes the concern of unwitting future incest (Kahn 2000). In recent years, ultraorthodox Jewish Israeli couples have typically purchased donor sperm abroad via the Internet. Single and lesbian women who appreciate knowing more details about potential sperm donors also tend to prefer international sperm banks. Once again, the Israeli state, in support of this form of third-party reproductive assistance, has set a fast-track procedure for individuals to import the donor sperm of one's choice.

Having said this, there is one instance in which paternity concerns are real and cannot be feigned. This is in the transmission of "Cohen" or "Levi," elevated ritual statuses that are transferred patrilineally and carry ritual significance in ultraorthodox communities. Since a son conceived by sperm donation is not entitled to the father's Cohen or Levi label, the birth of a donor son would expose the father's infertility and treatment. Apparently, the stigma of infertility and donor insemination are so great in ultraorthodox communities that such couples would rather forgo the crucial commandment to reproduce, unless they can ensure that sperm donation results in the birth of a daughter. Increasingly, this is being done through government-approved preimplantation genetic sex selection (Hashiloni-Dolev et al. 2010), which allows such orthodox families to select only female embryos for conception.

Egg donation, in some ways, is even more problematic than sperm donation as a form of third-party reproductive assistance in Israel. In Judaism, it is the mother's Jewishness that ensures the Jewishness of the child. Egg donation, which separates the genetic mother from the gestational one, thus problematizes the matrilineal inheritance of a donor child's Jewish identity. Most rabbis consider the womb to be the decisive factor in the transmission of Jewishness, and therefore minimize the religious significance of the egg donor. Some of these rabbis actually prefer non-Jewish egg donors, again to remove the concern of future incest. Other rabbis, however, insist that both the womb and the egg must be those of Jewish women, in order to ensure the child's Jewishness.

Egg donation is rare in Israel, even though it is legal. Israeli women who require donor eggs must usually search for egg donation in other countries. Women who endorse the stricter religious view usually seek the eggs of Jewish women, mostly in the United States. Yet, the high prices charged for American Jewish eggs ($30,000 to $50,000) may prevent Israeli Jewish couples from obtaining those American eggs, even in cases where they believe in the importance of Jewish genetic origin in defining a child's identity (Nahman 2006). Most Israelis end up opting for the more readily available supply of eggs from non-Jewish donors, usually purchased in Eastern Europe (Nahman 2011, 2013). The Israeli state, for its part, approves of both these modes of egg donation and accepts the resulting children as fully Jewish Israelis.

Interestingly, surrogacy is legal in Israel, but only for heterosexual couples (Teman 2010). Singles and gay couples who wish to take this road to family formation need to travel abroad. In the past few years, gay male couples in Israel have made extensive use of overseas surrogacy options (Farber 2014). As in all other modes of third-party reproduction, the child's birth certificate records the names of the social parents only, and carries no sign of the biological parents, including the egg donor and the gestational surrogate (who may be the same person or two different women).

In general, these gay surrogate families instantiate many of the general characteristics of Israeli families. The popular attempt to have twins by surrogacy maximizes the enormous financial investment, but also embodies the desire to have "a full family" rather than raising an only child. Bearing in mind that the state funds IVF up to the birth of two live children, the contemporary Israeli family is thought of as having at least two children to be whole. Gay men's effort to found such normative nuclear families reveals the strength of this norm beyond heteronormative couples. Furthermore, gay men have consistently described how the baby's birth via surrogacy has brought them closer to their extended families. These nontraditional families are often actively supported by their traditional, sometimes religious, parents and relatives. Similar accounts have been provided by single and lesbian mothers in Israel who have used ARTs to found their own families. This intensified closeness suggests that in family-centered Israel, becoming a parent is, in and of itself, a "normalizing" transition to full adult personhood.

Throughout Israel's active ART scene, then, it is the parents' desires and hopes that are the focus of attention, while the best interests of the donor or surrogate child are secondary in most ethical and clinical discussions. Furthermore, the presence and acceptance of all forms of assisted reproduction and family formations does not mean that these forms are of equal status. IVF and ICSI using a married couple's own gametes is free of charge, while donor sperm, which presents no threat to the child's Jewish identity, is not state funded, although it is relatively inexpensive. Egg donation, a more complex technology both clinically and religiously, costs three to six times the average Israeli monthly salary, placing this technology beyond the reach of many couples and older single women, whose salaries, on average, are about a third lower than men's. Finally, the most expensive ART is gestational surrogacy, which is not funded by the Israeli state and is not allowed for gay men within their own country. In this respect, Israel's generous funding of IVF and ICSI for married infertile couples, but not for non-traditional uses of ART, has led to a two-tiered system of reproduction and kinship, where biologically based, heteronormative families are definitely privileged.

22.8   Concluding Comparisons

In conclusion, it is fair to say that the globalization of ARTs to the Middle East has reinforced the biogenetic element of kinship and relatedness, even in the countries of Israel and Iran, where third-party reproductive assistance is allowed. In Israel, usually perceived as the most "democratic" and "progressive" country in the Middle East, all forms of ART are allowed by law, but only those that perpetuate biologically related, heteronormative, married family forms are actively encouraged and generously funded by the state. Similarly, in Shia Iran – which is rarely viewed as "progressive" and is usually cast by the Israeli government as a stronghold of fanaticism and oppression – all manner of ARTs are being allowed, just as in Israel. Yet, infertile Iranian couples often choose the closest possible, genetically related donors to preserve a semblance of *nasab*, or biogenetic relatedness. Such preservation of *nasab* is a religious and cultural mandate in the Sunni Muslim countries as well, where preservation of paternity, patrilineage, and biological kinship more generally are all deemed to be critical moral imperatives. This aim for biogenetic kinship – or at least partial biogenetic kinship through the use of ARTs – in all of these countries bespeaks the inferiority of social parenthood, and the problems that men in particular have in accepting social fatherhood without true biological paternity.

At the same time, third-party reproductive assistance is beginning to destabilize notions of biogenetic relatedness, especially for Middle Eastern women, who are increasingly turning to egg donation to become mothers. Women, their husbands, their clinicians, *and* their clerics are increasingly invoking innovative measures to make egg donation religiously and culturally acceptable. In the Muslim world, this includes new instantiations of the ancient practice of milk kinship, as well as temporary marriages and "as if" polygyny. In Israel, the religious validity of non-Jewish donor eggs has been accepted by wide swaths of Israeli society, including many rabbis, who have reinforced the sanctity of Jewish wombs in conferring Jewishness to donor offspring.

What is most remarkable about many of these biotechnological developments is that they have been incorporated under a variety of political and religious systems in the Middle East. Shia-dominant Iran is a theocracy, in which religious officials play key roles in both government administration and management of medical ethics. Turkey is a presumably secular country, but one that is now governed by an openly Muslim Sunni political party. Sunni Arab countries are politically diverse, but have been remarkably convergent in their attitudes toward ARTs, including the widely enforced religious ban on third-party assisted reproduction. Israel is one of the few formal democracies in the region, but it is a state defined on religious grounds as Jewish, with religious parties and authorities concentrating considerable political power and authority.

In all of these diverse political systems, the religious establishment plays a critical role in the reproductive medical sector, with medical practitioners effectively educating the religious leaders about assisted reproduction, thereby influencing the decisions of the religious authorities. Perhaps because of this medical influence, the prominence of religious authority does not necessarily translate into ART conservatism. All of these Middle Eastern settings have been quick to endorse assisted reproduction. Whether due to the power of pronatalism, the high prevalence of both male and female infertility, or the ban on adoption in most Muslim countries, each Middle Eastern setting described in this chapter has developed an active, prosperous ART industry. In some cases such as Israel and Turkey, public funding has been provided, leading to a major boost in local ART consumption. But even in the purportedly "conservative" Arab countries, infertile couples have been more than willing to pay for ARTs, in order to achieve norms of two children per family, a contemporary state of affairs reflected above in Table 22.1. Furthermore, a few Arab countries (e.g., Egypt, United Arab Emirates), as well as Iran, have provided partial public financing of ARTs, either through government hospitals or some form of insurance funding.

Table 22.2 provides a summary of current ART permissions and prohibitions in the countries described and compared in this chapter. As the table shows, in each setting, the state, in conjunction with religious authorities, attempts to contain the revolutionary potential of ARTs in one way or another. Although Israel is clearly the most permissive ART regime, Iran is close behind, and both abide by the still worldwide ethical ban on human reproductive cloning, which entails the autonomous asexual reproduction of offspring who are the genetic clones of their parents.

Table 22.2 *Middle Eastern assisted reproductive technologies: permissions and prohibitions**

Procedure	Iran	Sunni countries	Turkey	Israel
Anonymous third-party reproductive assistance	+	+	–	+
Cryopreservation (freezing) of embryos	+	+	+	+
Cryopreservation of gametes (sperm and egg freezing)	+	+	+	+
Donation of embryos	+	+	–	+
Donation of gametes	+	+	–	+
Embryo banks	+	+	+	+
Embryo couriers	+	+	+	+
Embryo transfer	+	+	+	+
Experimentation on the embryo	+	+	–	+
Gender (sex) selection	+	+	–	+
Intracytoplasmic sperm injection (ICSI)	+	+	+	+
Intrauterine insemination (IUI)	+	+	+	+
In vitro fertilization (IVF)	+	+	+	+
Multifetal pregnancy reduction (MFPR)	+	+	+	+
Gestational surrogacy	+	+	–	–
Gestational surrogacy by a polygynous co-wife	+	+	–	–
Posthumous insemination	+	+	–	+
Preimplantation genetic diagnosis (PGD)	+	+	+	+
Reproductive cloning	–	+	–	–
Same-sex couples using ART	–	+	–	+
Single women using ART	–	+	–	+
Surrogacy via IVF	+	+	–	+
Therapeutic stem cell cloning (from human embryos)	+	+	–	+

* The categories in this table are adapted from Jones et al. (2010).

Although Iran is often cast in Western media as one of the most conservative countries of the Middle East, Table 22.2 proves that its ART regime is surprisingly permissive, allowing virtually all of the ARTs, as long as these are used within the bounds of marriage. Indeed, in the Muslim world in general, it is fair to state that both governments and religious establishments have prioritized marriage as the most important ART kinship form. Even in Iran, where the boundaries of both marriage and *nasab* are being stretched, Shia religious and legal forces mandate the containment of ARTs within marriage, just as the Sunni establishment does in neighboring Arab countries and Turkey. Although Islam is popularly conceived of as a religion that undermines conjugal bonds – by allowing men's relatively free access to polygyny and divorce (Charrad 2001) – marriage within Islam is held up as "half of the religion." Marriage itself is also the major point of wealth transfer between the generations (Singerman 2007). Thus, in general, Muslims take the call to marriage quite seriously, and families often intervene to prevent divorce (Inhorn 2003, 2012). Within this "very married" Middle East – indeed, one of the "most married" regions of the world, with more than 90 percent of adults marrying at some point in their lives – marriage is being reinforced by the presence of ARTs, technologies that are truly focused on the "couple." Reciprocally, the desire of many infertile Muslim couples to "save" their marriages is fueling the tremendous growth and success of the ART sector in both Sunni- and Shia-dominant regions of the Muslim world.

Even in Israel, where third-party assisted reproduction and non-traditional family forms are subsumed within the prevailing ART regime, the normative aspirations of ART-seeking Israelis, their IVF doctors, and the rabbinical and state authorities who regulate these technologies are nonetheless all highly family centered, if not "couple" centered per se. This "focus on the family" in Israeli assisted reproduction is ultimately supportive of a rather conservative and pronatalist cultural ethos, in which individuals who do not conceive their own families are left behind. Indeed, the quest of nontraditional Israeli individuals – including single and gay men and women – for acceptance and integration into mainstream circles does little to challenge traditional family norms.

In short, the globalization of ARTs into diverse regions of the Middle East serves as a potent reminder that kinship matters – very much, indeed – and that new reproductive technologies with potentially transgressive social potential often still serve to reinscribe fundamental principles of kinship and family life. A Middle Eastern comparison juxtaposing Jewish versus Muslim, Sunni versus Shia, secular versus theocratic, and "conservative" versus "progressive" forces also proves that many of these dualisms require our scholarly interrogation. In matters of kinship and assisted reproduction, the convergences between countries such as Israel and Iran are more apparent than the divergences, a finding that may be counterintuitive but helpful in deconstructing prevalent Middle Eastern stereotypes.

Acknowledgments

We thank Sandra Bamford for inviting us to be part of this volume. This chapter was previously published as "Assisted Reproduction and Middle East Kinship: A Middle East Comparison," *Reproductive BioMedicine and Society Online* 4 (2017): 41–51. We thank Elsevier for open-access reuse permission.

References

Abbasi-Shavazi, J. M., P. McDonald and M. Hosseini-Chavoshi. 2008. "Modernization or Cultural Maintenance: The Practice of Consanguineous Marriage in Iran." *Journal of Biosocial Science* 40(6): 911–933.

Al-Torki, S. 1980. "Milk Kinship in Arabic Society: An Unexplored Problem in the Ethnography of Marriage." *Ethnology* 19(2): 233–244.

Arda, B. 2007. "The Importance of Secularism in Medical Ethics: The Turkish Example." *Reproductive BioMedicine Online* 14(Suppl. 1): 24–28.

Bargach, J. 2002. *Orphans of Islam: Family, Abandonment and Secret Adoption in Morocco*. Lanham, MD: Rowman and Littlefield.

Baykal, B., C. Korkmaz, S. T. Ceyhan, U. Goktolga and I. Baser. 2008. "Opinions of Infertile Turkish Women on Gamete Donation and Gestational Surrogacy." *Fertility and Sterility* 89: 817–822.

Birenbaum-Carmeli, D. 1997. "Pioneering Procreation: Israel's First Test-Tube Baby." *Science As Culture* 6: 525–540.

    2004. " 'Cheaper Than a Newcomer': On the Political Economy of IVF in Israel." *The Sociology of Health and Illness* 26(7): 897–924.

Birenbaum-Carmeli, D., Y. S. Carmeli and R. Cohen. 2000. " 'Our First IVF Baby': Israel's and Canada's Press Coverage of Procreative Technology." *International Journal of Sociology and Social Policy* 20(7): 1–38.

Birenbaum-Carmeli, D., Y. S. Carmeli and H. Yavetz. 2000. "Secrecy among Israeli Recipients of Donor Insemination." *Politics and the Life Sciences* 19(1): 69–76.

Birenbaum-Carmeli, D., Y. Diamand and M. Abu Yaman. 2014. "On Fatherhood in a Conflict Zone: Gaza Fathers and Their Children's Cancer Treatments." In *Globalized Fatherhood*, ed. Marcia C. Inhorn, Wendy Chavkin and Jose-Alberto Navarro, 243–263. New York: Berghahn Books.

Boivin, J., I. Bunting, J. A. Collins and K. G. Nygren. 2007. "International Estimates of Infertility Prevalence and Treatment-Seeking: Potential Need and Demand for Infertility Medical Care." *Human Reproduction* 22: 1506–1512.

Carmeli, Y. S. and D. Birenbaum-Carmeli. 2000. "Ritualizing the 'Natural Family': Secrecy in Israeli Donor Insemination." *Science As Culture* 9(3): 301–325.

Carmeli, Y. S., D. Birenbaum-Carmeli, I. Madgar and R. Weissenberg. 2001. "Donor Insemination in Israel: Recipients' Choices of Donors." *The Journal of Reproductive Medicine* 46(8): 757–763.

Charrad, M. 2001. *States and Women's Rights: The Making of Postcolonial Tunisia, Algeria, and Morocco*. Berkeley, CA: University of California Press.

Clarke, M. 2006. "Shi'ite Perspectives on Kinship and New Reproductive Technologies." *ISIM Newsletter* 17: 26–27.

    2009. *Islam and New Kinship: Reproductive Technology and the Shariah in Lebanon*. New York: Berghahn Books.

Collins, J. A. 2002. "An International Survey of the Health Economics of IVF and ICSI." *Human Reproductive Update* 8: 265–277.

De Geyter, C. 2018. "More Than 8 Million Babies Born from IVF since the World's First in 1978." European Society of Human Reproduction and

Embryology Press Release. www.eshre.eu/ESHRE2018/Media/ESHRE-2018-Press-releases/De-Geyter.aspx, accessed October 26, 2018.

Eberstadt, N. and A. Shah. 2012. "Fertility Decline in the Muslim World." *Policy Review* 173: 29–44.

Farber, A. R. 2014. Surrogacy and Fatherhood among Homosexual Couples in Israel. MA Thesis, University of Haifa.

Farhi, J. and A. Ben Haroush. 2011. "Distribution of Causes of Infertility in Patients Attending Primary Fertility Clinics in Israel." *Israel Medical Association Journal* 13(1): 51–54.

Franklin, S. B. 2012. "Five Million Miracle Babies Later." In *Reproductive Technologies As Global Form: Ethnographies of Knowledge, Practices, and Transnational Encounters*, ed. Michi Knecht, Maren Klotz and Stefan Beck, 27–60. Berlin: Campus Verlag.

Garmaroudi Naef, S. 2012. "Gestational Surrogacy in Iran: Uterine Kinship in Shia Thought and Practice." In *Islam and Assisted Reproductive Technologies: Sunni and Shia Perspectives*, ed. Marcia C. Inhorn and Soraya Tremayne, 157–193. New York: Berghahn Books.

Gnoth, C., B. Maxrath, T. Skonieczny, K. Friol, C. Godehardt and J. Tigges. 2011. "Final ART Success Rates: A 10 Years Survey." *Human Reproduction* 26(8): 2239–2246.

Gürtin, Z. B. 2011. "Banning Reproductive Travel? Turkey's ART Legislation and Third-Party Assisted Reproduction." *Reproductive Biomedicine Online* 23: 555–565.

2012. "Assisted Reproduction in Secular Turkey: Regulation, Rhetoric, and the Role of Religion." In *Islam and Assisted Reproductive Technologies: Sunni and Shia Perspectives*, ed. Marcia C. Inhorn and Soraya Tremayne, 285–311. New York: Berghahn Books.

2014. "Assumed, Promised, Forbidden: Infertility, IVF and Fatherhood in Turkey." In *Globalized Fatherhood*, ed. Marcia C. Inhorn, Wendy Chavkin and Jose-Alberto Navarro, 223–242. New York: Berghahn Books.

Gürtin, Zeynep, Marcia C. Inhorn and Soraya Tremayne. 2015. "Islam and Assisted Reproduction in the Middle East: Comparing 'Secular' Turkey, Shia Iran, and the Sunni Arab World." In *The Changing World Religion Map: Sacred Places, Identities, Practices and Politics*, ed. Stanley D. Brunn, 3137–3153. New York: Springer.

Haeri, S. 1989. *Law of Desire: Temporary Marriage in Shi'i Iran*. Syracuse, NY: Syracuse University Press.

Hashiloni-Dolev Y., G. Hirsh-Yechzkel, V. Boyko, T. Wainstock, E. Schiff and L. Lerner-Geva. 2010. "Attitudes toward Sex Selection: A Survey among Potential Users in Israel." *Prenatal Diagnosis* 30(11): 1019–1025.

Inhorn, M. C. 1996. *Infertility and Patriarchy: The Cultural Politics of Gender and Family Life in Egypt*. Philadelphia, PA: University of Pennsylvania Press.

2003. *Local Babies, Global Science: Gender, Religion, and In Vitro Fertilization in Egypt*. New York: Routledge.

2006. "Making Muslim Babies: IVF and Gamete Donation in Sunni and Shi'a Islam." *Culture, Medicine, and Psychiatry* 30(4): 427–450.

2012. *The New Arab Man: Emergent Masculinities, Technologies, and Islam in the Middle East*. Princeton, NJ: Princeton University Press.

2014. "New Arab Fatherhood: Emergent Masculinities, Male Infertility, and Assisted Reproduction." In *Globalized Fatherhood*, ed. Marcia C. Inhorn, Wendy Chavkin and Jose-Alberto Navarro, 243–263. New York: Berghahn Books.

2015. *Cosmopolitan Conceptions: IVF Sojourns in Global Dubai*. Durham, NC: Duke University Press.

2018. "Fertility, Demography, and Masculinities in Arab Families: From 1950 to 2015 and Beyond." In *Arab Family Studies: Critical Reviews*, ed. Suad Joseph, 449–466. Syracuse, NY: Syracuse University Press.

Inhorn, M. C. and D. Birenbaum-Carmeli. 2008. "Assisted Reproductive Technologies and Culture Change." *Annual Review of Anthropology* 37: 177–196.

Inhorn, M. C., L. Kobeissi, Z. Nassar, D. Lakkis and M. H. Fakih. 2009. "Consanguinity and Family Clustering of Male Infertility in Lebanon." *Fertility and Sterility* 91(4): 1104–1109.

Inhorn, M. C. and P. Patrizio. 2015. "Infertility around the Globe: New Thinking on Gender, Reproductive Technologies, and Global Movements in the 21st Century." *Human Reproduction Update* 21(4): 411–426.

Inhorn, M. C., P. Patrizio and G. I. Serour. 2010. "Third-party Reproductive Assistance around the Mediterranean: Comparing Sunni Egypt, Catholic Italy and Multisectarian Lebanon." *Reproductive Biomedicine Online* 21(7): 848–853.

Inhorn, M. C. and S. Tremayne, eds. 2012. *Islam and Assisted Reproductive Technologies: Sunni and Shia Perspectives*. New York: Berghahn Books.

Isikoglu, M., Y. Senol, M. Berkkanoglu, K. Ozgur, L. Donmez and A. Stones-Abbasi. 2006. "Public Opinion Regarding Oocyte Donation in Turkey: First Data from a Secular Population among the Islamic World." *Human Reproduction* 21: 318–323.

Israel Ministry of Health. 2013. "In Vitro Fertilization (IVF) Treatments: AbsoluteNumbers,Percentages,Rates."www.health.gov.il/Publications Files/IVF1986_2012.pdf, accessed October 22, 2018.

Jones, H. W., I. Cooke, R. Kempers, P. Brinsden and D. Saunders. 2010. "International Federation of Fertility Societies: Surveillance 2010." www.iffs-reproduction.org/documents/IFFS_Surveillance_2010.pdf, accessed October 26, 2018.

Kahn, S. M. 2000. *Reproducing Jews: A Cultural Account of Assisted Conception in Israel*. Durham, NC: Duke University Press.

Khatib-Chahidi, J. 1982. "Sexual Prohibitions, Shared Space and Fictive Marriages." In *Women and Space: Ground Rules and Social Maps*, ed. S. Ardener, 112–134. London: Croom Helm.

1992. "Milk Kinship in Shi'ite Islamic Iran." In *The Anthropology of Breastfeeding: Natural Law or Social Construct*, ed. Vanessa Maher, 109–132. Oxford: Berg.

Kilic, S., M. Ucar, H. Yaren, M. Gulec, A. Atac, F. Demirel, C. Karabulut and O. Demirel. 2009. "Determination of the Attitudes of Turkish Infertile Women towards Surrogacy and Oocyte Donation." *Pakistan Journal of Medical Science* 25: 36–40.

Mascarenhas, M. N., S. R. Flaxman, T. Boerma, S. Vanderpoel and G. A. Stevens. 2012. "National, Regional, and Global Trends in Infertility Prevalence since 1990: A Systematic Analysis of 277 Health Surveys." *PLOS Medicine* 9: 1–12.

Moosa, E. 2003. "Human Cloning in Muslim Ethics." *Voices across Boundaries* (Fall): 23–26.

Nahman, Michal. 2006. "Materializing Israeliness: Difference and Mixture in Transnational Ova Donation." *Science As Culture* 15(3): 199–213.

2011. "Reverse Traffic: Intersecting Inequalities in Human Egg Donation." *Reproductive BioMedicine Online* 23(5): 626–633.

2013. *Extractions: An Ethnography of Reproductive Tourism*. Basingstoke: Palgrave Macmillan.

Nyboe Andersen, A., V. Goossens, L. Gianaroli, R. Felberbaum, J. de Mouzon and K. G. Nygren. 2007. "Assisted Reproductive Technology in Europe, 2003: Results Generated from European Registers by ESHRE." *Human Reproduction* 22(6): 1513–1525.

Presidency of Religious Affairs of the Republic of Turkey. 2006. "The Assessment of New Applications Discussed by Contemporary Medicine such as IVF and Stem Cell according to the Religion of Islam." Presidency of Religious Affairs of the Republic of Turkey, Ankara. www.diyanet.gov.tr/turkish/dy/KurulDetay.aspx?ID=1162, accessed October 26, 2018.

Schenker, J. G. 2003. "Legal Aspects of ART Practice in Israel." *Journal of Assisted Reproduction Genetics* 20(7): 250–259.

Sella, T., G. Chodick, E. Luenfeld and V. Shalev. 2011. "Further Evidence on the High Prevalence of Male Factor Infertility Diagnosis in Israel." *The Israel Medical Association Journal* 13(6): 386.

Serour, G. I. 2008. "Islamic Perspectives in Human Reproduction." *Reproductive BioMedicine Online* 17(Suppl. 3): 34–38.

Singerman, D. 2007. *The Economic Imperatives of Marriage: Emerging Practices and Identities among Youth in the Middle East*. Working Paper 6. Washington DC/Dubai: Wolfensohn Centre for Development and Dubai School of Government.

Sonbol, A. el A. 1995. "Adoption in Islamic Society: A Historical Survey." In *Children in the Muslim Middle East*, ed. Fernea Elizabeth Warnock, 45–67. Austin, TX: University of Texas Press.

Teman, E. 2010. *Birthing a Mother: The Surrogate Body and the Pregnant Self*. Berkeley, CA: University of California Press.

Tremayne, S. 2006. "Not All Muslims Are Luddites." *Anthropology Today* 22(93): 1–2.

————. 2009. "Law, Ethics, and Donor Technologies in Shia Iran." In *Assisting Reproduction, Testing Genes: Global Encounters with New Biotechnologies*, ed. Daphna Birenbaum-Carmeli and Marcia C. Inhorn, 144–163. New York: Berghahn Books.

————. 2012. "The 'Down Side' of Gamete Donation: Challenging 'Happy Family' Rhetoric in Iran." In *Islam and Assisted Reproductive Technologies: Sunni and Shia Perspectives*, ed. Marcia C. Inhorn and Soraya Tremayne, 130–156. New York: Berghahn Books.

————. 2015. "Whither Kinship? Assisted Reproductive Technologies and Relatedness in the Islamic Republic of Iran." In *Assisted Reproductive Technologies in the Third Phase: Global Encounters and Emerging Moral Worlds*, ed. Kate Hampshire and Bob Simpson, 69–82. New York: Berghahn Books.

Tremayne, S. and M. C. Inhorn. 2012. "Introduction: Islam and Assisted Reproductive Technologies." In *Islam and Assisted Reproductive Technologies: Sunni and Shia Perspectives*, ed. Marcia C. Inhorn and Soraya Tremayne, 1–21. New York: Berghahn Books.

United Nations. 2013. *World Population Prospects: The 2012 Revision*. New York: United Nations.

Urman, B. and K. Yakin. 2010. "New Turkish Legislation on Assisted Reproductive Techniques and Centres: A Step in the Right Direction?" *Reproductive BioMedicine Online* 21: 729–731.

White, J. B. 2002. *Islamist Mobilization in Turkey: A Study in Vernacular Politics*. Seattle, WA: University of Washington Press.

————. 2014. *Muslim Nationalism and the New Turks*. Princeton, NJ: Princeton University Press.

23

A Comparison of Kinship Understandings among Israeli and US Surrogates

Elly Teman and Zsuzsa Berend

23.1 Introduction

In his *Critique of the Study of Kinship*, Schneider (1984: 200) proposed that we take an ethnographic approach and examine "in detail how the natives themselves conceptualize, define, and describe" kinship and how it is constructed "in the context of their culture." Schneider (1984: vii) contended that the existence of kinship "depends on how it is defined" and that "its definition does not, nor can it, arise solely as a consequence of 'its' real nature." However, kinship is not simply a matter of definitions but also of actions; it is "constituted through certain kinds of acts" and is "carried out in acts that are *meant* and that have meaningful consequences" (Lambek 2013: 246, 247, emphasis in original).

Our two long-term ethnographic research projects on surrogacy, an assisted reproductive practice in which a woman agrees to carry, birth, and relinquish a baby to "intended parents" who financially compensate her for her efforts, offer thought-provoking comparisons about how surrogates create meanings and interpretations of kinship by drawing on relevant cultural understandings available to them in two different sociopolitical contexts. We conducted our research in Israel and the United States respectively (Berend 2016; Teman 2010a), two countries where the structural conditions in which surrogacy arrangements occur are strikingly different. Our exploration begins with a question: does the difference in sociopolitical and regulatory context shape surrogates' expectations about their relationship with the intended parents (IPs) and with the surrogacy-born baby?

Our findings suggest that beyond the many structural and cultural differences between US and Israeli surrogacy, there are intriguing similarities in the ways in which surrogates made sense of the practice and also of the relationship they had with their couple. As in new practices in general, the practitioners have to make sense of what they are doing, given that there is not much precedence to follow. Surrogates work out meanings and definitions of surrogacy in various ways: in cooperation with the IPs, on message boards in which shared ideas about kinship take root and are crystallized, and in explanations of their involvement in surrogacy to their families and others involved in their everyday lives. In the following, we will argue that surrogates' own conceptualizations of feelings and practices, negotiated and crystallized in interactions with IPs, fellow surrogates, and other involved parties, are central to understanding surrogacy. We found that in spite of regulatory differences in the two countries, Israeli and US surrogates similarly disclaim bonding with the fetus they carry for their couple and often bond with the couple instead. They are also adamant that they are not the mother of the surrogacy-born baby, although their reasons differ, reflecting the different historical and sociocultural contexts.

23.2   The Regulatory Context

In the United States, there is no federal law governing surrogacy; every state regulates it differently and some refrain from regulating it altogether. Some states, such as New York, enforce bans while others, such as California, allow commercial surrogacy and IPs are able to establish legal parental rights before the birth, thus allowing a commercial market of private surrogacy agencies and fertility clinics to prosper in what is viewed as a "surrogacy-friendly environment" without state interference. Specific regulations differ between states, but most of the states that allow commercial surrogacy do not limit who can contract a surrogate or require mandatory contracts or screening, enabling surrogates and IPs to negotiate the conditions of their arrangement either through an agency or lawyer or privately.

And in this state-by-state regulatory situation where some states do not regulate surrogacy at all, some allow it, and others criminalize it, threads on the Surrogate Mothers Online (SMO) boards reveal that agencies, clinics, IPs, and surrogates take it on themselves to mandate screening and define and try to enforce contracts, even when they are not legally binding. However, although there has been standardization of requirements and contractual specification, there is quite a lot of room for negotiations and compromises. Moreover, SMO threads reveal that potential surrogates or IPs who are rejected by one agency or clinic may, and often do, find alternatives.

Conversely, surrogacy in Israel is tightly monitored by the state under a comprehensive law. All surrogacy contracts undertaken in Israel must be centrally approved by a government-appointed committee before couples and surrogates are permitted to proceed. Both parties must be

Israeli citizens, share the same religion and cannot be related to one another. Restrictive regulations prohibit same-sex couples and single men and women from contracting a surrogate, limiting the option to married, heterosexually paired couples with one shared child or no children. The practice is not officially encouraged by the state but viewed as a "last resort" for genetic kinship and is limited in scope to couples wherein the female partner has no womb, has been repeatedly unsuccessful with other reproductive strategies, or is at severe health risk in pregnancy (Teman 2010a, 2010b). Only gestational surrogacy is allowed, and the intended father must provide the sperm. Once approved by the committee, contracts are legally valid and the children born are full citizens and the IPs are recognized as their parents once a parental order is granted following the birth.

23.3 Methods

Our comparison draws from each of our research projects on surrogate motherhood arrangements. The Israeli study, conducted between 1998 and 2006, used multi-sited ethnographic research, including in-depth, open-format interviews with 26 Jewish-Israeli gestational surrogates and 35 intended mothers. An additional 20 interviews with surrogates who had given birth in the past two years were conducted in the summer of 2016. At the time of the initial study, surrogates had to be single and raising at least one child, while IPs had to be married heterosexual couples, and have no or only one genetic offspring; since 2013 married surrogates have been permitted, and all surrogates interviewed in the 2016 study were married. During the years of the initial study, intended mothers usually provided their own ova and in a handful of cases donor ova were used.

As a result of this legal context, all of the surrogates in the Israeli study were Jewish-Israeli citizens and were contracted by heterosexual, married Jewish-Israeli couples; all were gestational surrogates, and all were single mothers raising their children on their own. All were screened psychologically and physically before contract approval and all lived within a few hours' driving distance of the IPs, enabling them to meet frequently during the pregnancy and accompany the surrogate to all medical appointments. The surrogates ranged in age from 23 to 40 years. All of the surrogates in the initial study expressed clear financial motivations for becoming surrogates, often reporting the difficulty of supporting their own children as single mothers as a primary motivation. Roughly half were from lower-class backgrounds; 30 percent identified as lower-middle class to middle class, and the rest were very poor. The percentage of this third group declined over the years because the approvals committee became hesitant to approve women who are in such severe financial situations (Teman 2010a). In the 2016 study, nearly half of the surrogates were motivated primarily by a desire to make a significant contribution to society and did not view payment as their primary motivation. They were also of relatively higher socioeconomic status than the surrogates in the initial study, and all were married.

The American study, conducted from 2002 to 2013, employed online ethnographic observation of discussion threads on www .surromomsonline.com (SMO), the largest and most important mediated public surrogacy website in the United States, in which surrogates and some IPs post stories, questions, information, and advice on over 30 forums. Online fieldwork was complemented with email exchanges with 35 surrogates recruited from SMO. Founded in 1997, SMO has grown tremendously over the years. Around 2013 most discussions relocated to Facebook groups, but SMO remained an important site for information. The overwhelming majority of surrogates participating on SMO live in the United States, and the sample from SMO included in this study contains only US surrogates, thus we refer to them throughout the article both as SMO and as the US surrogates. Nevertheless, it is important to point out that not all surrogates in the United States participate on SMO, although many read it for the rich and varied information available on the site.

Surrogates participating on SMO are from many different states across the United States; most are married, are a mix of traditional and gestational surrogates – although more often the latter, and some do both traditional and gestational "journeys" – who carry for single men, gay and heterosexual couples, frequently from another state or another country. Available statistics on US surrogacy are extremely unreliable. Agencies have no reporting obligation, independent online matching is on the rise, and clinics report fresh non-donor egg IVF cases, not surrogate-assisted reproduction. While there is no overall demographic information about SMO members, it is clear from discussions that the vast majority were Caucasian, many worked full time, mostly in secretarial and support jobs, and view themselves as middle class; most are married and have two to four children, although some are divorced. Surrogates frequently raised work-related topics, talked about their jobs, and advised one another about work-related contractual issues in surrogacy. They debated family matters, religious and moral questions, and communicated extensively about their financial situation, thereby providing rich data about the social and moral context in which they chose to become surrogates. This context is quite different from the Israeli one at the time of Teman's study; the majority of SMO surrogates are married, lower-middle to middle-class women, many of them employed in helping professions and pink-collar jobs.

These differences about the respective populations notwithstanding, we had adopted the same interpretive and analytic approach and used grounded theory to analyze the data. Both of us wanted to understand how surrogates themselves see the world and the meaning of surrogacy, whether these understandings are uncovered through interviews or worked out in online interactions among surrogates. The methods of both studies are expanded upon elsewhere (Berend 2016, 2010, 2012; Teman 2010a).

In the following, we lay out our argument along three common themes that arose in our interviews, which together create a shared statement about surrogacy that is voiced by our informants. Specifically, the surrogates in both studies view surrogacy as creating kinship relations. However, these relations are not between surrogate and baby, but between surrogate and IPs and between IPs and "their baby."

23.4 Surrogacy Is a Journey of Love

The first finding that emerged from our comparison was that the surrogates in both Israel and the United States defined surrogacy as a journey of love with moral consequences, such as creating a family and a relationship of potential closeness and intimacy between surrogate and IPs. We both found that surrogates firmly placed the creation of families through surrogacy in the context of intimacy, caring, and love. Surrogates in both social contexts viewed these acts of family creation as morally meaningful, thus refuting the common argument that surrogacy upsets the traditional moral framework – in which reproduction is regarded as a "natural fact" grounded in love, marriage, and sexual intercourse (Schneider 1968) – by commodifying bodies, babies, feelings, and values (Anderson 1990; Danna 2015; Dolgin 1990; Ketchum 1992).

Much of the literature on surrogacy, and much of the public debate, views the contractual nature of surrogacy as a sign of the commodification of life and the intrusion of the market into the "sacred" realm (Berend 2012), juxtaposing the "hostile worlds of the market versus family, money versus love, and public versus private domains" (Berend 2012; Zelizer 2000). Yet whereas public debate and the theoretical scholarship suggest that families have become a matter of choice rather than fate or contract rather than status (Rao 2003; Dolgin 1990), making surrogacy immoral and unethical (Markens 2007), the surrogates' construction of surrogacy as a journey of love stresses that their journey is a fated one. In both Israel and the United States, surrogates seemed to seek out IPs with whom they "clicked" – a concept that both Israeli and US surrogates used to describe the immediate emotional response they thought of as a signal or proof that the relationship "was meant to be" (Berend 2012; Teman 2010a). Surrogates in both settings described their journey in terms that are usually reserved for romantic relationships, applying similar idioms of "chemistry," "connection," and even "falling in love," to define the affinity they felt, or believed they felt, upon their first meeting, "virtual" or in person, with their IPs.

In most Israeli cases, the language of clicking and chemistry was reserved for the intended mother and excluded intended fathers. Israeli surrogate Masha remembered the first time she saw her intended mother, Tova: "The minute that our eyes met, there was chemistry. From the minute that we began to speak it felt like I was sitting with someone whom I had known for five years. I knew right then that she was the one." Chemistry, to the Israeli surrogates, was believed to be the defining element that could make or break a surrogacy arrangement, as Israeli surrogate Lihi noted: "Chemistry is something that you can't replace with anything else. It is like having chemistry with your spouse, you either have it or you don't. That's why I say, if I do it (surrogacy) for another couple it won't be the same."

Similarly, SMO is filled with countless excited posts by surrogates, describing the first meeting in the idiom of "chemistry," and wishing each other the best by ending their postings with "May you find your perfect match soon." SMO surrogate Marianne followed the advice to "listen to her heart" and wait for "the perfect couple," and was happy to report that she found them: "It was just like you all said, when you know you just know." SMO surrogates more often talked about clicking with the couple, although subsequently they usually strove to bond with the intended mother and emphasize their closeness with her.

In both cases, references to "chemistry" situate third-party procreation in the same context as is generally understood for "normal" procreation, i.e., the result of affinity and love rather than interest (Schneider 1968). One difference is Israeli surrogates' more pronounced emphasis on "clicking with" the intended mother; the likely main reason is that the Israeli surrogates at the time of the study were single mothers, thus the three-way reproduction structurally resembled an extramarital affair. US surrogates, on the other hand, are mostly married women whose husbands are involved in all surrogacy-related relationships and tasks (Berend 2012, 2016). There are many stories on SMO about the surrogate and her husband socializing with IPs as a couple. Surrogates especially love it when "the men hit it off."

Both Israeli and US surrogates spoke of their hesitation whether to "do it again" for a different couple. As Israeli surrogate Talia explained, "You only fall in love once for the first time." Likewise, an SMO surrogate who contemplated doing a second surrogacy posted on the message boards: "I have a very close relationship with [my former IPs], and like a marriage where a spouse has passed, I don't know if I can 'recapture' THAT relationship." Many others echoed this sentiment:

> My first journey was so wonderful. We are all best friends to this day. I knew I would never do a second surrogacy, because how could anything ever compare to my first IPs and our fantastic relationship? But when I was approached, and really started to think about it, I just

called my FIM [former intended mother] and we chatted about all my concerns. I NEVER wanted her or FIF [former intended father] or the twins to think they were anything less than the most special people in the world.

With few exceptions, we both found that surrogates often decided between two or more potential couples by relying on such intuitive recognition and familiarity. "Listen to your gut feelings," was oft-given advice on SMO. Surrogates described their first meetings with their IPs as fated, "love at first sight," and as a relationship that was "meant to be." US surrogates advocate careful research and clear thinking but the "heart" plays a decisive role in their chosen loyalties to IPs.

Israeli surrogates also described an "unexplainable connection" and a "shared fate" that they felt with their intended mother, and often relayed how they felt "close to" her or professed that they "really love her." Sally described her thoughts the night before her first meeting with the IPs much like one would describe a blind date: "I wondered what kind of couple they were ... They have to be a couple that get into your heart a little. I am not saying that I have to fall in love with them at first sight, but that they should get into the heart." In their first fateful encounter, Sally's expectations were fulfilled: "As soon as they came up the escalator I said 'this is the couple' ... And that was it. From that moment there was a 'click.' Just like that." Rinat described the "click" she immediately and intuitively felt with her intended mother as in terms of a fated match: "I was their fifty-first in number ... but there wasn't a 'click' [with the others], a connection like ours." She relayed how she had inexplicably recognized her intended mother Sarit from her distant perch at the window of her second story apartment: "And they came in the car, and she is looking, and I said to her, 'Sarit, I am here.' As if I had known her from somewhere ... and from then on she decided that I would be her surrogate."

Likewise, SMO surrogate Melissa remembered her first meeting with her IPs: "I fell in love with them the first time we met." Rene reminisced: "I was introduced to only one couple and that is where I stopped, I loved them from the start." SMO surrogates often describe the match as one that was destined: "We must have talked on the phone for hours. Right then I knew this was meant to be." When they encounter difficulties, SMO surrogates often express doubts whether they had been destined to be surrogates. "I decided that if I didn't feel a connection right away, it wasn't meant to be." SMO surrogates often write about the importance of knowing what they want and of "not settling" or compromising on important issues, but they also look for signs of inexplicable connections which help them decide: "This time around, I believe I talked to about five couples before finding Mr. and Mrs. Right." Surrogacy is considered a "job of the heart."

In both samples, the resemblance between surrogacy and dating was also evident in the women's descriptions of the way their relationship progressed. It may have begun with a "blind date" and their increased closeness similar to "falling in love," but after that it becomes an intense and intimate companionship. Both Israeli and US surrogates enthusiastically tell or post about long telephone conversations and email exchanges with their IPs in the course of which they talk about "just about everything," engaging in self-revelation, which has been the primary symbol of intimacy since the nineteenth century among middle-class Americans (Lystra 1989). Both Israeli and US surrogates often also speak about their relationship with their intended mother by drawing upon various available definitions of social relationships, at times "like a best friend" or "like sisters" or even twins. Israeli surrogates also compared their relationship with their intended mother to that of a "temporary marriage" and described an intimacy that was sometimes "closer than a husband and wife."

Surrogates' conceptualization of their "journey" as one of shared love is consistent with the understanding of procreation in US – and Western – culture (Schneider 1968). When surrogates evoke their love for the couple, or the couple's love for them, they are highlighting the moral, private, emotional, and unique nature of the relationship, elevating it above the contractual arrangement yet distinguishing it from family relatedness. The understanding of surrogacy as a "labor of love" counters the stigma of mercenary "baby production" and situates procreation in the private realm (Berend 2012).

In both cases, this definition of surrogacy as love sometimes leads to situations in which the surrogate sacrificed her own well-being for the couple and "their pregnancy." Several Israeli surrogates expressed their realization as they waited for committee approval, often up to six months, that the money they would receive would not compensate for all of the time they had "put their life on hold," as several women put it. Others delayed marriages to partners they had met while trying to conceive for their couple because the Israeli law prohibited married surrogates. Two surrogates who wanted another child themselves delayed conceiving in order to have "one more child" for their couple.

Sima, who had been waiting with her couple for close to a year to begin the medical process because committee approval had been delayed, described her hesitation to undergo the embryo transfer when it finally commenced. She recalled that she nearly asked the doctor not to do the transfer until she looked at her intended mother and felt she could not forsake her because of the sense of alliance that she had already developed toward her during the waiting period:

> The more I got to know her, the more I felt like I wanted to do this for her. Because she made me, in the way she treated me, feel close

to her ... I said that I felt a kind of shared fate with her. She made me feel that way. She got to me, as you say. So I did it for her, let's say.

Fear of losing this intimacy was constantly in the back of the surrogate's mind as they worried that their intended mother would not be interested in continuing their relationship. Israeli surrogate Tsila relayed two weeks after she gave birth to the surrogate baby: "the next day I cried a lot because I thought that I was losing a friend." Sapir similarly relayed her sense of anxiety over the approaching birth because she thought the intended mother might abandon her after the baby was born:

> When I gave birth, I became anxious and sort of depressed. Not because of what's-his-name, the baby or something, but because the whole thing was over ... I was really afraid that I was going to lose her ... So I started to cry in the [hospital] room, because it was over. Look, I was the center of everything for a year. And when I was hospitalized, I cried. I would cry at night, until the next day ... I cried over Shoshana, not the baby. So the next day Shoshana came when the welfare officer arrived, and Shoshana said that she didn't want to break it off and that calmed me down ... I can no longer imagine myself without speaking to Shoshana at least once a week. And it calms me down that I have permission from her to call her whenever I want, and even to visit her.

Similarly, SMO surrogates tended to make sacrifices for their couple; they sometimes agreed to having three or more embryos to be transferred because their IPs were "desperate for a baby," or carried twins or triplets to provide their couple with "a whole family." Many lowered their compensation, decided to forgo some reimbursements, and used their own sick-days at work for surrogacy-related appointments to save money for their IPs, and researched cost-saving options in general. SMO surrogates discussed feeling ambivalent or bad about charging fees to IPs and at times agreed to lesser terms than they originally asked for. When these sacrifices go unappreciated by the IPs, surrogates can be very hurt. Christie, who "put so much time and effort" into making her IPs parents, was "very torn" she had tried not to mind that some payments were not forthcoming. "Because I love my IPs, I have let a lot of things slide financially, because really ... it wasn't about the money to me ... but now ... I am hurt."

Many SMO surrogates report a sense of loss and sadness after the birth: "I can feel our relationship changing. The calls are less often and shorter. The distance has begun." Some surrogates were disappointed, even depressed; others were resigned: "There is nothing wrong with feeling pain during or after surrogacy. LOVE is painful, no?" Fellow surrogates on SMO very often provided the acknowledgment and praise when the couple failed to do so, thus providing the recognition surrogates wished for. SMO discussions also helped redefine the rewards as the "knowledge that you created precious life" rather than IPs' gratitude and friendship.

For both the Israeli and the SMO surrogates, remaining in touch after the baby was born constituted acknowledgment from the IPs of the surrogate's contribution (gestating the baby and her sacrifices during the process) and that she herself as a person was valued beyond the monetary payment. In both settings, surrogates wanted to believe that these chosen loyalties were "thicker than blood." Surrogates in both samples felt immense pride in having been a surrogate especially, but not only, when acknowledgment was forthcoming. They did not keep surrogacy a secret, and continued to view surrogacy as part of their identity in subsequent years.

Israeli surrogate Sally told of her experience two years after her surrogacy was over when she worked in an office supply store. She told everyone she met about having been a surrogate, and was amazed by the reactions of complete strangers to her after she told them about having been a surrogate: "Everyone says 'kol hakavod' [good for you], what a mitzvah [moral deed] you have done." US surrogates were similarly proud of their achievement. Many women said that surrogacy is a good way to teach their children the value of altruism. When surrogacy was not well received by some family members, women often wrote disparagingly about these relatives, describing them as "selfish" and lacking empathy. Some surrogates started "screw you" threads where women who had some falling-out with family members over surrogacy could post their stories and support one another. Thus surrogates exercised choice in their relationships even when relatedness was a given. They were the happiest when their IPs showed continued loyalty: "they are my real family, even better than my own family." However, their own and other SMO surrogates' experiences also teach US surrogates to uphold the moral value of creating families even when some others may not. Sally, SMO moderator and surrogate to eight babies, expressed this stance:

> Don't stop giving the love that you so want to give ... Even the most perfect journey is never PERFECT! IPs obviously go into surrogacy with intent of starting a family. Some will keep us in their lives and some will not ... I always trust my intuition. The beauty of assisting others in creating family is beyond words for me.

23.5 Surrogates Carry Other People's Children

The second similarity is that in both studies surrogates adamantly insist that they do not bond with the babies they carried for their IPs. The reason in both settings is that surrogates did not see themselves as the mother of this baby, and most surrogates professed not developing the emotions that they believed women usually develop when carrying their "own" child: "It's not mine and that is why I didn't have the kinds of feelings you'd expect." Interestingly, as we will discuss below, both Israeli and US surrogates often contrast their "natural" maternal feelings during their own pregnancies with the lack of bonding during their surrogate "journeys." By highlighting the difference between their own and the surrogate pregnancy, they also make a strong claim about motherhood, namely, that they are not the mother of the surrogate baby.

Surrogates thus rejected popularly held notions about the naturalistic assumption that mother love and maternal bonding are universally and intrinsically rooted in the nurturing relationship between the pregnant woman and her child (Lauritzen 1993; Rothman 2000). Although scholars have repeatedly challenged this bonding theory, suggesting that women's emotional attachment to the babies they bear and acceptance of the maternal role are far from instinctive (Ivry 2010; Scheper-Hughes 1992), the assumption that "normal" women "naturally" bond with the children they bear is still a widely held belief in the public sphere and frames much of the research on surrogacy (Teman 2008).

Whereas much of the scholarship assumes that since pregnant women are "naturally" predisposed toward bonding, surrogates will suffer feelings of regret, loss, and depression after relinquishment (Teman 2008), surrogates such as Israeli surrogate Rinat, viewed their lack of bonding with the surrogate baby as "natural." Drawing on understandings that bonding with one's own babies is normal, Rinat claimed that she naturally bonded with her own but not with the surrogacy-born baby. Comparing her feelings toward the baby she carried as a surrogate and the baby she subsequently carried for herself, Rinat explained: "You have to understand that the feelings were [in surrogacy] completely different. For instance now (in her subsequent pregnancy with her own child) I feel that it is my heart and that it is all mine."

Recalling the first time she saw the baby she bore for her couple, she relayed: "(I felt) nothing! I also thought that when I saw him I would remember, but nothing ... I took him and kissed him and played with him. And it was fun ... It was just like my nephew coming in here, or my neighbor's son." US surrogates also talk about how the "surrobaby" behaved very differently in utero from the surrogate's own children, and that they nurture and love the baby the way they love a relative's or friend's child. "It is like I feel toward my brother's child; I love him and protect him but I'm not his mother." Other SMO surrogates were even more emphatic:

> I have NO feelings of "mother" towards her ... It is so very hard to explain. In a very large way I am very happy to feel this way. I do not in any way feel like I am giving up a child. I am giving a child to her

parents after nine months of helping her grow. I have said from the beginning and to anyone who might listen that this is NOT my child.

A traditional surrogate was equally firm that she was not the baby's mother:

This child in my womb is NOT mine. I am nurturing him or her for the time being, but upon birth, he or she will go to their parents where they belong. I am of the belief that the egg used in conceiving this baby was meant for my IPs from before we even knew we'd do this surrogacy. I just don't want anyone thinking this is my baby. I guess I shouldn't care what anyone thinks, as I KNOW what is true.

Both Israeli and US surrogates often compare surrogacy to "babysitting" – it is a nurturing relationship that entails responsibilities but does not make the child yours. "I relate my feelings towards this little girl I'm carrying as about the same as I feel towards the little girl I nanny for. I care for her well-being but I have no maternal feelings," wrote Jenny on SMO. Israeli surrogate Sapir explained:

I don't see myself as a second mother. Because … nothing in the child belongs to me. It is as if I would go now, and I would tell you, Elly, watch my child for me. It is just like that. It is from the beginning (literally, from the belly and birth), the original child of Shoshana and Itamar. So I didn't feel any (connection).

This and similar formulations assert that the IPs' dream and desire to become parents is more central to surrogates' gestational labor.

Both Israeli and US surrogates are resolute that their role is to help the baby's parents realize their "dream." As Tara relayed on SMO: "We carry children for the intention of making a family that's not for ourselves." All surrogates on SMO insist that the child always *belongs* to the IPs: "We are all carrying someone else's CHILD!" Both the Israeli and the SMO surrogates maintained that the goal of surrogacy is to make parents and create families. Given that assisted reproduction "does not automatically assist the making of parents," rather, it "assists the making of children" (Strathern 1992: 21), surrogates' emphasis on "making a family" shifts the emphasis from the baby the surrogate gestates to the family the IPs wish for. The endeavor to "make families" assumes IPs' relatedness to the not-yet existing children while also clearly drawing the boundary between the IPs' and the surrogate's family.

One way of designating parenthood in both contexts was to "share" the pregnancy and the birth as much as possible with the IPs, insisting it was "their" pregnancy rather than the surrogates'. In Israel, where surrogates and couples were able to physically meet throughout the pregnancy because of the short geographical distance between them, surrogates often looked for creative and intimate ways to share the pregnancy as much as possible with their intended mother (Teman 2010a). Israeli surrogate Orna relayed how she tried to help her intended mother "feel like she was pregnant" by sharing even the most visceral bodily functions, such as vomiting, dizziness, and physical pain with her:

> Look, throughout the pregnancy, I really tried to pass her all sorts of feelings so that she could, so to speak, feel like she was pregnant. I mean, if I had a headache, or I didn't sleep at night, or the fetus was kicking, moving, it pained me or whatever. I would call her and say, "she kicked me and it hurts." Then she would say, "okay, now which side hurts." I said, "left. Say it hurts you too." And she would yell, "ay, ay, ay" on the phone … and in the beginning when I had dizziness and vomiting, I would call her and say, "I feel yucky," and she would say, "I will go vomit instead of you." And she really felt like it belonged to her. Like she was pregnant. Because I shared everything with her.

Israeli surrogates also worked out the designation of the pregnancy and the baby by enabling the intended mother to participate in all medical appointments and by making sure she "carried" the responsibility for making the appointments, filing and bringing the necessary documents, and speaking to the doctor. Masha explained:

> It was important to me that she be present at all of the ultrasounds. Because it was important to me that she go through the whole experience and that she see the whole experience … I have no problem with a woman coming in (to the vaginal ultrasound) … About those things, I made sure that Tova took part in everything. Because it is really important to me that she go through and feel the whole experience exactly as I do. That is the way I wanted it, that she be my partner, as much as possible.

As the pregnancy progressed, Israeli surrogates developed a sense of sharing their body with the intended mother and of "making" her into a mother. It was not uncommon for Israeli surrogates to describe their body and the intended mother's body during surrogacy as "one body" or for them to describe the pregnancy as distanced from the surrogates body and vicariously "carried" by the intended mother.

US surrogates extensively discussed pregnancy-sharing ideas on SMO; geographic distance often makes frequent physical contact impossible. When they were physically near the IPs, both Israeli and US surrogates urged their couples to lay a hand on the stomach and feel the baby move, to attend medical appointments and scheduled sonograms for them to "visit with the baby." However, whereas Israeli surrogates were more intensely geared toward sharing the manifestations of pregnant embodiment and the experience of pregnancy with the intended mother, SMO surrogates, even when they lived geographically close, were more focused on sharing their privileged access to the fetus and enabling the IPs to be present for and bond with "their baby." Some surrogates sent weekly letters to their couple in the baby's name, reporting from the fetus' perspective, as the following example, an SMO post by a surrogate, shows:

> Hey Mom and Dad it's "Winston,"
>   We are officially 16 weeks or 4 months pregnant!!! Only 6 more till I meet you!!! Can't wait. I am 4 1/2 inches long (head to bottom) and 3 1/2 ounces, about the size of an avocado … My head up straighter (can hear mom right now "Sit up straight dear") than it has been … Ears are close to their final position, too. (I guess I can't say huh when you tell me to clean my room) … Maybe when I see y'all on the 22nd you can hear my heart beating through Liz's tummy!!!! … I've even started growing toenails (can't wait for my big sister to paint them if I am a girl). I am moving around a whole bunch and Liz is starting to feel it especially after she eats!!! She can't feel it on the outside yet but can't wait for you to feel me saying hi to you on the tummy. I am behaving myself and not giving her any trouble.

When geographical distance was greater, or IPs were unable to attend doctors' appointments, US surrogates often sent ultrasound images and the fetus' tape-recorded heartbeat. Others called their IPs and put their cell phone close to the monitor so that the couple could hear it in real time. Some surrogates kept and shared their journals of "the IPs' pregnancy." Another popular idea of how to encourage bonding was to play IPs' voice-recorded stories to the fetus so that it would "know its parents." There were some discussions about whether it was safe to put headphones directly on one's belly, and about methods to avoid intruding on the privacy of these times of intimacy between IPs and their fetus-babies.

After enabling their couple "to be as pregnant as possible," both Israeli and US surrogates wanted to give the IPs privileged access to the birth because it is "their birth" and "their baby." In both samples, surrogates spoke of rituals of participation, and IPs sometimes cut the umbilical cord. In nearly all Israeli cases, the intended mother attended the birth alongside the surrogate, even if it was a cesarean delivery. Surrogates reported how the intended mother held their hand, "helped" her push out the baby, and in some instances displayed couvade symptoms in identification with the surrogate's labor. US surrogates want their couple to be there at the delivery and are devastated when this does not happen. On SMO, the consensus was that surrogates should include IPs in the birth and the assumption is that IPs want to be there. Fellow surrogates were incensed when Bobbie said she did not want her IPs to be present at birth because she was very shy and private. They called her "selfish" and "unsympathetic," depriving her IPs of seeing "their child born." "They may not be carrying the baby but it's still their pregnancy too."

23.6 We Are Not the Mom

The third similarity, briefly referenced above, is that surrogates do not view themselves as the mother of the surrogate baby. With this claim surrogates refute widespread assumptions that the surrogate who carries and gives birth to the baby must be its mother and that it is morally wrong not to acknowledge her maternity and even detrimental to her and the resulting child (Anderson 1990, 2000; Danna 2015; Rothman 2000).

As we discussed before, neither Israeli nor US surrogates consider gestation to be consequential for motherhood; however, they have differing views about the role of genetics. Israeli surrogates firmly distinguished between the potentiality of wombs versus eggs in creating kin ties and emotional bonds between women and the babies they carry. They considered the egg to be inalienably associated with personhood and self and the vehicle for the creation of kin ties, whereas the womb was denuded of personal traits and separated from the kin line. Israeli surrogate Sapir, for instance, decided to become a surrogate based on her view that gestation did not "involve" her personally in the way that traditional surrogacy would have:

> If it was something that I was involved in then I would have immediately rejected the option … I mean like if it was my egg, if this child had part of me … So they told me no, that it is a couple that cannot have children because the woman has a problem with her womb. But she has eggs and it is just, you just have to carry it (the pregnancy). So the process looked really good in my eyes.

Like Sapir, Israeli surrogates were quick to emphasize that the baby they carried for their couple was not "created from me," "is a stranger," "is not mine." They were particularly adamant in stressing that the baby did not share their "blood" and were nearly all horrified by the idea of traditional surrogacy, which they believed would be "giving away my own child." They drew a sharp distinction between gestation and genetics; the former is neutral, while the latter is considered the basis of parenthood.

Accordingly, even as they stressed their genetic distance from the fetus, Israeli surrogates emphasized that they were "carrying" not just a baby but also the genetic lineage of the IPs. Significantly, even in the five cases in Teman's study in which a donor egg was used, it was kept a highly protected secret and surrogates, as well as intended mothers, stressed the genetic link to the intended father as encapsulating the continuity of the IPs' kin line. It was common for the Israeli surrogates to define their role in surrogacy as creating a "continuing generation" (*dor hemshech*) for their couple, a common cultural idiom that refers not only to a family's personal continuity, but also abstractly to the continuity of the Jewish-Israeli nation, which is dependent upon its coming generations (Hazelton 1977). As Israeli surrogate Orna said, "This couple has no continuing generation and if they don't have a child then they will simply be erased from this earth."

Israeli surrogates' insistence on the genetic idiom of a "continuing generation" must also be viewed in the sociopolitical context of the Israeli nation's struggle for survival, the reality of war, the biblical imperative, and the collective calling to replace the murder of six million Jews in the Holocaust (Teman 2010b). In this pronatalist context, motherhood is a basic status and role for women and "non-natalist" voices are seldom heard in public and private arenas (Donath 2010). Giving birth to a baby for a childless couple is thus endowing the intended mother with her "entry ticket" into the collective as well as contributing to the growth of the Jewish population within the context of a "demographic war" being played out as part of the Israeli–Palestinian conflict.

Such meanings were implied in Israeli surrogates' ideas about their role as surrogates. For example, Neta saw herself as "doing a moral deed [*mitzvah*] … it is helping a dynasty, the continuation, it is making life continue. That is the biggest mitzvah that can be. And especially since it was a son." Neta's use of the term "mitzvah" captures the higher meaning of her surrogate role. Used in Hebrew to denote the performance of a moral deed and colloquially as an act of human kindness, a *mitzvah* also refers to the 613 commandments given in the Torah which Jews are obligated to perform as their religious duty. Neta's elevation of surrogacy to the status of a *mitzvah* connotes the fulfillment of her moral duty as a Jew. Moreover, her indication of the particular social value of a son, who can carry on the family name and can also be a soldier for the nation, suggests that by carrying the IPs' genetic offspring, her surrogacy contributed to the continuity of the collective.

In her discussion of the privileging of genetic kinship in Israeli law and medical practice, Birenbaum-Carmeli suggests that genetic relatedness is promoted as fundamental to the Israeli construction of a "naturalized," "gene-based" notion of Jewish identity and the notion of Israel's Jewish collectivity as biologically related kin (Birenbaum-Carmeli 2008: 1023). She argues that non-genetic forms of kinship, such as adoption, are widely marginalized in Israel by laypersons, medical practitioners and by the state because they are perceived as a challenge to the "natural family" paradigm. It is only by demarcating genetic kinship as superior to its alternatives that national interests can be upheld. In view of this metonymic significance of genetics, it appears that for Israeli surrogates, the preservation of genetic continuity is part of an ideological discourse of collective regeneration supported by state political interests; by so vehemently protecting maternity's rootedness in a geneticized notion of "the natural family," the Israeli surrogates are protecting the state's interest in preserving a touchstone of the Jewish-Israeli collective.

SMO surrogates, on the other hand, do not treat the egg as the repository of personhood and kin ties and certainly do not view genetics as symbols of national continuity. In keeping with the privatized US understandings of social well-being, surrogates regard the family as the basic unit of society and emphasize that good, loving, stable families are the foundation of social progress. Helping people who need help is also considered a positive civic activity; seeing private charitable volunteering as the solution for social problems has a long history in the US. Accordingly, surrogates sometimes frame their assistance as akin to charitable activities. "I can't afford to give much to charity right now, and I don't have a lot of free time to volunteer. I figure surrogacy is one way I can contribute positively." Many others explained that they decided to become surrogates because "I could feel like I was really making a difference in the world." These somewhat vague expressions indicate that being useful in the world and helping couples become parents, i.e., the public and private sides of "usefulness," are connected but not in specific nation-building ways.

SMO surrogates also assert that meritorious behavior should reap its reward; thus IPs who are successful and well-established and do everything to have a baby deserve to be parents. "We found the perfect couple who we know are amazing parents! I have always wanted to help the world become a better place," Anne explained her decision. Surrogates frequently talk about how unfair it is that young unwed women have babies without even wanting them and how wanted and much-loved babies are precious. They also imply that such young and unwed mothers do not contribute to a better, more stable society. In the US sociopolitical context this juxtaposition signifies middle-class values and stances about marriage, childbearing, and the merits of planning and "hard work."

Surrogates argue that "wanted" children will be happier and healthier adults than "unwanted" children.

> To find out that your parents wanted you to be here so much that they were willing to have someone else bring you into this world would, I think, be ... easier to hear than your birth parents not wanting you or not being able to take care of you and giving you away ... I think it could definitely be traumatic to find out that you were not wanted.

Genetic parenthood is not a guarantee of good parenthood; love, care, and preparation for it are. "Almost anyone can use their DNA to produce a child ... not everyone can be a true guardian, friend, or care giver to a child." Discussions reveal that surrogates see choice as central in both relatedness and relationships. According to surrogates, not wanting to be the mother is an ethical choice in surrogacy, the opposite of not wanting one's own child: "this baby is not mine, it was planned by its parents from the beginning; I didn't just get pregnant and decide not to keep him!"

Given that genetics and thus eggs are not necessarily central to parenthood and relatedness and certainly not of nationhood, some surrogates are egg donors themselves, and many others have IPs who use an egg donor. Quite a few traditional surrogates say that they are "egg donor and gestational surrogate in one," thus reframing traditional surrogacy in the idiom of donation. Since SMO was the main source of information and support for both traditional and gestational surrogates who discuss and debate issues together, it is not surprising that they have established a common ground, one that preferences intentionality, regarding kinship conceptualizations in surrogacy. Also, some gestational surrogates offer their eggs after failed attempts and become traditional surrogates and some do both gestational and traditional journeys; gestational and traditional surrogates are not two separate groups.

Since many IPs end up using donated gametes, gestational surrogates on SMO cannot lean too heavily on the fact that they are not genetically related to the fetus because not infrequently neither are the IPs. Yet, whether there is a genetic link to the baby or not, SMO surrogates are adamant that the surrogate is "obviously" not the mother while the IPs are unquestionably the parents: "Surrogacy revolves around intent. A surrogate mother intentionally gets pregnant and carries a child for someone else. The father of my current IM's [intended mother's] future children is a sperm donor. If things don't work out, and she chooses to move on to an egg donor, she will still be the child's mother in my eyes."

There is overwhelming agreement on SMO that IPs' desire and love for the baby-to-be is the main unifying feature of surrogacy. On this view, intent, love, and parenting makes parents, not gestation or DNA. Desire for children, coupled with the acts of parenting, is a firmer basis of parenthood, according to SMO surrogates, than genetic relatedness. "My children are mine because of the relationship I've built with them over time. I really don't think that contributing some DNA makes someone 'mine.' Parenting makes a parent, IMO [in my opinion], not biology." The surrogate's role, accordingly, is to help the IPs realize their dream: "He was created between the love of his mother and father. I was just the middle man." Thus SMO surrogates, whether gestational or traditional, are in agreement that the babies they carry belong to the couple who desired them and will parent them. According to them, "it shouldn't matter if the child is biologically related to you or not. You went into the agreement with the intention to make a child for another family." A surrogate who did both gestational and traditional journeys summed it up: "We all know the biology involved, but that doesn't change whose children they are or how I feel about them."

By juxtaposing the Israeli surrogates' promotion of genetic kinship with US surrogates' dismissal of genetics in favor of love and care within each country's larger sociopolitical context of procreation, it becomes clear that definitions of kinship carry cultural and sociopolitical meanings and that more is at stake in these definitions than meets the eye. It is by carefully defining surrogacy through geneticized ideas about kinship that Israeli surrogates shape their role into one of value to the Jewish collective. For US surrogates, genes can be dismissed because what is important is the IPs' desire to become parents; and the surrogates' to help them. Thus, surrogates are fulfilling the private dream of the IPs as well as their own to "make a difference," creating "good," "chosen," and "deserving" families.

23.7 Conclusion

We began this chapter with the question: does the difference in socio-political and regulatory context give rise to different expectations among surrogates about their relationship with the IPs and with the surrogacy-born baby? Through a comparative exploration of our ethnographic studies of surrogacy in the United States and in Israel, we have argued that beyond the many structural and cultural differences between US and Israeli surrogacy, surrogates create a common set of understandings of the practice and also of the relationship they had with their couple. These shared understandings, elicited by taking the empirical experience and understandings of surrogates themselves seriously, refute long-held convictions about gestation creating kin ties and about pregnancy "naturally" leading to in-utero bonding with the fetus. The ethnographic data from our studies suggest that surrogates view surrogacy as a journey of love, they do not bond with the babies they carry but do bond or hope to bond with the IPs, and they do not consider themselves the mother of the baby. Surrogates want to be appreciated and acknowledged by their couple for their contribution both during the pregnancy and after the birth. When couples were less than grateful after birth, surrogates often felt betrayed. Both Israeli and US surrogates considered continued contact with the couple as confirmation that the morally significant act of assisting reproduction gives rise to "ties that bind."

Our studies reveal that for surrogates, whether kinship is understood to be based on genetics (Israel) or on intent (SMO), it is also and most importantly based on love and care. For the surrogates in both studies, maternity is not an automatic outcome of pregnancy; indeed, gestation does not create kin ties at all. Moreover, bonding with the fetus is revealed as not a universal emotional outcome of pregnancy but a choice. Surrogates in both contexts hold that bonding with other people's children as if they were one's own is morally wrong, while bonding with their couple is the logical outcome of the intense and intimate process of collaborative baby making. "Fictive kin" ties and a lasting solidarity between surrogates and IPs is the surrogate dream in most cases.

It may be easy to dismiss surrogates' accounts as false consciousness, or point out the rare newspaper article about a surrogate who decided to "keep the baby," but if we want to understand surrogacy, we should consider empirical data. The two studies together show that both Israeli and US surrogates consider surrogacy as a morally meaningful undertaking that creates babies and families; surrogates "nurture parents," not just "their babies." They bond or hope to bond with the IPs rather than the babies whom they do not consider their own. According to surrogates, "surrobabies" are precious and always belong to the IPs; surrogates help create these babies for their couple who want to parent them. Ironically, surrogates' own understandings and actions ultimately uphold the "sanctity" of the nuclear family rather than undermine the "moral order" critics see as threatened. When we consider empirical evidence we find that surrogates' accounts are important data for the ongoing redefinitions and acts of kinship in ways that can be made intelligible in their cultural and sociopolitical contexts.

References

Anderson, E. 1990. "Is Women's Labor a Commodity?" *Philosophy and Public Affairs* 19(1): 71–92.

2000. "Why Commercial Surrogate Motherhood Unethically Commodifies Women and Children: Reply to McLachlan and Swales." *Health Care Analysis* 8(1): 1–26.

Berend, Z. 2010. "Surrogate Losses: Understandings of Pregnancy Loss and Assisted Reproduction among Surrogate Mothers." *Medical Anthropology Quarterly* 24(2): 240–262.

2012. "The Romance of Surrogacy." *Sociological Forum* 27(4): 913–936.

2016. *The Online World of Surrogacy*. New York/London: Berghahn Books.

Birenbaum-Carmeli, D. 2009. "The Politics of 'The Natural Family' in Israel: State Policy and Kinship Ideologies." *Social Science and Medicine* 69: 1018–1024.

Danna, D. 2015. *Contract Children: Questioning Surrogacy*. Stuttgart: ibidem-Verlag/ibidem Press.

Dolgin, J. L. 1990. "Status and Contract in Surrogate Motherhood: An Illumination of the Surrogacy Debate." *Buffalo Law Review* 38(2): 515–550.

Donath, O. 2010. "Pro-Natalism and Its 'Cracks': Narratives of Reproduction and Childfree Lifestyles in Israel [in Hebrew]." *Israeli Sociology* 11(2): 417–439.

Hazelton, L. 1977. *Israeli Women: The Reality behind the Myths*. New York: Simon & Schuster.

Ivry, T. 2010. *Embodying Culture: Pregnancy in Japan and Israel*. New Brunswick, NJ: Rutgers University Press.

Ketchum, S. A. 1992. "Selling Babies and Selling Bodies." In *Feminist Perspectives in Medical Ethics*, ed. H. B. Holmes and L. M. Purdy, 284–294. Bloomington, IN: Indiana University Press.

Lambek, M. 2013. "Kinship, Modernity, and the Immodern." In *Vital Relations: Modernity and the Persistent Life of Kinship*, ed. S. McKinnon and F. Cannell, 241–260. Santa Fe, NM: School for Advanced Research Press.

Lauritzen, P. 1993. *Pursuing Parenthood: Ethical Issues in Assisted Reproduction.* Bloomington, IN: Indiana University Press.

Lystra, K. 1989. *Searching the Heart: Women, Men, and Romantic Love in Nineteenth-Century America.* New York: Oxford University Press.

Markens, S. 2007. *Surrogate Motherhood and the Politics of Reproduction.* Berkeley, CA: University of California Press.

Rao, R. 2003. "Surrogacy Law in the United States: The Outcome of Ambivalence." In *Surrogate Motherhood: International Perspectives*, ed. R. Cook, S. D. Sclater and F. Kaganas, 23–35. Oxford/Portland, OR: Hart Press.

Rothman, B. K. 2000. *Recreating Motherhood.* New Brunswick, NJ: Rutgers University Press.

Scheper-Hughes, N. 1992. *Death without Weeping: The Violence of Everyday Life in Brazil.* Berkeley, CA: University of California Press.

Schneider, D. M. 1968. *American Kinship: A Cultural Account.* Englewood Cliffs, NJ: Prentice- Hall.

1984. *A Critique of the Study of Kinship.* Ann Arbor, MI: University of Michigan Press.

Strathern, M. 1992. *After Nature: English Kinship in the Late Twentieth Century.* Cambridge: Cambridge University Press.

Teman, E. 2008. "The Social Construction of Surrogacy Research: An Anthropological Critique of the Psychosocial Scholarship on Surrogate Motherhood." *Social Science and Medicine* 67(7): 1104–1112.

2010a. *Birthing a Mother: The Surrogate Body and the Pregnant Self.* Berkeley, CA: University of California Press.

2010b. "The Last Outpost of the Nuclear Family: A Cultural Critique of Israeli Surrogacy Policy." In *Kin, Gene, Community: Reproductive Technology among Jewish Israelis*, ed. D. Birenbaum-Carmeli and Y. Carmeli, 107–126. Oxford: Berghahn Books.

Zelizer, V. 2000. "The Purchase of Intimacy." *Law & Social Inquiry* 25(3): 817–848.

24

Self, Personhood, and Belonging: The Role of Technology in Childhood Disability

Gail Landsman

24.1 Introduction

Who counts as a member of the family? Which characteristics threaten eligibility for kinship and belonging? As new technologies enter and take root in the reproductive realm, agonizing moral quandaries emerge and have effects that extend well beyond the individuals who actually utilize the technologies. A robust literature in the anthropology of reproduction has documented ways prenatal diagnostic technologies enter into and are enmeshed with specificities of place and history.

However, despite prenatal testing, selective abortion, and public health initiatives, children continue to be born and diagnosed with disabilities. The prevalence of childhood disability has risen steadily in the United States (Halfon et al. 2012), transformed by technological innovation itself. As Wise (2012: 174) points out, technologies may be "shifting mortality into chronic morbidity." Improvements in neo-natal care and medical management of conditions that were once fatal have resulted in more children with severe health conditions surviving, but at high risk for disability; at the same time, a rise in preterm births has increased the risk of neurological and developmental disorders, including cerebral palsy, ADHD, and sensory and intellectual impairments (Halfon et al. 2012). The increase in preterm births, as well as in low birth weight, has been attributed to the growing use of assisted reproductive technologies and resultant multiple gestations (Wise 2012). In addition, technologies of postnatal testing create the category of "patients-in-waiting," including those newborns currently asymptomatic, yet having markers, albeit often ambiguous, of disease

(Timmermans and Buchbinder 2010). With the birth of a child diagnosed with or at risk for disabilities, intensive engagement with technologies may have just begun.

Thus while I begin with discussion of the cultural contexts within which prenatal diagnostic technologies are utilized, the concern of this chapter is not with making the choice to use or refuse these technologies or selective abortion in the prenatal period, but rather on the relationship of technologies, personhood, and disability, *after* a child with disability – a child few would actively choose – is born. This, the unsought, unexpected encounter with disability, I have argued elsewhere, draws American mothers into what is at its heart, a most anthropological experience. For a mother of a child recently diagnosed with or at risk for disability, what had once been the "Other" is now a member of the family.

> And like an anthropologist in a new field site seeking to make sense of profound difference within a common humanity, such a mother, too, becomes engaged in a meaning-making, interpretive process, seeking to find, and often to advocate for, the personhood of a child whose life is routinely devalued, and indeed once might have been devalued by the mother herself.
>
> *(Landsman 2009: 3)*

In what follows I focus on the technologies with which families engage – diagnostic, therapeutic, and assistive – in this meaning-making process, and explore how such technologies are implicated in culturally specific attempts to prevent, normalize, and redefine childhood disability.

24.2 Diagnostic Technologies: Mother's Role in Disability

In her moving account of selective reproduction in North Vietnam, Gammeltoft (2014) points out how very much is at stake in a woman's pregnancy: "not only the coming-into-being of her child but also her own coming-into-being as a member of local moral communities" (2014: 83). The birth of a healthy, normal child will provide her with respect and a secure place within her household; the birth of a disabled child may "undermine her social existence, placing her on the margins of her family and community" (2014: 81). Belonging, Gammeltoft argues, is tenuous, vulnerable. Gossip about reproductive misfortune is rampant, with not only exposure to the defoliant Agent Orange, but also mothers' behaviors – being too focused on work, taking cold showers, getting sick, or failing to get prenatal care – often blamed for their child's misfortunes. Disabled children in North Vietnam are considered innocents, whose anomalous bodies and/or minds expose the moral failings of parents and/ or of distant ancestors.

In the "disability-suffering equation," North Vietnamese parents of disabled children, their extended family, and the children themselves are considered doomed to suffer (Gammeltoft 2014: 181). It is therefore considered a woman's moral responsibility to her unborn child and to her extended family to act to avoid this fate through prenatal testing, especially ultrasound, and selective abortion; for once born, the disabled child is deemed incomplete – loved and cared for, but not an individual capable of becoming a person (Gammeltoft 2008, 2014).

In Israel as well, ultrasound is embraced, and "the prospect of reproductive misfortune is the fabric through which pregnancies ... are navigated by doctors and women" (Ivry 2009: 189). Fetal imagery in Israel as in other parts of the world enables separation of mother and fetus; but unlike in the Euro-American context, it does not do so through the creation of fetal subjects whose health is threatened by their mothers. Rather, in Israel it is the fetus that is construed as the threat. In what Ivry dubs "the ultrasonic picture show" – study days sponsored by medical centers – women are shown ultrasound pictures of deformed fetuses, and "are understood, and are told to understand themselves, as being in the process of carrying a potential fetal catastrophe" (2009: 199). Termination of a deformed fetus is widely considered responsible maternal behavior in Israel. For the ultraorthodox Jewish woman in Israel however, this is not an option. Ultrasound findings force her to imagine giving birth to a disabled baby, her "God-sent ordeal" (Ivry, Teman and Frumkin 2011).

Shift now to the contemporary United States. Companies with names such as "Peek A Baby," "First Look Sonogram," "The Belly Factory," and "Fetal Studio," offer "keepsake" sonograms, elective 2D, 3D, and 4D ultrasound sessions to which family and friends can be invited to watch on large projection screens. A 3D ultrasound provides a realistic surface image of the fetus as a still photo; 4D ultrasound is a video loop that shows the fetus moving. To create a better viewing experience, companies suggest eating or drinking something cold or sweet prior to the session to get the baby moving. Facilities offer packages that may include CDs of 3D images, DVDs set to music, and ultrasound streaming services that transmit real-time ultrasound video of the fetus to computers elsewhere throughout the country or world.

"Gender reveal parties," in which the gender of the baby, sometimes already known by the parents-to-be, but sometimes written down and enclosed in a sealed envelope to be opened at the party, are made possible by ultrasound. Websites, social media, and party stores offer ideas for such parties, such as the use of food dye to color the inside of a cake blue or pink or opening a box revealing blue or pink balloons. Gender reveal parties and baby showers can also be part of keepsake ultrasound viewings, either in an ultrasound office or with the use of a portable ultrasound machine brought to the customer's chosen location. Shops on Internet marketplaces sell a range of items using ultrasound pictures, including ultrasound pillows, key rings, necklaces, and various kinds of "ultrasound art."

In 2004 the FDA issued a warning for women to avoid keepsake images, updating the statement in December of 2014; while acknowledging that fetal imaging can promote bonding between parents and fetus, the FDA expressed concern that there are no controls on how long the fetus is exposed to ultrasound in a session or how many sessions may be held. The agency warns that ultrasound waves are capable of heating tissues slightly, and can produce pockets of gas in body fluids or tissues (cavitation), the long-term consequences of which are unknown (USFDA 2014). Nevertheless, the practice continues in most states.

Client reviews published on ultrasound websites reveal the way the visualizing technology has been incorporated into the experience of pregnancy as a kin-making process.

> Your tech showed us some amazing things and it was fun to ... see his cute little feet and watch the heart beat. But he would not show us the front of his face no matter what we did. So the tech had us come back (for free) a few days later and there he was smiling at us looking just like his dad!!
>
> *(Samantha T., The Belly Factory)*

> Huge room with couches plenty of space for the whole family. Very friendly staff. Can't wait to go back & take my 2 little girls to see their baby sister!!
>
> *(Liptrap, Peekaboo3D)*

Many websites provide "before and after" photos comparing pictures of newborn infants to those of 3D ultrasound taken earlier at the studio. Similarities validate that the fetal images seen on the screen represent "real" babies, complete with family resemblances, i.e., with kinship connections to those already established as full persons and family members. "SEE ME LIVE! GOD's BLESSINGS BEFORE AND AFTER" proclaims the home page of "InfantSee4D." It shows an image of a 2D ultrasound, a 3D/4D ultrasound, and a live baby with the words "ME!" At the bottom of the page is written "Mommy & Daddy, Come See Me at InfantSee4D." Personhood, agency, and kinship for the fetus are here assumed and celebrated.

Yet personhood is not an all or nothing proposition; it can be diminished by a diagnosis of disability. Mothers of newborns with diagnosed disabilities describe choosing not to send out birth announcements, not receiving congratulations, having the baby talked about as if it were not really human, being treated by others as if they had never even been pregnant, and feeling as if they missed the experience of "real" motherhood. Fetal "persons" in the womb may become "non-persons" or "less-than" full-persons after birth (Landsman 2009).

24.3   The Age of Perfect Babies

"Keepsake" ultrasound with its souvenir DVDs and "first baby pictures" is not diagnostic, and may, as the governor of Connecticut warned in banning the practice in 2009, lead to false reassurances that "all was well with the baby" (State of Connecticut 2009). Parent comments on ultrasound websites often express such reassurances of perfection: "We did the first one at 15 weeks 2 days, and it was so amazing and reassuring to see him absolutely perfect even so early on."

The images of deformed fetuses that haunt Israeli women or North Vietnamese families during the ultrasound experience are absent in "keepsake" ultrasound materials. But this is *not* the case for public health campaigns and advice provided during prenatal visits in the United States, where indeed the prospect of fetal abnormality is made to loom large for those who might indulge in inappropriate behaviors.

In the United States, individual mothers, through their individual choices, are understood to pose threats to the unborn baby. The "Mommy Don't" campaign, in which the fetus pleads to the pregnant woman not to smoke, drink alcohol, or use drugs, is but one such example (Landsman 2009: 23–39). In another example, "Maribel's Story," a fotonovela and flyer produced by the Food and Drug Administration, tells the tragic story of how eating Queso Fresco (a Mexican-style soft cheese popular among Latinas in the United States) made from unpasteurized milk led a pregnant woman, Maribel, to contract listeriosis, which harmed her unborn baby, leading to stillbirth. "All she wanted was to eat cheese that tasted like the kind made in Mexico," a character remarks as she relates the events, and warns that "eating Queso Fresco like we used to isn't worth the risk" (USFDA 2011).

While many recent public health campaigns are framed in terms of what one *should* do rather than on what one *shouldn't*, the implication is still that "the birth of a healthy (i.e., non-disabled) child is within the control of a woman who behaves appropriately and who seeks and complies with professional medical care during pregnancy" (Landsman 2009: 28). Women in the United States do envision babies with deformities, but largely do not envision them as their own. Such babies are imagined to be children born to ignorant or irresponsible women, to drug users, teenagers, or those without access to prenatal care.

The range of dos and don'ts during pregnancy is now quite extensive, and public health campaigns have been expanded to cover the period before pregnancy. The Centers for Disease Control and Prevention's preconception plan campaign asks women to "Show Your Love!" by a host of behaviors to be implemented *before* pregnancy, including to be active, take folic acid, avoid toxic chemicals at home and work, not use street drugs or prescription medications prescribed for others, stop partner violence and protect oneself from sexually transmitted diseases. Women who also dutifully follow medical advice *during* pregnancy to avoid alcohol, unpasteurized soft cheeses, fish containing high amounts of mercury, raw sprouts, excessive caffeine, illegal and prescription drugs, smoking, second-hand smoke, cat litter, exposure to insecticides and solvents, abusive relationships, hot baths, dental X-rays, etc., and who eat a "healthy" diet including vitamins with folic acid, and who utilize the increasing number of recommended routine prenatal screening tests and receive results which do not indicate birth defects, often believe that they have successfully secured the birth of a "normal" baby. Pregnant women and their families can then engage in ultrasound for fun, reassurance, entertainment, and bonding. Although requiring women to navigate through ever increasing amounts of information and dangers, the availability of prenatal testing, selective abortion, and expert knowledge regarding the impact of maternal behavior on pregnancy outcome continues to affect expectations that with responsible motherly diligence and self-sacrifice, the birth of a "perfect" child is attainable.

The flip side of this expectation is that for a woman in the United States encountering a diagnosis of disability for her child *after* it is born, prenatal diagnostic testing and public health information have placed an implicit responsibility on her, as an individual, for the child's disability. While for Vietnamese women, as Gammeltoft explains, the diagnosis of disability leads parents to the question "How must we have lived?" the question asked by an American woman is "What must I have done wrong?"

I conducted a study of 60 women in upstate New York encountering a diagnosis of disability for their child during newborn follow-up and evaluations for early intervention, observing evaluations, carrying out open-ended interviews within a month of the evaluation, and second interviews with one-third of the mothers a year later (Landsman 2009). In initial interviews I asked women to explain what brought them to have their child evaluated. While I never asked women about their prenatal consumption practices, almost all brought up the subject themselves. Most described reviewing their pregnancies after the diagnosis. Women recalled with precision exactly how and when they had failed, usually inadvertently, to comply with rules of vigilant consumption – an alcoholic drink at a party before knowing she was pregnant, taking one Tylenol, eating fast food, getting a vaccination prior to entering college without realizing she was pregnant at the time. But most women, after intense searching, could not locate any "failure" on their part; they faced the profound and confusing situation of having "done everything right" but still having a child diagnosed with a disability.

How does one make sense of this apparently incongruent outcome, one in which the personhood of the child and the motherhood of the woman are both diminished despite the latter's having exercised conscious control over her choices? Some mothers emplot their children's lives in a narrative of progress and of "developmental delay," a temporarily slower pace along a normal course (Landsman 2003, 2009). Many of these same women reframe uncertainty positively as open-ended futures, requesting information from medical professionals while nevertheless rejecting prognoses that predetermine final outcomes. They construct narratives of hope in which children overcome disability and become publicly valued as "miracle babies," "survivors," "fighters," and/or as children whose unique strengths are recognized by parents and in the future will come to prove doctors' dismal predictions wrong.

Studies of parents whose children receive positive findings during postnatal testing for genetic disorders suggest that such testing destabilizes previous expectations of a "perfect" baby, leading to uncertainty and heightened vigilance (Buchbinder and Timmermans 2011), but also provide similar accounts in which parents revalue that uncertainty, and as time goes on, weigh their own intimate, personalized knowledge of their child against knowledge based on diagnostic technologies (McLaughlin and Clavering 2012; McLaughlin 2014; Whitmarsh et al. 2007). After a diagnosis, parents often explore Internet sites where they find images of children with marked abnormalities, or may be put in touch with families whose children are visibly affected by the same condition. The implication that in the future their own child will look like that and less like themselves is disturbing, suggesting that the "similar and normal child is easier to place within the boundaries of what it is to be human and what it is to be a kinship member" (McLaughlin and Clavering 2012: 471). However, a test's definitive diagnosis does not equate to a definitive prognosis; it rarely can predict the course of disease or development for any individual child.

> While parents find that uncertainty frustrating, it is the presence of uncertainty throughout the diagnostic process which allows them, and others, to exercise their own judgment based on their position within kinship worlds. It is the uncertainty contained within the diagnostic process which enables all concerned to creatively engage with the child in such a way that escapes "fixing" her or him into the category of the "genetically other."
>
> *(McLaughlin and Clavering 2012: 471)*

Because correlation of postnatal genetic findings to current symptoms is weak, parents' relational understandings can encompass both the concept that the child's body is different from the norm, perhaps more similar to others than to biological kin, *and* that the body is still in process and the future open (McLaughlin 2014).

24.4   Therapeutic Technologies: Pillow Angels and Ransom Notes

As parents negotiate the meaning of a child's diagnosis and imagine a range of alternative outcomes, they often seek or are directed by early intervention programs and medical professionals toward treatments. Cure-seeking efforts however, do not preclude parents' rejection of the medical model that locates a deficit within the child. Thus, many North American mothers of disabled children appear to be paradoxically saying to their disabled child both "I love you the way you are," and "I would do anything to change you." How do parents engaged in such an enterprise give meaning to their efforts and make sense of their child's self?

Using archival data from two public controversies, interview data from my ethnographic study of 60 mothers of very young disabled children, and data I collected in interviews and focus groups of eight sets of parents of children diagnosed with and engaged in an intervention program for Asperger's syndrome, I explore competing public and family discourses on what constitutes the "true" self of a disabled child. (The newest version of the *Diagnostic and Statistical Manual of Mental Disorders*, the DSM V, released in May 2013, subsumes Asperger's syndrome under the umbrella term autism spectrum disorder.) Pseudonyms are used for interviewees.

24.4.1   Pillow Angels: Controversy over the Ashley Treatment

The "Ashley Treatment" is a combination of medical procedures performed at Seattle Children's Hospital on a profoundly disabled girl. Ashley is described by her parents as a "Pillow Angel," a well-loved sweet child who stays wherever they place her (Ashley's Mom and Dad 2007). In a summary diagram they present on their blog (www.pillowangel.org), "Pillow Angels" are presented as forming a new category of disability brought about by medical advancements enabling survival. Those in the new category are described as "permanently unabled," "profoundly dependent on their caregivers & profoundly precious to their families." Ashley is tube-fed. She does not speak, nor can she hold a toy or change position. Ashley's parents expressed concern that as Ashley got physically larger she would be more difficult to care for at home as well as to transport. Continued growth, they argued, would restrict her participation in family life. Ashley's mother sought interventions to arrest Ashley's adult height and weight, procedures that were approved by the hospitals' ethics committee.

Ashley's treatment became public when her doctors described it in a published article in which they also recommended that, after proper screening and informed consent, the therapy should be an option available to non-ambulatory children with severe, combined neurological and cognitive impairment (Gunther and Diekema 2006). High doses of estrogen closed Ashley's growth plates, which reduced her projected height by about 13 inches. For the purpose of eliminating menstruation and its associated discomfort, Ashley's uterus was surgically removed, although the hospital later acknowledged that in carrying out a hysterectomy on a developmentally disabled six-year-old without court authorization, it had violated state law. Ashley's breast buds were also surgically removed. Her parents reasoned that as their daughter would never breastfeed a baby, she had no need of breasts, and they projected that having large breasts (which run in the family) would be uncomfortable, especially when she is being secured with straps in a wheelchair. Additionally, Ashley's parents raised the issue that breasts, when touched while she was being moved or handled could "sexualize" the girl towards her caregiver.

In an email interview carried out over several weeks in 2012 for *The Guardian*, Ashley's father revealed that six other families who had been in touch with him and his wife had concluded similar treatments for their "pillow angels" in the last few years, and that at least as many treatments were in progress. A private "pillow angels quality of life support group" had formed to discuss the treatment and share ideas (Pilkington 2012). Parents in New Zealand also had the Ashley Treatment carried out on their daughter, Charley, and their story was documented on video for a New Zealand TV news show (TVNZ 2014). The interviewer noted that some would say that because of the treatment their daughter has "missed out on her right to be a fully grown woman"; Charley's mother responded, "She missed out on that the day she was born," seemingly equating woman-hood with cognitive status. As in the case with Ashley, the New Zealand parents frame the treatment as a way to keep their disabled child a par-ticipant in family life; as parents age, the growth attenuation treatment makes caring for her at home more feasible.

Regardless of stated intentions, as a result of the procedures, with the treatment, Ashley, like Charley, could now physically appear to be a child, her parents' "Pillow Angel," forever. In his interview with *The Guardian*, Ashley's father continued to refer to her in this way, stating that "Ashley's life may be very limited, *but like any baby*, novelty attracts her attention" (italics added).

Commentary after the publication of the Ashley Treatment exposed competing views of what constitutes being a good parent for a disabled child. Disability rights activist John Hockenberry (2007) argued that the treatment both violates the personhood of the child and voids the par-ental relationship:

> Regardless of their love and affection for their daughter their deci-sion to remove her breasts and uterus and maintain her in a state of pre-puberty is not a parental decision. It is more the kind of control one might enforce on a pet to manage the relationship. It is some-thing a farmer managing the productivity of his or her operation would naturally enforce on livestock. This would be done humanely, morally, and no-doubt with considerable tender affection and love for the subjects. There would be no outcry and no controversy, yet no one would confuse these acts of husbandry as parenthood.

A 20-person working group convened by the Hastings Center found some common ground in their appreciation that approaches that favor and those that oppose growth attenuation treatment each "support the child's flourishing within the family." But differences remained unresolved around a central issue.

> The differences within our working group relate to attitudes toward our own bodies and toward those of our children. Whereas some emphasize the moral importance of learning to accept our (and our children's) bodies as they are, others emphasize the moral importance of shaping our (and our children's) bodies to advance our (and their) interests.
>
> *(Wilford et al. 2010: 29)*

Neither adult nor child, before or after the treatment, Ashley seems to defy classification (Battles and Manderson 2008: 223), yet action was taken to reduce ambiguity. In response to criticism that the treatment assaults the dignity of disabled people, physician Gunther asked, "Is there more dignity in having to hoist a full-grown body in harness and chains from bed to bath to wheelchair?" "Ashley," Gunther argued, "will always have the mind of an infant, and now she will be able to stay where she belongs – in the arms of the family that loves her" (quoted in Gibbs 2007). While this presents as an affirmation of parental love and family life, underlying the question is the assumption that the combination of adulthood and cognitive impairment is inherently demeaning.

Bioethicist Peter Singer rejects the very premise of the debate over dignity. Three-month-old babies, he states, "are adorable but not dignified. Nor do I believe that getting bigger and older, while remaining at the same mental level, would do anything to change that" (Singer 2007). Ashley's parents agreed, and quote George Dvorsky (2006), a member of the Board of Directors for the Institute for Ethics and Emerging Technologies, who wrote on his own blog, "The estrogen treatment is not what is grotesque here. Rather, it is the prospect of having a full-grown and fertile woman endowed with the mind of a baby."

These positions contend that low cognitive function within an adult body precludes dignity. In their article, Ashley's parents state that given her mental age, "a 9 and a half year old body is more appropriate" and provides her not only more dignity but more "integrity than a full grown female body" (www.pillowangel.org). Framed within a medical model, the individual is here both the source of the problem and the site of intervention in pursuit of normalcy. In the diagram, under the heading of "Sizing for Wellness" is listed "Physical self closer to cognitive self." Through the "Ashley Treatment," body and mind are made to appear consistent with one another. Ashley's mind – the locus of self – cannot be brought to an adult level; in the next best approximation of normalcy, her body is medically and surgically altered to ensure its perpetual childlike appearance (Landsman 2009).

24.4.2   Ransom Notes: The Self As Hostage

While the Ashley Treatment makes body and mind consistent by implementing changes to the child's body, the New York University Child Study Center's short-lived Ransom Notes campaign seemed to suggest creating consistency of mind and body through changes to the child's *mind*. It played on a medical model discourse to which mothers are commonly exposed: that their child's true identity has tragically been trapped by a disability separate from the self.

The New York University Child Study Center's well-intentioned, but ultimately short-lived and demeaning 2007 campaign was intended to boost public awareness about children's untreated psychiatric disorders. Rates of diagnosis of behavioral, emotional, and neural developmental disorders have risen dramatically, with changing screening procedures and diagnostic criteria, in addition to increased prenatal exposure to various environmental toxins among possible factors (Halfon et al. 2012).

The New York University Child Study Center's ad campaign took the form of "ransom notes," in which disabilities were portrayed as kidnappers, holding children hostage. One ad ran "We have your son. We will make sure he will not be able to care for himself or interact socially as long as he lives. This is only the beginning." The note is signed "Autism." The text of another ad reads, "We are in possession of your son. We are making him squirm and fidget until he is a detriment to himself and those around him. Ignore this and your kid will pay … ADHD." Yet another states "We have your son. We are destroying his ability for social interaction and driving him into a life of complete isolation. It's up to you now … Asperger's Syndrome" (The Gimp Parade 2007).

The ad campaign, discontinued in response to criticism from both disability rights' and parents' organizations, had played on parents' fears and the notion that a normal child lies within or elsewhere, trapped and in need of rescue through strategies that intervene to return the child to normalcy. Such strategies would therefore result in the child's true self eventually becoming apparent in the body of the child they are currently raising.

Mothers of newly diagnosed children I interviewed did sometimes make reference to their hopes for "pulling" a child "out of autism." Mothers of the elementary school children with Asperger's syndrome enrolled in the treatment program suggested that they feel they *should* be able to separate their child's self from the impairment. Yet they clearly struggled with how to do so. Commenting on reading about Asperger's syndrome, with which her son was diagnosed, one mother said, "I was like 'yeah,

okay he does this and this.' Some eight-year-old kids do this and it is difficult sometimes to know what is the Asperger and what is Mark." Another
mother reflects, "There are some behaviors, I don't know whether it's just
an eight-year-old driving his mother nuts or if it's an Asperger's thing."
"I'm just trying to learn," explains another parent; "When do I say 'well
this is an Asperger's thing going on and we just need to do this differently
than other folks,' versus 'no, this is just an 11-year-old boy acting out or
whatever and we need to just react the way we would to any'? So, I'm not
sure how to do that."

Parents in the study consistently described the goal of treatment in
terms of providing strategies to make their child happier and able to be
a full participant in social life. As one mother describes, "Now is the time
that the kids are going to start picking and bullying and he gets so very
upset with that. He needs to learn how to handle himself, and like I said,
interacting with people would be a very big start." Billy's mother explains
through this story:

> Last Halloween he was phantom of the opera and so he had a phantom
> of the opera half mask but it covered both eyes and half his face.
> He was playing with some neighborhood kids and came in crying
> and wanted his mask. And I said – I got it out for him and I said,
> "What's the matter with you?" He said, "Oh, they're being mean to
> me." And I said "Then don't play with them anymore." "No, they're
> my friends." This is another thing; part of it is he'll do anything to
> have friends. He'll let them beat him up to be friends with him. Well,
> evidently, there was a toy gun and they kept holding it to his head
> saying they were going to shoot him in the head. Well, I said "you're
> not playing with them anymore." He wanted – his feelings – he was
> so upset that – but, he still wanted to play with them because they
> were his friends. Do you understand? But, he was crying so hard, he
> wanted the mask, so they wouldn't see him cry. That's when I called
> Andrea [a psychologist leading the group]. I'm like, "Help! I need help
> here." And I went into the school and I said, "don't you understand,
> this is what we're dealing with here? A kid that is so tortured and
> wants friends so bad but can't relate to them, that he would wear a
> mask so they won't see him cry."

This mother attempted to engage the school system, but to no avail.
"The school said it's not their problem … Academically – they said, if he's
doing fine academically, that's all they want to hear." This is a common
theme in mothers' stories. Changing other people seems daunting,
so attempting to change the child's abilities has, often with parents'
ambivalence and frustration, become the default position. As one mother
explained about what she hoped to get out of the therapy her son was
receiving, "I would like him to experience being able to meet someone

and talk or whatever. Just that part. In life you have to deal with people all the time and he needs those skills." Another similarly expressed a desire for her son to build social skills that would make his life easier.

> I just want him to be able to cope every day; be able to learn how to talk to people, you know. The personal space is a good one. He will learn how far to stand from someone. He will learn, you know, when some – how to hold a conversation, that type of thing. But, see, it doesn't work because he told us that himself.

Other mothers, explaining their goals for the program, similarly tempered their comments with awareness that the child him/herself could not be changed: "He has really no social clue. He gets it, but he doesn't internalize it. It's not in his hard wiring." A mother of a child who believes he is a firefighter, and goes to school each day dressed as one, tells this story:

> Now one of his meltdowns was he was in the garage playing with a little friend and he had closed the door because the trucks were back in the station so he closed the door on a little boy. Okay? And he didn't get hurt, but when I went out there to talk to him about it, I couldn't even talk to him. He was yelling – he was screaming at me because he was the captain of the station, I'm just a volunteer. "This is a paid fire department. You are a volunteer. You shouldn't even be here and besides I'm the captain and I decide when the door closes." I'm like "Stop, stop, this is reality here." He didn't get it. That's his reality.

"The thing is," another mother stated, "I can't change my son, I can only change how I deal with him."

In response to the New York University Ransom Notes Campaign, various groups issued statements of protest. The Autistic Self-Advocacy Network, which promotes the concept of neurodiversity, reprinted Jim Sinclair's statement:

> It is not possible to separate autism from the person. Therefore, when parents say, "I wish my child did not have autism," what they're really saying is, "I wish the autistic child I have did not exist and I had a different (non-autistic) child instead." Read that again. This is what we hear when you mourn over our existence. This is what we hear when you pray for a cure. This is what we know, when you tell us of your fondest hopes and dreams for us: that your greatest wish is that one day we will cease to be, and strangers you can love will move in behind our faces.

In seeking increased participation in treatment programs, the Ransom Notes Campaign bet on the assumption that parents would indeed hold to such desires of replacement. Yet parent blogs also buzzed with anger on just this point, and in response the ads were pulled in just over two weeks. Most parents I had interviewed, while engaging their child in therapies such as applied behavior analysis or dramatic play therapy, nevertheless also described their child's personality as inherently integrated with the autistic spectrum, and often, linked to an endearing uniqueness.

> Mark is very strong willed. He is messy. He is disorganized. I know that is Asperger, but it is also Mark.

> It wears me out. I wouldn't have it – I mean, would I have it any other way? I don't know. I can't imagine Billy any other way. I mean, Billy's just Billy.

> I think Asperger's *is* kind of his personality because listening to other parents I was like "wow! John is just like that!"

> It's really, when you first hear information like that, you're heart is – you know, the wind is really knocked out of your sails – but it's not so bad. I mean, he's my kid. Would I imagine him differently? I can't imagine him differently. Would I have asked for this? No, but, can I imagine him differently? I can't. You know, I'm getting all teary.

> What would he be like if those things were different? I do not think that a lot. Yeah, Yeah. You know, I'd like to see these things be easier for him, but would I take away the way that he loves to read and what he knows and how he memorizes things and that really awful third-grade sense of humor? No. The umpteenth Star Wars joke is okay. I mean that's my kid.

> Rather than think about what would he be like if he didn't have this, I just accept that, well, he does have it and this is the way he is, and this is – and it's not as if he has a disorder that could be magically lifted away to reveal some different boy because that's not – that's a part of his personality. This isn't something like your hair is dyed green, but it will grow out and your own self will be revealed. This is him. I mean his hair *is* green.

Parents have access to a variety of public discourses on the relation of body, mind, disability, and self with which to make sense of their child. The Ashley Treatment presumes the possibility that a body may inaccurately represent the mind it contains; the proposed treatment rectifies this by replacing a changing, growing body with a body that is, presumably like Ashley's true self, perpetually childlike. The Ransom Note Campaign on the other hand presupposes that a child's body may contain within it an inaccurate representation of the child's self. The treatment encouraged by the campaign would therefore have parents replace the disabled mind with the child's "true" self currently held hostage by the disability.

In pursuing or accepting therapeutic interventions for children with cognitive and behavioral differences, parents see themselves as taking pragmatic action but do not necessarily believe that there is an objective deficit that lies within the child that can or should be cured. Rather many recognize a child whose self is inherently integrated with disability but living in a world in which such a child is at a painful disadvantage. The perspective revealed in parents' narratives is that "good" parents take action to reduce that disadvantage.

24.5 Assistive Technologies: Connectivity and Assemblages

So how are good parents to proceed? Therapeutic technologies and treatments like those described above represent attempts to intervene directly in the physical and behavioral processes of the disabled child; disabled bodies and minds are seen as anomalous, yet to some extent "fixable," i.e., able to be made to appear or act more "normal." For children with physical disabilities, traditional treatments have been conducted under the "assumption that a reduction in impairment necessarily equates to improved quality of life" (Gibson and Teachman 2012: 474), and with a clinical focus on either repairing the biological body and/or helping the child to adapt to the environment through maximizing what abilities remain (2012: 476). Physical therapy's traditional approach thus sought to normalize movement patterns by changing the child. This perspective, however, coexists with a trend in rehabilitation therapies toward modifying factors that are *external* to the child as a means for achieving successful movement (Wiart and Darrah 2002: 492). Parents negotiate both these perspectives as they engage with assistive technologies for their child.

First encounters with such technologies are often with manufacturers' websites or literature obtained from physicians and therapists. Critical discourse analysis of promotional materials for hearing aids and for robotic gait training technologies designed to help children attain a gait pattern approximating normal, "reproduce powerful discourses ... that define what counts as failure or success, inclusion or exclusion, and normal and abnormal" (Phelan, Wright and Gibson 2014: 1076), and reinforce perceptions of self as Other. Materials incorporate pictures of mothers with children, representing societal expectations that good parents work toward goals of normalization (Phelan, Wright and Gibson 2014).

Some mothers in my study of newly diagnosed infants and toddlers referenced materials they had read on brain plasticity, seeing themselves as "synapse builders" who could help a child with developmental delay catch up or at least mitigate disability through therapies and hard work (Landsman 2003, 2009). Many mothers expressed the view that there was a limited window of time in which to make positive changes in the child, and that it was their job to do so. Relating a doctor's visit, a mother explained:

> He said, everything that you're ever going to do to change what he is, is going to be done within the next five years ... he said, your brain and my brain, your information goes from A to B. He said Joey's brain, it goes from A to X to J, then maybe to B ... and ... it may never go A to B, but you can shorten it, and he said that can only happen between now and the age of five, so I was like, geez. You don't give me a lot of time to fix it. You could spend the first six months figuring it all out.

Parents generally attributed improvements to the mother's faith that her child could still change and her commitment of time and energy, often with the help of therapists, in working toward that outcome. For parents and therapists working with children with mobility impairments, independent walking in particular has been a high priority goal. In this view, then, adoption of certain assistive technologies – a power wheelchair, for instance – represents failure, an inability to bring the child to a state of "normal." Perhaps the most publically recognizable signifier of disability, a power wheelchair marks a child as deficient and permanently "less." It is the technology of last resort, for use only when hope of walking has faded.

My youngest daughter, DJ, has cerebral palsy (CP), significantly affecting her gross and fine motor skills, as well as her speech. Years ago, as she was preparing to enter kindergarten, I took her to a rehabilitation hospital to be evaluated for a manual wheelchair. Over the course of the afternoon, every component of the emerging chair – tires, wheel rims, hand rims, frame, brakes, armrests, foot plates, lateral supports, elements of the seating system, angles at which components would be placed, etc. – was selected specifically so as to create a chair that was as maneuverable by her as possible; even so, DJ was able to move the chair only a few inches at a time, and unevenly at that. The wheelchair specialist turned to me and asked why I was getting my daughter a manual chair instead of a power chair. I suspect I answered in terms of wanting her to retain and develop her strength and independence. The rehab specialist then responded with what I experienced as a haunting accusation: "*You* don't use every ounce of your energy to get across the room, why should *she*?" To this I had no good answer, only additional, unvoiced questions: who and what was this wheelchair about? What should a "good" mother do?

Now 23 years old, my daughter DJ loves that story. She, like other children and young adults with cerebral palsy, is aware of the symbolic value walking holds in our culture, but does not necessarily subscribe to it herself. During a presentation she gave at a health sciences class at a local college, she was asked if it bothered her that she could not walk; I awaited her answer with intrigue. Her response, slowly and painstakingly spelled out on her augmentative communication device, was simply "I have always had CP." In short, for her there is no sense of loss. Not walking is not particularly tragic, but rather quite ordinary. By the same token, she recognizes that had she been a different person, a person who had previously walked independently, she might experience not being able to walk quite differently.

Many parents fear that powered mobility will impede development of a child's independent walking skills (Burne and Breaux 2013; Wiart and Darrah 2002; Wiart et al. 2004), and like me, postpone the purchase. A study of Canadian children's and parents' beliefs regarding the value of walking revealed that children with CP regarded walking primarily as exercise rather than as functional; for their parents, on the other hand, a reduction in interventions directed toward independent walking provoked feelings of guilt for abandoning hope (Gibson et al. 2011). In an article in a magazine marketed to parents of disabled children, the authors acknowledge that to parents "the wheelchair itself may represent a sense of 'giving up' or a reliance on technology that is not wanted" (Burne and Breaux 2013: 32). The power wheelchair suggests not just the child's lack of linear progress toward the desired goal of independent walking, but a parent's *own* failure to maintain hope for "independent" mobility. Over time, powered mobility may be reinterpreted as just a different route to a child's independence. And it may also, as I discuss below, open opportunities for transforming meanings of dependence and independence, and indeed, of the relations of technology and personhood with disability.

My daughter now has her power wheelchair. She is in the chair when she attends classes at community college, and when she goes to the movies or bowling with friends. She sits in it as she controls her communication device through the same joystick that controls the power chair's movement. Absent technical glitches, no one need push it for her. In this sense, it offers independence. But she also sits in a *manual* chair when using her laptop computer where she types with an adapted keyboard resting on the attached tray. She is often not in any chair at all, and "knee walks" around the house; she also does Zumba at the YMCA and dances to music at home or in other settings on her knees. When we are traveling, DJ is in a special stroller that can fold and fit into the trunk of a taxicab. During physical therapy DJ may walk supported by a sling and metal frame in a gait trainer or with the smaller "Rifton TRAM" device. Perhaps the most often used means of her movement, other than knee walking, is assisted walking with someone supporting her from behind; I usually put my arms under her armpits and lean in with my left shoulder to support and stabilize her, but each carer – family members or various aides or a friend – will position themselves in whatever way works best for them in the situation in which they find themselves. Many configurations allow for mobility.

The choice of which particular combination of assistive technologies and bodies to form is contextual and collaboratively reached based on a range of issues including accessibility of the particular space, the weather, parking, terrain, purpose of the activity, a judgment of what is publicly acceptable in the setting, and a particular carer's comfort level and training. My daughter, her assistive technologies, her parents, and her aides thus move into and out of various "assemblages" in ways that Gibson, Carnevale and King (2012) argue trouble our dichotomies of independence/dependence, normal/disabled, and challenge our concept of the bounded, autonomous self.

Through a case study of a 12-year-old girl, "Mimi," and her mother, they explore two such assemblages – Mimi/wheelchair, and Mimi/mom/ (dad). Mimi breathes with a tracheotomy tube and ventilator and receives nutrition through a gastronomy tube. Her mother provides most of the assistance with activities of daily living. Elsewhere, Gibson (2006) analyzes three other examples – man–dog, man–machine, and woman–woman–man "connectivities" – as a means to reframe as connection what has usually been interpreted as dependencies inherent in the disability experience. In the case of Mimi (and, I would argue, my daughter), "assistive technologies and her parents can be viewed as assemblages of bodies/technologies/subjectivities that together achieve a set of practices" (Gibson, Carnevale and King 2012: 1894). When Mimi expresses concern about how students in the high school she is soon to attend will respond to her wheelchair, she explains that "It is just part of me," and "This is what makes me me" (2012: 1896). The authors argue that rather than considering her wheelchair to be a technology that is added to an essential self, Mimi understands that her " 'technobody' is one variant in an array of bodily configurations that is part of the human condition" (2012: 1896).

As the authors explain, there is also a mom/Mimi assemblage that is more maneuverable in some settings, and although disabling in some ways to the mother, it enables Mimi's mother to have her daughter at home instead of an institution and thereby to "do family" (2012: 1897). By examining these couplings, they argue, we can see at work a kind of confusion of boundaries in which the body is never complete and bounded. The "valorization of independence" in both the rehabilitation profession and North American life "has as its starting point the assumption that we are separate and distinct from other beings and things" (2012: 1895). In the assemblages they describe in Mimi's life, in which Mimi and her mother are not only interdependent but in which their selves merge and disconnect, in turn connecting to other selves and machines, there are not clear distinctions between persons or between persons and technologies.

The typical trajectory expected by a Western parent is to nurture a child from total dependence to eventual autonomy and independence. Rehabilitation therapies, educational systems, and media encourage families of disabled children to judge the latter developmental outcome a success, and indeed, to seek to emulate this trajectory even if travel along it is delayed or temporarily rerouted. In an article focusing on families of learning-disabled children, Rapp and Ginsburg (2011) note that experience of family life with disability "reverberates" through the life cycle. Children with learning disabilities "stay young" longer and so too their parents do not move through the normal domestic life cycle with the same rhythm and choices; for instance they may spend hours helping with or supervising their teenager's homework in a way that would typically be done with younger students (2011: 386), or adjust their work schedules and career decisions around different childcare responsibilities and acquired disability expertise and commitment to advocacy.

For children with profound disabilities and their parents, however, I suggest that the trajectory of child rearing may not only be different from the norm in its pacing and choices. The intimate engagement with assistive technologies and with other bodies lends itself, over time, to the kind of reimagining of dependency as connectivity proposed by Gibson and her colleagues, and indeed to a blurring of boundaries that challenges concepts of bounded selves.

As an example, I again use my daughter DJ, who requires assistance with all activities of daily living; someone must feed her, dress her, bathe her, brush her teeth and her hair, put her on the toilet, and wipe her after a bowel movement. These caring responsibilities for a 23-year-old now seem routine, and although time-consuming and constraining, otherwise unremarkable. That was not always the case. When DJ started menstruating, my husband felt unsure and "on new ground" caring for her; I recall with laughter his confusion that "the blood doesn't stop even after I wipe!" He has long since crossed a gendered boundary and ventured into what was then new territory, one in which physical contact is far greater and modesty far less than he could ever imagine with our older daughter. However, as 12-year-old Mimi reminds us, the need for assistance, whether in the form of technology or people, is part of the human condition. "I'm normal," she is recorded saying. "Treat me the same. We're all human. We can all get hurt" (Gibson, Carnevale and King 2012: 1896).

Over time my husband and I have watched DJ develop her own criteria for categories of people who can, without intrusion upon her sense of modesty or privacy, see her naked, take her to the bathroom, and/or feed her, and those who cannot. She understands that her categories do not coincide with those of typical others, and when training new aides will always reassure them about what does and does not bother her. When the mother of DJ's best friend asked to learn how to take her to the bathroom, DJ without apparent second thought agreed; she could now sleep over at the friend's house, an advantage that for all participants outweighed any other considerations. Yet in truth it seems other considerations were not weighed at all. To value exclusively autonomous or independent forms of participation denies the variability of participation preferences that exist among disabled people (Mirza, Magasi and Hammel 2016).

Disability makes more visible the situational permeability of bodily boundaries. In writing about my two daughters at DJ's senior solo dance performance at a historic local theater, a newspaper sports reporter used the analogy of teammates. In the article he explains how DJ's older sister Jessie had always assisted DJ in ballet class; when Jessie left home, mom took over in classes but Jessie always returned, learning the dance on the fly in order to perform with DJ on stage. Posting a video of the dance, he also writes about the sisters' last ever performance together, Jessie's twentieth appearance on stage, and DJ's fifteenth.

> With Jessie supporting under her arms or around her waist, D.J. is able to move, to glide, to dance in ways she can do by herself only in her head. They have done this for years, but the routine of all the routines doesn't make them any less of a remarkable tandem …
>
> The simple act of lifting her clasped hands above her head is a chore; she will use her left hand, the one she has the most control over, to lift and guide her right. But there she is, her sister by her side, in front of more than a thousand. The passion makes all the necessary effort worthwhile.
>
> Then you think of the sister on stage with her, and how theirs is a story of teammates accomplishing something stunning that neither could do on their own. The Reinhardts represent why it's vital for any team in or out of sports to trust and support each other – in this case physically as much as metaphorically.
>
> *(McGuire 2011)*

The reporter identifies the DJ/sister assemblage not in terms of dependency, but of connectivity; the sisters ("teammates") accomplish something neither could do alone. However, some assemblages are better received than others. During interviews mothers of infants who used visible technologies reported stares and feelings of accusation. A mother of premature twins explained how when she takes her daughter, whose head is partially shaved and has an nasogastric tube (used for feeding) taped on her face, out in public people "gawk" and ask what's wrong. "What do you tell those people?" I asked her. "I always say 'there's nothing wrong with her. She had brain surgery the other day.'" Another mother, whose child had a shunt inserted to drain fluid in the brain, described her husband's suggested response to the frustrating stares and questions about what's wrong with their daughter: "Say 'skiing accident.'" Sarcastic responses are one among many strategies by which parents resist the negative connotations of the infant/medical technology assemblage that to strangers reads as defect.

Another example is alternative and augmentative communication (AAC) devices, intended to enable people without speech or whose speech is unintelligible to communicate independently. People may access a device through direct selection (touch), switch, joystick, head pointer, or eye gaze. However, using a high-tech speech-generating device, especially for a person with motor control difficulties, is substantially slower than a typical person using natural speech. As mobility with a power wheelchair may violate norms of independence, communication using AAC devices may violate temporal norms. The standard wait time provided to a student to answer a question in school is less than one second (Keene 2014: 68). In typical conversations if wait time is much longer than that, the listener may assume the AAC user does not know the answer, or that the person is cognitively impaired; in such cases, the interlocutor will often speak in exaggerated, simplified "baby" talk or turn their attention to another person.

Paterson (2012) describes situations in which the communication partner attempts to anticipate what the speech-impaired person attempts to say, when s/he in fact does not know. The conversation goes awry, not because the partner can't understand, but because "the interlocutor is policed by temporal norms of communication into declining to take the time to ascertain what is being said" (2012: 170). Parents have similarly described as a major barrier and "worst scenario" that communication partners just walk away while a child is still preparing a message (McNaughton et al. 2008). To alert a communication partner that she is actually engaged in the conversation, my daughter has programmed a button on her device to speak the sentence "Please wait while I type." Nevertheless, many speakers are uncomfortable with silence and will fill wait time by carrying on separate conversations while she completes her message.

A panel of AAC users was held as a pre-conference session of the International Society of Augmentative and Alternative Communication (ISAAC) conference I attended in Pittsburgh in 2012. The audience members were knowledgeable and interested in AAC. Nevertheless, while some panelists were still preparing responses to the first question, audience members asked new questions from the floor and conversed. By the time a panelist had prepared a comment on their device, the response was no longer relevant; the conversation had moved on. Device users appeared out of sync with natural speakers, and the conventions of normal conversational turn-taking proceeded among speakers to the exclusion of those who used devices. The disabled person/AAC device assemblage, theoretically functional, was nevertheless devalued and marginalized.

Paterson argues that everyday "codes of conduct" have proscribed schedules and rhythms that inherently disadvantage the speech-impaired person. As independence is valorized in Western society, so too is speed. In a situation in which a speech-impaired person attempts a conversation with an unfamiliar interlocutor, the latter, Paterson claims, takes for granted that a conversation will be an inefficient use of time. "The person with speech impairment *disappears* for the stranger because they are a 'waste of time' and the person with speech impairment 'dys-appears' (for themselves) because they are in an immanent moment of obvious and palpable exclusion in which their social worth has been denied" (2012: 169). "Dys-appearance" is used by Paterson to refer to moments when the impaired body is "stunned into its own recognition" by disablism (2012: 165). These are also the moments when parents of speech-impaired children step in to repair the conversation, often "translating" for their children or filling the gaps with other, perhaps unrelated conversations to keep the attention of the interlocutor while the child formulates a response on a device; in such a way a parent attempts to head off both the child's disappearance for the stranger and its dys-appearance for the child him/herself.

It is perhaps not surprising then, that research suggests that making AAC more successful requires not only efforts aimed at the individual with speech impairment, but at communication partners. This might include, for instance, providing classmates strategies for initiating and responding to communicative attempts by AAC users (Calculator and Black 2009), encouraging understandings by typical peers of the barriers of AAC communication and of how AAC systems work (King and Fahsl 2012), creating tools that help neurotypical "children to approach their autistic peers in 'autistically appropriate' ways" (Mankoff, Hayes and Kasnitz 2010: 6), and promoting multimodal communication (King and Fahsl 2012). Of critical importance is to teach communication partners to increase wait time (Kent-Walsh and McNaughton 2005; Mathis, Sutherland and McAuliffe 2011), thereby helping to subvert the temporal norms of communication that are, as Paterson reminds us, informed by non-impaired carnality.

If communication is indeed a process during which partners continually influence each other (Kent-Walsh and McNaughton 2005), the successes and limitations of communication technology is a useful site to examine the implications of our concept of the bounded self. Expansion of the speech-impaired person/AAC assemblage to include the human communication partner recognizes the porousness of selves, and the consequences of making, and of all too often failing to make, connectivities. Regardless of whether a device is used, it takes time and effort to understand those with speech impairment, as it does for those with speech difference to communicate. Communication in such a situation is an act of interdependence. "What more precious resources do we need and offer than time and effort?" ask Kasnitz and Block (2012: 198).

Many individuals who appear "dependent" on AAC choose not to utilize their devices at home or with friends, family or carers who understand their speech. Some use what anthropologist Devva Kasnitz terms "revoicing," as she does in conference presentations (Kasnitz and Block 2012). My daughter and I instinctively developed a similar process, in which she speaks, looks to me and waits while I speak (revoice) what I believe she has said, then either verifies my understanding by continuing to speak or lets me know I have misunderstood. In the latter case, she repeats or provides "clues" by offering a different word, spelling, or gesture until I show I understand and have revoiced it for others to hear. I am struck by how often people are surprised at my ability to understand my daughter and by what she has said. Given her anomalous appearance and the time and energy required of both of us to engage in conversation, revoicing establishes what is not immediately obvious to others – her full personhood and her identity as someone with something to say.

When speaking with a human helper, "the two are a duet. The speech-impaired person articulates *with* the helper," explain Kasnitz and Block (2012: 203). Technologies that would incorporate into a portable device the specific expertise of such human helpers are being explored. For example, one device currently being developed is called Talkitt. It is calibrated by recording a sound made by the speech-impaired person, which is then associated by a carer with the text intended by the speaker and typed into a device. When spoken again, the unintelligible vocal pattern would be recognized by the device, and its meaning, previously translated by the caregiver, spoken aloud by text-to-speech technology (Rubin, personal communication 2015). A variety of barriers remain to the success of such a device for a wide range of people, particularly for those whose speech is inconsistent, but the concept is an intriguing attempt to develop the ability to carry in a machine the specific knowledge gleaned from a longstanding human relationship. For some it promises independence in communication while also suggesting acknowledgment of connectivities as a disabled person/technology/carer assemblage comes into being.

24.6 Conclusions

Underlying the relationship of childhood disability and technology are questions of kinship and belonging. Technology can reveal, celebrate, and share family resemblances and connections. But when birth goes awry and a diagnosis of disability is made, mothers in the United States bear ultimate and individual responsibility. A disabled baby in the United States is the embodiment not just of its parents' kin relations, but of its mother's choices.

Having brought into the world a child judged as less than a full person, a mother may acknowledge the loss of experience of what many define as "real" motherhood. But what is at stake is less her own place within a web of kinship, than that of her child's. When asked what were their greatest fears for their disabled child, most mothers in my study of newly diagnosed children responded not in terms of whether their child would be cured, but whether they would experience love, family, and social acceptance. Would the child marry, they wondered. Would they get to create their own family, or would they spend a life alone? Thus begins for many parents the struggle to establish and sustain the personhood of their child, the public recognition of the child as having social value and as worthy, now and in the future, of membership in family and community.

Therapeutic interventions directed at factors internal to the child are for many parents the default mode of action in this struggle. They attempt to fix the child to fit expectations of normalcy, whether a match of physical and mental "selves," or the ability to mimic socially appropriate behavior or movement patterns. Although the purpose of asserting a child's personhood may be to assure their participation in social life and ideally to reproduce family, the expected route to do so in the United States, perhaps ironically, is by moving the child toward independence and autonomy. With varying levels of success, assistive technologies and human connections are explored and utilized by families working toward reaching these goals. In that process, however, new possibilities can be found for reframing disability, self, and personhood. A child's use of an augmentative communication device or a power wheelchair can variously be understood as a means of achieving independence, a parent's giving up hope for their child to ever do so, or a reframing of norms of communication and mobility in an embrace of the variety of possible configurations of human forms.

There is no one approach to technology and disability taken by parents or by members of the disability community. There is, for example, currently debate over changing the universal blue and white accessibility logo from an icon of a person sitting in wheelchair to a more dynamic image of a person leaning forward and actively wheeling him/herself. The debate reflects concern with the stigma of disability and its associated technology around the twin American values of independence and speed. The goal of the changed logo is to shift from an image of dependency to independent agency; the new person/wheelchair icon reflects movement and speed. Does this help destigmatize disability as a whole, or does it continue to valorize independence and speed, further marginalizing those whose lives, marked by assistive technologies, appear deficient by such standards? The debate over the effect of the new icon is not only about the role of symbols in perceptions, but about the varied meanings of the relationship of personhood, technology, and disability.

Technology, which affects the prevalence of, and blame for, childhood disability, also provides tools used by parents in attempts to normalize disabled children and help ensure them a place in the world. But intimate interconnections among technologies, disabled children, and human carers also provide opportunities to transform families' experiences of childhood disability, and may come to affect our very definitions of disability and our conceptions of what it means to be human.

References

Ashley's Mom and Dad. 2007, updated 2012. "The Ashley Treatment, Towards a Better Quality of Life for Pillow Angels." www.pillowangel. org, accessed June 1, 2015.

Battles, Heather and Lenore Manderson. 2008. "The Ashley Treatment: Furthering the Anthropology of/on Disability." *Medical Anthropology* 27(3): 219–226.

Buchbinder, Mara and Stefan Timmermans. 2011. "Medical Technologies and the Dream of the Perfect Newborn." *Medical Anthropology* 30(1): 56–80.

Burne, Brian and Becky Breaux. May 2013. "Power Wheelchairs: Young Children." *EP Magazine*, 32–34.

Calculator, Stephen and Tibbany Black. 2009. "Validation of an Inventory of Best Practices in the Provision of Augmentative and Alternative Communication Services to Students with Severe Disabilities in General Education Classrooms." *American Journal of Speech-Language Pathology* 18: 329–342.

Dvorsky, G. 2006. "Helping Families Care for the Helpless." http:// sentientdevelopments.blogspot.com/2006/11helping-families-care-for-helpless_06.html, accessed June 26, 2007.

Gammeltoft, Tine. 2008. "Childhood Disability and Parental Moral Responsibility in Northern Vietnam: Towards Ethnographies of Intercorporeality." *Journal of the Royal Anthropological Institute* 14(4): 826–842.

    2014. *Haunting Images: A Cultural Account of Selective Reproduction in Vietnam.* Berkeley, CA: University of California Press.

Gibbs, N. January 2007. "Pillow Angel Ethics." *Time Magazine Online.* http://content.time.com/time/nation/article/0,8599,1574851,00.html, accessed April 4, 2007.

Gibson, Barbara. 2006. "Disability, Connectivity and Transgressing the Autonomous Body." *Journal of Medical Humanities* 27: 187–196.

Gibson, Barbara, Franco Carnevale and Gillian King. 2012. "This Is My Way: Reimagining Disability, In/dependence and Interconnectedness of Persons and Assistive Technologies." *Disability and Rehabilitation* 34(2): 1894–1899.

Gibson, Barbara and Gail Teachman. 2012. "Critical Approaches in Physical Therapy Research: Investigating the Symbolic Value of Walking." *Physiotherapy Theory and Practice* 28(6): 474–484.

Gibson, B. P., G. Teachman, V. Wright, D. Fehlings, N. I. Young and P. McKeever. 2011. "Children's and Parent's Beliefs Regarding the Value of Walking: Rehabilitation Implications for Children with Cerebral Palsy." *Child Care, Health and Development* 38(1): 61–69.

Gimp Parade. 2007. The Ransom Notes Campaign. http://thegimpparade. blogspot.com/2007/12/ransom-notes-campaign.html, accessed December 24, 2007.

Gunther, D. F. and D. S. Diekema. 2006. "Attenuating Growth in Children with Profound Developmental Disability: A New Approach to an Old Dilemma." *Archives of Pediatrics and Adolescent Medicine* 160(10): 1013–1017.

Halfon, Neal, Amy Houtrow, Kandyce Larson and Paul Newacheck. 2012. "The Changing Landscape of Disability in Childhood." *The Future of Children* 22(1): 13–42.

Hockenberry, John. 2007. "Ashley X: Straight on til Mourning." Posted on The Gimp Parade, February 23, 2007. http://thegimpparade.blogspot. com/2007/02/Saturday-slumgullion-29.html, accessed June 29, 2007.

Ivry, Tsipy. 2009. "The Ultrasonic Picture Show and the Politics of Threatened Life." *Medical Anthropology Quarterly* 23(3): 189–211.

Ivry, Tsipy, Elly Teman and Ayala Frumkin. 2011. "God-sent Ordeals and Their Discontents: Ultra-orthodox Jewish Women Negotiate Prenatal Testing." *Social Science & Medicine* 72: 1527–1533.

Kasnitz, Devva and Pamela Block. 2012. "Participation, Time, Effort, and Speech Disability Justice." In *Politics of Occupation-Centered Practice: Reflections on Occupational Engagement across Cultures*, ed. Nick Pollard and Dikaios Sakellariou, 197–216. Chichester: Wiley-Blackwell.

Keene, Ellin. 2014. "All the Time They Need." *Educational Leadership* 72(3): 64–71.

Kent-Walsh, Jennifer and David McNaughton. 2005. "Communication Partner Instruction on AAC: Present Practices and Future Directions." *Augmentative and Alternative Communication* 21(3): 195–204.

King, Amie and Allison Fahsl. 2012. "Supporting Social Competence in Children Who Use Augmentative and Alternative Communication." *Teaching Exceptional Children* 45(1): 42–49.

Landsman, Gail. 2003. "Emplotting Children's Lives: Developmental Delay vs Disability." *Social Science & Medicine* 56: 1947–1960.

2009. *Reconstructing Motherhood and Disability in the Age of Perfect Babies.* New York: Routledge.

Liptap, Amanda. http://peek3d.com/category/testimonial, accessed April 4, 2015.

Mankoff, Jennifer, Gillian Hayes and Devva Kasnitz. 2010. "Disability Studies As a Source of Critical Inquiry for the Field of Assistive Technology." *Proceedings of the 12th International ACM SIGACCESS Conference on Computers and Accessibility* 2010: 3–10.

McGuire, Mark. 2011. "They're the Ultimate Teammates." *Albany Times Union.* www.timesunion.com/sports/article/They-re-the-ultimate-teammates-1412561.php, accessed June 9, 2011.

McLaughlin, Janice. 2014. "Digital Imagery and Child Embodiment in Paediatric Genetics: Sources and Relationships of Meaning." *Sociology* 48(2): 216–232.

McLauglin, Janice and Emma Clavering. 2012. "Visualising Difference, Similarity and Belonging in Paediatric Genetics." *Sociology of Health Illness* 34(3): 459–474.

McNaughton, David, Tracy Rackensperger, Elizabeth Bender Wood, Carole Krezman, Michael Williams and Janice Light. 2008. " 'A Child Needs to Be Given a Chance to Succeed': Parents of Individuals Who Use AAC Describe the Benefits and Challenges of Learning AAC Technologies." *Augmentative and Alternative Communication* 24(1): 43–55.

Mathis, Hilary, Dean Sutherland and Megan McAuliffe. 2011. "The Effect of Pause Time upon the Communicative Interactions of Young People Who Use Augmentative and Alternative Communication." *International Journal of Speech-Language Pathology* 13(5): 411–421.

Mirza, Mansha, Susan Magasi and Joy Hammel. 2016. "Soul Searching Occupations: Critical Reflections on Occupational Therapy's Commitment to Social Justice, Disability Rights, and Participation." In *Occupying Disability: Critical Approaches to Community, Justice, and Decolonizing Disability*, ed. Pamela Block, Devva Kasnitz, Akemi Nishida and Nick Pollard, 159–174. Heidelberg: Springer.

Paterson, Kevin. 2012. "It's About Time! Understanding the Experience of Speech Impairment." In *Routledge Handbook of Disability Studies*, ed. Nick Watson, Alan Roulstone and Carol Thomas, 165–177. London: Routledge.

Phelan, Sharon, Virginia Wright and Barbara Gibson. 2014. "Representations of Disability and Normality in Rehabilitation Technology Promotional Materials." *Disability and Rehabilitation* 36(24): 2072–2079.

Pilkington, Ed. 15 Mar. 2012. "The Ashley Treatment: 'Her Life Is As Good As We Can Possibly Make It.'" *The Guardian.* www.theguardian.com/society/2012/mar/15/ashley-treatment-email-exchange, accessed June 1, 2015.

Rapp, Rayna and Faye Ginsburg. 2011. "Reverberations: Disability and the New Kinship Imaginary." *Anthropological Quarterly* 86(2): 379–410.

Singer, Peter. 26 Jan. 2007. "A Convenient Truth" [Op-Ed]. *The New York Times.*

State of Connecticut. 2009. "Governor Rell Signs Bill Limiting Obstetric Ultrasounds to Medically Necessary Procedures," June 24. www.ct.gov/governorrell/cwp/view.asp?A=3675&Q=442298&pp=12&n=1, accessed June 2, 2015.

Timmermans, Stefan and Mara Buchbinder. 2010. "Patients-in Waiting: Living between Sickness and Health in the Genomics Era." *Journal of Health and Social Behavior* 51(4): 408–423.

TVNZ. 2014. "Charley Girl." http://tvnz.co.nz/sunday-news/charley-girl-video-5974811, accessed June 1, 2015.

US Food and Drug Administration. 2011. "Maribel's Story: How Eating Queso Fresco Harmed Her Unborn Baby." www.fda.gov/Food/FoodborneIllnessContaminants/PeopleAtRisk/ucm106727.htm, accessed June 2, 2015.

   2014. "Avoid Fetal Keepsake Images," Heartbeat Monitors. www.fda.gov/ForConsumers/ConsumerUpdates/ucm095508.htm, accessed June 2, 2015.

Whitmarsh, Ian, Arlene Davis, Debra Skinner and Donald Bailey, Jr. 2007. "A Place for Genetic Uncertainty: Parents Valuing an Unknown in the Meaning of Disease." *Social Science & Medicine* 65: 1082–1093.

Wiart, L. and J. Darrah. 2002. "Changing Philosophical Perspectives on the Management of Children with Physical Disabilities: Their Effect on the Use of Powered Mobility." *Disability and Rehabilitation* 24(9): 492–498.

Wiart, Lesley, Johanna Darrah, Vivien Hollis, Al Cook and Laura May. 2004. "Mothers' Perceptions of Their Children's Use of Powered Mobility." *Physical Occupational Therapy in Pediatrics* 24(4): 3–21.

Wilford, Benjamin, Paul Steven Miller, Carolyn Korfiatis, Douglas Diekema, Denise Dudzinski, Sara Goering, and the Seattle Growth Attenuation and Ethics Working Group. 2010. "Navigating Growth Attenuation in Children with Profound Disabilities: Children's Interests, Family Decision-Making, and Community Concerns." *Hastings Center Report* 40(6): 27–40.

Wise, Paul. 2012. "Emerging Technologies and Their Impact on Disability." *The Future of Children* 22(1): 169–191.

25

Paid and Unpaid Labor: Pregnancy and Surrogacy in Anthropological Studies of Reproduction

Tsipy Ivry and Elly Teman[1]

25.1 Introduction

What would the sight of premature babies in their incubators at the NICU (Neonatal Intensive Care Unit) raise in a pregnant woman toward the end of term: anxiety about premature birth? A plea for the well-being of her unborn baby? Hopes for a safe delivery? While the latter surfaced among the women who participated in the "guided tour of delivery rooms" documented by one of us in 2001 in a Jerusalem hospital (Ivry 2010a), it was one woman's cynical response that captured our attention and became an entry point into our 15-year-long conversation about the meaning of metaphorical cross-references between pregnancy and surrogacy in Israel and beyond.

The "guided tour of delivery rooms" was organized by a childbirth instructor, whom we call Ruth, as part of a "childbirth preparation course" that she taught. After a lengthy exploration of the birthing rooms and the procedures surrounding hospital birth, Ruth took the expectant parents to the NICU, just across the corridor, to assure them that lest any problem arises with a newborn baby, the medical team can respond immediately because of the NICU's proximity. While the pregnant women and their partners were looking around at the beeping, wired incubators amazed by the tiny preemies they held, she remarked: "A day in the NICU costs $20,000. It is good to have national health insurance (to pay for it)." Tsila, a pregnant woman accompanied by her husband, responded cynically: "Can you imagine the state paying us $20,000 for every day of gestation?"

Tsila's sardonic remark illustrates how surrogacy can become a useful metaphor for thinking about "normal" pregnancy. The sight of incubators mirrors her own (albeit unpaid) gestational labor, rather than raising anxieties about fetal health; incubators, as she reminds us, are substitutes for the long-term gestational labor women do for free. Given that few Israeli women see surrogacy as a desirable way to make a living, we ask: what makes a woman who is eight months pregnant – with a child she conceived naturally within a heterosexual relationship – fantasize about being paid by the state for her gestational labor?

As Tsila explained to Tsipy later, she felt that the physical and mental hardships that she has undergone in the course of her pregnancy, which was medically categorized as "low-risk," go largely unacknowledged; rather than longing to be paid for her gestational efforts, this was her way to draw attention to them. Tsila's sentiment seemed even more striking to us when considered together with the idea expressed by the majority of surrogates in Elly's study, who reported never having had their pregnancies be received as "so important" as when they were surrogates. Comparing between their pregnancies with their "own children" and the surrogate pregnancy, they would note with poignant humor that no one commended them on their "hard work" during their own pregnancies but that in surrogacy, as surrogate Shahar noted, "everyone said what an amazing thing I am doing."

While these remarks provide rare moments of explicit protest against the invisibility of women's reproductive labor in "normal" pregnancies, our individual ethnographic research projects on pregnancy and surrogacy in Israel have taught us that more is at stake in the cross-references between surrogacy and normal pregnancy for Jewish-Israeli women.

In this chapter we put our separate ethnographic studies side by side. Tsipy's study was a comparative project looking at the cultural construction of pregnancy in Japan and Israel during the first decade of the twenty-first century. Based on a multi-sited approach, the study combined participant observation in Japanese and Israeli hospitals, birth preparation courses, "fun days" for pregnant women, textual analysis of popular pregnancy books, interviews with Israeli and Japanese women about their pregnancy experiences and interviews with Israeli and Japanese obstetrician-gynecologists. Fieldwork and interviews in arenas of pregnancy and prenatal care in Japan were conducted by Tsipy in Japanese, fieldwork and interviews in Israel were conducted in Hebrew. In this essay we mention the Japanese ethnography only briefly in order to highlight – by way of cultural comparison – the particularity of the Israeli culture of pregnancy which is our focus here.

Elly's study focused on the cultural construction of surrogacy in Israel. A multi-sited approach was also taken in this study, combining participant observation at birth celebrations, support group meetings for surrogates, observations of written exchanges on an online message board for surrogates and intended mothers and at their in-person gatherings, and interviews with surrogates and intended mothers, fathers, and professionals involved in Israeli surrogacy. Fieldwork and interviews were conducted by Elly in Hebrew. Both studies were published as ethnographies (Ivry 2010a; Teman 2010).

Bringing both these studies into this essay, we outline the cultural theories of procreation, embodied experiences and emotional postures that facilitate the cross-references between pregnancy and surrogacy. We argue that just as surrogacy becomes a useful metaphor for thinking about "normal" Israeli pregnancy, the features of "normal" Israeli pregnancy become a useful resource for women who actually become surrogates to draw upon while navigating the emotional and embodied dimensions of the surrogate pregnancy. Our explorations contribute to the ongoing scholarly endeavor to better understand pregnancy and to better understand surrogacy by looking at both as mutually constituted vis-à-vis one another in local sociocultural and political settings. Interestingly, the scholarship on reproduction echoes the observations of the pregnant women quoted above in that it becomes particularly interested in daily experiences of pregnancy when women get paid for their gestational labor.

25.2   Pregnancy and the Anthropology of New Reproductive Technologies

The rapidly expanding literature on the anthropology of reproduction and new reproductive technologies has been hesitant to consider pregnancy as a meaningful unit of analysis, let alone as a primary focus of scholarly concern. The few anthropological studies focused on experiences of normal pregnancy in industrial societies emphasize sensations of somatic transformation into an unfamiliar body (Bailey 2001; Han 2014), the liminality of pregnancy in the public sphere (Longhurst 2001) and the ways in which liminality is managed through rituals of consumer culture (Han 2014). Interestingly, this literature depicts Western pregnant women as consumers rather than as producers or laborers; their intensive long-term somatic and emotional efforts are documented and discussed – but are rarely acknowledged as laborious (cf. Ivry 2015). With few exceptions (Ivry 2010a), gestation is rarely theorized within a broader matrix of relations of production.

Other than the few examples cited above, anthropologists of reproduction have been much more concerned with the new ways in which women's reproductive capacities have been mediated, manipulated, substituted, and bypassed by the new reproductive technologies (NRTs). Indeed, the social scientific explorations of human reproduction that emerged at the intersection of feminist theory, medical anthropology, and science studies during the late 1980s were initiated in response to the growing availability and routinization of NRTs – assisted conception, donor technologies, and PND (Prenatal Diagnosis) – throughout the affluent West and beyond. It was women's encounters with reproductive technologies and medical interventions, rather than the everyday, embodied, and emotional experiences of "normal" gestation, that became the ultimate perspective from which to study the meaning of "reproduction" (cf. Morgan 1990).

Consequently, over the past four decades feminist and anthropological studies of reproduction have drawn attention to the effects of NRTs. When discussing pregnancy, these studies explore the transformative technologies that affect pregnancy, such as ultrasound. Scholars working in Europe and America claim that obstetrical ultrasound imaging has replaced the realization of pregnancy through quickening (Georges 1996). It is argued that the routinized use of sonograms is increasingly transforming fetuses into fully-fledged patients, whose rights might conflict with the pregnant woman's rights and which render women's bodies increasingly permeable and transparent (Mitchell 2001; Taylor 2008). The mother's body has become "an empty space," writes Barbara Katz-Rothman (Rothman 1986: 114); and Rosalind Pollack-Petcheksy (1987: 270), analyzing the uses of ultrasonic imagery in antiabortion propaganda, has poignantly commented on the deadly consequences of "the denial of the womb."

In addition, scholars documenting the routinization of prenatal diagnosis have shown how women's experiences of normal pregnancy are increasingly complicated by the need to contemplate the prospect of fetuses diagnosed or "suspected of" fetal anomalies. Amniocentesis has made pregnancy "tentative" (Rothman 1993) and pushes women who face post-diagnostic decisions about terminating their pregnancy to become "moral pioneers" (Gammeltoft 2014; Ivry 2010a; Rapp 1999). Much of the scholarship concentrates on the experiences of men and women trying to achieve conception. Anthropological inquiry into the assisted conceptive technology of IVF, in particular, has illuminated the ordeals of women and men seeking technological assistance in their quest for biological parenthood around the globe (Bharadwaj 2006; Inhorn 2003; Roberts 2012; Thompson 2005). Israel, well known for having the highest number of IVF clinics per capita in the world, has attracted a considerable amount of scholarly attention on this topic (Birenbaum-Carmeli 2004; Ivry 2010b; Kahn 2000; Teman 2010).

Of special significance when considering the scholarship on reproductive technologies is the work of Sarah Franklin, who has drawn on her extensive array of ethnographic and historical explorations of assisted conception in the UK to argue, together with Marilyn Strathern, that reproductive technologies are transforming our understandings of "the facts of life," together with notions of "nature" and "culture." Whereas IVF has been conceptualized in the public media as "giving nature a helping hand," Franklin argues that the effect is bidirectional: technologically assisted conception is increasingly becoming the primary frame of reference from which "natural conception" is understood (Franklin

1998, 2013; Strathern 1992). In other words, spontaneous conception is increasingly being imagined as if it has occurred in a petri dish; both "assisted" and "unassisted" conception are understood as increasingly complicated processes with high failure rates, and are envisioned in ever greater detail. It is with this focus on bidirectional imaginings that we turn to a short review of recent ethnographic research on surrogacy, arguing that a similar pattern is emerging. However, the ways in which scholars apply a specific set of terminology to surrogacy to consider it as "labor" – is making it seem as though only surrogates do such laborious gestational "work."

25.3   Surrogacy, Labor, and Embodiment

Within the intellectual legacy that privileges the technological above the "regular" in terms of scholarly interest in reproduction, the commercial surrogacy industry has been singled out as the height of the feminist nightmare about reproductive technologies gone awry. Radical feminist theorists of the 1980s–1990s advocated strongly against surrogacy, viewing it as a form of subordination and exploitation of women's bodies under patriarchal technological regimes comparable to prostitution and slavery (Corea 1985; Farquhar 1996; Klein 1992; Raymond 1993; Rothman 2000; Rowland 1992). As this scholarship gained traction, surrogacy became widely understood as erasing women's subjectivity and turning surrogates and the babies they produce into objects to be bought and sold as commodities. Importantly, the scholarship on surrogacy has consistently differentiated surrogate pregnancies from "normal" pregnancies, with the former constituted as an urgent bioethical problem.

Although a handful of ethnographic studies of commercial surrogacy arrangements in the US and Israel have attempted to illuminate the human subjects behind the bioethical scandals and to problematize surrogates' victimization (Berend 2010; Ragoné 1994, 1999; Roberts 1998a, 1998b; Teman 2010), most of the scholarly interest in surrogacy has remained theoretical and focused on its moral and ethical repercussions and on the question of exploitation. The same persistent and familiar moral anxieties about surrogacy as exploitation are reverberated in the current upsurge in ethnographic studies of surrogacy in India, but are now further augmented by the crossing of racial and national boundaries. These surrogacy arrangements emerging in the southern hemisphere mirror postcolonial power relations between the wealthy West and economically disadvantaged female citizens of the developing world.

This recent stream of studies on surrogacy in India continue earlier ethnographically bound attempts to complicate our understanding of surrogacy beyond exploitation and commodification by suggesting we consider surrogacy against the backdrop of other occupational opportunities in the Indian labor market; a common argument is that surrogacy can be understood as paid "biological labor" as well as "unpaid emotional work" (Crozier, Johnson and Hajzler 2014). Vora (2012) discusses surrogacy as a new form of "biological and affective labor," comparing it to another form of outsourced "service work," namely, call center work. What these types of "work" have in common, Vora suggests, is the "labor of producing and transferring human vital energy directly to a consumer" (2012: 682). Likewise, Pande (2010) creates an analogy between Indian surrogates and factory workers, emphasizing the construction of both as disciplined subjects and cheap global laborers, but adding to the surrogate's docility the qualities of selflessness and nurturance that make her a "perfect mother worker." She stresses the duality of the surrogate's "reproductive labor" by pointing out not only that surrogacy is "work" but also the labor of childbirth.

Finally, Rudrappa (2009, 2012) suggests that surrogacy may offer poor Indian women better working conditions than those they encounter in the job market. She argues that women in Bangalore working in the garment industry, who suffer daily sexual harassment and work to exhaustion in factories, feel that their lives are bettered by surrogacy. As surrogates they can stay indoors, away from uninvited touch, eat properly, and eventually, if they carry to term, get paid – enough to buy a desired house and/or pay for their children's education – and thus fulfill their motherly duties to their children and families. The anti-natalist Indian government is not interested in encouraging these women to contribute their own "product" of gestation – their genetic children – to society, and most surrogates interviewed by Rudrappa had been sterilized after they had two children as part of the Indian policy to reduce population size. However, the state and private medical clinics are highly interested in their reproductive service work so that the potential profitability of their "otherwise unused uterus," as Vora (2013: s104) puts it, does not go to waste.

In hindsight, while this new anthropological and sociological literature on surrogacy continues to challenge the notion of surrogates as predestined victims of exploitation by comparing it to other forms of outsourced labor, it has rarely questioned the singling out of surrogate pregnancy experiences as *profoundly different* from those of ordinary pregnancy. In other words, it seems that the division between paid and unpaid reproductive labor – echoing concordant divisions between unusual vs. ordinary, unethical vs. ethical, exploitative or abusive vs. fair, artificial vs. natural, and finally exotic and requiring explanation vs. taken for granted and uninteresting – has creeped into the assumptions underlying the choice and design of the research apparatus and into the theoretical orientations of ethnographers of reproduction. As a result, while scholars seem to be increasingly drawn to the topic of Indian surrogacy, we remain with relatively little understanding of the local cultures of pregnancy on which surrogate arrangements draw. Studies of pregnancy, on the other hand, pay sporadic attention to the implications of the gendered division of labor in a society on the embodied aspects of gestational labor; neither do they give due attention to the exploitative potential that such divisions engender.

Our ethnographies of paid and unpaid gestational labor in Israel, when put side by side, suggest that a consideration of bidirectional allusions between surrogacy and normal pregnancy, with close attention to the somatic modes of gestation in each, are pertinent for promoting a deeper understanding of these reproductive practices. It is only by meeting halfway between these two units of analysis – pregnancy and surrogacy – within local, sociopolitical, and cultural contexts, that their co-construction can be realized and that we can truly view culture "at work."

25.4   The Jewish-Israeli Version of the "Tentative Pregnancy"

An initial sense of culture at work can be gained from brief consideration of the strategies used in Israel by stores selling baby supplies to attract prospective parents. All of the successful chain stores in Israel that sell baby furniture and clothing invite expectant parents to make a "birth order" prior to the baby's due date. Expectant parents choose all of the furniture and supplies they will need immediately following delivery, but put down only a small deposit and leave the order at the store until after a live baby is ready to be taken home. A widespread local belief is that one should not assume that the journey of pregnancy will result in a live and healthy baby. Accordingly, one should not share the name of the baby before birth, or visibly prepare necessary equipment in advance. This conditional version of consumption echoes a broader conception of pregnancy as a highly tentative stage of reproduction in contemporary Jewish-Israeli culture, in striking contrast to the ways in which pregnancy was conceptualized in Tsipy's fieldwork in Japan as an early stage of parenting (Ivry 2010a). Conditional consumption toward the end of term in Israel is but one manifestation of the tentativeness of pregnancy in Israel.

The accounts of the pregnant Israeli women that Tsipy interviewed, all of whom experienced normal "low-risk" pregnancies, did not uniformly adhere to the cultural imperative of unpreparedness; all of them, however, dealt with it to some degree throughout their pregnancies. While some women completely refrained from any preparations, others, particularly second and third-time mothers – would use "compromising" strategies to have the cake – remain unprepared – and eat it too. Aya, for example, an educational psychologist and a pregnant woman in her thirties, who was a mother of a five-month-old at the time of interview, told Tsipy:

When I was in my eighth month of pregnancy, I saw a pair of two wonderful bottles on sale at the supermarket. I wanted to buy them but I could not. So I phoned my friend and we agreed that she would buy them for me and keep them at her house until I give birth.

While many Japanese "mothers" already prepare baby clothes for their unborn babies from the fifth month (Ivry 2010a), and American "expectant mothers" celebrate baby showers – events that "carry tremendous emotional importance for the nascent mother" (Davis-Floyd 1992: 36; also see Han 2014) – during the seventh month of pregnancy, this Israeli pregnant woman is too frightened to buy a pair of bottles even when the birth is rapidly approaching.

Carmela was a 33-year-old pregnant woman and the mother of a three-year-old child. She grew up in Argentina and immigrated to Israel in her twenties and was perplexed when she encountered the imperative of unpreparedness.

In Argentina, the room is ready for the baby beforehand. Everything! The bed and the sheets and everything. Here, nothing. Don't open up the bed. It's wrong [If you make an order], everything should stay at the store. With my first baby, it was strange … I think it is superstition … has to do with the fear that you will come back home without a baby, God forbid [*has vehalila*] … as if it would hurt less … I live here so I've become integrated, but I don't understand why preparing a bed for a baby is [forbidden] … Maybe it brings bad luck? … Maybe this way you'll be less disappointed? If you're expecting the worst, then if nothing happens everything will be all right. Maybe it's wrong to expect too much, maybe you shouldn't hope. This is fear. The fewer the expectations, the fewer the disappointments … now I understand, and I live here, so I behave the way people behave here … But yes, I washed the [baby's] clothes and put them in the drawers, but I won't open the bed, that's for sure; only the clothes. In the previous pregnancy I had a bed, but it was folded and I even had a mattress … Some people, you know, wouldn't dare even to do this.

Carmela narrates a pregnancy haunted by preeminent catastrophe. It takes a daring individual to contest this state of mind. Even Carmela, who referred to the cult of unpreparedness as "superstitious" and was intimately acquainted with a different understanding of pregnancy, resists quietly.

Notions of pregnancy as threatened by misfortune can be traced back many centuries before the advent of modern medicine, to Mediterranean ideas about the evil eye and the necessity to protect pregnant women from its potential damage (Sered 2000; Teman 2008) and it is beyond the scope of this essay to account for this national paradigm of thinking through a master-script of the existential threat that it echoes (see Ivry

2010a). However, the contemporary version of the threatened pregnancy owes much of its power to the local version of prenatal care in Israel and particularly to the advent of prenatal diagnosis of fetal anomalies.

25.5   Prenatal Diagnosis and the Fetal Suspect

Information about the ever-proliferating technological means to diagnose genetic and chromosomal fetal abnormalities permeates the Israeli public sphere; unlike Euro-American public spheres, there is no immediate association in the Jewish-Israeli media between prenatal diagnosis and neo-eugenics and thus little bioethical public debate. The standard "test basket" that is provided as part of the national health insurance standard prenatal care guidelines includes a larger number of fetal screening options than are offered in European and US prenatal healthcare systems. The Israeli routine includes testing late into the pregnancy and is backed up by a law legalizing abortions of fetuses diagnosed with fetal anomalies with no limit on the kind of anomaly or gestational age at the time of termination.

Israeli ob-gyns – increasingly threatened by wrongful birth lawsuits – tend to encourage women to undergo as many tests as possible "just for their peace of mind." Every new test that is invented is quickly "marketed" and doctors not only inform their patients about each new test, but some even accept women as patients on the condition that they will undergo these screenings, including invasive tests like amniocentesis that carry a significant risk of miscarriage. Israeli practitioners also claim that their detection rates are higher compared to their colleagues overseas because they have reached a higher level of expertise due to the proliferation of testing.

Thus women who were experiencing normal "low-risk" pregnancies found themselves confronted, in the course of routine medical care, with information about myriad reproductive misfortunes, emphasizing the prospect of carrying a child with an anomaly. The abundance of information on fetal abnormalities had a direct effect on couples' attitudes toward the pregnancy. As Dr. Yaloom, a gynecologist at a major Israeli hospital stated:

> Couples come to me, so I tell them, "Listen, there is this test for cystic fibrosis, and that test for something else, and this and that" … and I watch them and see how slowly the "wind deflates from their sails" and they were so excited about this baby.

Far from empowering expectant parents, the information that excited couples are given regarding prenatal diagnosis has the power to douse their spirit. Taken literally, Dr. Yaloom's image echoes the devastation and disappointment of those who were on the brink of taking flight, but after losing their confidence become immobilized. While some pregnant women may become engaged in an endless search for medical information, Tsipy also interviewed a few women who consciously minimized exposure to biomedical information for the sake of their emotional well-being. However, the latter had to exert much effort to block the flood of anxiety-provoking information that seemed to swamp them.

Consequently, in the Israeli setting, technologies such as obstetric ultrasound – theorized in Euro-American and Canadian settings as enhancing fetal subjectivity – seemed to have less of a "bonding" effect (Mitchell 2001; Taylor 2008), and were instead often regarded apprehensively, as in the scene described by first-time mother-to-be Neta:

> We entered the darkened room, and the doctor did the ultrasound examination. He said, "Look, what a nice face this fetus has, let's try to see what the sex of the fetus is." So my husband said, "First tell me if everything is okay and then tell us the sex."

Neta's husband attempts to suspend fetal subjectivity in the face of its enhanced visibility. For him the fear of fetal abnormalities is stronger than the technological "bonding" mechanism and the doctor's "bonding" efforts in this case.

Quite an ambiguous image of the "fetal suspect" arises from an examination of women's accounts of their pregnancies. Women may undergo frequent ultrasounds, and yet suspend "babyhood." Aya, who was quoted above, told Tsipy that she asked her doctor to prescribe as many ultrasounds as he possibly could for her in order to appease her anxieties about fetal anomaly.

TSIPY: How did you feel about seeing your baby so often?

AYA: Well, what do you mean? The fetus? The ultrasound relaxed me, seeing the fetus, and being told that everything is okay, but I was too busy with the ongoing things of pregnancy. I did not let myself fantasize about the baby until very late, maybe the eighth month. I did not let myself think about how it is going to be. I am always so surprised at women who fantasize a lot during pregnancy. How dare they? So many things, so many accidents can happen.

While Tsipy explicitly asks Aya about her "baby" in the above quoted exchange, what Aya sees on the ultrasound screen is a "fetus," still a remote entity. The enhanced visibility of the fetus does not "connect" Aya emotionally to her fetus. Instead, Aya's narrative is informed by a grammar of thinking that presupposes the preeminence of a reproductive catastrophe. Aya continued:

> I think I had mixed feelings, a mixture of excitement on the one hand and on the other hand a very big fear. Should I be happy and hope?

> Could I allow myself to expect too much? Because of my work I know about all kinds of syndromes in children, and all kinds of problems, so I did not let myself fantasize about how all this (having a baby) was going to be.

At this point Aya proceeded to tell Tsipy about the bottles that she asked her friend to buy for her. Aya's story is one of "hesitant-bonding." Her hesitance is directly linked to her negotiations with the notion of impending reproductive catastrophe; she is afraid to become too attached to the fetus because of a variety of possible "accidents" that might occur during the pregnancy.

Formulated from the time of inception as an entity that needs to be tested, scrutinized, and peered at before it can be deemed worthy of acceptance, the Israeli unborn baby emerges not so much as a baby but rather as a "suspect" of investigation. While many pregnancy guides in Tsipy's Japanese study conveyed a fully-fledged baby often from as early as the first trimester of gestation, pregnancy guides written in Hebrew refer to [fetuses] up to the last trimester of pregnancy. In fact, the reference to "fetus" can be found up until the birth itself. Ruth, the childbirth educator quoted above, explained in her birth preparation class to an audience of women approaching the end of term:

> The word fetus [ubar] stems from the Hebrew root for passing or transience [o'ver]. The fetus is transferred into a baby [ha'ubar o'ver lihiyot tinok] through the birth. Husbands should always remind their wives and keep in mind that the birth passes [overet].

25.6 "Geneticism," the Trivialization of Gestational Contributions to Fetal Health, and the "Divided Pregnancy"

Beyond suspension of prenatal bonding, the full thrust of the "worst case scenario" and its "fetal suspect" is in their ability to instigate separation of women's pregnancies into two distinct realms, fetus vs. pregnancy, with far-reaching implications on pregnancy outcomes. While the fetus is screened, tested, and "investigated" throughout for inborn anomalies emphasizing the determinant role of genes and chromosomes for fetal health, the effects of women's nutrition, physical activity, and myriad somatic and emotional dimensions of gestation are marginalized by medical practitioners as well as by women themselves, as discussed below (Ivry 2010a).

The cultural specificity of the emphasis on genes and chromosomes in Israeli prenatal care stands out when contrasted with Tsipy's findings on Japanese prenatal care. Japanese ob-gyns emphasized the various ways different kinds of environmental conditions – nutrition quality, weight gain pattern, maternal physical activity and stress levels, exposure to noise and air pollution – matter to fetal health. They saw the maternal body as an ecosystem encapsulating the unborn child, and made the pregnant mother responsible for controlling the entry of external substances into this maternal ecosystem. The Japanese ob-gyns that Tsipy spoke to during the first decade of the twenty-first century were hesitant to discuss prenatal diagnosis despite guidelines that instructed them to discuss it with women over age 35.

Israeli medical practitioners never skipped a discussion of a long list of prenatal diagnostic tests with their patients regardless of a patient's age, however, they rarely discussed issues of nutrition with women whose pregnancies were categorized as "low-risk," neither did they discuss preventive measures against excessive weight gain. This is in spite of the fact that, as Japanese doctors often point out, weight gain can have far-reaching effects on the well-being of women during pregnancy, and that it effects the rate of complicated deliveries. Tsipy called the Japanese prenatal regime she documented during the previous decade "environmentalism," and contrasted it with Israeli "geneticism."

In both the regimes of "geneticism" and "environmentalism" women were held responsible for fetal health, but were expected to pursue different strategies to succeed. Israeli women, terrorized by the specter of anomalous fetuses, were pushed toward performing responsible motherhood via selective technologies. Japanese women were encouraged instead to "make" a healthy baby through various nurturant practices exercising "embodied responsibilities" (Ivry 2007). Importantly, while Japanese women were encouraged to contact their physician should any unusual somatic sensation emerge in order to negate the possibility that fetal health may be endangered, Israeli women were relatively slow to interpret pain and discomfort during gestation as having anything to do with fetal well-being due to their attempt "not to make a fuss" over physical challenges of gestation.

Carmit, a 28-year-old secretary, experienced in her second pregnancy preterm labor contractions in her seventh month. Still, it took her a few days of pain and self-prescribed attempts to relieve it until she eventually decided to see a doctor. When the doctor prescribed bed-rest as a preventive measure against preterm birth, Carmit was reluctant to conceive it as an indication of a serious medical condition and after a while returned to her job and worked until the end of term.

Mira, a 27-year-old graphic designer, told of an ordeal that started in her fourth month of pregnancy, when her doctor prescribed iron pills. With hindsight, it became clear to her that these pills gradually caused her to dehydrate, which eventually led to preterm labor. This complication happened slowly, developing over as long as a month of suffering, during which Mira complained of not being able to eat and drink and of continuous diarrhea. She went to seek the advice of her doctor, who merely told her that her symptoms were "natural effects that happen during pregnancy." Although she felt strongly that something was clearly wrong, her family, and her female relatives in particular, all of whom had experienced pregnancy and birth, discouraged her from becoming alarmed at her sensations. Her mother, grandmother, and aunts said, "This is natural; it's because of the pregnancy. You'll see, you'll suffer from these symptoms until the end of your pregnancy."

Both Carmela and Mira initially rendered the pain to be their own individual pain – having nothing to do with fetal well-being – and developed a sort of "heroic deafness" towards their bodily sensations. This enabled them, at least temporarily, to carry on with their daily tasks and particularly allowed them to fulfill their commitments to their paid job despite pain and discomfort.

The above stories, when juxtaposed with the accounts of Japanese women who were quick to report any unusual sensation to their doctors, illuminate the importance of the positioning of gestation vis-à-vis work – both in the sense of paid occupation, and as a metaphor for somatic and emotional effort – to the understanding and treatment of pregnant women in a given cultural setting. Each regime of truth – Israeli geneticism and the Japanese ecosystemic understanding of pregnancy – conceptualized gestation vis-à-vis work. In Japanese arenas, where women were understood as literally the makers of their babies and where gestation was understood as a crucial determinant of fetal health, women were encouraged ultimately to quit their paid jobs in the labor market in order to be able to devote time and energy to their gestational work. They were understood not as quitting their jobs upon pregnancy but as switching from one job to another. The pregnant body was conceptualized as an "important body" (taisetsuna karada) and they were expected to nurture it carefully according to doctors' detailed instructions about nutrition and physical activity for the sake of the unborn baby's health.

In the Israeli arena, on the other hand, women's bodies were conceived as considerably less relevant to fetal health. The latter was rather determined by genes and chromosomes more or less around the time of conception; Israeli women were ultimately expected to continue fulfilling their commitments to their paid jobs until the end of term. While the Japanese theories of procreation suggest that there are ample ways to make or at least improve fetal health through responsible gestational efforts, in the Israeli realm there is no way to make a healthy baby in the contemporary Israeli medical and lay truth regimes, only to use technologies to select the healthy babies who are allowed to be born.

In other words, while in the environmental vision of gestation the pregnant body is an all-encompassing ecosystem, the geneticist vision of gestation renders the pregnant body as a receptacle of a "ready-made" baby. At its extreme, such a model not only denies women maternal agency, its implications for women's embodied experiences of pregnancy can be farreaching. While some of the Israeli women interviewed actively tried to resist the specter of genetic fatalism, and carefully, as if on tip toes, tried to foster relations with the fetus through embodied sensations, others were completely taken over by the script of threatening catastrophe to the extent of consciously working to ignore somatic sensations that attest to the existence of a living being within them. Ora, a 34-year-old mother of a 10-year-old child and in her second pregnancy, described her denial of somatic sensations eloquently.

ORA: I did not become attached to this pregnancy from the beginning. I felt him moving very early in the pregnancy, as early as the third month, but I ignored it. I said, "I don't want to feel anything. I want nothing. I want to know that everything is O.K. and then … maybe."

TSIPY: What do you mean exactly by "I did not become attached?"

ORA: The simplest thing. If I felt a movement, I ignored it, I felt nothing. It was just a muscle that moved … I said, "I feel nothing," because if they told me to abort, that is, if they told me that the fetus had a terrible disease and I have to abort it, what then?

Ora speaks of an attempt to detach herself from the pregnancy. This detachment is a familiar "emotional posture" (Ivry 2010a) that women become skilled in assuming during pregnancy, a social resource that is readily available for use. This "emotional posture" works as a defensive strategy keeping the divided person "immune" from unpleasant surprises, so that catastrophe does not befall them unexpectedly. In the next section, we argue that Israeli surrogates draw upon this cultural script and upon these techniques of detachment in order to navigate the surrogate pregnancy.

25.7 How the Cultural Script of Israeli Pregnancy Constructs Surrogacy

We suggest that this particular way in which pregnancy is constructed in Israel serves as an embodied posture, or even a cultural toolkit, from which surrogates draw in their navigation of the emotional complexities and boundary negotiations that surrogacy entails. In other words, it is on the backdrop of the "divided pregnancy" and the distancing of the "fetus" in the cultural construction of normative pregnancy that surrogates in Israel find the process culturally palatable; surrogacy fits almost seamlessly with the way pregnancy is conceptualized, making it less "strange" and perhaps more easily manageable. Surrogacy forms the practical realization or somatic materialization of the divided pregnancy.

First, surrogates draw upon the trivialization of pregnancy in order to "prove" to themselves and to others that they are not the one "creating" this baby but that they are merely "hosting" an already-formed embryo implanted artificially in their womb which then develops into a fetus. Einat, a surrogate, claimed along these lines that she was "only" providing shelter and warmth for the fetus: "I always say that it is like an oven. The ingredients are already mixed. You just put the dough in and heat it until it becomes bread."

Likewise, surrogates drew upon similar idioms to trivialize their contribution and to distance any possible emotional attachment that they believed they might develop towards the fetus. While "normally" pregnant women in Tsipy's study viewed their own lack of bonding as an issue and made strategic efforts to overcome it and to become more connected, surrogates viewed non-bonding as a mental and emotional goal to be achieved through conscious effort. Orna, a surrogate, explains:

> You have to remind yourself all the time that you are providing nothing more than a hothouse for him (the fetus) ... like a hotel in which one stays and leaves without feeling. I put it in my head that it won't have any physical or mental effects on me. That it would have no influence on me, and the fact is that it worked ... I had no feelings, no side effects ... I didn't feel like I was pregnant. It's just like it's called, an inn [*pundak*]. It's a boarding house for nine months.

Orna explains her emotional distance from the fetus by employing a direct and literal interpretation of popular images of surrogacy in the Israeli public sphere, referring to herself with the popular Hebrew term "pundekait" which relates to the surrogate as a female innkeeper or host, rather than a "substitute mother" as the term "surrogate mother" implies. While a major line of the feminist critique of surrogacy suggests that the practice reduces women to nothing more than "living laboratories" or "human incubators," Orna subversively employs the idioms of "hotel," "inn," and "boarding house" to achieve her goal of distancing the pregnancy, the fetus, and the possible maternal sentiments she believes could occur in pregnancy. The divided pregnancy and the trivialized pregnancy become grounds for her to purposely constitute her body as merely a site for the pregnancy to be hosted; the public image of surrogacy as innkeeping has materialized in her own perception of her body during surrogacy, and she embraces this image to make her point.

Orna's affirmation that she "didn't feel like she was pregnant" also echoed the sentiments of other surrogates, who imagined the pregnancy occurring in a space outside or alongside their "personal body." In this manner, the "divided pregnancy" that is part of the cultural script for "normal" pregnancy becomes a vehicle for imagining the pregnancy as completely detached from the surrogate's personal space. Orna continued:

> So I was like this. Me (points to her chest and above), not me (indicates area from chest to mid-thigh). Completely disconnected. I totally disconnected myself from the stomach. I mean, whatever I felt in my stomach, I didn't feel. I mean, I was always saying that I am divided

in three. From here to here is me, from here to here isn't me, from here to here is me.

Orna developed the "art of detachment" by pushing the notion of division in "normal" Israeli pregnancy further and using it to deconstruct her own body. Note that her body is divided into three parts, but conceptually she is divided into two: her personal self and the part of her body that she has divided off in order to gestate the fetus. The "divided pregnancy" literally manifests itself in her body. Other surrogates "mapped" their bodies into an even more intricate "body map" of separate and connected parts. They personalized their "heart," their "soul," their "blood," and their "egg/ova" while distancing their "brain," which was "artificially" commanded during surrogacy by doctors and medication, as well as their womb, or belly area, which were, as one surrogate summed it up, not "the same womb and emotions that is was when my own son was there."

Bringing the "divided pregnancy" further into acute materialization, surrogates spoke of how the surrogacy pregnancy acted differently than their "own body" acted during their previous pregnancies; cramps and contractions occurred in different parts of the body and at different intensities, cravings were for foods that proved this pregnancy's otherness, gestation and labor lasted comparatively longer or shorter than "their own," and weight was lost more quickly, while milk "dried up." Several surrogates claimed that their pregnant bellies went unnoticed by colleagues and even by their own children, or unrecognized as pregnancy in the public arena, up through the end of the gestational period, suggesting that "no one noticed that I was pregnant" or that they did not walk or stand like a pregnant woman.

Likewise, the distancing and division of the pregnancy enabled the surrogates to imagine it nearer to the intended mother's body, to verbally share bodily sensations with her associated with the pregnancy, and to virtually transfer, or "shift," the pregnant body to her (see Teman 2009, 2010). Surrogates spoke of the pregnancy they had distanced from their self being manifested upon the intended mother's body. One surrogate claimed that she did not gain a significant amount of weight during surrogacy and that her stomach remained small throughout, but that her intended mother had gained 13 kilograms and looked bloated "like she was pregnant herself." Others spoke of their intended mother's "sympathy pains," of telepathy between them, or the intended mother's intuitive knowledge of what she was feeling in the body, and even of sharing the pregnant body as "two who are one."

Yet even as the surrogate distances the pregnancy and "shares" it with the intended mother, the fetus remains distanced from them both. None of the surrogates in Elly's study felt that they had established any degree of maternal bond with the fetus they carried, and most of them reported that delivering the baby was the most exciting and satisfying moment of the process. Batya, a surrogate, explained that she intentionally looked away from the ultrasound screen in order to distance herself from the belly and its contents:

> In my subconscious, I said that it isn't mine, and I didn't become attached to him [the fetus]. I didn't have any connection to him, and that's it! I don't bond with the fetus! Even in the ultrasound, I wouldn't look. He [the doctor] would say to me, he is in such and such week … she has a girl … I didn't connect at all. Not at all … I would look to the side … It didn't interest me … because I said that it is just a fetus that I won't have in the end … I knew that it wouldn't stay with me in the end. And that it wouldn't be part of me. So why become connected to it?

On the other side of the coin, the intended mothers' intention to become a mother through surrogacy was also not enough to overcome the cultural script, or "mental posture" of hesitancy to bond. Most of the intended mothers had manifested the "worst-case scenario" fear of disappointment to an extreme, after undergoing multiple miscarriages or failed IVF attempts before approaching surrogacy. Yael, an intended mother, expressed this sentiment in the sixth month of her surrogate's pregnancy:

> I am afraid to become too attached because of what happened last time [miscarriage] … I am afraid to even be happy. Afraid to bond and just afraid … Every day that passes I say thank G-d that everything is okay … Every time the phone rings my heart jumps … Every time [the surrogate] calls, she says, "Yael, don't be scared, everything is okay, I just called to say …" There is this fear until he comes out into the world alive and whole.

Sounding much like the "normally" pregnant women in Tsipy's study, Yael spoke of how she hesitantly looked in the window of the baby supply store, only finally entering it to look around near the end of her surrogate's pregnancy. None of the intended mothers prepared the baby's room before the birth, none shared the name, and many kept the pregnancy secret until a very late stage of surrogacy for fear that even sharing the "good news" might cause something to go wrong.

Surrogacy as a multiply divided enterprise reached a climax in the notion of the lonely fetus. While the surrogate divides herself conceptually from the fetus and from the part of her body in which she carries it, the intended mother is physically divided from the fetus. In this light, Sima, a surrogate, expressed her concern that no one was bonding with the baby she carried:

> (Four months into the pregnancy) I told her what a strange situation this was. That I was trying so hard to ignore my stomach and she was keeping her distance. No one was bonding with them (the twins she carried). No one was touching, talking to them.

25.8   Discussion: Towards a Cross-Inspiration between Studies of Paid and Unpaid Gestational Labor

Having juxtaposed Israeli women's accounts of unpaid and paid gestational labor, let us now return to our opening question: what makes a woman who is eight months pregnant – with a child she conceived naturally within a heterosexual relationship – fantasize about being paid by the state for her gestational labor? A two-fold answer emerges from our juxtaposition: one at the level of local contemporary Jewish-Israeli culture, the other at the level of the assumptions underlying much of the scholarship on the anthropology of reproduction and NRTs.

At the level of contemporary Jewish-Israeli culture, surrogacy and pregnancy arise as mutually constituted within a common cultural setting. Just as surrogates draw on the cultural script of regular pregnancy to construct their detachment from the fetus and the distancing of the pregnancy, surrogacy also serves as a metaphor for Israeli women's construction of "normal" pregnancy. Moreover, the Israeli geneticized understanding of procreation – with its tendency to disregard the contribution of the gestational process to the making of the fetus, rendering women's bodies as merely receptacles of ready-made unborn babies – lends itself particularly well to gestational surrogacy. However, while it would be tempting to analyze the cross-references between unpaid gestation and surrogacy as a phenomenon particular to the Jewish-Israeli setting, we argue that such cross-references deserve serious consideration beyond the Israeli arena.

Accordingly, we suggest rethinking transnational surrogacy in India with due attention to local cultures of pregnancy; we must consider that the women who travel from villages to the different cities of this large country to become surrogates do not conceptualize pregnancy completely anew just because they are surrogates and are "trained" or "coached" to see their pregnancy as "work." Instead, it is pertinent to consider that they have experienced their previous pregnancies in local cultural arenas in which pregnant bodies are conceptualized and treated in culturally specific ways, in which mythological and spiritual and even astrological beliefs may matter, and where local folklore, language, metaphor, and stories, as well as myriad other factors, give pregnancy a particular flavor. But the Indian surrogacy studies rarely consider local idioms, understandings, and practices of normative pregnancy in the specific enclaves in which surrogacy is practiced.

Yet, cultures of pregnancy are obviously at work there too: local theories of procreation and beliefs about the making of kinship ties, reproductive metaphors, practices and rituals of pregnancy and birth emerge sporadically in the background of each of the surrogacy studies discussed. Nevertheless, even when these surface, the culturally embedded experiences of pregnancy are overlooked. Pande (2009) quotes surrogates talking about the blood, sweat, and tears shed during surrogate gestation, but she analyzes these references to the body in terms of kinship understandings and paid labor. Deomampo (2013) looks at the restrictive surveillance, immobility, and compulsory docility of surrogates temporarily housed in rented apartments away from their homes, but this is as far as the attention to pregnant embodiment reaches. The lack of attention to the embodiment of culture leaves important questions unaddressed. For instance, what are the implications, in the Indian case, of the incongruence between the two different cultural theories of procreation – one that constructs women's somatic and emotional contribution through gestation to the making of the new human being, and the other that geneticizes kinship and renders pregnant women as receptacles of ready-made babies – on surrogates' embodied experiences of gestation? How do surrogates interpret embodied sensations of gestation now that their "sweat" and "blood" goes into a baby that they will not raise? Do they ever attempt to "remap" their bodies in the way that Israeli surrogates do in order to distance the unborn baby? Do they attempt to "other" the baby through other cognitive mechanisms, for example, giving differential meaning to nutrition prescribed during surrogacy as opposed to their nutritional intake in their previous pregnancies? What are the somatic effects of physical segregation and what effects do surrogates expect them to have on the pregnancy and the unborn baby? If surrogacy is discussed as a unit of analysis completely separate from "normal" pregnancy, then the cultural conceptions that shape them both bidirectionally are eclipsed.

An additional array of important questions may come to mind when rethinking surrogacy through the literature on reproductive technologies. There is little consideration of the implications of prenatal diagnosis and ultrasound on the experiences of surrogates and intended parents involved in these arrangements, despite the centrality of these technologies in the anthropology of reproduction scholarship on non-surrogate pregnancy. This splitting of the scholarship on surrogacy and on regular pregnancy makes it seem as though ultrasound has profound effects solely in the context of normal pregnancies and PND only makes regular pregnant women into "moral pioneers." Do surrogates in India just sit passively during ultrasounds because it is their "work?" Do fetal anomalies never occur? If they do occur, which model of kinship is drawn upon to make sense of the anomaly and by whom? Is the surrogate cleared of any blame because she is "just a receptacle?" Or is she to blame because it is her gestational effort? Are decisions never made to terminate, and do these not affect the bodies and emotions of surrogates who have shed their sweat and blood to make an (anomalous) baby?

Furthermore, in line with our contention that the bidirectional influence of "normal" pregnancy and surrogate gestation should be considered, why is surrogacy theorized with such revelation as "paid" and "unpaid," "affective," "emotional," and "biological" labor without consideration of the scholarship on regular pregnancy as "hard work" (Ivry 2010a)? Conceptualizing surrogacy in terms of the "global division of reproductive labor" (i.e., Vora 2012) means writing out not only the considerable

volume of domestic surrogacy arrangements – Indian surrogates gestating for Indian childless couples – but also the ongoing somatic and
emotional efforts and the ongoing gestational labor that the vast majority
of women the world over are doing for free. Silencing the ongoing efforts
of unpaid reproductive laborers means that the multiple dimensions of
social, economic, and emotional exploitation of unpaid pregnant women,
as well as the sociocultural and economic conditions for acknowledging
their efforts, go under-theorized. Moreover, the physical effects of the
acknowledgment or dis-acknowledgment of these gestational efforts on
pregnancy outcomes remain under-theorized. Elly found that surrogates
did not receive due acknowledgment of their gift if they did not manage
to carry to term, but what about the effects of dis-acknowledgment of
women's "hard work" gestating "ordinary" pregnancies?

It remains true, at the beginning of the third millennium, that any
living human being will have been gestated for some months inside a
woman's body. This includes premature babies, and babies who have
been conceived through surrogacy agreements. Not even "test-tube
babies" are actually gestated in test tubes. Long-term reproductive labor
is still required of women – in neoliberal social orders where commodi-
fied modes of reproduction are burgeoning as in prior social orders – for
humans to come into being.

Regardless of whether pregnancy suggests a risk-taking behavior – an
ordeal of survival in the face of a preeminent reproductive catastrophe
(as is likely to happen in Israel) or a nurturing activity associated with
child rearing (as is likely in Japan) – in neither case is pregnancy a matter
of "expecting," with its implication of a state of waiting for the drama
of the birth to come. In both cases, pregnancy is a mentally and physically demanding way of being, and often an energy-consuming project
of meaning making. Thus pregnancy is "pregnant with meaning": it
emerges as a key site for understanding wider dimensions of the embodiment of culture (Ivry 2010a).

Let us clarify that when we advocate for closer attention to local cultures
this is not to insinuate the notion of culture – as an insular entity – held
by classical anthropologists. Rather we suggest a fine-tuning between
considerations of local and global modes of meaning making as well as
local and global modes of subsistence, production, consumption, and the
moral economies they entangle.

When we advocate for greater attention to "ordinary" pregnancies,
we are suggesting a finer balance between studies of "exotic" high-tech
transnational reproductive practices, and studies of the less exotic but
widespread, long-term, demanding, somatic and emotional effort of
gestational labor required to bring new human beings into being. It is
only by understanding the embodied and affective "labor" of everyday
pregnancy that we can try to comprehend the "reproductive work" of
"global" surrogates. Finally, since paid and unpaid gestational labor are

not mutually exclusive phenomena, much insight can be gained from cross-inspiration between anthropological literature on both.

Note

1. Equal first authors.

References

Bailey, Lucy. 2001. "Gender Shows: First-Time Mothers and Embodied Selves." *Gender & Society* 15(1): 110–129.

Berend, Zsuzsa. 2010. "Surrogate Losses: Understandings of Pregnancy Loss and Assisted Reproduction among Surrogate Mothers." *Medical Anthropology Quarterly* 24(2): 240–262.

Bharadwaj, Aditya. 2006. "Sacred Conceptions: Clinical Theodicies, Uncertain Science, and Technologies of Procreation in India." *Culture, Medicine and Psychiatry* 30: 451–465.

Birenbaum-Carmeli, Daphna. 2004. "'Cheaper Than a Newcomer': On the Political Economy of IVF in Israel." *Sociology of Health and Illness* 26(7): 897–924.

Corea, Gena. 1985. *The Mother Machine: Reproductive Technologies from Artificial Insemination to Artificial Wombs*. New York: Harper & Row.

Crozier, G. K. D., Jennifer L. Johnson and Christopher Hajzler. 2014. "At the Intersections of Emotional and Biological Labor: Understanding Commercial Surrogacy As Social Reproduction." *International Journal of Feminist Approaches to Bioethics* 7(2): 45–74.

Davis-Floyd, R. 1992. *Birth as an American Rite of Passage*. Berkeley, CA: University of California Press.

Deomampo, Daisy. 2013. "Gendered Geographies of Reproductive Tourism." *Gender & Society* 27(4): 514–537.

Farquhar, Dion. 1996. *The Other Machine: Discourse and Reproductive Technologies*. New York: Routledge.

Franklin, Sarah. 1998. *Embodied Progress: A Cultural Account of Assisted Conception*. Abingdon: Routledge.

2013. "Conception through a Looking Glass: The Paradox of IVF." *Reproductive Biomedicine Online* 27(6): 747–755.

Gammeltoft, Tine M. 2014. *Haunting Images: A Cultural Account of Selective Reproduction in Vietnam*. Berkeley, CA: University of California Press.

Georges, E. 1996. "Fetal Ultrasound Imaging and the Production of Authoritative Knowledge in Greece." *Medical Anthropology Quarterly* 10(2): 157–175.

Han, Sallie. 2014. *Pregnancy in Practice: Expectation and Experience in the Contemporary US*. London: Berghahn Books.

Inhorn, Marcia. 2003. *Local Babies, Global Science: Gender, Religion and In Vitro Fertilization in Egypt.* New York: Routledge.

Ivry, Tsipy. 2007. "Embodied Responsibilities: Pregnancy in the Eyes of Japanese Ob-Gyns." *Sociology of Health and Illness* 29(2): 251–274.

2010a. *Embodying Culture: Pregnancy in Japan and Israel.* New Brunswick, NJ: Rutgers University Press.

2010b. "Kosher Medicine and Medicalized Halacha: An Exploration of Triadic Relations among Israeli Rabbis, Doctors, and Infertility Patients." *American Ethnologist* 37(4): 662–680.

2015. "The Pregnancy Manifesto: Notes on How to Extract Reproduction from the Petri Dish." *Medical Anthropology* 34(3): 274–289.

Kahn, Susan Martha. 2000. *Reproducing Jews: A Cultural Account of Assisted Conception in Israel.* Durham, NC: Duke University Press.

Klein, Renate. 1992. *The Ultimate Colonisation: Reproductive and Genetic Engineering.* Dublin: Attic Press.

Longhurst, Robyn. 2001. "Breaking Corporeal Boundaries: Pregnant Bodies in Public Places." In *Contested Bodies*, ed. R. Holliday and J. Hassard, 81–94. London: Routledge.

Mitchell, L. M. 2001. *Baby's First Picture: Ultrasound and the Politics of Fetal Subjects.* Toronto: University of Toronto Press.

Morgan, L. M. 1990. "The Medicalization of Anthropology: A Critical Perspective on the Critical-Clinical Debate." *Social Science and Medicine* 30: 945–950.

Pande, Amrita. 2009. "It May Be Her Eggs but It Is My Blood: Surrogates and Everyday Forms of Kinship in India." *Qualitative Sociology* 32(4): 379–397.

2010. "Commercial Surrogacy in India: Manufacturing the Perfect Mother Worker." *Signs: Journal of Women in Culture and Society* 35(4): 969–992.

Pollack Petchesky, Rosalind. 1987. "Fetal Images: The Power of Visual Culture in the Politics of Reproduction." *Feminist Studies* 13(2): 263–292.

Ragoné, Helena. 1994. *Surrogate Motherhood: Conception in the Heart.* Boulder, CO: Westview Press.

1999. "Surrogate Motherhood, Gamete Donation, and Constructions of Altruism." In *Transformative Motherhood: On Giving and Getting in a Consumer Culture*, ed. L. L. Layne, 65–88. New York: New York University Press.

Rapp, Rayna. 1999. *Testing Women, Testing the Fetus: The Social Impact of Amniocentesis in America.* New York: Routledge.

Raymond, Janice G. 1993. *Women As Wombs : Reproductive Technologies and the Battle over Women's Freedom.* San Francisco, CA: HarperSanFrancisco.

Roberts, Elizabeth F. S. 1998a. "Examining Surrogacy Discourses: Between Feminine Power and Exploitation." In *Small Wars: The Cultural Politics of Childhood*, ed. N. Scheper-Hughes and C. F. Sargent, 93–110. Los Angeles, CA: University of California Press.

1998b. "Native Narratives of Connectedness: Surrogate Motherhood and Technology." In *Cyborg Babies: From Techno-Sex to Techno-Tots*, ed. J. Dumit and R. Davis-Floyd, 193–211. New York: Routledge.

2012. *God's Laboratory: Assisted Reproduction in the Andes*. Berkeley, CA: University of California Press.

Rothman, Barbara Katz. 1986. *The Tentative Pregnancy: Prenatal Diagnosis and the Future of Motherhood*. New York: Viking.

1993. *The Tentative Pregnancy: How Amniocentesis Changes the Experience of Motherhood*. New York: Norton.

2000. *Recreating Motherhood*. New Brunswick, NJ: Rutgers University Press.

Rowland, Robyn. 1992. *Living Laboratories: Woman and Reproductive Technologies*. Bloomington, IN: University of Indiana Press.

Rudrappa, Sharmila. 2009. "Working India's Reproduction Assembly Line: Surrogacy and Reproductive Rights?" *Western Humanities Review* 66(3): 77–102.

2012. "India's Reproductive Assembly Line." *Contexts* 11(2): 22–27.

Sered, Susan Starr. 2000. *What Makes Women Sick?: Maternity, Modesty and Militarism in Israeli Society*. Hanover, NH: Brandeis University Press.

Strathern, Marilyn. 1992. *Reproducing the Future: Essays on Anthropology, Kinship and the New Reproductive Technologies*. Manchester: Manchester University Press.

Taylor, Janelle S. 2008. *The Public Life of the Fetal Sonogram: Technology, Consumption, and the Politics of Reproduction*. New Brunswick, NJ: Rutgers University Press.

Teman, Elly. 2008. "The Red String: The Cultural History of a Jewish Folk Symbol." In *Jewishness: Expression, Identity, and Representation*, ed. S. J. Bronner, 29–57. Oxford: Littman Library of Jewish Civilization.

2009. "Embodying Surrogate Motherhood: Pregnancy As a Dyadic Body Project." *Body & Society* 15(3): 47–57.

2010. *Birthing a Mother: The Surrogate Body and the Pregnant Self*. Berkeley, CA: University of California Press.

Thompson, Charis. 2005. *Making Parents: The Ontological Choreography of Reproductive Technologies*. Cambridge, MA: The MIT Press.

Vora, Kalindi. 2012. "Limits of 'Labor': Accounting for Affect and the Biological in Transnational Surrogacy and Service Work." *South Atlantic Quarterly* 111(2): 681–700.

2013. "Potential, Risk, and Return in Transnational Indian Gestational Surrogacy." *Current Anthropology* 54(7): s97–106.

Part VI

Kinship and the Nation-State

26

Reading the Contested Forms of Nation through the Contested Forms of Kinship and Marriage

Susan McKinnon

From at least the nineteenth century, social theorists have largely argued that an historical alignment of values between the domestic, political, and economic orders were disjoined through two distinctions that brought into being the contours of modernity, the nation-state, the market economy, and, we could say as well, the discipline of anthropology, itself. The first distinguishes between kin-based societies (where political, economic, and religious relations are all understood to be organized through relations between kin and *kin groups*) and state-based societies (where political and economic relations are understood to be organized by relations between *individuals* – free of entanglements of kinship and ordered by territory, secular law, contract, and the market). The second makes an analogous distinction, *within* state-based societies, between the relations of kinship and those of politics and economics (McKinnon and Cannell 2013). While domestic relations are seen as necessarily embedded in the structures of the political economy, the gauge of "modernity" is precisely what Latour (1993) might call a "magico-purificatory" taboo on – or injunction against – the influence of family status on political and economic relations (McKinnon 2013).

Anthropology was, of course, founded on this distinction between kin-based and state-based societies; and, on the whole, even when anthropologists turned their attention to the latter, they generally continued to presuppose rather than question the narratives of evolution – and later, those of development and modernization – that were founded on this double distinction. In anthropology, the very meaning of "kinship" has depended on this twined distinction and its accompanying associations and values. That is, the anthropological study of kinship has been shaped by what is a particular historical and cultural narrative masquerading as the necessary and inevitable result of a more or less universal process of development and modernization.

This chapter challenges the oppositional framework that presumes that, within contemporary nation-states, the entanglement of kinship and nation – institutionally or ideologically – should be seen as a sign of backwardness or of an incomplete process of modernization and development. Indeed, I argue that kinship remains central to articulating citizenship and national belonging as well as to articulating the core values that organize diverse nation-states. This is the case not only in explicitly tribal states or states where national belonging is conceived in terms of a singular ethnic descent line and/or where the family is the basic social and political unit, but also, seemingly paradoxically, for those states that presume the primacy of the individual as the basic social and political unit.

In this chapter, I consider how different forms of kinship – particularly different forms of marriage – are inextricably bound up with the meaning, signification, and realization of different forms of political governance distinguished by their relative emphasis on the value of the family group or the individual, hierarchy or equality, divine providence or free will, and religious or secular/contract law. That is, different forms of kinship and marriage are central to imagining the contours of different economic and political regimes, and they are at the center of contestations between hegemonic Euro-American and other narratives of modernity and the constitution of the nation-state. I look at debates about the value and place of different kinship/nation formations primarily in nineteenth-century United States, and, in particular, I consider the articulations between kinship/nation as they are manifest in contestations about polygamy vs. monogamy as well as kin marriage vs. non-kin marriage; and I examine how these contestations are central to the ways in which differential values noted above are brought into being. I also follow the reverberations of these nineteenth-century understandings as they manifest themselves in one example of the contemporary debates about kin marriage.

26.1   Individual vs. Family As the Unit of the Nation

How do people imagine both the unity of a nation and the quality of the relations people have to one another and to the nation-state? While some argue that the fundamental unit and ideology of the modern nation are the individual and individualism, it is evident that not all contemporary nations are organized in such terms; some are constructed out of the building blocks of family (including lineage, clan, or tribe) and of particular forms of marriage. What are we to make of such contemporary facts?

In *Nationalism and the Politics of Culture in Quebec* (1988), Richard Handler argues that nationalism "is an ideology of individuated being. It is thus a variety of Western individualism, the dominant, encompassing ideology of modern societies" (1988: 50). Indeed, for Handler, a modern nation can be understood through two manifestations of the ideology of individualism: as a collective individual and as a collection of individuals. Images of the nation as a "living" collective individual "convey a sense of wholeness and boundedness. They establish the integral, irreducible nature of the collectivity as an existent entity" (1988: 40) – indeed, as a naturalized entity. As such, the nation bears the qualities of an individual: "it can be said to have a soul, spirit, and personality" – a "national character" or a species type – and a national will, freedom of choice, and an "ability to control its own destiny" (1988: 41). As a collection of individuals, the nation is composed of individuals who are "all characterized by the same specific qualities. They are equivalent to one another, and to the generic type" (1988: 43) that is characteristic of the nation. From the hegemonic Western perspective, what counts as a modern nation therefore is marked by the fact that it is seen as a collection of generically equivalent individuals and seen, itself, as a collective individual.

Yet in the contemporary world there are nations that see themselves as fully modern in which the structure and ideology of family, lineage, clan, or tribe – not the individual – are the basic building blocks of the nation. Thus, there are the "tribal modern" states of the Gulf region (Cooke 2014; Herb 1999), such as Oman, where citizenship depends upon membership in a tribe. Or there are the "family nations," like Japan, in which the family "household" (*koseki*) is the legal unit of the nation (Alexi, personal communication). Or the states like Israel, in which a particular ethnic/religious lineage stands as the structural core and rationale for its existence. Or there are states, like Kazakhstan, where "modern clan politics" are inextricably bound up with particular state formations (Schatz 2004: 19).

So entrenched is the narrative of the *transition* from kin-based societies to nation-states, and the presumption of their categorical opposition, that any overlap between the two is taken – from a Western perspective, at least – as a sign of backwardness. Thus, to the extent that a nation-state is organized in terms of relations between kinship groups (not individuals), and by relations of hierarchy (not equality), and by religious (not secular) law, it is seen as less than fully modern. As Edward Schatz notes, from the perspective of political science:

> The picture of identity politics that prevails among political scientists is this: the forces of modernization (urbanization, industrialization, mass literacy, and education) dissolve group boundaries. Studies of nationalism in particular imply that subnational divisions (ethnic groups or kinship-based clans) progressively fade from social and political importance. When outcomes deviate from this core expectation – that is when subnational identities remain important – this is usually explained to be the result of incomplete homogenizing pressures.
>
> *(2004: 4)*

From a Western perspective, such nations are temporally distanced (Fabian 1983) from so-called modern nations and seen as backward relics of the past. Theories of development and modernization perfectly reproduce, in this way, the logic of nineteenth-century evolutionary theory (McKinnon 2001, 2013).

In face of this reinvention of evolutionary theory manifest in Western assumptions of what counts as a truly modern nation, I wish to make two points. First, rather than see the differences in national constitution as indicative of an evolutionary or developmental trajectory, I see them as indicative of the differential and highly contested values and ideologies through which contemporary nation-states are constituted. To brand one as modern and another as backward ranks them according to an ethnocentric logic, but it does not help us understand the varieties of contemporary nation-states. Second, whether the unit of contemporary nations is understood to be the individual or a kin group of one or another kind, the primary question I wish to address in this chapter is how particular forms of kinship and marriage are themselves used as analogues through which to imagine the constitutive values that are seen as essential to the formation of a modern nation-state. I argue that particular forms of political governance (democracy, theocracy, monarchy) are brought into being in relation to particular forms of kinship (nuclear vs. extended family, shallow vs. deep descent lines) and marriage (monogamy vs. polygamy, non-kin vs. kin marriage, companionate/contract vs. arranged/coerced marriage). Rather than see these necessarily as different markers along a universal evolutionary movement inevitably unfolding towards a state of "modernity," I see them as evidence of deeply contested values about the nature of human relations – both domestic and political – that have long been at the core of culture wars in the United States and in the global politics of colonial and postcolonial conflicts.

26.2   Imagining National Unity through Familial Hierarchy and Equality

How then might we understand this relation between the domestic and the political, between the forms of kinship and marriage and the forms of nation and political governance – the separation of which was itself supposed to be a signifier of modernity? How might we understand both the unity of the nation or family and the character of the social relations within the nation or family?

In the late 1960s, David Schneider argued that the domain of American kinship could be analyzed in terms of a set of distinctive features: those defined by nature (or biology, substance), which included "natural" illegitimate children; those defined by law (or cultural code for conduct, choice), which included relations by marriage, fosterage, and adoption;

and those defined by both nature and law, biology and code for conduct, substance and choice – which he somewhat confusingly called relations "by blood" and which included relations between (grand)parents and (grand)children and between siblings, cousins, etc. (1968: 28). The unity of the family, he argued, was characterized by the symbols of sexual intercourse, love, and diffuse enduring solidarity (1968). Carrying his cultural analysis further – and crossing domains to follow the symbolic logic of these distinctive symbols and distinctive features wherever they might go – Schneider (1969) found that, at what he called the "pure cultural level," these distinctive features (nature and law, substance and code for conduct) and the symbolic logic of diffuse enduring solidarity could also be seen to define the citizenship in the US nation and also, although in different ways, membership in certain religions, specifically Christianity and Judaism.

Schneider's analysis accomplished several important things. First, it read cultural symbols across domains – kinship, nationality, and religion – that were usually analyzed separately; second, it pointed to the ways in which the symbolic unity and solidarity of family, nation, and religion could be configured in relation to one another; and, third, it called attention to the ways in which kinship (and nationality and religion) could be seen as either given (in nature) or made (as the work of human activity) or both. However, in part because of peculiar theoretical distinctions he made – between what he called the "pure" and "conglomerate" level of cultural analysis – Schneider missed the symbolic import of gender, sexuality, age, and race in delineating hierarchies within the symbolic unity of kinship, nationality, and religion.

Feminist anthropologists were quick to point out that, even within Western nations, the picture of the nation as composed of generic, equivalent individuals hardly held up when viewed from the position of women. They emphasized that the structure of both the family and the nation (not to mention religion) had to be seen as fundamentally gendered (not to mention racialized). As Anne McClintock notes:

> In post-French Revolution Europe, women were not incorporated directly into the nation state as citizens, but only indirectly through men, as dependent members of the family in private and public law. The Code Napoleon was the first modern statute to decree that the wife's nationality should follow her husband's, an example other European countries briskly followed. A woman's political relation to the nation was submerged as a social relation to a man through marriage. For women, citizenship in the nation was mediated by the marriage relation within the family.
>
> *(1993: 65)*

In the United States, for instance, laws of coverture shaped women's civil and economic rights, in some aspects, well into the twentieth century. In the spring of 1907, for instance, the United States Congress passed a law that declared that "any American woman who marries a foreigner shall take the nationality of her husband," and on March 2 the federal government summarily denationalized and denaturalized thousands of American women for marrying foreign citizens. There were no exceptions to this rule. Choice of a spouse was the overriding determinant of a married woman's citizenship, and the assumption of her husband's nationality was an unwritten part of a woman's nuptial contract (Bredbenner 1998: 4). It was not until 1934 that this provision of "derivative nationality" and "gender-based double standards in the country's nationality laws" were overturned (Bredbenner 1998: 7).

Taking account of such inequalities and challenging the notion of the family or the nation as composed of generic equivalent individuals, feminist anthropologists and kinship theorists have focused on the gendered hierarchies of family and national belonging and how the two coincide to naturalize relations of hierarchy within unity. Both Anne McClintock (1993) and Carol Delaney (1995) argue that it is precisely the extent to which kinship is seen as a natural (biological) relation that it can be used analogically to naturalize relations in other social domains, such as that of the nation. As a model for the nation, the family provides not only a symbol of a seemingly natural unity and a collective whole, characterized by diffuse, enduring solidarity, but also a symbol of hierarchy and differential power through symbolic analogues with age, gender, and marital relations with the family. As McClintock notes, "the family offered an indispensable figure for sanctioning social hierarchy within a putative organic unity of interests. Since the subordination of woman to man, and child to adult, was deemed a natural fact, other forms of social hierarchy could be depicted in familial terms to guarantee social difference as a category of nature" (1993: 63; see also Delaney 1995: 178).

McClintock goes on to suggest that the family also provided analogies for the differential relations between peoples and nations in colonial and postcolonial narratives of progress and evolutionary development.

> Since children "naturally" progress into adults, projecting the family image on to national and imperial "Progress" enabled what was often murderously violent change to be legitimized as the progressive unfolding of natural decree. National or imperial intervention could be figured as an organic non-revolutionary progression that naturally contained hierarchy within unity: paternal fathers ruling benignly over immature children.
>
> *(1993: 64)*

Often racialized, relations within and between nations in colonial and postcolonial contexts were thus also essentialized by reference to the naturalized relations of gender, age, descent, and marriage within the family to justify relations of colonial – and putatively of evolutionary and developmental – difference between peoples and nations (Heng and Devan 1992 and others).

Within the history of gender, kinship, and race studies, the power of the idea of de/naturalization entailed two analytic moves. The first, of course, was to denaturalize the claims that differences in gender, kinship, and race are biologically determined and to understand these as culturally, not naturally, constructed categories. The second was to analyze the means by which, in culturally particular contexts and in culturally particular ways, they had come to be naturalized in the first place. Sylvia Yanagisako and Carol Delaney took up this question in the introduction to their volume, *Naturalizing Power: Essays in Feminist Cultural Analysis* (1995).

> If the meanings of "male" and "female" are not ... just about natural differences, this prompts us to explore the ways in which these meanings articulate with other inequalities which are supposedly structured by other differences. We need to ask not only how these other inequalities are themselves naturalized – i.e., made to appear the logical outgrowths of other "facts of life" – but how their distinctiveness from gender is naturalized.
>
> *(Yanagisako and Delaney 1995: 11)*

They argue, ultimately, that it is the taboo on reading across domains – particularly those domains such as science and religion that appear to represent universal truths above and beyond human agency (Yanagisako and Delaney 1995: 13) – that prevents us from seeing the concordance of inequalities across domains that serves to naturalize hierarchical relations.

In this chapter, I build on this imperative to read across domains to probe how the figure of hierarchy within unity is naturalized by concordances between family and nation. However, I take two further steps. First, I want to think about the ways in which not only hierarchy in unity but also equality in unity is brought into being and naturalized through such concordances. Second, I want to understand not only the spaces of concordance between the values that organize family, nation, and particular forms of political governance, but also those spaces of discordance – where the values that organize the family and the nation are explicitly different. These latter can either be sites of naturalization or present an opportunity for challenge and denaturalization. To explore these possibilities, I turn to nineteenth-century America.

26.3 Contested Forms of Marriage and Political Governance in Nineteenth-Century America

In 1856, the first Republican Party national convention adopted a platform that called for the abolition of the "twin relics of barbarism" – slavery and polygamy – thereby announcing its intention to radically reform these "peculiar domestic institutions" in the United States (Gordon 2002: 55). In the following two years, 1857 and 1858, Dr. Samuel Merrifield Bemiss published two reports (the latter commissioned by the nascent American Medical Association) on what he – and two decades later, Lewis Henry Morgan (1877) – would call the "evil effects" of marriages of consanguinity, a domestic institution that had been both common and highly valued up to that time in America.

The history of the United States might be seen as a sustained, if always unsteady and deeply contested, revolt against a British and early colonial patriarchal order that established a concordance in the values of hierarchy, holism, and divine or natural law across domestic, political, and religious institutions: that is, the same values organized the religious relation between god and man, the political relation between sovereign and subject, the domestic relations between husband and wife and between parents and children (Cott 2000: 13; Dolgin 1997; Grossberg 1985). In the post-revolutionary United States, the ideals of individualism, equality, consent, and contract came to be seen as appropriate to the governance of political and economic relations and – as Michael Grossberg (1985) and Nancy Cott (2000) tell us – they also increasingly came to be seen as appropriate to the domestic relations of kinship and marriage, which had heretofore remained governed by the patriarchal principles of hierarchy, holism, and divine or natural law. However, the degree of this domestic transformation was highly contested. Indeed, it could be said that the question of whether domestic relations should remain distinctly shaped and governed by patriarchal principles or rather be reconfigured by the same values of the post-revolutionary political and economic order has remained at the heart of the "culture wars" in America. One could say that they actually began in the post-revolutionary era (Grossberg 1985) and have extended up to the present in the contemporary debates about rights of privacy, birth control, abortion, and gay marriage (Dolgin 1997; Santorum 2005).

But over the second half of the nineteenth century, Americans expended an extraordinary amount of blood, treasure, and scientific, legislative, judicial, and literary effort to effect the prohibition of several "domestic institutions" – slavery, polygamy, cousin marriage, and nepotism – whose reliance on values of hierarchy, inequality, family privilege, coercion, and divine law had come to be seen as too inconsistent with and corrosive of ideals of equality, individualism, choice, and secular contract law central to post-revolutionary ideals of political governance, not to mention "free" economic labor.

In this section, I want to focus on the two forms of marriage that came under attack and were subject to intense and virulent campaigns of prohibition during the last half of the nineteenth century in the United States. I do this as a way of getting at the densely intertwined relationship between contours of kinship and marriage and those of nation. It is precisely through the contrast that was established in the late nineteenth century between polygamy and theocracy and between cousin marriage and monarchy that a deep association between monogamy and secular democracy was wrought (here "secular" needs to be read as Christian Protestant).

In a "modern" world where matters of kinship and marriage are presumed to be separated from those of economics and politics, it is hard to comprehend just how densely intertwined ideas and practices relating to kinship and marriage were with different religious and political ideologies of what might constitute a modern, "civilized" nation-state (Cott 2000; McKinnon and Cannell 2013). And, in a world where monogamy and non-kin marriages are (pretty much) settled norms associated with "modern," democratic societies, it is perhaps hard to comprehend just how many marital forms jostled with monogamy and non-kin marriage for attention in nineteenth-century America.

Mormon polygamy, Shaker celibacy, Oneida group marriage, "free lovers," and Owenite and Fourierist communitarian relations, cousin and double cousin marriage, and sibling-set exchange articulated not only different ideals about the shape of domestic relations, but also different ideals about the values through which the nation and economic and property relations should be constituted (Cott 2000: 68–74; Cross 1950; Foster 1991). Although many positions were staked out in this unsettled territory, at the very core, the issue was whether marriage, labor, and government should be organized through the values of family status or individual merit, of hierarchy or equality, and of coercion or free will. The radical reformist agendas of the newly formed Republican Party as much as the newly formed American Medical Association asserted national ideals of individualism, equality, and free will by articulating a link between monogamy and (secular/Protestant) democracy; and they set themselves in opposition to hierarchy, family status, and coercion by articulating the links between polygamy and theocracy as well as cousin marriage and monarchy – not to mention slavery and patriarchal society.

26.4 Polygamy/Theocracy and Monogamy/Democracy

In considering the contest over polygamy in mid to late nineteenth-century America, I focus not on the complex question of religious freedom, but rather on three issues that relate centrally to the theme of this chapter: first, the manifestation of religious hierarchy in both domestic and political institutions; which entailed, second, the question of whether the unit of domestic, religious, and political institutions should be the family or the individual; and third, the question of whether women under polygamy were necessarily coerced into marriage. One of the most striking aspects about the nineteenth-century debate over polygamy is that both those for and those against polygamy agreed upon a central proposition: that there should be an *integral and necessary connection between marriage, religion, and forms of political governance* – that is, in Sarah Barringer Gordon's words, that "commitment to one or the other form of marriage *shaped* public as well as private life" (Gordon 2002: 5, emphasis added; see also Cott 2000: 10, 21, 114). However, they violently disagreed on the character of the values that should underlie these relations.

Opponents of polygamy railed against the hierarchical – that is, explicitly patriarchal – order that was at the core of both the Mormon family and Mormon theocracy. They considered three aspects of Mormon life – plural "Patriarchal Marriage," the patriarch's absolute authority over his wives, and the religious elders' tight control over governmental institutions in the Utah Territory – to be the foundation for despotism in both the domestic and political arenas. Cott notes that "the thematic equivalency between polygamy, despotism, and coercion on the one side and between monogamy, political liberty, and consent on the other resonated through the political culture of the United States all during the ... [nineteenth] century" (2000: 23).

Central to opponents' perception of the hierarchical order of Mormon domestic, religious, and political relations was the individual's – and particularly the woman's – encompassment within the family and her submission to the authority of her husband. Not only a woman's status but, indeed, her very salvation, depended upon her position within a family and upon her submission to her husband. Gordon observes:

> Only in families (rather than as individuals) could Mormons achieve the highest level of salvation, known as "exaltation." Control of families living in the Principle, the most exalted of all structures of governance, was clearly and unequivocally vested in husbands. Patriarchal governance required a husband to command obedience, to preserve harmony among wives, and to ensure the celestial progress of wives (and children) *through his own exaltation* after death.
>
> *(2002: 105, emphasis added)*

While Brigham Young preached that such command was *not* tyrannical but simply an application of "the principles of our religion, which, in their very nature, are bound to make those who will be guided by them healthy, wealthy and wise" (Gordon 2002: 105), opponents nevertheless saw Mormon polygamy as a form of tyranny and despotism. For instance, political theorist Francis Lieber argued that "*polygamy **led to** 'the patriarchal principle* ... which, when applied to large communities, fetters the people in stationary despotism, while that principle cannot exist long in monogamy'" (Gordon 2002: 81, emphasis added; see also Cott 2000: 114–115). Here, both equality and individual agency were understood to be sacrificed to the hierarchical values of divinely ordained patriarchy – the key to domestic, political, and indeed eternal salvational order. Opponents contrasted the hierarchical encompassment of individuals – particularly women – within the family and under the despotic lordship of the polygamous father/husband with the (relative!) individualistic equality and free will of monogamous marriage.

At the center of this portrait of Mormon domestic, economic, and political tyranny stood the contrast between coercion and force on the one hand, and choice, free will, and voluntarism, on the other. Opponents took it as self-evident that women under polygamy could not possibly exercise individual choice, free will, or the voluntarism that they deemed necessary to Protestant Christian marriage, religious freedom, free labor, and democratic political engagement. Accordingly, women under polygamy were often referred to as "white slaves" – mirroring the "black slaves" that together constituted the "twin relics of barbarism," against which the Republican Party had set itself. Under both regimes, the enslaved were incapable of the free choice that, under the Northern political order, was considered essential to free marital, labor, and political relations.

Mormons, however, countered that "consent" was fundamental both to polygamous marriage and to the theocratic order of the Utah Territory. But opponents of polygamy did not perceive the Mormon concept of consent to be the same as the non-Mormon (i.e., Protestant) legal and political concept of free will, choice, or voluntarism (Gordon 2002: 93). As Gordon elucidates, the Saints

> ... made their most important choice when they testified to the truth of the New Dispensation. From this life-changing decision, others flowed. Mormons were expected to either "take sides with the mother of harlots, and with her monogamy, and celibacy, and prostitution, or take sides with the Almighty, and with His holy law of polygamy, and sexual purity." ... Free consent to marriage was essential and evidence of the faith necessary to assure exaltation in the celestial worlds. But consent occurred within the faith; the capacity to affirm the doctrines central to the faith – including plural marriage – was the core freedom granted to all Saints.

(2002: 93)

As much as the Saints conceptualized polygamy as integral to Mormon theocracy, so too did their opponents understand monogamy as the foundation of liberty and democracy. Indeed, as Cott argues, the founders of the Republic, drawing upon

> ... the French Enlightenment author the Baron de Montesquieu, whose *Spirit of the Laws* influenced central tenets of American republicanism ... learned to think of marriage and the form of government as mirroring each other ... Their Montesquieuan thinking tied the

institution of Christian-modeled monogamy to the kind of polity they envisioned; as a voluntary union based on consent, marriage paralleled the new government.

(2000: 10)

Despite the evident contradictions with coverture and other gender inequalities, nineteenth-century novelists and politicians in the North saw the hierarchical patriarchal order of Mormon polygamists and theocrats as a stark contrast to the relative egalitarian and individualistic order that they conceived to be vital to monogamy, religious disestablishment, and democracy. Gordon notes that "Popular novelist Metta Victor explained to her readers in 1856 that monogamous marriage was essential to 'the spirit and intent of that Constitution which is to perpetuate the republic, and render it, in truth, the refuge for the oppressed, the *home* of liberty'" (Gordon 2002: 29). The opponents of polygamy asserted that monogamous "marriage was not only a component of *human happiness* but of the *Constitution itself*. The right to emotional and spiritual fulfillment, conceived as the 'spirit and intent of th[e] Constitution,' they argued, was integral to the novelists' claim that polygamy entailed an illegitimate exercise of authority" (Gordon 2002: 51–52).

Central to the Republican platform against both polygamy and slavery was the critique of a hierarchical social order that presumed Mormon wives, like Southern slaves, were coerced into a state of enslavement. This state denied them the choice and free will that was *as necessary* to monogamy as it was to religious disestablishment, to free labor, and to democratic institutions. In the campaign against polygamy, Gordon suggests, the Republican reformers "were committed to the release of fetters on human progress, to the onward march of civilization through the purification of marriage to protect and promote freedom, democracy, and equality – all in a constitutional system that integrated [Protestant] Christianity and political liberty" (2002: 83).

What is interesting for my purposes here is the fact that the contours and values of particular forms of marriage not only *parallel* those of particular forms of national governance, but were also actually understood to *engender* them.

26.5   Kin Marriage/Monarchy and Non-Kin Marriage/Democracy

Unlike the case of polygamy, where polygamy's link through religious hierarchy to theocracy was the central concern, with cousin marriage the main issue was the link between cousin marriage – through inherited family status and wealth – to political manifestations of royalty, aristocracy, and monarchy. This connection was articulated through ideas about heredity and relative health and disease – which were thought about in terms of humors and temperaments (since the language of genetics and germ theory of disease had not yet come into being). The cultural logic of the debate focused on whether the "intensification" of temperaments attributed to "in-and-in marriage" (or the inbreeding of animals) resulted in beneficial enhancements of desirable traits or in a morbid intensification of familial temperamental peculiarities and diseases and the overall degeneration of familial lines. Opponents of cousin marriage associated the degeneration assumed to follow from "in-marriage" with the inevitable decline of hierarchical monarchies while they linked the vitality of "out-marriage" to the enviable rise of egalitarian democracies – in particular, the American Republic.

Opponents of cousin marriage focused their attention upon European royalty and aristocracy and their American avatars, whose repeated and reckless propensities to marry "in-and-in," they assumed, were driven by concerns for consolidating both wealth and rank. In the March 1855 edition of the *Nashville Journal of Medicine and Surgery*, for instance, F. E. H. Steger, of Maysville, Alabama, made evident his utter contempt for the Spanish monarchy. "From the time of Charles 5th," Steger argued, the Spanish monarchs "selected wives, often near relatives, from considerations of mere personal aggrandizement ... and the consequence has been that the race is, as it ought to be, nearly extinct, exhibiting to the world a *beautiful specimen* of a queen in the person of the present lecherous fugitive!" (1855: 191, emphasis in original). Dr. Charles Caldwell, of Kentucky, suggested that one of the causes of degeneracy in the European nobility is a "long perseverance in family alliances" (1834: 31).

> Witness the present royal families of Europe, that, from sceptered pride, and state policy, have long intermarried with each other. They can now scarcely muster heirs, in the direct line to occupy their thrones – and such heirs that, the whole of them united, would not form a well-gifted man! ... Yet, those families, now so degenerate, were once signalized for high and noble qualities ... and were, on that account, clad in purple, and decorated with crowns ... Of the nobility of Portugal, I might observe the same. They were once the pride of Europe. But, by intermarriages, continued for centuries, they are now a most degenerate race.
>
> *(Caldwell 1834: 31–32)*

Within the United States, itself, those families with aristocratic pretentions came under the same criticism as the European royalty. Quoting a gentleman from Fredericksburg, Virginia, the Reverend Charles Brooks of Medford, Massachusetts, commented upon the consequences of the inmarrying, property-preserving predilections of the Virginia aristocracy:

> A certain family of wealth and respectability have intermarried for many generations, until there cannot be found in three or four of

them a sound man or woman. One has sore eyes, another scrofula, a third is idiotic, a fourth blind, a fifth bandy-legged, a sixth with a head about as large as a turnip, with not one out of the number exempt from physical or mental defects. Yet they persevere in intermarrying, although these monuments are constantly before them.

(1856: 240)

For these authors, it goes without saying that such aristocracies – in which the family is turned in on itself, in which wealth and status are valued above all else, and in which political hierarchy is the accepted norm – are doomed to extinction before the superior vigor of the outbred democratic republics.

In the American political context, in which progress was measured, in part, by the move away from hierarchical monarchies toward egalitarian democratic republics, commentators drew a direct relationship between out-breeding and mixing of populations, on the one hand, and progress and the evolution of society, on the other. Dr. Samuel Bemiss (1857: 377) imagined that "history will … sustain the opinion that the most vigorous people have sprung from the ingrafting of nations differing in constitution and temperament from each other. I believe … that the extraordinary activity and energy of the American people are due to the composite nature of their blood."

Some commentators conjured up an image of the hierarchical implications of "inbreeding" in the production of monstrous races of supermen that were anathema to democratic principles. Edward Crossman expressed his deep concern with extending the practice of livestock inbreeding to humans. He asked:

But are the same results desirable in the reproduction of the human race? Is it not directly the contrary? Is not the man the best citizen, whose mental and bodily powers are most evenly balanced? Would the idea of maintaining through successive generations distinct breeds of statesmen, physicians, clergymen, soldiers, prize-fighters, and jockeys, be agreeable to our notions of civilization? No! what we desire is to maintain the members of the human family as far as possible in equilibrium; to advance in the mass, to progress altogether [sic]; but to check the development in individuals of exaggerated characteristics either of mind or of body, and to banish amongst us the seeds of damage and decay.

(1861: 402)

The vision evoked by the opponents of cousin marriage is one of a democratic dystopia, where individuals are bred to caste positions, where individual choice yields to biological manipulation, where the equality of the Republican mass yields to the hierarchical disparities of wealth and breeding, and where the very equilibrium required for health, well-being, and progress is bent away toward commercial profit.

In an outburst of nationalist optimism, Reverend Brooks articulates the extent of the beneficial consequences that he imagines to be derived from the mixing of populations (when, that is, it is limited to the "Caucasian race") and the connection between the vitality of this mixing and the vitality of a Republican and Christian government.

> Will not our country furnish the most wonderful example of the effects of intermarriages with different castes of the Caucasian race? When the people of these United States become a mixture of English, Scotch, Irish, Germans, and French, will they exhibit a strength of body and an intelligence of mind, a true inborn energy and moral power, which do not equally signalize either of the nations from whom they sprang? Under the fostering care of a truly republican and Christian government, will they advance in science, arts, agriculture, commerce, and manufactures, and all the blessings of a religious civilization and political equality, as no one of their parent nations has? Let us hope that it is the appointed destiny of our free and prosperous land, to exhibit a higher development of human attributes than has yet blessed or astonished mankind.
>
> *(Brooks 1856: 246)*

In the complex racial politics of antebellum America, however, this wildly positive assessment of the consequences of out-marriage had its limits. Both those for and against cousin marriage situated their arguments in relation to their perception of the negative exception of racial difference, which was informed by the debate about the monogenetic or polygenetic origins of humans. After arguing that human vigor and progress clearly followed from the "ingrafting of nations differing in constitution and temperament," Dr. Bemiss is quick to qualify the positive implications of such mixing. He suggests:

> This rule, however, seems subject to some qualification; for there certainly exist strong reasons to believe that matrimonial alliances between the greatest possible contrast to be found on our globe – the negro and Caucasian races, for instance – are not favourable to the most vigorous propagation of the species. I do not look upon mulattoes as hybrids, but think they exhibit less of vigor and vital force than are found in crosses where there is less contrast.
>
> *(Bemiss 1857: 377)*

The comment that he does "not look upon mulattoes as hybrid" indicates that Bemiss does not conceive of the races as different species, as the polygenesists would. However, he clearly sees interracial unions as resulting in diminished vitality and vigor.

In sum, the debate about cousin marriage in nineteenth-century America explicitly linked forms of marriage and forms of political governance. Cousin (or "in-and-in") marriage – which tied individuals back into networks of kin and intensified not only temperaments but also relative family wealth and aristocratic status – was seen as inherently connected to monarchical forms of governance and the social hierarchies that they perpetuated. In the American context, over the nineteenth century, cousin marriage was reconceptualized as central to an outdated, hierarchical form of domestic and political governance that was inimical to the egalitarian principles of the democratic republic. Non-kin marriages (or the mixings entailed in "out-marriages"), by contrast, were thought to ensure a healthy equilibrium of temperaments – both individually and politically – and to establish a level, democratic political and economic playing field on which individuals could be equal, and the masses as a whole could progress together. Here, again, the contours of marriage were the necessary and inextricable foundation for the contours of political and national formations. Yet, if the positive injunction to marry out was understood to level the political and economic playing field and to define the vitality of egalitarian republican governance, the negative prohibition on marrying "out" across the racial color line reinforced the grounds for racial inequality and marked the limits of republican equality, democratic ideals, and national belonging.

26.6 Contemporary Reverberations of the Cousin Marriage Debate

The relationship between monogamy and non-kin marriage and the egalitarian ideals of democracy is so well established in contemporary Euro-American societies that it is hardly remarkable. Indeed, this relationship has become such an implicit part of what counts as "modern," that the stigmatization of polygamy and cousin marriage is central to narratives of development and very much part of modernization efforts, at least in Western-leaning nations.

One can see the cousin marriage debate resurface in two contexts: in relation to Western neo-imperial "national building" efforts abroad (McKinnon 2013: 39–41); and in relation to the influx of immigrant populations at home. Very often, in both of these contexts, the current debate is also implicitly one that poses Christian and Muslim ideals and practices in stark opposition to one another again within a developmental frame that – at least from a Christian point of view – presupposes particular ideals and practices (individualism, equality, free will, secular law) as inherently "modern" and others (presumed to be organized in terms of familism, hierarchy, coercion, and religious law) as inherently "backward."

In this section I take one example of how the nineteenth-century debates about cousin marriage continue to reverberate in the political economy of the contemporary global relations: that is, the controversy about cousin marriage that has been ignited by the high rates of cousin marriage (and its presumed consequences) among "Pakistani Muslims" in Britain. This debate should be read against the very different history of (English, Christian) cousin marriage in Britain, where it remains legal. In his book on cousin marriage – *Incest and Influence: The Private Life of Bourgeois England* (2009) – Adam Kuper argues that, although cousin marriage (and sibling-set exchange) had a long history among royalty and aristocrats in Britain in the nineteenth century, it became a critical force in consolidating (very public) political, economic, and intellectual relations among an emergent upper middle class. Kuper outlines the importance of cousin marriages and sibling-set exchanges to the rise of Quaker (Barclays) and Jewish (Rothschild) banking houses, of manufacturing concerns (such as Wedgewood pottery), of multigenerational intellectual, political, and/or religious networks (such as those of the Darwins or of the Clapham Sect) and, more broadly, of relations that crisscross all these concerns – as is evident in the entangled genealogies of the Wedgewood, Darwin, and Allen families, linked by generations of cousin marriage and sibling-set exchange (Kuper 2009: 107–178; Kuper 2001, 2002; and see Sabean and Teuscher 2007 for a comparative history of cousin marriage in Europe). As in the United States, the very fabric of British political, economic, intellectual, and religious life was stitched together through repeated cousin marriages and sibling-set exchanges in the nineteenth century and up to World War I (Kuper 2009: 251–256). After World War I, cousin marriage in England declined precipitously: by the 1930s, only one marriage in 6,000 was with a first cousin (Kuper 2009: 251). Kuper cites a number of causes for the waning of cousin marriage in England. There was a complex set of trends and transformations in English society that set the stage for the decline: the liberalization of the business environment, the flourishing of the stock exchange, the decline of family firms in the postwar depression, demographic changes (including the loss of marriageable men in the war and smaller family size), and universal adult franchise (2009: 251–253). These broader sociological trends were complemented by arguments – entangled in the rise of eugenics in the 1920s and 1930s – that "cousin marriages should be discouraged because of their link to recessive [genetic] disorders" (2009: 249–250). Despite the fact that the genetic argument generally overstated the modest risks of cousin marriage,[1] "these scientific concerns passed into the general culture" (Kuper 2009: 250) and gave scientific authority to what was otherwise a broader cultural trend against cousin marriage. In the UK, cousin marriage went out with a whimper, not a bang. It was never prohibited; it simply waned.

When the concern over cousin marriage emerged in relation to the influx of "Pakistani Muslims" in Britain in the late twentieth century, the tenor of the debate was quite different and the positive history of cousin marriage in Britain was conveniently forgotten. Although the category of "British Pakistani Muslims" is internally highly differentiated – from diverse regions and with diverse marital practices (Shaw 2001: 316–317) – it is nevertheless clear that consanguineous marriages among this population run as high as 55–69 percent of all marriages and that the percentage has, at least among some populations, increased rather than decreased subsequent to immigration to Britain (Shaw 2001: 318–320; 2009). Alison Shaw has articulated a number of reasons for the high rates of cousin marriage among British Pakistani Muslims, including positive cultural values relating to: the equality of endogamous (vs. exogamous) marriages; continued obligations to kin (vs. individual autonomy); maintaining relations with kin in the country of origin; forging economic alliances; facilitating immigration; and the sentimental, emotional connections between siblings and their children (Shaw 2001, 2006, 2009).

In the first decade of the twenty-first century, the cities of Bradford and Birmingham captured public attention due to the high rate of prenatal and infant mortality and morbidity – particularly of genetic recessive disorders – among the resident population of Pakistani Muslims and the presumed correlation between consanguineous marriages and the emergence of these health problems. While there does, indeed, seem to be a correlation between the high incidence of these cousin marriages and an increased risk of prenatal and infant mortality and genetic recessive disorders, the exact rate of that risk and its relation to a complex variety of other sociological (and non-genetic) factors – including class, occupation, environmental factors, discrimination, inequities in access to health-care services, etc. – are matters of considerable debate. Also, a subject of hot debate is the solution to these health risks – from the outright ban on cousin marriage, on the one end, to genetic counseling, on the other. Alison Shaw (2001, 2006, 2009) has provided an outstanding, detailed, and sensitive analysis of the ethnographic, medical, and political complexities of this situation. For the purposes of this chapter, I am, however, less interested in the specific statistics of rates and risks and more interested in the way in which the specter of cousin marriage immediately became entangled in discourses about modernity, specifically about Pakistani Muslims' ability to assimilate to British cultural and political values, and about their readiness to participate in forms of democratic forms of governance.

Debates about cousin marriage have surfaced periodically over the past couple of decades. However, beginning in 2005 and again in 2008, two British MPs, Ann Cryer and Phil Woolas – each with significant Pakistani populations among their constituencies – raised a cry against cousin marriage or what Woolas called the "elephant in the room" (Driscoll 2008; see also Butt 2005; Gadher, Morgan and Oliver 2008; Shaw 2009; Sparrow 2008). Woolas told the *Sunday Times*: "If you have a child with your cousin, the likelihood is there'll be a genetic problem. The issue we need to debate is first-cousin marriages, whereby a lot of arranged marriages are with first cousins and that produces lots of genetic problems in terms of disability" (Sparrow 2008). A reporter for *The Guardian* noted:

> [Cryer] stressed that she was only talking about "certain sections" of the Pakistani community. The problem related to families who engaged in "trans-continental marriages" because most of those marriages were between cousins. There was often "a price to pay," she went on. "The price to pay is often babies being born dead, or babies being born very early or babies being born with very severe genetically-transmitted disorders."
>
> *(Sparrow 2008)*

Despite their unquestioning conflation of genetic and other causes of morbidity and mortality, their automatic assumption that cousin marriages are arranged marriages, and that the problematic cousin marriages are transcontinental (as opposed to within Britain), the MPs' rhetoric was relatively subdued.

Less so was what followed. Commenting on the MPs' discussion of cousin marriage, Jasvinder Sanghera, a director of a local health trust in Derby who testified before the MPs, equated cousin marriage with forced marriage, blood feuds, disappearing girls, and cheating the immigration system (Driscoll 2008), and he went on to assert a link between cousin marriage and a backwardness that is both foreign and deeply antithetical to British values.

> These babies would not exist if it were not for the importing of traditional rural customs that should have no place in modern Britain. Every day I come face to face with the pain and distress caused by teenagers being forced into marriages with people they have never met in order to "honor" pledges made when they were babies ... The "logic" behind first-cousin marriages is keeping the bloodline clean. Blood feuds can be started if such arrangements are not honored.
>
> *(Driscoll 2008)*

Here, cousin marriage is seen as inherently patriarchal, coercive, lacking in individual free will, and inherently turned in toward particularistic interests of family rather than society at large.

Two years later, in 2010, Baroness Deech – a family law professor, cross-bencher, and Chair of the Human Fertilisation and Embryology Authority for eight years – elaborated on some of these themes in the third of a three-part lecture series. In a preview of the lecture, Frances Gibb writes that Baroness Deech

> ... will note that the practice [of cousin marriage] has always been associated with immigrants and the poor and is "at odds with freedom of choice, romantic love and integration." But factors linked to cousin

marriage in the British immigrant community are working against what she calls its "otherwise inevitable decline." One is finance: such marriages can be arranged to settle debts. Another is financial support of relatives abroad. A third is that it provides a "ready-made framework of supportive family members for a new immigrant spouse"; and a fourth is that it enables relatives to migrate to Britain as a fiancé or spouse. In the Middle East, it is also said to underpin clan loyalty and to accompany nepotism, she argues. But cousin marriage can be a barrier to integration of immigrant communities and "arguably to democracy as we know it abroad."

(2010; see also Alidina and Walji 2010; Beckford 2010; Shaw 2009)

In the absence of any historical memory of the importance of cousin marriage to the consolidation of progressive social, economic, and intellectual transformations in nineteenth-century Britain, cousin marriage, here, becomes shorthand for an immigrant population that is hopelessly backward; perversely and willfully resistant to the core values of British culture, modernity, and democracy (individualism, choice, gender equality, etc.); and stubbornly adherent to patriarchy, inbreeding, clannishness, and nepotism. Not only do these immigrants refuse to assimilate into the mainstream of their host country, they also shamelessly take advantage of open immigration policies and health-care services, placing an undue burden on the British taxpayers and irrationally risking the health of their own children. These concerns about cousin marriage in contemporary Britain echo those that were expressed in nineteenth-century America, only here they have become more explicitly targeted against a population of Muslim immigrants as a way of articulating who does and does not have the necessary values to participate in a supposedly secular, egalitarian, democratic society.

26.7 Conclusion

Ultimately, over the course of the late nineteenth and early twentieth century in America, slavery was abolished, polygamy was banned, overt theocracy was thwarted, cousin marriage was prohibited in 31 states and widely stigmatized across the United States, and laws against nepotism in government began to be put in place. However, none of these outcomes was achieved without tremendous contestation and a considerable amount of cultural, scientific, legislative, judicial – indeed military – effort to attempt to consolidate a moral consensus about the forms of marriage, political governance, and economic relations that would and would not be tolerated in the United States.

In this chapter, I have attempted to show why marriage taboos and prescriptions mattered so much to the articulation of nineteenth-century political ideals concerning what America, as a "modern" nation, should look like; and I have provided one example of the ways in which the nineteenth-century revaluation of cousin marriage in America has reverberated in contemporary debates about modernity and national belonging. I would like to make several points concerning the significance of this history for kinship theory, for understanding the relation between kinship and nation, and for contemporary theories of development and modernity.

First, the nineteenth-century debates about polygamy, monogamy, and cousin marriage challenge narratives of social evolution, development, and modernity that presume a separation between the values and institutional arrangements of kinship and marriage, on the one hand, and economics and politics, on the other (McKinnon and Cannell 2013). Indeed, these historical events demonstrate that Americans perceived an inextricable bond between domestic and political/economic formations not only in those they struggled to prohibit but also in those they endeavored to make central to their vision of the nation. Moreover, it is worth noting that nineteenth-century Americans perceived the forms of kinship and marriage not simply as parallel but also as foundational to the forms of political governance.

Second, some anthropologists – beginning with David Schneider and moving through a number of feminist and other anthropologists – have explored the conceptual relationship between kinship, nation, and citizenship. However, they have mostly done so by attending to ideas about procreation and descent. Here I would like to point to the important ways in which different forms of marriage are conceptually central to imagining and contesting different forms of governance and to ideas about what counts as a "modern" nation.

Finally, contestations over forms of kinship and marriage are ways of talking about contestations over the values that are at the heart of national being and about who does and does not belong within a particular nation. Contests about forms of governance and nation are fought through contests about forms of kinship and marriage because the latter are seen as inseparable from the former. This is the case as much today as in the nineteenth century.

Note

1. Kuper (2009: 250–251) sums up the recent scientific understandings of the risks of cousin marriage in this way: "The chances of birth defects and of infant mortality are roughly doubled for the children of first cousins, but in normal circumstances that means that only an additional 2 percent of children may be affected. According to the geneticists A. H. Bittles and U. E. Markov, 'The risks to the offspring of inbred unions generally are within the limits of acceptability … In the United States, the National Society of Genetic Counselors recently convened a panel

of experts to review the risks of first-cousin marriage. They reported that the small background risk of congenital defects is raised by some 1.7–2 percent in the case of children of first cousins. There is also an additional 4.4 percent chance of pre-reproductive mortality (Bennett Motulsky, Hudgins et al. 2002).' The risks are significantly higher, however, if cousin marriages are repeated over several generations."

References

Alidina, Rizwan and Mohamed Walji. 17 Sept. 2010. "Cousin Marriages: A Question of Understanding." *The Guardian*. www.theguardian.com/commentisfree/2010/sep/17/cousin-marriages-understanding-health-risks, accessed August 7, 2015.

Beckford, Martin. 23 Mar. 2010. "Baroness Deech: Risks of Cousin Marriage Not Discussed for Fear of Offending Muslims." *The Telegraph*. www.telegraph.co.uk/news/religion/7497906/Baroness-Deech-Risks-of-cousin-marriage-not-discussed-for-fear-of-offending-Muslims.html, accessed August 7, 2015.

Bemiss, Samuel Merrifield. 1857. "On Marriages of Consanguinity." *Journal of Psychological Medicine and Mental Pathology* 10: 369–379.

——— 1858. "Report on the Influence of Marriages of Consanguinity upon Offspring." *Transactions of the American Medical Association* 11: 319–425.

Bennett, Robin L, Arno G. Motulsky, Alan Bittles, Louanne Hudgins, et al. 2002. "Genetic Couselling and Screening of Consanguineous Couples and Their Offspring: Recommendations of the National Society of Genetic Counselors." *Journal of Genetic Counseling* 11(2): 97–119.

Bredbenner, Candice Lewis. 1998. *A Nationality of Her Own: Women, Marriage, and the Law of Citizenship*. Berkeley, CA: University of California Press.

Brooks, Charles, Rev. 1856. "Laws of Reproduction, Considered with Particular Reference to the Intermarriage of First-Cousins." *Proceedings of the American Association for the Advancement of Science*, 236–246.

Butt, Riazat. 15 Nov. 2005. "British Pakistanis Should Stop Marrying Cousins, Says MP." *The Guardian*. www.theguardian.com/politics/2005/nov/16/immigrationpolicy.politics, accessed August 7, 2015.

Caldwell, Charles. 1834. *Thoughts on Physical Education: Being a Discourse Delivered to a Convention of Teachers in Lexington, KY., on the 6th and 7th of Nov., 1833*. Boston, MA: Marsh, Capen and Lyon.

Cooke, Miriam. 2014. *Tribal Modern: Branding New Nations in the Arab Gulf*. Berkeley, CA: University of California Press.

Cott, Nancy F. 2000. *Public Vows: A History of Marriage and the Nation*. Cambridge, MA: Harvard University Press.

Cross, Whitney R. 1950. *The Burned-Over District: The Social and Intellectual History of Enthusiastic Religion in Western New York, 1800–1850*. Ithaca, NY: Cornell University Press.

Crossman, Edward. 1861. "On Intermarriage of Relations As a Cause of Degeneracy of Offspring." *British Medical Journal* 1: 401–402.

Delaney, Carol. 1995. "Father State, Motherland, and the Birth of Modern Turkey." In *Naturalizing Power: Essays in Feminist Cultural Analysis*, ed. Sylvia Yanagisako and Carol Delaney, 177–200. New York: Routledge.

Dolgin, Janet L. 1997. *Defining the Family: Law, Technology, and Reproduction in an Uneasy Age.* New York: New York University Press.

Driscoll, Margarette. 17 Feb. 2008. "It's Tradition, Not Religion, That Wrecks So Many Lives." *The Sunday Times.* www.freerepublic.com/focus/f-news/1972391/posts, accessed August 8, 2015.

Fabian, Johannes. 1983. *Time and the Other: How Anthropology Makes Its Object.* New York: Columbia University Press.

Foster, Lawrence. 1991. *Women, Family, and Utopia: Communal Experiments of the Shakers, the Oneida Community, and the Mormons.* Syracuse, NY: Syracuse University Press.

Gadher, Dipesh, Christopher Morgan and Jonathan Oliver. 10 Feb. 2008. "Minister Warns of 'Inbred' Muslims." *The Sunday Times.* www.thesundaytimes.co.uk/sto/Test/politics/article80421.ece, accessed August 7, 2015.

Gibb, Frances. 20 Mar. 2010. "Rise in Marriages between Cousins 'Is Putting Children's Health at Risk.'" *The Times.* www.timesonline.co.uk/tol/news/uk/health/article7069255.ece, accessed February 13, 2011.

Gordon, Sarah Barringer. 2002. *The Mormon Question: Polygamy and Constitutional Conflict in Nineteenth-Century America.* Chapel Hill, NC: University of North Carolina Press.

Grossberg, Michael. 1985. *Governing the Hearth: Law and the Family in Nineteenth-Century America.* Chapel Hill, NC: University of North Carolina Press.

Handler, Richard. 1988. *Nationalism and the Politics of Culture in Quebec.* Madison, WI: University of Wisconsin Press.

Heng, Geraldine and Janadas Devan. 1992. "State Fatherhood: The Politics of Nationalism, Sexuality, and Race in Singapore." In *Nationalisms and Sexualities*, ed. Andres Parker, Mary Russo, Doris Sommer and Patricia Yaeger, 343–364. New York: Routledge.

Herb, Michael. 1999. *All in the Family: Absolutism, Revolution, and Democracy in the Middle Eastern Monarchies.* Albany, NY: State University of New York.

Kuper, Adam. 2001. "Fraternity and Endogamy: The House of Rothschild." *Social Anthropology* 9(3): 273–287.

———. 2002. "Incest, Cousin Marriage, and the Origin of the Human Sciences in Nineteenth-Century England." *Past and Present* 174: 158–183.

———. 2009. *Incest and Influence: The Private Life of Bourgeois England.* Cambridge, MA: Harvard University Press.

Latour, Bruno. 1993. *We Have Never Been Modern.* Cambridge, MA: Harvard University Press.

McClintock, Anne. 1993. "Family Feuds: Gender, Nationalism and the Family." *Feminist Review* 44: 61–80.

McKinnon, Susan. 2001. "The Economies of Kinship and the Paternity of Culture: Origin Stories in Kinship Theory." In *Relative Values: Reconfiguring Kinship Studies*, ed. Sarah Franklin and Susan McKinnon, 277–301. Durham, NC: Duke University Press.

——— 2013. "Kinship within and beyond the 'Movement of Progressive Societies.'" In *Vital Relations: Modernity and the Persistent Life of Kinship*, ed. Susan McKinnon and Fenella Cannell, 39–62. Santa Fe, NM: School for Advanced Research Press.

McKinnon, Susan and Fenella Cannell. 2013. "The Difference Kinship Makes." In *Vital Relations: Modernity and the Persistent Life of Kinship*, ed. Susan McKinnon and Fenella Cannell, 3–38. Santa Fe, NM: School for Advanced Research Press.

Morgan, Lewis Henry. 1877. *Ancient Society; or, Researches in the Lines of Human Progress from Savagery through Barbarism to Civilization*. New York: Henry Holt.

Sabean, David Warren and Simon Teuscher. 2007 "Kinship in Europe: A New Approach to Long-Term Development." In *Kinship in Europe: Approaches to Long-Term Development (1300–1900)*, ed. David Warren Sabean, Simon Teuscher and Jon Mathieu, 1–32. New York: Berghahn Books.

Santorum, Rick. 2005. *It Takes a Family: Conservatism and the Common Good*. Wilmington, DE: ISI Books.

Schatz, Edward. 2004. *Modern Clan Politics: The Power of "Blood" in Kazakhstan and Beyond*. Seattle, WA: University of Washington Press.

Schneider, David M. 1968. *American Kinship: A Cultural Account*. Englewood Cliffs, NJ: Prentice-Hall.

——— 1969. "Kinship, Nationality and Religion in American Culture: Toward a Definition of Kinship." In *Forms of Symbolic Action* (Proceedings of the 1969 Annual Spring Meeting of the American Ethnological Society), 116–125. Seattle, WA: University of Washington Press.

Shaw, Alison. 2001. "Kinship, Cultural Preference and Immigration: Consanguineous Marriage among British Pakistanis." *Journal of the Royal Anthropological Institute* 7(2): 315–334.

——— 2006. "*Rishtas*: Adding Emotion to Strategy in Understanding British Pakistani Transnational Marriages." *Global Networks* 6(4): 405–421.

——— 2009. *Negotiating Risk: British Pakistani Experiences of Genetics*. New York: Berghahn Books.

Sparrow, Andrew. 11 Feb. 2008. "Backing for Minister over First-Cousin Marriage Comments." *The Guardian*. www.guardian.co.uk/politics/2008/feb11/religion.medicalscience, accessed November 8, 2010.

Steger, F. E. H. 1855. "Hereditary Transmission of Disease." *Nashville Journal of Medicine and Surgery* 8(3): 177–191.

Yanagisako, Sylvia and Carol Delaney. 1995. "Naturalizing Power." In *Naturalizing Power: Essays in Feminist Cultural Analysis*, ed. Sylvia Yanagisako and Carol Delaney, 1–22. New York: Routledge.

27

The Prison as a Technology of Care in Northeast Brazil

Hollis Moore

27.1 Introduction: A Preference for Prison

Andreia is an Afro-Brazilian woman in her early fifties. She lives in her very own concrete house which is one of her proudest accomplishments. Andreia and her relations built it, bit by bit, on recently invaded land on the margins of an already peripheral neighborhood located in the vicinity of the state of Bahia's largest prison compound.[1] Andreia's oldest daughter, Neguinha (a diminutive meaning "blackie"), is a pre-trial detainee at this compound's only prison for women. During one of my visits to Andreia's house, she shows me a stack of dog-eared family photos. She pauses on an old photo of Neguinha, tapping it as she tells me her daughter's hearing has been scheduled and that she could be released next month. I smile enthusiastically, saying: "I hope all goes well and she returns home soon." I quickly learn, however, that Andreia is not eagerly anticipating Neguinha's release:

> I'd rather her be in prison than on the street because she doesn't stay here [at home]. On the street, she's eating, drinking. There [in prison] she isn't going to die. I prefer her there, in prison ... I can sleep without worrying about her.

How does a mother come to value her daughter's imprisonment positively? In this chapter, I answer this question as I show how, in a context of profound insecurity, the prison emerges as a technology of care. I use this term to refer to the way carceral subjects[2] use the prison – a pervasive feature of their social landscape – to fend off (or exploit) crises in order to achieve social reproduction at the level of the household.

When household social reproduction is threatened, one possible intervention is "habilitation" (Waldram 2012: 101) or, more specifically, the cultivation/restoration of appropriate levels of consideration among relatives perceived to be deficient in this regard. Deficient consideration is problematic from the perspective of household reproduction insofar as consideration "denotes recognition of what one has received, allowing for active entry into the symbolic cycle of reproduction of the family, the kinship network, and society" (Hita 2008: 27). In short, "consideration" implies acknowledgment and enactment of "mutuality of being" (Sahlins 2013) – that is, participating in one another's existence, being deeply interconnected, and having a sense of shared fate. Crucially, this quality of being is not an inevitable concomitant of Brazilian kinship; it is both constitutive, and a *potential* consequence, of kinship.

Consideration is an emic concept through which Brazilians conceptualize their degree of relatedness with others. It is "a fundamental concept of the Brazilian social world" (da Matta 1991: 64) that is integral to the kinship system. According to Hita, this principle is:

> ... the third term – together with consanguinity and affinity – ... through which mechanisms of selection, integration and exclusion are activated, mediating relationships of affinity, friendship, neighbourhood, god-parenthood or belonging to a group, and transforming the fictitious relative into an effective or operational one. This dilutes the efficacy of the principle of blood and institutes the modality of "choice" through which the *relative* "in principle" may become an effective relative.
>
> *(Hita 2008: 4–5)*

Through consideration, neighbors may become co-parents; friends may become siblings; affines may become close relatives; and children's caregivers may become aunts or even mothers. Indeed, many Brazilians speak of having multiple mothers, for example, "the mother who nursed me, the mother who raised me and the mother who gave birth to me" (research participant quoted by Fonseca 2006). In short, through consideration, a person who is unrelated according to criteria of consanguinity or affinity may come to be viewed, and treated, "*as if s/he were consanguineous*" (Hita 2008: 4–5). Consideration also shapes and orders consanguineal relationships. Not all blood relatives are considered equally (Marcellin 1999: 21). For example, a granddaughter who was (specially) considered by her recently deceased grandmother might expect to receive a greater inheritance than other kin.

This formulation is apt but does not address problems of worrying and caring that persist even though some adults and children cannot be relied upon to conduct themselves in a manner commensurate with a social position of consideration. Yet, persistently uncooperative – or even harmful – (in)action by problematic relatives does not mechanically result in a negation of consideration. People who have nurtured and raised youth who fail to properly reciprocate consideration, often continue to extend care, in the hope that one day troubled relatives will learn to feel and behave differently. Kin speak proudly of the presence of consideration (an unambiguously good thing) and bemoan its absence. Betrayals of supposed-intimates, for instance, might be explained with reference to a "*falta de consideração*" (dearth of consideration). Similarly, an adult son who supports his crack-cocaine habit by repeatedly selling the household cooking-gas canister might be said to take this harmful action because drugs have diminished his consideration: "when he smokes he *nem considera ninguém* [doesn't consider anybody]."

Although carceral subjects do not explicitly characterize imprisonment as a means to cultivate consideration, I observed numerous people operationalizing it in this way. "Improper" or "insufficient" consideration is a high-stakes issue with which research participants grapple incessantly. Criminalized kin are disproportionately vulnerable to a number of losses: loss of material goods through an increased vulnerability to criminal victimization; loss of respectability which can negatively impact employment, housing, inclusion in mutual support networks, and other dimensions of personal security; loss of freedom through incarceration; and loss of life through extralegal state-meted punishments or the violence of acquaintances/rivals. Because having consideration means sharing responsibility for one another's well-being as well as sharing a mutual susceptibility to harm – relatives of consideration share an "interdependent existence" in which they live each other's lives and die each other's deaths (Sahlins 2013: 24) – the vulnerabilities experienced by considered criminals are shared, at least to some degree, by their relations. It is in light of these dynamics that some people respond to the incarceration of dangerous/endangered kin as an opportunity to habilitate – rouse recognition and consideration – and avoid (further) losses.

This chapter contributes to the anthropology of kinship by exploring the importance of a *carceral safety net* as a technology of care that prison visitors weave and wield to save and enhance the interdependent lives of kin. The manner in which carceral subjects engage a repressive state institution to keep life going is fundamentally connected to ambivalence in kinship (Peletz 2000), an understudied dimension of sociality.

27.2 Ambivalence in Kinship and the Prison

Many scholars writing on kinship have tended to emphasize its "positive" rather than its "negative" aspects (Carsten 2013: 246; Strathern 2014). I take inspiration from those who attend to its ambivalence (Das 1995; Han 2011; Lambek 2011; Peletz 2000; Reece 2016; Schuster 2015; Strong 2016). The prevalence of ambivalence within the institution of the family, a primary site of socialization, anticipates carceral subjects' engagements with the prison and, perhaps, the state more broadly.

Many carceral subjects, especially young people and females, have considerable experience living in a highly ambivalent state of interdependence with dangerous/endangered yet "considered" kin and dependence upon more powerful, abusive relations (i.e., patrons, parents, partners, etc.). Arguably, such experiences encourage carceral subjects to understand the prison – a powerful and harmful institution – as a potential resource in social reproductive struggles. Concerned kin are able to "outsource" coercion of deficient relatives to the state, harnessing spatial and relational constraints of imprisonment to cultivate reciprocal consideration. Insofar as women are disproportionately harmed and hemmed in by the double-edged qualities of kinship in patriarchal Brazil, they appear to be more inclined to endure the pains of imprisonment in order to realize projects.[3]

In Northeast Brazil, gender matters greatly in terms of personal (and familial) securitization strategies. Here I am referring to attempts to meet basic needs of sustenance, shelter, restoration, and physical security (both in the short and longer term). Bahia's sex/gender system (McCallum 1999), including but not limited to the sexual division of labor,[4] contributes to the feminization of poverty. Women, especially young women who are childless or mothers of small, dependent children, are often compelled to access crucial resources through sexual and/or conjugal relationships with men. Alternatively, or additionally, they may seek support through other relationships with more powerful actors (e.g. employment or other patronage relations).

Eliciting support from powerful and abusive intimates and institutions is one of several classed and gendered strategies that Bahian carceral subjects, especially women, use to live with – and through – insecurity. I consider how this strategy, which I refer to as "appropriative endurance," as well as strategies of "containment" and "relational intervention," shape and are shaped by state-led practices of punishment. In short, the strategy of containment encompasses tactical inaction, self-restraint, and the confinement of self and others. Violence reduction is an important outcome of such efforts. Relational intervention refers to poor Bahians' attempts to survive or improve their lot by reworking relatedness. Common practices such as relocation (or internal migration), joining an Evangelical church,[5] and child circulation (Fonseca 1986, 2006) may be viewed as instances of this strategy insofar as their value derives, in large part, from a dual process of separation from some relations and integration with others.

Andreia's life history serves as the backbone of the present analysis. I draw on portions of this life history to foreground key dimensions of insecurity within the perilous milieu of Salvador's low-income urban periphery. Andreia's life history also provides a window onto strategies employed by carceral subjects, particularly women, to contend with these intersecting insecurities and (re)make a familial life. I argue that sedimented experiences of living with and through insecurity condition the emergence of the prison as a technology of care. And, somewhat counterintuitively, the prison as technology of care has the potential to help Andreia realize two critical components of household social reproduction: (1) day-to-day survival of members; and (2) the intergenerational transmission of knowledge, values, practices, and affects. Women like Andreia – so often cast out of homes and excluded from the protections of citizenship – extend care not only despite criminalization and imprisonment but because of it, nurturing intimate solidarities that are a condition of livable lives. Their creative engagements with carceral institutions, that are supposedly no more than disciplinary or harmful, challenge popular and scholarly discourses about the Brazilian poor, family (dis)connections, and the ramifications of carceral expansion.

27.3 Imprisonment As an Alternative to Death

The day I first met Andreia, she was waiting outside the women's prison to visit Neguinha. She was sitting on a narrow retaining wall, nibbling on a kola nut and talking with a couple of other mother-visitors. These three women were commiserating over the recent, violent deaths of their sons. A few months earlier, Andreia's son was killed by police. The women's conversation was interrupted when a rat moved through the gutter beneath them, splashing their dangling flip-flop-clad feet. This shifted their discussion away from lethal interpersonal violence to another area of concern: inadequate housing. Andreia expressed frustration that the floor of her house was still unfinished; she has found snakes and other pests inside. The son who had helped most with her house was the one who had just been killed.

This scene serves as a reminder that carceral subjects face enormous challenges stemming from sources other than the prison. And, as I will show, the prison can be mobilized to address these. Moreover, meanings of imprisonment are forged in light of the experienced inter-relatedness *and distinction* of carceral and "non-carceral" (in)securities, spaces, and institutions. It is precisely because the prison is *not* synonymous with the street (or the house) that creative social actors might come to value it. Although scholars of "hyperincarceration" tend to theorize the contemporary prison as one functional element of an integrated system of neoliberal penality, we cannot grasp how the prison is deployed as a technology of care if we do not attend to the meaningful distinctions people draw, for example, between the prison and the street or imprisonment and extralegal police violence – carceral versus "capital" punishment.

27.4   Livelihood, Belonging, and Practices of Imprisonment

Neguinha's imprisonment is not the first time that Andreia has engaged the prison to respond to violence, deprivation, "lack of consideration," and a resultant crisis of social reproduction. Andreia came of age in Northeast Brazil – one of the poorest regions of the country – during the military dictatorship (1964–1985). In the early 1960s, when she was a toddler, her family joined waves of landless peasants migrating from Bahia's rural interior to the urbanizing outskirts of Salvador, the state capital. Scheper-Hughes' research on the everyday violence of infant mortality in a neighboring northeastern state provides us with a sense of what life and death were like for the rural poor in the wake of development interventions that forced small farmers off the land:

> Now they were seasonal contract workers, earning roughly a dollar a day to cut and sack cane … For these people, who lacked water, electricity, and sanitation, and faced daily food scarcities, epidemics, and military police violence, premature death was an everyday occurrence.
>
> *(Scheper-Hughes 2015: 271)*

Life would not have been significantly easier for those who migrated to growing cities in search of jobs that, for the most part, did not exist.

Andreia's family settled in a shantytown erected on invaded land. Her stepfather worked as a mechanic and her mother ran a vending stall. Andreia is the oldest of her mother's seven children who lived past infancy – the only child born *"fora de casal"* (of a different father). She suspects that her paternity is the reason why she was ultimately expelled from the household. When she was 13, her mother threw her out on the pretense that she was no longer a virgin (an accusation that Andreia vehemently denies to this day). As Andreia told me about this formative experience of familial disaggregation she expressed a deep sense of injustice: "My mother *never* helped me – only my children help. My son worked and always helped me but then the police killed him."

After Andreia was cast out of the family home, she joined the already-crowded household of Dona Amelia (the mother of a friend). Practices of imprisonment enabled Dona Amelia to sustain the household. Andreia explains:

> Dona Amelia didn't work but she did visit a prisoner. Back then the prison wasn't like it is now. They [the prisoners] grew beans, rice, and corn. When I was around 18, Dona Amelia brought me along on a visit to see her husband. She put me out there so I could meet someone as well. Then, the help [*ajuda*] Dona Amelia earned [*ganhava*], I earned as well. In order to earn you had to have someone, there [at the prison].

As a youth, Andreia managed to endure a patterned form of gendered abandonment with the assistance of a mutual support network shored up by the prison. Through the tutelage of Dona Amelia, Andreia learned to enact practices of imprisonment through which she could secure a livelihood and her belonging in a family home. Today, 40 years later, she visits her eldest daughter at the same penal compound she first visited as a young woman. And, once again, she is able to make these visits into earning opportunities with the potential to productively integrate a problematically uncontained woman (Neguinha) into the moral domain of family home.

Andreia walks to and from the penal compound. One rainy day, after her regular visit, I offered to pay both of our bus fares back to her neighborhood. She politely declined my offer. Instead, we made the wet and slippery journey by foot, as Andreia collected discarded bottles and cans along the way. As we walked and Andreia "hunted" recyclables for resale, she spoke about – and demonstrated – her high level of consideration within the area where she has lived, off and on, for half a century.

She points out a little shop and explains that, due to her relationship of consideration with the owner, she is able to take items on credit and sell them, at a small profit, to people at the prison. For example, a large clear resealable plastic container (like Tupperware) can be sold for R $15 at the prison. After repaying the shopkeeper R $10, Andreia would be left with R $5 cash-in-hand (the same amount as the cost of two adult bus fares). There is a good market for transparent resealable plastic containers which visitors use to transport home-cooked meals into the prison. With Neguinha's assistance, Andreia also sells mail-order hygiene and beauty products (e.g., Avon) to prisoners and their visitors.

Andreia uses the cash acquired through these various ventures to meet the daily needs of her household. At the time of my research, Andreia was unmarried, providing for two of her surviving seven children and two of her grandchildren – Neguinha's sons. When pervasive insecurities and present (inter-)personal trajectories threaten to undermine familial continuity and flourishing, exposing members (and the group) to fatal risks, imprisonment may represent an opportunity. In this sense, practices of imprisonment have the potential to yield more than financial benefits; to engage the prison as a technology of care is to mobilize this institution toward ends that exceed mere survival. Andreia's Tupperware and cosmetics enterprises integrate Neguinha into a network of close cooperation – a key condition of consideration (Hita 2008: 4–5). It is important to point out that Neguinha was not a contributing, cooperating member of her mother's household prior to her incarceration. Andreia describes the situation which, if left unremedied, could be unsustainable:

> I don't bring [Neguinha's] sons to visit her [in prison] ... She is a
> mother who, outside [prison] doesn't care for her children. If she

made an effort I would make it happen … I've taken care of the boys since before Neguinha was in prison. She has a baby and leaves it here while it's still wet. She heads for the street. She does not have love for her children. She has some other children that she'll bring here for me to raise. I'll raise them in the way and according to the conditions that I can manage.

Beyond enabling the poor to access day-to-day necessities of life, practices of imprisonment might support kinship projects that seek to cultivate moral subjectivity and, thereby, "[bring] about an [improved] eventual everyday from within the actual everyday" (Das 2012: 134). Counterintuitively, Neguinha becomes a contributing member of the household when she is imprisoned. The depth and durability of this transformation will be tested when she is eventually released.

Before returning to Andreia's efforts to habilitate Neguinha, I unpack the three social reproductive strategies outlined above (viz. relational intervention, appropriative endurance, and containment), revealing conditions under which the prison as a technology of care becomes both necessary and thinkable. Bahia's carceral subjects weave these everyday strategies through the warp of imprisonment to produce a carceral safety net that permits continued kinship and enlivens hope for the future.

27.5   Relational Intervention

Andreia continued to live with Dona Amelia and visit a male prisoner until, at age 19, she lost her virginity to a man she met at the beach. This sexual encounter developed into an effective marriage,[6] at which point it was no longer necessary or appropriate for Andreia to keep visiting the prisoner she had met through Dona Amelia.

Andreia cohabitated with her new husband until he abandoned her and left her, again, in search of housing. Although marriages (and procreative sex) should, ideally, yield houses which women (and children of the union) retain in the event of a separation (Moore 2017), this outcome is far from guaranteed. In cases where a lasting house is not established – e.g., because of virilocal residence within an extended-family household or because the conjugal couple rents (or borrows) a space – ex-wives are entitled to very little. Among Bahian carceral subjects, serial marriages tend to correspond with high levels of residential mobility and housing insecurity – a pattern that exacerbates the overall perilousness of life for women (and their dependents).

Andreia, at age 22, quickly met a new man after the dissolution of her first marriage. This man impregnated her but resisted "taking responsibility." He did not marry Andreia (that is, he did not cohabitate with her) or sufficiently provide for her and their unborn child. Perhaps he would have eventually, but we will never know: he was killed when Andreia was seven months pregnant with Neguinha. Neguinha's father died fighting, with a weapon in his hand, after having instigated a *briga* (street confrontation – see Linger 1992) with two brothers. As Andreia explains it, this death was all too predictable: he "was *valentão* [very macho], he showed up at parties looking for a fight."

At the time of Neguinha's father's death, Andreia was staying with an aunt and a female cousin. According to Andreia, this cousin encouraged her to do many *coisas erradas* (wrong things) to support herself and her newborn. For example, Andreia went to work with her cousin at a bar where the female proprietor tasked them with the job of increasing sales by flirting and, at times, "prostituting" themselves.

According to Andreia, the owner of the bar "liked women" and was displeased when her cousin entered a relationship with a man. Eventually, this tense situation erupted in violent conflict during which Andreia's cousin attacked their boss with a broken bottle, severely injuring the women. As police arrived at the bloody scene, Andreia hid in the nearby forest with baby Neguinha. Ultimately, she managed to escape this incident unscathed, uncharged, and unemployed. To maintain her small family dyad, Andreia made the "structured choice" (Wesely 2006) to relocate to Salvador's city center.

This micro-migration distanced Andreia – both physically and symbolically – from people and places associated with her lover's death, her disreputable employment at the bar, and her cousin's criminalized violence. At the same time, Andreia's relocation put her in proximity to the affluent, relatively powerful citizens of the capital's so-called "noble neighborhoods." From this sociospatial location, Andreia arranged live-in domestic work as a nanny and found a woman to care for Neguinha for a fee.

I interpret Andreia's relocation to the city center as a relational intervention. At once, the move brought Andreia into the orbit of people who could materially and symbolically support her moral striving and away from dangerous/endangered kin. Closeness to such kin increases one's vulnerability to external dangers (e.g., violent police or vengeful enemies) as well as to the threat of personal criminalization or "demoralization." Conversely, employment as a live-in domestic worker in the feminized, moral domain of an affluent familial home conveys a certain degree of respectability (as indexed by proper gendered containment within a house) while opening up the possibility of patron–client exchanges and the kind of "insurance" this represents.

Andreia's life history demonstrates that thick relational ties can insulate people from the oppressive relations of an exploitative and racist society but also increase exposure to harmful situations, forces, and practices. Her account of this period of her life emphasizes how she was drawn, by obligations toward her infant daughter and proximity to dangerous/

endangered intimates such as her cousin, into risky gender deviant performances (viz. heavy drinking and promiscuity in a masculinized street-like domain). Although, in this case, Andreia was able to ameliorate her circumstances and support an ethical project by altering her primary relationships, the possibility of relational intervention is not always available or desirable. Often, to cope with a harmful social order, people, especially women, endure abuses perpetrated by intimates, managing to turn injurious kinship configurations to their slight advantage. The following account provides a window onto this strategy of appropriative endurance.

27.6   Appropriative Endurance

Andreia's life has been characterized by extreme housing instability. Until she was finally able to construct her own house, she often found herself living, *de favor*, in the houses of others. At other times, she was able to access the money required to rent a room and carve out a degree of familial autonomy. This pattern, of moving from one precarious living situation to another, was interrupted when an ex-husband returned from protracted out-of-state travels with a desire to reunite. The once-estranged couple reconciled and their second marriage lasted 12 years, begetting two children. For over a decade, Andreia and her husband worked together at one of Salvador's largest open-air markets, living together with Andreia's children, in a room located in the rear section of her husband's brother's home. Such residential arrangements – where a nuclear family occupies one room in the crowded house of relatives, utilizing the kitchen and bathroom facilities of the main house – are a common response to economic constraint. Andreia recalls her longest marriage as "good" but not without its challenges. Her husband was a heavy drug user. Additionally, throughout this marriage, Andreia was routinely "mistreated" (raped) by her brother-in-law (the homeowner).

During one of my visits to Andreia's home, when we had just finished discussing this exceptionally stable period of her life – and the bitter compromises it entailed – her abusive ex-brother-in-law – now a frail, elderly man – actually appeared on her doorstep.

> The old man lingers at the door, complaining about his struggle to obtain disability payments. Uninvited, he enters and takes a seat. When conversation turns to the issue of violent police, he declines to comment, saying that such talk could have consequences. Shortly after his arrival, he leaves. As he turns and makes his way down the crumbling dirt road, Andreia raises her eyebrows and bulges out her eyes. "What is it?" I ask. At first, she doesn't respond. Only when he is well out of earshot does she finally speak: "That's him, the guy I was *just* telling you about!"

Andreia took some satisfaction from the eerily timed visit of her repeat rapist, treating his appearance as an authentication of everything she had been telling me. For my part, when I recall the way he perched shirtless and uninvited on the arm of Andreia's plastic-covered sofa – next to her children and grandchildren – I am still struck by the intimacy of violence. Not only Andreia's resilience, but her ongoing capacity to turn the co-presence of an abuser to her slight advantage is noteworthy. She marshaled this man's unsettling presence as irrefutable evidence of her honesty and status as a mature *sofredora* – a woman who has suffered and knows how to properly and productively *contain* her suffering (see Mayblin 2010). This brings us to the strategy of containment, a strategy which often complements appropriative endurance but which is not reducible to it.

27.7 Gendered Violence and Containment

In Northeast Brazil, the sex/gender system marks women as in need of containment and control (both self-control and control by dominant others) (McCallum 1999; Mayblin 2010). Both men and women are understood to embody forces and desires (e.g., a sexual drive). But, whereas men are expected and encouraged to be mobile and free to realize these desires, women are to exhibit restraint. Women's sexuality, speech, anger, and violence must be contained, especially in light of males' anticipated violent reactions to provocation. As McCallum notes,

> [t]here is an urgency to this multiple imprisonment within a self-containing body ... women and their offspring, through their endless financial demands upon the man, can bring him to his knees, socially, economically, psychologically. He must be free to go out and battle in the world, earn money, spend it on drinking with his mates, or on sexual adventures. To return to his condition as husband-provider-father must be his own choice. If a woman "provokes" him (*provocar*) ... and, uncontained, dares question the trajectory of his body in the world beyond the house, what better means of reply than lashing out at her verbally and even physically?[7] The blows serve to force her to contain herself again – *ficar na dela* (keep herself to herself, not react). And indeed, the need to keep oneself to oneself is constantly reiterated in day-to-day living in Salvador ... Both men and women constantly need to restrain themselves in daily life in Salvador. But the onus is often on the woman to deflect another's provocation. The act of self-control is one way that female gender is constituted.
>
> *(1999: 284)*

Women are not only expected to preempt intimate partner violence by containing their own urges within themselves but also feel pressure to keep themselves and their family members (especially young children and daughters) cloistered within the feminized domain of the house and away from the unsafe and criminogenic masculinized domain of the street. This is a near impossible task insofar as poor women are often required to support their households financially by engaging in extra-domestic income-generating activities. When women are drawn out of the house to make ends meet, many have no choice but to leave children and adolescents unsupervised. This presents a dilemma which some women respond to by locking children/youth inside the house during their absences.

Ideas about gender shape interpersonal violence as well as nonviolent behaviors and efforts to avoid confrontation. Yet, the everyday work of nurture and preempting or limiting harm has not been fully examined by anthropologists who have placed more emphasis on aggression and violence (Van Esterik 2007). At the same time, accounts of kinship that view "family" as convivial community (Edwards and Strathern 2000: 152) tend to neglect negative corollaries of kinship (i.e., differentiation, hierarchy, exclusion, and abuse) and thus fail to acknowledge household solidarity and sociability as effects of laborious and uncertain accomplishment. Thus, I foreground the commonplace feminized strategy of containment to highlight ways in which female carceral subjects in particular enhance personal/familial safety through self-restraint, deliberate inaction, and the spatial-symbolic confinement of self and others.

State-led imprisonment might be said to complement enactments of strategic containment in at least two senses. First, women regularly sublimate their own impulses and "[continue] to behave normally" (Mayblin 2010: 74), to avoid provoking dangerous intimates to violence. This form of self-restraint can stabilize volatile domestic situations, maintain life-sustaining mutual support networks, and forestall retributive cycles of violence. Moreover, in Northeast Brazil, women (particularly older women) are able to accomplish morality by suffering well, namely by containing their own suffering (by publicizing their suffering in conventionally subtle ways) and bearing suffering on behalf of others (Mayblin 2010: 67–93). By assuming the role of the paradigmatic self-sacrificing mother, women are able to symbolically capitalize on their suffering in a manner that enables them to transfigure and deal with problems and foster productive social relations (Mayblin 2010: 92–93). Certainly, the indignities of prison visitation represent an opportunity for women to suffer well and, thus, negotiate dilemmas and deficient kinship relations.

Second, the strategy of containment can exceed self-government when, for example, it involves the spatio-symbolic containment and physical constraint of others within the moral domain of the house. This externalized version of strategic containment has both practical and ethical dimensions. Containing self and family members within the house serves to establish respectable femininity (a good reputation is believed to reduce the chances of victimization – see Rebhun, personal communication, January 23, 2016; Arias and Rodrigues 2006). Additionally, domestic spaces are generally understood to be safer – less rife with lethal hazards – than the street. Finally, fostering an intimate's orientation toward the house and household as opposed to the street and peers – by regulating movement between and within these domains – represents a means by which poor Brazilians seek to reinforce relations' investment in the family's collective well-being as well as prevent intimates from becoming self-identified criminals destined for arrest or premature death. While penal confinement is clearly less compatible with respectable femininity than encompassment within a family home, state-enforced punitive containment nonetheless limits prisoners' physical access to (and perhaps their personal investment in and public association with) the dangerous and demoralizing domain of the street.

Andreia's practical understanding of the prison as a protective and ethical technology bears a certain resemblance to, and affinity with, strategic containment. Andreia is able to exploit Neguinha's unfreedom of mobility and association to effect habilitation – the prison substituting for the house and standing in opposition to the street – while avoiding the antagonism and resentments that would likely be generated if she were the one required to police and punish Neguinha. Furthermore, by making the sacrifice to submit to the excruciating ritual of *revista íntima* (strip and body cavity searches required of visitors each time they enter the prison), and bearing the burden of visitation properly, Andreia is enacting a moral(izing) performance of containment. Her engagements with state-led confinement provide grist for the mill of "socially productive suffering narratives" (Mayblin 2010) with the potential to provoke consideration in Neguinha.

It is important to consider the broader context of gendered violence (and its containment) in which the prison emerges as a technology of care because quotidian efforts to address the specter of immanent and imminent interpersonal violence condition the crafting of a carceral safety net. A key dimension of this context is not only the opposition of house and street (Da Matta 1997), which informs practices of containment, but also the opposition of prison and street. This latter opposition is embedded in research participants' experiences of a corresponding pair of state-led mechanisms of control: imprisonment and policing. Police and prisons are differentiated on the basis of the lethality of the former and the relative survivability of the latter. This conceptualization of the world has implications for the enactment of the social reproductive strategies I have been discussing, particularly as these are brought to bear on interactions with state actors and institutions.

The state of Bahia has an alarmingly high rate of police killings. In 2010, in Salvador and its surrounding metropolitan region (the Região Metropolitana de Salvador or RMS), police killed at least 187 people.[8] The

RMS has a population of almost 4 million people, which is roughly the same population size as that of Los Angeles, California. In 2016, the Los Angeles Police Department led US police forces in fatal shootings, with a total of 19.[9] Within Brazil, the possibility of being killed by the police in Salvador, Bahia's capital, is at least three times higher than in the city of São Paulo, which is notorious for its high rates of police violence (Brinks 2008: 223). And, within Bahia, as elsewhere in Brazil and Latin America (e.g., Goldstein 2003), the poor, who endure the worst living conditions, are the social group most susceptible to violent crime, including police brutality. In 2000, the total rate of homicides in some of Salvador's low-income neighborhoods was in excess of 100/100,000 (as compared to 20/100,000 for the city's general population) (Viana et al. 2011).[10]

Importantly, these homicide rates do not include most police killings which tend to be classified as *autos de resistência* (AR – acts of resistance to arrest) as opposed to homicides. When police killings are categorized in daily security bulletins as acts of resistance, the dead person is designated as the "author" rather than the victim of the act. In the first half of 2011 Salvador and the RMS had 1,114 homicides (including 77 categorized as acts of resistance). This means that at least 6.7 percent of violent deaths were authored by police (Torres and Uchôa 2011). When we consider that only 25 percent of homicides in Bahia are "solved" (where the author of the act is identified) (Torres and Uchôa 2012) and there is abundant evidence of police participation in "off-duty" extermination groups engaged in social cleansing (or "private justice") (Brinks 2008), we may logically estimate that so-called acts of resistance actually constitute only a portion of police-authored killings.[11] Yet, despite numerous cases of police killings every year, it is difficult to encounter a single instance in which a police officer has been convicted of murder (Brinks 2008: 224). In what follows, I examine how police violence is "contained" by carceral subjects and how it shapes their ongoing engagements with the prison. Specifically, I describe Andreia's efforts to keep life going in the wake of her son's death, surfacing her hard work of self-restraint and inaction. Although such achievements leave little obvious trace, they are essential to living as kin in a perilous urban setting.

27.8 Containing Violence: "They Killed My Son … and I Did Nothing"

In October 2010, both Andreia and her neighbor, Natália, lost their sons. Here is Andreia's account of these interrelated events; I have quoted her at length.

> Natália's sons smoked a lot [marijuana, possibly crack]. Those two liked to kill as well. Another son worked in this business of the

police – he also likes to kill. The problem grew and grew. One of Natália's sons would go to the *BR* [nearby highway] to rob people. The police caught him and killed him. Her other son sold a refrigerator and headed down to the *boca* [drug selling/consumption point] to smoke. On his way down, *malandros* [crooks, deadbeats, streetwise scoundrels] grabbed him, stole his money, and killed him.

I saw Natália crying. I arrived and everything was stopped, folks were just watching. I went and spoke with my son [Anderson, who was eventually killed]. I told him that something happened down below. He said he didn't see anything. I was headed toward my house when a *colega* [acquaintance] explained what had happened. I returned to tell my son. I went back [to where many residents were gathered] and Natália – the mother – started crying again. She just kept crying "my son, oh my son!"

I had never lost a son but I felt it [Natália's pain]. I hugged her, calmed her down *not knowing* that her husband would send a bunch of police to kill *my* son – really not to kill my son but to kill the traffickers (but that day my son was down there).

Natália's son died on the 1st. On the 6th … they [police] killed my son and one other boy … On that day, my son was with someone who sold *porqueria* [filth, drugs] – my son didn't sell, he smoked [marijuana] and hung out with some folks who sell – you see? The police came, it was a total siege. My son ran and they shot him in the chest.

At the time of my first recorded interview with Andreia, ten months had passed since Anderson's death. Although she had repeatedly asked God to remove her pain, so far, her prayers had gone unanswered:

My tears don't stop … the death of a son is excruciating. There are times when I don't feel that he died. There are times that I feel he will still arrive at home. It's hard, it's hard … It's lunch time and I don't have a plate of food for my son. At times, I leave a little bit of food in the pan thinking it's for him, that he'll arrive. But he won't arrive so it's very hard … it's a torment.

The death of Andreia's unarmed son was categorized as an AR and was not investigated. This catastrophe and its implications haunt Andreia. I was able to observe, firsthand, the frequency with which she spontaneously referenced (or was wordlessly affected by) the violent death of her son. This loss seemed to permeate every moment and dimension of her life, coloring her experiences of the most mundane tasks and, arguably, informing her approach to the imprisonment of "dangerous/endangered kin." Anderson's death is especially significant to Andreia, not only because he was her son, but also because he was a worker. The significance of this status is captured by a striking scene that unfolded during a visit to Andreia's home.

In the midst of a conversation about Andreia's work history, she rose abruptly from the table, disappearing into the bedroom. Moments later, she emerged brandishing a worn, canary-yellow T-shirt emblazoned with the logo of a major chain of electronics stores (Ricardo Eletro). Andreia held the shirt up and said: "You see? He was a worker! A worker – not a bandit! He worked here, this is his uniform. He worked, he helped me." Anderson worked, formally, in the service sector and contributed to the household. Unlike two of his older siblings – Neguinha and his brother Alan – Anderson had not "chosen the wrong path": he was a worker not a bandit.[12] This is what Andreia pronounced, and sought to convince me of, as she proffered Anderson's uniform as proof, proof of her son's status and as a sign of the (former) goodness of their mutually entwined lives.

Within the prison–neighborhood nexus, it is difficult to identify Anderson as a worker given dominant systems of categorization. Prevailing logic casts such identification as oxymoronic. Simply put, moral (non-criminal) conduct is supposed to insulate *favela* residents from violent victimization. Recognizing the victim of an extrajudicial execution as a "worker" would destabilize the "myth of personal security" (Arias and Rodrigues 2006),[13] a powerful ideology that undergirds any limited sense of security enjoyed by vulnerable people like Andreia. This myth orients local securitization strategies and provides people with some sense of control over their safety. The pervasiveness and utility of this myth mean that Anderson's status as a worker may be called into question by the fact of his extrajudicial execution. Death-by-police can fix the deceased's marginal status in the eyes of neighbors whose own mental well-being depends upon the perpetuation of the myth of personal security. Public "confirmation" of one dead person's marginality can tarnish the reputation of their closest relations, rendering these friends and family members more vulnerable to various possible harms than they were before.

To some extent, Andreia's status as a creator of workers was shaken when Anderson's shooting symbolically repositioned her as the mother of a dead bandit, a disreputable status that can exacerbate her personal/ familial insecurity and constrain her agentive capacity. Following Andreia's insistences upon Anderson's decency, as she painstakingly folded her dead son's yellow uniform, she reflected on why, after his death, she "did nothing":

> I desired to go to the television station to get it off my chest, to speak [to make a public denunciation] … but I didn't … I wanted to go to the newspaper, say that they killed my innocent son … it's just that we have to *entregar tudo nas mãos de Deus* [surrender everything into God's hands].
>
> Also, my acquaintance died because of a haircut … the police came late at night and killed everyone in the house. I – *here* – don't have any security. As if I'm going to speak out and go looking for a problem

with the police. They'll come and kill me as well. My acquaintance [from nearby] had his own razor to cut people's hair. A guy got his hair cut but didn't want to pay so he went ... and complained [to the police] that the barber had threatened him with a revolver. The police came and abused the barber, they threw hot oil at him. It was on television ... The police were expelled [lost their jobs] but then they returned on a night patrol, invaded the house, and killed everyone inside. Because of this I'm afraid to take measures and turn in the police who killed my young son.

It came out on *Bocão* [popular news program] that my son wasn't *do mal* [evil], he was *gente fina* [a great guy]. It came on *Na Mira* [another popular news program] that he was a good son, and he really was. I am certain that God will give me victory.[14]

Andreia's extensive classed experience of police violence; her gendered obligations as a primary caregiver and breadwinner; and the unraveling of a major orienting myth have combined to deter her from denouncing those responsible for the death of her son. Andreia does not know what the outcome of a complaint would be, though she has good reason to suspect that taking such measures could be risky. And, if she were to be killed or injured, what would become of her children and grandchildren? Although Andreia asserts that she "did nothing," her deliberate inaction is better understood in terms of the strategy of containment. Andreia sought to endure this crisis and keep familial life going by repressing a strong urge to cause problems for the police and the neighbor, Natália, who she also blames.

27.9   Criminal Kin: Dangerous and Endangered Intimates

At the same time that Andreia was mourning Anderson's unjust death, contending with Neguinha's imprisonment, and helping me with my research, her oldest son, Alan, went missing. Alan drinks heavily, uses drugs, and is involved, at least to some degree, in "the world of crime." After two days of unanswered calls to Alan, still unable to locate her "problematic son," Andreia told me,

I'm not going to lie. If [Alan] were also imprisoned I wouldn't worry. Because, when he's free ... he only wants to be up to something. [In an unpleasant, aggressive voice she imitates her son:] "*tou pra matar, pra morrer!*" ["I'm for killing, for dying"] ... If you [Hollis] were a lawyer I still wouldn't get him out [of prison], no way.

The scope of this chapter does not permit further discussion of the unfolding of Alan's disappearance. I only raise this issue to point out that Andreia, deeply concerned about the undetermined fate of this criminal of consideration, has expressed a preference for prison which has come to represent the possibility of survival, thicker ties, and familial futurity. This shows that Andreia's opposition to police and trafficker violence extends beyond its application to "innocent" worker-victims like Anderson. She also disapproves of arbitrary lethal responses to "real" criminals like Alan and Neguinha. Quite simply, mutuality of being is not necessarily negated by criminalization. However, criminalization can certainly act as a countervailing force to consideration and pose a threat to household security and social reproduction.

It is not my intention to fortify harmful stereotypes by portraying the urban poor as uniformly "involved" in the "world of crime." However, analytic room must be allowed for the possibility of criminal involvement.[15] Indeed, many of my research participants are seriously preoccupied with: (a) how to prevent oneself and those one "considers" from becoming (presumed) criminals; and (b) how to manage or reverse processes of criminalization once these have begun. In emic terms, resistance to actual "involvement" in the world of crime is expressed in talk of two paths: *o caminho errado* (the wrong path) and *o caminho certo* (the right path). These alternative paths anticipate disparate futures. The wrong path leads to "*cadeia ou caixão*" (jail or a coffin – see Figure 27.1) while the right path represents the cultivation of moral subjectivity and a route to improved personal/familial security and well-being. Importantly, Andreia's creative engagement of the prison as a technology of care registers a parsing of possible outcomes of the wrong path. That is, *cadeia* is vastly preferable to *caixão* precisely because carceral containment affords the possibility that considered criminals might, one day, take the right path.

Criminalized kin are not typically regarded as inveterate criminals by their intimates. Rather, carceral subjects usually conceptualize criminality as an achieved and fluctuating status. Specifically, they tend to attribute criminalization to particular relational configurations which

CRACK É CADEIA OU CAIXÃO.

SEM CONSUMO O TRÁFICO PARA.

Figure 27.1 Public service announcement displayed around Salvador at the time of the field-work. The anti-drug campaign's alliterative warning – that consumption of crack-cocaine will result in death or imprisonment – reflects and reinforces a commonly expressed local perception about the consequences of involvement in the drug trade generally and use of crack-cocaine specifically

may be intervened in. Unfortunately, the local theory of criminal becoming which underlies the perceived mutability of criminal status (and empowers people like Andreia to engage in habilitation) also represents a threatening cause of exclusion. Considered criminals threaten to contaminate (or criminalize) those people they are closest to. And, the danger presented by a spreading stain of criminalization is enormous. One of the most pressing challenges confronted by research participants is the problem of how to care for criminalized kin while striving to sustain a good family into the future. The prison, qua technology of care, presents one possible solution to this high-stakes puzzle.

27.10   *Cadeia* As Technology of Care

It has been established that, for much of her life, Andreia has managed to "earn" in and through the prison. In moments of extreme deprivation and uncertainty, when life-sustaining ties have been strained or severed, Andreia has engaged in – securitizing, sustaining – practices of imprisonment. But, the prison does not simply enable subsistence; nor is this institution best understood as an always already-present safety net. Certainly, this is not how imprisonment is experienced by research participants like Andreia. Rather, carceral subjects who manage to derive modest benefits from the prison must actively and creatively weave a carceral safety net from a tangle of thin and frayed threads; they must learn to cast this net in order to capture resources and "social-capitalize" on the coercive capture of dangerous/endangered criminal kin.

In the final section of this chapter, I explore the prison as a technology of care. I begin by fleshing out the details of Andreia's present situation that have not yet been established in previous sections. Particularly, I attend to one of Andreia's greatest accomplishments – her *casa própria* (own house). After more than four decades, Andreia has finally managed to *produce* a material legacy, a manifestation of her ceaseless labor that cannot be ignored. Andreia has now achieved the status of *dona da casa* (lit. female owner of the house). Yet, these gains are still quite fragile, threatened by forces largely beyond Andreia's control and by considered criminals – one vector of insecurity over which Andreia may be able to exert at least some influence.

In a previous section, we learned of the abuse Andreia endured during her 12-year-long marriage. Andreia left the home of her abusive ex-brother-in-law and ended her marriage when she heard of a land invasion occurring on the margins of the neighborhood where she grew up. In my terms, this move may be conceptualized as a form of relational intervention. When Andreia "invaded" the land, the area where her house now stands was "*mata pura*" (pure bush).

Over the years, since clearing and claiming a small plot of land, little by little and with a great deal of sacrifice and support from her earning children (including Anderson and Alan), Andreia has built her house. She was able to access a windfall of building materials (and construction labor) through a now-ended romantic relationship that commenced around the time she joined the invasion. This romantic union also begot Andreia's two youngest children. Although this man ultimately abandoned Andreia (and their two children), Andreia has managed to retain the house he helped her construct. With a modest sense of pride, Andreia describes her *casa própria*:

> It was a *barraco* (hut, shanty) made of paper and plastic. There was a project to fix the [nearby] road and I started to like one of the workers. He started to help me with materials for the house. He helped me with everything. Then he went elsewhere for work and married another woman. The house is *feinha* [ugly modified by the diminutive] but it's mine. I don't pay rent. I don't pay electricity – it's *de gato* (pirated). I don't have any way to pay so I [did it this way]. The water is also *de gato*. I don't have a [working] refrigerator.

Although Andreia has managed to secure housing, which is a major accomplishment, she still faces a number of challenges and uncertainties. Currently, two issues in particular are causing her extreme anxiety: the death of Anderson and the unaccounted-for absence of her son Alan. In contrast, Neguinha's imprisonment does not bother Andreia. In fact, Neguinha's carceral confinement diminishes Andreia's worry and constitutes a rather unexpected source of hope.

This is the fourth time Neguinha has been imprisoned. In the past, prior to Anderson's death, Andreia expended great effort and scarce resources to secure Neguinha's release.

> My oldest son [Alan] gave me a big television on Mother's Day. I had to give it to a lawyer to get Neguinha out [of prison the first time]. Then she ended up in prison again – she'd stolen again. I gave R $20, R $100, R $30, R $40 to the lawyer and got her out *again and again*. But, it looks as if she likes it in there [prison]; she does the same thing *again and again*. If she didn't like it, it only would've been the one time – so this time I'll leave her there.

As Andreia puts it, "this time" she has stopped fighting to bring her daughter home. While Andreia may have stopped resisting Neguinha's imprisonment, it would be erroneous to presume that she has abandoned her daughter as a lost cause. Andreia comes to value Neguinha's imprisonment, in part, because it keeps her daughter relatively safe (away from hazards associated with the street). But, Neguinha's imprisonment also represents an opportunity for longer-lasting change. Andreia endures the indignity of prison visitation, appropriating the institution as a tool of

containment and relational intervention through which she might cultivate Neguinha's moral subjectivity and shore up the security and futurity
of their shared family. That is, Andreia makes use of the simultaneously
disintegrative and integrative effects of incarceration to rework relatedness and thereby effect habilitation.

Reworking relatedness entails a dual process of separation and integration. Avoiding or altogether abandoning certain social contexts removes
or distances a person from one web of relations and implants them in
another. This is seen to alter the arrangement of interpersonal influences
and, thus, have the power to transform the conduct and character of deficient subjects.

The idea that shifting social context can transform subjects and not
simply alter the situations they find themselves in is crucial. Certainly,
some relational interventions need not work at this deeper level to be
effective. For example, I observed numerous "spatial-relational fixes"
that involved removing a person from an immediate danger posed by an
unpaid debt, a spurned lover, a *rixa* (feud), a warrant, *alemães* (enemies),
etc. Through the creation of distance and the passage of time, threats may
be mitigated without transforming the person/group served by the intervention. However, in a great many cases, there is hope that relational
interventions will yield deeper, longer-lasting results.

The transformative capacity of relational interventions presupposes a
relational/processual theory of (de)moralization. This theory underlies
the aforementioned local perspective on criminality – namely, that thick
ties to criminals constitute vectors not only of misfortune, but of criminalization as well. In Bahia's prison–neighborhood nexus, friendships,
romances, kinship, and cohabitation are regularly cited to explain why
a particular person has taken "the wrong path." Consider Andreia's
remarks about Neguinha:

> Neguinha goes to houses where she shouldn't go, houses where *gente*
> [folks] sell *porcaria*, houses that have a bunch of women thieves who
> don't like to work – they like to go to stores and fill their bags without
> paying. Neguinha *caí presa* [lit. fell prisoner] because of this, because
> *quem esta no meio de quem que não presta não presta também* [those who
> are in the middle of those who are of no use are also of no use].

Neguinha's imprisonment has the potential to facilitate the cultivation
of moral subjectivity insofar as it separates her from deviant, unruly
"friends" and renders her receptive to rebuilding her relationship with
Andreia. During biweekly visits, mother and daughter spend time
together talking, eating, working, and extending small acts of care. This
conviviality – and the cooperation involved in Andreia and Neguinha's
Tupperware and Avon enterprises – is a precondition of consideration.
And, the elicitation of proper consideration is a crucial component of the
perseverance and well-being of the household over time.

I conclude this section by quoting Andreia at length. The following excerpts of our interview were voiced moments after Andreia declared that she prefers Neguinha in prison. Her remarks speak to the essential link between consideration and household reproduction and register Andreia's frustration and uncertainty about her ambivalent familial life.

> From the bottom of my heart – if I am lying may God punish me – if I were to begin my life today I wouldn't want any children. I would not want children because they don't obey, they don't respect; because I have suffered. We fight to raise our children. I am 51 years old and they are already raised – one is 20, another is 28, another is 30. I order them to work: "You want money? You really like money? Go work!" I fought and I fought *correndo atrás* [running around, going after things] to provide for them. I take in laundry to earn R $5, R $10.
>
> In the beginning, I didn't even go to visit Neguinha [in prison]. After three or four months, I went. But, I earn – like I showed you – R $5–10, R $15–20, R $20–25. I bring products for her to resell [inside the prison]. This money that she gives me is a help. But, I'm still enraged that she prefers to stay there than [here] at home …
>
> My life is a sacrifice. It's very difficult but, even so, *esta dando pra viver* [it's worth living] because people seek to help me. They keep their cans and bottles [to give me]. I go out at night with my grandsons hunting [recyclables] around here. I'm able to raise my children. My son that the police killed helped me but the police got him and killed him so I don't have a way of getting money any longer …
>
> I used to receive "*bolsa escola*" [government social transfers currently titled "*bolsa família*"] but my card was blocked because they keep track of the children's school attendance. My grandson – who Neguinha registered at the prison – was registered with the incorrect age. He's 8 years old but his identification says that he's 10. He's not in school because of this confusion.

Note how the prison continues to have negative connotations: Andreia is enraged by her daughter's "preference" for the prison over home. Moreover, a paperwork error by prison social workers has prevented a child from attending school and blocked Andreia's access to crucial cash transfer payments. Even as Andreia creatively weaves a carceral safety net that offers some real benefits, she remains largely overwhelmed by other challenges (viz. economic insecurity and extreme yet warranted concern for her children and grandchildren). Although Andreia is willing to experiment with the prison as a means to morally remake Neguinha so that her eldest daughter might one day become a contributing member of the household, this result is far from guaranteed. Yet, minimally, the prison is serving as a refuge, protecting Neguinha from the perils of the street and alleviating Andreia's well-founded anxieties about kin who have gone astray. As such, Neguinha's preventative detention represents a favorable sort of indeterminacy. Perhaps Neguinha will live long enough that appropriate levels of consideration for her mother, her children, and other relatives might be drawn out. The possibility is retained as long as Neguinha is in a *cadeia* (prison) and not a *caixão* (coffin).

27.11 Conclusion: Ambivalent Outcomes of Social Reproduction

Andreia's story exemplifies that imprisonment – like extralegal police violence – is an institution that structures the everyday lives of those who inhabit Salvador's urban periphery, a group that is disproportionately criminalized and penalized. Yet, like Neguinha's post-release path, the cumulative result of this structuring is still undetermined. To conclude this chapter, I turn to a final vignette which underlines the processual, indeterminate, and ambivalent character of both Andreia's familial life story and the carceral normalization of which it is a part.

Some time after my first major interview with Andreia, we reconnected in the waiting area outside the women's prison. On this occasion, Andreia was accompanied by her 16-year-old daughter, Ana. Ana is tall, shapely, neatly dressed, and meticulously groomed. She is "a very pretty *Neguinha*," her mother remarks. As the pair waits to be admitted to the prison, a young man wearing a paint-spattered blue work uniform passes by, stealing a glance at Ana. Moments later he reappears and approaches us, now proffering a bible with an ornately carved and painted wooden cover. He passes the book to Ana who receives it without hesitation. She runs her fingers appreciatively over the handiwork before returning it.

Although only a few words are exchanged before the man departs, much is communicated: (1) this man is interested in Ana; (2) he is not only dressed as a worker, he is clearly a talented craftsman; (3) he identifies as *fiel* (a faithful Christian). What Ana doesn't initially realize is that this man is also a prisoner. When this fact registers, she asks why he is outside. I explain the system of *Fardos Azuis* (lit. Blue Uniforms – refers to a special group of male prisoners, from a neighboring "maximum-security" prison, who are assigned to work detail and permitted to circulate, relatively unsupervised, throughout the penal compound) and Andreia nods knowingly in agreement, adding: "it means he has good behavior."

A kindly guard named Iris steps out of the reception area to smoke a cigarette. She asks why Ana is not in school today, a Wednesday. Andreia explains that Ana attends school at night because she is behind, "she lost three years." Ana is in the fourth grade. Whereas Andreia is pleased that Ana is studying, "to be someone a little better and never fall into this life," the guard expresses concern, asking how Ana fell so far behind. Andreia's initial response is oblique: "*Falar é facil, não é Dona Iris?*" ("Talk is easy, isn't it Dona Iris?"). Then Andreia elaborates. Like other women

I have met in Salvador's prison–neighborhood nexus, she struggled to "*tirar identidade*" (obtain an identity document), which is a requirement of school enrollment. Andreia says that it would have cost R $22 to obtain the document and she simply didn't have the "conditions." Although there are laws and policies in place to ensure that all citizens are able to obtain identity cards, accomplishing this task nonetheless requires outputs of already scarce energy, time, and money (e.g., bus fare and the cost of photographs).

In addition to this obstacle, Andreia identifies another factor under-lying Ana's years-long absence from school: "She didn't go because she didn't have ID and she only had a small notebook. She was ashamed – the other students would mock and tease her. Now she has a beautiful note-book!" Indeed, the prohibitive expense of school uniforms and supplies was a common theme of conversation.

The guard finishes her cigarette and I continue to chat with Andreia and Ana as they await processing. Ana, echoing a sentiment I have heard her mother express, tells me she doesn't plan on having any children of her own. In the future, she hopes to become a dentist or a professional singer. She already sings evangelical music which she prefers to Catholic and Jehovah Witness music ("too boring!") as well as *pagode* (a form of samba that is massively popular, and locally produced, in the state of Bahia). According to Ana, "*Pagode é tudo baixaria* [is wholly 'vulgar'], the lyrics are all about sex."

By the time that Andreia and Ana's number is finally called by an on-duty guard, Ana is having second thoughts about entering the prison. She does not want to endure the *revista íntima*, even the less-invasive strip search version that is required of minors. Minors are searched in the presence of their parent. They must remove their clothing and take down their underwear. Ana pulls up the hem of her denim skirt a couple of inches to reveal a pair of shorts declaring, "I even shower in my under-wear. I don't want to show myself." Andreia beseeches the guards to allow her daughter to enter without being searched: "My daughter is a virgin." Eventually, a compromise is struck and Ana is permitted to enter only as far as the gated entrance to the patio/cell-block area. From this supervised location, she will be able to spend a few moments talking, through bars, to her older sister.

For Ana, imprisonment is not yet entirely "normal"; she is certainly not accustomed to visiting prisons. Yet, this normalization process is already underway and, arguably, is furthered during the quasi-visit I have just described. Chatting with a charming *crente* convict and undertaking her initiation to visitation with her practiced mother helps to "dispel the sense of apprehension inherent to an unfamiliar institution" (Cunha 2008: 332) and nourish receptiveness to the radical – or at least ambiva-lent – opportunities prisons and prisoners might represent. Although the prison indubitably harms, carceral subjects have reason to imagine the separation and containment it effects might be productively endured and marshaled as a habilitative relational intervention. Like the ambivalent institution of the family, the prison too can be *made* to do more than simply harm. As a technology of care deployed by concerned kin, the prison becomes an unexpected catalyst of reciprocal consideration or "enduring, diffuse solidarity" (Schneider 1980) among relatives.

Notes

1. In my descriptions, I use the present tense when I am able to draw directly from my field notes. The field notes used here were recorded in 2010 and 2011.
2. Carceral subjects are those most affected by uneven carceral expansion: (ex-)prisoners, visitors, and non-visitors – people with an imprisoned relation who do not visit.
3. Although I observed men and women engaging in what might be thought of as "carceral habilitation," the vast majority of prison visitors are female. At the prisons where I conducted research, including one prison for men and one prison for women, approximately 90 percent of visitors are female.
4. Importantly, in Brazil, women are primarily responsible for educating and caring for children (Rebhun 1999: 119–120).
5. Goldstein (2013 [2003]) explores young women's structured choice to become *crentes* (lit. believers, refers primarily to Pentecostals) – or "convert" to evangelical Protestantism – in a Rio shantytown. In Brazil, and across Latin America, Pentecostals are predominantly female, outnumbering males by a ratio of two to one (Chesnut 1997: 22). Goldstein shows how women's "fluctuating religious fervor" (2013 [2003]: 220) is connected to their relatedness with dangerous/ endangered (and later dead) crime-involved men. Identification as *crente* is "at least partly influenced by a desire to distance themselves (and potentially their partners) from the real or potential conflicts in which the men were enmeshed" (2013 [2003]: 220).
6. I use the term marriage as most research participants do – to refer to the union of a cohabitating couple.
7. Historically, when a Brazilian man killed his wife or lover, he could often escape punishment by invoking the "defense of honor" or defense of "violent emotion" (similar to temporary insanity in the United States). Defense of honor was equated with self-defense justifications of murder. Although the first penal code of the Brazilian empire abolished this legal privilege, it remained a customary defense that could be used in murder trials. Indeed, over the years, its uses expanded to protect, for example, husbands who killed wives merely on the suspicion of her unfaithfulness (Page 1996: 255). By the

late 1970s, people began to protest jury verdicts that resulted in the acquittal of men who had killed their wives (Hautzinger 2007: 185). In 1991, Brazil's Supreme Court ruled that a man can no longer kill his wife and win acquittal on the ground of "legitimate defense of honor" (Brooke 1991: n.p.). However, on retrial, a judge permitted the defense of honor, the jury acquitted the defendant, and, under the law, no appeal was permitted (Page 1996: 255). By the 2000s, all-women police stations, specializing in attending to women, were operating throughout Brazil. As Hautzinger notes, "[t]he principal rationale for instituting the [Women's Police Stations] was to intervene in the impunity that male offenders typically experienced in the Brazilian law enforcement and legal system" (2007: 2).

8. That is, 187 deaths were classified as acts of resistance to arrest.

9. www.washingtonpost.com/graphics/national/police-shootings-2016/, accessed June 1, 2018.

10. Between 2000 and 2006, Salvador's homicide rate increased by 98.5 percent (to 39.7/100,000) (Viana et al. 2011). Between 2006 and 2010 this rate increased by an additional 70 percent (to 62/100,000) (O Correio 2011). Note, the United Nations considers a homicide rate of 12/100,000 to be "acceptable."

11. A review of the major newspapers from 1996 through 1999 found that 15 percent of Salvador's "homicides" in those years were attributed to the police while 8 percent were attributed to "extermination groups engaged in social cleansing" (Brinks 2008: 224).

12. See Millar's (2014) overview of the symbolic value of the worker (viz. the formally employed worker) in Brazil's moral order (also see Goldstein 2003; and Penglase 2009). In short, in the 1930s, President Getúlio Vargas exalted "the worker" as the model Brazilian citizen and, generated "a worker–criminal dichotomy that continues to function" (Millar 2014: 41). Today, in the context of intense public anxiety about violent street crime connected to drug trafficking, Salvador's poor frequently evoke the worker–marginal or worker–bandit dichotomies.

13. Arias and Rodrigues (2006) argue that people who have no choice but to live in dangerous places (viz. Rio's *favelas*) deal with fear of physical violence by cultivating a powerful ideology that says those who conduct themselves appropriately will be respected and insulated from harm. Respect is thought to hinge on whether or not you drink, smoke, sniff, or engage in sexual impropriety. Arias and Rodrigues refer to this local understanding of security as a "myth" because, in actuality, uses of violence are strategic and tend to reflect the relative power – versus moral status – of the perpetrator and victim.

14. Although Andreia professes her faith in divine justice throughout our interview, it emerges that she is experiencing an intense crisis of faith. She speaks extensively about how she had to leave her church

following the death of her son (because she could not stand to be there with Natália, the neighbor who she blames for Anderson's death) and has questioned her status as a true believer (*crente*) because she feels rage and *murmura* (murmurs) too much.

15. The nature of my research design has meant that most of my study participants are either engaged in criminalized activities or are intimately connected to criminals. I cannot ignore the struggles and strivings of those for whom criminality is a deeply personal challenge or possibility.

References

Arias, Enrique Desmond and Corinne Davis Rodrigues. 2006. "The Myth of Personal Security: Criminal Gangs, Dispute Resolution, and Identity in Rio de Janeiro's Favelas." *Latin American Politics and Society* 48(4): 53–81.

Brinks, Daniel. 2008. *Police Violence in the Americas: The Judicial Response to Police Killings in Latin America: Inequality and the Rule of Law*. Cambridge: Cambridge University Press.

Brooke, James. 29 Mar. 1991. "'Honor' Killing of Wives Is Outlawed in Brazil." *The New York Times*. www.nytimes.com/1991/03/29/us/honor-killing-of-wives-is-outlawed-in-brazil.html, accessed June 1, 2018.

Carsten, Janet. 2013. "What Kinship Does – and How." *HAU: Journal of Ethnographic Theory* 3(2): 245–251.

Chesnut, R. Andrew. 1997. *Born Again in Brazil: The Pentecostal Boom and the Pathogens of Poverty*. New Brunswick, NJ: Rutgers University Press.

Cunha, Manuela Ivone P. 2008. "Closed Circuits: Kinship, Neighbourhood and Incarceration in Urban Portugal." *Ethnography* 9(3): 325–350.

Da Matta, Roberto. 1991. *Carnivals, Rogues, and Heroes: An Interpretation of the Brazilian Dilemma*. Notre Dame, IN: University of Notre Dame Press.

   1997. *A casa e a rua: Espaço, cidadania, mulher e a morte no Brasil*. Rio de Janeiro: Rocco.

Das, Veena. 1995. *Critical Events: An Anthropological Perspective on Contemporary India*. Delhi: Oxford University Press.

   2012. "Ordinary Ethics." In *A Companion to Moral Anthropology*, ed. Didier Fassin, 133–149. Hoboken, NJ: Wiley Blackwell.

Edwards, Jeanette and Marilyn Strathern. 2000. "Including Our Own." In *Cultures of Relatedness: New Approaches to the Study of Kinship*, ed. Janet Carsten, 149–166. Cambridge: Cambridge University Press.

Fonseca, Claudia. 1986. "Orphanages, Foundlings, and Foster Mothers: The System of Child Circulation in a Brazilian Squatter Settlement." *Anthropological Quarterly* 59(1): 15–27.

   2006. "Da circulação de crianças à adoção internacional: questões de pertencimento e posse." *Cadernos Pagu* 26: 11–43.

Goldstein, Donna M. 2013 [2003]. *Laughter Out of Place: Race, Class, Violence, and Sexuality in a Rio Shantytown*. Berkeley, CA: University of California Press.

Han, Clara. 2011. "Symptoms of Another Life: Time, Possibility, and Domestic Relations in Chile's Credit Economy." *Cultural Anthropology* 26(1): 7–32.

Hautzinger, Sarah. 2007. *Violence in the City of Women: Police and Batterers in Bahia, Brazil*. Berkeley, CA: University of California Press.

Hita, Maria Gabriela. 2008. "Ownership, Appropriation and the Reproduction Cycle of Afro-Descendent Houses in Salvador, Bahia." Ownership and Appropriation Conference, Association of Social Anthropologists of the UK and the Commonwealth Conference, University of Auckland, 2008.

Lambek, Michael. 2011. "Kinship As Gift and Theft: Acts of Succession in Mayotte and Ancient Israel." *American Ethnologist* 38(1): 2–16.

Linger, Daniel Touro. 1992. *Dangerous Encounters: Meanings of Violence in a Brazilian City*. Stanford, CA: Stanford University Press.

McCallum, Cecilia. 1999. "Restraining Women: Gender, Sexuality and Modernity in Salvador da Bahia." *Bulletin of Latin American Research* 18(3): 275–293.

Marcellin, Louis Herns. 1999. "A linguagem da casa entre os negros no recôncavo baiano." *Mana* 5(2): 31–60.

Mayblin, Maya. 2010. *Gender, Catholicism, and Morality in Brazil: Virtuous Husbands, Powerful Wives*. New York: Palgrave Macmillan.

Millar, Kathleen M. 2014. "The Precarious Present: Wageless Labor and Disrupted Life in Rio De Janeiro, Brazil." *Cultural Anthropology* 29(1): 32–53.

Moore, Hollis. 2017. Imprisonment and (Un)Relatedness in Northeast Brazil. PhD Dissertation, University of Toronto.

O Correio. 7 Feb. 2011. "Violència registrada em Salvador é destaque no Jornal Nacional." *O Correio*. www.correio24horas.com.br/noticia/nid/violencia-registrada-em-salvador-e-destaque-no-jornal-nacional/, accessed November 1, 2018.

Page, Joseph A. 1996. *The Brazilians*. Boston, MA: Da Capo Press.

Peletz, Michael. 2000. "Ambivalence in Kinship since the 1940s." In *Relative Values: Reconfiguring Kinship Studies*, ed. Sarah Franklin and Susan McKinnon, 413–444. Durham, NC: Duke University Press.

Penglase, Ben. 2009. "States of Insecurity: Everyday Emergencies, Public Secrets, and Drug Trafficker Power in a Brazilian Favela." *PoLAR: Political and Legal Anthropology Review* 32(1): 47–63.

Rebhun, L. A. 1999. *The Heart Is Unknown Country: Love in the Changing Economy of Northeast Brazil*. Stanford, CA: Stanford University Press.

Reece, Koreen. 2016. "A Familiar Crisis: Kinship and Intervention in Botswana's Time of AIDS." Paper delivered at AAA 2016 Annual Meeting for the Kinship and Crisis Panel.

Sahlins, Marshall. 2013. *What Kinship Is – and Is Not*. Chicago, IL: University of Chicago Press.

Scheper-Hughes, Nancy. 2015. "Death Squads and Vigilante Politics in Democratic Northeast Brazil." In *Violence at the Urban Margins*, ed. Javier Auyero, Phillipe Bourgois and Nancy Scheper-Hughes, 266–304. New York: Oxford University Press.

Schneider, David Murray. 1980. *American Kinship: A Cultural Account*. Chicago, IL: University of Chicago Press.

Schuster, Caroline. 2015. *Social Collateral: Women and Microfinance in Paraguay's Smuggling Economy*. Berkeley, CA: University of California Press.

Strathern, Marilyn. 2014. "Reading Relations Backwards." *Journal of the Royal Anthropological Institute* 20(1): 3–19.

Strong, Thomas. 2016. "The Axiom of Enmity: A Papua New Guinea Example." Paper delivered at AAA 2016 Annual Meeting for the Kinship and Crisis Panel.

Torres, Juan and Victor Uchôa. 14 July 2011. "Policiais mataram 77 pessoas em Salvador e RMS de janeiro a junho." *O Correio*. www.correio24horas.com.br/noticia/nid/policiais-mataram-77-pessoas-em-salvador-e-rms-de-janeiro-a-junho/, accessed November 1, 2018.

5 Jan. 2012. "Salvador e RMS tiveram 2.037 mortos por homicídio no ano passado." *O Correio*. www.correio24horas.com.br/noticia/nid/salvador-e-rms-tiveram-2037-mortos-por-homicidio-no-ano-passado/, accessed November 1, 2018.

Van Esterik, Penny. 2007. "Advocacy." www.yorku.ca/esterik/advocacy.html, accessed June 1, 2018.

Viana, L. A. C., M. D. C. N. Costa, J. S. Paim and L. M. Vieira-da-Silva. 2011. "Social Inequalities and the Rise in Violent Deaths in Salvador, Bahia State, Brazil: 2000–2006." *Cadernos de saude publica*, 27(supl. 2): s298–s308.

Waldram, James. 2012. *Hound Pound Narrative: Sexual Offender Habilitation and the Anthropology of Therapeutic Intervention*. Berkeley, CA: University of California Press.

Wesely, Jennifer K. 2006. "Considering the Context of Women's Violence: Gender, Lived Experiences, and Cumulative Victimization." *Feminist Criminology* 1(4): 303–328.

28

The Interface between Kinship and Politics in Three Different Social Settings

Signe Howell

The relationship between a society's particular political organization and its kinship system was a topic that was central in the early years of British Social Anthropology, arguably reaching its high point in Evans-Pritchard's study of the Nuer segmentary system (1940). In the seminal volume *African Political Systems* edited by Evans-Pritchard and Meyer Fortes (also 1940), they, surprisingly, argue for a separation between kinship and politics.

> We must here distinguish between the set of relationships linking the individual to other persons and to particular social units through the transient, bilateral family, which we shall call the kinship system, and the segmentary system of permanent, unilateral descent groups, which we call the lineage system. Only the latter establishes corporate units with political functions. In both groups of societies kinship and domestic ties have an important role in the lives of individuals, but their relation to the political system is of a secondary order.
>
> *(1940: 6)*

This separation of narrowly defined kinship from politics and the division into types seems rather spurious today, but it continued to be influential in British anthropology. In his review of the history of British Anthropology, Kuper expresses surprise at how the presence or absence of descent groups was selected as primary criterion for the classification of political systems (1973: 110; Thelen and Alber 2017). With a few notable exceptions such as Edmund Leach's famous monograph *Political Systems of Highland Burma* (1954), the anthropology of politics and kinship has tended to develop along their separate paths. Attempts to bring them together have resurfaced recently[1] and are proving fruitful, not least as the rigid separation between state and non-state societies is being challenged and new light is being shed on other longstanding dichotomies such as public and private, traditional and modern.

In this chapter I shall continue these recent investigations concerning the relationship between kinship and politics. I shall approach the topic through an examination of three very different ethnographic settings that I have studied; different in terms of their symbolic as well as socio-political orders.[2] These are, first, the hunting-gathering egalitarian Chewong of the Malaysian rain forest, whose kinship system is bilateral and whose jural-political reference point is placed outside the narrow human domain and extends into the world of animated forest beings and objects. Second, I discuss the socially stratified Indonesian Lio, whose kinship system is pretty close to an empirical example of an elementary structure as described by Lévi-Strauss (1948) – but is also much more than he imagined – practicing prescriptive matrilateral cross-cousin marriage with all that it entails in terms of political, ritual, and symbolic life. The Lio are settled agriculturalists. Third, I consider contemporary Norway; a modern democratic nation-state whose legal system shapes and regulates the kinship system, but which is nevertheless an open system responding to changes in public values. I will give some details about the pertinent points regarding the interface of politics and kinships in each case.

I take kinship to be about codified relatedness between significant others in one's social environment that somehow, though far from exclusively and in a variety of ways, is predicated upon biological connectedness. "Mutuality of being" or "mutuality of existence" as suggested by Sahlins (2013: 28) as a definition for kinship is relevant for the social reality of all my three cases, but that does not mean that bodily, or biological, origin is irrelevant. While social categories give rise to rules and expectations for behavior regardless of the actual status of the bodily relatedness of their members, the body frequently acts as a template.

Kinship is about jural factors. Jural pertains to the rights and obligations governed and sanctioned by rules or by laws. Jural in my usage implies politics – but it is also about much more, such as notions of personhood and the principle, value, and practice of sociality. Politics for present purposes is, minimally, about the theory and practice of influencing people at a community or individual level and about the jural rules that legitimize the exercise of authority and sanctions. My overall argument is that somehow kinship and politics are mutually implicated – probably everywhere, but certainly in my three examples.

In order to narrow the discussion and make the project more easily comparative, I concentrate on the jural aspects of kinship and the politics of procreation. That means a slant towards kinship as jural practice. In my three empirical examples the interface between moral doctrines and jural doctrines is not clear-cut. While each example highlights some basic similarities, they also demonstrate radical differences in ontology and epistemology and ensuing practice.

My starting point will be the ontology and epistemology in each case: how socio-political phenomena are manifestations of root assumptions about the nature of people and things in the world and their relationship within the total schema. I will look at the significance attributed to biological and social relatedness, at practices of kinning, notions of belonging, the sociopolitical role of descent and marriage, and the underlying values of practices performed by sociopolitical institutions as these affect the practice of kinship – and, in turn, are influenced by the kinship system. Procreation includes conception, birthing, marriage, parenthood, residence, inheritance (of status and property). Although the modes vary, in no society is the birthing of children left to chance or completely to individual choice. As the politics of sex and gender are integral to kinship, procreation is always a matter of social concern which has political ramifications. I shall outline the relationship between kinship and politics in each case.

My general argument will be that, while there is indeed a relationship between politics and kinship, there is no necessary correlation between a particular kinship order and a sociopolitical organization. Cognatic or bilateral kinship is found in societies with sociopolitical stratification,[3] and egalitarian social forms may have complex patrilineal kinship systems.[4] Indeed, the famous example from Highland Burma (Leach 1954) makes this abundantly clear. Here society oscillates between an egalitarian (*gumlao*) form of social organization and a stratified (*gumsa*) form, but both are hypogamous.

According to Barnard and Good, marriage rules are not purely theoretical constructs or arbitrary cultural preferences; they are expressions of political and economic ideology (1984: 136). They point out that while Lévi-Strauss devoted his influential work to the problem of the choice of spouse he, according to Meillassoux, did not "consider the central problem of kinship, which is the destination of the offspring" (1984: 131). This is an interesting critique of Lévi-Strauss and one that I will take account of in this chapter. To varying degrees and with different evaluative manifestations, the destination of offspring is certainly a political issue for the hierarchical patrilineal Lio where marriage exchanges are highly structured; much less so for the egalitarian bilateral Chewong; and the destination of children arises in contemporary democratic Norway primarily on occasions of "personal crisis"; that is, in cases of involuntary childlessness, divorce, parental abuse, and same-sex marriage. Closely related to the destination of children is the question of rights in children. I will consider both within an overall frame of values.

28.1 Chewong

Although they represent a most unusual example of the interface between kinship and politics, being a prime example of "anarchic solidarity" (cf. Gibson and Sillander 2012), my first example is Chewong, a small hunting-gathering-shifting cultivating group of people who live in

Peninsular Malaysia (Howell, e.g., 1984, 1985, 2011, 2013). I start with Chewong precisely because the paucity of familiar social and symbolic categories throw into sharp relief how metaphysical schemata nevertheless order sociality and relatedness.

Chewong adhere to a strong egalitarian ethos that permeates their social and symbolic classification and daily practice. There are no leaders and no system of coercion. Political life is ego-centered and relations are transitive. Their kinship system is very simple: cognatic/bilateral, with shallow memories of ancestors and negative marriage rules.[5] The Chewong cognatic kinship system is, in its structure, analogous to their egalitarian sociopolitical order. It is inclusive, that is, everyone is a relative and everyone is known to everyone else. Marriage and procreation are largely, but not completely, left to the individual. Kinship is important in placing individuals in relation to others and in defining belonging and it gives rise to loose and flexible group formations. As conception is the result of repeated deposit of the father's sperm mixed with the mothers' blood, bodily connection to parents is not doubted, but this fact carries little importance beyond the question of marriage partner.

Marriage between children of sisters is strongly valued while that between children of brothers is not allowed. There is thus a slight patrifocus in an otherwise thoroughgoing egalitarian ethos. Marriage between children of a brother–sister pair is common. Groups of brothers often marry groups of sisters. With a preferred uxorilocal residence for the first few years after a marriage, this means that a group of married sisters who live with their parents form a loose group in which the parents-in-law command some respect. Although humans have no authority over others, the relationship between a man and his father- and mother-in-law is one of some restriction and mutual avoidance. He may not address either by their proper name but always employs their nickname, or refers to them as mother/father of wife. The parents refer to their son/daughter-in-law as the "husband/wife of x." This affinal relationship alone employs reciprocally the polite term of address (as in *vous*, not *tu*).[6] Once a child is born, the young couple may decide to move elsewhere. Actual performance of these relationships is determined by the personality of those concerned. It is of less politico-jural significance than that between the humans and nonhumans as manifested and enacted through the cosmo-rules as outlined below.[7]

Kin relatedness contributes little in defining interaction in terms of rights and obligations. Chewong live according to a sharing ethos that includes all Chewong (i.e., kin status in some way or other) who happen to be in one's vicinity when there is something to share. The boundary of kinship is the boundary of the Chewong world, but this world includes many more than the 400 human beings. Their environment is animated with a large number of "spiritual beings" (conscious, sentient, nonhuman beings and material objects) that interact with humans (Howell 1986,

2013). The forest is thus very much alive with significant others that are integral to Chewong sociality and who enter directly into the daily life of humans and are party to the constitution of persons and the moral/jural order. The politico-jural principle is anchored in the relationship between humans and non-Chewong worlds.

Although, seemingly, people can do pretty much as they please in terms of activities in the forest and the settlement, their activities are nevertheless framed and constrained by a number of prescriptions and proscriptions that I call cosmo-rules because they are predicated upon the Chewong relationship with their cosmos. As their social world extends into their forest environment nonhuman sentient beings constitute the medium for performing repercussions for the breach of these rules. This usually manifests itself in the form of illness or personal mishap of some kind. Sometimes not only the perpetrator is "punished," but punishment may extend to the whole settlement (the temporary corporate group). Authority is thus located outside the purely human social world, and anchored within the extended human/animated nonhuman world. The nonhuman beings associated with specific cosmo-rules constitute a major part of the politico-jural world of the Chewong. Daily activities such as hunting, gathering, cooking, and sharing are all predicated upon one or more cosmo-rule. They are thus far from neutral activities but embedded within the cosmology through the rules. Cosmo-rules, I suggest, are central to the cognitive process by which the Chewong understand themselves. Children learn them while young. Interestingly, the cosmo-rules do not organize marriage and procreation beyond the negative marriage rules. Those who engage in prohibited marriage or sexual relations are struck by lightning sent by the Thunder spirit. The two cosmo-rules *maro* and *punén* that specify the sharing ideology (requiring that all food brought to a settlement must be shared among all present), together constitute society in so far as they formulate the moral basis for its very existence, emphasizing the kinned relatedness of all within the extended social universe with its ensuing moral obligations. In other words, jural factors are based in the worlds of spirits, not in the narrow human world.

Authority is thus located outside the purely human social world. Humans and nonhumans are in a continuous exchange relationship of correct behavior framed by cosmo-rules. Transgressions are punished on the basis of these rules. The nonhuman beings associated with specific cosmo-rules thus constitute a major part of the political world of the Chewong. The cosmo-rules are central to how the Chewong understand themselves, their notion of personhood, and their subjectivity. Theirs may be thought of as an extended kin network – although Chewong themselves do not talk explicitly in these terms. However, their particular understanding of relatedness and sociality is replicated in the numerous animated worlds in the forest that are invisible to all but shamans. Individual Chewong may contract a relationship of spouse with one such being who then becomes his or her spirit-guide and assists at times of stress.

Divorce is rare and up to the parties concerned. The destination of children is not an issue; usually they will live with their biological parents until they get married. They may, however, move around to live with others in the settlement or elsewhere, and orphans tend to move in with a sibling of one of their parents. Interestingly, and in strong contrast to the Lio and Norway, the notion of rights in a child is not present.

On the face of it, Chewong kinship and Chewong politics are extremely simple and laissez-faire. If a conflict arises, some of those involved will choose to move away rather than confront the rest. Removal from potential conflict is characteristic of Chewong social and political life. However, I wish to suggest that, as Valeri argued for taboos among the Huaulu, the very process of Chewong subject formation by means of cosmo-rules and their semantic and moral connotations, is sufficient to create the system of power by which their lives are ruled (cf. Lansing 2003: 373).[8]

28.2   Lio

My second example concerns the Lio who are settled agriculturalists in the highlands of Flores, Eastern Indonesia. Lio represent an extreme contrast to Chewong. Theirs is a highly stratified sociopolitical organization that is constituted through kinship and which is predicated upon the cosmogenic past through patrilineal and (less obvious, but no less important) matrilineal descent (Howell 1995a). There are structural distinctions between the aristocratic patrilineal descent groups and the commoners and between men and women – relations that are anchored in and legitimized through, their ontology and metaphysics. Authority is exercised by religio-political priest-leaders (*mosa laki*) whose status and role are achieved by virtue of correct descent and marriage, and the jural rules that give rise to their authority are predicated upon the situation of the cosmogenic past (Howell 1986). What matters is to belong to clans that can be traced back to the ancestors, those who descended from the sacred mountain to initiate sociopolitical life as it is known today and to marry according to correct procedure that means "following the path" of one's parents. The Lio kinship system is close to an "elementary structure" (Lévi-Strauss 1949) with prescriptive matrilateral cross-cousin marriage – a system that is inseparable from their political organization. Thus, kinship frames all social interaction. Kinship concerns pervade every aspect of social organization, constituting subjectivity and sociality. Unlike the Chewong, procreation and the destiny of children is not left to circumstances or individual choice, but are controlled by the priest-leaders through complex jural rules regarding descent and marriage. Procreative practices affect not only human fertility, but also that of the land.

Since the institution of priest-leaders is a constituent of Lio institutions and sociality, I will limit my discussion of the system to an examination of them. To become a priest-leader, a man obtains his wife from not only the same patriclan, but also patrilineage as did his father, his father's father and so on back to the origins of time, although the system is classificatory, not narrowly biological. However, it is not just a question of descent and marriage, but also of gift exchange (*belis*) between the two groups of wife-givers and wife-receivers (Howell 1986). Only by presenting and receiving the required alliance gift[9] are rights in the woman fully transferred to her husband's clan and she may perform the ritual acts of a female priest-leader of his clan. She and the gifts follow the "same path" as the wives before her. Their children are eligible to continue the path for the next generation. As I argue that ritual is deeply implicated in political life, this demonstrates the entangled reality of kinship and politics. This aspect of the kinship/alliance system of many societies in Eastern Indonesia has not been brought out previously.

Ideally there are seven patriclans in each self-governing village domain. These are hierarchically ordered. One wields overall authority, namely the trunk priest-leader who encompasses the rest in the sense that he is the ultimate mediator between the original ancestors and chief deities and as such is responsible for the well-being of the whole population, not just those who belong to his House.[10] He performs all the important rituals in connection with the communal flow of life, such as the elaborate annual agricultural ceremonies, the rebuilding of the Lio temple and the care of the sacred objects kept inside the temple, major sacrificial events, and marriage negotiations. He also wields ultimate power over matters that concern the whole community, such as serving as a judge in conflicts that were not resolved at a lower level in the hierarchy and deciding (in the old days) on going to war with neighboring communities. Lio kinship is an example of a house-based society, corresponding to Lévi-Strauss' characterization of the house as "category, building, idea and value" (Howell 1995b). I have argued that it is best understood as a life-promoting community in a broad sense, and that the priest-leader couple is the personified manifestation of the House in matters of ritual and political practices. In all these matters Lio differ radically from the Chewong. The Lio jural system and authority are internal to the human Lio social organization whereas in the case of the Chewong it is, as I have argued, (narrowly defined) external to it.

Priest-leaders are also the caretakers of all House land, which they may distribute to the households that belong to it. Land is part of Lio personhood and it is apt to state that land owns people, not the other way round. It is not alienable. Land owns people through the category of priest-leader and the quality of the relationship between priest-leaders and the spirits of the land determines the fertility of the land. The priest-leader couple performs clan agricultural ceremonies on behalf of all the farmers and they receive an annual tribute from every farmer. Again, the difference between Lio and Chewong is marked. With the latter all forest land and all forest produce belong to everyone for free exploitation. What matters is correct behavior within the forest and amongst themselves.

Marriage is pivotal in Lio political hierarchy, not just for the maintenance of relations between groups à la Lévi-Strauss, but also in terms of the destination of offspring as Meillassoux suggested. What matters in particular is the creation of proper offspring for the continuity of legitimate succession to priest-leadership. Wife-givers and wife-receivers repeat and reconfirm their relationship from generation to generation. The son of a priest-leader earmarked for succession must marry a woman from the same aristocratic sub-group of a clan that provided his mother (that is, his [classificatory] MBD). Only they can produce an offspring that will reproduce the power inherent to legitimate priest-leaders and be carried on to similar future marriages. When such a woman is married to her (classificatory) FZS from the same group as her father she will, ipso facto, become a female priest-leader, empowered to perform the required female religious and political tasks that accompany those of the husband. If the wife of a priest-leader is not of the correct category, or if wife-receivers default on the prestation of the various life-promoting occasions to their wife-givers, the woman cannot perform the task of a female priest-leader. These tasks are then performed by another woman who is in a correct relationship, but either married to another man or she is unmarried. If no such woman exists, a male relative in the wife-giving group may step in and be referred to as "the wife." In such cases biological sex is subordinated to gender considerations (Howell 1996). Similarly, if there is no male successor to an existing priest-leader (including his brothers), a woman may be elevated and perform the required duties. When performing her political or religious duties she is symbolically male and a man from the necessary wife-giving group will stand forth as her counterpart – the female priest-leader. So what matters is less the actual biology of the priest-leader couple but the fact of their kin and affinal position in relation to each other as gendered persons is appropriately positioned.

Lio children are kinned (Howell 2003) into an understanding of their descent relationships and into their potential future affinal relationships. The kinship and alliance system may be construed as being the process by which the Lio "subject is brought into existence, in the sense of the knowing and embodied self ... the 'person' also constructs the subject in the second sense of the word; one who is subject to a system of power" (Lansing 2003: 373). Lio children learn early how their particular kin status will determine in large measure their future sociopolitical status. This applies especially to sons and daughters of priest-leaders who are more constrained in the selection of their future spouse. They are already earmarked at birth. Whether they actually marry the appointed woman/man or not is irrelevant for the operation of the system. As I have shown, substitutes may be activated on required occasions. Lio understandings of sociality, perhaps more than that of Chewong and Norwegians, may be thought of as an example of what Strathern has termed dividuals (Strathern 1988), whereby the boundaries between people are not static, but fluid. Personhood crosses the bodily boundaries of those related through descent or marriage in such a way that they may be interpreted as dividuals within a highly structured kinship classification system that is maintained through the prescribed gift exchanges rather than as bounded individuals.

Thus Lio kinship and politics are two sides of the same coin. As opposed to the Chewong, whose behavior is framed only by cosmo-rules whereby repercussions of breaches are exercised by external agents, Lio are constrained by the constituting significance of the sociopolitical life of the cosmogenic past which limits and directs peoples' movements and choices in most parts of their daily life, marked most clearly in their prescribed behavior towards kin and affines. The larger relations of ancestry and descent as well as affinal connections are interjected into the politics of procreation.

28.3 Norway

My third example is that of contemporary Norway and it represents yet another very different scenario. Contemporary Norwegian society is an example of an egalitarian modern welfare state in which individual autonomy is highly valued and endorsed in legislation. Although Norwegian ideology is premised upon the right of the individual to choose his or her life and life partner, procreation is closely regulated by law – Norwegian family law and international conventions. Here we have an example of governmentality in Foucault's (1991) sense of the benevolent state exercising authority over people's personal lives for the intended benefit of all; what I call democratic absolutism. The state controls the meaning and practice of kinship and family and defines the relationship between biology, relatedness, and sociality, of belonging and nationality. But it seeks to do so in conformity with majority opinion. Biological connectedness is paramount in Norwegian thinking and the laws demonstrate this. Acceptable deviations are at the outset defined as "as-if" kinship, although once the legal requirements for transforming non-biological relations into legal kin relations are complete, the parties are henceforth treated as such. Similarly, same-sex marriage is today treated as "as-if" marriage.

Kinship is bilateral with, until recently, a clear patri-bias that was reflected in family law. This has changed in recent years in line with contemporary sexual politics. I will return to this later in this chapter. Kin relatedness is not institutionalized as a source of political power; its social ramifications do not usually extend beyond the nuclear family of parents and children. Affines are important socially and emotionally to a spouse, but not to his/her own kin. However, family life is highly valued and for a couple to have children is of the utmost importance as a source for personal satisfaction. This is clearly observable in the case of involuntary childlessness (Howell 2001, 2006). Marriage rules are negative and few and, beyond these, the choice of spouse is left entirely to the individual. But marriage and procreation practices are codified in law, and these laws are in constant process of change, especially as regard to sex and gender. The state, through the legislative procedure of Parliament, controls what category of person may marry what other category, and when natural biological procreation fails, the state controls which categories of person may seek alternative sources for obtaining a child, whether this be adoption, in vitro fertilization, egg or sperm donation, or surrogacy. Changes in the laws in these two regards are fraught with moral concerns and subject to serious and heated public debate (Melhuus 2012). Ultimate power lies in Parliament, but unlike the Lio, Norwegian values and practices concerning marriage and procreation are not predicated upon an understanding of the cosmogenic past, the replication of which is vital for the recreation of the future. Neither Lio nor Chewong have conceptual or moral space for changing the premises of procreation or correct behavior. Norwegian family law, by contrast, is subject to constant revisions in conformity with changes in social values (Howell 2009; Melhuus and Howell 2009; Strathern 1988). Norwegian citizens may argue for change in the laws that they regard as oppressive in some way or other – restricting individual freedom, and this has been happening during the past decade or so – especially with respect to same-sex marriage and "non-natural" procreation.

So, while kinship considerations may on the face of it seem irrelevant in the everyday life of most individual Norwegians today, details of marriage and procreation are in fact topics of great moral concern and public debate, rendering the interface between kinship and politics a particularly hot potato. Different political parties have different views. I will give a very brief review of some pertinent changes in Norwegian family law that will demonstrate that there is indeed an interactive relationship between kinship and politics in this country, although in a very different way from that of the Lio and Chewong.

There is a clear biological bias in popular and legal understandings of pregnancy and birth manifested in the idioms employed. For example, the popular practice of adopting a child from countries in the South as well as from Eastern Europe is embroiled in a long bureaucratic process wherein prospective parents, as well as the various agents involved employ the idiom of pregnancy and birth to the process. Thus a couple embarking upon an application to be granted the right to adopt refers to this as the pre-pregnancy stage, to be followed by the pregnancy stage when their application is accepted. When a particular child is allocated to a particular set of parents and they are given a photo and some details of him or her, the birthing has started. This stage is completed when the child is united with the adoptive parents and they have brought the child to their home (Howell 2006).

Legal marriage is foundational to procreation as well as to adult partnership and carries social as well as economic advantages for the parties concerned. For example, a woman who is not married to the man she lives with may find that she inherits nothing upon her partner's death unless he has made a will. Were she married without children, she would be entitled to everything, and minimally half if there are children. Biological children, including, interestingly, any biological children a man may have from a previous informal relationship, on the other hand, have the same inheritance rights as children of legal marriage. The law manages divorce and specifies childcare after a divorce. Only legally married parents have visitation rights and duty to support a child after a breakdown in the relationship. Three major changes in family law occurred in 1978, 1985, and 1986. First, the abortion law of 1978 allowed abortion on demand whether the woman was married or not. Contraception was also made freely available. Second, the law of inheritance of family farms (*odelsrett*, English *allodium title*) of 1985 changed the right to inherit from the firstborn son to the firstborn child regardless of sex. This law (much as Lio understanding) that links land and patrilineal persons in an intimate relationship goes back to Viking times. Third, the Adoption Law of 1986 made adopted children legal children on par with biological children.

The destination of offspring (viz. Meillassoux) and the rights to a child become an issue on the occasion of divorce. Custody is legally binding and only legal parents have visiting rights following a divorce. Although mothers tend to have custody, showing a bias toward the perceived superiority of the mother role (2012 and see below), fathers increasingly demand a share, and the law allows for equal share of maintenance. The dogma of the "best interest of the child" is at the basis of all child politics in Norway – be it conception, birth, care, and residence. As most women and men today work outside the home, the question of who will look after the children has become another topic for heated debate. Many argue that the mother should stay at home until the child is at least two years old. Others demand public kindergarten facilities from the age of one. A large public demand for 100 percent pre-school facilities has been met by the previous and current government with promises to provide good quality publically funded kindergarten from the age of one to six. Approximately 80 percent of children in the appropriate age group today attend full-time pre-school. This practice clearly affects attitudes to parenthood and family.

With the arrival of various forms of new reproductive technology, the state has become very active in regulating the practice, i.e., what kinds of practices should be allowed and who should be entitled to use them.

This is a large and complicated topic and I will just mention a couple of the most pertinent concerns. Today, egg donation is still not allowed nor is surrogacy, but sperm donation is, marking a special moral emphasis upon motherhood that sets it apart from fatherhood. However, biology retains its superior position as a defining part of relatedness. A sperm donor cannot achieve anonymity and a child conceived by sperm donation has the right to know the identity of the donor upon reaching the age of maturity. The same applies to adopted children.

Issues of sex and gender became central in these debates when homosexuals demanded the right to marry, to adopt and to receive reproductive assistance. The law has moved slowly from allowing same-sex couples to enter into legal partnership to legal marriage in 2009. However, religious politics is more restrictive and many church communities do not allow same-sex church marriage. As far as adoption and assisted reproduction are concerned the law has changed from restricting these practices to legally married heterosexual couples alone, to allowing single men and women to apply to adopt, and same-sex married couples may adopt inside Norway, but not children from overseas. Lesbian married couples, but not male same-sex couples, may receive assisted conception. There is thus a continued sexual imbalance in Norwegian family law which contributes to the constitution of actual family and kinship relations. A so-called co-mother of a lesbian couple has no rights unless she is registered as a legal co- or stepmother (www.llh.no/nor/homofil). Thus we can see that legislation prevents some categories of people from being free to choose their spouse or to choose to have a child.

Norwegian political life is not based on, or directly related to, the Norwegian kinship order – although kinship practices influence much political debate. Norway is a democratic welfare state in which the rights of the individual are central to political ideology regardless of descent or political party. However, the politics of kinship and procreation are profoundly controlled through the elected Parliament who formulate and pass laws in line with contemporary thinking. With new options for contracting marriage and producing children, the state has involved itself actively in ensuring that these practices are performed in conformity with current opinion as well as with an aim to shape future opinion in line with what is regarded as desirable. In this sense kinship and politics are mutually implicated and should be studied as part of one cultural domain.

It is a truism to say that the politics of procreation must, in some way or other, also be about the politics of sex and of gender. In many so-called traditional societies, such as Chewong and Lio, biological sex and social gender are collapsed into one conceptual category, while in contemporary Norway the picture is more complicated. The difference in this regard has ramifications for the ideology and practice of marriage and procreation. Both Chewong and Lio are adamant that their social world is made up of men and women – biologically and sociologically. Neither has classi-ficatory space for homosexuality. Neither tolerates anything other than formalized heterosexual relationships.[11] That makes procreation a matter of the right man and woman getting together in a relationship we can call "marriage." Following the "sexual revolution" and gay politics in Norway, and in the wake of heated public debate, Norwegian law today allows marriage between same-sex couples. Having cast that particular dice, it follows that the right to have children cannot be denied any married couple. But, as I have shown, the law is more complicated in the case of same-sex couples than heterosexual couples. Fraught sexual politics appear in the question of birth-leave and state financial support. While all political parties agree that the father ought to be actively involved in the care of a baby, they differ as to how to implement this. The Left insists that it can only be achieved through legislation, while the Right argues for leaving it up to the couples themselves. At the moment the parents have to share the leave with the father taking a minimum of full ten weeks leave in order to obtain maximum financial benefits.

28.4   Conclusion

Politics (as much as economics and religion) and kinship are more obvi-ously closely part of each other in many communities in countries in the South than they are in the contemporary North. Nevertheless, the procreative domain is regulated in all three societies, whether by norms – however loosely defined and adhered to – or by codified laws. The power to influence, control, and punish also varies: from cosmo-rules and super-natural external retribution among the Chewong; to intervention by priest-leaders whose authority is based on correct descent and marriage as replication and continuation of the first humans among the Lio; to various forms of legally binding codes and sanctions in Norway.

Chewong and Lio are examples of what Dumont (1982) has termed hol-istic societies in which the whole is more highly valued than the indi-viduals within it. Contemporary Norwegian society is an example of an individualistic society in which the individual represents the dom-inant value upon which the politics of the society is constituted. These differences have profound effects on the imaginaries and practices of kinship and politics.

Regardless of an actual kinship order, kin are always part of each other; in some way or other "the mutuality of being" (Sahlins 2013) is operative everywhere. With the hierarchical Lio, kin are also part of the ancestors. The particularity of that relationship determines status in Lio society and determines to what extent someone may exercise influ-ence over others. Politics and kinship are both internal to Lio order. The Chewong social world with an egalitarian ethos that values autonomy also displays a profound sense of communality, the outer boundary of which coincides with their animated forest environment. Their person-hood is extended into the world of animate nonhuman others which through the cosmo-rules is the source of praxis. Politics is external to the purely human domain but internal to the wider animated environ-ment. In Norwegian ideology the individual is granted dominant value. Freedom to choose one's lifecourse is highly valued and runs through pol-itical life. Nevertheless, the state regulates the procreative domain. While the Norwegian state and its laws are subject to constant challenge and revision as the result of public demand; ideologically speaking Chewong cosmo-rules are constant – as is the Lio ontological schema.

Lio political life is profoundly intertwined with their kinship and alliance system. It is difficult to state which is determining which. Rather, kinship and politics are two sides of the same coin. In contrast, kin related-ness does not organize sociopolitical life among the Chewong. Chewong behavior is framed and constrained by cosmo-rules, breaches of which are punished by external agents. Lio practices are framed and constrained by the constituting significance of the sociopolitical life of the cosmogenic past reproduced in the present and which limits peoples' movements and choices in most parts of their daily lives, marked most clearly in their prescribed behavior towards kin and affines. In Norwegian ideology the individual is granted dominant value. Nevertheless, the state regulates the procreative domain, arguably representing an external agency much as the animated forest beings do in the Chewong world.

Notes

1. Tatjana Thelen and Erdmute Alber organized in Berlin in 2014 a con-ference entitled *Doing Politics – Making Kinship* in which the aim was to "bring the two subdisciplines into closer communication, thus enab-ling a new holism in the anthropology of holism and belonging." My chapter here is a reworked version of my unpublished presentation at the conference.
2. Fieldwork with Chewong carried out between 1977 and 1979 and in 1981, followed by numerous shorter visits, the last one in 2010. Fieldwork with Lio undertaken in 1984, 1986, 1989, 1994, 2001. Fieldwork on transnational adoption in Norway started in 1999 and continued through 2008.
3. For example, countries in Western Europe, Maori.
4. For example Australian aboriginals and several Amazonian societies such as Piaroa and Tri.
5. Marriage between parents' children and between siblings is forbidden. Marriage with the child of someone with whom one's mother has had a previous sexual relationship is similarly so.

6. I suggest this practice may be related to the fact that in marriage a person often changes the status of previous relationships, namely from kin to affine (e.g., from aunt and uncle to mother/father in-law).

7. Since this chapter went to press, Sahlins (2017) published his controversial article "The original political society" in which he argues that there are no true egalitarian social forms; they are all subordinate to a cosmic polity of divinities, ancestors etc. One of his empirical examples is Chewong (see my reply Howell 2017).

8. Lansing's article discusses Valeri's work on the Huaulu, a group of people on the Indonesian island Seram. I found the discussion of relevance for my analysis of both Chewong and Lio – although for different reasons.

9. I call the gift exchange system an alliance exchange system, not just marriage exchange because it is activated on a number of life-giving occasions beyond marriage, such as the birth of a child or the death of a close relative from the clan of the wife-receiver/wife-taker, the rebuilding of a clan house of the wife-receiver/wife-giver clan, etc. Wife-receivers must give gold, money, buffalos, and pigs. Wife-givers reciprocate by giving cloth, rice, and palm wine.

10. Specific function is associated with particular priest-leaders and these are ranked in importance. For example, the priest-leader of war is number two, the priest-leader of performing sacrificial acts is number three, and the priest-leader of fertility (human and agriculture) is number four. Other functions vary between domains. In addition to his special function, a clan priest-leader has authority over all clan members and can exercise this unless the matter is of communal relevance when the trunk priest-leader superimposes him.

11. I never observed any signs of homosexual practice during my fieldwork with Chewong or Lio and attempts to elicit opinions on such practice came to nothing. Of course this does not mean that it is not practiced, but it is not socially acknowledged.

References

Barnard, A. and A. Good. 1984. *Research Practices in the Study of Kinship*. London: Academic Press.

Dumont, L. 1982. "On Value" (Radcliffe brown Lecture 1980). *Proceedings of the British Academy* 66: 207–241.

Evans-Pritchard, E. E. 1940. *The Nuer*. Oxford: Clarendon Press.

Fortes, M. and E. E. Evans-Pritchard, eds. 1940. *African Political Systems*. Oxford: Oxford University Press.

Foucault, M. 1991. "Governmentality." In *The Foucault Effect: Studies in Governmentality*, ed. G. Burchell, C. Gordon and P. Miller, 87–104. Chicago, IL: University of Chicago Press.

Gibson, T. and K. Sillander, eds. 2011. *Anarchic Solidarity: Autonomy, Equality, and Fellowship in Southeast Asia*. New Haven, CT: Yale University Press.

Howell, S. 1984. *Society and Cosmos: Chewong of Peninsular Malaysia*. Oxford: Oxford University Press. (New paperback ed. Chicago, IL: University of Chicago Press. 1989.)

1985. "Equality and Hierarchy in Chewong Classification." In *Context and Levels*, ed. R. H. Barnes, D. De Coppet and R. J. Parkin, 167–180. JASO Occasional Paper, 4. Oxford: JASO.

1986. "Of Persons and Things: Exchange and Valuables among the Lio of Eastern Indonesia." *MAN* (n.s.) 24: 419–438.

1995a. "Rethinking the Mother's Brother." *Indonesia Circle*. November.

1995b. "The Lio House: Building, Category, Idea, Value." In *About the House: Levi-Strauss and Beyond*, ed. J. Carsten and S. Hugh-Jones, 149–169. Cambridge: Cambridge University Press.

1996. "Many Contexts, Many Meanings? Gendered Values among the Lio of Indonesia." *Journal of the Royal Anthropological Institute* (incorporating *MAN*) 2(2): 253–269.

2001. "Self-Conscious Kinship: Some Contested Values in Norwegian Transnational Adoption." In *Relative Values: Reconfiguring Kinship Studies*, ed. S. Franklin and S. McKinnon, 203–223. Durham, NC: Duke University Press.

2003. "Kinning: The Creation of Life Trajectories in Transnational Adoptive Families." *Journal of the Royal Anthropological Institute* (incorporating *MAN*) 9(3): 465–484.

2006. *The Kinning of Foreigners: Transnational Adoption in a Global Perspective*. Oxford/New York: Berghahn Books.

2009. "Accelerated Globalisation and the Conflicts of Values Seen through the Lens of Transnational Adoption: A Comparative Perspective." In *The Anthropology of Moralities*, ed. Monica Heintz, 81–101. Oxford/New York: Berghahn Books.

2011. "Sources of Sociality in a Cosmological Frame: Chewong, Peninsular Malaysia." In *Anarchic Solidarity: Autonomy, Equality, and Fellowship in Southeast Asia*, ed. T. Gibson and K. Sillander, 40–61. New Haven, CT: Yale University Press.

2013. "Knowledge, Morality and Causality in a 'Luckless' Society." *Social Analysis* 56(1): 133–147.

2017. "Rules without Rulers?" HAU: *Journal of Etnographic Theory* 7(3): 1–5.

Kuper, A. 1973. *Anthropologists and Anthropology: The British School 1922–1972*. London: Alan Lane.

Lansing, J. S. 2003. "The Cognitive Machinery of Paoer: Reflections on Valeri's 'The Forest of Taboos.'" *American Ethnologist* 30(3): 372–380.

Leach, E. 1954. *Political Systems of Highland Burma: A Study of Kachin Social Structure*. London: Bell.

Lévi-Strauss, C. 1969 [1949]. *The Elementary Structures of Kinship*. Boston, MA: Beacon Press.

Melhuus, M. 2012. *Problems of Conception: Issues of Law, Biotechnology, Individuals and Kinship*. Oxford: Berghahn Books.

Melhuus, M. and S. Howell. 2009. "Adoption and Assisted Conception: One Universe of Unnatural Procreation. An Examination of Norwegian Legislation." In *European Kinship in the Age of Biotechnology*, ed. Jeanette Edwards and Carles Salazar, 144–161. Oxford/New York: Berghahn Books.

Sahlins, M. 2013. *What Kinship Is – and Is Not*. Chicago, IL: University of Chicago Press.

2017. "The Original Political Society." HAU: *Journal of Etnographic Theory* 7(2): 1–36.

Strathern, M. 1988. *The Gender of the Gift: Problems with Women and Problems with Society in Melanesia*. Berkeley, CA: University of California Press.

Thelen, T and E. Alber, eds. 2017. *Reconnecting State and Kinship*. Philadelphia, PA: Penn Press.

29

A Global Family: Kinship, Nations, and Transnational Organizations in Botswana's Time of AIDS

Koreen M. Reece

Motse o lwapeng. "The village is in the home."

"This week, Batswana have welcomed into their family twenty-nine ambassadors from Canada. In diplomatic work, relations can be nurtured at a personal level; nation-states are composed of individuals, and the international system is composed of nation-states, so it follows that individual relations facilitate better international relations." The Deputy Permanent Secretary for Botswana's Ministry of Foreign Affairs stood at a makeshift podium, incongruous in his sharp business suit among the trees. Flanking him to his right sat a small phalanx of similarly well-dressed officials, suited or uniformed, the women wearing high heels in spite of the deep sand. To his left ran a long, open white tent, under which a handful of other elite figures sat on office chairs at long tables covered in cloth and bright Botswana-blue bunting, fronted by an impressive display of baskets, gourds, and woven mats. Facing the tent, across an open performance area, three rows of Canadian high school students wearing tailored shirts and skirts of blue German-print cloth shifted uncomfortably in small iron chairs brought from a local primary school for the occasion. Everyone else – a crowd of people from the nearest village, including elders, young men and women, and gaggles of children – sat and stood around the edges, behind the ranks of officials and Canadians.

We were an unlikely group in an unlikely spot. We sat in a wooded area next to a deep, dry riverbed in a remote corner of the country. A well-established national nongovernmental organization (NGO) had acquired the area as a campsite in which to host therapeutic retreats for children orphaned by Botswana's ongoing AIDS epidemic. The program had been modeled explicitly on the tradition of initiation, a practice which had long since lapsed in most of the areas the NGO served; but the NGO's proposals also cast the retreats explicitly as a means of "creating kin." I had helped broker the government's partnership with the NGO in my previous work as a technical advisor at Botswana's Department of Social Services, and had attended trainings and retreats in the past. The program now spanned the country, and was being implemented by government social workers in half of the nation's administrative districts.

The Canadian students, looking alternately bored and bewildered as the speeches wore on, had fundraised to help build a meeting hall to be used for ceremonies at the new campsite, modeled on a *kgotla* (customary court). They'd come for a week to help finish its construction, and an agreement had been struck to mark the occasion with an official opening event. A remarkable number of senior civil servants – from the local administration and schools in the nearby village, from the District Council and Land Board in the regional center (a couple of hours' drive away), and from the Department of Social Services, the Ministries of Foreign Affairs and Local Government in distant Gaborone – had found their ways along the red, sandy roads and down the narrow track that led into the site. Many had come a day's drive from the capital; others had come during the week to camp and help with the work of finishing the site and preparing for the event, much as they might have done for a wedding or funeral. Given my longstanding relationships with both Social Services and the NGO, and given I was Canadian too, I was invited to tag along.

The Deputy Permanent Secretary had moved on to the President's goals for national development, and was appreciating the Canadian group for situating their work so well within them. "That these students can demonstrate this kind of love and care for other human beings gives me hope that coming generations will inherit a more caring world," he continued. "I wish to pay a special tribute to the parents of these young people ... we hold in high esteem parents who can allow their small children to travel to a far place and live among strangers for a week." He spun together development goals, love and care, inheritance, global humanitarianism, parenthood, and cultural exchange as effortlessly as he had envisioned ambassadors in families in his opening lines.

As he finished his speech, the first of six local choirs danced and sang their way into the performance area to the shouts and ululations of the audience. The choir, singing a greeting song for *bagolo* (the elders), faced the podium and tent, until an enterprising social worker noticed the disappointed expressions of the Canadian contingent and induced the choir to shift so that they could be seen by everyone at the same time. They sang "*Modimo, o thusa bana ga ba na batsadi*" – "God, help the children without parents." The song was the first reference to the children for whom the campsite had been built, and evoked their helplessness, vulnerability, and isolation, as well as the potential threat they posed to the nation's future. It stood in stark contrast to the vibrant, interconnected global family the previous speaker had conjured.

The song's tropes were familiar enough. Botswana has been facing one of the world's worst AIDS epidemics for nearly 30 years, in spite of its relative wealth and stability, and notwithstanding its proactive response to the spread of the disease. The epidemic is frequently cast as a crisis – not just in public health terms, but in humanitarian terms and in terms of its effects on Botswana's long-term development as well. Above all, it is cast as a crisis of the family. Total family breakdown is often assumed to be both cause and inevitable effect of the epidemic, and the "orphan crisis" and "crisis of care" that are imagined to threaten the economic, political, and social survival of the nation are situated firmly in the home. As such, the family is the primary target of a vast array of interventions undertaken by the Botswana government, NGOs, transnational organizations and donors in response to AIDS – making it an unexpectedly apt site for investigating the state, humanitarian, and development interventions, and the links and distinctions between kinship and politics on local and transnational levels.

In this chapter, I follow the lead of Susan McKinnon and Fennella Cannell (2013), who call attention to the "persistent life" of kinship in the economic, political, and religious projects of "modern" states, corporations, churches, and other agencies. They point out that any distinction between these "domains" is ideological, not given, and requires significant boundary-making work – in spite of which, a deep interdependence remains (2013: 11). I add that the "kinship and marriage coordinates of Western liberal, supposedly secular, individualistic, democratic states" (2013: 25) become especially evident in both the local and transnational humanitarian and development programs those states, and their civil society counterparts, fund or initiate. Many of these interventions explicitly or implicitly take the rehabilitation of families, and their transformation into a "modern" kin ideal, as a primary aim; and they draw out the "kinship coordinates" of the communities and states in which they intervene in response. Kinship, in these contexts, offers the primary terms in and practices by which the boundary work distinguishing public from private is undertaken and contested – not just by families, but by states, NGOs, and transnational agencies as well.

By drawing together the domestic and the political in this way, I do not seek a return to understandings of African societies as "premodern"; nor do I aspire to the corollary characterizations of African politics as predominantly kin-based (cf. Evans-Pritchard and Fortes 1940; Schapera 1970). Rather, I suggest that we might reconceptualize *all* public, political institutions and work – including those we are accustomed to exceptionalizing as "Western" and "modern" – as being fundamentally informed by kinship ideals and practices, and in constant negotiation with both. The practice of politics and governance does not simply arise out of kin practice (Schapera 1940), but neither does it simply act upon families (Kuper 1975). It does both, describing a constant dialectic between the state and home, the public and the domestic; and this interdependence has taken on transnational implications, brought into sharp relief in the era of AIDS intervention.

In spite of its prominence as a site of intervention, anthropological accounts of humanitarian and development programs have generally overlooked the family, focusing instead on institutional actors, the production of human universals and futures, and emergent forms of governance (Ticktin 2014; Fassin 2012). Indeed, the tendency to avoid families and the micro-processes of relatedness as objects of study suggests an uncanny echo of development and humanitarian organizational practice and discourse itself, in which kin relations have been viewed as encumbrances, threats, and even cause for suspicion (Redfield 2012: 362). And yet the notion of family, like that of humanity, remains "meaningful across political, religious, and social divides" (Ticktin and Feldman 2010: 1) – a key trope in imagining human universality, vested with a variety of shifting, unstable meanings, which are nonetheless effectively deployed to a wide range of political ends (Tsing 2005: 8). The humanitarian imperative to provide care for strangers (Redfield and Bornstein 2011; Redfield 2012), for example, evoked so explicitly by the Deputy Permanent Secretary above, is underpinned by the conviction that when those who should ordinarily care for people – namely, their families – can't, or won't, "society, either through philanthropy or the state, [is] obliged to stand in" (Fassin 2013: 118). In this sense, the principles of humanitarian intervention and government are subtly but deeply informed by expectations, ideologies, and practices of kinship. Like humanitarianism, kinship marks "a particularly charged terrain between politics and ethics" (Redfield and Bornstein 2011: 25), drawing together affect and value, rights and obligations, the moral and the political, and bridging the paradoxes they present in similar ways (Fassin 2012: 3). On this reading, the family itself emerges as not only a target, but a sphere of humanitarian governance (Fassin 2012).

Much has been said about the anti-politics of humanitarian and development interventions (Ferguson 1994; Ticktin 2011), but comparatively little has been said about the work to which families and kinship specifically are put in those anti-politics. I suggest that the family provides a key depoliticizing, dehistoricizing, and universalizing space in and through which an international humanitarian community – a global family – can construct itself (compare Malkki's description of refugees in these terms,

1996: 378). As both the Deputy Permanent Secretary's speech and the choir's performance above indicate, many intervening agencies turn first to the discourse of family when seeking to downplay and obscure fundamentally political or economic aims. The family provides a powerful organizational metaphor that government, NGOs, and donors can – and do – tap into as a means of naturalizing their work, relationships, and power. But attempts to operationalize kinship to the ends of governance are frequently foiled by the "superfluity … and excess" of kinship (Lambek 2013: 255; cf. Ticktin and Feldman 2010: 5). Kinship is, after all, more than a metaphor; and I argue that it features powerfully in the daily practice and lived experience of "official" spaces. Government and NGO programs that intervene in the family, attempting to contain and reshape it, are themselves saturated with and animated by kinship ideals and practice. Kinship is, in this sense, as crucial to understanding development and humanitarian programs as development and humanitarianism are to understanding kinship.

Below, I demonstrate the distinct ways in which government social work interventions and NGO programs attempt to bureaucratize and managerialize the family and household, seeking to absorb them into public projects in a way that produces a clear distinction between the domestic and the political, and explicitly prioritizes the latter. These efforts, of course, are frequently frustrated, given the capacity of families to evade and overwhelm the constraints of bureaucratic systems (Lambek 2013: 255). I suggest that such failures may also index the subtle but pervasive domestication of public projects and workplaces, the everyday experiences and relationships of which are suffused by kinship ideals and practices. This suffusion blurs distinctions between the domestic and the political, disrupting and inverting hierarchies between them – while introducing different modes of distinction in turn. Indeed, kin-like relationships between institutional actors seem to emerge. It is with this framing that I suggest we might best understand the proverb that opens this piece: to say *motse o lwapeng* – the village is in the *lelwapa* (lit. courtyard; also family) – is to suggest that the village is grounded in, sustained by, and even encompassed by the home.[1] I contend that the shape and meaning of the public sphere, and the power in its politics, emanates above all from this specific relationship with the family.

29.1   Social Work

"Do you have the death certificate?" Goitse asked the hunched, slightly bewildered-looking man who sat across the desk from her, next to two teenagers in their school jumpers. He shook his head, saying he'd already given copies to his local social worker. "Birth certificates?" she pursued, nodding towards the students while picking up her mobile phone and dialing. These he provided, looking askance at her phone. She pulled out a file in which to record them. Meanwhile, her call having gone through, she began berating another social worker for his missing registration statistics. She handed the birth certificates back, and still on the phone, told the client, "You'll have to come back with certified copies of those and the death certificate. I'll be in touch to call the children for therapy." He nodded, looking a little perplexed at the mention of therapy. "They're already registered for the food basket, don't worry," Goitse added, going back to her phone call. The man nodded and sighed, ushering the teenagers out.

I had just arrived at the District Council Social and Community Development (S&CD) office to meet with Goitse, who was head of the area's orphan care program. We had known each other for years, dating back to my time working as a technical advisor with the Department of Social Services. Initially I had stayed outside her office, seated on one of the long benches that lined the hallway, waiting for her to finish with her clients. The benches were crowded with people that day, many of whom looked as if they had been waiting for hours: men with their heads tipped back against the wall, women with their heads scarved and their arms crossed, grandmothers trying to contain the impatience of small children. It was reminiscent of many other S&CD offices I had visited around the country. Spotted by one of Goitse's colleagues, I was encouraged to go straight in.

After she finished her call, I asked Goitse about the register of birth certificates. She explained that the children we'd just seen had been registered as orphans recently, and had brought in their certificates in response to a government push to ensure that all orphaned and vulnerable children had their identity documents in order. "I don't know who that man was who came with them," she added, sounding a bit suspicious. "There were issues. I can see them." I asked what she meant. "Just, problems," she answered. "It can be anything. People these days lack parenting skills, they don't know how to care for children," she added.

Before she could expand, another young man came in, holding a file. She seemed to know him, and invited him to sit down. He had dark bags under his eyes, and handed her a death certificate. She looked over the certificate, and asked him in Setswana about the illness it recorded. He began speaking about his grandmother, who had died the week previously, and the pain she had experienced in her legs – until he was interrupted by a phone call. Goitse answered, and conducted a lengthy conversation about the availability of a government house she hoped to move in to while her client waited. When she put down the phone, Goitse noted that the death certificate listed cardiac congestion and asked the young man whether he understood what that was. He shook his head, and said it just seemed that she had given up and died. The phone rang again. The man sat patiently. Another social worker came in with forms for school uniforms that needed signing off. Goitse – on the phone still – refused, saying there was no money left; the social worker pleaded with her, calling his clients *bongwanake*, my children, and insisting they wouldn't be able to go to school without the uniforms. Goitse signed the forms, protesting. As he left, the social worker asked Goitse to loan him 200 Pula (roughly £20) to pay his water bills; this request she refused flatly, but only, she reassured him, because she had not yet paid her own.

Once the social worker had left, Goitse turned her attention back to the young man, noting the number of the death certificate in a spreadsheet. "They did something when they were taking those mourning clothes from her," the young man added obscurely, looking troubled. Goitse did not register the comment, nor ask what or whom he meant. She handed him back the death certificate, and thanked him, and then got up promptly. "I'm coming," she said to me, and then went. I didn't see her again until the end of the day.

I attended Goitse's office frequently, and like most S&CD offices, it was predictably hectic. There were four officers assigned to it, though it was clearly meant for one. They squeezed between shelving, filing cabinets, and computers, ranged along both sides of a broad L-shaped desk that bisected the room, occasionally shuffling over to make room for clients. They were seldom all there at once; more often they were one or two, with others' coats or handbags left on the desk to signify their presence while they were off seeing to administrative responsibilities – or at one of the frequent meetings, trainings, workshops, or conferences to which they were called and sent by a bewildering array of bosses and supervisors. Almost as frequently, they would be out paying their utility bills or the monthly interest on lay-by purchases, buying snacks to share, picking up things for their children, or making visits to colleagues. The door was kept closed, but the traffic in and out was constant: people looking for forms, calling people to meetings, dropping off statistics, being sent for fresh *diphaphata* (bread), or just popping their heads in to say hello, ask favors, or borrow sugar and tea (for which the officemates contributed jointly). At the same time, there were clients bringing letters and documentation, or lodging concerns around property grabbing, the illness and death of parents, or the welfare of their children. Meanwhile, the social workers whose office it was held meetings for their *metshelo*, or small-scale savings groups (which often included other officemates); conducted phone conversations with creditors and debtors, their landlords, or their children's schools; or called friends, partners, and even pastors for guidance in dealing with difficult issues in their relationships. And they did all of these things freely, in front of me and one another, and occasionally in front of clients as well. The office was a curiously private, public space; or a curiously public, private space – in many ways like the *lelwapa*, or courtyard, that stands at the heart of most Tswana homes.

The Department of Social and Community Development had a vast range of responsibilities. At village level, each office had perhaps one or two social workers, but hundreds of clients, sometimes spread across several communities. Clients ranged from destitute families and orphaned children to the HIV-positive and World War II veterans. Social workers were responsible for assessing and registering clients; for administering food baskets, via local shops; for paying school fees, arranging school placements, school uniforms, and transport for children; for providing adequate shelter and clothing; and, nominally at least, for offering psychosocial support and counseling. They were mandated to undertake direct intervention in families, and to remove children in cases of neglect, abuse, or violent conflict; and they were responsible for arranging foster or institutional care, and the subsequent rebuilding of the family as well. While these duties already represented an overstuffed portfolio, social workers were also responsible for the oversight of Village Development Committees and other local development initiatives, as well as the organization of most major commemorative events. District-level offices, like Goitse's, not only coordinated village offices, but oversaw their budgets, reporting, and training, linking them both with District Councils and, at national level, the Department of Social Services. They also handled cases directly, or on referral.

At both levels, social workers were swamped. Their powers were sweeping, grounded in recognition of their professional training and expertise, and the potential scope of their access to the family was unparalleled by any other "super-familial" actor. But they frequently complained of being stuck in the office, bound to the administrative imperatives of their work, and unable to practice what they saw as their core responsibility – namely, the psychosocial support of their clients. As we saw briefly above, the policy environment in which they worked prioritized the filling of forms and registers, the collection and assessment of certificates, the maintaining of detailed case files, the processing of statistics and wrangling over money for the basic goods to which clients were entitled. It was work, in other words, more concerned with the bureaucratization of clients and their families than anything else. Drawing on the history and practices of colonial governance, it sought to situate clients in a network of documents, and to trace and define their familial relationships in the same way; and it tied access to a vast range of material support to this bureaucratic recognizability. While social workers chafed under this bureaucratization, it was nonetheless key to their greatest professional capacity to provide care – which Batswana locate in the provision of material goods, and the work of acquiring and looking after them (see Klaits 2010). This care provision, formalized bureaucratically, was crucial in connecting social workers to their clients while simultaneously distinguishing them, ultimately positioning the state in a position of power over the home.[2]

Goitse's reflections on her clients evinced a common professionalizing discourse, used both to describe the extent of breakdown in the Tswana family and to justify intervention. Many social workers I knew complained – always in English – of a "lack of parenting skills" among their clients' families. Alternatively, they spoke of parents misunderstanding children's developmental and emotional needs, or having a poor grasp of basic psychology, all of which rendered them less capable of providing love and care (especially if the children were not "theirs"). This discourse was another key means of distinguishing family and state, rooted in an alternative framework – drawn from dominant social work, public health, humanitarian and development discourse – for understanding the problems facing families, and their appropriate solutions. In the exchanges narrated above, for example, Goitse does not register her client's suspicions about his dead grandmother's mourning clothes, which among Batswana would have connoted a fear of potential witchcraft. As well as they understood it in personal terms from their own families, Batswana social workers seldom made room for witchcraft as a legitimate risk to be addressed in a professional context. Instead, problems were traced to latent psychological or emotional stress caused by an inability to express grief, trauma, or other feelings – although, as has been amply described elsewhere, Batswana generally consider the expression of pain and other negative emotions to be *more* dangerous than its containment (Durham 2002; Durham and Klaits 2002; Klaits 2010). Social workers focus on the clear identification, expression, and resolution of issues that arise – a focus that echoes the bureaucratic work of recognition and authorization for which they are responsible, but that stands in stark contrast to the careful containment of recognition and expression, and the emphasis on *ir*resolution, that families routinely bring to similar issues (which we will revisit below; see also Reece 2019).

Michael Lambek (2013) notes that the "shift to new forms of authorization or recognition is the biggest transformation of kinship to take place under modernity" (2013: 250). As the examples above illustrate, it is a shift that has become even more marked in Botswana's time of AIDS. Bureaucratic and professional recognition might well, as Lambek suggests, be acts of kinship (2013: 249–250). And yet, a certain myopia belies that possibility. Goitse did not recognize the man who brought the first two clients I found in her office, though she claimed to recognize the risk of "problems" he posed; she recognized the second, but did not recognize the concern he registered about the behavior of relatives at his grandmother's funeral. Goitse could "see" potential issues, but not always the networks of kin in which they were emplaced. The government social work perspective, in other words, was oriented towards recognizing problems and seeking their bureaucratic solutions, but not the relationships that contextualize (and generate) those problems. In this sense, I suggest that while negotiating bureaucratic recognition may be an act of kinship, it is an act of kinship between those who negotiate it (the two men above, or the parents and grandparents waiting outside the office) and those for whom it is negotiated (the teenagers, the children outside), rather than between those people and the state. Family, in other words, may accede to a degree of bureaucratization and professionalization, and in this sense their acts of kinship may also be acts of state-making; but at the same time, their relationships evade and remain obscure to the state, and are actively distinguished from it, refusing it any place in their kin-making (Lambek 2013: 250–251, 255–256).

Of course, as the office slice of life presented above suggests, social workers are not simply bureaucratic machines. They challenge and unsettle their own bureaucratizing work, primarily through gestures of domestication, in which the office is rendered home-like (not unlike the domestications of Malaysian blood banks described in Carsten 2013). I see domestication working in two ways in Goitse's office. First, Goitse and her colleagues used their shared workspace, undertook their work, and related to one another in ways distinctly reminiscent of life in the *lelwapa* (courtyard), deploying a number of what Frederick Klaits has characterized as "housing activities" (though not nearly all; Klaits 2010: 31). Thus, for example, they were in constant movement, visiting colleagues elsewhere in the office and around the district. They contributed together for certain food staples, fetched meals together and for one another, and ate together, all in ways reminiscent of the management of food at home. The youngest were called and sent to buy or fetch things, or to call others. And the social workers drew clients into these dynamics as a matter of course, continuing to undertake their homework in the clients' presence. Social workers often spoke of child clients as *bongwanake*, my children; my former supervisor at Social Services frequently referred to himself as the uncle of Botswana's orphans. Of course, clients were often bewildered by this treatment, and seldom engaged in it reciprocally. Rather, they behaved like guests in someone's yard, surrounded by the business of family but careful to exclude themselves from it.

Second, Goitse and her colleagues prioritized their duties to their own families over their professional duties while in the office – and this prioritization was generally accepted among the social workers as a responsible one. Goitse's phone calls above were partly work related, but largely related to securing housing for herself and her family, or arranging for problems to be fixed at home. I visited the office several times, and each time I would be invited to accompany the others as they went to pay their bills, to negotiate with Water Affairs over a broken pipe, to buy their children clothing, or to pick up groceries – all of which errands were undertaken in the middle of the day, and usually took hours. I was often hesitant, and asked whether we shouldn't be in the office; but I was scoffed at, and reminded that these errands could only be run during office hours, and obviously took priority. Discussion gravitated around life at home; conversations conducted with spouses, partners, and children over the phone were frank and direct, regardless of the audience in the office. The prioritization of home-work made the office a highly home-oriented space, and subtly blurred the lines between the two. These domesticating practices served simultaneously to naturalize the bureaucratizing project for which the social workers were responsible, and to subvert it – particularly when clients or NGO workers judged the behavior inappropriate to a government office, as they often did.

In many ways, the working conditions, aims and programs of the NGO world diverge sharply from those of the social work office. And yet, I suggest, similar dynamics – of bureaucratizing the family, on the one hand, and of domesticating the workplace, on the other – are at work, marking similar distinctions, blurrings, and subversions between the familial and the political. I turn next to a visit I made to a local NGO to interrogate this possibility.

29.2 Home Visits

Tsholo filled me in as we bumped our way along a meandering dirt road in the organization's spacious, logo-plastered combi van. "The girl's parents died," she began.

> So she left their village and came here looking for work, maybe as a maid for somebody. At first it was fine, she was living with a family, cooking for them, caring for the children. They didn't pay her much but she had a place to stay, and food. But then her sister came looking for her. After some time the family felt it was too much and kicked them out.

The yard to which we were making our way was the last stop in what was clearly the NGO's grand tour. It had begun at the orphan care center, with its impressive hall, kitchen, classrooms, and office block; and it had featured not only an introduction to the children, but an opportunity to participate in some large-group singing and playing with them. The project had been conceived and founded by a European, was heavily funded by European development agencies and supported by many resident expats from Europe, Britain, and America. But on a day-to-day basis, Tsholo and her husband – both from the village themselves – ran the show. The tour emphasized the ways in which children were being helped with their schooling and life skills and given opportunities to develop their talents, as well as being fed and allowed to play. Throughout, Tsholo spoke about the center's clientele as "our children." I was struck by the reach the NGO had achieved; but the model, and even the tour, was familiar to me from dozens of other NGOs I had visited. Indeed, I had led similar tours myself, having previously volunteered in a center structured in a similar way. Whether because she acknowledged that shared experience, or whether it was part of the tour, Tsholo was fairly frank about the family we visited last.

"The social workers had heard about them but weren't doing much," she continued. The NGO fell under the auspices of Goitse's office, and the two agencies held the majority of their orphaned clients in common. They sometimes worked together on cases, though on the whole they shared very little information. "S&CD found the small ones a place at school, but you know they were hardly eating, only the meal they got at the center," Tsholo continued.

> The social workers were looking for a plot for them but not managing. We worked together with them on that one, going to Land Board. Then they found this plot, but *hei*! So far! how are the children supposed to get to school? Then they couldn't find transport for them, so for a long time we were coming here to pick them to school ourselves.

There were broad stretches of dusty scrub between the few cleared yards around us. Where people had built, their houses were clearly newer: many were still unpainted, or unplastered, and some had only reached window level. Children stopped their play to watch us pass.

"At least we managed to find some money for building. S&CD managed with some, and then there was this foreign volunteer with us who did a lot of fundraising from her family and friends. But when the house was finished! *Owai* ... Relatives started pitching up from everywhere," Tsholo continued. I admitted I had been wondering about them; previously unmentioned or unknown family members had a habit of gradually over-populating such tales. I asked whether anyone had tried to find extended family in the girls' home village before the building had begun. Tsholo shrugged.

> We didn't know anything about them. But as soon as the house was there ... ! *Ija!* This other uncle came with the wife, they have two children; then the other cousin came; plus the three children that were here already. Now there are eight people in a little two-and-half [room house], and lots of others coming and going. Nobody is working, you know, and the food basket from S&CD is not enough. We took the older girl back to school but now she's fallen pregnant, imagine ... she is still *motsetse* (confined) in the house by now.

She gestured up ahead a little, where the house had come into view. It was a neatly painted two-and-a-half – named for the two bedrooms standing out on either side of a much smaller, recessed "half" room, each with its own door leading in from a narrow stoop. The house sat in the back of a fenced, cleared yard, swept smooth. We turned into the gate, and one of several children in the yard ran up to open it. As we pulled through and wheeled in front of the house, Tsholo leaned over me to shout a greeting at the small group of women and children washing clothes under a tree. "I don't know those ones," she commented, somewhat suspicious. She came to a halt in front of the stoop, where a young woman looked up from her sweeping and smiled at us shyly.

Unusually, we didn't get out of the combi. Tsholo explained that we were just passing by, and then asked after the girl who had just given birth. The young woman chatted readily but somewhat apologetically, casting me uncertain smiles throughout – we had not been introduced, which made us both hesitant. The new mother was fine, and the baby was healthy. They were hoping she could go back to school in the next term. Shortly thereafter we were headed out again, saying goodbye to everyone we had greeted on the way in. Their expressions were impassive.

A substantial variety and number of NGO interventions target children and their families in Botswana. I was tasked to establish a unit to identify and coordinate them at Social Services in 2005, and a rapid assessment I ran then uncovered no fewer than 220 orphan care projects – as most called themselves – nationwide. They ranged from preschools to therapy camps, from sexual abstinence programs to residential places of safety, from community mobilization programs to income-generation projects. Some involved one person handing out donations; others, a committee of local volunteers conducting events, or a group of professionals creating training curricula. But by far the majority – the sought-after ideal, and often the best-funded – operated on the drop-in center model, like Tsholo's. These centers might run all-day preschools, but they were predominantly set up for after-school care, and usually welcomed orphaned children and youth of school-going age for several hours every afternoon.

NGOs – like S&CD offices – also have registration processes, and their means of bureaucratizing the family linked closely to the social workers'. S&CD offices often referred client families to local NGOs, which may request similar documentation (birth certificates, death certificates, and so on), keep parallel registers, and maintain case files of their own. Families that approach NGOs first, as many do, are usually referred to S&CD in the same way. NGOs, in this sense, play a key, complementary role in securing and extending the government's bureaucratization project.

NGO staff and volunteers, however, are often able to take a much more hands-on approach to their work – though even this hands-on work tends to link to the bureaucratization project described in the first section. Tsholo's narration of the NGO's work with the girl they found focuses primarily on navigating governmental systems: bringing her to the attention of the social workers, helping them advocate to the Land Board, working with them to access funds for building a house, and so on. In this sense, I suggest, NGO work is often primarily managerial; it seeks to steer clients (and by extension their families) through government bureaucratic systems, to advocate for, advise, and direct them, and to make them bureaucratically visible and manageable in turn. The NGO's other main work lies in temporarily filling the gaps in that project: feeding the children until they receive their food baskets, driving them to school until transport is supplied, and supplementing the building fund with the help of international donors. NGOs play a critical role in making the government bureaucratization project work in practice, in regularizing its access to clients, and in coordinating the range of institutions and people involved.

That said, much of the work NGOs do is not with families at all, but exclusively with orphaned clients, at least to begin with. And this focus strongly influences the dynamics of domestication evident in NGOs, which diverge somewhat from those of their social work counterparts. Of course, many of the same domesticating practices as those we saw with the social workers above are also at work in NGOs: staff and volunteers are frequently on the move, visiting clients, colleagues, stakeholders, and donors; they call and send junior staff and children on errands, make visits, eat together, contribute various forms of care (whether through fundraising, or cooking, or joint upkeep of the center), undertake nearly continuous building projects, and so on. And they draw their clients into all of these processes to an even greater extent than social workers do, given that they are usually together for several hours every day. NGO staff also bring their home lives into the workplace in similar ways: phone call interventions, errands for home being run in tandem with errands for work, and the gathering of excess donations for kin at home are all common. Indeed, as in Tsholo's case above, many NGOs are managed by married couples; frequently their children are in attendance, and extended kin are tapped to help with the day-to-day running of the project, making the presence of the family even more dominant in NGO workplaces than elsewhere.

The fact that many orphan care projects are run as "family businesses," as one friend put it, speaks to the other major way in which they are domesticated: they are often conceptualized as independent *gae*, or homes, into which clients could be drawn. Many NGO coordinators I knew insisted on being identified by parental epithets at work, and were called *mmago* or *rrago*, mother-of or father-of. While they would have been called by these teknonyms elsewhere in the community, using them in a work environment underscored the familial terms in which they imagined their projects. These appellations were attached exclusively to the names of the coordinators' own children, but the coordinators themselves generally encouraged other children at the center to take them as parents or family; and as we have seen above, they used the possessive "my" or "our" for the children, reciprocally.

Beyond naming, the spatialities of the center are strongly reminiscent of the *gae* as well. The center bears strong symbolic resonance with the *lelwapa*, or courtyard, bracketed by offices and activity centers rather than bedrooms; indeed, larger centers generally paved a *lelwapa* of their own. Tsholo's tour took us to affiliated income-generation projects and building sites, which bore a geographical relationship to the center that echoed the relationships families traced between their farmlands, cattleposts, and *lelwapa*, as well. Notably, all were sites where NGO staff and clients might be based (or "stay"), among which they would frequently need to be called and sent, and where they might be seen to be doing care work (of cooking, for example, gardening, building, or looking after children) – as would be expected of the places that comprise the *gae*. At the same time, clients' family homes became marginal, offshoots of the center's *lelwapa* among which the center-family might move, and at which the children might stay, but ultimately disconnected from and secondary to the center itself.

But for all that the NGO is modeled upon, draws in, and even attempts to replace the home, it is also sharply distinguished and segregated from family. The NGO's assessment of the girl they found under the tree as family-less indexes a disconnect similar to the social workers' above, which extends through the provision of well-meant material resources and opportunities. While the NGO sees a lost child, they struggle to see the family relationships in which she is situated until they reveal themselves; and even then, those relationships are constituted mostly as a problem or threat. The inherent risks that are likely to accrue to the girl because of the NGO's intervention – she now owns a fully finished house while still at school, for which she owes virtually no obligation – in terms of jealousy, or the management of claims made by extended family members that she may be understood to have scorned (Klaits 2010: Introduction), go unanticipated. The latter risk in particular had already ripened into a silent tension between Tsholo and the extended family, marked by their evident mutual suspicion and the awkwardness with which we were received in the yard.

In spite of the differences in their approaches, then, the parallel projects evident in S&CD offices and NGOs – of bureaucratizing the family, on the one hand, and of domesticating the workplace, on the other – both seem to encounter the same difficulties. Both projects offer the promise of naturalizing the work and roles of these agencies, while containing the problematic disorder and breakdown of the Tswana family; but client families thoroughly evade them, and the agencies' approaches undermine such naturalizing effects as their efforts might have had. To further unpack these dynamics, I return to the opening ceremony with which the chapter began, to question what sorts of relationships are performed, what those relationships might tell us about the influences at work in the disruptions we have described above, and what can be deduced about the links between kinship and politics.

29.3   An Opening Ceremony, Revisited

The choir finished their rousing performance, weaving their way off the sandy stage and singing until they broke formation and dispersed among the audience. From the podium, the master of ceremonies thanked them warmly, and welcomed the lead teacher of the Canadian school group to speak next.

The lead teacher was a contentious figure. The previous day he had insisted on separating food and water for his students from the water supplied for everyone else at the remote campsite, suspecting theft. Senior government figures watched with a mix of dismay and bemused resignation as he first berated the NGO director, and then instructed his students to relocate dozens of water bottles from the kitchen into their tents. Now at the podium in his custom-tailored German-print T-shirt and a baseball cap, he consulted with the translator to ensure that he would be translated phrase by phrase. After speaking of the retreat campsite as a "humanitarian project" that represented strengthened bonds between Botswana and Canada, the teacher thanked the host NGO and government departments and ministries in a perfunctory, non-differentiating fashion. He added offhandedly, "We consider everyone here to be like surrogate parents for us." The translator followed with, "*Re le tsa jaaka batsadi ba rona tota tota*" – "we take you like our real, real parents."

He then called all 29 of his students in front of the podium – though it meant their backs were to the dignitaries and most of the community, and they faced only the VIPs under the tent – and presented them as the best Canada had to offer. They were a visibly diverse group, as the lineup was meant to emphasize: of largely South Asian, Southeast Asian, Chinese, and mixed European descent. He intoned: "A country without its culture is lost." It was a common enough sentiment for Batswana; but attached to such a diverse group of children, from a place no one knew much about – but which presumably had greater prosperity and fewer social ills to cure – it caused apparent confusion. The teacher elaborated a vision of what defined Canada as a nation: multiculturalism, a history of peacekeeping instead of war, the assurance of equality for all. "We teach our children to celebrate other cultures and values," he explained, describing his students as the future leaders of Canada, and adding: "They are an example of what youth should be throughout the world ... committed to making change." The students tried to look grave and inspiring. Behind them, many in the crowd looked politely baffled. On the one hand, the audience was being encouraged to preserve their culture; on the other, they were being encouraged to adopt a rather inscrutable but ostensibly successful Canadian model. On the one hand, these children had respected and taken their hosts as parents; on the other, they seemed to suggest that parents were incidental or unnecessary to the exemplary individuals these children had already become. The twinned tropes of culture and family had been deployed as a means of reproducing a privileged subject-ivity for the Canadian students.[3] I thought back to the teacher's comment to his students late the night before, which I had overheard from across the campsite: "I'll be honest with you, I don't really care about Botswana or Botswanans or whatever. The important thing here is you guys, and the experience you're getting."

The Canadian teacher stepped down from the podium, leaving it to the last and most highly ranked speaker – the Assistant Minister of Local Government, a ministry that oversaw everything from Social Services to District Councils and village administrations. He made his way out from under the VIP tent, dressed in sharp khaki trousers and a multi-pocketed photographer's vest. Flashing a good-humored smile, he waved away the translator jovially and settled in at the podium. He began with an unex-pected injunction: "I would like to invite you all to rise, and observe a moment of silence for those orphans we have lost to HIV and to abuse."

His somber invitation – in English – caught us all a little off-guard, though we rose and bowed our heads dutifully. For all my years attending such ceremonies and events, I had never heard such a discursive combin-ation of catastrophes. Holding orphans up for pity over the loss of their parents and the assumed neglect of their overburdened families, and rallying cries to rescue them and, through them, the future of the nation, constituted the usual rhetoric (much as it has in South Africa; Fassin 2013: 112). But in the context of successful programs in the free provision of antiretroviral medication (ARVs) and the prevention of mother-to-child transmission, orphanhood was seldom posed as a cause of HIV infection in Botswana, and links between orphanhood and death were virtually never made. While abuse was connected with orphanhood frequently enough, and had become a major focus of social services discourse, I'd never heard it connected to death, either. The request for silence was unsettling in the complexity of social ills it subsumed; and more than that, it was jarring in its dislocation from the reality to which most of us in the audience were accustomed, in what felt like a dramatic inflation of the stakes of orphanhood in particular.

The Assistant Minister continued a while in English, congratulating the Canadian students, and their parents, for the spirit of love and giving they had shown, and calling upon all present to learn from their example. He did not bother to translate. Before long, however, he had shifted into Setswana, and had begun a different speech altogether. The exhortative thrust of this parallel speech was *kgokgontsho ya bana*, child abuse; and on this topic the Assistant Minister spoke at great length, with great con-viction and passion. He confronted his audience: "Child abuse is there in our homes and families, though we are turning a blind eye to it and pretending it is not. Men! Uncles! Check yourselves! Check yourselves, look into your hearts." It was a deliberate echo of the nationwide HIV/ AIDS behavior change campaign launched a few years previously, dubbed

Oicheke! – Check yourself! (USAID 2010). "We appreciate these Canadian children for coming to look after our children," he continued, still in Setswana; "but we have a responsibility to look after our children too, so that one day they might go to Canada to help children there, or even to any other place in the world." He did not bother to translate this part of the speech either.

It was a spellbinding oration. The audience, however, did not look altogether impressed. The ranks of community members listened attentively but wore bland expressions. Children continued to run in and out, and choir members joked with one another on the sidelines. The Canadian contingent had begun to glaze over; most looked bored, some frustrated. Just at the point where he had almost lost them, the Assistant Minister switched back into English – to describe his hope that one day, one of the Canadian students before him would meet a doctor on their travels, and find that he had grown up in Botswana, had attended a camp run in the very place they sat now, had come to grips with his loss and grief, had found hope, a sense of self and direction, and had made something of his life. The students lifted their heads, and some began to smile warmly. They were, of course, unable to decipher the strange double register that had emerged: in Setswana, families were abusive, irresponsible, corrupted, and broken; in English, they were sources of love, giving, and hope for the future.

Shortly after the speeches were finished, the cooks and several volunteers from the village nearby called the Canadian students to help serve up the enormous meal that had been prepared – a task that befitted children and young people at such a gathering, and a gesture of inclusion. Their lead teacher was outraged, refused his meal in protest, and insisted the students sit and allow themselves to be served like the VIPs. Everyone dispersed soon afterwards, the community members walking up the dusty road back to their homes and the government officials heading off in convoys of white four-by-four trucks. I learned later that the event, and the Canadians' week-long visit, had cost the host NGO in Botswana more than three times as much as the students had fundraised – running into hundreds of thousands of Pula (or tens of thousands of pounds). It cost Social Services as much again, in officers' hours, petrol, food, and so on; and both Foreign Affairs and the District Council would have had similar bills. I was shocked, but my friends at Social Services and the NGO shrugged it off. "If someone was giving me only five pula I would still do everything to appreciate them," one insisted.

The speeches recounted above, like the speech given at the outset of the chapter, provide a sense of how discursively entangled the family is with the state, development, humanitarianism, and transnational politics. Community, national, and international relations are all – often awkwardly – cast in the idiom of family, with a special emphasis on parents and children. International diplomacy is framed as a familial fostering of ambassadors; humanitarian work is cast in terms of love, care, and the inheritance of future generations. The NGO takes as its explicit mission the creation of kin for and among orphans, implicitly replacing lost parents. The Canadian students are thanked in part through their parents, acknowledge their hosts as parents, and are appreciated for helping raise Batswana children – a network of relatedness within and against which they then define their culture and nationhood. As Elana Shever (2013) notes of national sentiments – to which we might easily add humanitarian, development, and NGO sentiments more broadly – they "rest on a trope of familial bonds as the authentic basis for solidarity, care, obligation, and sacrifice" (2013: 88); and this trope works to refigure an otherwise distinctly odd combination of characters in Botswana's backwoods, loosely and temporarily bound by circumstance and charity, as natural, unified, and enduring.

At the same time, these discursive formulations work to separate the event's participants, and establish the terms on which they can relate. As Didier Fassin notes, compassion performed in public spaces "is … always directed from above to below" (2012: 4), both presupposing and reproducing inequality. It produces precarious lives, in the sense of "lives that are not guaranteed but bestowed," by "protecting and revealing them" (2012: 4). The sharpest separation made is between the NGO, government ministries, and Canadian students on the one hand – sources of compassion – and the families in attendance, whose lives these figures seek to protect and reveal, on the other. The Assistant Minister cast aspersions on his entire Setswana-speaking audience by purporting to publicly expose the abuse in their homes, upbraiding them collectively for their inability to look after their own children as well as the Canadian students – themselves children – could. The Tswana families (especially their men, their uncles) were thereby infantilized, cast beneath the protective elderhood first of the juvenile Canadian contingent, and secondarily of the government and NGO agencies that recruited their assistance. The Canadian teacher's speech, while accepting the group's Batswana hosts as surrogate parents, underlined this infantilization by emphasizing the students' superior agency in addressing issues that afflicted the community. Meanwhile, both the Assistant Minister and Deputy Permanent Secretary – when speaking in English – were careful to cast themselves and their agencies as the equals or elders of the Canadian group, whether thanking the students through their parents or positioning themselves as temporary parents in turn. And both deployed parallel professional discourses – one framed around international relations; the other in terms of social work assessments of societal dysfunction and its remedy – that reinforced this claim to equal consideration, by establishing a suitable distinction between the corrupted, suspect realm of the family and the advanced, modern realm of the state. This distinction echoed those made by the Canadian teacher, whose reference to family was peremptory, and quickly superceded by a lengthy rumination on the Canadian nation, establishing common ground among the speakers and their agencies from which the families in whose mould they had earlier cast themselves were explicitly excluded. All of the speakers, in other words, were engaged in a similar form of the boundary-making work that McKinnon and Cannell (2013) suggest indicates the ideological distinction of politics from kinship.

These discursive deployments and reframings of kinship are typical of a social welfare, development, and humanitarian genre, as well as being familiar ways of speaking about the state. But to the extent that they organize ways of relating, they are more than simply metaphorical. Indeed, a closer look at the unfolding of the event demonstrates uncanny parallels with kinship practice, as well as discourse – much as we saw in our examination of social work offices and NGO centers above. Echoes of wedding celebrations are perhaps most obvious: the white tent, housing *bagolo* (elders) around which the event was oriented (here ministers instead of spouses and their parents); the ranging of celebrants around an open *lelwapa* or courtyard-like space; the speeches, introducing key figures in terms of their relatedness to one another; the collective contributions of money, goods, and work appropriate to a celebration, for entertainment, and for food sufficient to feed a village of guests are all reminiscent of a wedding celebration (see van Dijk 2010). Like a wedding feast, the opening ceremony sought to perform the success and generative power of key relationships, while attempting to extend that success and remake those relationships in clear ways that distinguished them from the collected invitees.

In the process, the Tswana family is curiously marginalized, destabilized, even demonized. The campsite itself is geographically removed not only from local families, but from the families of children the NGO serves. Actual parents and children sit on the edges of the ceremony, moving in and out – but, unusually, have no real role to play in the proceedings. The only mention made of them is either in terms of orphans having lost parents to disease, or in terms of the collapse and corruption of their relationships, beset by death, loss, abuse, and the constant threat of harm. And for all the appreciation afforded the Canadian students and the NGO for their help, it is the Tswana family that bears the blame and responsibility for its own dissolution.

In discourse and practice alike, then, it seems that both the state and NGOs are involved in processes characteristic of Tswana kinship. They are engaged in a form of state-making, or NGO-making, and the making of a shared public sphere, *through* family and kinship processes, and by relating to Tswana families in specific ways. And these processes are curiously effective in legitimizing these agencies as political entities, and in naturalizing and solidifying their relationships with each other. Their legitimacy is modeled on kinship ideals, and is drawn from an apparent involvement in the day-to-day practice of kinship, though primarily geared towards building relationships with other "super-familial" actors, at local, national, and transnational levels. As distinct as the spheres of policy and practice in the public sector may be (Mosse 2004), they seem to be bound by an idiom and logic of kinship. At the same time, these institutions are explicitly excluded from kin-making as such. Instead, the speakers' deployment of the logic, idiom, and practice of kinship *separates* them from the sphere of the family, over which they attempt to assert authority but to which they enjoy little real access.

That the kinship processes I have described should prove so pivotal on a macropolitical scale is further indication of the fundamental importance of kinship practice in organizational and political practice – not simply at village level, but nationally and transnationally as well.

The question of what the kinship logic that binds these agencies together *is* goes beyond the scope of this chapter, but as a gesture in that direction, I suggest one key characteristic is multiplicity. In the speeches above, as in the disjunctions evident between social work offices, NGOs, and families "on the ground," a certain mutual misunderstanding is patent. While the Canadian head teacher imagines his hosts as "surrogate parents," for example, his translator understands them as real parents; and the links the teacher makes between individuals, culture, and nations against that backdrop visibly perplexes his audience. The Assistant Minister's assessment of family breakdown, and his moment of silence for "lost orphans," strikes a similarly confusing note. At the same time, the speakers, social workers, and NGO volunteers profiled above describe ideas of family in terms of love and care, or normative parent–child relationships, in ways that give the impression that they believe they are all referencing the same, universal notion of family. I suggest that these misunderstandings are the result of a proliferation and confusion of multiple models of kinship at work in the discourses above, and in the intervention practices explored in earlier sections of this chapter. State and NGO interventions weave together, take apart, and move between what we might understand broadly as Tswana and Euro-American understandings of kinship – familiar enough to one another to be mutually recognizable, but disparate enough to be jarring. In this sense, it is worth considering political institutions as "site[s] of contention ... between competing normative ideas" (Bierschenk and Olivier de Sardan 2014: 6) of kinship, as much as governance or bureaucracy.

Where kinship seems to provide a common basis of mutual understanding and relating, then – a natural, shared ideal, a common emotional register, and a familiar set of practices – it also provides a muddled and contradictory field of experience. Taken together with its persistent and yet evasive presence in our visits to S&CD and the local NGO above, I suggest this multiplicity positions kinship as encompassing of the political, institutional realm. Kinship encompasses the political not because it taps into a naturalized, universal process, but because it *doesn't* – though political perspectives on families expect it to do so. And this is especially evident in transnationally informed contexts like the ceremony above. Where kinship is invoked to naturalize and stabilize institutionalized claims of power, its multiplicity instead makes them awkward and unnatural, and *de*stabilizes them. Kinship, understood thus, does not simply evade or overwhelm bureaucratic attempts to contain it; it underpins those attempts, saturates their logic, and disrupts them from within, often rendering them ineffective. And it is in this sense that I suggest kinship – as discourse, ideal, and practice – should be understood as crucial to the political dynamics of governments, NGOs, and donor agencies alike.

29.4   Conclusion

At the opening ceremony described above, the families of the *motse*, or village, ranged around the outside of the event, an undifferentiated mass of variously engaged witnesses to the agencies' main act. The NGO, ministry representatives, and Canadian students seemed to take these families as context and backdrop: a potential challenge or threat, an audience to whom exhortations might be made and for whom responsibility must be borne, but entities unquestionably separate from and marginal to the performance itself. And yet, as we have seen above, it is these very families – and the shadow audiences of Canadian families behind them – against, through, and within which that performance was defined, and around which it was oriented. More than that, it is the micropractices of relatedness common to those families through and within which the everyday work of NGOs and ministries alike is conducted.

It is not simply that powerful national and transnational political forces exert unidirectional influence on the Tswana family, then – as Isaac Schapera (1940: 346–357) feared in the colonial era, and as public health, humanitarian and development interventions assume in seeking to address Botswana's AIDS pandemic. And it is not simply that the Tswana family exerts counter-influences of its own. Rather, the "domains" of kinship and politics (McKinnon and Cannell 2013) – produced in state, NGO, and social sciences discourse alike – are inseparable, in practice as much as idiom; each can only be meaningfully and fully understood in terms of the other, with attention to the ways in which people actively distinguish, conflate, and prioritize them.

Anthropological analyses of development, humanitarianism, and public health have tended to ignore the family, taking for granted that the domestic is distinct from and incidental to the political, and reproducing that distinction in turn. And yet families mark a key sphere in which humanitarianism, development, and public health concerns inevitably converge (*pace* Redfield and Bornstein 2011: 4). They are targeted by such a diverse and vast array of interventions in part because they provide a context, discourse, and set of practices by which the states, NGOs, and other agencies that run those interventions can produce and reproduce themselves, while simultaneously elevating themselves above the family and naturalizing their power and relationships. And the hierarchies generated between family, NGO, and state in turn provide a framework for reproducing, depoliticizing, and naturalizing global inequalities between nations. At the same time, the ways in which kinship practices and ideologies saturate the work of these agencies serves to blur and shift the distinctions they seek to make, to invert and denaturalize the hierarchies they assert, and ultimately to disrupt the work they undertake, in part by excluding them from the family as such. These dynamics frequently underpin the unintended consequences for which such interventions are notorious, and any serious attempt to make sense of the complex legacies of intervention – especially in contexts of crisis – requires that we expand our frame of reference to incorporate the family accordingly.

Notes

1. Isaac Schapera interprets the same proverb more narrowly, to mean "a man's social standing and influence are ... determined by his reputation as a host" (Schapera 1940: 170). My reinterpretation here aligns with his structuralist accounts of the deep links between politics and kinship among the chiefly families of the Kgatla (Schapera 1970), but extends it to include a much wider array of families and political institutions.
2. Building on Max Weber's assessment of bureaucracy as an explicit project of separating the private sphere from the public sphere, Thomas Bierschenk and Jean-Pierre Olivier de Sardan (2014: 11) also describe social welfare provision as a key mechanism of bureaucratization and distinction making in African states.
3. I thank Sandra Bamford for pointing out this dynamic.

References

Bierschenk, T. and J.-P. Olivier de Sardan. 2014. *States at Work: Dynamics of African Bureaucracies*. Leiden: Brill.

Carsten, J. 2013. "Ghosts, Commensality, and Scuba Diving: Tracing Kinship and Sociality in Clinical Pathology Labs and Blood Banks in Penang." In *Vital Relations: Modernity and the Persistent Life of Kinship*, ed. Susan McKinnon and Fennella Cannell, 109–130. Santa Fe, NM: School for Advanced Research Press.

Durham, D. 2002. "Love and Jealousy in the Space of Death." *Ethnos* 67(2): 155–179.

Durham, D. and F. Klaits. 2002. "Funerals and the Public Space of Sentiment in Botswana." *Journal of Southern African Studies* 28(4): 773–791.

Evans-Pritchard, E. E. and M. Fortes. 1940. *African Political Systems*. Oxford: Oxford University Press.

Fassin, D. 2012. *Humanitarian Reason: A Moral History of the Present*. Translated by R. Gomme. Berkeley, CA: University of California Press.

———. 2013. "Children As Victims: The Moral Economy of Childhood in the Times of AIDS." In *When People Come First: Critical Studies in Global Health*, ed. J. Biehl and A. Petryna, 109–130. Princeton, NJ: Princeton University Press.

Ferguson, J. 1994. *The Anti-Politics Machine: "Development," Depoliticization, and Bureaucratic Power in Lesotho*. Minneapolis, MN: University of Minnesota Press.

Klaits, F. 2010. *Death in a Church of Life: Moral Passion during Botswana's Time of AIDS*. London: University of California Press.

Kuper, A. 1975. "The Social Structure of the Sotho-Speaking Peoples of Southern Africa: Part I and Part II." *Journal of the International African Institute* 45(1): 67–81, 139–149.

Lambek, M. 2013. "Kinship, Modernity, and the Immodern." In *Vital Relations: Modernity and the Persistent Life of Kinship*, ed. S. McKinnon and F. Cannell, 241–260. Santa Fe, NM: School for Advanced Research Press.

McKinnon, S. and F. Cannell. 2013. "Introduction." In *Vital Relations: Modernity and the Persistent Life of Kinship*, ed. S. McKinnon and F. Cannell, 14–49. Santa Fe, NM: School for Advanced Research Press.

Malkki, L. 1996. "Speechless Emissaries: Refugees, Humanitarianism, and Dehistoricisation." *Cultural Anthropology* 11(3): 377–404.

Mosse, D. 2004. "Is Good Policy Unimplementable? Reflections on the Ethnography of Aid Policy and Practice." *Development and Change* 35(4): 639–671.

Redfield, P. 2012. "The Unbearable Lightness of Ex-pats: Double Binds of Humanitarian Mobility." *Cultural Anthropology* 27(2): 358–382.

Redfield, P. and E. Bornstein. 2011. "An Introduction to the Anthropology of Humanitarianism." In *Forces of Compassion: Humanitarianism between Ethics and Politics*, ed. P. Redfield and E. Bornstein, 3–30. Santa Fe, NM: School for Advanced Research Press.

Reece, K. 2019. " 'We Are Seeing Things': Recognition, Risk, and Reproducing Kinship in Botswana's Time of AIDS. *Africa* 89(1).

Schapera, I. 1940. *Married Life in an African Tribe*. London: Faber and Faber.

———. 1970. *Tribal Innovators: Tswana Chiefs and Social Change, 1795–1940*. London: The Athlone Press.

Shever, E. 2013. " 'I Am a Petroleum Product': Making Kinship Work on the Patagonian Frontier." In *Vital Relations: Modernity and the Persistent Life of*

Kinship, ed. S. McKinnon and F. Cannell, 85–108. Santa Fe, NM: School for Advanced Research Press.

Ticktin, M. 2011. *Casualties of Care: Immigration and the Politics of Humanitarianism in France*. Berkeley, CA: University of California Press.

    2014. "Transnational Humanitarianism." *Annual Review of Anthropology* 43: 273–89.

Ticktin, M. and I. Feldman. 2010. *In the Name of Humanity: The Government of Threat and Care*. Durham, NC: Duke University Press.

Tsing, A. L. 2005. *Friction: An Ethnography of Global Connection*. Princeton, NJ: Princeton University Press.

USAID. 2010. AIDSTAR-One Case Study Series: The O Icheke Campaign, Botswana. https://aidsfree.usaid.gov/resources/o-icheke-campaign-botswana, accessed July 17, 2017.

Van Dijk, R. 2010. "Marriage, Commodification and the Romantic Ethic in Botswana." In *Markets of Well-Being: Navigating Health and Healing in Africa*, ed. M. Dekker and R. van Dijk, 282–306. Leiden: Brill.

30

Kinship, World Religions, and the Nation-State

Fenella Cannell

30.1 Ethnographic Introduction: Two Visions and an American Family

"Let me tell you the story about Eric," said Cathy.

> It's a long story. I had Heather and she was a sweet, perfect little girl. Then I had Karen, and Karen was, for the first three or four years of her life … an unhappy child. She cried all the time, on and on [with colic and different transient problems] … So at that point, I said, I really don't want to have any more children. But I knew that I ought to have another child, because childbirth is actually very easy for me, and I knew that would be the right thing to do. But I don't even *like* babies – I mean, I love to hold them, and then give them back to someone else! Like, "Here, take it!" – but I don't like *caring* for babies. But then I said; Well, all right. But I made a prayer to God, and I said, OK God, I'll have another baby. But please let it be a boy (because we wanted a boy for Dave) and please, let it be a good one.
>
> So then I got pregnant, and my mother-in-law called me, and she said, "I had the strangest dream." She said she was in a huge place that looked like a planetarium, with the planets each spinning around, and that the roof kept opening and closing, and a voice was saying things like; "Here's a girl for Steve and Pattie." And then the roof opened, and it said, "Here's a boy for Dave and Cathy – and he's a good one."
>
> So when I heard that, I thought, Hallelujah! You know – my prayers have really been answered.
>
> So then I was pregnant, and when I was five months I found out it was Brooke, you know – it was a girl.[1] And for about two months after that I was just incredibly angry, you know, and part of why I was so angry was because I knew there was still this boy to come.

I didn't want four children; I wasn't even sure I wanted *three* kids, let alone four.

But then something happened, and I really started to love Brooke; in fact, of all of them, I think Brooke is the one I really loved even before she was born ... I don't know why; I think a lot of it is just to do with Brooke, actually, with who she is ... and I really loved her. Then I said to God, "Ok, I know what you want me to do, but I'm sorry, forget the Celestial Kingdom, I give up on it. I'm just not going to do it, OK, God?" Then I put it off for a number of years. By the time Eric was born, Brooke was five and Heather was ten ... I wanted to keep my nice, peaceful life ...

But then one night, I woke up in the middle of the night, and I knew there was someone in the room, standing next to the bed. And not being a very spiritual person, I didn't talk to this angelic presence or anything.[2] I just stuck my head under the pillow ... like, "Leave me alone!" But I knew who it was; it was Eric. And I knew that this was one last plea for me to do what was right. And so, then I was, "Alright." And I got pregnant. But all the way through my pregnancy, I was really not reconciled to it at all; I was really fighting it. The night before Eric was born, you know, I was out here [makes gestures of very pregnant belly] and I turned to [Dave] and said [crying] "I just don't want to do this!"

And it was interesting, because of the way I felt, I sought a lot of priesthood blessings during my pregnancy, and ... they were all very accepting and very comforting. Not one of them was like, "Get a grip!" They all kept telling me, "Don't worry; when this baby is born, you will love him and everything will be just fine."

And when Eric was born, the moment I saw him, you know, I just loved him. He was everything we had been promised. He's such a wonderful little boy; so kind and loving and obedient ... and from that I know that God loves me *personally* and knows what is best for me *personally*, even when it isn't what I want ... It's interesting, you know; it was a step by step process, and we had to go all the way through it ... If I had had Eric first, I would *never* have had Brooke. And we had to have Brooke because of who Brooke is; we *needed* Brooke.[3]

Cathy's story was one of many told to me by American Latter-day Saint (LDS) women during my fieldwork, which speaks to and from a repertoire of LDS maternal visions (Austin et al. 2012; Cannell 2005, 2013, in preparation). I was drawn to work with Latter-day Saints ("Mormons") in part because of the ways in which their attitudes to both kinship and religion are constructed in a very unusual relationship to the modern – in this case the American – nation-state (Cannell 2017a, 2017b). For Latter-day Saints, kinship and religion are coterminous and absolutely implicated in each other. As Mormonism's most thoughtful scholars have long noted

(Davies 2000; Shipps 1987: 148–149) one of the most distinctive features of Mormonism viewed from the perspective of other forms of Christianity, is that it understands salvation, in its highest form, to be collective. For Latter-day Saints, while the individual person can attain the life everlasting, the real joy of heaven and the real purpose of human existence resides in the attempt to get to heaven together with your family – if possible, *all* your family, down to every long-lost fourth cousin, every elderly great aunt who maybe doesn't go to church much anymore, and beyond. Latter-day Saints value the nuclear family but also the extended family, and the whole network of what anthropologists call cognatic kinship, as sacred.

This concept of familial salvation as the highest form of salvation is sometimes referred to by Latter-day Saints as "exaltation" (Church of Jesus Christ of Latter-day Saints 2011: chapter 47). For members of the church, this collective heaven, while it takes the coordinated efforts of church and family, rests ultimately on individual free will, which is centrally important in LDS doctrine. Mormon teenagers are enjoined to "Choose the Right," a phrase which often appears on wristbands, mugs, and other small personal items frequently given as gifts and available on LDS commercial websites. God ("Heavenly Father") intended every human being to live in the right way and so come into his or her true inheritance, life eternal in the highest of Mormon heavens, the Celestial Kingdom, but he requires the cooperation of each one of us. If every person does their part, every kinship relationship on earth can be eternalized and given a life everlasting; kinship, as well as the individual, can be resurrected. Further, kinship in the Celestial Kingdom will not be fixed and finished; Mormon married couples who reach the Celestial Kingdom will undergo a kind of apotheosis, and will become the parents of "spirit children"; new souls who will eventually people worlds to come (Cannell 2005; Davies 2000, 2003, 2010; Givens 2004, 2012).

Reaching further even than the extended family, LDS missionary work is ultimately dedicated to trying to save every soul, past and present, living and dead, for whom recoverable records are available in the world.[4] Through rituals of vicarious baptism, the dead as well as the living can be given the opportunity to choose the right beyond the grave, and so to enter the highest heaven. For Latter-day Saints, it is extremely important that no person who has ever lived should be denied this chance and therefore they devote tremendous effort and energy to "temple work" on behalf of unknown as well as known others; every person in every record, they reason, is *somebody's* family.

At the same time, LDS doctrine and revelation teach that there is a world *before* earthly birth as well as a world after earthly death. All the people who will ever be born on this earth already exist, and are waiting in "spirit" form, as Cathy's son Eric was waiting, for someone to become their earthly mother. Since Mormonism does not regard spirit and matter as each other's opposites (Givens 2014), the development from "spirit" form through earthly form to resurrected bodily life is regarded as a progressive development of matter through different stages; the body develops towards its intended glory in parallel with the learning process of each individual. Mormon mothers, when they give birth, are therefore not only laboring to bring an infant into the world; they are laboring to open a gateway between parts of the universe and stages of the human soul, according to the divine plan. It is primarily for this reason that women such as Cathy are attuned to a sense of obligation as to how many children they should carry and birth which exceeds their own personal preference.

As Cathy's story shows – and as I have considered elsewhere in relation to its implications for LDS understandings of adoption (Cannell 2013) – the idea of a premortal existence also allows Latter-day Saints to think of their earthly familial relationships as reflecting sacred acts of intentionality that lie outside this visible life. People often consider that relationships in this world – including both kin relations and friendships – reflect a commitment people have made to each other premortally, although they also think that, given human failings, not all such commitments are fulfilled as they ought to be, in this life.

That kinship and religion are profoundly mutually constitutive is one of the distinctive qualities of LDS life and the focus of my own research work with LDS interlocutors and friends. Clearly, all these people are modern Americans; Latter-day Saints construct their lives according to distinctive practices,[5] but these are not practices that would mark them out, to the outside observers' eye, as readily identifiable. They do not wear "old-fashioned" clothing on a daily basis; they are not opposed to the use of computers, modern vehicles, or modern medical science. They have a church which is now highly centralized and whose staff, not unlike many modern corporations, include a public relations department and legal and financial experts. Some critics of the church indeed claim that contemporary Mormonism has lost the distinctiveness that characterized its nineteenth-century origins. Looked at from another viewpoint, however, the ways in which kinship and vision inhere in each other in Latter-day Saint experience and narrative is highly atypical of the ways in which modern Americans expect to live.

It is a central assumption of many classic strands of theoretical writing about modernity and the modern nation, that both what we call "kinship" and what we call "religion" have receded in importance in contemporary life, compared to the determining force of "politics" and "economics" (McKinnon and Cannell 2013). I would argue that this is not the case. Although it is often further assumed that "kinship" and "religion" are clearly separate areas of modern life, and that it is quite obvious what each of these means, I suggest that in fact the opposite is true; kinship and religion are often bound up together in practice, and it is by no means always clear where one stops and the other begins. This may be true, from an analytic viewpoint, both for people who say they are "religious" and for people who say they are "not religious," although that distinction as made by an anthropologist's interlocutors is clearly also a very important ethnographic fact, itself reflecting a specific social history in relation to these categories (Cannell 2011: 475–476). I have followed various ethnographic and theoretical arguments in this terrain in relation to two different modern nation-states, the United States, where I have worked with Latter-day Saints, and the United Kingdom where I have worked with amateur genealogists and with users of Anglican cathedral spaces (Cannell 2010, 2013). For present purposes, I will simply note that the formal relationship between the nation-state and religion is, of course, quite different in these two countries; while England still has an established church, the Church of England, headed by the monarch (but much modified by modern Parliamentary democracy, multiculturalism, and the decline of regular church attendance), the US Constitution provides for the separation of state and religion and the freedom of religion (albeit many commentators have identified an in-practice "state religion" in the United States and more tolerance for some religious traditions than for others.) Nevertheless, notable overlap or ambiguity between kinship practices and religious practices can be observed in both national settings.

The title of this section of the *Handbook*, on which subject I have been asked to write, presents a certain conceptual challenge. By linking together kinship, world religions, and the nation-state, it might be taken to imply that we know what each of these terms means, and that there is a clear and readily definable relationship between them. Just the reverse, however, is the case. In the practice of our discipline at present, each of the constituent terms of this title has come to be understood as more and more problematic. Max Weber is the major theorist whose work is above all associated with the idea of 'world religions' – defined as salvationist, often with an ascetic orientation or division of labor between ascetic specialists and lay people, as expansive, as characterized by the development of an internally coherent doctrine (e.g., Weber 1991 [1915]). Weber's discussions are complex and his exact meaning can be interpreted in different ways. Most people these days are not entirely confident in declaring what a "world religion" might be. The long-running and intense debates that have been held over the existence or non-existence of something called "kinship" are well known, and have been explored elsewhere (Bamford and Leach 2009; Carsten 2000; Franklin and McKinnon 2001; Sahlins 2011a, 2011b; Strathern 1980, 1988, 1992; Schneider 1984; Yanagisako and Delaney 1995). "The nation-state" might appear at first glance to be the most stable of the set of terms in question, but is in fact also contentious in several different ways. The relationship between "the nation-state" and "religion," for example, is precisely at issue in the long-running discussions about "secularization" and "the secular" (e.g., Casanova 1994; Taylor 2007; Asad 1993, 2003). The question of whether "the state" should be viewed for analytic purposes as a discrete or a homogeneous entity has been raised by a number of anthropologists, as has the issue of whether "political" forces have any kind of causal priority in human life, or whether these can be meaningfully separated from, in particular, economic forces and the dependence of many nation-states on different kinds of capitalist production or forms defined by their opposition to capitalist processes.

At the back of all these definitional issues stand even more general questions. Foundational theorists in anthropology have sometimes suggested that it is from the relations between "kinship," "world religions," and "the nation-state" that something fundamental can be understood about the nature of the modern world. The legacies of these ideas therefore condition the way that anthropologists view their own discipline's relationship with "modernity." As an anthropologist, what does one understand by modernity? Is it a real state of transformed being or set of definable institutional shifts? Is it finally reducible to capitalism or other forms of economic life? Does its key importance lie in the contrasts various analysts in social science have drawn with "tradition" – perhaps particularly in the realm of kinship (McKinnon 2013)? Or is modernity above all an idea to which we come to subscribe; a myth or an ideology which – like all ideas – comes to have real effects in the world because we believe in it, and act as though it were true and inevitable (Cannell 2010, 2011)? The relative explanatory weight accorded by different writers to the terms "kinship," "world religions," and "the nation-state" can be diagnostic of these different approaches.

Given the potential range of this topic I will not pretend to a comprehensive literature review of these terms in this chapter. In even the necessarily selective account given here, I rely on the work of many colleagues writing on kinship, including but not limited to the editor of and contributors to the present volume (see also Bamford and Leach 2009; Feeley-Harnik 1999, 2001a, 2001b, 2013), and my coeditor and contributors to the volume *Vital Relations: Modernity and the Persistence of Kinship* (McKinnon and Cannell 2013).

30.2 Nation-States and Their Rivals

We might proceed via some historical background to the Mormon ethnography with which I started. The most widespread misconception about contemporary Latter-day Saints (as many members of the church are only too keenly aware) is that they practice polygamy. In fact, "plural marriage" (LDS polygamy) was held as a religious and virtuous ideal during the mid-nineteenth century, and publically practiced by perhaps

20–30 percent of church members between about 1850 and 1890, when the practice was permanently suspended by church leaders. Present-day polygamists belong not to the official LDS church, but to smaller independent groups who broke away from the main church at that time. Within the official present-day LDS church, polygamy would be grounds for excommunication.

Religious polygamy remains an object of fascination for observers precisely because it is perceived as a highly anomalous practice for citizens of a modern nation-state. Polygamy provokes comment because it unsettles the often unacknowledged norms by which kinship, religion, and the state are defined and coexist in the American polity. Polygamy is not considered "civilized" or normative as a mode for organizing kinship; it does not align itself with state laws on marriage. On the other hand, it describes itself as a form of *marriage*, rather than as a private, sexual choice, or relationship lifestyle (as polyamory is described).[6] Critics of the LDS church may also tend to assume that polygamy is a culturally "primitive" or "backward" practice, to argue that it inherently demeans women, to make sensational and voyeuristic claims about the sex lives of polygamous persons, and/or – given that Latter-day Saints adamantly identify themselves as true Christians – to feel that it threatens mainstream Christian definitions of marriage as a sacrament intended to join one man with one woman. Although there are relatively few contemporary polygamists in the United States, the practice continues to have a disproportionate capacity to unsettle people, visible most recently in the ways in which some US activists used polygamy as code or analogue for the campaigns for and against equal (gay) marriage (Bennion 2012; Serjeant 2009). Even the idea of polygamy (or indeed, polygamy in popular fiction and entertainment) raises the specter of a challenge to the state's monopoly power to define the status of its citizens.

Anti-polygamy campaigners and critics of Mormonism in the nineteenth century also claimed that polygamy was backward, primitive,[7] oppressive to women and children, unsuitable for civilized people in the modern world and un-Christian. Gordon (2002) has shown how LDS polygamy also became a target for the expanding nineteenth-century American state. Latter-day Saints had hoped to establish the legality of plural marriage under state law in Utah (then a Territory) and under the freedom of religion guaranteed in the Constitution (see also Flake 2003). Most nineteenth-century Americans continued to agree in theory with the constitutional principle of religious freedom, and also with the idea that marriage was a sacramental institution – that is, a bond created by divine power through ritual and religious authority, rather than being only a contract in law. However, in practice the developing governmental and legal system increasingly registered the need for the civil control of the institution of marriage. Marriage was understood as "vital to the welfare of all society" in so far as it "connected the authority of fathers and husbands" (the male electorate) with the sexual, fiscal, and moral regulation of households within the nation, with social reproduction and with public order (Gordon 2002: 138). By the 1880s, "[m]arriage and its attendant legal protections were simply too vitally important as a matter of politics to be relinquished back to ecclesiastical control" (Gordon 2002: 140). In addition, the social organization of Latter-day Saints through kinship was perceived as threatening to the state in other ways; polygamous Utah Mormons were seen as clannish, nepotistic, and likely to favor their own at the expense of other citizens. They were also seen as "inherently expansionist" (Gordon 2002: 143) – that is, as likely to encroach on their neighbors if left unchecked – and seen to run their own affairs so theocratically as to impinge on the legitimate role of the Federal state. The language of the primitive, exclusive kinship-based "clan" coexisted throughout the century in variable ways with the language of the sect or cult, headed by religious "despots," as ways of evoking what was wrong with Mormonism in the minds of non-Mormon American critics.

As historians have demonstrated, "Political power was the essence of the problem" (Gordon 2002: 143). It is notable and important that the nineteenth-century US state did not simply invoke a secularist agenda in its attack on Mormonism, despite the constitutional separation of church and state. Rather, what occurred was a continued acknowledgment of the higher powers of Christian faith, coupled with the effective narrowing of the definition of what "Christianity" meant. Christianity came to be defined within evolving American law according to implicitly Protestant models, which gradually marginalized and finally excluded alternate claims including those of Mormonism. The ending of polygamy became the condition on which Utah was granted statehood by the Federal government, and the grounds for the admission of LDS senators, with complex consequences for the LDS church as it adjusted its narratives and perspectives to this far-reaching change (Flake 2003). While the US state relied on increasingly narrower definitions of what counted as "Christian," the LDS church responded by continuing to defend the sacredness of its leadership and organization despite structural change. Latter-day Saints understand that their church is marked out by the gift of present-day revelation; its leaders are both presidents and prophets, and are given revelation for the survival and good of the whole church. The requirement to live in plurality was a revelation given to the founding prophet Joseph Smith; the requirement to end plurality for the survival of the church was a revelation given to the church president and prophet in 1890, Wilford Woodruff.

The situation was therefore quite complex; clearly, the US state was treating the Mormon church as a rival, attacking both its religious/sacramental prerogatives and its kinship practices. As Gordon notes, "there is no escaping the fact that the power deployed was secular, and the power attacked was religious" (Gordon 2002: 140). The LDS church, despite the teaching on continuous revelation, has struggled since that date with ambiguities about the change of direction in its doctrine and religious organization, as both external critics and members have tried to decide whether or not the end of polygamy represented a loss of sacredness and a fracture in the church's essential fabric. At the same time, neither the attack on nor the defense of the Mormon church could be reduced to a simple advance of secular values; the state sought to identify itself with a majoritarian form of American Protestantism, while the LDS church sought to sustain its own definitions of the continuity of radical revealed authority. Depending on the perspective taken by a commentator, it is possible either to stress the losses of religious charisma that resulted from the end of polygamy, or the continuities and developments in profound experiences of kinship as sacred in the present day which, my own ethnography records, and which remain foundational for ordinary Latter-day Saints.[8]

The example of American Mormonism provides a very striking instance of a way of life in which kinship and religion are deeply codeterminant for a group of people within a contemporary nation-state, and also provide an apparently unavoidable provocation to the state. Mormonism is unusual in part in offering a highly explicit *doctrine* of the mutuality of kinship and religion. This is especially unusual within the repertoire of Christianity. Christianity has been considered, above all, a religion in which loyalty to kin should be qualified or sometimes superceded by loyalty to religious community and vocation, in which those who love Christ are commanded to be ready to leave father, mother or spouse to enter the discipleship of Jesus (e.g., Luke 14: 25–27). It has also been one of the world religions in which sexual celibacy has been cultivated as a form of asceticism pleasing to God, at least for those with a special religious vocation. In anthropology and sociology, this ascetic view of Christianity has been reinforced by readings of Weber, for whom of course "ascetic" action in the world as opposed to "mystical" withdrawal from the world is a development of religious value-making with highly significant historical consequences, especially in Europe (Weber 1991 [1915]; 1991 [c.1920]). A long-established trend in the literature on modern Europe and the United States, in particular, offered a teleological reading of Weber, in which was embedded an ascetic understanding of what Christianity was and what its effects might be. Christianity was ascetic; ascetic action was key to Western European Protestantism; ascetic Protestantism in combination with mercantile capitalism produced, through an irony of history, the iron carapace of modern capitalism and bureaucracy, and the conversion of the originally religious sense of "vocation" into one of the internalized self-disciplinary practices that helped sustain all these (Weber 2001 [c.1930]). The teleological emphasis here was misleading in a number of respects (Cannell 2010) but the tendency to identify Christianity as a world religion "against kinship" has only rather recently begun to be qualified in the literature (Thomas, Malik and Wellman 2017).

Outside Christian contexts, the notion that kinship practice might be the terrain of the sacred (or vice versa) within modern nation-states is less unfamiliar. Seeman (2017), while warning against a crude contrast between Judaism and Christianity in this regard, sets out some of the parameters of Jewish American kinship identity. Leite (2017) considers the situation of people wishing to reclaim a "lost" Jewish identity as Portuguese Marranos, navigating complex paths to belonging through often fragile or challenged claims to Marrano ancestry. Liberatore (2016) follows the crossover between ideas of heaven and dreams of an ideal husband for young Muslim women in London.

Recent ethnographies of nation-states outside Europe and America have also illuminated the ways in which an overlapping terrain of kinship and religion may exist in tension with the contemporary state. In this context, ethnographies of India have been particularly illuminating. The postcolonial Indian nation-state, like many contemporary Western states, defines itself as "secular." However, Indian constitutional secularity is constituted differently than any form of secular government in the West; drawing originally on a self-definition of the postcolonial independent state as being putatively at an equal distance from any of the subcontinent's religions (rather than, as is often implied in the West, as being the successor to religion regarded as of the past) (Cannell 2010). New ethnography, such as that by Pool (2016), suggests that the state is considered, related to, and invoked through a "vernacular secular" which is inflected by assumptions drawn from Hindu caste understandings, even for Indian Muslims, who may share some elements of self-understanding with Hindu neighbors while defining themselves contrastively with respect to others. The Indian "secular" state therefore does not constitute itself completely independently of Hindu understandings any more than the American state constitutes itself autonomously from Christian understandings.

The work of Laura Bear (2007, 2013, 2015) on contemporary India explores the inseparability of kinship from religion, economics, and politics in various contexts, recently through a consideration of the mainly Hindu workers in the shipbuilding industry of Kolkata. Although working within an internationally owned industry attuned to neoliberalism, the workers of the Hooghly river continue to link the process of shipbuilding to other processes, including religious pujas, through which their own bodies, kin relations, and neighborhoods are made and sustained (Bear 2013). Bear's first book on Anglo-Indian railway workers (Bear 2007) makes these interdependencies clear in a different way. As citizens, Anglo-Indians inherit a doubly excluded position from the colonial period; claims to recognition of their kinship to or descent from British citizens are precarious and hedged with racialized exclusionary and restrictive practices. Even during the colonial period, the British state required difficult and sometimes impossible forms of bureaucratic proof from Anglo-Indians which were productive of great anxiety given how much depended on them in terms of job security, permission for children to attend school abroad, and other forms of access to the UK that defined life chances as well as confirming identity. Within post-independence India, however, Anglo-Indians are also excluded from full belonging because of the ways in which logics of caste (or exclusion from caste for Muslims, dalits, and other groups) are enfolded within categories of citizenship and define modalities of access to state-controlled resources. Bear describes the ways in which Anglo-Indians work to articulate a space of habitation in the face of these two exclusions, in part through their adherence to Roman Catholicism, which as in other colonial and postcolonial contexts, offers an alternative form of Christian identification to the dominant Protestantism of the colonial power. Anglo-Indians, Bear tells us, often see benign ghosts who create "connections between generations founded on the idea of a Catholic community of" connections to the space of the railway colony and "a return to self-being that is impossible to effect in other contexts" (Bear 2007: 271).

Mody's (2008) ethnography of interfaith marriage in contemporary India offers another set of insights into tensions between the modern state, on the one hand, and the grounds of self-making located in kinship and religion combined on the other hand. Marriage in India continues to be freighted with importance not derived from the state. As Mody notes, marriages are still viewed as having profound moral and religious significance. Within the Hindu and caste perspective they are: "an instrument for the pursuance of higher goals in life [dharma] rather than ... a means for personal gratification" (Mody 2008: 16, quoting Basu 2007: 24). Marriage, Mody reminds us, makes kin, within relations that are essentially hierarchical because they are caste based. Muslim marriages are conceptually equal as a means of differentiation from caste, but are still endogamous to the religion (Mody 2008: 24–25). Kin-making through marriage is a collective and soteriological enterprise, a process of alliance, and marriages should therefore be arranged by adult representatives of the group.

Couples who wish to enter into love marriages do not, Mody finds, want to overturn all these grounds of social being, but simply to renegotiate the boundaries at which they apply. Most couples would like to have their unions accepted and approved by their elders and their extended family, and they often stress the ways in which they are, despite a difference in faith, otherwise highly compatible according to criteria that their parents would also recognize. Such couples, however, are obliged to resort to the Civil Marriage Act of 1872, which was introduced by secularist reformers under British colonial rule, in an attempt to deal with situations that fell between the delegated jurisdictions of India's faith communities. The act, confusingly compiled and unevenly applied in the courts – where it may often be subject to the preferences of senior members of different faith groups – creates a landscape of contradictions, in which many young couples become lost. Hindu nationalism and contemporary communalism create further hazards for interfaith marriage. But as Mody notes, although these marriages and attempted marriages may become intensely politicized, the intentions of those who enter into them are not directly political; addressing themselves to state law in an attempt to negotiate the restrictions imposed by faith and family, young couples instead come to be subjected to other, often arbitrarily applied, national agendas. The rise of Hindu nationalist politics has only intensified these pressures and entanglements (Mody 2008).

The complex, diverse, and unpredictable ways in which kinship, religion, and the modern nation-state can become engaged with each other are, therefore, clearly evidenced in the ethnographic record. It is also clear that the contemporary nation-state is frequently in tension with kinship and religion considered together, as an alternative or partly alternative space for the making of persons and relations between persons. Michael Lambek (2013) offers an incisive description:

> Kinship is never the sole discourse and practice of person-making in any society. The big shift in modernity [compared to traditional societies] comes less with respect to abandoning kinship for other forms of personhood than with the state's role in legitimating the making of new persons, a role it appropriates largely from what has been called religion but which, from a certain angle and in some societies more than others, could be seen simply as undifferentiated from kinship in the first place ... If we take ritual seriously, as an intrinsic part of kinship, then we sharpen our understanding of what is lost – and perhaps gained – when the state steps in and replaces religious ritual with law.
>
> *(Lambek 2013: 256)*

Lambek's account, in an important essay, includes a particularly useful definition of kinship as a distinctively generative, or relation-making activity. Lambek points out that kinship terms, used for instance as terms of address (say, "Mother!"), are performative both in constituting a kin relation between the speaker and the addressee, and also in implying and enacting further kinds of relationality beyond this dyad (for instance, the existence of a father). As Lambek draws out the implications of this thought:

> In modernity, kinship is found alongside many other disciplines or discourses of person-making (Hacking 1999), but it is perhaps the only one that is intrinsically relational. Kinship does not "make up persons" as monads, but as always already invested in webs of relatedness. It

is so thoroughly relational because new kin are related not only to those who produce them but also to those people's relations, in turn. Kin relations are ever-ramifying and auto-productive.

(Lambek 2013: 256)

Or, as he also puts it, kinship is "immoderate" and "immodern." Modern states and their bureaucracies prefer to have a monopoly on the definition of persons, and to identify them in ways that are fixed and unambiguous. Kinship, however, "escapes laws that attempt to pin it down" (Lambek 2013: 256). It is felt and defined in ways that are often multiple, overlapping pathways of relatedness, and asserted or denied in ways that seem irrational, otiose, contradictory, or ambiguous from the point of view of the modern state. It is also freighted with excessive meanings, perhaps especially in the modern world, and becomes what Lambek, quoting Arendt, calls a "'romanticised object[s]' to which all kinds of excess causality are attributed" (Lambek 2013: 242).

30.3 Theoretical Occlusions

It has, however, been difficult until fairly recently to hold all these terms together within a theoretical framing. It has been hard both to see that kinship (and religion) might have properties that are not completely defined and subordinated to modern state processes, and that kinship and religion might often be coextensive in the modern world.

The reasons for these difficulties are rooted very far back in the theoretical development of the foundational social sciences, and one key factor here has been the one-time dominance, and later persistent half-life of teleological accounts of modernity. Across a wide range of different authors the claim has been made, either explicitly or implicitly, that what we call kinship and religion come to be less important in modernity, compared to what we call politics and economics. Susan McKinnon (2013) has incisively identified and described the ways in which this trope has unfolded through anthropological theories of kinship in the work of Maine, Tönnies, Weber, Lévi-Strauss, and beyond. What was originally a nineteenth-century social evolutionary paradigm concerning the supposed historical advances of human civilization traveled sometimes almost invisibly into kinship theories which most often did not intend to reproduce it. For McKinnon, kinship theory has too often rested on a mythologized contrast between traditional and modern societies. Traditional societies were assumed to be crucially organized through kinship forms understood implicitly by their analysts as "natural." Modern, complex, and industrial societies were portrayed by contrast as transcending these primitive modes of social organization and replacing them with other, culturally made ideas and institutions that had freed themselves of their determination by natural kinship (McKinnon 2013: 60). In some formulations of this view, kinship was encapsulated by the modern state, so that kinship – often recast as family or domestic life in relation to a more powerful public or jural domain – becomes subordinated to the workings of the state, which has annexed many of its functions.

Building on the work of many previous anthropologists of kinship including the feminist anthropology of Collier and Yanagisako (1987), Susan McKinnon and I "question[ed] the core presumption in the narratives of modernity; that kinship has been effectively cordoned off in the domestic domain and has become irrelevant to the operations of modern economic and political institutions" (McKinnon and Cannell 2013: 12). Relying on the work of our contributors Bear (2013), Bodenhorn (2013), Carsten (2013), and Rutherford (2013), Feeley-Harnik (2013), Lambek (2013), Shever (2013), and Yanagisako (2013), we questioned the language of social domains through which theories of modernity had been developed and expressed, and challenged both the idea of the supercession of kinship as a social force in the modern world, and "the fundamental validity of the narrative structure of modernity altogether" (McKinnon and Cannell 2013: 12). We and our contributors argued that "the nature of kinship ... should not be presupposed but should rather be the focus of historical and ethnographic enquiry" (McKinnon and Cannell 2013: 13). In the ethnographic work represented in this volume, our authors in fact traced the interpolation of kinship idioms with modern shipbuilding, international textile manufacture, nationalist oil production, migration policies at the US/Mexico border, laboratory work in Malaysia, climate change debates in the United States, and many other contexts.

One contribution of the volume was to "contest[s] the idea that kinship is a social formation that can be understood exclusively as either historically prior to or structurally subordinate to the nation-state and that the nation (or state) can be conceptualized apart from its entanglements with kinship ... the reigning understanding of a nation-state needs to be questioned" (McKinnon and Cannell 2013: 24). We argued that the relationship between nation and kinship goes well beyond the merely metaphorical; that is, beyond ways in which nations may borrow the language of kinship to generate their own logics and loyalties (Schneider 1980 [1969]).[9] Second, we questioned the assumption that nation-states are based on the unit of the individual citizen, and the corresponding tendency for analysts to be blind to actual kinship processes still at work within modern nation-states. Third, we followed Lambek's argument, already referred to above, that kinship is not in fact encapsulated and subordinated within the modern state; "kinship is not separate, because it is embedded in the fundamental actions of the state" – including all those actions by which the state asserts the right to make and recognize persons and relations between persons – "and it is not subordinate, because it is part and parcel of what the state is and means" (Lambek quoted in McKinnon and Cannell 2013: 26).

We have noted that kinship and religion are treated in teleological modernization theory, as the two domains that have become subordinated to modern states and economies that claim to transcend them. We have also noted that in fact, kinship and religion are often constituted in the same practices, including performative speech and ritual, and that therefore they overlap considerably, or may even sometimes be virtually coextensive, in modern states. Nevertheless, there are some contexts in modern practice and in theories of modernity, in which a strong distinction may be made between the two domains. It is my view (Cannell 2013) that this kind of distinction has left a deep impression in certain kinds of anthropological writing on kinship.

A contrast, rather than a parallel, is made between kinship and religion when kinship is considered in relation to science. From the viewpoint of a modern science defining itself as concerned with the material world, kinship is "real" while religion is "unreal." Kinship, for different kinds of scientists, can be viewed as an expression of the real in the sense of material, physical, and natural forces that may be glossed and elaborated by human culture but are not ultimately controlled by human culture, such as "the selfish gene" in the understanding of Richard Dawkins (2006 [1976]). It is interesting to note how often ethnographies of kinship – especially kinship concerned with any kinds of modern scientific or medical intervention such as IVF – have tended to treat their subject as though it had obviously nothing to do with religion, or as though any emergence of a religious theme or reference in this context were purely metaphorical, or else anomalous (Cannell 2013: 230–232). A rich vein of ethnographic work on kinship in modern states, concerned with the medical mastery of the body, has therefore tended to be in conversation primarily with other work on similar themes, and not in conversation with any literature that considers religion.[10]

Religion is figured as what has been superceded by science in modernity, just as the traditional (kin-based) state is figured as what has been superceded by the nation-state in modernity. In discussions of medicalized kinship, however, the body and its materiality become the terrain on which this transcendence is played out; we see modern knowledge apparently mastering nature rather than traditional culture apparently being mastered by it. In this context, the medicalized human body stands as the guarantor of both the reality and the modernity of the processes under consideration.

Schneider (1980 [1969]) famously described the importance of idioms of the mastery of nature in underpinning American kinship as a cultural construct. His work (and that of Marilyn Strathern and others) has prompted us to be sensitive to the ways in which a specific idea of nature is itself part of our own culture in places that inherit legacies of Western philosophy. Nevertheless, it seems to me that if we allow the anthropological study of "kinship" to be placed in a conceptual enclave that divides it from "religion," we inadvertently reproduce some of those ways of thinking, and we do not take account of the kinds of lived complexities which in fact permeate experience in nation-states.

In an earlier essay on Mormon polygamy and its implications for anthropology (Cannell 2013), I argued that Schneider's own account of American kinship is itself blind to aspects of the social salience and historical production of the analytic categories he uses. Schneider's research method for his famous study appears, in particular, to have proceeded in such a way as to flatten the nuance of what his interlocutors had to say about religion in relation to kinship. Readers will recall that Schneider's respondents frequently invoked their own background to citizenship, often describing themselves by reference to both faith and ethnicity, as in "Jewish-American" or "Italian-[Catholic]-American." Schneider downplayed these self descriptions because he wanted to draw out the commonalities in all his interlocutors' accounts of, for example, motherhood, and particularly the ways that these commonalities rested on the nature/culture trope with which he was concerned. One does not have to claim that these commonalities did not exist, however, to say that viewed from another perspective the distinctions Schneider's respondents were making could be equally constitutive of the kinship they were living.

As we know from many anthropological accounts, religion is also about the making of persons and the relations between persons, including in some cases relations between the living and the dead, and/or the living and the divine (Orsi 2005, 2016.) But these dimensions of lived relationality will be made to disappear if the analyst has in advance decided to make a strong separation between kinship on the one hand and religion on the other. It is my view that Schneider's theoretical apparatus in *American Kinship*, as well as his methodology, has this effect. Schneider's nature/culture distinction is pitched at a level of generality which does not inquire about the particular kinds of work and experience that belong to religion. His categories of "blood" and "the law" viewed as the cultural constructs of which American kinship is made, are strongly de-historicized and are presented as though derived solely from the 1960s survey data on which his study is based. However, a brief consideration of the example of American Mormon doctrine and polygamy with which we began this chapter, offers us a corrective to this view. To follow the history of the Federal government's suppression of Mormon religious kinship is to see definitions of the law of God, the law of man, and the permissible character of genealogical relatedness ("blood") all in processes of considerable contestation and change over the long nineteenth century and beyond. The category distinctions which Schneider used were, in effect, the definitions created and imposed by the largely Protestant American majority whose view of the world was victorious in this battle. But although they won at the level of the state and its laws, the majority did not thereby create a perfectly homogeneous American experience, which is what some readings of Schneider's work might tend to suggest. Many other alternate American kinships also existed historically and still exist in part or whole today for some American citizens, as the work of Gillian Feeley-Harnik teaches us.[11]

This kind of approach to kinship, which divides it from the topic of religion and in effect re-naturalizes that distinction by invoking kinship's supposed "materiality," is, I would argue, the correlate of secularization debates as they have figured in the anthropology of religion. The claim, or assumption, has often been made that modernity would inevitably involve a decline in religious engagement and a withdrawal of religion from the public into the private sphere. Proceeding by what Charles Taylor calls "subtraction stories" (Taylor 2007: 530–531), secularization theorists have claimed in many interrelated ways that modernity is the state in which we live when various primitive, mistaken, and irrational elements of human life and thinking are given up. In this view, religion figures centrally as what is to be given up, because it is associated with an infantile or dependent condition of the human person, as well as being associated with a primitive or uncivilized early period of human history, technological inadequacy, superstitious, authoritarian, corrupt, or irrational systems and institutions, and so on. Both the infantile and the primitive aspects of human life are understood as rather shameful conditions which it is imperative to overcome. Thus the new atheist movement (drawing however as Taylor points out rather directly but not necessarily consciously on Nietzsche), advocates as the fulfillment of human being a thorough embracing of modern scientific knowledge, especially on human evolution, combined with a heroic determination to face the fact that man is alone in the universe, devoid of any quasi-parental divinities taking an interest in his sufferings or his fate (Taylor 2007: 583).

These orientations give a heroic status to the individual, conceived as the (loosely) Nietzschean superman in unflinching engagement with the real, and also give privileged status to the material world, because the modern person is invited and required to experience the disaggregation of what is real from what is superstitious or imaginary. This effort of absolute distinction, attempted but never fully achieved, underwrites these myths and narratives of the modern (see also Latour 1993).

As we noted above, all the terms of the title of this article were famously discussed by Max Weber, and together they constituted much of what Weber had to say about modernity, including many of his insights into the ways in which modern persons have to live with profound experiences of loss of meaning, compared to those in traditional societies and in archaic times. I have argued elsewhere (Cannell 2010) that when

Weber is read, as he often has been, as promoting a teleological view of modernity, he is misunderstood. Weber certainly felt that many aspects of modernity were unavoidable, and he drew on Nietzsche in so far as he was required, as a social scientist, to think unflinchingly about reality as he understood it – whatever the personal and emotional cost might be. Weber, however, did not take a triumphalist tone when writing about modern experience, or about changes or apparent declines in religious engagement and practice in the modern world. His writing is therefore to be distinguished from branches of later secularization literature in which the end of religion in modernity is either deemed to be an inevitable and universal aspect of social change, or else is considered and described as obviously a "good thing" (Boyer 2001) – for instance, as a form of liberation from previous intellectual confusion, or from oppressive religious authorities and structures. We do not need to deny that either intellectual confusion or oppressive religious structures have existed in the past and continue to exist today, to wish to take a more nuanced approach to the value of religious life for human beings in society. Weber's own tonality in writing about religion in the modern world is complex and often ambivalent, holding in view the tragic elements of human loss that are entailed, and never simply celebrating scientific, bureaucratic, or economic "progress." Neither does Weber propose that modernity will take the same route in all other parts of the world as it has taken in Western Europe, or result therefore in a homogeneous form of universal modernity. On the contrary, Weber's insistence that historical processes of "rationalization" (in his meaning; i.e., the gradual acquisition of internal coherence within any system of thought) proceed through the interaction between value systems particular to different world religions, and developing economic systems, suggests that diverse and multiple forms of modernity are likely to be the outcome. It is true that Weber does appear to consider religious modalities attuned to action (what he calls "asceticism") as more likely to create engagements with economic change than religious modalities attuned to contemplation (what he calls "mysticism"), which allows for the possibility of a predictive reading, but it is also true that he identified European Calvinist and Lutheran Protestant asceticism as exceptional in their orientation to action in the world ("outworldly asceticism") and that therefore the complex synergy that Weber famously proposes in which a strict Puritanism ironically lent energy and values over time to the development of capitalism (2001 [c.1930]) is best understood as a *unique* historical instance in Weber's thought, and not as predictive of forms or directions that the intersection between world religions and the modernizing state and economy might take in other times and places (Weber 1991 [1915], 1991 [c.1920], 1991 [1922], 2001 [c.1930]).

Despite this, there have been many and very influential readings of Weber which take him to offer a view of modernity as inevitable, and as likely to proceed universally along the lines he traced historically in

Western Europe. This kind of reading has not only insisted that modernity will always be (or become) more secular, but has also had the second effect of reading Protestantism (and sometimes, by analogy, other world religions) "backwards" as a kind of historical staging post on the way to a secular destination that is allegedly known in advance (Cannell 2006, 2010). This view has had a number of effects on anthropological writing, of which I have argued elsewhere one has been the accidental over-privileging of views of Christianity which are too narrowly based on the characteristics of Protestantism (Cannell 2005, 2006). If, in the history of the suppression of American Mormon polygamy we can see unfolding an insistence on defining "Christian values" in terms of what were actually Protestant norms, so also in anthropological writing and theory, Protestant themes have sometimes tended to become too prominent, excluding our view of other experiences and processes. There are many contexts, including the Dutch Calvinist Protestant missionization of Sumba, described by Webb Keane (2007), in which these are actually the values in question for the actors with whom anthropologists are concerned. However, in doing as Keane then does and extrapolating from his Sumbanese/Calvinist encounter to a general theory of "Christian Moderns," we have to exercise caution not to lose sight of other ways of being Christian, and therefore other ways of being modern. It might be argued that the recent – and richly illuminating – anthropological interest in both the "individual" and the definitive lessons to be learned from the issue of "material religion" takes its cue from Protestant ideas – and ideas about the importance of the Protestant model – which are also bound up in partly submerged claims about the place of Protestantism in processes of secularization and modernity. It may indeed be partly for this reason that some of the ethnography which is most valuable in thinking about the intersection between religion, kinship, and the nation-state actually derives from contexts outside this form of majoritarian Protestantism, whether non-Protestant Christianities such as Roman Catholicism or Mormonism, or non-Christian salvationist religions, including Judaism and Hinduism.

The value of the work of Talal Asad is amply acknowledged by many of the writers referenced above, and particularly by Michael Lambek in the seminal essay here described. Interestingly, though, Asad seems in some respects also to have reproduced a tacit apparent division between kinship and religion, if only because he rarely explicitly names or addresses the topic of kinship when talking about the anthropological category of the religious (Asad 1993) or about the processes of secularization and the creation of an ideology of the secular as real, which he considers to be inseparable from the making of the modern Western nation-state (Asad 2003). In fact, kinship in Asad's writing figures most prominently perhaps in the famous discussion of the shift in Egyptian marriage laws in the British colonial period (Asad 2003: 206–246) but even here not as a leading category; it is not a topic that is foregrounded when Asad talks about the historical or the contemporary West. The exception to this is Asad's discussion of the work of Pamela Klassen on contemporary American birthing practices as "Blessed Events" (Asad 2003: 87–89; Klassen 2001). Klassen's ethnography, to my eye, clearly suggests, like other ethnography cited here, the experiential inseparability of kinship and religion in modern American life, including for people who do not define themselves as "religious." Asad, however, considers the work under the rubric of his category of "passionate agency" – that is, the valuation of forms of human experience, including the positive value of suffering in certain conditions – as these are outlawed by liberal post-enlightenment Western states and by international agreements such as human rights legislation. Asad's main point is that these constraints on the recognition of agency exclude and tacitly coerce actors within other traditions, including religious ascetic traditions, an observation that he rightly connects with the negative stereotyping of Muslims in America and Europe, but which could also be applied to persons of many other backgrounds. The cue to consider what directions "passionate agency" might take within European modern life (despite its negation by the state) is, however, not fully taken up or explored by Asad himself. Asad also discusses these issues under the term "human life" rather than the term kinship, which again creates a disconnect between the topic of kinship and the context of modern nation-states, and which has also prompted Veena Das (2006) to note, in response to Asad's rather dyadic contrast between Western liberal secularism and Islamic tradition, that there are, in fact, multiple understandings of human life in the world, including Hindu paradigms which fit neither model proposed in Asad's work.

30.4 The Sense of the State

It is often the case that a particular area of difficulty in anthropological theory yields to a convergence of thinkers who are each moving towards it from slightly different directions. Bearing in mind that the conceptual division between anthropologists of kinship and of religion is itself, I have suggested, part of the problem of myths of modernity, we can note that the question of the relationship between kinship, religion, and the nation-state in modernity seems to be such an instance. The critique of secularist paradigms – and also of buried Protestant normativities in the description of modern experience – has been the angle of approach on this problem taken from the anthropology of religion. Writing on the anthropology of kinship has, however, also recently offered its own approach towards what seem to me to be congruent conclusions, albeit drawing on a different literature. Marshall Sahlins (2011a, 2011b) – building on his earlier critiques of sociobiology and his insightful account of "the native anthropology of Western cosmology" (Sahlins, 1996) – offered a highly illuminating and nuanced defense of the possibility of retaining a general definition of the category of kinship, despite the widely acknowledged variability of the terms on which such a category can be based, particularly the category of "nature." For Sahlins, "mutuality of being" is a definition which can permit all this variation without self-contradiction, including, for instance, the notoriously non-Western ontologies of Amazonian life often described as "perspectivism." In making this argument, Sahlins draws persuasively on the work of Vivieros de Castro (2009) who argued that kinship can be understood as like gift giving and (with caveats) magic, in so far as it expresses the creation of relationality through human intentionality (Sahlins 2011b: 239).

Sahlins' formulation "mutuality of being" is helpful for anthropologists also interested in religious dimensions of life, since it readily allows for the description and perception of such mutuality between all kinds of persons, across the boundaries of death, the distinction between the human and the divine, or indeed (as in the Amazon and, according to Feeley-Harnik, also in a different way in modern America and England) across species. Viveiros de Castro refers to "magic" and therefore brings to mind "traditional" rather than "world religion" or "state" contexts, but we have already argued, following Lambek, that the distinctions between the ways in which societies draw on kinship relations in modern and traditional contexts can be greatly overstated. Like the amendment of secularization theory, a more flexible definition of kinship permits us to escape the problem of operating with categories that have already been limited by narratives and myths about modernity and its purifications, and permits anthropologists to speak to each other about the experience of people in modern states across supposedly mutually exclusive domains.

None of this, of course, is new, as nothing ever is. For those unpersuaded by a less "rationalist" view of Max Weber, one might note Robert Bellah's interesting essay on a lesser-known aspect of Weber's discussions of modernity and its complexities (Bellah 1997). Weber was considering the displacement of religious affect into alternate areas of modern life, including art and erotic love, without reaching any optimistic conclusions about the capacity of either to sustain human fulfillment without some form of coercion. He also noted the tendency for modern states to ally themselves with highly selective versions of religious and kinship actions, for example by integrating certain definitions of permissible marriage. Perhaps more unexpectedly – or not, considering Weber's own background and his respect for the faith of his wife and cousin Marianne – Weber concluded that one potentiality of world religions as he understood them was the generalization of "brotherly love" from a care and compassion supposedly extended only to (blood) kin in primitive societies, to a potentially infinite audience of one's fellow humans. Despite his pessimism about what either politics or religion could do in the darkening context of the twentieth-century state, it seems that Weber continued to place some hope in the idea of a compassionate human capacity for "world denying love." Although still within a certain social evolutionist framing, therefore, it seems that Weber was himself alert to the possible complex mutual constitution of "kinship" and "religion" in the modern state of his day.

In my view, then, Lambek is right in suggesting that kinship is both an "immoderate" and an "immodern" object; although it may exist within a context of state biopolitics, it can never be limited to or by the biopolitical (Lambek 2013: 256). I would add just two concluding notes to this: the first is that in my view "religion" is also both "immoderate" and "immodern" in a similar sense, and the second is that, returning to the point powerfully made by McKinnon, we should try never to assume in advance what the mutual relations might be between what we call kinship, religion, and the nation-state. The literature I have drawn on suggests how powerful the "sense of the state" is as lived reality, and yet how complex and variable the inhabitations of reality are in relation to states around the world. These experiences are not reducible to "modernization" considered as a homogeneous or unidirectional process. Even in the small sample of examples it has been possible to offer here, we can see both that as Mody says, citizens may act in relation to their understanding of kinship/religion, but be inadvertently drawn into the political, or else, as in my Mormon example but also in contexts beyond this, people may – despite the continuing oppressive potentials of religious institutions and hierarchies – consciously find and pursue alternate ways of being human through kinship and religious life that do not conform to the definitions required by the modern nation-state, and continue to make, although unevenly, certain kinds of spaces within it.

Notes

1. This implies that Cathy, like most American women, had amniocentesis (see Rapp 1999).
2. Angels, as messengers from the divine, in Mormonism, can be understood as either premortal spirits or resurrected beings; in this case, the spirit of Cathy's son is obviously premortal. There can also be postmortal (not-yet resurrected) messengers, but it is my impression that these sacred messengers are less often referred to as "angels," perhaps because they tend to be known (deceased) individuals who are referred to by name or relationship, or as ancestors.
3. For a full discussion of this ethnography and Mormon motherhood visions see Cannell (in preparation).
4. Latter-day Saints are well aware that the records of many lives have been lost or destroyed. They speculate that these records will be recovered during the millennium, with the help of specific early-resurrected persons, for instance, Biblical Abraham.

5. Including rules of modesty in conduct and dress, and dietary prohibitions among others.

6. Polygamy, being evidently a contractual relationship, is also excluded from the forms of social recognition now afforded to identities of personal sexual orientation or gender identity.

7. As Gordon (2002) demonstrates, polygamy was also implicated in anxieties about and debates over slavery and its abolition, although the racialized elements of the discourse were usually implicit.

8. Here I differ in emphasis from the conclusion reached by Gordon, who stresses loss of religious charisma compared to the nineteenth century, and regards the continuities as more attenuated (Gordon 2002).

9. This article can only gesture towards the ways in which it is artificial also to separate discussions of religion, kinship, and politics from discussion of modern economics. The work of Sylvia Yanagisako (2002) offers a lucid critique of Weber's view that kinship did not structure modern capitalism through her ethnography of Italian family textile manufacture; the work of Laura Bear (2015), and Elana Shever (2012) considers kinship in relation to neoliberalism and state capitalism respectively.

10. Important partial exceptions may be Marcia Inhorn's discussion of Arab hegemonic masculinity and lineal kinship in relation to assisted reproduction practices in the Arab world (Inhorn 2012) and Elizabeth Robert's discussion of acceptance of IVF in Andean Ecuador despite the formal opposition of the Catholic church (Roberts 2012). It is notable that both studies concern contexts in which anthropologists acknowledge that formal religious authority continues to influence states and law-making.

11. Feeley-Harnik's profound and nuanced accounts of changes in American and English understandings of kinship between humans and relatedness between species acknowledge many such alternate kinships, and kinship thinking in question, for example in the work of Lewis Henry Morgan and his Iroquois interlocutors.

References

Asad, Talal. 1993. *Genealogies of Religion: Discipline and Reasons of Power in Christianity and Islam*. Baltimore, MD: Johns Hopkins University Press.
    2003. *Formations of the Secular: Christianity, Islam, Modernity*. Stanford, CA: Stanford University Press.
Austin Felice, Lani Axman, Heather Farrell, Robyn Allgood and Sheridan Ripley. 2012. *The Gift of Giving Life: Rediscovering the Divine Nature of Pregnancy and Birth*. Culver City, CA: Madison and West Publishing.
Bamford, Sandra and James Leach, eds. 2009. *Kinship and Beyond: The Genealogical Model Reconsidered*. New York: Berghahn Books.

Basu, Paul. 2007. *Highland Homecomings: Genealogy and Heritage Tourism in the Scottish Diaspora*. New York: Routledge.

Bear, Laura. 2007. *Lines of the Nation: Indian Railway Workers, Bureaucracy and the Intimate Historical Self*. New York/Chichester, West Sussex: Columbia University Press.

2013. "'This Body Is Our Body': Vishwakarma Puja, the Social Debts of Kinship and Theologies of Materiality in a Neoliberal Shipyard." In *Vital Relations: Modernity and the Persistent Life of Kinship*, ed. Susan McKinnon and Fenella Cannell, 155–179. Santa Fe, NM: School for Advanced Research Press.

2015. *Navigating Austerity: Currents of Debt along a South Asian River*. Stanford, CA: Stanford University Press.

Bellah, Robert. 1997. "Max Weber and World-Denying Love: A Look at the Historical Sociology of Religion." Humanities Center and Burke Leadership on Religion and Society, University of California, San Diego, CA. October 30. www.robertbellah.com/articles_3.htm, accessed October 4, 2017.

Bennion, Janet. 2012. *Polygamy in Primetime*. Lebanon, NH: Brandeis University Press, an imprint of the University Press of New England.

Bodenhorn, Barbara. 2013. "On the Road Again: Movement, Marriage, Mestizaje and the Race of Kinship." In *Vital Relations: Modernity and the Persistent Life of Kinship*, ed. Susan McKinnon and Fenella Cannell, 131–154. Santa Fe, NM: School for Advanced Research Press.

Boyer, Pascal. 2001. *Religion Explained: The Evolutionary Origins of Religious Thought*. New York: Basic Books.

Cannell, Fenella. 2005. "The Christianity of Anthropology." Malinowski Memorial Lecture, May 20, 2005. *Journal of the Royal Anthropological Institute* (n.s.) 11(2): 335–356.

2006. *The Anthropology of Christianity*. Durham, NC/London: Duke University Press.

2010. "The Anthropology of Secularism." *Annual Review of Anthropology* 39: 85–100.

2011. "English Ancestors: The Moral Possibilities of Popular Genealogy." *Journal of the Royal Anthropological Institute* (n.s.) 17(3): 462–480.

2013. "The Re-Enchantment of Kinship." In *Vital Relations: Modernity and the Persistent Life of Kinship*, ed. Susan McKinnon and Fenella Cannell, 217–240. Santa Fe, NM: School for Advanced Research Press.

2017a. "Forever Families: Christian Individualism, Mormonism and Collective Salvation." In *New Directions in Spiritual Kinship: Sacred Ties across the Abrahamic Religions*, ed. Todne Thomas, Asiya Malik and Rose Wellman, 151–169. New York: Palgrave Macmillan.

2017b. "Mormonism and Anthropology: On Ways of Knowing." In *Mormon Studies Review* 4(1): article 2. https://scholarsarchive.byu.edu/msr2/vol4/iss1/2, accessed November 13, 2018.

In preparation. *Book of Life: Mormon Sacred Kinship in Modern America*.

Carsten, Janet. 2000. *Cultures of Relatedness: New Approaches to the Study of Kinship*. Cambridge: Cambridge University Press.

2013. "Ghosts, Commensality and Scuba Diving: Tracing Kinship and Sociality in Clinical Pathology." In *Vital Relations: Modernity and the Persistent Life of Kinship*, ed. Susan McKinnon and Fenella Cannell, 217–240. Santa Fe, NM: School for Advanced Research Press.

Casanova, Jose. 1994. *Public Religions in the Modern World*. Chicago, IL: University of Chicago Press.

Church of Jesus Christ of Latter-day Saints. 2011. *Gospel Principles*. www.lds.org/manual/gospel-principles/chapter-47-exaltation?lang=eng, accessed January 8, 2017.

Collier, Jane and Sylvia Junko Yanagisako, eds. 1987. *Gender and Kinship: Essays toward a Unified Analysis*. Stanford, CA: Stanford University Press.

Das, Veena. 2006. "Secularism and the Argument from Nature." In *Powers of the Secular Modern: Talal Asad and His Interlocutors*, ed. David Scott and Charles Hirschkind, 93–112. Stanford, CA: Stanford University Press.

Davies, Douglas. 2000. *The Mormon Culture of Salvation*. Farnham: Ashgate.

2003. *An Introduction to Mormonism*. Cambridge: Cambridge University Press.

2010. *Joseph Smith, Jesus and Satanic Opposition: Atonement, Evil and the Mormon Vision*. Farnham: Ashgate.

Dawkins, Richard. 2006 [1976]. *The Selfish Gene*, 30th anniversary ed. Oxford: Oxford University Press.

Feeley-Harnik, Gillian. 1999. "Communities of Blood": The Natural History of Kinship in Nineteenth-Century America." *Comparative Studies in Society and History* 41(2): 215–262.

2001a. "The Ethnography of Creation: Lewis Henry Morgan and the American Beaver." In *Relative Values: Reconfiguring Kinship Studies*, ed. S. Franklin and S. McKinnon, 54–84. Durham, NC: Duke University Press.

2001b. "The Mystery of Life in All Its Forms: Religious Dimensions of Culture in Early American Anthropology." In *Religion and Cultural Studies*, ed. S. Mizurchi, 140–191. Princeton, NJ: Princeton University Press.

2013. "Placing the Dead: Slavery, Kinship and Free Labor in Pre- and Post-Civil War America." In *Vital Relations: Modernity and the Persistent Life of Kinship*, ed. S. McKinnon and F. Cannell, 179–217. Santa Fe, NM: School for Advanced Research Press.

Flake, Kathleen. 2003. *The Politics of American Religious Identity: The Seating of Senato Reedr Smoot, Mormon Apostle*. Chapel Hill, NC: University of North Carolina Press.

Franklin, Sarah and Susan McKinnon, eds. 2001. *Relative Values: Reconfiguring Kinship Studies*. Durham, NC: Duke University Press.

Givens, Terryl. 2004. *Latter-Day Saint Experience in America*. Westport, CT: Greenwood Press.

2012. *When Souls Had Wings: Pre-Mortal Existence in Western Thought*. New York: Oxford University Press.

2014. *Wrestling the Angel: The Foundations of Mormon Thought.* New York: Oxford University Press.

Gordon, Sarah Barringer. 2002. *The Mormon Question: Polygamy and Constitutional Conflict in Nineteenth Century America.* Chapel Hill, NC: University of North Carolina Press.

Hacking, Ian. 1999. *The Social Construction of What?* Harvard, MA: Harvard University Press.

Inhorn, Marcia. 2012. *The New Arab Man: Emergent Masculinities, Technologies and Islam in the Middle East.* Princeton, NJ: Princeton University Press.

Keane, Webb. 2007. *Christian Moderns: Freedom and Fetish in the Mission Encounter.* Berkeley/Los Angeles, CA: University of California Press.

Klassen, Pamela. 2001. *Blessed Events: Religion and Home Birth in America.* Princeton, NJ: Princeton University Press.

Lambek, Michael. 2013. "Kinship, Modernity and the Immodern." In *Vital Relations: Modernity and the Persistent Life of Kinship*, ed. S. McKinnon and F. Cannell, 241–260. Santa Fe, NM: School for Advanced Research Press.

Latour, Bruno.1993. *We Have Never Been Modern.* Translated by Catherine Porter. Cambridge, MA: Harvard University Press.

Leite, Naomi. 2017. *Unorthodox Kin: Portuguese Marranos and the Global Search for Belonging.* Berkeley, CA: University of California Press.

Liberatore, Giulia. 2016. "Imagining an Ideal Husband: Marriage As a Site of Aspiration among Pious Somali Women in London." *Anthropological Quarterly* 69(3): 781–821.

McKinnon, Susan. 2013. "Kinship within and beyond the 'Movement of Progressive Societies.'" In *Vital Relations: Modernity and the Persistent Life of Kinship*, ed. Susan McKinnon and Fenella Cannell, 39–62. Santa Fe, NM: School for Advanced Research Press.

McKinnon, Susan and Fenella Cannell. 2013. "The Difference Kinship Makes." In *Vital Relations: Modernity and the Persistent Life of Kinship*, ed. S. McKinnon and F. Cannell, 3–38. Santa Fe, NM: School for Advanced Research Press.

Mody, Perveez. 2008. *The Intimate State: Love-Marriage and the Law in Delhi.* New York: Routledge.

Orsi, Robert. 2005. *Between Heaven and Earth: The Religious Worlds People Make and the Scholars Who Study Them.* Princeton, NJ: Princeton University Press.

2016. *History and Presence.* Cambridge, MA: Belknap.

Pool, Fernande. 2016. The Ethical life of Muslims in Secular India: Islamic Reformism in West Bengal. PhD Thesis, London School of Economics.

Rapp, Rayna. 1999. *Testing Women, Testing the Fetus: The Social Impact of Amniocentesis in America.* New York: Routledge.

Roberts, Elizabeth. 2012. *God's Laboratory: Assisted Reproduction in the Andes.* Berkeley, CA: University of California Press.

Rutherford, Danilyn. 2013. "Kinship and Catastrophe: Global Warming and the Rhetoric of Descent." In *Vital Relations: Modernity and the*

Persistent Life of Kinship, ed. Susan McKinnon and Fenella Cannell, 261–283. Santa Fe, NM: School for Advanced Research Press.

Sahlins, Marshall. 1996. "The Sadness of Sweetness: The Native Anthropology of Western Cosmology." *Current Anthropology* 77(3): 395–428.

2011a. "What Kinship Is" (Part 1). *Journal of the Royal Anthropological Institute* 17(1): 2–19.

2011b. "What Kinship Is" (Part 2). *Journal of the Royal Anthropological Institute* 17(2): 227–242.

Schneider, David. 1980 [1969]. *American Kinship: A Cultural Account.* Chicago, IL: University of Chicago Press.

1984. *A Critique of the Study of Kinship.* Ann Arbor, MI: University of Michigan Press.

Seeman, Don. 2017. "Kinship As Ethical Relation: A Critique of the Spiritual Kinship Paradigm." In *New Directions in Spiritual Kinship: Sacred Ties Across the Abrahamic Religions*, ed. T. Thomas, A. Malik and R. Wellman, 85–108. New York: Palgrave Macmillan.

Serjeant, Jill. 16 Dec. 2009. "'Big Love' Returns to TV with Provocative Gay Story." Reuters. www.reuters.com/article/us-biglove/big-love-returns-to-tv-with-provocative-gay-story-idUSTRE5BF5O520091216, accessed November 3, 2018.

Shever, Elana. 2012. *Resources for Reform: Oil and Neoliberalism in Argentina.* Stanford, CA: Stanford University Press.

2013. "'I Am a Petroleum Product': Making Kinship Work on the Patagonian Frontier." In *Vital Relations: Modernity and the Persistent Life of Kinship*, ed. Susan McKinnon and Fenella Cannell, 85–109. Santa Fe, NM: School for Advanced Research Press.

Shipps, Jan. 1987. *Mormonism: The Story of a New Religious Tradition.* Urbana and Chicago, IL: University of Illinois Press.

Strathern, Marilyn. 1980. "No Nature, No Culture: The Hagen Case." In *Nature, Culture and Gender*, ed. C. MacCormack and M. Strathern, 174–222. Cambridge: Cambridge University Press.

1988. *The Gender of the Gift: Problems with Women and Problems with Society in Melanesia.* Berkeley, CA: University of California Press.

1992. *After Nature: English Kinship in the Late Twentieth Century.* Cambridge: Cambridge University Press.

Taylor, Charles. 2007. *A Secular Age.* Cambridge, MA: Harvard University Press.

Thomas, Todne, Asiya Malik and Rose Wellman, eds. 2017. *New Directions in Spiritual Kinship: Sacred Ties across the Abrahamic Religions.* New York: Palgrave Macmillan.

Vivieros de Castro, Eduardo. 2009. "The Gift and the Given: Three Nano-Essays on Kinship and Magic." In *Kinship and Beyond: The Genealogical Model Reconsidered*, ed. S. Bamford and J. Leach, 237–268. New York: Berghahn.

Weber, Max. 1991 [1915]. "Religious Rejections of the World and Their Directions." (*Zwischenbetrachtung*). In *From Max Weber: Essays in Sociology*, ed. H. Gerth and C. Wright Mills, 323–363. New York: Routledge.

——— 1991. [c.1920]. "The Protestant Sects and the Spirit of Capitalism." In *From Max Weber: Essays in Sociology*, ed. H. Gerth and C. Wright Mills, 302–322. New York: Routledge.

——— 1991. [1922]. "Science As a Vocation." In *From Max Weber: Essays in Sociology*, ed. H. Gerth and C. Wright Mills, 129–156. New York: Routledge.

——— 2001. [c.1930]. *The Protestant Ethic and the Spirit of Capitalism*. Translated by T. Parsons from a German original c.1904. London: Routledge.

Yanagisako, Sylvia. 2002. *Producing Culture and Capital: Family Firms in Italy*. Princeton, NJ: Princeton University Press.

——— 2013. "Transnational Family Capitalism: Producing 'Made in Italy' in China." In *Vital Relations: Modernity and the Persistent Life of Kinship*, ed. Susan McKinnon and Fenella Cannell, 63–84. Santa Fe, NM: School for Advanced Research Press.

Yanagisako, Sylvia and Carole Delaney, eds. 1995. *Naturalizing Power: Essays in Feminist Cultural Analysis*. New York: Routledge.

Index